A COMMONWEALTH OF HOPE

A Commonwealth of Hope

AUGUSTINE'S POLITICAL THOUGHT

MICHAEL LAMB

PRINCETON UNIVERSITY PRESS

PRINCETON & OXFORD

Published by Princeton University Press
41 William Street, Princeton, New Jersey 08540
99 Banbury Road, Oxford OX2 6JX

press.princeton.edu

All Rights Reserved

Library of Congress Cataloging-in-Publication Data

Names: Lamb, Michael, 1982– author.
Title: A commonwealth of hope : Augustine's political thought / Michael Lamb.
Description: Princeton, New Jersey : Princeton University Press, [2022] |
    Includes bibliographical references and index.
Identifiers: LCCN 2021048327 (print) | LCCN 2021048328 (ebook) |
    ISBN 9780691226330 (Print : acid-free paper) | ISBN 9780691226354 (eBook)
Subjects: LCSH: Augustine, of Hippo, Saint, 354–430—Political and social views. |
    Political science—Philosophy—History. | Christianity and politics. |
    BISAC: PHILOSOPHY / Political | RELIGION / Theology
Classification: LCC JC121.A8 L36 2022 (print) | LCC JC121.A8 (ebook) |
    DDC 320.092–dc23/eng/20220213
LC record available at https://lccn.loc.gov/2021048327
LC ebook record available at https://lccn.loc.gov/2021048328

British Library Cataloging-in-Publication Data is available

Editorial: Rob Tempio and Chloe Coy
Production Editorial: Kathleen Cioffi
Jacket Design: Heather Hansen
Production: Erin Suydam
Publicity: Alyssa Sanford and Charlotte Coyne
Copyeditor: Hank Southgate

Jacket image: Jean-Claude Golvin (b. 1942), watercolor painting of Hippo Regius, ancient name of the modern city of Annaba, Algeria. Musée départemental Arles Antique © Jean-Claude Golvin / Éditions Errance

This book has been composed in Arno

Printed on acid-free paper. ∞

Printed in the United States of America

10 9 8 7 6 5 4 3 2 1

For my parents,
Ken and Angela Lamb,
who taught me how to hope

CONTENTS

Why Augustine? Why Hope?

AUGUSTINE OF HIPPO is one of the most influential thinkers in the history of political thought. A North African bishop and theologian who lived in the Roman Empire at the turn of the fifth century and was later recognized as a saint in the Catholic Church, Augustine served as an essential bridge connecting Greek and Roman philosophy with medieval Christianity.[1] One prominent political theorist describes him as "the first and perhaps the greatest of Christian synthesizers."[2] Another observes that "Augustine's importance to the subsequent history of Europe is impossible to exaggerate."[3] Even fierce critics acknowledge the extent of his influence.[4] Apart from perhaps Plato, Aristotle, and Cicero, no other ancient thinker has had more influence on Western politics.[5]

Much of Augustine's influence came through appropriations by medieval philosophers and theologians.[6] Roughly 80 percent of Peter Lombard's *Sentences*, a widely used textbook in the medieval period that became a required source for lectures and commentaries for students seeking to become professors of theology, consists of quotations from Augustine.[7] One of those students was Thomas Aquinas, who did more than anyone to integrate Aristotelian ethics with Augustinian Christianity.[8]

Augustine's impact has not been limited to the Roman Catholic Church.[9] From the beginning of the Reformation, Protestants have drawn on Augustine to advance their accounts of theology and politics. Before posting *The Ninety-Five Theses*, Martin Luther was a friar and priest in the Order of St. Augustine and held a chair established by the Order at the University of Wittenberg, which identified Augustine as its patron saint.[10] Luther quoted Augustine extensively throughout his works and, like Aquinas, had studied Lombard's *Sentences*, noting on the first page of his copy that "Augustine can never be praised enough."[11] Similarly, John Calvin referred explicitly to Augustine approximately

1,700 times and quoted, paraphrased, or alluded to him an additional 2,400 times.[12] "Augustine is so completely of our persuasion," Calvin wrote, "that if I should have to make written profession, it would be quite enough to present a composition made up entirely of excerpts from his writings."[13]

Prominent political thinkers have also engaged deeply, if sometimes critically, with Augustinian ideas.[14] In Italy, Dante drew on Augustine's *Confessions* to inform his spiritual autobiography and laced *The Divine Comedy* with themes of love, history, and politics drawn from Augustine's *City of God*.[15] In England, John Milton not only integrated Augustinian accounts of creation, free will, and the Fall into his "Augustinian epic," *Paradise Lost*, but also cited passages from *City of God* to challenge opponents who had used Augustine instead to defend the divine right of kings.[16] In France, Christine de Pizan invoked Augustine's *City of God* to call medieval princes to virtue and construct a "City of Ladies" to elevate the virtues of women,[17] while Jean-Jacques Rousseau wrote his *Confessions* as a direct reply to Augustine's.[18] In early America, one scholar suggests, Augustine might have "exerted the greatest single influence upon Puritan thought next to that of the Bible itself."[19] Later, another scholar notes, some African Americans looked to Augustine as one of the "specifically African classical forbearers" whose work informed and inspired their own.[20]

Augustine's complex legacy extends into contemporary political theory.[21] It is striking to see how many prominent political theorists—both religious and secular—engage Augustine's work. These include representatives of the most influential strands of contemporary political theory: liberalism,[22] conservatism,[23] communitarianism,[24] realism,[25] republicanism,[26] and radical democracy.[27] The sheer variety of these accounts reveals the "Proteanism" of Augustine's authority.[28] Even if many of these theorists contest Augustinian ideas, the fact that they take up his work at all highlights the need to continue grappling with him.[29]

Augustine's political influence is not confined to the academy. Public intellectuals ranging from David Brooks, E. J. Dionne, and Jon Meacham to Roosevelt Montás, Cornel West, and Molly Worthen have invoked Augustine in their analyses of religion, politics, and culture,[30] while politicians, pundits, and public officials have occasionally trotted out Augustine to defend public policy positions. After the terrorist attacks of September 11, 2001, Jean Bethke Elshtain cited Augustine to provide intellectual support for the Bush Administration's decision to invade Iraq, while opponents invoked Augustine to challenge the decision.[31] In 2008, the Speaker of the US House of Representatives, Nancy

Pelosi, made national news when she recruited Augustine to defend her pro-choice stance on abortion in the first trimester, while pro-life Catholics cited Augustine's authority to contest Pelosi's claims.[32] US President Barack Obama enlisted Augustine's understanding of "just war" to defend his administration's use of drones, a statement that led one philosopher to wonder if the policy could be reduced to the question "What Would Augustine Do?"[33] More recently, President Joe Biden cited Augustine's vision of the commonwealth in his inaugural address to encourage Americans to unite around "common objects" of love, while critics quoted passages from City of God to suggest that Biden "misreads Augustine."[34]

Augustine's authority is apparent in the Christian church and broader public culture. Before becoming Pope Benedict XVI, Joseph Ratzinger wrote his dissertation on Augustine, and Pope Francis has described Augustine as one of his favorite saints.[35] Within the Anglican Church, Rowan Williams wrote extensively about Augustine's moral and political theology before serving as the Archbishop of Canterbury.[36] Meanwhile, universities and monasteries claim their place in the Augustinian tradition, while scholars have highlighted Augustine's relevance for politics, psychology, philosophy, literature, history, science, education, and environmental studies.[37] Even poets, artists, and musicians see Augustine as a muse. How many other thinkers are the subject of poems by Henry Wadsworth Longfellow and Mary Oliver and ballads by Bob Dylan and Sting?[38]

Yet, if modern political culture remains in the "shadow of Augustine," as one scholar put it,[39] this Augustine is largely an Augustine of shadows. Darkness and pessimism prevail. The world is a vale of tears, and government is nothing but a remedy for sin. Politics remains tragic, limited, and hostage to necessity. Citizens must either do the "lesser evil" so that good may come or retreat from politics altogether, finding refuge in an otherworldly vision of heaven or the purity of the institutional church.

This was the portrait of Augustine I encountered in college. As I read fragments of City of God, I learned more about Augustine's "two cities"—the earthly and the heavenly—and how this contrast was intended to direct us away from the world and toward heaven. The picture that emerged was of an otherworldly, sin-obsessed pessimist who encourages us to renounce the world and seek the City of God.

As I pursued graduate work, however, a more complex image of Augustine began to take shape in my mind. Here was a thinker who grew up in a rural farming community in North Africa on the edges of the empire, far away from the center of "civilization" in Rome.[40] His father, Patricius, was Roman, and his mother, Monica, was likely Berber, so Augustine was of mixed ancestry, and his family was what we might now call middle-class.[41] Augustine excelled in school, but his family's resources were limited.[42] He was able to pursue further study only because a patron, Romanianus, supported his education.[43] In Carthage, Augustine became the top student in rhetoric,[44] and after teaching in Carthage, Thagaste, and Rome, he was appointed the imperial professor of rhetoric in Milan, a prestigious position that one commentator compares to "the endowed chair of government at Harvard."[45] Augustine had an ambition to become a lawyer and serve in political office, potentially as governor of a local province, but after two years in the rough-and-tumble world of the imperial court, he became disillusioned with politics and accused rhetoricians of being more committed to flattery than telling the truth.[46] So, in the process of converting to Christianity in 386, he abandoned his political ambitions and retreated to a friend's villa in Cassiciacum, where he enjoyed philosophical dialogues with close friends and family. He wrote about the happy life and sketched plans to develop an entire curriculum in the liberal arts.[47] But he would not stay long in his retreat. After being baptized by Ambrose in Milan and spending another year in Rome, he returned home to North Africa,[48] where for roughly forty years he served his people and his place, teaching farmers, merchants, and monks in Hippo, advocating on behalf of the poor and vulnerable, writing letters, sermons, and books on theology, ethics, and politics, and encouraging diverse citizens to share a common life together. For me—a student of political theory who grew up on a small farm in rural Tennessee, received a scholarship to a liberal arts college that my family could not otherwise afford, took a leave from graduate school to manage political campaigns, and returned to study politics, ethics, and religion with a desire to go back to my home region to teach and write—Augustine's life acquired a relevance that was missing, even as some of his complicities and commitments came to seem more disturbing than before.

As I took more courses and analyzed sermons, letters, and treatises often neglected in political theory, I also began to suspect that the pessimism often associated with his name was anachronistic. I kept coming across passages explicitly extolling the virtue of hope or implicitly designed to encourage his readers cultivate it. But I could not discover a single book-length treatment of Augustine's account of hope in English. So I set out to write such an account, one both sensitive to his historical context and concerns and capable of correcting, or at least complicating, the received image of his pessimism.

On the question of hope, Augustine is an especially valuable, if unlikely, ally in our contemporary moment. In the face of political division, racial injustice, economic inequality, and ecological devastation, many citizens are understandably tempted to despair, wondering if politics can offer any hope in our troubled times. Others are tempted to downplay, neglect, or reject the real challenges we face. Augustine offers another way. He criticizes pride, presumption, and the lust for domination while also resisting cynicism, resignation, and despair. Recognizing both the limits and possibilities of politics, he encourages a realistic hope for a better form of community not only in heaven but on earth and actively works to instantiate it through his service and citizenship. By holding together a robust critique of injustice with a legitimate hope for concord, he shows the importance of finding the mean between presumption and despair. Despite my many disagreements with him, I have found this feature of his work instructive, even inspiring.

To uncover this account, I will need to challenge the pessimistic reading of Augustine, integrate evidence from multiple sources, reexamine overlooked texts, and revisit more familiar ones, all while questioning some assumptions that most interpreters have taken for granted. Throughout, I will try to view Augustine's all-too-familiar ideas as if for the first time. As he himself once asked, "Isn't that what happens when we show beautiful scenes which we have often gone past with a careless glance, but which give us fresh joy as we share others' joy on first seeing them? . . . The more, by the bond of love, we enter into each other's mind, the more even old things become new for us again."[49] My hope in this book is to make Augustine new for us again.

A COMMONWEALTH OF HOPE

Beyond Pessimism

> If St. Augustine were to appear today and enjoy as little authority as his
> modern defenders he would not accomplish anything.
>
> —BLAISE PASCAL, *PENSÉES*, §517[1]

AUGUSTINE LOVED MOSAICS. A popular form of Roman art in North Africa,
mosaics adorned the homes of wealthy citizens and lined the floors of many
churches, including Augustine's basilica in Hippo.[2] In an early dialogue, Augustine adopts the mosaic as a metaphor for the universe, admonishing those
whose fixation on evil blinds them to the beauty of the larger pattern. These
cynics are like art critics who, "confined to surveying a single section of a
mosaic floor, looked at it too closely, and then blamed the artisan for being
ignorant of order and composition."[3] "In reality," Augustine writes, "it is [the
viewer] himself who, in concentrating on an apparently disordered variety of
small colored cubes, failed to notice the larger mosaic work" and see how the
"apparent disorder of the elements really comes together into the unity of a
beautiful portrait."[4]

The same selective vision afflicts many interpretations of Augustine in political theory. Fixating on small, colorful fragments of Augustine's texts, particularly
his account of evil, most political theorists neglect the larger patterns of the
Augustinian mosaic and emphasize one theme: pessimism. John Rawls describes Augustine as one of "the two dark minds in Western thought."[5] Annette
Baier numbers him among the "pessimists" about human love.[6] Bertrand Russell
suggests that his "ferocious" fixation on sin "made his life stern and his philosophy inhuman."[7] Even Reinhold Niebuhr, who considered Augustine "a more
reliable guide than any known thinker," concedes his realism is "excessive."[8]

Undoubtedly, Augustine provides evidence to support this interpretation. At times, the *Confessions* can read like a personal indictment of sin, and the first ten books of *City of God* prosecute a scathing polemic against imperial Rome, assailing the Romans' "lust for domination" and prideful pursuit of this-worldly glory.[9] Throughout *City of God*, Augustine laments the "miserable condition of this life," bemoaning the "darkness" and "undoubted evils" that accompany political affairs.[10] In Book 22.22–23, he compiles a lengthy list of the "many and grave evils" that beset human affairs, going so far as to describe our condition as "a hell on earth."[11]

If these passages were not enough to justify a "picture of a man pessimistic about politics,"[12] historical interpreters have added fuel (and sometimes brimstone) to Augustine's fire. Augustine's emphasis on sin inspired Protestant reformers such as Luther and Calvin, who insisted on the depths of depravity and necessity of grace, as well as Puritan preachers such as Jonathan Edwards, whom one scholar has described as the "American Augustine."[13] According to prominent accounts of these interpreters, Augustine teaches followers to renounce the world and turn toward the City of God.[14]

This portrait of pessimism dominates Augustine's reception in contemporary political theory. Hannah Arendt complains that Augustine makes a "desert out of the world," stripping the world of its value and politics of its significance.[15] Following Arendt, Martha Nussbaum argues that Augustine's "perverse" view of sin and "otherworldly" longing for the heavenly city deny the reality of human goodness and discourage this-worldly striving, supplying a "politics of shame" rather than a politics of hope.[16] David Billings concedes that "Augustine's eschatological ends do provide a kind of hope," but it is not "political hope."[17] For Billings, Augustine's hope is not "for the world" but "against" it.[18]

Standard accounts tend to affirm this interpretation, which means Augustine is "usually numbered among the pessimists."[19] If he offers any hope, most assume, it is a hope for heaven, not politics. As Eric Gregory notes, many interpreters cast Augustine as "the patron saint of a dour and otherworldly pessimism which emphasizes the radical limits of politics and virtue as compared to a heavenly city."[20]

Many of Augustine's most faithful interpreters have done little to challenge this consensus. Few scholars explore Augustine's account of hope or its implications for politics.[21] There is not even an entry for "hope" in a respected Augustinian encyclopedia.[22] One commentator begins his "history of hope" with Aquinas instead of Augustine,[23] and those who advance an Augustinian account of hope rarely cite the Bishop of Hippo, relying as much on Barth, Marcel, and Moltmann as Augustine himself.[24]

Meanwhile, many of Augustine's defenders appropriate his pessimism to chasten political hope and emphasize the limits of politics. Reinhold Niebuhr draws on Augustine to highlight the realities of evil and resist utopian forms of political idealism.[25] Herbert Deane describes Augustine's "grim" pessimism as his most enduring contribution to political theory,[26] and Judith Shklar praises Augustine as one of the intellectual "giants" who gave "injustice its due."[27] More recently, Jean Bethke Elshtain, Patrick Deneen, and William Galston have cited Augustinian authority to emphasize the limits of politics over its possibilities, while Peter Iver Kaufman has defended "a politically pessimistic Augustine" against more hopeful alternatives.[28]

While realists parlay Augustine's pessimism to chasten political hope, communitarians summon Augustine to advance an even more radical critique of contemporary politics. Alasdair MacIntyre draws on an Augustinian strand of Thomism to indict contemporary liberalism, arguing that the "Augustinian alternative" eclipses liberal accounts of justice.[29] John Milbank appropriates Augustine's notion of the "two cities" to impugn secularism's "ontology of violence" and encourage Christians to retreat from the diseased body politic into the purifying body of Christ.[30] And Stanley Hauerwas recruits the bishop to cast the church as the "only true political society," a "contrast" society that exposes secular politics as dominating and destructive.[31] Rather than engaging fully in practical politics, Hauerwas counsels Christians to first "be the church," assuming a status as "resident aliens" as they sojourn toward their home in heaven.[32] In the hands of defenders as well as detractors, Augustine is presented as a pessimist about this-worldly politics.

I. Why Pessimism?

Accounts of Augustine's pessimism are often fueled by the assumption that, for Augustine, earthly goods, and hence political goods, have little or no value. A central aim of this book is to challenge this assumption about the value of political goods and the pessimism it underwrites. Advancing this alternative account requires analyzing subtler assumptions that inform the prevailing view. Recognizing various methodological temptations can alert us to the interpretative ruts that can seduce all of us who read Augustine in the wake of this tradition.

Historical Context

The historical context of Augustine's most influential political interpreters may help to explain their emphasis on his pessimism. Following World Wars I and II, the Holocaust, and the Gulag, in the midst of what Isaiah Berlin describes as the "most terrible century in Western history," it is no surprise that twentieth-century political theorists find Augustine most useful for thinking about sin, evil, and domination.[33]

John Rawls, who finished his senior thesis in December 1942—just months before he enlisted as a soldier in World War II—makes use of Augustine to highlight the evils of the age. Noting that Augustine is "always acute in his analysis of pride," Rawls draws on Augustinian insights to diagnose the "egotism" of Nazism, which he describes as "pride in its most demonic form."[34]

Augustinian interpreters with Jewish and European roots were particularly influenced by the horrors of concentration camps, genocide, and war. As a Jewish scholar who escaped Nazi Germany while threatened with arrest, Arendt was deeply affected by both world wars and the Holocaust,[35] as was Judith Shklar, a refugee of the Holocaust.[36] Given their personal experiences and intellectual context, it is easy to see why Arendt and Shklar draw on Augustinian ideas to highlight the depth of evil and injustice.[37] As Arendt wrote in 1954, Augustine is "the one great thinker who lived in a period in which, in some respects, resembled our own more than any other in recorded history, and who in addition wrote under the full impact of a catastrophic end which perhaps resembles the end to which we have come."[38]

A year earlier in 1953, Reinhold Niebuhr published his famous essay "Augustine's Political Realism," which is still one of the most influential sources for understanding Augustine's political theory.[39] Describing Augustine as "the first great 'realist' in Western history," Niebuhr argues that Augustine's vision of the earthly city and "biblical" view of "human selfhood" highlight the distorting influence of "pride" and the "social factions, tensions, and competitions which we know to be well-nigh universal on every level of community."[40] Ultimately, Niebuhr concludes that "[a] generation which finds its communities imperiled and in decay . . . might well take counsel of Augustine in solving its perplexities."[41]

The influence of historical context is even more explicit in Herbert Deane's *The Political and Social Ideas of St. Augustine*, published in 1963, which is perhaps the most influential interpretation of Augustine within political theory.[42] "In our own century," Deane writes, "when, once more, men have been

compelled to recognize the almost incredible brutalities of which human beings are capable, especially when they struggle for political power and military domination, it is no accident that Augustinian pessimism and realism
have enjoyed a considerable revival among both theologians and secular
thinkers."[43] For Deane, an awareness of how "pride" and the "more obvious
vices of avarice, lust for domination, and hatred, can lead men and nations to
perpetrate enormous crimes" explains "why pessimistic analysts of human
nature and of society and politics have received increasing attention during
the last two decades, and why Augustine's views are entitled to our serious
consideration."[44]

Selective Interpretations

This historical context informed interpreters' selective focus on passages that
emphasize evil, sin, and self-interest. In Augustine's case, textual selectivity is
understandable, even inevitable.[45] After all, Augustine composed 113 books,
hundreds of letters, and thousands of sermons, leaving a total of five million
words that, as one scholar calculated, equals "a three-hundred page printed
book every year for almost forty years."[46] Even Augustine's first biographer,
Possidius, notes his friend's prodigious output: "As for all that he dictated and
published, and all the debates in the cathedral that were taken down and revised . . . there are so many that there is hardly a student who has been able to
read and get acquainted with them all."[47] Almost two hundred years later,
Isidore of Seville insisted that anyone claiming to have read all of Augustine's
works was lying.[48]

Given the volume of Augustine's corpus, political theorists tend to focus
on City of God, which many assume, with Arendt, to be Augustine's "only political treatise."[49] Yet City of God is almost 1,200 pages, and it is not simply
"political." The vast majority of Augustine's magnum opus is focused on historical and theological topics that may seem irrelevant to modern political
interpreters. As a result, political theorists typically focus on selected passages,
what Jean Bethke Elshtain describes as "Augustine Lite."[50] Most concentrate
on Book 19, the "locus classicus of political Augustinianism."[51] Here, Augustine describes the "great evils" of the earthly city, laments the realities of war
and limits of peace, and offers his alternative definition of a commonwealth.[52]
Book 19 provides a useful "microcosm of Augustine's social thought,"[53] and, at
just over fifty pages, it is ideal reading for an introductory course in political
theory.[54] While Book 19 includes some of Augustine's most constructive

theorizing about politics, however, a narrow focus on the darker and more cautionary passages can license an exaggerated emphasis on Augustine's pessimism and ignore how his more theological texts shape, qualify, and amplify his political ideas.[55] This neglect is particularly relevant for his account of hope, which is scattered throughout sermons, commentaries, and treatises rarely read or analyzed in political theory. If interpreters focus on Book 19 of *City of God* and neglect these more theological texts, it is easy to see why they think Augustine is a pessimist.

Recently, a handful of scholars in theology and religious studies have highlighted the moral and political importance of Augustine's sermons and letters, uncovering a more complex, subtle, and interesting portrait than the one associated with more systematic treatises.[56] The sermons and letters provide a glimpse of the bishop addressing diverse audiences with different modes of argument and authority, applying his ideas discriminately to concrete cases, and advising audiences in ways that are attuned to their specific roles, needs, and circumstances.[57] These texts reveal how Augustine's historical, social, and theological contexts shape his moral and political vision and illuminate the conceptual, interpretative, and political resources that more holistic readings make available, particularly for his account of hope.

Disciplinary Specialization

Unfortunately, recent work on Augustine's sermons, letters, and theological treatises by scholars in theology and religious studies has not yet been taken up in political theory, which points to another feature of modern academic life that feeds selective interpretations: disciplinary specialization. Many political theorists look only to Book 19 because they assume that Augustine's "political theory" can be isolated from his larger theological purposes and that any consideration of his theology belongs properly to the disciplines of theology and religious studies rather than political science.[58] But Augustine lived in an age before academic specialization. His views on politics cannot be easily excised from his reflections on religion, ethics, and theology. Contemporary accounts that ignore this intersection tend to furnish distorted and decontextualized interpretations that obscure how Augustine's more "theological" texts inform his "political" thought.[59]

Disciplinary boundaries also lead political theorists to overlook relevant secondary scholarship. Over the last twenty years, scholars in theology and religious studies have inaugurated a renaissance in Augustinian studies, producing a spate of new books analyzing Augustine's moral and political thought. But the Augustinian moment is only beginning in political theory. With some notable exceptions,[60] there have been few book-length treatments of Augustine within political theory in the last three decades. Recommended reading lists at top PhD programs and introductory chapters in textbooks still draw heavily from the work of Niebuhr and Deane in the 1950s and 1960s, leaving many interpretations outdated and devoid of recent contributions from other disciplines.[61] As a result, pessimistic interpretations continue to dominate the field.

A Lutheran Lens

Finally, and perhaps most subtly, most political theorists tend to interpret Augustine directly or indirectly through a Lutheran lens. Luther drew heavily upon Augustine's anti-Pelagian writings regarding the depth of human sin and necessity of God's grace, central themes in the Reformer's critique of works-righteousness and doctrine of salvation by grace alone.[62] Because of Luther's extensive influence, this selective interpretation informed many accounts of Augustine in the early modern period and beyond, especially within the Protestant tradition. Whether or not these later interpretations accurately reflect Luther's, they had the effect of hardening a picture of Augustine as a pessimist about human sin, agency, and politics.[63]

Scholars have traced the influence of this "lopsided Augustinianism"[64] or "hyper-Augustinianism"[65] in modern theology, philosophy, and political thought, highlighting how a Lutheran skepticism toward pagan virtue and emphasis on human depravity informed later thinkers. The legacy of "hyper-Augustinianism" also extends into contemporary political theory. It is striking to consider how many of Augustine's most influential political interpreters are shaped by Lutheran sources.[66]

Arendt wrote her dissertation on Augustine in Germany in the early twentieth century when Lutheran influences were pervasive. While she mentions Luther only in passing in her dissertation, she makes the connection more explicit in a short essay on the 1,500th anniversary of Augustine's death in 1930, a year after she submitted her dissertation.[67] There, she reclaims Augustine for a Protestant tradition in which he remains "largely forgotten."[68] Noting how Luther "appealed to Augustine's authority and felt himself to be following in Augustine's footsteps," Arendt highlights how Luther's Augustinianism shaped Protestantism.[69]

Nussbaum's Lutheran reading of Augustine emerges more indirectly through the secondary sources she cites. In addition to relying on Arendt, Nussbaum derives several criticisms from Nietzsche's scathing attack on Christianity, which, notably, targeted a Lutheran strand of Augustinian Christianity that emphasized human sin and divine grace.[70] Nietzsche repeatedly associates Augustine with Luther and describes Augustine as the archetype of a *"vulgarized* Platonism" that devalues the world in pursuit of otherworldly aims.[71] In similar fashion, Nussbaum cites Nietzsche's critique of Platonism just before criticizing Augustine's form of Christian Platonism.[72] Elsewhere, she quotes Nietzsche to argue that an Augustinian "[l]onging for the other world puts people to sleep in this world."[73] Nussbaum's Augustine is refracted through Nietzsche's Lutheran lens.

Niebuhr inherits his Lutheran commitments more directly. He grew up in the German Evangelical Synod of North America, a Christian denomination that combined Lutheran and Reformed theology.[74] Raised by a father who was a prominent Synod pastor and a mother who was the daughter of a Synod missionary, Niebuhr attended a Synod elementary school and a Synod boarding school for part of high school, graduated from the denomination's seminary, and later served as the pastor of Synod congregations.[75] Once he began teaching at Union Theological Seminary in 1928, Luther's influence became more pronounced in his theological vision and textual interpretation, including of Augustine.[76] Niebuhr was especially drawn to Lutheran understandings of sin and grace but not the Reformer's approach to politics.[77] In several works, he notes similarities between Augustine's and Luther's Christian realism, observing that both were "too consistent to give a true picture of either human nature or the human community" and thus generated a sense of "defeatism" and "despair" about the world.[78] Niebuhr criticizes Augustine and Luther for their overemphasis on sin and dualistic accounts of love, which, in Augustine's case, Niebuhr attributes to Neoplatonic influences.[79] Notably, Niebuhr's critique of Augustine's Neoplatonism is influenced heavily by Anders Nygren, a Lutheran theologian and bishop whose influential book *Agape and Eros* targets Augustine's account of love.[80] Both Niebuhr's religious background and theological sources shaped his desire to resist what Robin Lovin describes as the "consistent pessimism of Augustinian-Lutheran theology."[81]

While John Rawls grew up in the Episcopal Church and even considered attending seminary,[82] his account of Augustine is shaped significantly by Lutheran sources.[83] Among the "chief sources" of his senior thesis, Rawls lists Luther just under the Bible, followed by Emil Brunner, a neoorthodox

Reformed theologian with strong Lutheran tendencies; the philosopher Philip Leon; Niebuhr; and Nygren.[84] It is no surprise that Rawls emphasizes the aspects of Augustine most attractive to Lutherans, including a conception of sin as a form of "pride," a "more pessimistic view of human nature," an anti-Pelagian emphasis on grace, and a conception of justification by faith alone.[85] Rawls's Lutheran inheritance informs also his criticisms of Augustine, which draw heavily on the work of Brunner, the theologian he "learned the most from," and Nygren's *Agape and Eros*, to which is he "very much indebted."[86]

Similarly, Herbert Deane compares Augustine's "somber and pessimistic portrait" of "fallen man" to the "views of human nature expressed by his followers at the time of the Reformation, Luther and Calvin, and by Machiavelli and Hobbes."[87] Deane emphasizes how Luther and other modern thinkers revived an Augustinian "tradition of political realism" that attends to the "darker aspects of political life."[88] For Deane, the imprint is unmistakable: "The Lutheran and Calvinist views of human nature and of political authority carry clear marks of their Augustinian origin."[89] Given Deane's influence in contemporary political theory, his Luther-informed view of Augustine's "grim realism" has become a filter through which much of Augustine's thought is read.[90]

If this Lutheran reading affects the content of prevailing interpretations, it may also shape their underlying interpretative method.[91] A Lutheran view of justification by faith alone prioritizes the intellectual content of belief: having faith becomes less about practicing certain liturgies and rituals and more about possessing the proper set of beliefs about God, Christ, and salvation. Thus, when Luther and his followers draw on Augustine to support their Protestant view, they focus primarily on Augustine's theological doctrines and utterances and downplay his implicit rhetorical and philosophical practices, which often owe as much to pagan philosophers as to Christian theologians. This Lutheran emphasis on orthodoxy (right belief) rather than orthopraxy (right practice) may inform methods of textual interpretation. Eschewing the idea that ordinary believers need priests to interpret scripture authoritatively, many Protestant Reformers held that the truths of sacred texts are accessible to any person who can read or hear them. In some cases, this view may fuel a methodological assumption that texts have a literal meaning that can be discerned through a direct and straightforward reading, which can cause a text's rhetorical, pedagogical, or contextual features to fall out of view.

This way of reading is especially problematic for understanding Augustine's "pessimistic" passages, which, I will argue in chapters 6 and 7, should not be taken simply as literal utterances of Augustine's doctrinal views but as rhetorical exercises intended to shape the character of his audiences. There, I attribute the tendency to reduce texts to their propositional content primarily to dominant modes of interpretation in modern philosophy, but a Lutheran framework of interpretation may reinforce this approach, particularly when combined with early modern skepticism toward rhetoric and an Enlightenment focus on the propositional content of authors' intended meanings.[92]

II. Toward an Augustinian Account of Hope

In what follows, I develop an alternative interpretation that unsettles these common ways of reading—or misreading—Augustine as a pessimist. Situating Augustine's thought within his historical, rhetorical, and religious contexts and gleaning insights from treatises, sermons, and letters often neglected in political theory, I recover Augustine's conception of hope as a virtue that finds a way between vices of presumption and despair and trouble the simplistic dichotomy between optimism and pessimism often imposed on his thought. By offering a nuanced account of this virtue, I seek to make a novel contribution to Augustinian studies while illuminating how interdisciplinary engagement across the humanities can inform our understanding of Augustine. In particular, I lift new research from religious studies, theology, philosophy, rhetoric, and classics into political theory to highlight its relevance for contemporary politics.[93] I also amplify and extend these interpretations in new and politically relevant ways by integrating resources from political theory to advance original accounts of Augustinian concepts that have long been misconstrued, obscured, or ignored.

This interdisciplinary integration offers several advantages. First, it furnishes a more faithful and holistic account of Augustine's political thought, which he never considered to be separate from his reflections on religion, ethics, and theology. A central claim of this book is that decontextualized interpretations are partly responsible for the distorted portraits that prevail in political theory. Situating Augustine within his historical, political, rhetorical, and religious contexts chastens temptations toward reductionism.[94]

Second, careful attention to Augustine's more theological texts and contexts reveals how he develops, refines, and extends key political concepts in texts rarely read in political theory. Expanding the range of relevant texts is especially important for recovering Augustine's account of hope, which is developed in less familiar sermons, letters, and treatises. An interdisciplinary engagement with these texts can both broaden our understanding of Augustinian hope and uncover resources that can enrich the theory and practice of political hope in our time.

Finally, attending to Augustine's religious commitments can enable critical engagement with Augustinians on their own terms. In particular, adducing distinctively Augustinian reasons for citizens to engage in public life and seek common objects of hope with diverse citizens can deflate critiques from communitarians such as Milbank and Hauerwas who claim Augustinian authority to indict contemporary democracy. Whether intentionally or not, these influential thinkers may have fueled much of the withdrawal and resentment common among some religious citizens with Augustinian sympathies.[95] An alternative interpretation can show these citizens that they need not forfeit their religious commitments to participate in public life. Rather, engagement in public life can provide opportunities for citizens to develop and exercise virtues in ways that can express and even deepen their faith.[96]

From the opposite angle, attending carefully to Augustine's moral and theological commitments can help secular political theorists see that Augustinianism need not license otherworldly escape or political passivity. A rich engagement with Augustine's political thought can instead highlight important points of convergence among diverse scholars and citizens, both religious and secular. Such convergence is particularly important in a context where much of the resentment toward secular political theory has emerged from critics claiming Augustinian authority. An account that highlights sources of common ground has the potential to reduce resentment and unite citizens around common hopes.

Augustine's political thought, of course, does not map neatly onto contemporary categories.[97] Augustine was not a democrat, much less a liberal or radical one.[98] He never explicitly advocated a democratic regime, and as a citizen of the Roman Empire, he might have doubted that the large-scale transformation of political institutions was possible.[99] Although he had views on which kinds of laws and institutions were just or unjust and sometimes made efforts to change the laws or moderate their enforcement,[100] he focused his efforts more on transforming the character of leaders and citizens than on reforming the institutions of government.[101] He saw reordering the loves and hopes of citizens as fundamental for the work of forming and reforming institutions.[102]

Augustine also held beliefs and accepted practices that I find deeply disturbing. He held patriarchal views about women.[103] He defended the use of coercion to compel religious dissenters to return to orthodoxy as understood by the Catholic Church.[104] He not only accepted the institution of slavery but also used it as a metaphor to describe human beings' relation to God.[105] In recent and ongoing work, scholars are interrogating, contextualizing, and evaluating Augustine's positions and legacy on these and related issues.[106] This important work will generate critical debates about how we understand Augustine in his historical context and how contemporary thinkers might appropriate, criticize, or resist his ideas in our modern context. As this work continues to emerge, it will be vital to consider how it shapes our understanding of Augustine's political thought and its relevance for contemporary politics.

This book is concerned with somewhat different problems in the ideological appropriation of Augustine, problems that have less to do with his complicity in structural injustice than with his alleged pessimism regarding politics. "Augustinian pessimism" is a major ideological option in recent political thought. Its defenders have largely neglected the issue of complicity, but many of them have projected their own assumptions and concerns onto his writings anachronistically and then drawn dubious conclusions about the use of force and the limits of politics.[107] Meanwhile, assuming that the pessimists have Augustine right, his detractors have, understandably, dismissed him as a resource for contemporary political theory. I claim that Augustine did not actually encourage political pessimism or passivity. In his work as bishop, theologian, and citizen, he advocated and modeled engagement in public life, frequently collaborating with other citizens, pastors, and political leaders to reduce poverty, fight injustice, and resist domination by wealthy and powerful elites.[108] Of course, his efforts to preserve freedom, equality, and community fall short of contemporary civic ideals and modern assumptions about the possibility of systematic change. But understanding his political ideas and example in his historical context makes it harder for contemporary interpreters to parlay his "pessimism" in ours. Attending to some of the conceptual and contextual complexities of Augustine's political thought illuminates a more hopeful, this-worldly Augustine who encourages diverse citizens to share common objects of hope, even as they cast their ultimate hopes on different horizons.

To advance this account, part I, "The Virtue of Hope," specifies Augustine's understanding of hope's proper objects and grounds. In his most systematic discussion in the *Enchiridion*, a "handbook" on faith, hope, and love, Augustine examines the relations among these concepts before offering a more detailed exposition of each.[109] In chapter 1, I follow his lead, reconstructing his grammar of hope by considering its relations to faith and love. By explicating Augustine's implicit distinctions and supplementing the *Enchiridion*'s analysis with insights from sermons and commentaries, I show how faith supplies hope with grounds for belief, while love confers the motivating power that propels hope's pursuit. Against critics who reduce hope to either faith or love, I highlight why hope remains conceptually distinct and functionally necessary: hope supplements faith with motivation and provides love with the resolve needed to endure time's difficulties and delays.

Chapters 2 and 3 consider the relationship between hope and love to illuminate the proper objects of hope and challenge political interpreters who dismiss Augustinian hope as otherworldly. Since many of these criticisms emerge from anxieties about Augustine's "order of love," chapter 2 draws on research in theology and religious studies to offer a more subtle interpretation that encourages love for temporal goods as long as it is "rightly ordered." Chapter 3 applies this order of love to reconstruct Augustine's implicit "order of hope." Gleaning insights from neglected texts, I argue that Augustine allows a robust hope for temporal goods as long as it is rightly ordered and avoids opposing forms of disorder—the vices of presumption and despair. Since the order of hope has gone unnoticed by contemporary interpreters, this account seeks to make a novel contribution to Augustinian studies while providing a useful way to conceptualize the relationship between proximate and ultimate objects of hope. I also highlight the moral, spiritual, and social practices that Augustine deems necessary to cultivate this virtue and resist its corresponding vices.

If chapters 2 and 3 analyze hope's objects, the next two chapters consider its grounds. For Augustine, as for Paul, faith supplies the "substance of things hoped for, the conviction of things that are not seen."[110] In chapter 4, I survey various meanings of faith in Augustine's works and examine his account of reason and authority as the dual bases of faith. Drawing on contemporary epistemology and philosophy of religion, I show that Augustine's reasoning is often characterized by a "default and challenge" structure that allows belief or trust in an authority unless or until there are sufficient reasons to abandon or adapt it. This underappreciated aspect of Augustine's account provides a helpful conceptual framework for understanding the grounds of faith and, by extension, the grounds of hope, which are the subject of chapter 5. There, I draw on Augustine's account of faith to reconstruct the grounds of hope and show how he affirms the legitimacy of hoping in both God and neighbor to achieve future goods. For Augustine, hope typically involves hoping *in* another to attain what we hope *for*.[111]

Part II, "The Rhetoric of Hope," extends this analysis by elevating an undervalued aspect of Augustine's life and work: his training as a rhetorician.

Situating his work within an ancient tradition of philosophy as a "way of life,"[112] chapter 6 illuminates how he employs rhetoric both to "instruct" and "encourage" audiences, an aspect of his texts often missed by political interpreters. To illustrate, I focus on the pedagogical purposes of Augustine's most rhetorical texts, his sermons to the people. Applying research in classics, theology, philosophy, rhetoric, and religious studies to his homilies on hope, I explore how his sermons make moral and civic education accessible to those who had been denied access to elite institutions in the Roman Empire. Situating Augustine's sermons within his rhetorical, political, and pedagogical contexts not only deflates concerns about his otherworldly rhetoric but also reveals his homilies as strikingly egalitarian pedagogies of hope.

Lest interpreters assume that Augustine confines his use of rhetoric to his sermons, chapter 7 shows how he employs similar pedagogical strategies in his most overtly political work, City of God. Taking up a passage from Book 22 frequently cited as evidence of Augustine's pessimism, I argue that this passage should instead be interpreted as a moral and spiritual exercise of hope, one that uses intentional rhetoric and a default and challenge structure of reasoning to help readers resist presumption and despair. Reading Augustine rhetorically affords a more nuanced vision of the City of God, including its infamous account of evil in Book 19.

Part III, "The Politics of Hope," considers whether and how distinctly political goods can be proper objects of Augustinian hope. Against those who assume that hope for the heavenly city is otherworldly and antipolitical, chapter 8 shows how Augustine encourages diverse citizens to share common objects of hope in the "secular age." Against Augustinian realists who defer the eschaton to an indefinite future and Augustinian communitarians who confine the heavenly city to the institutional church, I argue that Augustine counsels diverse citizens to seek the shared goods of the commonwealth, especially civic peace. I conclude by examining how Augustine's emphasis on common objects of hope offers resources for political deliberation in the face of disagreement and alerts citizens to the temptations that accompany the pursuit of common goods.

Chapter 9 explores how Augustine exemplifies political hope in his own life. Drawing on his correspondence with Roman officials, Christian bishops, and personal acquaintances, I argue that Augustine's letters reveal a bishop committed to active citizenship in the Roman Empire, one who often uses his persuasive skills, political influence, and ecclesial connections to advise political leaders and advocate on behalf of society's most vulnerable people, including those who were poor, imprisoned, and enslaved. Considering Augustine's example of citizenship casts new light on his political thought and challenges those who summon his authority to recommend worldly withdrawal or ecclesial isolationism.

Finally, chapter 10 considers whether an Augustinian virtue of hope can also be cultivated by non-Christian citizens or whether a purely civic virtue is doomed to remain at best a "splendid vice." Analyzing Augustine's vexed discussion of "pagan virtue,"[113] I explore multiple ways of interpreting key texts and propose a new interpretation that recognizes the possibility of genuine civic virtues in non-Christians. Attending to Augustine's concerns about pride and domination, I argue that genuine civic virtue depends on the interconnected virtues of piety and humility, both of which chasten the vices of presumption and despair. Recovering these interconnected virtues moves us beyond entrenched disputes about the splendid vices and highlights how piety and humility can help both Christians and non-Christians develop the virtue of hope.

Throughout the book, I mostly attempt to interpret and analyze Augustine's commitments in ways he could acknowledge and accept as his own.[114] Occasionally, I also interpret Augustine's commitments in relation to views and distinctions that he could not have used or imagined in his own time—for example, when drawing on contemporary epistemology and philosophy of religion to make explicit his "default and challenge" structure of reasoning in chapter 4 or when applying Cass Sunstein's idea of "incompletely theorized agreement" to illuminate his view of the commonwealth in chapter 8. These latter interpretations still aim to describe the conceptual content of Augustine's commitments but in ways that can be understood and evaluated by contemporary audiences.[115]

While the primary aim of this book is to offer a more contextualized interpretation of Augustine's thought on its own terms to resist mischaracterizations of his "pessimism," this detailed historical work does not thereby reduce Augustine to a historical artifact. Instead, it makes his thought *more* relevant to contemporary politics and political theory than accounts that strip him from his contexts.[116] In the conclusion, I gesture toward several ways the alternative account of Augustine offered here might inform efforts to nurture a commonwealth of hope in our own time.

While Augustine's account of hope offers useful conceptual and normative resources for contemporary politics, he also gives us plenty to dispute, resist, and reject. My aim is neither to lionize the saint nor sanitize the sinner.

Fortunately, Augustine recognizes that fidelity does not require uncritical allegiance: "I would not want anyone to embrace all my views in order to be my follower, but only those points on which he sees that I am not mistaken."[117] Throughout his vast corpus, Augustine consistently invites conversation and correction,[118] and he celebrates the fact that there is more than one valid way to interpret texts: "I would hope to have written in such a way that if anyone else had in the light of truth seen some other valid meaning, that too should not be excluded, but present itself as a possible way of understanding in what I had said."[119] As we explore the neglected patterns of Augustine's mosaic, may we remain attentive to that Augustinian hope.

PART I

The Virtue of Hope

1

A Conceptual Grammar

ON FAITH, HOPE, AND LOVE

[L]ove cannot exist without hope nor hope without love, nor can either
exist without faith.

—AUGUSTINE, *ENCHIRIDION*, 2.8

AROUND 420 CE, Laurentius, the brother of a Catholic imperial official, wrote
to Augustine requesting an *enchiridion*—a "handbook"—on the Christian
faith.[1] Laurentius solicited Augustine's guidance on a host of theological questions: "[W]hat we should seek above all, what we should chiefly avoid because
of the various heresies there are, to what extent reason comes to the support
of religion, what lies outside the scope of reason and belongs to faith alone,
what should be held first and last, what the whole body of doctrine amounts
to, and what is a sure and suitable foundation of Catholic faith."[2] In the
Enchiridion, sometimes called *On Faith, Hope, and Charity*,[3] Augustine offers
a straightforward response: "Without a doubt you will know all these things
for which you are looking if you take care to know what should be believed,
hoped for, and loved. These are the most important things, or rather the only
things, that are to be followed in religion."[4]

The *Enchiridion* offers a helpful starting point for our inquiry. In this short
handbook, Augustine offers his most systematic and influential account of
hope, explaining the relations among faith, hope, and love and devoting a section to the proper objects of hope.[5] Thomas Aquinas draws on the *Enchiridion*
to develop his account of hope as a virtue,[6] while contemporary interpreters
invoke it to inform theirs.[7] Strikingly, critics cite the same text to *deny* that

hope is a virtue.[8] Careful attention to the *Enchiridion*, then, can illuminate Augustine's understanding of hope while offering critical purchase on important interpretative disputes.

Political interpreters interested in Augustine's account of hope may find his brief treatment disappointing. Of the articles enumerated by the editors, Augustine devotes 105 primarily to faith but only five to charity and three to hope, leading one commentator to describe hope as the "most elusive" of the three.[9] Since the *Enchiridion* can only take us so far, we must also extend the range of relevant texts to discover how Augustine understands the concept of hope. As he suggests elsewhere, "[A] considerable part of discovery is to know what you are looking for."[10]

Most of Augustine's discussions of hope are deposited throughout theological treatises, sermons, and letters often overlooked in political theory. Yet, even when we examine these texts, we encounter interpretative difficulties. Augustine does not offer a comprehensive discussion of hope in any one text, nor does he give an explicit definition. His rhetorical and pedagogical purposes make conceptual reconstruction difficult. As James O'Donnell argues, Augustine is more like a "jazz improvisationalist" than an analytic philosopher: in his preaching and prose, he responds to current events as they are happening, writing in multiple genres for multiple audiences, all while adapting to his audience's mood, "repeating old themes but never in the same way."[11] Augustine's "jazzy style" means that he offers few precise formulations or definitions.[12] Some scholars even suggest he is "intentionally ambiguous and inconsistent in his use of terminology" to emphasize the limits of language, reveal new interpretative horizons, and prevent concepts from being reified through overuse.[13] Whether intentional or not, Augustine's dynamic language creates difficulties for interpreters seeking to understand the structure, function, and meaning of a concept like hope. The Bishop of Hippo cares more about teaching his audiences how to hope than explaining its conceptual structure.

To reconstruct his account, I will follow Augustine where his language leads, noting distinctions, variations, and applications that give content to his conception. Often, this effort requires integrating other texts to illuminate an interpretative puzzle or making explicit what Augustine only leaves implicit or assumes his audiences will know. Lest critics worry that such explication is unfaithful to Augustine, the bishop himself recommends this procedure: "Any interpretation of an obscure passage should . . . be confirmed by the testimony of manifest facts or by other passages where the meaning is not in the least open to doubt. In this way we shall, by the investigation of several views, either arrive at the meaning intended by whoever wrote the passage, or, failing this, the examination of a profoundly obscure passage will lead to the statement of a number of other truths."[14] My hope is that assembling relevant views from Augustine will illuminate the meanings of obscure passages and potentially lead to the statement of other truths.

Fortunately, Augustine provides useful conceptual content in his discussions of faith, hope, and love. Chapters 2–5 explore the objects of these virtues in more detail. This chapter considers Augustine's basic conceptual grammar. Part I focuses on faith and hope while part II analyzes hope's relation to love. Attending to distinctions between these concepts provides critical leverage on the structure and function of Augustinian hope while challenging interpreters who assume that hope can be reduced to either faith or love. This account will offer a useful framework for analyzing Augustine's account of virtue, rhetoric, and politics in the remainder of this book.

I. Faith and Hope

In the *Enchiridion*, Augustine identifies "rational distinctions" between faith (*fides*), hope (*spes*), and love (*caritas, amor, dilectio*) by appealing to biblical interpretation and practicing a kind of premodern ordinary language analysis.[15] In addition to citing meanings implied by Paul, Augustine points to what is "rightly said" in the larger public culture and considers whether it would "be right to criticize" particular expressions as "inconsistent" with the proper use of those terms.[16] Augustine invokes linguistic practices of holding speakers responsible for a particular use of a word or concept and then determines proper use by acknowledging what is socially recognized as a legitimate meaning of a term. To highlight the distinction between hope and fear, for example, he contrasts Lucan's statement, "Give hope to the fearful," with one from Virgil, who, "though a better poet, speaks inaccurately when he says, 'Had I been able to hope for this one sorrow.'"[17] According to Augustine, Virgil wrongly implies that one can hope for an object that causes fear or sorrow. This is why "teachers of grammar use his line as an example to illustrate the improper use of words and comment that 'he said 'hope' instead of 'fear.'"[18] Augustine's use of ordinary language analysis here to develop a conceptual grammar prefigures the work of Ludwig Wittgenstein.[19]

For our purposes, it is notable that Augustine bases his account of proper use not only on the words of religious authorities but on examples from "pagan" writers and the linguistic practices shared by Christians and pagans alike. This recognition will be significant when we examine the controversial debate about "pagan virtue" in chapter 10 and consider how Augustine uses the same procedure to define piety.[20] For now, this analysis illuminates Augustine's method of differentiating hope from faith and love.

Augustine identifies several features of hope. First, hope requires *belief* or *trust* in the existence or possibility of an object: "What is there that we can hope for without believing in it?"[21] Hope, in other words, presupposes epistemic grounds that an object can be realized or attained: an object must be believed or perceived to be possible in order to be an object of hope. For Augustine, faith (*fides*) supplies the "evidence" that justifies hope in the "unseen." Augustine follows Hebrews 11:1, which defines faith as "the substance of things hoped for, the conviction of things not seen."[22] Faith supplies the ground of hope, a belief or trust in the possibility of its object.

Possibility, however, does not entail full presence or possession. Augustine quotes Romans 8:24–25, a passage he cites some 130 times: "Now hope that is seen is not hope. For who hopes for what is seen? But if we hope for what we do not see, we wait for it with patience."[23] If we see or possess what we hope for, we can no longer be said to "hope" for it. Rather, we find joy or rest in it. Both hope and faith, then, share a common belief in the "unseen," objects that are possible but not fully present or possessed.[24]

Augustine recognizes that we might "see" some goods partially but not fully. He frequently quotes 1 Corinthians 13:12: "Now we see through a glass, darkly; but then face to face."[25] Later, I will argue that Augustine's participationist ontology and inaugurated eschatology imply that human beings may be able to *partially realize* some objects of eternal hope here and now, but only in an imperfect way. Because these hopes are not fully realized, their presence or possession still remains somewhat uncertain and "unseen."

That hope implies uncertainty or incompleteness helps to distinguish Augustinian hope from a conception popular in contemporary culture. Today, many people equate hope with blind or shallow optimism, a sunny disposition or confident expectation that some good will certainly come about or that a particular object will certainly be realized.[26] This is not how Augustine understands hope. Rather, he conceives hope's objects as possible but uncertain: if objects are not "unseen," they are no longer proper objects of hope. Yet Augustine recognizes that hope's objects must not be so uncertain that they are *impossible*, for then we could not properly be said to hope at all.[27] Hope's dependence on faith for belief in an object's possibility thus distinguishes hope from mere wishing, which could be directed toward objects that are desirable but impossible. Faith and hope are based on reasons to believe that a particular object is possible.

Despite this shared feature, Augustine insists on making "a rational distinction between faith and hope" and giving them "different names."[28] Three features distinguish hope from faith. First, while we can have faith "in past realities, in present ones, and in future ones," we can hope "only for things that are in the future."[29] Hope's objects, in other words, are characterized by futurity: while we can hold beliefs about past, present, and future objects, we can be said to hope only for what is absent and not yet attained.[30]

Second, while we can have faith in "things that concern us, and in things that concern others," we can hope only for objects that "concern the one who is said to have hope in them."[31] Unfortunately, Augustine does not develop this distinction in detail. At first glance, he seems to imply that hope is self-regarding in a way faith is not, suggesting that one can hope for objects only for oneself. But this does not fit with what Augustine says in the *Enchiridion*'s conclusion, where he says he is "hoping for good" from Laurentius,[32] or what he says elsewhere about the propriety of hoping for the good of others.[33]

Aquinas addresses this potential inconsistency when endorsing Augustine's claim that hope concerns the one who hopes.[34] Aquinas distinguishes love, which "denotes union between lover and beloved," from hope, which "denotes a movement or a stretching forth of the appetite towards an arduous good." Love entails *joining* with its object and thus includes a direct regard for the friend as an "other self," but since hope has not yet achieved such union with its object, it involves a *movement* toward the object, making it more immediately about the subject who is moved by hope. Yet Aquinas recognizes that "we can hope for something, through something else being presupposed, and in this way its object can be something pertaining to someone else."[35] Thus, "if we presuppose the union of love with another, a man can hope for and desire something for another man, as for himself." In other words, if we are in a relationship of love or friendship, we can rightly be said to hope for things for the friend because they are an "other self," which entails that our hopes for them are hopes that, through our union, also concern us.[36] This interpretation makes sense of Augustine's claim that hope's objects "concern" the subject while allowing that one may desire a common good or a good for a friend, as Augustine consistently does.

This interpretation also illuminates the third distinction between hope and faith in the *Enchiridion*: while faith regards both "good things and bad," hope "is only for good things," things we desire or love.[37] This feature of hope reflects Augustine's eudaimonism, his belief that all human action is motivated by some good that constitutes or conduces to one's happiness or flourishing (*eudaimonia*).[38] Those with faith can have beliefs about objects they do not desire as a good conducive to happiness or flourishing. Hope, by contrast, seeks an object as *desirable*, an object cast under a description as good, and thus involves an affective *movement* toward its object. Augustine develops this distinction through several examples. He notes, for instance, that people of faith "believe in the punishments of the wicked, but without hoping for them."[39] Faith, in other words, can include beliefs about objects that are good or evil, whereas the objects of hope can be perceived only as good, objects that can be loved, willed, or desired. The desirability of hope's objects—and the affective stretching of hope toward union with its objects—distinguishes hope from faith.

Desirability also distinguishes hope from fear. Whereas hope causes us to pursue objects believed to be good, fear causes us to "run away" from objects believed to be evil. Augustine cites James 2:19: "Even the demons believe—and shudder."[40] He suggests that demons have a kind of belief or faith that a just God exists and will give the rewards or punishments others are due, but demons "do not hope or love but rather fear that which we hope for and love, believing that it will come about."[41] Fear, like hope, implies belief that a certain object is possible or true, but unlike hope, fear assumes the object is one of aversion, not attraction.[42] Objects of hope, by contrast, are perceived to be desirable, prompting a motivation to pursue the object rather than withdraw from it.

Recognizing the desirability of hope's objects is important for contemporary debates about hope in politics. In *Democratic Faith*, Patrick Deneen appropriates an Augustinian virtue of hope to chasten democratic faith, arguing that Augustine's hope is "oriented ultimately toward the divine, not the secular."[43] Deneen supports his case by drawing on Augustine's analysis in the *Enchiridion*. Although he acknowledges Augustine's clear distinction between hope and faith, Deneen suggests the distinction is insignificant. Upon "close examination," he concludes, "hope seems to be a subset of faith": "Faith represents the belief in that which exists in any temporality and which has as its object things that may be either good or bad; hope represents only the belief of a happy outcome in the future. Hope is a form of faith, finally, but assumes only certain features of faith—those that are most positive and, because they are oriented toward the future, least provable from the standpoint of sensory evidence."[44] Deneen uses this equation of religious hope and faith to emphasize the importance of hope for the heavenly city rather than "hope within the earthly sphere."[45]

Given Deneen's appropriation, it is perhaps no surprise that contemporary critics worry that Augustinian hope remains too otherworldly, dismissing it as a more "positive" and less "provable" form of faith. This is the criticism that Vincent Lloyd levels against both Deneen and Augustine. Engaging Deneen's account, Lloyd cites the *Enchiridion*'s claim that "objects of hope can only be good" to deny that hope is a virtue and, in turn, to suggest that faith offers a more realistic political posture.[46] Because faith's objects can be "both good and evil," faith "grapples with the realities of the world without solace in any fantasy of escape," whereas hope's focus only on good things in the future denies the "tragedy," "failure," and "loss" that accompany moral and political life.[47] According to Lloyd, "The virtue of faith requires acknowledging the tragic. The rhetoric of hope persuades by eliding the tragic. The virtue of faith involves mourning, but the rhetoric of hope conjures an object which can never be lost."[48] For Lloyd, then, hope fuels a shallow and sentimental form of otherworldly enchantment that denies the truth of tragedy and the reality of this-worldly evil. "Hope is not a virtue," he concludes, "it is a rhetorical technique."[49] While Lloyd acknowledges that citizens need a virtue to help them persevere through adversity and conflict, he attributes this resolve to faith, not hope: "Whatever remainder of hope there is beyond its rhetorical nature is the virtue of faith, but often there is no remainder."[50]

Lloyd is right to recognize the dangers of any rhetoric of hope detached from reality, but his rejection of hope as a virtue is too quick, not least because his account—following Deneen's—rests on a mistaken interpretation of Augustine. In highlighting Augustine's claim that hope regards "good" things while faith regards both the good and bad, both Deneen and Lloyd seem to assume that objects of faith and hope are both objects of mere belief.[51] This assumption licenses Deneen's claim that hope is a "subset" of faith with objects that are "most positive" and "least provable,"[52] an interpretation Lloyd follows. On this reading, the only difference between the two is that faith allows beliefs about positive and negative realities that can be past, present, and future, while hope involves beliefs only about positive realities in the future. This interpretation enables Deneen to cast Augustinian hope as otherworldly and encourages Lloyd, in response, to reject any virtue of hope that ignores this-worldly tragedy, those "negative" realities that only faith recognizes. Both Deneen and Lloyd agree on their interpretation of Augustine; they simply take different normative stances toward it.

Their shared interpretation, however, skates over several crucial distinctions in Augustine's account.[53] First, consider the difference between hope and faith. While hope depends on a prior act of faith to supply epistemic evidence that an unseen object is possible, hope also involves an affective movement or desire toward that object in a way that faith does not. Augustine does not present the distinction in such explicit terms in the *Enchiridion*, but his contrast between hope and fear suggests the difference.[54] People who have faith can believe objects are either good or bad, but they will be motivated differently depending on what they believe. If they believe that an object is possible but good, they will have *hope*—they will be motivated by attraction. If they believe that an object is possible but bad, they will have *fear*—they will be motivated by aversion. This is why "demons believe—and shudder."

That faith can license either hope or fear suggests that faith, as a matter of mere belief, does not necessarily involve an affective movement or desire for an object in the way that hope does. In saying that hope regards "only good things," Augustine is not dismissing the reality of evil, the presence of tragedy, or the necessity of conflict, nor is he saying that hope is simply "more positive" than faith, as Deneen and Lloyd assume. Rather, he is suggesting that evil and tragedy are not objects one properly *hopes* for; they are objects one *fears*. Augustine's reference to "good things" simply refers to the formal specifications of hope's objects as desirable. As a concept that involves affection (*affectus*) or a movement of will (*motus, voluntas*), hope is focused on forming the proper motivational, affective, or volitional responses toward the objects believed through faith. By contrast, as a concept that focuses primarily on epistemic concerns, faith involves forming proper beliefs about certain objects rather than motivating one to pursue or avoid them. Because Deneen and Lloyd do not attend to the conceptual assumptions underwriting these distinctions, their reading reinforces the common assumption that Augustinian hope remains an otherworldly form of optimism, which leaves the virtue of hope vulnerable to attack. Augustine's distinction between hope and faith, however, suggests that two virtues serve different conceptual and psychological functions.

Several of Augustine's sermons make these functional distinctions more explicit. Rehearsing Hebrews 11:1's definition of faith as the "ground of things hoped for, the conviction of things which cannot be seen," Augustine argues in Sermon 359A that faith supplies hope with belief, while hope supplements faith with movement: "How after all, when you're walking somewhere, will you even move your feet, if you have no hope of ever getting there?"[55] As a potentially inert form of belief, faith must rely on hope to motivate the pursuit of difficult goods. Without hope, those who have the right belief would lack the constancy and resolve to sustain the "hard work of the journey."[56] "Take away hope," Augustine concludes, "and faith falters."[57]

Augustine develops this functional distinction between faith and hope further in a sermon on Psalm 31. Discussing an apparent dispute between Paul and James on justification by faith or works, Augustine argues that an act of faith must precede any good work since a person has no way to achieve good ends unless he understands what he is "aiming" at and "whether he is directing his efforts toward the right harbor, like a skilled pilot."[58] Since a belief or vision of an end is required before we can be motivated to hope or desire it, faith precedes hope. But, echoing James, Augustine argues that faith is "dead" if it does not "issue in right action," becoming a "barren, dried-up root that never produced fruit."[59] To avoid becoming "sterile," faith must work through hope and love: "If faith is devoid of the will to love, it will equally be devoid of good actions. But don't spend too much time thinking about the works that proceed from faith: add hope and the will to love to your faith, and you will have no need to ask yourself what kind of works you should perform. This deliberative love cannot remain idle."[60]

Augustine goes on to describe hope as the "middle term" between faith and love. Pointing to parallels between two passages in the Pauline epistles, Augustine grafts the triad of "faith, hope, and love" in 1 Corinthians 13:13 onto 1 Timothy 1:5's triad of "single-hearted charity, a good conscience, and unfeigned faith." Since the parallels between charity and faith are obvious, Augustine explains why hope correlates with "a good conscience": "[A]nyone who wants to have good hope needs to have a good conscience, and to have a good conscience we must both believe and work. So from this middle term, hope, we can work backward to the beginning, that is, to faith; and forward to the end, which is charity."[61]

That hope provides conceptual and functional connections between faith and love has an important implication: it entails that, by asking what we hope for, we can determine what we believe and what we love. As a "middle term," hope provides an entry into both faith and love and enables us to infer what one believes and loves from what one hopes.[62] In chapter 8, I argue that hope's function as a middle term offers valuable conceptual and discursive resources for an Augustinian account of politics. For now, I highlight the connection to call attention to a central feature of Augustinian ethics: the virtuous life is not simply a matter of having the right beliefs; it also requires having the right ends, motivations, and affections that in turn prompt right action and good work. This is an important reminder for contemporary moral and political theory, which tends to prioritize rational justifications and epistemic rationality over concerns about virtue, desire, and affection.[63] Simply having the right beliefs about democracy, justice, or liberty will not be sufficient to motivate citizens to pursue these goods in concrete circumstances, particularly when they encounter obstacles or opposition. Human beings need virtues, desires, and affections to motivate, guide, and sustain action in the face of difficulties and delays. Faith without hope and love is dead.[64]

II. Hope and Love

That hope supplements faith with a motivation, however, might threaten hope's reduction from a different direction. If hope's movement toward an object of faith requires an act of will, a kind of love or desire,[65] then hope depends motivationally on love: "[Y]ou can't even hope for anything you don't love. Love, you see, kindles hope, hope shines through love."[66] Love provides hope with its volitional force, motivating us to pursue specific objects as ends that we desire as good. Without love, there would be no desire to prompt hope. If faith without hope and love is dead, hope without love is stillborn.

Hope's dependence on love highlights a fundamental feature of Augustine's eudaimonism: love is the fundamental affection, the spring of all emotion and action. All movements, actions, and affections are motivated by a love or desire for a particular object judged or perceived to be good. Indeed, Augustine often describes loves as "weights" that move us toward or away from certain objects, as the weight of bodies moves them toward their resting place: "For the weight of bodies is, as it were, their love, whether they are carried downwards by gravity or upwards by their lightness. For the body is carried by its weight wherever it is carried, just as the soul is carried by its love."[67] In *City of God*, Augustine identifies the weight of love with acts of the will, arguing that all emotions or affections reflect some kind of love:

> The will is engaged in all of them; indeed, they are no more than acts of the will. For what is desire and joy but an act of the will in agreement with what we wish for? And what is fear and grief but an act of the will in disagreement with what we do not wish for? . . . [U]niversally, as a man's will is attracted or repelled by the various things which are pursued or avoided, so it changes and turns into emotions of one kind or another.[68]

Given the centrality of love, it is no surprise that Augustinian hope also relies on love's motivating force. As Augustine writes in the *Enchiridion*, hope "cannot exist without love."[69]

In the *Enchiridion*, however, love not only prompts hope but also perfects it. Citing Paul's claim that charity is the "greatest" of the virtues, Augustine argues that love is the ultimate determinant of one's character and the consummation of virtue:

> [T]he greater it is in a person, the better is that person in whom it is. For when we ask whether somebody is a good person, we are not asking what he believes or hopes for but what he loves. For one who rightly loves without doubt rightly believes and hopes, and one who does not love believes in vain, even if the things he believes are true; he hopes in vain, even if the things for which he hopes are those which, according to our teaching, belong to true happiness, unless he also believes and hopes that if he asks he may also be given the ability to love.[70]

Ultimately, the virtue of love provides hope with its final end and completion: "[F]aith is succeeded by sight and hope succeeded by the thing hoped for, charity succeeded by nothing at all."[71] When faith and hope achieve their objects, they dissolve; we have no reason to have faith or hope when the unpossessed is possessed, when the absent is present, when the unseen is seen. This is why Augustine believes there will be no faith and hope in heaven: we can have faith and hope only for objects that are uncertain and unseen.[72] But perfect love will abide:

> Over and above faith and hope there is a third virtue: charity. It is nobler than faith and hope. Faith is directed to things not seen as yet, and once they are seen it will be succeeded by vision. Hope is focused on things not yet possessed, and once the realization comes, hope will exist no more, because we shall not hope for the reality but embrace it. But charity can only go on increasing.[73]

Eternal love is hope's ultimate end, both its telos and terminus.

That hope depends on love for its prompting and perfection raises an important question: if love constitutes hope's perfection, should we simply reduce hope to a form of love? Augustine suggests not. Insisting that these virtues remain "somewhat different," he states that "love cannot exist without hope."[74] Unfortunately, in the *Enchiridion*, he does not say more about *how* love depends on hope, but examining what he says elsewhere can reveal what he means.

In Sermon 359A, Augustine distinguishes two kinds of love: "Love expressed in desire is one thing, love satisfied by sight another": "Your love, when you desire, is aimed at arriving; your love, when you see, at staying."[75] The first love is the love that prompts hope: it is the *desire* for goods that are future, possible, but not yet possessed, a desire that aims at "arriving" at the hoped-for good. The second love—the love satisfied by sight—characterizes perfect love: it is the *joy* that "rests" in or "enjoys" the goods possessed. The second love—the joy of resting in communion with the beloved—perfects or completes hope, while the first love—the desire for the beloved—prompts it.

Although Augustine believes the enjoyment of God in perfect love is the ultimate object of hope and the end of all virtues, he recognizes this perfect union is only possible in eternity when human beings will no longer be burdened by fallibility, finitude, and sin. Within time, human beings need the "in-between virtues," "the virtues proper to this present life,"[76] to direct them toward this ultimate good and to prompt and perfect their acts of union with God and neighbor.[77] Hope is one of these in-between virtues. Without hope, human beings would lack the motivation and resolve to patiently endure the difficulties and delays that accompany the pursuit of difficult future goods here and now.[78] They would fail to do the work necessary to achieve their objects. Indeed, for Augustine, the virtue of hope is necessary precisely because perfect love of God and neighbor is not possible in this life: "[I]n this condition, those very virtues than which nothing better or more advantageous is found in man clearly attest to his misery precisely by the great assistance that they give him in the midst of perils, hardships, and sorrows."[79] On this side of the eschaton, the function of the virtue of hope is to help human beings endure these hardships and pursue goods with patience and perseverance in the face of time's difficulties and delays.[80] When human beings attain these goods and enjoy union with what they hope for, they will no longer need hope to direct and sustain them; they will rest joyfully in communion with the hoped-for good. Until then, they need the virtue of hope to "stretch" and sustain them as they pursue a future that remains unseen.[81]

Given hope's temporal necessity, some interpreters have elevated it as the paradigmatic virtue of Augustinian pilgrims. "Hope," Robert Markus argues, "is the characteristic virtue of the wayfarer: by this he is anchored to his real home."[82] Markus devotes an entire chapter to Augustinian hope in his influential *Saeculum*, suggesting that Augustine's hope is focused primarily on an eschatological reality deferred until the final judgment, when perfect love of God will be fully and completed realized.[83] Until then, temporal hope is what sustains the pursuit of eternal love. Markus is right to affirm the value of hope for the eschaton, but he downplays the ways in which Augustine believes hope can help facilitate love of neighbor *within time*. As we will see in the following chapters, Augustine argues that trusting and hoping in another person is often the only way to forge a friendship of love.

In light of this interdependence, Eric Gregory criticizes Markus's realist vision of political Augustinianism for minimizing hope's relation to love.[84] Challenging accounts that focus on either hope or justice, Gregory elevates love as the "central virtue" of an Augustinian political morality: "Love proves to be a concept rich enough to include both hope and justice."[85] I share Gregory's endorsement of love as the fundamental Augustinian virtue, yet love's centrality does not exclude the necessity of hope. Gregory recognizes this: "Features of each type [of Augustinian liberalism] can support one another, and there are fluid elements in each type's paradigmatic virtue."[86] Gregory goes on to offer a more sustained and detailed discussion of love's relation to justice, but he does not devote as much attention to hope.[87] My aim in chapters 2 and 3 is to extend Gregory's analysis of love to hope.

Conclusion

My purpose in this chapter has been to draw on neglected texts to reconstruct Augustine's conceptual grammar and challenge interpretations that elide distinctions that Augustine draws. Recognizing the relations among faith, hope, and love permits a tentative specification of hope's structure and function.

For Augustine, hope is the orientation of will toward objects that are *good, future, possible,* yet *not fully possessed,* objects that engage our desire and spark an affective movement for union with what we love. For belief in the possibility of these objects, hope relies on an act on faith, but faith is not sufficient to supply hope with the affective or volitional movement toward its objects. Hope also depends on love. Without faith and love, hope would lack both its ground and its goal. But without hope, faith and love would lack their middle term, the motivational impulse that moves human beings toward their hoped-for goods within their time-bound existence. On this side of the eschaton, the three concepts remain conceptually distinct but functionally interdependent.

The relations among the concepts can supply a grasp of hope's basic structure, but as Augustine recognizes, specifying and evaluating the content of hope requires examining hope's particular objects and grounds. This is how Augustine proceeds in the *Enchiridion*. He begins by briefly explaining the conceptual relations among faith, hope, and love before analyzing the "objects of each of these three, that is, what we should believe, what we should hope for, and what we should love."[88] To follow Augustine, we must now explore hope's proper objects and grounds.

2

Against Otherworldliness

THE ORDER OF LOVE

I am not saying that you should have no loves; I simply want your loves to be
properly ordered.

—AUGUSTINE, SERMON 335C.13, IN *POLITICAL WRITINGS*, 59

AUGUSTINE IDENTIFIES hope as necessary for the good life but recognizes
that simply possessing hope is insufficient: "It makes a difference, you see,
what you believe, what you hope, what you love."[1] The purpose of the next two
chapters is to assess what Augustine thinks we ought to hope for and how we
ought to hope for it.

Identifying hope's proper objects requires addressing an anxiety common
among Augustine's critics, particularly in political theory. Many interpreters
worry that Augustine's excessively otherworldly hope denies any legitimate
hope for temporal goods, including the goods of politics. These complaints
often arise from more fundamental anxieties about the "otherworldliness" of
Augustinian love. Because Augustine discourages love for temporal goods,
critics assume he refuses any hope for temporal life on earth. This suspicion
underwrites objections from Hannah Arendt and Martha Nussbaum, but
David Billings makes it most explicit. "Augustine cannot develop an adequate
view of politics," Billings argues, "because loving the world for its own sake is
idolatry and secular (worldly) events cannot attain true significance."[2] Thus,
"while Augustine's eschatological ends do provide a kind of hope, they do not
provide political hope—i.e. a hope that can sustain and enrich political action."[3] Notice the assumption here: because Augustine does not countenance

32

any love of the world or recognize the significance of worldly events, he cannot commend any hope for this-worldly politics. For Billings, "Augustine offers a hope against the world (with its great calamities and frightful evils) rather than a hope for the world."[4]

In this chapter, I attempt to dispel this otherworldly anxiety by challenging the assumptions that support it. The argument unfolds in two parts. Part I sets forth Augustine's famous and controversial discussion of the "order of love" (*ordo amoris*) and examines criticisms from three prominent political interpreters—Arendt, Nussbaum, and Niebuhr—who worry that Augustine's order of love instrumentalizes the neighbor and evacuates the world of its value. Part II challenges this interpretation by synthesizing and integrating recent scholarship in theology and religious studies to advance an alternative account of the "order of love." By illuminating Augustine's participationist ontology and highlighting how his order of love is as focused as much on moral psychology as metaphysics, I show how he allows love for temporal goods as long as that love is properly ordered. In chapter 3, I draw on this order of love to reconstruct Augustine's implicit order of hope.

I. The Order of Love

Augustine's most influential account of the "order of love" appears in *On Christian Teaching*, where he endorses the "double-love" commandment from Matthew 22:37–40: "'You shall love the Lord your God with all your heart and with all your soul and with all your mind,' and, 'you shall love your neighbor as yourself. On these two commandments depend the entire law and the prophets.'"[5] After commending this "twofold love of God and of one's neighbor," Augustine explains how to fulfill the commandment:

> The person who lives a just and holy life is one who is a sound judge of these things. He is also a person who has ordered his love, so that he does not love what it is wrong to love, or fail to love what should be loved, or love too much what should be loved less (or love too little what should be loved more), or love two things equally if one of them should be loved either less or more than the other, or love things either more or less if they should be loved equally.[6]

To determine which objects to love and how to love them, Augustine employs a famous distinction between "use" (*usus/uti*) and "enjoyment" (*fruitio/frui*):

> There are some things which are to be enjoyed, some which are to be used, and some whose function is both to enjoy and use. Those which are to be enjoyed make us happy; those which are to be used assist us and give us a boost, so to speak, as we press on towards our happiness, so that we may reach and hold fast to the things that make us happy. And we, placed as we are among things of both kinds, both enjoy and use them; but if we choose to enjoy things that are to be used, our advance is impeded and sometimes even diverted, and we are held back, or even put off, from attaining things which are to be enjoyed.[7]

Augustine goes on to clarify what use and enjoyment entail: "To enjoy something is to hold fast to it in love for its own sake. To use something is to apply whatever it may be to the purpose of obtaining what you love—if indeed it is something that ought to be loved."[8] He adds that "[t]he improper use of something should be termed abuse."[9]

With this account in view, Augustine emphasizes that the supreme good to be "enjoyed" is God, the "supremely excellent and immortal being": "[I]t is only the eternal and unchangeable things which I mentioned that are to be enjoyed; other things are to be used so that we may attain the full enjoyment of those things."[10] Human beings should love only God for God's sake; all other objects must be "used" to "enjoy" God.[11]

As Augustine recognizes and critics hasten to highlight, the priority of God in the order of love raises the "important question" (*magna quaestio*) of "whether humans should enjoy one another or use one another, or both":

> We have been commanded to love one another [John 13:34; 15:12, 17], but the question is whether one person should be loved by another on his own account or for some other reason. If on his own account, we enjoy him; if for some other reason, we use him. In my opinion, he should be loved for another reason. For if something is to be loved on its own account, it is made to constitute the happy life, even if it is not as yet the reality but the hope of it which consoles us at this time.[12]

Thus, Augustine concludes, "a person who loves his neighbor properly should, in concert with him, aim to love God with all his heart, all his soul, and all his mind. In this way, loving him as he would himself, he relates his love of himself and his neighbor entirely to the love of God, which allows not the slightest trickle to flow away from it and thereby diminish it."[13] In other words, the love of neighbor and other temporal goods must always be "related" or "referred" to God,[14] or as Augustine says in later formulations, they must be loved "in" God.[15]

Political Critics of an Otherworldly Augustine

To contemporary readers, especially those with Kantian sensibilities, Augustine's discussion of "use" and "enjoyment" can seem like a blatant violation of the categorical imperative, encouraging citizens to exploit the world and treat their fellow human beings as mere means to their ends.[16] Arendt, for example, argues that Augustine tends "to strip the world and all temporal things of their value and to make them relative."[17] As a result, Augustine's account of love drains this-worldly life of significance, requiring that we "stand against the world, not simply without it."[18] Moreover, his injunction to "use" other human beings to enjoy God instrumentalizes our neighbors, making them into mere "means and tools" rather than ends in themselves.[19] By Arendt's lights, Augustine's neighbor becomes either an instrument that enables us to love God or a "constant reminder of [our] sin" that directs us to the heavenly city.[20] Either way, we no longer love our neighbor qua neighbor or individual qua individual. Rather, we love what is "eternal" in them.[21] Loving our neighbor becomes "only an occasion to love God."[22]

Martha Nussbaum presses similar charges. While she praises Augustine's efforts to restore "compassion, along with other emotions, to a place of centrality in the earthly life," she complains that Augustine's vision of Christian love remains too transcendent and otherworldly.[23] Targeting his contrast between "human or earthly love" and "Christian love, whose core is the love of God," Nussbaum argues that Augustine "repudiates the one and urges us, disdaining it, to cultivate the other."[24] Citing Arendt, she suggests the "insistent otherworldly direction of this longing" denies the value of this-worldly striving and eclipses human individuality.[25] For Nussbaum, "it is a little unclear what role is left . . . for loving real-life individual people. For what one loves above all in them is the presence of God and the hope of salvation."[26] Ultimately, Augustine's attempt to "direct longing away from this-worldly virtue" encourages passivity in politics and complicity in evil.[27] Rather than "taking action as best we can," Nussbaum concludes, Augustine simply admonishes us to "cover ourselves, mourn, and wait."[28]

Critics are not alone in raising suspicions about Augustine's order of love. Even an Augustinian as influential as Reinhold Niebuhr identifies "several grave errors in Augustine's account of love."[29] In particular, Niebuhr argues that Augustine instrumentalizes the neighbor: "The love of the neighbor is for him not part of a double love commandment, but merely the instrument of a single love commandment which bids us flee all mortality, including the neighbor, in favor of the immutable good."[30] Niebuhr blames this flight on a lingering Neoplatonic focus on the nature of love's objects: "[T]he emphasis lies always upon the worthiness or unworthiness of the object of our love; the insistence is that only God and not some mutable 'good' or person is worthy of our love."[31] While Niebuhr concedes this formula is "a safeguard against all forms of idolatry," he suggests that "using" the neighbor and earthly goods to enjoy God denies human individuality and trivializes the value of temporal goods.[32] While Augustine is "too much the Christian to engage in a consistent mystic depreciation of the responsibilities and joys of this earthly life," he nonetheless insists on "performing these tasks for the ultimate, rather than the immediate end."[33] Like Arendt, Nussbaum, and Billings, Niebuhr concludes that Augustinian love, taken on its own, furnishes a world-denying pessimism.

These objections threaten to undermine any plausible Augustinian hope for politics. If Augustine's order of love instrumentalizes the neighbor and deserts the world, it is difficult to see how he can countenance any hope for this-worldly politics. While Augustine's rhetoric occasionally supports such readings, influential scholars in theology and religious studies have recently challenged this interpretation of the order of love, offering more subtle accounts that allow an expansive love of temporal goods, including the goods of politics. Unfortunately, this scholarship has yet to penetrate political theory. By lifting this alternative account into the discipline and showing its wide acceptance among scholars, I hope to challenge prevailing interpretations of Augustine's otherworldliness and open new vistas on his political thought.

II. The Order of Love Reconsidered

Three assumptions tend to underwrite otherworldly interpretations of Augustine's order of love. The first is the view that the metaphysical nature of love's objects—their "worthiness or unworthiness," to quote Niebuhr—solely determines love's moral quality.[34] Because an infinite, eternal, and unchanging God is the most perfect being, God is the highest object of love, and since temporal goods are subject to contingency, fortune, and finitude, they cannot provide the security that eternal goods can.[35] To realize their ultimate good, human beings should turn away from fleeting goods and toward the eternal God. Any love of the world "for its own sake" is, as Billings suggests, "idolatry."[36]

This concern about idolatry licenses a second assumption, namely, that love of eternal and temporal goods is mutually exclusive or competitive. Human beings must enjoy either God or neighbor; they cannot love both fully for their own sake.[37] This assumption is evident not only in Billings's concerns about idolatry, but in Nussbaum's suggestion that Augustine "repudiates" "human or earthly love" and "urges us, disdaining it, to cultivate [love of God]."[38] As Eric Gregory observes, the assumption behind such complaints is that Augustine endorses a "competitive tournament of loves between God and the world."[39]

This either-or account of love fuels a third assumption about Augustine's distinction between "use" and "enjoyment." Most interpreters, including both defenders and detractors, view this relation as a means-end relation and read it through a distinctly Kantian lens, assuming Augustine requires that we "use" temporal goods and human neighbors instrumentally as mere "means and tools" to "enjoy" eternal ends.[40] Critics then indict Augustine for denying that the neighbor and the world have any intrinsic value, leveling charges of ethical instrumentalism and political pessimism.

Recently, scholars in theology and religious studies, including Eric Gregory, Charles Mathewes, Sarah Stewart-Kroeker, and Rowan Williams, among others, have challenged these assumptions by denying the implicit metaphysical and eschatological dualism they impute to Augustine.[41] Augustine's God is not located simply in some "transcendent region" or "absolute future," as Arendt and Nussbaum assume.[42] Rather, God is "Being itself," the "author and creator of everything."[43] If God is the "true ground" of all being, then God is not completely separate from the world; rather, everything that exists has its being because it participates in God's being.[44] While Augustine insists on preserving a distinction between creature and Creator,[45] he maintains that human beings have their being because they participate in the ultimate source of being.[46]

This participationist ontology also informs Augustine's understanding of goodness. If everything has its being because it participates in God's being, which is ultimately good, then everything that exists also participates in God's goodness: "We exist because he is good, and we are good to the extent that we exist."[47] Or as he writes elsewhere, "Existence as such is good, and supreme existence is the chief good. . . . Every good thing is either God or derived from God. Therefore even the lowest form is God."[48] It follows that, for Augustine, "[e]verything that exists is good."[49]

As a Christian, Augustine grounds his participationist ontology in Christology. For Augustine, what enables humans to participate in God is not simply that God is the source of all being and goodness, but also that God, through

Christ, participated in humanity and entered the world in time. As both human and divine, Christ becomes the "mediator" between humans and God, incarnating love and enabling humans to participate in the supreme good.[50] For Augustine, this mediation is related to imitation. Humans can approach God by coming to "resemble" God, and they can resemble God by imitating Christ the "mediator," who resembles both God and humanity.[51] By imitating Christ, human beings can come to love what Christ loves and in the way that Christ loves and thereby more fully participate in God's being and goodness.[52]

This participationist ontology has radical implications for understanding Augustine's order of love. First, it challenges critics' first assumption that the metaphysical status of love's objects determines their moral quality.[53] Rather than quarantining God to some transcendent realm and denying the goods of the world, Augustine suggests a more fundamental continuity between heaven and earth, time and eternity. If everything that exists is, in some way, good, then even finite, temporal goods partake in God's goodness. Temporal goods are still *goods*.[54] As Augustine writes, "Whatever God has made is good. Some are great goods, some are small goods, but all are good. Some are celestial good things, some are earthly good things; some are spiritual goods, some are bodily goods; some are eternal goods, some are temporal goods. But they are all good, because the one who is good made them good."[55] In *City of God*, Augustine even rejects the claim that "the goods which [the earthly] city desires are not goods; for, in its own human fashion, even that city is better when it possesses them than when it does not. . . . These goods are goods, and they are without doubt gifts of God."[56]

If Augustine's participationist ontology undermines critics' first assumption about the metaphysical and moral status of temporal goods, it also challenges their second assumption about Augustine's either-or account of love. If human beings participate in God's being and goodness, then loving God does not necessarily crowd out, or compete with, love of neighbor or the world. In loving temporal goods properly, human beings also love God; the two loves are not mutually exclusive.[57] On this account, God is not an "object" like other objects.[58] Rather than constituting a completely *external good* separate from human agency, Jennifer Herdt argues, God is, in a sense, *internal* to all that we do and are.[59] An either-or account of love fails to register the continuity implicit in Augustine's participationist ontology.

The primary problem is not with the metaphysical status of temporal goods, but with human beings who love them in an inordinate or disordered way.[60] As Augustine says of the "miser" who loves money, the "fault . . . lies not with the gold, but with the man; and this is true of every created thing: though it is good, it can be loved well or ill; well when the proper order is observed, and ill when that order is disturbed."[61] Thus, Augustine concludes, "a brief and true definition of virtue is 'rightly ordered love.'"[62]

If virtue is "rightly ordered love," it follows that vice is disordered love, a *privation* or *perversion* of goodness.[63] Challenging the Manichean view of good and evil as competing forces in the world, Augustine argues that if God is all-good, then everything that God creates, including the material world, must be good since God could not be responsible for creating anything evil.[64] Even the nature of the devil is, in one sense, good.[65] For Augustine, evil is not an independent force that competes with goodness, but a deficiency or negation of goodness, either a turning away from what is good (privation) or the wrongful use of a good for improper ends (perversion).[66] Evil is an effect not of God but of the free will of rational creatures.[67]

The ontological and moral priority of goodness over evil furnishes what Gregory describes as a psychological "dialectic" between love and sin, virtue and vice.[68] Since sin reflects the privation or perversion of love, love has ontological, moral, and psychological priority over sin: without a movement of love, there would be no sin. Yet, because love can become disordered, love is always threatened by sin, the human tendency to love a good insufficiently or perversely.[69] In this life, love risks becoming deficient or excessive, and virtue remains threatened by temptations toward privation or perversion.[70] As a result, one function of a virtue is to help human beings resist temptations toward vice.[71]

Augustine is especially concerned about the vice of pride (*superbia*), or perverse self-love, which breeds a "lust for domination" (*libido dominandi*) that drives human beings to grasp temporal goods for their own purposes.[72] Under the sway of pride, human beings assume they are self-sufficient and self-sustaining sources of their own being and goodness, putting themselves in the place of God and seeking to place others under their power.[73] "[W]hat is pride," Augustine asks, "but an appetite for a perverse kind of elevation? For it is a perverse kind of elevation indeed to forsake the foundation upon which the mind should rest, and to become and remain, as it were, one's own foundation."[74] In *City of God*, Augustine attributes the Fall to this prideful assumption of self-sufficiency, which denies the ways human beings participate in God's being and goodness:

Adam and Eve would have been better fitted to resemble gods if they had clung in obedience to the highest and true ground of their being, and not, in their pride, made themselves their own ground. For created gods are not gods in their own true nature, but by participation in the true God. By striving after more, man is diminished; when he takes delight in his own self-sufficiency, he falls away from the One who truly suffices him.[75]

For Augustine, pride causes human beings to grasp at temporal goods and dominate their neighbors for private purposes rather than participate in a good that everyone can share in common.[76]

This fundamental distinction between the private and the common distinguishes the "two loves" that define Augustine's "two cities": "of which one is holy, the other unclean, one social, the other private, one taking thought for the common good because of the companionship in the upper regions, the other putting even what is common at its own personal disposal because of its lordly arrogance."[77] What distinguishes the "earthly city" is that its members reject the common good and grasp at merely private goods, which leads to pride and domination.[78] Echoing Platonic concerns about "graspingness" (*pleonexia*) and Roman concerns about "domination" (*dominatio*), Augustine describes the "lust for domination" as the expression of the earthly city's pride.[79] "For pride hates a fellowship of equality under God and wishes to impose its own dominion upon its equals, in place of God's rule."[80] Augustine impugns the pride and lust for domination of pagan Rome, where the lust for glory fueled imperial ambitions.[81] Ultimately, pride drove their insatiable lust for domination, creating a "city which aims at dominion, which holds nations in enslavement, but is itself dominated by that very lust of domination."[82] For Augustine, domination is the ultimate consequence of sin, the personal and political manifestation of perverse love.

Gregory draws on this concern about pride and domination to furnish an alternative understanding of Augustine's order of love. When viewed in light of the dialectic between love and sin, the primary function of the order of love is moral as much as metaphysical: Augustine's "philosophical and theological energies are devoted more to *how* one is to love in an actively ordering way rather than to an abstract metaphysical speculation on *what* one is to consider as appropriate objects of love."[83] Mathewes concurs: the order of love "is more dispositional than metaphysical: Augustine does not want us not to love the world, but rather to change how we love it, as a whole and in its component parts."[84] Rather than providing a doctrine that derives the moral value of love's objects from their metaphysical status, Augustine supplies a moral and spiritual practice intended to chasten the pride that leads human beings to love temporal goods perversely. As Augustine preaches, "I am not saying that you should have no loves; I simply want your loves to be properly ordered."[85]

This focus on moral psychology disrupts critics' third assumption that Augustine's injunction to "use" temporal goods to "enjoy" God instrumentalizes the neighbor and deserts the world. The order of love has the opposite aim: it seeks to prevent idolatry and chasten the lust for domination, functioning as a regulative ideal that checks tendencies to harm, dominate, and possess others.[86] As Rowan Williams writes, "The language of *uti* is designed to warn against an attitude towards any finite person or object that terminates their meaning in their capacity to satisfy my desire, that treats them as the end of desire, conceiving my meaning in terms of them and theirs in terms of me."[87] This view is evident in Augustine's suggestion to "use" rather than "enjoy" our neighbors, for when we "enjoy" our human neighbors, we rest in them as our ultimate end, believing they "constitute the happy life," the final object of our satisfaction.[88] By enjoining us to love neighbors "in God" or to "use" rather than "enjoy" them, Gregory concludes, Augustine's order of love "aims to morally protect the neighbor from the self's prideful distortion that the neighbor exists only in terms of one's own ends, or that the neighbor is a threat to the self's relation to this infinite God."[89] Loving others "in God" or "for God's sake" encourages prideful human beings to recognize that temporal goods and human neighbors are not theirs to abuse, dominate, or possess.[90]

Drawing on a similar insight, John Bowlin describes the act of referring love of human neighbors and temporal goods to God in terms of "truthful description."[91] "The problem with friends," Bowlin argues, "is not that they divert love from its proper, eternal object to something transient. No, the problem is with us, with our inability to love friends aright, as they should be loved, as they deserved to be loved."[92] Referring loves to God helps us give a truthful description of our neighbor's proper relation to God and reality and then act properly under that description:

> Friends will not be loved as they deserve to be loved if they are cast under a false description, one that erases their relation to God, to the truth. A true description will accent the fact that they are fallen creatures whose goodness comes from God and whose salvation depends on God's love for them. It will also attend to everything else about them that is true and relevant: that they cannot be a substitute for God, that they are mortal, that they are not extensions of ourselves, or instruments of our aims, that they are both

creatures of a certain kind and individuals with specific quirks, characteristics, and defining features.[93]

"Referring" neighbors and worldly goods to God means referring them to the
facts about their existence, to the truth about their dependence, mortality, and
individuality.[94]

Bowlin's account of truthful description will become relevant again in chapter 10 when we evaluate Augustine's analysis of "pagan virtue." Here, I highlight
it to show how Augustine's participationist ontology is put to moral purpose:
if human beings are not independent sources of being and goodness but utterly dependent on God, they are not self-sufficient, and their neighbors are
not theirs to dominate or possess. They could not even imagine their neighbors, much less truthfully describe them, without acknowledging dependence
on God. Understood this way, an Augustinian order of love neither denies
individuality nor eclipses the neighbor. Instead, it attempts to preserve neighbors from human tendencies to violate, dominate, or control.

The order of love also frees human beings to enjoy temporal goods more
fully as they enter into relationship with God and neighbor.[95] This relational,
intersubjective account of love is at the center of Augustine's moral and theological vision.[96] By loving others in God, human beings forgo competing with
others to participate with them in a good they share in common.[97] Instead of
excluding love of temporal goods, ordering love to God enables a more capacious love of temporal goods:

> A man's possession of goodness is in no way lessened by the advent or
> continued presence of a sharer in it. On the contrary, goodness is a posses-
> sion which is enjoyed more fully in proportion to the concord that exists
> between partners united in charity. He who refuses to enjoy this possession
> in partnership will not enjoy it at all; and a man will find that he possesses
> it more abundantly in proportion to the fullness with which he loves his
> partner in it.[98]

By loving temporal goods "in God" or "on account of" God, partners united
in charity and concord can love "in the way" God or Christ loves.[99] Human
beings can love God and neighbor, eternal and temporal goods, with "one and
the same love."[100]

This focus on participation challenges a merely instrumental, means-end
account of the relationship between temporal and eternal goods. Instead, a
participationist ontology suggests that properly loving the neighbor and

temporal goods in an ordinate way can be partly *constitutive* of loving God.[101] The relation is even a reinforcing one, strengthening love of God by enabling a more complete participation in a common good that both the lover and beloved share.[102] The constitutive and reinforcing dynamics of *ordo amoris* cannot be reduced to the instrumental, means-ends reasoning usually foisted onto his conception of "use" and "enjoyment."

Augustine's original Latin supports this more capacious conception.[103] According to one commentator,

> *Uti* and *frui* are . . . not closed and rigid terms. We will understand Augustine's meaning better if we bear in mind that he is a rhetorician. His form of argument is not that of a systematic philosophical presentation and investigation; rather, it is a looser form of discussion in which ideas are more fully developed as the discussion progresses. Augustine does not define the concepts *uti* and *frui* rigidly at the outset and then systematically apply them to problems of Christian love; rather, he works with the terms, creating new meaning as the conversation progresses.[104]

As we have seen—and will see again in chapter 6—the former professor of rhetoric has the same fluid and dialectical understanding of hope.

Moreover, the Latin meaning of *uti* does not bear the weight of Kantian interpretations. William Riordan O'Connor highlights Augustine's definition of use and enjoyment in *The Trinity*:

> To use something is to put it at the will's disposal; to enjoy it is to use it with an actual, not merely anticipated joy. Hence everyone who enjoys, uses; for he puts something at the disposal of the will for purposes of enjoyment. But not everyone who uses, enjoys, not if he wants what he puts at the disposal of the will for the sake of something else and not for its own.[105]

According to O'Connor, "Augustine's own definition of use merely means to take up something into the power of the will, i.e., to apply the will to something, consciously to allow the will to become engaged with it. This in itself does *not* dictate an instrumental attitude."[106] This reading fits with Augustine's suggestions that God "uses" human beings[107] and that a relation of "use" is the bond of love that joins the members of the Trinity.[108] In these contexts, "use" is not instrumental or exploitative but describes a relation to goods pursued for the sake of something else, as constitutive parts of a larger whole.[109]

Given this alternative account and the influence of Kantian renderings, it is perhaps best to recast Augustine's use/enjoyment distinction as his way of referring to *proximate* and *ultimate* objects.[110] To *use* a good is to relate to it as a proximate object, to will it for the sake of something else, a part of attaining what can be enjoyed. In most cases, to *enjoy* a good is to rest in a good obtained, or to seek a good as a distant or ultimate end, the *terminus* of one's desire and pursuit.[111] While many influential interpreters map this distinction onto an instrumentalist interpretation of "means" and "ends,"[112] a more accurate account renders the proximate/ultimate object distinction in terms of *parts* and *wholes*—proximate goods that participate, or take part in, the ultimate unity of the whole.[113] On this account, to "use" neighbors or temporal goods is not to treat them as mere means, but to recognize them as parts of creation whose being and goodness depend on God and cannot be merely ordered to one's own selfish ends. This interpretation discourages instrumentalizing and dominating relations with the neighbor and the world and thereby authorizes a more positive view of temporal goods than critics assume. Loving the neighbor and the world for their "own sake" is not necessarily "idolatry," as Billings claims.[114] Rather, because the neighbor and the world have their being and goodness in God, human beings can love them as part of God's creation and in the "spirit" that God loves them.[115]

In one sermon, Augustine explicates 1 John 4:20 to suggest it is impossible to love the invisible God without loving the visible neighbor: "[I]f you do not love the brother whom you see, how can you love God, whom you do not see?"[116] Properly loving the neighbor simply *is* loving God: "Does he who loves his brother also love God? It must be that he loves God; it must be that he loves love itself. . . . By loving love he loves God. . . . If God is love, whoever loves love loves God."[117] In this context, love of neighbor does not compete with love of God but partly constitutes it. To adapt a phrase from Benjamin Elijah Mays in another context, these loves are "inseparable"—love of God and love of neighbor are "one love."[118]

Augustine extends this insight by frequent appeal to Matthew 25, which, Raymond Canning notes, appears more than 275 times in his writings.[119] Matthew 25 suggests that those who love the "least of these"—the hungry and homeless, the sick and naked, the stranger and prisoner—love God properly and will receive eternal life, even if they do not consciously realize they are loving God. However, those who consciously believe in God but do not love the "least of these" will not receive eternal life.[120] Augustine frequently invokes this passage to direct attention toward the neighbor here and now:

Now here we are already, by God's goodness, in winter. Think about the poor, how Christ in his nakedness is to be clothed. . . . Listen to the judgment he is going to pass: *When you did it for one of these least of mine, you did it for me* (Mt 25:40). You are all looking forward to greeting Christ seated in heaven. Attend to him lying under the arches, attend to him hungry, attend to him shivering with cold, attend to him needy, attend to him a foreigner. Do it, if it's already your practice; do it, if it isn't your practice.[121]

By identifying God in the neighbor and recognizing the neighbor as part of God's whole, Augustine calls listeners to a more holistic and capacious love, not to an instrumentalizing or selfish egoism. The commandments to love God and neighbor, Augustine says, "cannot exist without each other."[122]

For my purposes, Augustine's frequent use of Matthew 25 is relevant for two other reasons. First, Matthew 25 suggests that rightly ordered love is not a sentimental attitude or affection but is expressed in action and developed through practice, an insight Augustine emphasizes in several sermons. "[I]f you believe something else, hope for something else, love something else, you must prove it by your life, demonstrate it by your actions."[123] To "live in faith" is to develop a faith that "gathers to itself hope and the decision to love and begins to express itself in good actions."[124] Elsewhere, Augustine uses agricultural metaphors to encourage congregants, including many farmers, "not to come fruitlessly to church by hearing so many good things and yet not acting well."[125] Instead, "let a wonderfully abundant crop of good works spring up in your characters and your lives as in good soil, and so you may look forward to the coming of the farmer, who is now preparing a barn to put you in."[126] Augustine's repeated emphasis on knowing someone by their "fruits" is significant. As I will argue in chapter 8, Augustine's insistence that love finds its completion in action allows us to make inferences about what we love—and hope—by looking to actions rather than simply inquiring into mental states. This account offers a more expansive understanding of how diverse citizens can share common objects of love and hope.

Second, Matthew 25 implies that what makes human beings virtuous is not that they *consciously know* they are loving God as their ultimate end, but that they *actually* are loving God by loving the neighbor.[127] Augustine's reliance on Matthew 25 suggests the quality of love is not reducible to subjective knowledge or belief but to one's objective participation in goodness.[128] On this view, "referring" one's love to God does not necessarily entail having God consciously "in mind" in every act of love. An act of referral need not always be subjectively conscious for one to participate in God. Augustine suggests as much in Letter 155, where he argues that "our character is usually judged not from what we *know*, but from what we *love*."[129] He shares a similar sentiment in *City of God*: "[I]t is not he who *knows* what is good who is justly called a good man, but he who *loves* it."[130] If human beings love the neighbor or temporal goods properly, then they participate in the love of God, whether or not they have God in mind when they act. As I will argue in chapter 10, this more inclusive account of properly ordered love unsettles prevailing interpretations of Augustine's critique of "pagan virtue."

Conclusion

Augustine's order of love is not otherworldly or instrumentalizing. Contrary to what critics assume, Augustine does not measure love by the metaphysical status of its objects, assume love of God and neighbor are mutually exclusive, or counsel human beings to "use" others instrumentally to "enjoy" God. Augustine seems more concerned about the moral psychology of love than the metaphysical status of love's objects, and he believes loving the visible neighbor can be one way to love the invisible God. Since temporal goods and human neighbors participate in God's goodness, Augustine encourages love for them as long as that love is properly ordered. And if Augustinian love is not as otherworldly as critics assume, Augustinian hope need not be either. Augustine's explicit order of love supplies a model for reconstructing his implicit order of hope.

3

Between Presumption and Despair

THE ORDER OF HOPE

There are two things . . . that kill souls, either despair or perverse hope.

—AUGUSTINE, SERMON 87.10

HOPE DEPENDS fundamentally on the movement of love. Indeed, for Augustine, "hope cannot exist without love."[1] This claim coheres with Augustine's view that all virtues and affections find their unity in love.[2] As we saw in chapter 1, hope is a kind of love for a future good that is desirable and possible to attain but not yet fully present or possessed. Hope is a love for objects cast under this description.

If love is virtuous when it is properly ordered, so, too, are the other emotions or affections that depend on love: "[T]hese feelings are bad if the love is bad, and good if it is good."[3] As an *emotion* or *affection*, hope can be good or bad depending on whether it is directed toward good or bad objects or pursued in good or bad ways. As a *virtue*, hope can only be directed toward the right objects in the right ways. The affection of hope thus requires the virtue to properly direct it toward the good. For Augustine, the virtue of hope is the good quality of the soul that properly disposes human beings to desire future possible goods in the right ways and in the right order. The virtue of hope consists in rightly ordered hope.

Unfortunately, Augustine never develops an "order of hope" in such explicit terms. Although he understands hope to be both an affection and a virtue, he often uses "hope" (*spes*) interchangeably to refer to one or the other, without making the difference clear or explicit. But when we examine his treatises, sermons, and letters, we discover resources for explicating an implicit order of hope, which can illuminate Augustine's distinctive understanding of hope and its relevance for politics.

But first it is necessary to note one complication. Augustine often uses the same verbal formulation to refer both to *objects of desire* (what we hope *for*) and *agents of assistance* (whom we hope *in*). In *Summa Theologica*, Aquinas describes this as the twofold object of hope—"the good which it intends to obtain, and the help by which that good is obtained."[4] Augustine does not provide such precision or specificity, but he implicitly recognizes the difference in an exposition of the Lord's Prayer, his paradigmatic practice of hope: "[W]hen you make your appeal, there are two things to beware of: asking for what you shouldn't ask and asking for it from someone you shouldn't ask it from."[5] Here, Augustine suggests properly ordered hope requires *hoping for* the right objects in proper measure and *hoping in* the right agents of assistance in proper measure. But unlike Aquinas, Augustine rarely distinguishes this twofold object. Sometimes, he even conflates them, describing what it means to "hope *in* the Lord" by identifying the goods one ought to hope *for*.[6] Reconstructing an Augustinian order of hope, then, requires exploring whether Augustine permits hope *for* both temporal objects of desire and *in* temporal agents of assistance. I will consider hope in temporal agents of assistance in chapter 5. Here, I will focus on what we may hope for.

Part I builds on distinctions in Augustine's order of love to reconstruct his implicit order of hope, an aspect of his thought that has gone unnoticed by scholars of Augustine. Drawing on neglected texts and Augustine's implicit practices, I argue that Augustine allows and even encourages hope for temporal goods as long as this hope is properly ordered. Part II fills out this order of hope by specifying corresponding forms of disorder—the vices of presumption and despair. Augustine's virtue of hope finds a way between these vices. Finally, part III explores the moral and spiritual practices that Augustine recommends for cultivating this virtue and resisting opposing vices. Since these implicit pedagogical practices are often overlooked by interpreters who focus only on his explicit doctrinal utterances, I argue that a more contextualized account affirms that Augustine cares as much about *how* we hope as *what* we hope for.

I. Hope for Eternal and Temporal Goods

The *Enchiridion* provides a useful place to start. In his short section on hope, Augustine appeals to the Lord's Prayer to identify "what we should hope for."[7] The first three petitions—*Hallowed be your name, your kingdom come, your will be done, on earth as it is in heaven*—identify hopes for "eternal gifts" that "will endure perfectly and immortally in our spirit and body."[8] Importantly, Augustine does not locate these eternal goods in an otherworldly realm or defer their enjoyment to an eschatological afterlife. Rather, he suggests we can begin experiencing these eternal gifts here and now: "[T]hey begin here and as we progress they grow in us, but once they are perfect, which is something we must hope for in the next life, they will be possessed forever."[9] By indicating that we can already begin to experience the eternal goods we hope for, Augustine challenges the either/or dualism that locates eternal goods in a purely transcendent realm. Instead, he suggests we can already begin to participate in the heavenly city by hoping properly for eternal goods and, to some significant extent, by beginning to enjoy them.[10]

While eternal goods are the ultimate objects of hope, Augustine does not exclude hope for temporal goods.[11] He identifies temporal goods as proper, if proximate, objects of hope in the last four petitions of the Lord's Prayer—*Give us this day our daily bread, and forgive us our debts as we also forgive our debtors, and do not bring us to the time of trial, but deliver us from the evil one.*[12] These petitions identify temporal goods that are "necessary for acquiring the eternal gifts" and "concern our needs in the present life."[13] We need "daily bread" in "sufficient quantity to meet the needs of body and soul," and we need the "forgiveness of sins" and deliverance from "trial" and "evil" here and now since that is when "sins are committed" and temptations "lure or drive us" to do wrong.[14] Since these goods are necessary for pilgrimage toward the heavenly city, they do not necessarily conflict or compete with eternal goods. Rather, hoping for these temporal goods can be a proximate part of realizing the ultimate end.[15]

Given common interpretations in political theory, Augustine's inclusion of hope for temporal goods is worth highlighting. It is an aspect of the *Enchiridion*, for example, that Deneen neglects. In emphasizing hope in God rather than human beings, Deneen downplays the fact that Augustine acknowledges the legitimacy of hoping for temporal goods. Instead, Deneen seems to assume a strict separation between the "eternal" and "earthly," "divine" and "secular," that remains in tension with Augustine's account in the *Enchiridion*.[16]

Augustine takes a similar approach in an exposition of Psalm 129, where he explicitly acknowledges the permissibility of hoping for temporal goods: "Am I condemning hope for worldly advantages, if God is besought to grant them? No, but there is another kind of hope proper to Israel. It is not Israel's true calling to hope for riches or bodily health or an abundance of earthly assets, *as though such things were its supreme good.*"[17] This last phrase is significant: it implies that Augustine allows hope for certain temporal goods as long we do not hope for them as our supreme good or ultimate source of happiness.

In places, Augustine even suggests we can hope for some temporal goods for their own sake. In Letter 130 to Proba, as in the *Enchiridion*, he specifies objects of hope and desire by appealing to the Lord's Prayer,[18] and he identifies good "health" and "friendship" as temporal goods properly sought "for their own sake" (*propter se*).[19] He goes on to acknowledge that human beings may also hope for "a sufficient amount of necessary goods . . . sought not for their own sake but for the sake of [health and friendship], when they are sought in a proper fashion."[20] Among these other goods he includes "temporal well-being" and even "honors and positions of power."[21] "Yes," Augustine affirms, "it is proper to will these things if it is their responsibility to provide for those who live subject to them, not on account of these things themselves but on account of another good that comes from them," namely, the temporal well-being of the community.[22] But he insists that these temporal goods must only be proximate objects to be used rather than ultimate ends to be enjoyed. This admonition reflects Augustine's concerns about pride and domination: if honors and positions of power are "desired on account of an empty pride over their superiority and on account of the superfluous or even harmful pomp of vanity, it is not proper."[23] But "if they desire for themselves and for theirs a sufficient amount of necessary things and do not desire any more, they do not desire improperly."[24] While Augustine suggests that human beings ought to "prefer eternal to temporal things" and love them "on account of" God, he still permits hoping for temporal goods for the sake of health or friendship, as long as this hope does not become disordered or perverse.[25]

Augustine's emphasis on hoping for such temporal goods in "proper fashion" highlights a crucial feature of his account. To be virtuous, hope, like love, must be properly ordered. Strikingly, Augustine applies the same distinctions to hope that he uses to explicate his order of love.

In Sermon 157, he invokes the distinction between use and enjoyment in the context of hope rather than love. He praises those who are "hoping for eternal things which we cannot see" and admonishes those who are "hooked on temporal things that can be seen."[26] For Augustine, the problem is that those who "never stop hoping for temporal things . . . are frequently disappointed in [their] hopes": they "never stop being excited by them before they come, being corrupted by them when they come, being tormented by them when they've gone."[27] Augustine encourages his audience to hope for "eternal things," which "won't pass away when they come; because in fact they don't even come, but are always abiding, always there."[28] Yet he acknowledges that those who hope for eternal goods should not abandon hopes for temporal goods if they are properly ordered: "We too make *use* of them according to the needs of our journey; but we don't set our heart's *joy* on them, in case when they collapse we should be buried in the ruins. You see, we make *use* of this world *as though we were not using it,* in order to reach the one who made this world, and remain in him, *enjoying* his eternity."[29] Here, Augustine employs the use/enjoyment distinction to chasten listeners against hoping for proximate, temporal goods as their supreme good or ultimate end.

These texts show that Augustine allows, and even encourages, hope for temporal goods and earthly assets, including "life itself and . . . the wholeness of mind and body," friendships that are not "bounded by narrow limits," and positions of honor and power that can be used to preserve temporal well-being.[30] Augustine emphasizes that hopes for these goods must be "referred" ultimately to God,[31] but if we apply an alternative account of the order of love and recognize how temporal goods can participate in God's goodness, hoping for temporal goods can be a way to hope for eternal goods as long as this hope is properly ordered.

Of course, Augustine recognizes that cultivating, exercising, and sustaining properly ordered hope will not be easy. Given human limitations and the vicissitudes of fortune, the virtue of hope will always be accompanied by temptations toward privation or perversion. To understand what the order of hope entails, then, we must consider corresponding forms of disorder: the vices of presumption and despair.

II. Between Presumption and Despair

In Sermon 87, Augustine identifies "two evils" that "kill souls": "despair" (*desperatio*) and "perverse hope" (*peruersa spes*).[32] For Augustine, despair is the vice of deficiency, the privation of hope. To experience *desperatio* is literally to be "without hope," which Augustine considers a great evil: "[I]t is bad to have no hope now, for anyone who has no hope here will not have the reality hereafter. We must have hope during this present life."[33] Indeed, Augustine adds, "To call someone hopeless is a way of insulting him; we sometimes curse somebody by saying he is hopeless."[34] Why? Because despair causes us to withdraw from the good rather than "stretch" toward it in hope.[35] When we despair, we lose the capacity to patiently endure the difficulties and delays associated with attaining a future good, especially eternal fellowship with God.[36]

Like hope, despair can have two different objects, one related to the object of desire (what we hope for) and one related to the agent of assistance (whom we hope in). Most often, Augustine discusses despair in relation to eternal goods—hope *for* eternal life or hope *in* God. Those who despair typically give up the hope for eternal life, assuming they do not have the ability to attain it or that God will not be willing to offer assistance or mercy in their pursuit. "A person who does not believe that his sins can be forgiven," Augustine writes, "is made worse by despair, feeling that nothing better awaits him than to be wicked, since he has no faith in the results of being converted."[37] Augustine often ascribes the vice of despair to those with a false self-estimation, distorted vision, or deficient faith, those who "think about the evil things they have done" and "assume that they can't be pardoned."[38] The despairing fail to see themselves and the world rightly and thus fail to act with a truthful description of it, which causes them to withdraw from future goods that are within reach.

For Augustine, such despair typically has one of two effects. The despairing either sink into a debilitating "desperation" and slothful "lethargy" where they are not motivated to act at all, or they recklessly pursue other vices, believing that the certainty of eternal punishment licenses some form of "temporal enjoyment."[39] Augustine sometimes compares these despairing souls to Roman gladiators destined to die in the arena. Because they have "no hope of being spared," they either "look for a way to die" or "do not hesitate to commit a foul," using violent force without hesitation or constraint.[40] Either way, the despairing enter a "deep and dizzy whirlpool" where they "turn their backs" on God and fall "into various sins and vicious forms of behavior."[41]

Augustine does not often discuss despair in relation to temporal goods, but given his participationist ontology and implicit order of hope, it is possible to identify the causes and effects of despair in relation to temporal goods. Accordingly, the despairing either fail to hope sufficiently for goods that are possible and necessary for this temporal life (goods such as health, friendship, and temporal well-being), or else they fail to hope sufficiently in their neighbors and friends to achieve such goods. Such despair results from distorted vision or deficient faith, either the belief that their own deficiency prevents them from realizing difficult goods in the face of the obstacles, or the belief that their friends and neighbors lack either the ability or willingness to help them achieve these goods. Either way, despair distorts their motivation and causes them to retreat from the good. They sink into a slothful lethargy that discourages any effort to overcome obstacles, or they recklessly pursue less worthy goods or private goods that can be attained by isolated individuals rather than common goods that require the cooperation of friends. In both cases, the privation of hope prevents them from achieving difficult future goods.

If despair is the vice of deficiency, presumption (*praesumptio*) is the vice of excess, the perversion of hope.[42] Those who escape despair must "be careful they don't tumble into another whirlpool, and find that having been unable to die from despair, they now die from perverse hope," which is "equally pernicious."[43] By "perverse hope," Augustine means a kind of presumption, which characterizes those who "hope in the wrong way," hoping "too much" for certain goods that are not appropriate or possible, or "too much" in someone's assistance to achieve them.[44]

Augustine identifies forms of perverse hope in relation to both objects of desire and agents of assistance.[45] He notes, for example, that hope can become perverse if it is a "hope for something unworthy, even though you hope for it from God."[46] Augustine does not say what makes an object "unworthy," but elsewhere, he gives the example of hoping in God for "death" or "harm" to one's enemies, which cannot be ordered to love of God or neighbor.[47] The implication is that "unworthy" objects are not genuine goods: they cannot be referred to God.[48] Elsewhere, he suggests hope can also become perverse or "false" (*spem falsam*) when it assumes "more than the facts warranted."[49] Here presumption entails an excessive epistemic confidence in the possibility of realizing a certain good, which affects one's motivation to pursue it. Thus, presumption, like despair, can entail apathy or recklessness: the presumptuous either assume they have already attained their object of hope and need to do nothing more to achieve it, or they rush headlong into its pursuit without a proper estimation of the potential risks.[50] In this way, presumption, like despair, reflects a distorted vision of reality, a kind of self-deception that causes us to hope for objects under a false description.[51]

As with despair, Augustine usually discusses presumption in relation to eternal goods, but his analysis can be extended to temporal goods. In regard to objects of desire, the presumptuous person is one who hopes for temporal goods that are impossible or improper, either hoping more than the evidence warrants or hoping for objects that are not genuine goods. In regard to agents of assistance, the presumptuous person is one who hopes too much in another's help, presuming either that no further effort is needed to achieve a difficult good or that others have the ability to assist when they do not. In all these cases, presumption presupposes false belief or excessive pride. For Augustine, such perverse hope is as dangerous as despair.[52] The "right sort of hope" finds a middle way between presumption and despair.[53]

Augustine, of course, never develops an explicit "doctrine of the mean" in his account of virtue. He likely only read a smattering of Aristotle and probably only the *Categories*.[54] His acquaintance with Aristotelian accounts of virtue would have most likely come secondhand through Roman interpreters, especially Cicero, who appropriates the Aristotelian concept of the mean—the "intermediate course between too much and too little"—when discussing virtues that relate to the emotions and affections.[55] Strikingly, Cicero gestures toward such a mean when discussing the virtue of "magnanimity" or "greatness of spirit": "When anyone does undertake public business, he should remember to reflect not only on how honourable that is, but also on whether he has the capacity to succeed. Here he must take thought so that indolence does not make him despair prematurely, nor greed spur him to over-confidence."[56] Though Augustine does not mention this Ciceronian passage in his sermons on hope, the structure of his concept, if not the object, is similar: hope emerges as a way between presumption and despair.[57] As he writes in a commentary on the Gospel of John, "We are in danger, therefore, from either side, from hope and from despair, contradictory things, contradictory emotions.... The one lot are killed by despair, the other by hope. The spirit vacillates between hope and despair. You need to be afraid of being killed by hope, in case by harbouring too great a hope of mercy you come under judgement. You need to be afraid on the other hand of being killed by despair, in case by thinking that it's too late for you to be pardoned for your serious offences, you fail to repent, and encounter the judge, Wisdom, who says, 'And I shall mock your affliction' [Prov 1:26]."[58] Here, then, the virtuous mean is between despair, on the one hand, and presumption, or "too great a hope," on the other.

That the virtue of hope is surrounded by vices on both sides fits with Augustine's dialectic of love and sin, where virtue is always accompanied by temptations toward vice.[59] In one sermon, for example, he describes temptations toward presumption and despair as "two siren voices, each opposed to the other, but both dangerous, which lure people to destruction."[60] Presumption and despair are each like a self-consuming "whirlpool" (*uoraginem*), warping a person's entire character and creating bonds of habit that are hard to alter or escape.[61] Moreover, if virtues aid the ascent to wisdom, vices, like whirlpools, cause human beings to curve in on themselves, plunging them into a downward spiral and pulling them farther away from God and the Good.[62]

For Augustine, "good hope" avoids the whirlpools of presumption and despair.[63]

That Augustine uses maritime metaphors to describe these vices is not accidental. Many of his allusions recall Greek and Roman myths that would have been familiar to his audiences, who, like Odysseus, would have wanted to avoid sin's "sirens" and find a way between the Scylla of presumption and the Charybdis of despair.[64] Such maritime allusions also reflect Augustine's vision of the pilgrim sojourning toward the City of God, a theme that pervades his corpus.[65] Recalling both ancient philosophical connections between travel and *theoria* and religious traditions of pilgrimage to sacred sites, Augustine's pilgrimage motif would have been especially resonant with his audience in Hippo, a port city home to sailors and merchants who regularly traveled by sea.[66] For many of them, the need to sustain hope amidst life's "storms" would not have been simply a metaphor.[67] To counsel those in such storms, Augustine recalls Paul's description of hope as an "anchor of the soul" to discourage pilgrims from being battered onto the shores of presumption or despair:

> [B]y fixing our hope up above, we have set it like an anchor on firm ground, able to hold against any of the stormy waves of this world, not by our own strength but by that of the one in whom this anchor of our hope has been fixed. Having caused us to hope, after all, he will not disappoint us, but will in due course give us the reality [*res*] in exchange for the hope [*spes*].[68]

Like an anchor, the virtue of hope stabilizes the soul, giving pilgrims the ability to resist temptation and endure trial with steady resolve and perseverance. Although this hope achieves its stability by being anchored ultimately in God, Augustine's implicit order of hope suggests that this time-bound virtue also allows hope for temporal goods, ordering them in ways that prevent human beings from drowning in presumption or despair.

Hope among the Virtues

To avoid these vices, hope requires the cooperation of other virtues. In the previous two chapters, I showed how hope depends on the virtues of faith and love. I will explore hope's relationship to faith further in the next two chapters. In addition to these virtues, Augustine follows his Greek and Roman predecessors in affirming the importance of the four cardinal virtues—temperance, fortitude, justice, and prudence. In *City of God*, when engaging Roman interlocutors, he emphasizes the functions of these virtues in terms his interlocutors would recognize and even endorse. For example, he defines temperance as the virtue that "bridles lusts of the flesh," fortitude as the virtue that enables us to "endure" difficulties "with patience," justice as the virtue that functions "to give to each his due," and prudence as the virtue that assists in "distinguishing good things from bad."[69] All four of these virtues, he argues, are "necessary for this mortal life."[70]

Yet, unlike his predecessors, Augustine locates the unity of these virtues not in prudence but in love.[71] Each virtue reflects a "certain varied disposition of love": "Temperance is love offering itself in its integrity to its beloved. Fortitude is love easily tolerating all things on account of the beloved. Justice is love serving the beloved alone and as a result ruling righteously. And prudence is love that wisely separates those things by which it is helped from those by which it is impeded."[72] Since Augustine identifies love of God as the ultimate aim, each of these virtues functions to direct human beings to God as "the highest good, the highest wisdom, and the highest harmony."[73] Here, in *A Catholic Way of Life*, a treatise written to lift up common Christian practices over against those of the Manicheans, he emphasizes the way virtues are ordered to love of God.[74]

While Augustine frequently discusses these cardinal virtues explicitly in relation to love, they are also relevant for hope. The virtue of hope needs the assistance of temperance to chasten presumption and moderate desires for specific temporal goods, fortitude to endure difficulties that prompt fear and tempt despair, justice to ensure that acts of hoping for goods and in others give them what they are due, and prudence to discern, deliberate, and judge which goods to pursue and how to pursue them in light of concrete circumstances. In turn, hope can assist temperance, fortitude, and justice by supplying the resolve needed to stretch toward difficult goods and enact these virtues over the long haul when presumption or despair might cause us to rest prematurely in our progress or give up on efforts to improve.[75] And hope can assist prudence by chastening the temptations that might distort our reasoning and judgment about future possible goods. These virtues are mutually reinforcing.

Given common misunderstandings of Augustine's order of love and hope, it is especially important to attend to the role of prudence—the virtue of careful discernment, good deliberation, and right judgment. Sometimes, Augustine's discussions of right order, especially when couched in terms of higher and lower goods, can seem straightforward and formulaic, as if his prescriptions can be read off from some metaphysical hierarchy of being or goodness.

While Augustine does acknowledge various "degrees of good" in his treatises, Joseph Clair shows that Augustine's order of love is much more "messy and complex" than any straightforward calculation of duty or assessment of a good's relative weight.[76] The order of love (and by extension, hope) is better understood as "a way of discernment," a practice of "discerning the good" and responding appropriately in light of a range of contingent circumstances, including one's roles and obligations.[77] As Augustine writes in his most famous account of the "order of love," the "person who lives a just and holy life is one who is a sound judge of these things."[78] Clair shows that ordering one's loves and hopes is not simply a matter of aligning desires with the metaphysical or moral status of eternal and temporal goods. It also requires the contextual discernment and sound judgment of prudence.[79]

The role of prudence is particularly important for understanding the virtue of hope. In contrast to contemporary accounts that tend to judge hope as good or bad in the abstract, an Augustinian account recognizes that judgments about particular objects of hope are contextual, reflecting the circumstances, roles, and obligations of particular individuals and occasions. What may appear to be hope in one case may actually reflect presumption or hide a deeper form of despair in another. To find the mean between these two vices requires prudence, which can aid hope in "distinguishing good things from bad" and taking "precautions against pitfalls," enabling us to identify and pursue proper objects of hope while avoiding its opposing vices.[80]

Augustine also emphasizes the importance of two other virtues that inform his distinctive order of hope—humility and piety—which often come packaged together in Augustine's texts.[81] In chapter 10, I will explore these virtues in more detail and explore how they might inform an Augustinian account of "pagan virtue." Here, I want to sketch how they assist the virtue of hope.

Humility (*humilitas*) involves a proper recognition of one's own limitations and weaknesses, which, for Augustine, make it an essential moral, political, and theological virtue.[82] If sin finds its ultimate source in pride, then humility is necessary to prevent loves from becoming disordered and dominating.[83] We can see this in Augustine's discussion of the Fall in *City of God*, where he attributes human sin ultimately to "pride" and an "appetite for a perverse kind of elevation,"[84] a prideful self-sufficiency that refuses relationships of dependence and resorts to domination "to secure the dependence of others."[85] Against this vice of "exaltation," Augustine lifts up the virtue of "humility" as the antidote to pride.[86] Humility is "most highly praised in the City of God and commended to the City of God during its pilgrimage in this world."[87] "The safe and true way to heaven," he affirms later, "is built by humility."[88]

As the virtue that calls attention to human limitations and weaknesses, humility serves to chasten temptations toward presumption. Human beings need humility to see the world rightly, recognize their weaknesses and limits, and be alert to the dangers of hoping too much for a specific good or too much in another's assistance. Without humility, hope can easily swell into presumption.

The virtue of piety (*pietas*) serves a similar function. In ancient Roman thought, piety is the virtue that encourages human beings to acknowledge their dependence on and duty toward others, including their family, friends, commonwealth, and the gods.[89] Tied to justice, piety involves giving others the grateful acknowledgment they are due for making our existence and development possible.[90] Augustine adapts this virtue for his Christian context, acknowledging that piety can legitimately be shown to one's parents or commonwealth but must ultimately be directed toward God, the source of all being and goodness.[91] For Augustine, piety disposes human beings to properly recognize their dependence on others and gratefully acknowledge the ultimate source of their being, goodness, and virtue in God. Pious people do not claim sole credit for their existence, virtues, or possessions but see these goods as gifts.[92] Importantly, like his Roman predecessors, Augustine tends to regard piety as a virtue or excellence of character, which does not consist simply in fleeting feelings toward another but in a disposition that issues in tangible acts of gratitude, service, and sacrifice toward those on whom one depends, acts that acknowledge and sustain the bonds of that relationship.[93] For Augustine, the enactment of piety explains why *pietas* is often used to describe "works of mercy" and "worship" since both express a grateful and just acknowledgment of dependence on others and the duties that accompany such dependence.[94]

The virtue of piety plays an essential role in supporting Augustine's virtue of hope. Acknowledging dependence on others can temper the presumption that virtue or goodness is the result of our own effort or achievement, thereby encouraging us to recognize our virtue and goodness as a gift. In this way, piety cooperates with humility to resist presumption. Piety can also stave off despair. By disposing us to properly acknowledge our reliance on others, piety reminds us that we are not alone, that we are related to, and dependent on, others who have contributed to our progress in the past. If they have helped before, they may be able to assist again. Piety and humility work together to help the hopeful resist presumption and despair.

III. Putting on Hope

If hope is the virtue that cooperates with other virtues to order the affections in ways that avoid presumption and despair, the function of the virtue will consist in helping its possessors resist these powerful temptations: "[W]hat is [virtue's] task in this world but to wage perpetual war against the vices?"[95] Although Augustine believes we "cannot manage to achieve [perfection] in our present life, no matter how much we may wish to," he insists we can make progress if, relying on God's grace, we can focus on the purification of our souls and the perfection of our virtues.[96] Moral, spiritual, and social practices play a crucial role in this progress, coming to virtue's aid in its war against vice.

Recognizing hope as a virtue that is cultivated and sustained through particular practices casts new light on Augustine's most important discussions of hope. Consider the *Enchiridion*, his most famous treatment of hope. Interpreters often read the *Enchiridion* as a "dogmatic-moral treatise," "compendium of Christian doctrine," or "systematic exposition of Christian dogma," a text where Augustine simply uses the Lord's Prayer to provide doctrinal scaffolding for his discussion of hope.[97] Reading the *Enchiridion* merely as an explication of theological doctrine can reinforce the view that what matters most for Augustine is what we hope for, not how we hope. But recognizing Augustine's emphasis on practices and attending to the pedagogical purposes of the *Enchiridion* reveals a more complex picture.

Consider the *Enchiridion*'s distinctive literary genre. Laurentius, recall, had requested a "handbook" of the Christian faith, an *enchiridion* that "can be carried in the hand, not to burden the bookshelves."[98] Throughout his reply, Augustine shows awareness of the genre's constraints and purposes, one of which is to encourage accessibility and repetition.[99] The very size of the handbook serves a pedagogical purpose: it allows the reader to have the book always on hand and read it repeatedly. "[I]f you have a copy of it at hand," he tells Laurentius, "you can easily turn to [the answers] and read them again."[100] The *Enchiridion* provides a kind of "catechism" meant to be practiced regularly so that its reader can cultivate the virtues of faith, hope, and love.[101]

Augustine recognizes, however, that his reader will not always have the book handy. He explicitly tells Laurentius that he has structured his reply to help him "remember" these insights, even if he does not have the *Enchiridion* in his possession.[102] This remark helps to explain Augustine's pedagogical choice to structure his exposition of hope by appealing to the Lord's Prayer. Because it is short, accessible, and easy to remember, the prayer functions as a useful mnemonic device to facilitate the cultivation of virtue: "Think of the Creed and the Lord's Prayer. What text is there that takes a shorter time to hear or to read? What is there that is easier to commit to memory?"[103] Memory, in this case, facilitates the repetition needed to cultivate the virtue, particularly for the majority of people in Augustine's time who were unable to read.[104]

Moreover, because the Lord's Prayer is a common part of religious services and daily rituals, it supplies frequent occasions for practitioners to evaluate their hopes in the context of community.[105] In the ecclesial context, the Lord's Prayer is both a spiritual and social practice, one that gains its force from the way it brings individuals together into shared community. If members of this community reflect on their hopes every time they hear or say the Lord's Prayer, this liturgical practice will serve to educate their attitudes and solidify their bonds of affection. With enough time and repetition, such a practice can help participants develop a virtue or habit that reflects properly ordered hope. As a result, the Lord's Prayer is not simply an analytical scaffolding device on which Augustine hangs his theological doctrines, as most interpreters assume, but a moral, spiritual, and social practice whose repetition can enable practitioners to reorder their hopes.

The pedagogical importance of the Lord's Prayer is clear in a series of sermons Augustine preached to those seeking baptism in the Catholic Church.[106] As lessons for beginners in the Christian faith, these sermons were part of an intentional form of spiritual and moral education for catechumens participating in a kind of late antique "confirmation class," where they learned about the religious faith they were planning to profess publicly during their baptism on Easter. During this preparatory process, Augustine and other priests "handed over" (*traditio*) the creeds, prayers, and sacred texts of the church, offering homiletic commentaries on their meaning and significance.[107] Catechumens would then memorize these texts, especially the Creed and the Lord's Prayer, and "give them back" (*redditio*) a week or two later during an examination. This process was meant to prepare them to say the Apostles' Creed on the day of baptism, "with everyone present listening."[108] In this context, Augustine did not hesitate to invoke this risk of public embarrassment to encourage catechumens to take their spiritual formation seriously. Steeped in a Roman culture that emphasized glory, he was not beyond appealing to an ecclesial "economy of esteem" to encourage progress in virtue.[109]

These sermons provide an illuminating look into how Augustine uses regular spiritual practices to help beginners cultivate the virtue of hope. Augustine typically begins his instruction by teaching beginners to learn the Creed, which he describes as the "short and grand rule" of the faith.[110] As in the *Enchiridion*, Augustine ties his discussion of the Creed to the virtue of faith, and since faith precedes hope, it is fitting that Augustine begins here. As he tells the catechumens, "The right order for your formation and for building you up in the Christian community is for you first to learn what you should believe, and afterward what you should pray for."[111] Augustine encourages these beginners to practice the Creed every day: "When you get up, when you go to bed, give back your creed, give it back to the Lord, remind yourselves of it, don't be tired of repeating it. Repetition is a good thing, to prevent forgetfulness creeping in." He specifically highlights how daily repetition can prompt reflection and self-examination: "Call your faith to mind, look at yourself; treat your creed as your own personal mirror. Observe yourself there, if you believe all the things you confess to believing, and rejoice every day in your faith." The Creed is like "the everyday clothes of your mind." If we "clothe" ourselves with the Creed and check ourselves daily in the "mirror," we will be able to "dress" ourselves in the virtue of faith.[112]

Jennifer Herdt identifies Augustine's advice to "put on" virtue as a significant feature of his "mimetic" account of moral formation.[113] As Herdt highlights, Augustine sought to "put on" the virtue of Christ. In one of his most famous moments of conversion in *Confessions*, Augustine is inspired to "take up and read" a random passage of the Gospel, alighting upon a passage from Paul: "Put on the Lord Jesus Christ, and make not provision for the flesh in its concupiscences."[114] The idea of "putting on virtue" suggests that human beings become virtuous, in part, by *imitating* virtuous exemplars and *acting* more virtuously, even if their internal states do not match their external behaviors. By "putting on" virtue and "clothing" themselves in Christ, Augustine suggests, human beings can become more like Christ.

In introductory sermons to catechumens, Augustine applies the same metaphors to moral formation, highlighting how imitating Christ, repeating the Creed, and participating in certain spiritual practices can enable Christians to "put on" the virtue of faith. He suggests a similar process with the Lord's Prayer. Explaining that he will test his students next week, he tells them to "fix this prayer as well firmly in your minds, because you are to give it back in a week's time."[115] Augustine proceeds to offer a theological exposition of the prayer, emphasizing again that the first three petitions refer to eternal goods and the last four to the temporal goods of our "daily life."[116] He encourages the class to say the prayer daily so they will remember and enact it: "[L]et's say it everyday, and let's mean what we say, and let's do what we say."[117] Practicing the Lord's Prayer every day will help them put on the virtue of hope so that they eventually habituate the proper disposition toward temporal and eternal goods. "This prayer can be a great encouragement to you; in it you may not only learn to ask God your Father who is in heaven for whatever you desire, but also learn what you ought to desire."[118] Augustine's attention to the practical, pedagogical features of the Lord's Prayer fits with an alternative emphasis on the moral psychology of hope. If hoping rightly requires not only hoping for the right objects but hoping in the right ways, the Lord's Prayer aids that practice.

One final feature of the Lord's Prayer reinforces these practices of moral formation: the prayer is the *Lord's* Prayer, a prayer that Jesus himself is reported to have prayed. Augustine makes much of this in his sermons. Sometimes, he mentions it to accent the prayer's efficacy or origins,[119] but often he refers to it to lift up Christ as a teacher and exemplar of virtuous hope.[120] In one sermon, he suggests that the Lord's Prayer is intended to help us "put on the image of the heavenly man, that is, of Christ."[121] In another sermon, he suggests that "the words our Lord Jesus Christ has taught us in his prayer give us the *forma* of true desires," the "model," "form," or "framework" of proper hopes.[122] For Augustine, Christ ultimately provides the "pattern" of virtuous hope.[123]

For my purposes, Augustine's emphasis on exemplarity in the Lord's Prayer is significant for two reasons. First, it shows that Augustine encourages audiences not only to learn a practice but also to imitate an exemplar, to model one who exemplifies properly ordered faith, hope, and love. This focus on imitation highlights Augustine's appropriation of a central element of the ancient virtue tradition and supports an alternative emphasis on the moral psychology of hope. In encouraging Christians to imitate Christ's prayer, Augustine is teaching them not only *what* to hope for, but *how* to hope, namely, in the way that Christ hoped. This is especially significant since, second, it shows that even Christ—even the one regarded as the Son of God—expressed and endorsed hopes for temporal goods such as daily bread. Even Christ was not so focused on eternal goods that he ignored the need to hope for temporal goods during his earthly life. Christ's example fits with an Augustinian order of hope that allows hope for temporal goods.

Conclusion

Contrary to what critics of Augustine's "otherworldly" hope assume, Augustine does not recommend that we abandon all hopes for temporal goods; he simply wants our hopes to be properly ordered. At times, he even suggests that hoping for temporal goods can be proximate parts of hoping for God, ways to participate in God's goodness here and now. His implicit order of hope does not deny the value of temporal goods but chastens disordered desires for them, providing a regulative ideal that discourages human beings from hoping for temporal goods too much or in the wrong ways. When supported and sustained by moral, spiritual, and social practices, hope can become a virtue that enables us to endure difficulties and resist temptations toward presumption and despair.

This account of Augustine's order of hope illuminates what human beings can hope for. Yet, as Augustine reminds us, hope depends not only on love but on faith. Understanding the virtue of hope thus requires analyzing Augustine's account of faith.

4

Faith in the Unseen

TRUSTING IN ANOTHER

[B]e ready to respond to everyone who asks us for an account of our
faith and hope.

—AUGUSTINE, LETTER 120.1.4, QUOTING 1 PETER 3:15

IF FAITH is the "substance of things hoped for, the conviction of things that
are not seen," then faith supplies hope with its grounds, the bases to believe
that hope's unseen objects are possible to attain and that specific agents of
assistance can potentially help to attain them.[1] To understand Augustine's account of hope, we must explore his conception of faith.

Political theorists do not typically devote attention to Augustine's account
of faith.[2] From Arendt and Nussbaum to Niebuhr and Shklar, most interpreters tend to focus either on Augustine's account of love or his analysis of sin.
They rarely engage a conception of faith that, to their minds, might seem beyond their disciplinary scope, too theological for their political purposes or
too peripheral to Augustine's vision of public life. In some cases, this neglect
may reflect a liberal separation between "public" and "private" that consigns
faith to the private sphere, relevant for individual believers but not the body
politic. Whatever the cause, the omission represents a missed opportunity to
understand a key concept in Augustine's thought, one that has significant implications not only for his account of hope but also for his practice of reasoning, rhetoric, and politics.

Unfortunately, Augustine is not always clear what he means by faith (*fides*).
He uses the term in various ways in different contexts. To elucidate his

meaning, I will distinguish his different uses and analyze their relations. Part I attempts this reconstructive task by identifying five forms of faith, many of which involve trusting in another. Augustine's account of faith is fundamentally relational. Part II considers how we might have faith in the "unseen" and on what grounds such faith rests, focusing on Augustine's account of reason and authority as the dual bases of faith. Part III extends this analysis by considering one of the most underappreciated aspects of Augustine's account: his default and challenge structure of reasoning, which holds that we can be entitled to beliefs based on authority until we have reasons to doubt, abandon, or adapt them. This default and challenge structure illuminates the conceptual structure of faith's grounds, informs the connection between faith and perseverance, and highlights the temporal, social, and dialogical dimensions of discursive reasoning. Part IV considers faith's connection to rhetoric, highlighting how his Greek, Roman, and Christian predecessors understand the close connection between reasoning, rhetoric, and trust. Augustine's highly relational form of faith depends on persuasion. With the grounds of faith in view, part V considers its objects. Analyzing *Faith in the Unseen*, a treatise often overlooked by political theorists, I show how Augustine acknowledges the permissibility of placing faith in human neighbors while recognizing how such acts of trust might become disordered. The next chapter considers how this account of faith supplies hope with its grounds.

I. Five Forms of Faith

Faith (*fides*) is a term with multiple meanings in Latin.[3] I focus on five ways that Augustine uses the term throughout his works.

First, faith can refer to a *belief that*, or *act of believing that*, something is true or possible. Augustine often connects the verb "to believe" (*credere*) to the noun for "faith" (*fides*), suggesting, for example, that "faith believes" (*fides credit*).[4] Following contemporary philosophers, we can call this *propositional faith* since it involves *believing that*, or *having faith that*, a particular proposition is true.[5] In this case, *fides* means having *faith that* God exists or Jesus is the Christ, or *faith that* a particular outcome is true or possible.[6] In contemporary accounts, propositional faith is the form of faith usually assumed. After the Reformation and Enlightenment recast traditional religious concepts in terms of belief and epistemic rationality, many simply assume "faith" is equivalent to a belief that something is true.[7] But premodern Roman and Christian thinkers like Augustine also understood faith in other ways.

Second, Augustine uses faith to refer to the *propositional content* or *object* of such beliefs—in Augustine's words, "what must be believed" or the "faith which is believed" (*fides quae creditur*).[8] We can call this *creedal faith*, the set of propositions, tenets, or doctrines that constitute *the* faith.[9] Throughout his texts, Augustine often refers to the "Christian faith" or "Catholic faith" to describe a general set of beliefs or doctrines.[10] Creedal faith is what Augustine has in mind when he ties *fides* to the Creed in the *Enchiridion* to specify the beliefs that Christians should hold.[11] Augustine describes the Creed as a "brief summary of the faith" and devotes an entire treatise to *Faith and the Creed*.[12]

For Augustine, both propositional and creedal faith often rely on a third kind of faith, *faith in* a particular person or their authority, testimony, or witness. We can call this *relational faith*, which involves *trusting in* another person or the *relationship of trust* that provides the context for this act.[13] Since we typically *believe that* something is true because we *trust in* another's testimony or authority, relational faith often underwrites other forms of faith.[14]

This relational form of *fides* was especially significant in Augustine's Roman context, where trust in others was among the foundational concepts of Roman social life.[15] Cicero, for example, describes *fides* as a precondition for justice and the basis of the reciprocal relationships that unite citizens in a commonwealth: "[T]here is nothing that holds together a political community more powerfully than good faith."[16] The same applies for friendship: "The foundation of the stability and constancy for which we look in friendship is faith [*fides*]."[17]

In her monumental study of Roman and Christian faith in the early empire, Teresa Morgan notes how Greek, Roman, and Jewish writers emphasized *fides* and its Greek antecedent, *pistis*, primarily as a form of trust. According to Morgan, *pistis/fides* "is, first and foremost, neither a body of beliefs nor a function of the heart or mind, but a relationship which creates community."[18] Morgan argues that the primary meaning of *pistis/fides* as trust in the early empire has been obscured by later interpreters who anachronistically read the New Testament backward through the language of interiority and propositional belief. Strikingly, Morgan attributes this misreading to the influence of Augustine, who distinguishes between the "faith which is believed" (*fides quae creditur*) and "the faith by which it is believed" (*fides qua creditur*).[19] The former refers to "the propositional content of faith," while the latter reflects the interior faith that "takes place in the heart and mind of the believer."[20] While Morgan acknowledges "Augustine only juxtaposes these phrases once, in passing, in *On the Trinity* (13.2.5)," she says that "[i]t is clear . . . from references to one or the other scattered throughout his works, that this bina-rism is ingrained in his thinking."[21]

Morgan is right that Augustine emphasizes interior belief and propositional faith more than earlier writers, but we must be careful not to read Augustine anachronistically through the lens of later interpreters or neglect the wider range of texts where he discusses *fides* in more relational terms.[22] As a rhetori-cian in the Roman empire who had read Cicero extensively and later served as an arbitrator of legal cases in the bishop's council, Augustine was immersed in the rhetorical, philosophical, political, and legal meanings of *fides* that Mor-gan surveys, and he frequently uses *fides* in the context of relationships of love and friendship, often with the same "language of inter-subjective relation-ships" that Morgan so deftly canvasses.[23] In *The Excellence of Marriage*, he dis-cusses the "fidelity" between married couples, describes how adultery consti-tutes a "betrayal of trust," and identifies *fides* as one of the key qualities of a marriage.[24] He offers similar reflections on marital "faith" and "fidelity" in *The Excellence of Widowhood*.[25] In *Faith in the Unseen*, he extends such "faith" to friendships, discussing how we must place our "trust" (*fides*) in friends and family.[26] In *The Advantage of Believing*, he affirms that friendship depends on trust in the unseen: "[F]riendship cannot exist unless we believe some things that cannot be proved for certain."[27] Here and elsewhere, he uses *fides* in ways similar to the Roman views he inherited, highlighting the value of the "higher faith, because of which [Christians] are called 'the faithful'" and "the kind of faith which is also called faith (or trust) in ordinary matters."[28] "If trust [*fides*] of this kind were to disappear from human affairs," he writes, "who would not be aware of the confusion and appalling upheaval which would follow? . . . Friendship as a whole would therefore disappear."[29] Thus, when we look be-yond the single distinction from *The Trinity* that Augustine makes "in pass-ing,"[30] we can find a richer and more complex account of faith rooted in rela-tionships of trust. For Augustine, faith is fundamentally a form of trust.[31]

The mutuality implicit in relational faith points to a fourth and closely re-lated kind of faith, what we can call *fidelity* or *faithfulness*.[32] Also common in Latin usage, fidelity involves acting in "good faith," or "keeping faith" with another person who has placed faith in us.[33] Relational faith is often depen-dent on such fidelity since we trust another because they are "faithful" or "act in good faith."[34] Such fidelity is at stake when someone has claimed to be a witness or authority on a particular matter, or when people choose to enter into a contract, covenant, or promise with another person. Augustine identi-fies fidelity as a particular good of human friendship and marriage[35] and an essential duty in keeping promises, even to one's enemies.[36] He also considers fidelity a basis for trusting in God's promises: "This will be brought about by God, the most almighty Founder of that City. For He has promised it, and He cannot lie; and He has shown His good faith by doing many things that He has promised, and many, indeed, that He has not promised."[37] In such cases, fidelity is a ground and source of other forms of faith.

Finally, Augustine sometimes identifies faith as a *virtue*, an interior quality of the soul that orients a person properly to what they believe or the other whom they trust, thereby producing appropriate acts of belief and trust that maintain and deepen a relationship of mutual love. Unlike singular acts of propositional or relational faith that could be false or inappropriate, the virtue of faith reflects a good quality of one's soul that is always appropriate, ordering particular acts of faith to their proper objects and grounds. While trusting in another is a characteristic act of this virtue, the virtue of faith is conceptually distinct from a mere act or attitude of faith. The virtue of faith involves not only cognitive attitudes of epistemic credence in an authority or proposition, but also an affective attitude toward what is believed or toward the one who is trusted. As Augustine writes, "[T]he very act of believing is nothing other than to think with assent," with "assent" constituting, in part, a volitional and affective commitment toward the object of one's belief or trust.[38] Because of such assent, the virtue of faith issues not merely in a cognitive act but an expression of hope and love, a steadfast commitment to the truth of what is held or the person whom is trusted.[39] Such affective and motivational force is missing from simple propositional faith, which is why, according to Augustine, "demons" can believe that God exists or that Jesus is the Christ, but lack the virtue of faith that draws them toward God.[40] They do not believe *in* God or Christ in a way that seeks union with them.[41] For this affective movement, the virtue of faith relies on the cooperation of hope and love, which, as discussed in chapter 1, supplement faith with motivation. The virtue of faith is what Augustine has in mind when he uses the triad of "faith, hope, and love,"[42] lists "faith" alongside other virtues,[43] and endorses biblical descriptions of "the faith that works through love" and "the faith from which the righteous now live."[44]

Unfortunately, Augustine does not always explain which form of faith he has in mind when he describes faith or belief, even within the same passage. In one paragraph in *Faith and the Creed*, for example, he refers to "believing in God the Father Almighty" (relational faith) in order "to believe that there is no creature which has not been created by his omnipotence" (propositional faith), a belief that he then connects with key components of "our faith" (creedal faith).[45] Similarly, throughout the *Enchiridion*, he often uses *fides* to refer to the belief that God exists (propositional faith), the set of beliefs that constitute the faith (creedal faith), and the disposition of the soul that orients the human intellect toward God (the virtue of faith).[46] Attending to how Augustine applies the concept can help us determine how he understands the complex relation between hope and faith.

II. Faith in the Unseen

Faith, Knowledge, and Credulity

Throughout his writings, Augustine frequently discusses faith as a form of partial vision.[47] What various forms of faith share is a belief in the "unseen," a belief that falls short of full and perfect knowledge of what can be "seen." Early in his career, Augustine uses this distinction between "believing" and "seeing" to distinguish faith from knowledge.[48] We have "knowledge" or "understanding" of an object when it is "seen" or "present" to us, when we can know it directly and have no doubt about its "reality" (*res*).[49] He gives the example of knowing that we exist, or that we intend something, because the idea is "present" to the "gaze of our mind"—we can "see" it with our "interior eyes."[50] His favorite example is seeing God "face to face" in eternity, where human beings can know "reality" and "see God as he is."[51]

In this life, however, this full and perfect vision eludes us; we can only see God "through a glass, darkly."[52] Faith is the most that finite human beings can muster on this side of the eschaton. For this reason, Augustine describes faith, in part, as an orientation toward objects absent and unseen. For things that are absent to the external senses or the interior gaze of the mind (such as the true intentions of a friend or true feelings of a spouse), faith or belief is typically the highest level of epistemic credence to which we are entitled. We cannot see others' inner states as we see our own mind; we can only believe or trust them on faith.[53] Faith involves belief in the unseen rather than perfect vision: "[B]y faith we believe what we do not see."[54]

Later, Augustine's views on the relationship between faith and knowledge shift. While he previously held that belief based on testimony does not constitute "knowledge," Matthew Siebert shows that he came to accept that some belief based on testimony could acquire the status of "knowledge."[55] Even here, Siebert acknowledges that Augustine's view of testimonial knowledge, at least in "human matters," tends to "leave room for theoretical doubt" while yielding "enough certainty that ordinarily it is not reasonable to be in any doubt."[56] Later in life, Augustine relaxes this position a bit, suggesting that belief in testimony does not achieve "certain knowledge" (*certissimam scientiam*) but can achieve a kind of "knowledge [*notitia*] through witnesses whom it is absurd not to believe."[57]

Importantly, even when he suggests that faith in the unseen does not achieve the certainty of knowledge, he does not hold faith to be groundless. Throughout his writings, he holds that faith must have rational grounds; otherwise, a belief might be false or misplaced. Thus, he distinguishes "believing" not only from "knowing" and "understanding," but also from possessing rash confidence or "credulity" (*credulitas*), which involves being too willing to believe any and every thing proposed.[58] Since a credulous person is indiscriminate toward truth and fails to differentiate proper beliefs from false or baseless ones, Augustine considers credulity a vice or defect.[59]

To avoid error or credulity, on what basis should a human being believe? Augustine typically identifies two sources of faith's grounds: authority and reason.[60] Understanding their dialectical relation can illuminate the grounds of faith and, by extension, hope.

The Priority of Authority

Augustine's views on the relationship between authority and reason are complex and often shift in light of his personal experiences and engagements with particular interlocutors.[61] Nonetheless, his analysis shares a basic consistency across various works that allows us to reconstruct the general contours of his account.

In Augustine's late antique context, reason was often assumed to be the most secure and direct source of understanding. The priority of reason was emphasized not only by Stoics and Platonists but also by Manicheans, an influential sect in which Augustine spent nine years as a "hearer" before becoming a Catholic.[62] The Manicheans criticized, and sometimes even mocked, the Catholic Church because they thought Catholics "were ordered to believe, but were not taught by most solid reason what the truth was."[63] As "a young man yearning for the truth," Augustine was initially drawn to the Manichean promise of rational understanding.[64] Later, he found it hollow. In recruiting followers and defending their faith, Manicheans, he came to believe, relied on "authority" more than "pure and simple reasoning," leaving a "wide discrepancy" between what they claimed on authority and what he was able to discern through reason.[65]

In contrast to the Manicheans, Augustine holds that belief in authority is often temporally prior to rational understanding: "Authority comes first in time, reason in the reality of things."[66] Augustine offers several explanations for authority's temporal priority, most of which reflect his understanding of human nature. He holds, for example, that access to some religious truths—such as the mysteries of the Trinity—is possible only through belief in authority. Humans simply cannot reason their way to divine truths, which are beyond the grasp of the human intellect.[67] In addition to being finite, the human intellect is also fallible, subject to the corrupting influences of sin and disordered love, which can create an "obstacle to our reaching eternal things."[68] As a result, human beings must initially rely on divine authority to purify their minds and prepare them to eventually approach the understanding provided by reason.[69] "There is no right way of entering into the true religion without believing things that all who live rightly and become worthy of it will understand and see for themselves later on, and without some submission to a certain weight of authority."[70] For Augustine, "faith prepares the ground for understanding."[71]

The necessity of believing first on authority is not only relevant to divine truths. It is simply how human beings learn.[72] Students who wish to learn literature cannot simply read the most difficult texts on their own; they need a teacher to instruct and guide them.[73] Infants do not come out of the womb able to reason through complex proofs or understand why they must believe some things; they believe on the authority of others. Even "the identity of their parents" is a matter of belief since infants cannot understand or prove who their parents are since "they retain no awareness of the period in question," but "nonetheless they are prepared to give their assent unhesitatingly to others who told them about it."[74] In many cases, Augustine argues, we have no other choice but to "believe without any hesitation, things that we admit we cannot know."[75]

The same applies in relationships with family and friends. We cannot know or see the interior will of friends, so we must trust them on the authority of their testimony and expressions of affection, which count as evidence they can be trusted, even if we do not "know" they can be. We put "faith in" a friend before we have "proof" they are actually a friend; we "believe" before we can "see."[76] The same is true of spouses, siblings, and relatives.[77] If we refuse "to believe what we cannot see," Augustine concludes, "human relationships [would be] thrown into chaos, and the foundations [would be] utterly swept away by our failure to trust the goodwill of people, a goodwill which is impossible for us to actually see."[78] Indeed, "absolutely nothing in human society would be safe if we decided not to believe anything that we cannot hold as evident."[79]

Even more mundane beliefs require faith in an authority without prior rational proof. We often believe in the existence of certain cities or places, not because we have visited them but because we trust in the testimony of others.[80] This is also true of many "events of world history," which we did not witness ourselves but nonetheless believe on the basis of testimony.[81] If we were unwilling to believe before we have rational proof in such cases, Augustine holds, we could scarcely believe or know much of what we take for granted every day.[82]

Forms of Authority

Throughout his works, Augustine identifies and relies on many different forms of authority as a basis for faith. Often, he frames these authorities in term of "testimony."[83] For those objects that cannot be known through the "testimony of our own senses," Augustine suggests that "we require the testimony of others," especially those who have seen or experienced the relevant events or causes of a belief firsthand.[84] Augustine emphasizes the authority of "witnesses" whose "testimonies" and "reports"—either verbal or written—reflect direct knowledge or experience.[85] Given his theological context, he often focuses on the authority of those who had firsthand knowledge of Jesus and can testify to his life and work,[86] but he also recognizes the importance of testimony in more mundane matters.[87] The weight given to a particular testimony depends on a range of factors, including the "reputation" of the authority and "acceptance" of the testimony by others.[88] On matters of faith, Augustine emphasizes the quantity and variety of people who accept the Catholic faith, which is supported by "wide acceptance of the report, strong in its unanimity and antiquity."[89] The Church's authority, he believes, is strengthened by the "great numbers of people" and "countless nations of the world" who accept its testimony.[90] And the Church's authority across time lends weight to its testimony: "From the apostolic throne, through the chain of succession of the bishops, it occupies the pinnacle of authority, acknowledged by the whole human race."[91] Here, Augustine exaggerates the Catholic Church's popularity in his age, but his emphasis on both the breadth and history of its witness testifies to the weight he places on "accepted views and recognized traditions of communities and nations."[92] For Augustine, history and tradition are relevant sources of authority.[93]

For Augustine, the most trustworthy authority is the "divine authority" of God revealed through scripture.[94] The scriptures are God's "divine testimonies," communicated through both words and signs, including the fulfillment of "prophecies" and performance of "miracles."[95] As he explains in relation to Genesis, the authority of scripture "is greater than all human ingenuity."[96] Therefore, it is not only permissible to believe scripture but "wrong *not* to believe this authority."[97] Often, Augustine suggests the Church has a role in mediating and reinforcing the authority of scripture, not least through the determination of "canonical" scriptures.[98] As he argues in Letter 147, "[I]f [a claim] is supported by the clear authority of those divine scriptures, namely, those that are called 'canonical' in the Church, it must be believed without any doubt."[99] Yet, even here, Augustine does not preclude the possibility of other grounds for faith. While a claim supported by scripture is assured, "you may believe or not believe other witnesses or testimonies by which you might be persuaded to believe something to the extent that you consider that they have or do not have sufficient weight to produce faith."[100]

Reason's Role

In each of these cases, belief in authority comes prior to reason. Yet Augustine does not thereby reject reason or hold reason to be incompatible with faith. He is no fideist. Any proposed opposition between reason and faith does not comport with God's creative act since reason is the capacity by which humans are made in God's image: "Mind, reason, judgment, which animals haven't got, nor have birds, nor have fishes. It is in this respect that we were made to the image of God. . . . So we ought above all else to cultivate in ourselves this quality in which we excel the beasts, and somehow or other refashion it and chisel it afresh."[101] If reason is the capacity that marks humans as made in God's image, humans should not abandon it, even in matters of faith.

Such a view informs Augustine's reply to Consentius's apparent fideism in Letter 120. Rejecting Consentius's conviction that "the truth about things divine must be attained more by faith than by reason," Augustine affirms the God-given capacity for reason: "Heaven forbid, after all, that God should hate in us that by which he made us more excellent than the other animals. Heaven forbid, I say, that we should believe in such a way that we do not accept or seek a rational account, since we could not even believe if we did not have rational souls."[102] While Augustine acknowledges that some reasoning can be "false," not all reasoning is.[103] Instead, the deliverances of reason can help to illuminate and reinforce what human beings believe by faith. Augustine thus seeks to offer a "rational account" of faith to Consentius so that "what you already hold with the firmness of faith you may also see with the light of reason."[104]

Augustine's reply to Consentius reflects one way in which reason relates to faith and authority: while belief in authority "comes first in time," rational understanding is the ultimate aim of belief, and reason, purified by faith, can help to achieve it.[105] "Authority demands belief and prepares man for reason. Reason leads to understanding and knowledge."[106] Reason, prompted and guided by faith, leads to the "fullness and perfection of knowledge," where faith finds its consummation and completion.[107]

Yet, even if authority is chronologically prior, "reason is not entirely absent from authority," Augustine argues, "for we have got to consider whom we have to believe."[108] In particular, human beings rely on reason to judge which authorities to trust and how much to trust them, which reflects a second way reason influences belief in authority. Augustine emphasizes such judgment in a letter to Paulina when he recommends that she make "distinctions" in her mind when evaluating the "authority of witnesses" and discerning whom to trust.[109] While Paulina should not hesitate to trust in the divine authority of the scriptures, she must judge how much to trust in the human authority of Augustine and Ambrose so she is "not misled in believing us more or less than [she] ought."[110] Elsewhere, Augustine warns against believing something without reason: "I have no wish that they should believe my words, unless I give reasons."[111] Belief in a human authority requires rational grounds.

In other texts, Augustine suggests that rational capacities are involved in judging not only who to believe, but what to believe.

> After all, who does not see that thinking comes before believing? No one, of course, believes anything unless he first thought that it should be believed. For, although certain thoughts fly quickly, even most swiftly, before the will to believe, and the will follows so soon afterward that it accompanies it as if it were united to it, it is nonetheless necessary that thought precede everything which we believe. In fact, the very act of believing is nothing other than to think with assent. . . . For, without thinking, there is no faith at all.[112]

In this anti-Pelagian text, Augustine holds that thinking itself is a gift of God, for "we are not 'sufficient to have a single thought as if from ourselves, but our sufficiency comes from God.'"[113] Nonetheless, he insists that grace prompts our rational capacities and thereby provides the "beginning of faith."[114]

Augustine makes a similar claim about a translation of Isaiah 7:9: "Unless you believe, you will not understand."[115] Augustine cites this passage frequently to affirm his conception of faith seeking understanding.[116] Yet, while holding that belief is often necessary for understanding, he concedes that unbelievers might need to "understand, in order to believe," for "unless they understand what I am saying, they cannot believe."[117] Augustine proposes that "we can accept both without argument": "Understand, in order to believe, *my word*; believe, in order to understand, *the word of God*."[118] Here, Augustine affirms that human beings must rely on faith to understand divine authority and on reason to understand and evaluate human authority.

Reason is also relevant in a third and final way: once human beings have been exposed to alternative beliefs or authorities, reason can help them discern whether to continue holding those beliefs, abandon those beliefs and accept alternative authorities, or revise their current beliefs in light of new arguments or evidence. This function of reason is implicit in Augustine's letter to Consentius. "[A]fter having been carefully instructed by reading or hearing other works," Augustine tells Consentius, "you yourself may more extensively correct your own statements made in another vein."[119] In other places, Augustine affirms that reason can prompt revision or correction, a view implicit in his frequent attempts to engage his interlocutors in terms of reason rather than authority.[120]

These texts reveal Augustine's complex and nuanced understanding of what one commentator describes as the "dialectic between authority and reason."[121] Given the limits of human knowledge, belief in authority can provide access to truths that are not attainable or demonstrable through reason, and it can prepare the mind to assent to truths that may at first seem inaccessible or unacceptable. Yet, if authority often precedes reason in time, reason can provide belief with its completion in knowledge and understanding. Reason informs which authorities to trust and which beliefs to affirm, and it enables us to confirm, abandon, or correct the beliefs we hold.[122]

III. A Default and Challenge Structure of Reasoning

This dialectic of reason and authority points to an aspect of Augustine's epistemology that has been underappreciated in secondary scholarship: a "default and challenge" structure of reasoning.[123] While Augustine holds that some things—such as the content of our mind—can be known directly and nondiscursively and that other things can be known through inductive inference, not every belief must be justified by an appeal to an priori reason or inference.[124] In many cases of discursive reasoning based on testimony, the authority of experience or testimony can, by default, supply rational grounds for belief and hope, grounds that can later be subject to rational evaluation, confirmation, or correction. Thus, rather than being required to provide reasons *before* assenting to a belief or proposition in every case, as is common in more foundationalist models, a default and challenge model allows a person to be entitled to hold a belief or invest trust based on a judgment of authority, experience, or reasoning until they encounter other authorities, experiences, or reasons that challenge their default belief.[125] This means that many default beliefs can be prima facie defeasible: we can be entitled to hold them until we have good reason to abandon, adapt, or revise them. Such beliefs can be described as "innocent until proven guilty."[126]

In a default and challenge model, challenges or "defeaters" are reasons that undermine the default belief. Scholars typically identify two types.[127] *Rebutting defeaters* challenge the default belief by providing overriding or outweighing reasons for another belief that is inconsistent with the default belief. Rebutting defeaters attempt to show that the default belief cannot be rationally maintained in light of the reasons that support the defeater. *Undercutting defeaters* challenge the default belief by undermining the reasons or grounds on which it rests. They undercut the authority, evidence, or reasoning that justifies the default belief. Both kinds of defeater constitute potential reasons to give up or adapt a default belief.

In the face of such challenges, a person may be able to adduce arguments or evidence that enables their default belief to survive the challenge—they may be able to *defeat the defeaters*.[128] For example, they may adduce additional evidence for their default belief, show the rebuttals to be mistaken or misplaced, demonstrate that the challenge does not actually relate to the belief in question, or undercut the authority, evidence, or reasoning on which the defeater is based. If they are able to rebut or undercut the potential challenge, they are rational in preserving their default belief and need not abandon it.

In other cases, opposing reasons may actually defeat or undercut the default belief. In such cases, it would be epistemically irrational to maintain it. A person should either give up the default belief, lessen one's degree of credence or commitment to it, or correct it to avoid the defeaters. To fail to abandon, adapt, or revise a belief in the face of a successful challenge would be rationally irresponsible.[129]

Augustine, of course, never explicitly describes his structure of epistemic entitlement in the language of contemporary epistemology, but it fits with the larger context of early Christianity. As Nicholas Wolterstorff emphasizes, a concern with providing foundational reasons to justify belief in God is a largely post-Enlightenment preoccupation: "Until the modern age, Christian apologetics consisted mainly not in giving or defending arguments *for* Christianity but rather in answering objections *to* Christianity."[130] Many early Christians saw the truth of Christianity as reasonable by default; their primary efforts were devoted to defeating any defeaters.

A default and challenge model would have been also available to Augustine in his late antique Roman context. Michael Williams notes a similar structure in the theories of "skeptical assent" held by the Academics and the doctrine of "tested impression" advocated by Carneades.[131] Augustine was aware of these doctrines and even briefly entertained Academic skepticism as his own position.[132] Although he eventually wrote a treatise against skepticism, he would have been familiar with its structure of justification, and even if he did not endorse its conclusions, he may have been informed by its mode of reasoning.[133] Indeed, part of his approach in *Against the Academicians* is to engage skeptics on their own terms by using the kinds of arguments and reasoning they found authoritative to show the inconsistency of their approach and defeat the "obstacle" that challenged his faith.[134]

Whether or not Augustine consciously adapted such a method, a default and challenge structure is implicit in the way he articulates the dialectic between authority and reason. He holds that we can be entitled to many default beliefs based on trust in authority until we are presented with reasons to doubt, abandon, or adapt those beliefs. If we have no reason to doubt those beliefs, we need not inquire into them.[135] In this way, Augustine does not require us to pursue or possess rational foundations for every belief before we accept it on authority. Many default beliefs are innocent until proven guilty.

Augustine's discussion of whether humans can see God or spiritual bodies in Letter 147 reflects this approach. He expresses an openness to argument but suggests he need not inquire into a topic he has no reason to doubt: "[S]ince I do not have any doubt that the nature of God is not seen in any location, I do not ask about it."[136] Yet, as he affirms in the next sentence, the strength of this default belief does not prevent him from being open to persuasion. "Now," he continues, "I am ready to hear with the peace of love from those who are able to prove through argument whether something that is not seen in a location can be seen by the eyes of the body."[137] Suggesting this question "must be examined with more care and concern," he proceeds to consider and then reject such a view.[138] Holding that one may "confirm" a belief "by the authority of other testimonies, that is, of the divine scriptures or of any others by which he is moved to belief,"[139] he draws on the scriptural testimony of Paul and Peter and the interpretative authority of Ambrose and Jerome to add weight to his default belief and stave off undercutting defeaters from "those who hold another view . . . so that they do not criticize such learned commentators on the divine scriptures."[140] In the next sentence, he challenges a potential rebutting defeater by showing how it involves contradictory assumptions.[141] Here, his reasoning reflects an implicit default and challenge structure, one that affirms a default belief and seeks to answer challenges by drawing on additional authorities to confirm the default belief and support it against rebutting and undercutting defeaters.

Augustine makes a default and challenge structure more explicit when describing his own method of reasoning in *Of True Religion*:

> I have given much consideration for a long time to the nature of the people I have met with either as carping critics or as genuine seekers of the truth. I have also considered my own case both when I was a critic and when I was a seeker; and I have come to the conclusion that this is the method I must use. Hold fast whatever truth you have been able to grasp, and attribute it to the Catholic Church. Reject what is false and pardon me who am but a man. What is doubtful believe until either reason teaches or authority lays down that it is to be rejected or that it is true, or that it has to be believed always. Listen to what follows as diligently and as piously as you can.[142]

Here, Augustine endorses a default and challenge structure, encouraging readers to hold firmly to what they believe to be true by authority until reason or authority defeats or confirms their default belief.

This default and challenge structure of reasoning has significant implications for how we understand the grounds of faith and, by extension, the grounds of hope. If we can be epistemically entitled to faith based on a belief in a credible authority, then faith does not require that we logically deduce reasons for faith before we believe, as long as we remain open to examining our beliefs in light of any subsequent reasons or counterevidence. Yet, even if faith can be initially based on a belief in authority, it does require that we are prepared to defend our faith (and our hope) with reasons, or else abandon or revise our beliefs. Citing 1 Peter 3:15, Augustine affirms that believers must "be ready to respond to everyone who asks us for an account of our faith and hope."[143]

The "Certainty" of Faith

The suggestion that Augustine might allow or even require a revision of faith based on an exchange of reasons raises an immediate issue. Augustine often talks about faith in God as "certain,"[144] but how can faith or belief be "certain" if, on a default and challenge model, it is subject to potential challenges?

One answer is that Augustine, like his interlocutors, does not always use terms precisely. Augustine writes about faith as a pastor and rhetorician, not as a systematic philosopher.[145] Furthermore, he acknowledges that ordinary usage often conflates "knowing" and "believing." In the *Retractions*, he clarifies this point in relation to his own usage in *The Advantage of Believing*:

> In truth, when we speak precisely, we mean that we know only what we grasp with the sound reason of mind. But when we use words better suited to common usage, as, indeed, Holy Scripture uses them, we should not hesitate to say that we know both what we perceive with our bodily senses and what we believe on the authority of trustworthy witnesses, provided, however, that we understand the difference between them.[146]

Augustine may be following common usage and the example of divine scripture in sometimes attributing the certainty of knowledge to faith.

A second and related possibility draws on his hint above about "worthy witnesses," particularly the witness of scripture. Augustine typically describes faith as certain in relation to trust or belief in God, whom he takes to be the most trustworthy witness whose word we should believe "without any doubt" (*sine ulla dubitatione*).[147] He does not attribute the same level of epistemic certainty to faith in human beings, whose witness and testimony are more susceptible to doubt.[148] This is clear when he compares the "firmness" of God's promise to the "weakness" of human beings.[149] Recognizing that a person can be "uncertain" about both God's will for him and his own will for himself, Augustine encourages him to "entrust his faith, hope, and love to the more firm rather than the less firm."[150] Even when referring to his own authority, he advises Paulina that she should "accept in faith these words in one way and the words of God in another."[151] Both passages acknowledge that the firmness of faith can come in degrees, which challenges the idea that firmness necessarily entails the highest levels of epistemic certainty. Accordingly, it is possible that Augustine, like Aquinas after him, holds that faith can be "certain" when it has a *source* or *cause* whose testimony or authority is beyond doubt—namely, God—but less certain in relation to its *object*, which, unlike an object of knowledge, remains unseen.[152]

Another way to address the puzzle is to suggest that it is no puzzle at all, at least if we avoid interpreting it anachronistically through post-Enlightenment understandings of "faith," "belief," and "certainty." Today, when many of us think about the "certainty" of faith or belief, we tend to assume that certainty refers to the level of epistemic credence one has in a belief. But Latin usages do not necessarily carry the same meaning. As discussed above, "faith" (*fides*) often referred to a relational form of "trust" in another, while "to believe" (*credere*) often meant to trust someone, invest loyalty or allegiance in another, or make a commitment to someone.[153] These terms do not simply connote cognitive categories; they also reflect the kind of affective and volitional investment that characterizes a relationship of trust or fidelity.[154] Moreover, in Latin, to describe faith or belief as "certain" does not necessarily refer to the highest level of epistemic confidence, although that is one potential meaning. *Certa* can also mean "determined," "resolved," "fixed," "settled," "purposed," "assured," "trustworthy," or "firm."[155] Some of these meanings—"settled," "assured," "trustworthy"— suggest high levels of credence without necessarily implying that a belief is beyond doubt, which would allow Augustine to describe faith as *certa* without thereby equating faith with knowledge. Other meanings—"determined," "resolved," "fixed," "purposed," "firm"—might fit more with a conception of "tenacity," "steadfastness," or "perseverance" than with levels of epistemic credence.[156] Wolterstorff suggests such a distinction when discussing the ambiguity around Calvin's notion of the "firmness of belief":

> By saying of someone that she believes something firmly one may mean that she believes it with a high level of confidence. But may one not also mean that she believes it tenaciously, steadfastly, perseveringly? Perhaps to believe it thus is to believe it and to be reluctant to give it up, to resist giving it up. It seems to me that the two phenomena are indeed distinct—that of believing something with a high level of confidence, and that of believing something tenaciously. One might tenaciously believe something in which one does not have a very high level of confidence; and one might be not at all tenacious in believing something in which one does have a high level of confidence.[157]

According to Wolterstorff, such a view does not necessarily exclude doubt but instead encourages Christians to "hold the faith tenaciously, with steadfastness, with perseverance,"[158] even in the face of doubt. Augustine, whose account of faith informed Calvin's,[159] may be operating with a similar focus on the tenacity, steadfastness, and perseverance of faith, one that tends to be obscured by a modern conception of faith as a primarily doxastic concept and of certainty as the highest level of epistemic credence. This emphasis can be seen when Augustine discusses how we "know whatever we hold *by faith un-feigned* (1 Tm 1:5)," for "even though we do not yet see it by vision we nonetheless already hold firmly to it by faith."[160] It also aligns with his acceptance of both translations of Isaiah 7:9: "'if you do not believe, you will not *understand*'" and "'if you do not believe, you will not *stand fast*.'" Both, he argues, "convey something important to those who read intelligently," indicating the need for faith both to lead to "understanding" and enable them to "hold fast to the truth" on their journey toward understanding.[161]

This interpretation is strengthened when we consider Augustine's consistent emphasis on the connection between faith and perseverance.[162] Augustine devotes an entire treatise, *The Gift of Perseverance*, to highlighting the need to rely on God's grace to persevere in faith until the end, and throughout his writings, he speaks of faith in relation to movement toward, or adherence to, God.[163] To have faith is not only to believe *that* God exists or believe *in* God but, on the basis of that belief, to *move* toward God as one would move toward a person whom one loves or trusts. Indeed, Augustine often uses active, biblical metaphors of movement ("we walk by faith, not by sight") when describing faith's commitment to its object.[164] Faith involves not simply passively trusting in another but making an active commitment to move toward that person in action or affection, even when the object is unseen.[165] While belief might mark the beginning of faith, it is not sufficient for its completion.[166] Affective and volitional commitment, informed by hope and love, enables those with the virtue of faith to maintain their adherence to God.

If faith informed by hope and love involves an affective and volitional movement toward God or another, then "perseverance" in faith is a necessary complement of belief. For Augustine, one cannot simply believe or trust in God; one must persevere in that belief and trust to move closer to God or keep from falling away. This is why Augustine emphasizes both "finding and holding to the truth" and highlights "the faith which perseveres and makes progress."[167] Faith requires the volitional complement of perseverance to increase and find completion in God, particularly in the face of human sin. Otherwise, faith will "falter in the midst of temptations and trials."[168]

Firm faith requires mutually reinforcing practices such as prayer to foster perseverance: "Faith pours out prayer, prayer being poured out obtains firmness for faith."[169] In this passage, "firmness" seems to be understood more in relation to persevering in adherence to God than holding high epistemic confidence about an unseen object. Indeed, Augustine holds that one can have "faith" even if it remains "incomplete," which is how he interprets the famous passage from Mark 9:24: "I believe, Lord; help my unbelief."[170] The man acted upon his faith in Jesus to heal his son while also acknowledging that his faith remained imperfect.[171] This passage shows the active and steadfast commitment involved in trusting in and relying on another, even when a belief is not held with epistemic certainty.

In this way, Augustine's account of faith as a form of persevering trust has much in common with nondoxastic accounts of faith in contemporary philosophy of religion. Perhaps most relevant is Daniel McKaughan's account of "relational faith," which identifies faith as an interpersonal form of trust in or reliance on another in the face of uncertainty, doubt, or difficulty.[172] Against prevailing doxastic accounts that emphasize the cognitive components of faith and cast it primarily as a form of propositional belief, McKaughan positions faith and faithfulness as forms of trust and trustworthiness involving affective and behavioral dimensions alongside cognitive ones.[173] McKaughan defines faith in terms of an "*active commitment*, which involves interpersonal trust or reliance and a commitment to remain actively involved in a relationship," a commitment that often manifests in behaviors such as following or relying on another.[174] McKaughan helpfully shows how such faith can be rational in the face of uncertainty and highlights how its value consists partly in enabling one to persevere in the face of challenges that might otherwise cause one to abandon an active commitment. For McKaughan, such perseverance is not unconditional. Rather, it requires a proper responsiveness to the value of one's objects and to available evidence that potentially supports or challenges faith, making it compatible with a default and challenge structure of reasoning.[175] McKaughan bolsters his account of relational faith by drawing on ancient Greek, Roman, and Christian understandings of *pistis/fides*.[176] Given what we have seen above, Augustine might provide another ancient source for McKaughan's account of relational faith and its "characteristic perseverance."[177]

Faithful Reasoning: Temporal, Social, Dialogical

One reason that persevering faith is compatible with a default and challenge structure is that epistemic entitlement has a *temporal* dimension. While human beings may be entitled to a belief at any one point in time, entitlement is an ongoing process. Until they achieve full and perfect vision of God, none of their beliefs will achieve the completion expected of full and perfect knowledge. So, depending on their epistemic context, they may be entitled to a belief or form of trust at one time but not another. Or they may *not* be entitled at one time but come to be entitled later, perhaps because they are persuaded by a friend or have a religious experience that supplies a reason to assent or place trust in another (such as Augustine's experience of hearing *tolle lege*—"Pick it up and read"—in the garden).[178] On this side of the eschaton, epistemic entitlement remains an iterative process. Human beings need perseverance to stand firm in the face of doubts and difficulties.

This diachronic dimension is an important aspect of the epistemic context for faith and perseverance. Once a person embarks on the path of faith and hope, they begin to acquire other epistemic, practical, and relational commitments that potentially reinforce a particular belief or practice, and this web of commitments can strengthen an entitlement to believe or trust in another.[179] In this context, defeaters must be weightier than they would have been had they arisen when the person first assented to the belief or placed trust in another. This temporal dimension fits with Augustine's frequent emphasis on "the beginning of faith."[180] As human beings grow in love toward God, their faith may be "increased," further strengthening their bond of trust and providing even more reason to trust.[181] This increase in faith reinforces their default commitment and fosters perseverance, making them more steadfast in the face of doubts or defeaters that may otherwise cause them to abandon belief.

The relational context of such entitlement is significant. The ongoing process of entitlement is not only temporal but *social*, an aspect often elided in contemporary philosophy. As Wolterstorff argues, the picture typically assumed in contemporary epistemology is that of a "*solitary* reactor," "a solitary person sitting in a chair passively receiving such sensory stimulation as comes his way, taking note of the beliefs that that stimulation evokes in him, recalling certain events from his past, observing what is going on in his mind, and drawing inferences."[182] Such a view leaves out the social context of the formation, maintenance, and revision of beliefs and the active ways that faith seeks understanding, often in community, rather than simply waiting for it arrive.

That inquiry is a distinctly social practice has several implications. First, practices of inquiry are themselves socially embedded.[183] We adopt particular ways of knowing and believing through particular practices that our community makes available to us: practices such as reading, reflecting, conversing, debating, or submitting ourselves to teaching and instruction. Often, these practices are inherited as part of a tradition passed down over generations. As Wolterstorff notes, while a tradition makes these practices "socially available" to its members, only some socially available practices will be "personally accessible" to a particular person within that tradition. Still fewer will be "personally acceptable" such that particular individuals would be willing to employ them as a practice of inquiry.[184]

Augustine provides an apt example. As the son of a Christian mother and pagan father in late antique Rome, he was heir to multiple traditions, including Christianity and the Roman forms of education that shaped his larger culture. This social context made certain practices of inquiry—the study of rhetoric and philosophy, the reading of texts, and debate and dialogue—socially available and personally accessible to him. But as he reports in Confessions, early in his life he found certain Christian practices of inquiry—such as prayer and the reading of scripture—personally unacceptable.[185] Seeing scripture as rhetorically and philosophically unrefined, he was drawn instead to philosophy. But in Milan, his social and epistemic context shifted. As he listened to the sermons of Ambrose and saw an example of Christian philosophical and rhetorical excellence, he began to embrace other practices of inquiry that he now found more acceptable, joining his love of philosophy with prayer and the reading of scripture, which transformed his faith and belief.[186] Even his famous hearing of tolle lege in the garden, which might seem like the most solitary of acts, was socially and linguistically mediated through the songs of the children in the fields and the practices of inquiry common to his tradition.[187] In addition to hearing the call through the linguistic forms he had inherited, he only knew to "pick it up and read" because reading scripture was part of his tradition's way of knowing God and because he had learned the story of St. Antony, who had heard a particular verse being read, took it as a direct message from God, and was "promptly converted" to Christianity.[188] Moreover, not only was Augustine's interpretation of tolle lege socially mediated, but it was also socially affirmed. Augustine reports that his experience was immediately affirmed by his friend, Alypius, who was with him in the garden and had been undergoing a similar process of conversion.[189] Even though Augustine ultimately attributes their conversions to God's grace, their experiences were mediated through social practices of inquiry made available within a particular community and tradition.

The social aspect of Augustine's journey of faith highlights another aspect of a default and challenge model: entitlement can be inherited from someone taken to be an authority.[190] Since a default and challenge model does not require identifying every justifying reason for a default belief before reasonably accepting it, one can rely on the authority or testimony of another who is entitled to the belief. Their entitlement licenses one to hold the default belief responsibly until it is defeated. In such cases, social relations of authority and responsibility contribute to the weight of one's entitlement.[191]

Augustine offers numerous examples throughout his work, perhaps most notably in his exchange with Honoratus in *The Advantage of Believing*. Augustine acknowledges that because he has "not actually seen Christ in the way he chose to appear to the human race," he has to rely on the "testimony" of others.[192] He recognizes his entitlement to belief is inherited: "I see that what I have believed is only the accepted views and recognized traditions of communities and nations."[193] But he argues that the entitlement to these views is strengthened by their "unanimity and antiquity": the "wide acceptance of the report" confers authority to the belief, and this authority is preserved in the Catholic Church, which stands out because it has the strongest "reputation" and "greatest numbers" of believers from various parts of the world.[194] While these factors do not offer "proof," Augustine suggests that the weight of their authority makes them "the most appropriate starting point for our inquiry."[195] For Augustine, the fact that the Christian faith has survived and secured wide acceptance in the face of potential defeaters lends weight to its authority.

The dialectical nature of justification highlights another social aspect of a default and challenge structure: its reasoning is *dialogical*. Being entitled to a particular belief involves being willing and able to give reasons when asked and to offer reasons when challenges are presented.[196] Posing a challenge to another's default belief also requires being willing to give reasons for the challenge.[197] One cannot make a successful challenge without being able to give reasons when pressed. This dialogical process involves exchanging reasons with actual or imagined interlocutors and holding ourselves and others responsible for giving reasons that meet any potential challenges.

Augustine embodies such dialogical reasoning in his own life. This is most evident in his *Retractions*, which supplies a vivid example of how dialogue with interlocutors leads him to examine his errors with "judicial severity" and revise his initial beliefs by acknowledging some of the truths expressed by critics.[198] Even his series of philosophical and religious conversions in *Confessions* reflect how he gives and exchanges reasons with various interlocutors. One reason why he could no longer remain a Manichean was because Faustus could not adequately reply to his challenges.[199] Augustine finds similar inconsistencies and deficiencies in the thought of the Academics and Platonists.[200]

Elsewhere, he explicitly invites correction from readers: "Let the reader, where we are equally confident, stride on with me; where we are equally puzzled, pause to investigate with me; where he finds himself in error, come to my side; where he finds me erring, call me to his side."[201] Or as he says more bluntly a few paragraphs later, "If I am being stupid in this, I hope anyone who has a better idea will correct me."[202] Augustine often expresses openness to correction as a bishop, acknowledging, for example, that he changed his belief about coercing Donatists after dialogues with fellow bishops in North Africa. Although he initially opposed coercion, he explains that "this opinion of mine was defeated, not by the words of its opponents, but by examples of those who offered proof [*demonstrantium*]."[203] Here, Augustine explains how dialogue with fellow bishops provided a challenge to his default beliefs and caused him to revise his belief based on the "proof" they provided.

In addition to illuminating Augustine's rational procedure, the dialogical aspect of a default and challenge structure casts new light on how he engages opponents. Strikingly, many of Augustine's treatises are written in response to opponents who have challenged his position or interlocutors who have requested further clarification. In works such as *City of God* or *On Christian Teaching*, he begins by responding to objections before advancing his more constructive claims, and he frequently anticipates additional objections and responds to each in detail.[204] While some may interpret Augustine's vigorous responses as the defensive retorts of a bishop obsessed with preserving Catholic authority, a default and challenge structure might help to explain why Augustine responds so comprehensively and vigorously. In many cases, he is offering defeaters to the defeaters, arguments intended to either rebut or undercut the objections and thus enable him to preserve his default belief. Even if his arguments do not always offer rational proof, they seek to provide evidence that supports his default belief and enables perseverance in the face of proposed challenges.

Importantly, Augustine often engages such exchanges in dialogical form. While this dialogical approach is especially apparent in letters where he directly addresses interlocutors,[205] it is also true of many treatises, including those where he analyzes or defends the Catholic faith. *Against the Academicians*, for example, is written explicitly as a dialogue between Augustine, Alypius, Licentius, and Trygetius at Cassiciacum. In this dialogue, as in others from his time in Cassiciacum, Augustine follows his Greek and Roman predecessors in using a dialogical account of objections and replies to advance his philosophical arguments and defend his beliefs against skeptical challenges.[206] He even frames his *Soliloquies* as a dialogue with his own reason rather than a monologue expressing his ideas and beliefs.[207]

A dialogical approach also characterizes some treatises not written explicitly as dialogues.[208] For example, in *Faith in the Unseen*, Augustine uses a form of direct address to engage skeptical readers. He begins by refuting opponents' objections to the Catholic faith and then defends the faith's authority and credibility, using an imagined dialogue to advance his claims.[209] Similarly, in *The Advantage of Believing*, he addresses his arguments to Honoratus, a Manichean whom he is trying to convert to Catholic Christianity. Throughout the treatise, he uses the tone of a friend, engaging in an imaginative set of dialogues to anticipate and reply to potential objections.[210] His aim is first to defeat the Manichean defeaters—to show Honoratus that belief in authority can be a secure foundation for faith and that the Manichean attacks are irrational.[211] He does this by offering both rebutting defeaters of the Manichean conclusions and undercutting defeaters that show their conclusions do not follow from their premises. As he explains in the conclusion, he attempts not to provide a complete defense of the Catholic faith but to make Honoratus "more receptive" to it: "I only wanted to weed out from you, if I could, the false opinions about Christian truths that were instilled in us through malice or ignorance and to raise your mind to learn certain great truths about God."[212] The argument aligns with a default and challenge structure of reasoning aimed at eliminating defeaters.

This structure also aligns with Augustine's frequent use of immanent critique to engage opponents. Rather than trying to first convince opponents on his terms or ask them to reason on neutral terms, he often engages the default authorities they already accept, drawing on sources they find personally accessible and acceptable. In asking whether he should engage Honoratus and other Manicheans by appeal to authority or reason, for example, he affirms that "authority precedes reason when we learn something," but since the Manicheans hold that "a reason must be given first," he agrees to "go along with them," even though reason is a "defective" starting point.[213] He makes a similar appeal in Book 19 of *City of God*, where he distinguishes the two cities "not only by calling upon divine authority, but also, for the sake of unbelievers, by making as much use of reason as possible."[214] Implicit in such immanent critique is Augustine's recognition that drawing on opponents' authorities is an effective way to rebut and undercut their arguments and defeat any defeaters they present. It is also an effective way to show respect and avoid domination. By appealing to opponents' authorities rather one's own, immanent critique respects their values, reasons, and commitments and engages them on terms they could accept as legitimate rather than arbitrary, which helps to avoid the arbitrary interference that constitutes domination.[215]

Augustine's emphasis on believing first on authority while being prepared to justify faith and hope with reasons, often dialogically through immanent critique, will have significant consequences for his account of political contestation and deliberation in chapter 8. Here, I want to focus on several implications for his understanding of faith, rhetoric, and persuasion. A default and challenge structure of reasoning provides further justification for his extensive use of rhetoric to form audiences' faith and hope.

IV. Faith, Rhetoric, and Trust

Augustine's Ancient Inheritance: From Pistis to Fides

To understand the connection between faith and rhetoric, it is helpful to consider the concepts and terms Augustine inherited from his Roman and Christian predecessors. In Latin, Romans used *fides* (faith) as a translation of the Greek *pistis*, which was commonly used in Greek philosophy, Hellenistic Jewish literature, and Greek versions of the Bible.[216] As scholars have shown, *pistis* and *fides* share a wide range of meanings: "'Trust,' 'trustworthiness,' 'honesty,' 'credibility,' 'faithfulness,' 'good faith,' 'confidence,' 'assurance,' 'pledge,' 'guarantee,' 'credit,' 'proof,' 'credence,' 'belief,' 'position of trust/trusteeship,' 'legal trust,' 'protection,' 'security.'"[217] *Pistis* can also refer to a "ground for faith," "evidence" that a person is trustworthy, or "proof" that an assertion is true.[218] Plato, for example, uses *pistis* to refer to grounds for believing in the soul's immortality or the gods' existence,[219] while Aristotle uses *pistis* to refer to a rhetorical "proof" or "means of persuasion."[220] Given Aristotle's influence on Greek and Roman rhetoric, this rhetorical meaning was particularly prevalent among many ancient philosophers and teachers of rhetoric.[221]

In his influential study, *Greek Rhetorical Origins of Christian Faith*, James Kinneavy traces the rhetorical meaning of *pistis* through discussions of faith in the New Testament.[222] Describing the teaching of rhetoric as a centerpiece of Greek, Roman, and Jewish schools of the time, Kinneavy notes how early Christian writers were thoroughly steeped in rhetorical arguments and methods in a Greek and Roman context that placed rhetoric at the center of education and culture.[223] As a result, the books of the New Testament are highly "rhetorical" texts.[224] Given the widespread lack of literacy in this period and the expense of producing written texts, the Bible "was more often heard when read aloud to a group than read privately," meaning that many writers intended it partly as a form of "speech."[225] Moreover, early Christians conceived the

New Testament as itself the "word" of God, a divine message conveyed to human beings. As Paul writes in Romans 10:11, "[F]aith comes from what is heard, and what is heard comes by the preaching of Christ," made available through scripture.[226] Most significantly, Christ is identified in the Gospel of John as the "Word" (*logos*) of God.[227] In ancient Greek, *logos* was also a form of *pistis*, one of the three means of persuasion commonly identified as essential to rhetoric. Here and elsewhere, God appears as a trustworthy and faithful communicator who shares his word to persuade human beings to come to faith and enter a trusting relationship with him.

Given the cultural milieu of early Christian writers and the influence of rhetoric in the larger culture, Kinneavy argues that there is a "strong probability" that the connection between faith, rhetoric, and persuasion informed how both the authors and audiences of Christian scriptures understood the uses of the *pistis*.[228] Kinneavy supports this conclusion by analyzing 491 occurrences of the noun (*pistis*) and verb (*pisteuein*) in the New Testament.[229] "[I]n many cases," Kinneavy concludes, "the word 'faith' translating *pistis* could just as well be translated 'persuasion,' and the word 'believed' translating the verb could just as easily be translated 'was persuaded.' Very few of the 491 occurrences resist a rhetorical analysis."[230]

This focus on rhetorical persuasion is supported by the way in which early Christian writers support appeals to faith (*pistis*) with reason and argument (*logos*). As George Kennedy has noted, early Christian writers do not simply rely on a proclamation of faith to persuade audiences. Frequently, their proclamation also attempts "to give a reason why the proclamation should be received and thus appeals, at least in part, to human rationality," often through the use of supporting reasons, examples, or authorities.[231] Teresa Morgan affirms this emphasis on reasoning, noting that scriptural writers did not require "a deliberately counter-rational 'leap of faith'" but typically supported proclamations of faith with appeals to reasons.[232] They wanted to convince audiences that trust in God "has solid foundations."[233]

A closer look at Hebrews 11:1 is illustrative, particularly since Augustine frequently invokes the passage to describe faith as the ground of hope, "the substance of things hoped for, the conviction of things that are not seen."[234] Though Augustine engaged the New Testament primarily through Latin translations, he also read Greek and occasionally consulted the Greek text to discern a potential meaning.[235] In the original Greek of Hebrews 11:1, *pistis* is the word for "faith," while *elegkos* is translated as "conviction," which, in a modern context, can often imply a propositional belief.[236] As Kinneavy observes, however, "The usual meaning of *elegkos* is an *argument* of disproof or refutation or else a testing or scrutiny."[237] In other words, *pistis* is functioning as "proof in the sense of evidence from which a conclusion is drawn,"[238] and, I would add, evidence that *defeats* a disproof or challenge to hope, the doubt that might arise from its object being "unseen." The implicit description of faith in Hebrews fits with the default and challenge structure of persuasion discussed above. Kinneavy notes that the examples of *pistis* that follow in the same chapter of Hebrews affirm the grounding relationship of faith to hope. "In each case of the entire chapter, the faith of the person mentioned allows that person (or group) to achieve something that seemed difficult or impossible."[239] In these instances, faith supplies the "substance" or "foundation" (*hypostatis*) of hope, the "ground," "proof," or "evidence" (*elegkos*) that defeats any defeaters and justifies hope for the unseen.[240]

As numerous scholars have argued, the Latin *fides* shares deep semantic and conceptual similarities with *pistis*, so much so that influential scholars often analyze them together.[241] Etymologically, *fides*, like *pistis*, derives from the *pith-* root in Greek, highlighting its connection to "persuasion."[242] *Fides* thus likely retained some of its earlier rhetorical connotations. According to Kennedy, "The acceptance of *pistis* to mean 'Christian faith' by the early Church implied at the very least that faith came from hearing speech, and provided a future opening for the acceptance of classic rhetoric within Christian discourse."[243] In late antiquity, Augustine did more than anyone to bring the resources of classical rhetoric into the Christian faith.

Rhetoric Human and Divine

Augustine's study of rhetoric was extensive. Before he became a pastor and theologian, Augustine won oratorical contests as a teenager and eventually emerged as the "ablest student in the school of rhetoric" at Carthage.[244] He went on to teach rhetoric in Thagaste, Carthage, Rome, and Milan, where, as the imperial professor of rhetoric, he gave orations before the emperor, taught rhetoric to the sons of Roman officials, and joined an elite group of government officers controlling the levers of imperial power.[245] Yet, after a year or two in Milan, he became frustrated by imperial politics and offered a scathing indictment of Roman rhetoricians, decrying his own work as that of a mere "word-peddler" (*venditor verborum*).[246] Although he eventually resigned his imperial post, he did not hesitate to employ the rhetorical devices he had perfected early in his career.[247] As Robert Dodaro writes, "Augustine never abandons the conviction, dear to classical rhetoricians, that human behaviour is largely conditioned by the effects of language on the soul."[248]

Augustine's most vigorous defense of rhetoric's effects on the soul appears in Book 4 of *On Christian Teaching*, a manual of Christian oratory written for educated bishops, preachers, and lay people.[249] Recognizing that rhetoric can be used "to give conviction to both truth and falsehood," he aims to give Christian teachers the tools to defend "true faith" against "error."[250] To this end, he introduces Cicero's three styles of rhetoric and shows how early Christian writers employ similar rhetorical forms in Christian scripture.[251] He is especially attentive to rhetoric in the epistles of Paul, whom Augustine praises for his "amazing combination of wisdom and eloquence."[252]

For Augustine, the supreme exemplar of rhetoric is not human but divine. As Dodaro shows convincingly, Augustine frequently presents God as the divine "orator" and scripture as "God's oratory," making an "analogy between the scriptures as a divine discourse and the role of political oratory in Roman society."[253] References to scripture as God's "divine discourse" or "divine eloquence" abound throughout Augustine's works,[254] highlighting his belief that "when those authors wrote their works, God Himself was speaking to them, or through them."[255] Elsewhere, Augustine describes the Old and New Testaments as a harmonious and unified "divine discourse," coming "as if from the mouth of one speaker."[256] Augustine even implies God employs some of the rhetorical strategies and figures of speech common to Roman rhetoricians.[257] If the scriptures reflect the "divine voice speaking through men"[258] who, in turn, frequently use rhetorical techniques to inspire faith, then, Dodaro argues, "God is the author of the scriptures in terms not only of their content, but of the rhetorical strategies which they employ."[259] According to Dodaro, "Augustine holds that the entire content of the scriptures can be interpreted through rhetorical theory."[260]

Following the examples of Greek, Roman, and Christian predecessors who connected *pistis* and *fides* with persuasion, Augustine's recognition of God as orator and scriptural writers as rhetoricians highlights the close connection between rhetoric, reasoning, and faith. If God uses rhetoric dialogically to inspire faith in others, it is not only permissible but proper for Christian teachers to follow God's divine lead. In this sense, Augustine sees rhetoric not as a mere ornament of speech or a clever way to engage audiences' emotions, but as an essential means of rationally persuading others to come to faith and hope. When he uses rhetoric for these purposes, he is using a justificatory strategy rooted in the authority of his own tradition, one that seeks either to persuade others that his faith and hope are properly grounded or to defeat any defeaters that attempt to rebut or undercut them. When combined with a default and challenge structure of reasoning, the use of rhetoric to secure entitlement for particular beliefs becomes a rationally justifiable means of grounding faith and hope, a way of providing evidence of the unseen.

The connection of *pistis/fides* to trust reinforces this view. The rhetorical power of persuasion often depended on the trustworthiness of the communicator. To put faith in another or be persuaded by their testimony, one must trust that they are acting in good faith and that what they report is true. This is one reason why ancient rhetoricians—from Aristotle to Quintilian—emphasized the "character" of the communicator as an effective means of persuasion.[261] Communicating that one is trustworthy is likely to increase the trust others place in the speaker. Augustine adopts this view, noting in *On Christian Teaching* that "the life of the speaker" is "[m]ore important than any amount of grandeur of style."[262]

In chapter 9, I will suggest that Augustine's own example of political hope functions as a rhetorical form of persuasion, but here, I want to note how Augustine applies the relationship between faith, rhetoric, and trust to God and Christ. For Augustine, the reason human beings can be persuaded by God and Christ is because they can trust God and Christ to be true to their word and act in good faith. God is trustworthy because God, in "good faith," has fulfilled God's promises.[263] Augustine especially emphasizes Christ's role as a "mediator" between God and human beings who encourages faithfulness to God.[264] As Morgan emphasizes, in ancient Rome "mediators" often acted as "go-betweens" in negotiations between two parties, and the most effective were those whom each side saw as "both trusting and trustworthy" and thus worthy of their "faith" (*pistis/fides*) as an "instrument of reconciliation."[265] New Testament writers apply this metaphor to describe Christ's reconciling work between God and humanity: through his life and death, Christ the mediator is able to effect justice and reconciliation because he is seen as "faithful to God and worthy of God's trust" and "trustworthy by human beings and trusted by them."[266] Strikingly, Augustine uses the metaphor of Christ as "mediator" throughout his most influential texts, including *City of God*, *Confessions*, and *The Trinity*.[267] Describing how God "speaks" to human beings through Christ, Augustine cites 1 Timothy 2:5 to emphasize how Christ, as the Word of God, serves as a "mediator" between God and humanity, who, "assuming humanity without putting aside His Godhood, established and founded this faith [*fides*], that man might find a way to man's God through

God made man."[268] As Dodaro observes, when Augustine describes Christ as a "mediator" who unites God and humanity, he frames "divine mediation" in "the metaphorical terms of a dialogue between Christ and the members of his body," where the "incarnation" is understood as a "divine discourse by which human beings are justified."[269] In this way, the metaphor of Christ as mediator unites multiples meanings of faith as belief, trust, and trustworthiness within the context of rhetoric and persuasion.[270]

For Augustine, then, to have faith is fundamentally to trust in another based on authority and reason, which cooperate to supply faith with its grounds. Given Augustine's default and challenge structure of reasoning, one is entitled to a default belief or trust based on reason or authority until a challenge rebuts or undercuts it. This means that the process of entitlement is a temporal, social, and dialogical process, requiring that one "be ready to respond to everyone who asks us for an account of our faith and hope."[271] Given the role of rhetoric in the Roman and Christian accounts of faith, such exchange of reasons often relied heavily on forms of persuasion. For Augustine, rhetoric is not necessarily a manipulative form of speech but a divinely inspired way to encourage faith and trust and to offer persuasive reasons that can justify a belief or defeat any potential defeaters to it. The most trustworthy communicators are those who inspire faith by speaking and living the truth and practicing fidelity in relation to those who trust them. This process of relying on them successfully strengthens the firmness of one's faith and enables faith to persevere.

V. Objects of Faith

The purpose so far has been to reconstruct how Augustine understands the grounds of faith—the basis on which we are entitled to believe or trust another. With this structure in view, we can now turn to the objects of faith—those whom we believe or trust.[272] Often, as in the case of God and Christ, the grounds and objects of faith are closely related: according to Augustine, human beings can believe in God and Christ because God's and Christ's words are trustworthy. Such faith is both directed toward God and Christ and grounded in their authority. Yet, conceptually, objects and grounds are distinct. One may believe in God, Christ, or even a human friend (an object) because another person has provided compelling testimony of their existence or trustworthiness (a ground). To understand Augustine's account of faith, then, we must consider its objects.

Faith in God and Christ

Most of the time, Augustine speaks of God or Christ as the primary object of faith. Sometimes, he speaks of God or Christ as the object of propositional faith, including the belief that God exists or that Christ has been resurrected.[273] But as discussed above, mere belief is insufficient for complete faith since "[e]ven the demons believe—and shudder."[274] While demons believe that God exists, they lack "the faith that works through love."[275] According to Eugene TeSelle, Augustine holds that believing *in* God (*credere in Deum*) entails more than simply believing God (*credere Deo*).[276] As Augustine writes, "[B] elieving in God . . . is a great deal more than believing what God says. We may often believe what some human being says, yet know that such a person is not to be believed in."[277] By contrast, Augustine holds that we should place our faith and hope "in God" so that we "cling by faith to God who effects the good works in such a way that we collaborate well with him."[278] Informed by love, faith in God involves a *relationship* of trust with God, a "personal adherence to God or movement toward God."[279] When humans have faith in God, Augustine believes, they become part of a relationship through which faith, hope, and love increase as they move closer to God.

Faith in the Human Neighbor

Augustine's understanding of faith in God and Christ merits an entire theological study, but since my focus here is primarily political, I want to explore an underexamined aspect of his account of faith: his recognition that other human beings can also be objects of faith or trust (*fides*).[280]

In part, this recognition reflects Augustine's participationist ontology, his belief that human beings have their very being and goodness because they participate in God's being and goodness. Since Augustine most often discusses this participationist ontology in relation to love of God and neighbor, I analyze it in detail in chapter 2, but here, I want to highlight its relevance to faith. If human beings, by nature, participate in God, then having faith in a trustworthy friend can be one way to participate in faith in God, who is the source of that friend's faithfulness.

Augustine suggests this idea in a conciliatory letter to Jerome. When describing how he has come to trust his most intimate friends, he identifies God as a source of his trust:

> I . . . feel that God is in that person to whom I abandon myself with security and in whom I find rest in security. And in that security I do not at all fear

that incertitude of tomorrow stemming from the human fragility that I lamented above. For, when I perceive that a man is aflame with Christian love and has become my loyal friend with that love, whatever of my plans and thoughts I entrust to him I do not entrust to a human being, but to him in whom he remains so that he is such a person. For *God is love, and he who remains in love remains in God, and God in him* (1 Jn 4:16).

Augustine suggests one can place faith in a friend who loves God because that friend has faith in God.

In Sermon 21, Augustine explicitly affirms the importance of placing faith in human beings. Noting that he is "not talking about that higher faith [*fides*], because of which you are called 'the faithful,'" he highlights the value of the "kind of faith which is called faith (or trust) [*fides*] in ordinary matters": "About this kind, of course I say too that your Lord enjoins it to you: not to cheat anyone, to keep faith in your business dealings, to keep faith with your wife in your bed."[281] Here, Augustine admonishes his congregants to cultivate the trust and fidelity that characterizes healthy social relationships.

Even when he writes to those outside the Catholic Church, Augustine recognizes that one may rightly place faith or trust (*fides*) in fellow human beings who are not necessarily Christian. This is most evident in *Faith in the Unseen*, a short treatise written sometime after 399, most likely between 420 and 425, around the time when Augustine wrote the *Enchiridion* and the last books of *City of God*.[282] *Faith in the Unseen* is an exhortation to Christian faith, a response to empiricist critics who challenge the reasonableness of faith in any object not perceived through the senses.[283] What is perhaps most interesting about Augustine's refutation is how he proceeds: he suggests that human beings can recognize the value and rationality of faith in an invisible God by recognizing the value and rationality of faith in visible neighbors. Since they cannot know the mind or heart of a friend through sense experience or introspection, a friend's intentions remain "unseen."[284] Yet the "fact remains that what you cannot see or hear or glimpse within yourself you nevertheless believe, lest your life be totally devoid of that friendship and the affection shown you by your friend remain unacknowledged on your part."[285] Indeed, placing faith in a stranger—trusting a potential friend—is the only way to develop a relationship of mutual love: "[W]hen you do entrust yourself to a friend in order to prove his friendship, you are actually putting your faith in him before you have proof that he is your friend."[286]

Augustine goes on to celebrate the value of such trust (*fides*):

> If trust of this kind were to disappear from human affairs, who would not
> be aware of the confusion and appalling upheaval which would follow?
> Since the love of which we speak is unseen, who then could enjoy the mu-
> tual love of another, if I do not feel bound to believe what I cannot see?
> Friendship as a whole would therefore disappear, because its essence is
> mutual love.[287]

Thus, to develop and preserve relationships of mutual love between spouses,
friends, and families, we must trust them, even without evidence that their
intentions are good or they will help us in times of need.[288]

To drive home the point, Augustine shifts away from philosophical claims
about the rationality of faith to highlight the faith implicit in ordinary social
practices, practices of reciprocating love with gratitude and goodwill, practices
that would not proceed if friends lacked trust in another's goodwill or assistance.
He highlights ordinary decisions to marry a spouse, bestow gifts on friends, and
offer grateful acknowledgment, all of which depend on faith in what cannot be
seen. Refusing faith in such cases "is not clever but despicable."[289] It undermines
the "goodwill" at the foundation of human relationships.[290]

With the importance of social trust established, Augustine draws an analogy between the rationality of faith in human friends and the rationality of
faith in God. Whether we accept his analogical argument or not, what is
important for my purposes is his recognition of the value of trusting in human
friends, which is often obscured or downplayed in interpretations of Augustine in political theory. If such trust can be the basis or foundation of hope,
then, as I will suggest in chapter 5, Augustine recognizes the value of hoping
not only in God but in neighbors, friends, and fellow citizens.

The Virtue of Faith

Even if Augustine permits placing faith in fellow human beings, he recognizes
that some propositional or relationship acts of faith, trust, and belief can be
disordered or false.[291] That is why he characterizes faith as a *virtue*, a disposition of the soul that orients our trust and belief to God and neighbor in appropriate ways. The virtue of faith is the "faith that works through love," the
virtue by which the "just" live.[292] Unfortunately, Augustine does not say much
explicitly about the virtue of faith. Most of his discussions simply assume a
conception of faith as a virtue; they do not spell it out. He does not devote

attention to explaining proper order as he does for love or explicitly identify particularly vices that oppose the virtue of faith as he does for hope. But in places, he does imply that there are vices that hinder faith, which would appear to have much in common with presumption and despair. More often, he characterizes these vices as the vices opposed to hope, but they are implicit in what he says about faith and thus help to inform the epistemic order and disorder that characterize the virtue of hope.

Augustine offers his most explicit discussion in *Against the Academicians*. Addressing Romanianus, he identifies "two defects and obstacles to finding truth": "(*i*) you may underrate yourself and despair of your ever finding the truth; or (*ii*) you believe yourself to have found it."[293] Augustine takes aim at both vices. Although initially enamored of Academic skepticism after falling into Manicheanism, Augustine came to reject skepticism as a counsel of "despair" since its arguments "instill a despair of finding truth and prevent a wise man from giving assent to anything or approving anything at all as clear and certain, since to them everything seems obscure and uncertain."[294] Because skeptics believe that human life is filled with uncertainty and that any error is sinful, they recommend refusing assent to any proposition lest it lead to error.[295] As a result, their position commends "despair" toward the truth, which, Augustine argues, is opposed to faith.[296] Despair constitutes an epistemic deficiency, a failure to believe what should be believed with assent.

As we saw in chapter 3, however, despair is not simply an epistemic vice. It also affects the motivation for pursuing truth. Despair causes human beings to become "lazy and utterly inactive."[297] It characterizes those "who seek the truth with no hope that they will find it and those who do not seek it at all."[298] Because the latter no longer believe truth is possible to achieve, they are no longer motivated to pursue it. Despair thus produces both an epistemic deficiency and a motivational privation that opposes the virtue of faith.

Overconfidence (*audacia*), akin to presumption, is the vice of those who, out of "vanity" (*uanitati*), hold false opinions to be true, reject true beliefs as false, and consider what is uncertain to be certain.[299] They are "overconfident" and assert rashly what they do not know to be true, which Augustine sometimes describes as "being opinionated" (*opinari*).[300] Being opinionated, he argues, is "bad for two reasons": "Those who are already convinced they know something are not able to learn about it, if learning about it becomes possible, and being hasty is in itself a sign of an ill-adjusted mind."[301] This means that the effects of rash assertion, as in the case of despair, are not only epistemic. Like prideful presumption, vain overconfidence diminishes the motivation to learn or seek the truth. As Augustine suggests, human beings, "having found a false opinion, do not search diligently for the truth if they search at all, and even turn away from the desire for searching."[302] As a virtue, faith, like hope, must avoid vices akin to presumption and despair.

Augustine argues that the virtue of faith avoids these vices because it only believes that which it has reason to believe. Believing is not virtuous "when something unfitting is believed about God or too easily believed about another person. In other matters there is nothing wrong with believing, provided one understands it is something one does not know."[303] Indeed, if a person recognizes "the great difference there is between thinking one knows something and believing on authority something one is aware that one does not know, then he will surely avoid mistakes and escape the charge of being proud and lacking in humanity."[304] In other words, he will maintain a proper faith that avoids the excesses of vain overconfidence and prideful presumption. As we will see below, Augustine's discussion of vices in the context of faith helps to illuminate the epistemic forms of disorder that oppose the virtue of hope.

Conclusion

The aim of this chapter has been to analyze Augustine's account of faith's objects and grounds. I have identified five forms of faith implicit in Augustine's writings and shown how most depend on a relational conception of faith as trust. I have also highlighted how both reason and authority supply faith with its grounds and argued that a default and challenge structure is implicit in Augustine's mode of reasoning. This structure not only illuminates neglected aspects of Augustine's concept of faith but also elevates Augustine as a relevant resource for contemporary epistemology and philosophy of religion. Scholars looking for ancient sources who offer philosophically sophisticated accounts of rational entitlement and relational faith can find an ally in Augustine.

One of the most striking features of Augustine's account of relational faith is that he recognizes the possibility of trusting not only in God or Christ, but also in fellow human beings, as long as such faith avoids corresponding forms of epistemic disorder—overconfidence or presumption, on the one hand, and despair, on the other. This reconstruction of Augustinian faith will inform my account of how Augustine uses rhetoric to reorder faith, hope, and love in chapters 6 and 7 and how he conceptualizes exchanging political reasons for hope in chapter 8. But first, we must explore how his account of faith illuminates the grounds of hope.

5

Hope in the Unseen

HOPING IN ANOTHER

What is there that we can hope for without believing in it?

—AUGUSTINE, *ENCHIRIDION*, 2.8

AUGUSTINE DOES NOT PROVIDE much detail on the grounds of hope. Most often, he simply assumes his audiences will ground their hope in proper faith without explaining how to make those judgments or discern which authorities to trust. But if faith is the "ground" or "substance of things hoped for,"[1] it is possible to reconstruct an account of hope's grounds from his analysis of faith.

Part I builds on the synthetic account of faith offered in chapter 4 to reconstruct the structure of hope's grounds, extending Augustine's dialectic of authority and reason and default and challenge structure of reasoning to hope. Part II shows how Augustine encourages hope not only in God but in human neighbors, drawing on his example from *Confessions* to illustrate. Part III revisits the vices of presumption and despair to demonstrate how they reflect epistemically disordered hopes. Taken together, this conceptual framework supplies analytical clarity on the grounds of Augustinian hope and informs the accounts of rhetoric and politics that follow.

I. The Grounds of Hope

As we saw in chapter 1, hope and faith share a common feature: both reflect a belief or trust in an object that is "unseen" and thus not yet present or possessed. This means that the virtue of hope, like faith, lacks the epistemic certainty of "knowledge" or "understanding," which obtains when objects are "seen." Yet, by extension, the virtue of hope also avoids gullibility or "credulity,"[2] a false hope that assumes any object is possible, even in the absence of good reasons. Hope must have proper grounds even if its future object remains unseen.

If faith provides the grounds for such hope and if faith is fundamentally relational, it follows that hope is also fundamentally relational. For Augustine, hoping *for* an object typically involves hoping *in* another, either explicitly or implicitly. Discerning in whom we may hope requires discerning whom we can trust.

Authority and Reason

As we saw in chapter 4, Augustine identifies two common grounds of faith—authority and reason—which, by extension, can supply grounds for hope. As in the case of faith, we may first come to hope in another based on their authority—for example, the fact that they are trusted by other reliable witnesses (testimony), have a record of helping and fulfilling their promises (history), are part of a community or tradition that places a priority on helping others and being worthy of trust (tradition), inhabit a particular relationship of responsibility to us (role), or possess a certain kind of virtue or goodwill toward us that makes them trustworthy to assist (character). Each of these forms of authority can provide grounds for hoping in another, but given our finitude in relation to the future, we cannot *prove* that others will offer assistance before we invest hope in them. To extend one of Augustine's examples, a traveler cannot know her friends will give reliable directions to a new city, but she can hope in those friends if she can judge them to be authoritative guides because other witnesses have reported successfully using their directions (testimony), they have a record of traveling to that city (history), they are part of a community that values being truthful and helping neighbors (tradition), they inhabit a relationship that makes them inclined to help (role), or they have goodwill toward her and thus will be unlikely to lead her astray (character). Each of these cases involves hoping in others' authority without having the ability to "see" their intentions or future actions before risking an act of hope.

Yet, as Augustine emphasizes in the case of faith, hope is not necessarily blind. Reason is also involved in forming judgments and offering assent. Reason enables us to discern and judge which authorities to hope in, how much to hope in them, and what we should hope them to do. In this way, reason informs our evaluation of the trustworthiness of an authority as a potential agent of assistance, not only before we hope in another but also afterward. It enables us to evaluate our experience of placing our hope in a particular person in a particular instance and to modify, confirm, or correct our hope accordingly. Through the use of reason, we can discern whether a particular act of hoping in another is wise, whether we ought to modify, revise, or correct our hope based on experience, or whether we ought to redirect our hopes to others who can assist. Reason can help to complete or perfect acts of hoping in another.

A Default and Challenge Structure of Hope

Implicit in this account is the default and challenge structure of reasoning discussed in the previous chapter. Most of the time, if our faculties are functioning properly, we are, by default, entitled to invest hope in another based on trustworthy evidence or authority. We need not have definitive *proof* that they are worthy of hope before we rationally hope in them, and we are justified in maintaining this hope until we have good reason to adapt or abandon it. Our defeasible hope can be innocent until proven guilty. But if we encounter evidence that potentially defeats the basis of our hope in another, either by offering overriding or outweighing evidence that is inconsistent with our default hope (a rebutting defeater) or undermining the grounds on which that hope rests (an undercutting defeater), then rationality requires that we either provide defeaters to the potential defeaters or revise, adapt, or abandon our default hope in response to the challenge.

The temporal dimension of this default and challenge structure entails that we may be entitled to a particular hope at one time but not others. It also entails that some defeaters must be weightier at some points than at others. If we have a long history of successfully hoping in another and relying on their assistance to achieve difficult goods—for example, when asking for directions to a new city—then any counterevidence that arises about that person's hope-worthiness might need to be more significant or serious to justify a correction or revision than it would have been without this history. This is one reason why some hopes can persevere in the face of potential challenges and need not fluctuate continuously with the shifting winds of counterevidence.

While the objects of hope are future and thus not epistemically "certain," Augustine often emphasizes that hope, like faith, can be "firm" (*firma*) or "certain" (*certa*), particularly when placed in God or Christ.[3] This view of hope's firmness or certainty is reinforced by the image of hope as an "anchor of the soul."[4] "[B]y fixing our hope up above," Augustine argues, "we have set it like an anchor on firm ground, able to hold against any of the stormy waves of this world, not by our own strength but by that of the one in whom this anchor of our hope has been fixed."[5]

The discussion of faith and perseverance within a default and challenge structure sheds light on how a hope directed toward a future object can be "certain." While hope in human neighbors might not have such stability, Augustine assumes that hope in God can be firmly anchored, persevering in the face of doubts and difficulties that threaten it. Citing Romans 8, he highlights Paul's plea that "the persecutions of this world be overcome through love, with an assured hope [spe certa] in the assistance of God."[6] In this context, the "certainty" that accompanies hope for a future good is not necessarily epistemic certainty about its object; it has as much to do with hoping in God with perseverance, which is why some scholars translate certa as "assured," "resolute," or "unwavering."[7] Here, the firmness of hope relates more to the source of the assistance (God) and to the tenacity and perseverance of hope maintained than levels of epistemic credence. This helps to explain why Augustine holds that hope can supply additional resolve and perseverance to faith: faith is "made solidly firm by hope."[8] A default and challenge structure of reasoning supports this emphasis on perseverance, highlighting how faith and hope can increase and be held more firmly over time.

In addition to having a temporal dimension, a default and challenge structure of hope also has a social dimension. To use Wolterstorff's terms, human beings are not solitary hopers; their hopes in others are always embedded in relationships, communities, and contexts that can make specific practices *socially available, personally accessible,* and *personally acceptable.*[9] This communal context is one reason why Augustine places so much emphasis on the church as a community of character. Given his theological commitments, he believes members will be better able to form good hopes in the context of a community with shared practices of inquiry and accountability to God and neighbor. Moreover, being part of the church enables members to inherit certain hopes through their communal formation and expression, providing authority to invest specific hopes on the authority of testimony and tradition. For Augustine, the "reputation" and "wide acceptance" of the Catholic Church is part of what yields weight to its authority, making it "the most appropriate starting point for our inquiry."[10]

Finally, a default and challenge structure of hope is thoroughly dialogical, requiring that we give and exchange reasons for our hope with others, including opponents who seek to challenge or defeat our hopes. For Augustine, this process of dialogical exchange, often by informed use of immanent critique and rhetorical persuasion, is what enables hope to persevere in the face of potential defeaters, offering responses to objections and challenges that threaten the grounds of hope. It also informs how human beings might persuade opponents with a different hope—by engaging them on their own terms and on the basis of authorities they accept. This dialogical approach to immanent critique and rhetorical persuasion will feature prominently in the analysis of Augustine's rhetoric and politics of hope in chapters 6–8. As we will see, Augustine employs a default and challenge structure of rhetorical reasoning in his sermons and treatises to acknowledge and then defeat the challenges and temptations that threaten to undermine a default hope. This dialogical process further grounds hope and increases its strength in the face of possible defeaters.

To summarize, if we extend Augustine's account of faith to hope, then hope's grounds can be specified as consisting in reasons for believing or trusting that a future good is possible and that an agent of assistance can help to achieve it. These default reasons are not epistemically certain. Since objects of hope are unseen, and since fallible and finite human beings may fail in their capacity to assist, there are always potential defeaters that threaten the grounds for hope. These defeaters might require abandoning an object of hope or redirecting hope to another who can assist. Yet, like prima facie reasons for a default belief, these reasons are also defeasible. We may be able to defeat the defeaters to preserve our default hope, adapt our default hope in light of the defeaters to avoid the challenge, or show that the challenge does not apply to the particular case in hand.

On this account, then, grounds for hope will consist in (1) a default entitlement or set of prima facie reasons for pursuing a particular object of hope and/or investing our hope in another who can assist that pursuit, and (2) in the case of potential defeaters, a set of prima facie reasons that rebut or undercut the defeaters or show the defeaters to be nondefinitive or nonapplicable.[11] While Augustine never specifies the grounds of hope in such analytical terms, the structure is implicit in his account.

II. Hoping in God and Neighbor

With the structure in view, we can now consider the agents of assistance in whom we hope. Augustine's hope typically involves hoping *in* someone to achieve what we hope *for*.

When Augustine identifies whom we should hope in, his admonitions almost always focus on hoping in God, particularly when he explicates scripture. He cites Psalm 129's call to "hope in the Lord" and frequently invokes Jeremiah 17:5: "[C]ursed is he who puts his hope in a man."[12] After citing Jeremiah in the *Enchiridion*, he argues that "anybody who trusts in himself is bound by the chain of this curse. So it is only from the Lord God that we must ask for any good deeds that we hope to do or any reward that we hope to receive for good deeds."[13]

Sometimes, Augustine seems to advise audiences to hope *in* God to discourage them from hoping *for* temporal goods too much or in the wrong ways. In explaining Psalm 129's counsel to "hope in the Lord," for example, he emphasizes objects of desire rather than agents of assistance, acknowledging that it is proper to hope for "riches or bodily health or an abundance of earthly assets," as long as one does not hope for these things as their "supreme good."[14] Here, the recommendation to hope for temporal goods "in God" parallels Augustine's encouragement to love the neighbor "in God": it discourages the tendency for human beings to see these goods as theirs to dominate or possess.

Most of the time, Augustine adjusts the formula, suggesting we should hope *in* God *for* temporal and eternal goods. In one sermon, for example, he encourages his listeners to "hope in God for God."[15] Here, the emphasis is on agents of assistance, and for Augustine, God is the ultimate helper. Consider his discussion of the Lord's Prayer. It is significant that he ties the virtue of hope to a *prayer*, a form of petition and supplication to God. For Augustine, prayer is a proper practice of hope: "[W]e must thirst in prayer as long as we live in hope and do not as yet see what we hope for."[16]

At first glance, these passages may suggest that Augustine prohibits any hope in temporal neighbors or fellow citizens. If this is so, Augustinian hope again becomes open to the charge of otherworldliness: hope can be virtuous only if it calls on the assistance of an otherworldly God who intervenes mysteriously in human affairs. Yet, if we draw an analogy between Augustine's order of love and implicit order of hope, this conclusion does not necessarily follow. The complaint relies on assuming that God is *separate* from other human beings, that hoping in God *competes with* or *excludes* hope in human neighbors. This either-or account is too simple. Given Augustine's participationist ontology, hoping in other human beings can also be a way to hope in God, as long as that hope is properly ordered.

Unfortunately, Augustine does not always make the propriety of hoping in a neighbor explicit. One reason may reflect his dialectic of virtue and vice. If hoping properly in another remains subject to temptations toward abuse, hoping in a neighbor to attain a good—particularly a good for oneself—may be particularly prone to instrumentalism or domination. When we hope in a neighbor to achieve a specific good, we may be especially tempted to use that neighbor for our own purposes rather than treating the neighbor with respect or hoping for a good that we share in common. As in the case of love, Augustine's insistence on hoping "in" God may function to chasten temptations to use a neighbor for selfish purposes.

A closer look at Augustine's discussions of hope affirms his concern about pride and domination. One feature is especially telling: when Augustine juxtaposes *hope in God* with *hope in human beings*, he almost always employs this formula to discourage hoping in *ourselves*, not in our neighbors or fellow citizens.[17] Even Augustine's connection between the virtue of hope and the Lord's Prayer reflects his concern about pride:

> Prayer itself reminds you that you need the help of your Lord in order not to place the hope of living well *in yourself*. For you are not praying now to receive the riches and honors of the present world or something pertaining to human vanity but that you might not enter into temptation, and if a human being could give that to himself by his own will, he would not ask for it by his prayers.[18]

Throughout discussions of hoping in God, Augustine seems more worried that we will rely too much on ourselves rather than hope too much in our neighbors, that we will see our own efforts as the source of virtue and not rely on the gift of grace.

Augustine is especially insistent that our own efforts are insufficient to attain *eternal* goods, which, he argues, can only be gifts from God. Many of his criticisms of pagans and Pelagians who hope in themselves relate to the presumption they can achieve eternal goods, such as salvation or moral perfection, through their own efforts.[19] In *City of God*, he describes "the adversaries of the City of God, who belong to Babylon" as those "who presume upon their own strength and glory in themselves and not in the Lord."[20] A similar concern is evident in his account of the order of love in *On Christian Teaching*. When he cites Jeremiah 17:5 to suggest "he who puts his hope in a man" is "cursed," he is challenging those who believe that "enjoying" the neighbor rather than God will constitute "the happy life."[21] The worry is not that they are wrong to love or hope in a human being, but that they hope in a human being for the *ultimate good* rather than *proximate goods*. The impropriety relates to pridefully hoping in one's own virtue or agency to attain eternal goods rather than relying on God.

Augustine's concern with pride may have been especially acute given that many Roman citizens, especially those influenced by Neoplatonic and Stoic philosophy, felt tempted to place hope in themselves. Peter Brown describes a striking mosaic on the dining room floor in one of the grandest houses in Bulla Regia, a town on Augustine's usual route to Carthage. Against a background of blue, gold letters proclaimed a motto written in Greek: *en seauto tas elpidas ekhe*: "Place your own hopes in your own self."[22] In one of his anti-Pelagian texts, Augustine quotes a similar line from Virgil's *Aeneid*—"Let each be his own hope"—and follows it with his common recourse to Jeremiah 17:5.[23] For Augustine, it is the presumption of self-sufficiency that made both paganism and Pelagianism so dangerous. In admonishing audiences to hope in God, he attempts to puncture the pride of those who believe they can achieve salvation and perfection solely through their own efforts.[24]

Even in places where Augustine diagnoses the dangers of hoping in other human beings rather than ourselves, he seems most concerned about pride and domination. In *On Christian Teaching*, for example, he distinguishes those who enjoy the neighbor "in God" from those who enjoy the neighbor "in ourselves," who "put our hopes of happiness on a human being or an angel."[25] One might expect Augustine to go on to describe the dangers that follow when we hope in human neighbors, but he does not. Instead, his concern focuses on the pride of those in whom we hope: "This is something that arrogant people and arrogant angels pride themselves on; they rejoice when the hopes of others are placed on them."[26] Here, Augustine seems more concerned about the moral psychology of hope and sin than the metaphysical standing of hope's objects.

If we expand the range of texts and attend to the implicit suggestions hovering below the surface, we find several passages where Augustine implicitly endorses hoping in neighbors and friends. Consider again *Faith in the Unseen*, where Augustine uses an analogy of placing faith in friends to justify the rationality of placing faith in God. In particular, Augustine identifies the friend—the human neighbor—as a proper object of faith and trust, a person on whom we can rely to realize difficult goods in "adverse circumstances."[27] While Augustine does not mention hope explicitly in this treatise, what he says about "faith in the unseen" also applies to "hope in the unseen," particularly given what he says in the *Enchiridion*, written around the same time. There, he claims that hope depends on a faith in the "unseen" to justify belief. The "fact that we

do not see either the things we believe in or those we hope for makes not seeing a feature that faith and hope have in common."[28] Given this commonality,
we can extend what Augustine says about trusting in one's friends to hoping
in one's friends, especially since hope adds to faith a desire for a difficult good.
Implicit in *Faith in the Unseen* is the assumption that what motivates trust in a
friend is a desire for goods that will emerge from that friendship, including
security for oneself and the relationship that friends share in common.[29] These
objects of social trust are objects not simply of faith but of desire and hope,
goods unseen and not yet possessed. Augustine's praise of social trust suggests
that one may properly hope in one's neighbors and friends, and if we take seriously Augustine's analogy between faith in God and faith in friends, we may
even learn how to trust and hope in God by trusting and hoping in our friends.
As in the case of love, hoping in visible neighbors can provide a way to hope
in the invisible God.

Confessions of Hope

Augustine's own development of hope in *Confessions* suggests such a dynamic.
Typically, *Confessions* is read as Augustine's autobiography, a series of sinful
confessions about his grief over the death of an unnamed friend, his infamous
theft of pears, and the lusts that lead him to pray, "Lord, make me chaste, but
not yet."[30] But sin is not all that Augustine confesses. He also confesses hope
and praise, for he realizes that God, and not he, is the author of his life.[31] As
Charles Mathewes argues, *Confessions* is not simply an autobiography but an
"anti-autobiography," a narrative that aims to undermine the "presumption of
beginning," the prideful idea that human beings are the sole sources of their
being and the sole authors of their lives.[32] According to Mathewes, Augustine's
recognition of his dependence on God explains why the first and last lines of
Book 1 are not assertions of self but hymns of praise: "Great are you, O Lord,
and exceedingly worthy of praise" (1.1); "this too is your gift to me—that I
exist" (1.20.31).[33] God is the source of Augustine's being and goodness who
helps to redirect his hopes.

Importantly, *Confessions* casts Augustine's spiritual transformation in terms
of hope (*spes*). Describing *Confessions* as Augustine's "story of hope," Edward
Brooks notes "68 occurrences of *spes* and its derivatives."[34] In the first few
books, Augustine explains how his hope was disordered. He "hoped to win
praise and honor," "reputation and wealth," but his "worldly hope" (*spes saeculi*)
was "empty" and "hollow" since it was motivated by his swollen pride and

directed to his private good.[35] His "self-sufficient arrogance" caused him to focus more on worldly glory than the glory of God.[36] "[D]ominated by a vain urge to excel," he turned away from God and others.[37] His "hope of academic success" even discouraged his mother from arranging a marriage for him: she feared "that if I were encumbered with a wife my hope could be dashed."[38]

The rest of *Confessions* tells the story of Augustine reordering his hopes by relying on God's assistance. It is God, the great physician, who heals his "conflicting urges," transforming "disintegration" into unity and infusing him with hope: "It is you, *you, Lord, who through hope establish me in unity*."[39] Slowly, as God becomes both the object and ground of Augustine's hope, he begins to long for eternal life: "This is my hope, for this I live: to contemplate the delight of the Lord."[40] According to Augustine, this hope is only possible because of God's assistance: God is the "helper" who transforms his sinful soul, sustaining his hope and forbidding him to "slump into despair and say, 'I can't.'"[41] Without God's grace, "no shred of hope would be left to us."[42] As the narrative proceeds, God becomes Augustine's "sole" object and source of hope.[43]

A brief glance at this rhetoric may reinforce otherworldly suspicions, suggesting that Augustine counsels us to hope only in God, not other human beings. But attending to the implicit practices that underwrite Augustine's narrative reveals a different story, one that suggests God's assistance does not compete with human assistance but works through it. This mediation of grace is apparent in how Augustine's own hope grows by relying on the instruction and example of his friends.[44]

In Milan, for example, Augustine seeks the assistance of Ambrose, "who was known throughout the world as one of the best of men."[45] Ambrose was a "devout worshipper" and "teacher of truth" whose "energetic preaching" and interpretative method helped Augustine read scripture less literally.[46] Before meeting Ambrose, Augustine "had given up hope of finding [truth]" in the Church and had developed an attitude of "despair."[47] Yet, while Augustine had initially approached Ambrose to learn rhetoric, the content of Ambrose's speech slowly "seeped" into his mind: "little by little, without knowing it," he "was drawing near" to salvation.[48] Ambrose, who bore "hope," modeled the virtue and provided scaffolding for Augustine to emulate it.[49]

Ambrose was not Augustine's only exemplar. Augustine also describes how Ambrose's mentor, Simplicianus, shared the story of Victorinus, the "deeply learned old man" whose "habit of reading holy scripture and intensively studying all of the Christian writings" led him to the Church.[50] After hearing this story, Augustine was "fired to imitate Victorinus," and a "new will had begun to emerge" in him.[51] Importantly, Augustine describes Victorinus as an exemplar of hope: "[T]he Lord God was his hope, and he had no eyes for vanities or lying follies."[52]

Augustine's most influential exemplar of hope was his mother, Monica, who nurtured Augustine's hope from an early age. Augustine explicitly commends Monica's "hope," along with "her virtues and her sincere faith," and praises her for holding out a vision of hope for him even when he could not see it.[53] Given Monica's influence on Augustine, it is perhaps fitting that he experiences his most powerful conversion in a conversation with her at Ostia. Leaning by a window overlooking the garden, Augustine and Monica "were alone, conferring very intimately" about deep theological questions, including "the light of present truth, the Truth which is yourself, what the eternal life of the saints would be like."[54] Their "colloquy" made their "longing yet more ardent toward *That Which Is*," and through "inward thought and wondering discourse on [God's] works," they arrived at the "summit" of their minds. In this mystical moment, they "touched the edge of [eternity] by the utmost leap of [their] hearts" before returning, "sighing and unsatisfied," to the "noise of articulate speech."[55] Augustine ultimately attributes this mystical vision to God, but it is no accident that Monica is a conduit of divine grace. By imitating Monica and engaging her in conversation, Augustine received a glimpse of God, which strengthened his hope.

In many ways, *Confessions* is a story of how Augustine learns to rely on— and hope in—his friends. Whether describing his theft of pears or his grief over the death of an unnamed friend, the first four books focus on stories of *disordered* friendships and thus Augustine's inordinate hope in his friends.[56] While many interpreters have taken these passages as evidence of Augustine's otherworldly denial of human friendship,[57] Eric Gregory suggests that such "episodes of regret are motivated by a moral concern with self-enclosure rather than a spirituality of otherworldly escapism."[58] Augustine's self-described failures do not consist merely in loving temporal friends but in trying to grasp these friends for himself, reducing friendship either to an abstract ideal or an instrumental mean to selfish ends.[59] As Gregory argues, Augustine's regret for weeping for a friend was not because "he loved his friend, a mortal creature, or even that he loved him intensely. It was that he loved him 'as though he would never die' (*Conf.* 4.6.11). To love in this way was to take possession of his friend . . . as his own—as belonging to him rather than God."[60] Augustine, then, does not deny the importance of hoping in friends but cautions against hoping in friends too much or for the wrong reasons.[61] In this context, it is significant that the next five books of the *Confessions* are largely testaments to the value of *good* friendships, friendships with Alypius, Monica, Adeodatus, and others who nurture Augustine's hope. Ultimately, friendship for Augustine is, as Gilbert Meilaender puts it, "a school of virtue,"[62] a source of hope that does not necessarily compete with hope in God. One lesson of *Confessions* is that hoping in one's friends can be a way to hope in God.

Augustine makes this more explicit in his preface to *On Christian Teaching*, written around the same time as *Confessions*. There, he celebrates the role of human teachers and friends as necessary to growth in "faith, hope, and love."[63] He even chastises those who presume their understanding of the divine scripture comes to them as a special, unmediated gift from God: "[A]lthough they have a perfect right to rejoice in their great gift from God they nevertheless learned even the alphabet with human help."[64] Challenging "Christians who congratulate themselves on a knowledge of the holy scriptures gained without any human guidance," Augustine argues that even biblical figures who were reportedly directed by angels or divine voices nevertheless received instruction through human teachers.[65] "All this could certainly have been done through an angel, but the human condition would be wretched indeed if God appeared unwilling to minister his word to human beings through human agency."[66] Moreover, he adds, "there would be no way for love, which ties people together in the bonds of unity, to make souls overflow and as it were intermingle with each other, if human beings learned nothing from other humans."[67] As in *Faith in the Unseen*, Augustine suggests that trusting and hoping in another's assistance—relying on another human being—can actually help to increase mutual love among friends and provide ways to participate in the love of God. Augustine's entire practice as a pastor, preacher, and teacher is predicated on this premise. If God were always to grant knowledge and virtue mysteriously, without the mediation of human teachers, Augustine's work would be unnecessary. Hoping in teachers, neighbors, and friends remains a proper part of learning how to hope in God.

To develop these arguments further would require exploring Augustine's complex views on the relations between grace and nature, divine agency and human agency. These questions are beyond the scope of this inquiry. For now, I simply want to show how Augustine allows and even encourages hope in human neighbors. In light of his implicit practice of developing the virtue through the assistance of teachers and exemplars, Augustine's explicit recommendation to hope in God, not in human beings, is motivated, in part, by his concerns about the moral psychology of pride and domination. As in the case of love, he seeks to discourage disordered hopes and chasten the lust for glory and domination, temptations that may be especially powerful when we rely on others' assistance or when others rely on us.

III. Presumption and Despair Again

This analysis reinforces the account of the order of hope offered in chapter 3. The virtue of hope requires avoiding the vices of presumption and despair, the "two evils" that oppose good hope.[68] As I argued above, both vices can reflect hope that is disordered either epistemically or volitionally: human beings can hope too much or too little for objects that are either good or bad (a form of volitional disorder), or they can hope too much or too little for objects that are possible or impossible to attain, or too much or too little in another's assistance to attain them (a form of epistemic disorder). Although Augustine's moral psychology does not provide a neat separation between the volitional or epistemic, considering hope's relationship with faith highlights the epistemic dimension.

Despair reflects an epistemic deficiency, a belief that an object of hope is not possible to attain or that a particular agent of assistance cannot help us attain it. It rests in a deficient or "cross-eyed faith" (*fidei oculis non rectis*) that fails to "[h]ope in the Lord" for "encouragement" (*exhortatione*), an image that emphasizes faith's connection to vision and hope's connection to encouragement.[69] Most often, Augustine refers to the despair of those who fail to hope properly in God for forgiveness or salvation, those who "think about the evil things they have done" and "assume they can't be pardoned."[70] They fail to hope adequately in God's mercy and assistance, or they lack an accurate estimation of themselves.[71] These people suffer from "unbelieving despair" (*infidelem desperationem*).[72]

Others suffer from "false hope" (*spem falsam*), a form of epistemic presumption that assumes "more than the facts warranted."[73] Their confidence in the possibility of an object, or in another's ability to assist, is perverse or excessive. They "hope for what is worth hoping for, but not from God, from whom you should hope for it."[74] Augustine gives the example of hoping for eternal life from "demons" or hoping for human life from "deaf and dumb idols."[75] He even suggests that the devil's "deadly tricks" present a "difficulty [that] is useful in ensuring that a person does not put hope in himself or in somebody else but rather in God, the hope of all who belong to him."[76] Augustine is especially concerned about those who presume they can achieve virtue, perfection, and salvation by hoping only in themselves. The presumptuous person

> exalts himself in rash self-assurance, trusting in his own strength of character, and mentally resolving to fulfill all the righteous requirements of the law and to carry out all it enjoins without offending in any point whatever. If such persons think they can keep their lives under their own control and slip up nowhere, fall short nowhere, with never a wobble, never a blurring of vision, and if they claim credit for themselves and their own strength of will, then even if they have carried out the whole program of righteous conduct as far as human eyes can discern, so that nothing in their lives can be faulted by other people, God nonetheless condemns their presumption and boastful pride.[77]

Here, Augustine identifies presumption with prideful perfectionism, but in the same sermon, he admonishes those who go to the opposite extreme, confessing their sin and weakness but presuming that God will be merciful no matter what they do. "[S]elf-deceived by presumption," these people make no effort to reform their character, seeking to enjoy "deadly delights" because they presume God will forgive them without any work or sacrifice on their part.[78] In all of these cases, presumption reflects a lack of humility and piety, the failure to recognize one's limits and dependency on others.[79] For both presumption and despair, a deficient or distorted faith leads to disordered hope. Here again, hope must rely on other virtues, especially prudence, humility, and piety, to discern in whom and how much to hope.

Conclusion

Drawing on the account of faith's objects and grounds from chapter 4, I have attempted to reconstruct an Augustinian account of hope's grounds. This account recognizes hope's reliance on faith and the ways hope can be rationally justified, often through a default and challenge structure that engages both reason and authority. Moreover, contrary to assumptions about Augustine's otherworldly account of hope, this account highlights how Augustine allows hope in human neighbors as long as that hope is properly ordered, which provides an epistemic supplement to the volitional account of hope analyzed in chapter 3. While Augustine may consider hope primarily as a form of love, the concept cannot be understood fully without also considering its complex relation to faith.

This analysis has significant implications for the arguments that follow. A default and challenge structure of reasoning, for example, will inform my account of Augustine's account and example of political engagement in chapters 8 and 9, highlighting the value of engaging diverse opponents on their own terms to challenge their default beliefs while exchanging reasons in turn. The close connection between faith, rhetoric, and reasoning also features centrally in the next two chapters. It highlights Augustine's extensive and sometimes excessive use of rhetoric not simply as a technique to elicit emotions but also as a rational strategy to supply grounds of hope that can defeat any defeaters. We can see Augustine's art of rhetoric at work in his homilies of hope.

PART II

The Rhetoric of Hope

6

Pedagogies of Hope

AUGUSTINE AND THE ART OF RHETORIC

On every question relating to moral life there is need not only for instruction but also for encouragement. With the instruction we will know what we ought to do, and with the encouragement we will be motivated to do what we know we ought to do.

—AUGUSTINE, *THE EXCELLENCE OF WIDOWHOOD*, 1.2

There is hardly anyone who has a true opinion of himself. Those who underestimate themselves need to be encouraged, those who overestimate themselves need to be repressed, so that the former will not break with despair and the latter will not crash through overconfidence.

—AUGUSTINE, *THE ADVANTAGE OF BELIEVING*, 10.24

AUGUSTINE WAS one of the most influential preachers in the Roman Empire.[1] Large crowds flocked to hear him in Hippo, and he was frequently invited to preach in churches across North Africa.[2] When he passed through towns on his travels, priests and parishioners often implored him to speak, sometimes more than once.[3] In his biography, Possidius counts Augustine's sermons among his most enduring legacies: "[N]o one can read what he wrote on theology without profit. But I think that those were able to profit still more who could hear him speak in church and see him with their own eyes and, above all, had some knowledge of him as he lived among his fellow men."[4]

According to scholarly estimates, Augustine gave thousands of sermons over his almost forty-year career as a bishop and priest.[5] Since he rarely used notes or wrote his homilies in advance, most of these sermons are lost. But thanks to scribes who recorded them and executors who preserved them, about one thousand sermons survive, constituting "the largest body of oratory surviving from any ancient speaker."[6] Despite this voluminous deposit and their central place in Augustine's life and work, his sermons remain significantly underanalyzed, especially in political theory, where scholars focus instead on more systematic treatises.[7] Part of my aim is to show how these neglected texts challenge prevailing interpretations of Augustine's pessimism and commend a more nuanced hope for temporal goods.

Not all of Augustine's sermons are so subtle. When we expand our interpretive scope, we also discover passages that seem to reinforce Augustine's otherworldly dualism and challenge the account of Augustinian hope I have advanced. Consider Sermon 313F, where Augustine warns against "worldly hopes": "These things are delightful, they're beautiful, they're good; seek the one who made them, he it is that is your hope. . . . Let him be your hope in the land of the dying, and he will be your portion in the land of the living."[8] In Sermon 198, Augustine exhorts listeners not to imitate pagans who "hope for the vanities of this age" but to be "true Christians" who "hope for eternal life."[9] Even in Sermon 157, where he applies the use/enjoyment distinction, Augustine encourages listeners not to hope for "temporal things that can be seen" but "eternal things" that cannot be seen.[10] At best, these passages threaten to expose Augustine as philosophically inconsistent; at worst, they convict him of the otherworldly escapism I have sought to challenge.

In chapter 3, I argued that distinguishing *properly ordered hope* for temporal goods from *perverse hope* for these goods can potentially resolve this apparent inconsistency. The distinction acknowledges that hope for temporal goods is not necessarily vicious and indeed can be virtuous if it avoids the vices of presumption and despair. Yet this conceptual point at times seems hard to square with Augustine's explicit admonitions. Is there a way to alleviate this tension while engaging a wider range of texts? This chapter suggests that attending to Augustine's art of rhetoric can help.

Unfortunately, few political interpreters recognize the rhetorical and pedagogical purposes implicit in Augustine's works. Whether consciously or not, many scholars project their modern understanding of philosophy as a theoretical discourse onto Augustine's more ancient form and neglect how he uses rhetoric to educate readers. Recognizing his rhetorical and pedagogical purposes, I believe, complicates influential interpretations of Augustine's pessimism and furnishes a more capacious vision of his moral and political thought.

This chapter explores Augustine's use of rhetoric in his homilies of hope. Part I examines recent scholarship on ancient philosophy as a "way of life" and situates Augustine within this tradition. Distinguishing ancient philosophy from modern forms, I show how the rhetorical and pedagogical strategies of ancient texts affect interpretations of their meaning. Since Augustine inherited this philosophical tradition from his Neoplatonic and Stoic predecessors, I argue that his texts also employ rhetoric to "instruct" and "encourage" readers.

Part II applies this pedagogically sensitive approach to Augustine's most rhetorical texts, his sermons to the people. Analyzing his homiletic practices, I explore how he uses rhetorical forms—exhortations, antitheses, and rhymes—to elicit and educate audiences' hope. By calling attention to the social, ecclesial, and educational functions of these sermons, I also show how he extends moral education to a broader and more diverse range of citizens, thereby challenging the elite forms of moral education dominant in the Roman Empire. When situated within their wider theological, social, and political contexts, Augustine's sermons reveal an egalitarian, dialogical impulse that complicates critiques of his "monological" and "totalizing" style.[11]

I. Philosophy as a Way of Life

Recently, scholars have offered radically new interpretations of ancient texts by situating them in their rhetorical and pedagogical contexts.[12] Pierre Hadot's account has been the most influential. In *Philosophy as a Way of Life*, Hadot argues that ancient philosophy was a "way of life," an "art of living" focused not only on defending abstract propositions but also on cultivating the virtue and vision needed to make moral, intellectual, and spiritual progress.[13] In contrast to modern conceptions of philosophy as a theoretical discourse or abstract mode of analysis, ancient authors saw philosophy more as a discipline "which had to be practiced at each instance, and the goal of which was to transform the whole of the individual's life."[14] To commend such discipline, many ancient philosophers relied not only on rational reflection but on "spiritual exercises," concrete philosophical and moral practices intended to cultivate specific virtues and guide the soul's ascent to higher levels of wisdom.[15] From meditation and memorization to reading and writing, these exercises aided the soul's progress as weight training increased an athlete's strength, growing intellectual and moral muscles through a rigorous form of training.[16] Various rhetorical and philosophical forms—from dialogues and treatises to poems and epistles—enhanced these exercises and encouraged the pursuit of wisdom. Many of these texts took the form of "protreptics" designed not only to teach readers about the good life but to exhort them to pursue it.[17] By addressing the whole of one's character, these protreptics commended a kind of moral education, an *askēsis*, aimed at perfecting vision, disciplining desire, and cultivating virtue.[18]

Recognizing philosophy as a "way of life" has significant implications for how we interpret ancient texts. If a text is not intended simply to expound timeless truths but to educate followers in a particular time and place, the text's historical, rhetorical, and pedagogical contexts will affect its meaning. Proper interpretation requires considering the conditions and constraints that shaped an author's pedagogical practices, from the norms associated with particular genres and rhetorical traditions to the moral commitments that defined a specific school of thought.[19] "Whether the goal was to convert, to console, to cure, or to exhort the audience," Hadot concludes, "the point was always and above all not to communicate to them some ready-made knowledge but to *form* them."[20]

Many modern interpreters neglect the rhetorical and pedagogical functions of ancient texts. Trained in a more abstract form of philosophy, contemporary political theorists often miss how ancient thinkers used rhetoric to transform audiences.[21] This temptation is especially strong when texts appear in a more "systematic" form, where abstract language, reasoned analysis, and a declarative style can seduce interpreters into assuming authors are operating within a modern theoretical discourse. As Hadot shows, however, even many seemingly "systematic" texts were "written not so much to inform the reader of a doctrinal content but to form him, to make him traverse a certain itinerary in the course of which he will make spiritual progress."[22] Augustine's works are no exception.

Instruction and Encouragement

Augustine knew the power of philosophical exhortation.[23] It was Cicero's exhortation to philosophy, the *Hortensius*, that first "fired [his] passion for the pursuit of wisdom."[24] After turning to *philosophia*, Augustine became especially enamored by the Neoplatonists, whose philosophy he found largely compatible with the Christian tradition.[25] Although he eventually distances himself from Neoplatonic emphases on the sufficiency of reason and the corruption of the body, he maintains aspects of his Platonic inheritance, arguing as late as *City of God* that "[n]o one has come closer to [Christianity] than the

Platonists."[26] Importantly, this Platonic tradition includes a distinct appreciation for philosophy as a way of life, what Augustine sometimes describes as the "art of living."[27] Plotinus, Porphyry, and other Neoplatonists employed a variety of exercises—including oral commentaries on texts, dialogues between teacher and pupil, and practices of attention—to teach new ideas and exhort practitioners to traverse an "itinerary" intended to purify their souls and enable their "ascent" toward the divine.[28] As scholars have long noted, Augustine incorporates this Neoplatonic way of life into his Christian vision of ascent.[29]

Less recognized is Augustine's appropriation of Stoic ideas and rhetorical practices.[30] Many interpreters—including Arendt, Rawls, Niebuhr, and even Nussbaum, an accomplished scholar of Hellenistic thought—reduce Augustine's classical influences to Neoplatonism and neglect how he adapts insights from Cicero, Seneca, and other Stoics to develop his moral and theological vision. In a recent book, Sarah Catherine Byers offers a detailed account of Augustine's "Stoic-Platonic synthesis," highlighting how he integrates Stoicism and Platonism into his Christian account of perception and moral motivation.[31] In particular, Byers shows how Augustine combines the Platonic notion that "love" motivates action with a Stoic account of how objects are loved under certain descriptions or "perceptions," particularly as "beautiful," "useful," or "good."[32] To encourage these perceptions, Augustine adapts Stoic rhetorical strategies and "cognitive therapies" to transform vision and redirect desire.[33] Byers is especially attentive to Augustine's use of "encouragement" or "exhortation" (exhortatio), a Stoic addition to the list of classical rhetorical forms.[34] Augustine often relies on "exhortation" to "arouse the will" of audiences, especially in his sermons, which are his most powerful "exercises in rhetoric."[35]

Augustine and Rhetoric

Augustine's use of exhortation reflects his philosophical influences and early education.[36] It is notable that Augustine first read Cicero's exhortation to philosophy while studying rhetoric,[37] which points to an aspect of late antiquity often ignored by many political interpreters: Augustine was steeped in a rhetorical culture where learning and practicing the art of rhetoric were essential parts of the curriculum.[38] As we saw in chapter 4, Augustine was a renowned student and teacher of rhetoric, eventually climbing to the heights of Roman intellectual and political life as the emperor's professor in Milan. Even after he abandoned his imperial post, he continued using his immense rhetorical skills. In debates with religious dissenters, councils with Catholic bishops, letters to

Roman officials, and sermons to Christian congregations, he exercised the arts of rhetoric with great frequency and skill. Ultimately, he knew that "one who tries to speak not only wisely but eloquently will be more useful if he can do both."[39]

Augustine's defense of rhetoric's moral purposes reflects his understanding of human nature and its two primary defects: ignorance (*ignorantia*) and weakness (*infirmitas*).[40] After the Fall, Augustine believed, human beings lack both the capacity to *know* fully what is good and the settled *will* to do it. As a result, moral education must address both needs: "On every question relating to moral life, there is need not only for instruction [*doctrina*] but also for encouragement [*exhortatio*]. With the instruction we will know what we ought to do, and with the encouragement we will be motivated to do what we know we ought to do."[41] In his own teaching, Augustine practiced both instruction and encouragement and counseled others to do the same.

Nowhere is this more evident than in Book 4 of *On Christian Teaching*.[42] Modeling the book in part on Cicero's rhetorical writings, Augustine appropriates the classical art of rhetoric to educate Christian orators in the spirit that Cicero had instructed Roman senators.[43] In particular, Augustine adapts Cicero's dictum that orators should speak so as to "instruct, delight, and move" their audiences.[44] While Augustine insists that "instruction" (*doctrina*) is "a matter of necessity," knowing what is right does not ensure people will do it: "[W]hen one is giving instruction about something that must be acted on, and one's aim is to produce this action, it is futile to persuade people of the truth of what is being said, and futile to give delight by the style one uses, if the learning process does not result in action."[45] Good teachers must also learn to delight and motivate their audiences: "A hearer must be delighted so that he can be gripped and made to listen, and moved so that he can be impelled to action."[46]

Augustine connects these three purposes of rhetoric—instructing, delighting, and motivating—to Cicero's three rhetorical styles: the restrained, mixed, and grand. While all three styles aim at "persuasion,"[47] each serves a different pedagogical purpose: "The eloquent speaker will be one who can treat small matters in a restrained style in order to instruct, intermediate matters in a mixed style in order to delight, and important matters in a grand style in order to move an audience."[48] Although all matters regarding the Christian life are "important" and merit the "grand style," it does not fit every pedagogical purpose.[49] When attempting to present "facts," analyze a "difficult and complicated matter," or solve "knotty problems," the restrained style is most fitting:

it produces the clarity and precision needed to analyze "factual evidence" and avoid rhetorical flights of emotion.[50] On its own, however, the restrained style is insufficient:

> To clarify disputed issues there must be rational argument and deployment of evidence. But if listeners have to be moved rather than instructed, in order to make them act decisively on the knowledge that they have and lend their assent to matters which they admit to be true, then greater powers of oratory are required. In such cases what one needs is entreaties, rebukes, rousing speeches, solemn admonitions, and all the other things which have the power to excite human emotions.[51]

The mixed and grand styles serve these functions. The pleasing ornament of the mixed style helps to secure the attention of the audience, especially when "censuring or praising something," while the affectively charged rhetoric of the grand style arouses emotion and inspires action.[52] For my purposes, it is significant that Augustine encourages "those who wish to speak eloquently and wisely" to combine the mixed and grand styles to exhort audiences to "love good behaviour and avoid the bad."[53] This pedagogical function will be relevant when we evaluate Augustine's rhetoric of hope.

Augustine's vigorous defense of rhetoric in *On Christian Teaching* highlights his complex pedagogical practices and the need to understand his teachings in light of their style.[54] Most political theorists, however, seldom read *On Christian Teaching*, which is typically perceived as a theological treatise. When they do, they tend to focus, with Arendt and Nussbaum, on Book 1, where Augustine offers a brief exposition of Christian doctrine and introduces his controversial "order of love." Rarely do they consider Augustine's teaching on interpretation or rhetoric in Books 2–4.[55]

Such neglect is at odds with recent methodological trends in the history of political thought. In the last few decades, intellectual historians have made profound interpretative innovations by attending to the rhetorical culture of prominent thinkers and situating authors' explicit ideas and utterances within their historical and rhetorical contexts.[56] By considering not only what an author is *saying* but also what an author is *doing* in saying it, they have shown how influential political philosophers unite "wisdom with eloquence" to persuade audiences, "arguing in such a way that . . . hearers are not only instructed in the virtues but incited to the performance of virtuous acts."[57] By attending to this connection between "reason" and "rhetoric," scholars have offered novel accounts of canonical thinkers such as Plato, Machiavelli, and Hobbes.[58] With a few notable exceptions, however, political theorists have not yet applied the same sensitivity to Augustine.[59]

In her dissertation, Arendt advances a "purely philosophical" interpretation of Augustine, adopting a stance of "intentional detachment" that eschews the rhetorical and "dogmatic elements" of his texts, along with the historical "evolutions" that shaped him.[60] Niebuhr focuses only on Augustine's attitudes and utterances, weaving together passages from treatises, sermons, and commentaries without considering their historical context or rhetorical effect.[61] The young Rawls makes similar use of Augustine in his undergraduate thesis.[62] Even when Rawls invokes Augustine's "personal experience," he does so to make a doctrinal point, arguing that Augustine defends "orthodox dogma" against Pelagian attack.[63] Deane is more attentive to Augustine's historical contexts, but he largely ignores his rhetorical and pedagogical contexts, assembling quotations from letters, sermons, and treatises without recognizing how their rhetorical styles or purposes shape their meaning.[64] Reducing many passages to their propositional content, he is more interested, as his title suggests, in the "political and social ideas of St. Augustine" than the bishop's implicit pedagogical practices.[65]

Perhaps most surprising is Nussbaum's insensitivity to Augustine's rhetorical forms. Nussbaum devotes an entire book to Hellenistic philosophy as a "therapy of desire," arguing that these texts can be fully understood only when interpreters are sensitive to their literary genres and the pedagogical purposes they serve.[66] Since she confines her study to a period between the late fourth century BCE and the first two centuries CE, it would be unfair to criticize her for neglecting a fifth-century thinker like Augustine.[67] But she does not simply neglect Augustine's account; she sets her account against it. Contrasting her "therapeutic" model to the Platonic approach, she suggests that Augustine's Christian Platonism relies on a rationalistic and dualistic deductivism that is incongruous with the more indirect and immanent forms of Hellenistic philosophy she prefers.[68] By focusing on Augustine's ideas and doctrines, Nussbaum neglects the possibility that Augustine may also be practicing a form of therapeutic philosophy.[69]

Recently, a number of scholars in classics, philosophy, theology, and religious studies have elevated the rhetorical and pedagogical functions of Augustine's theological and philosophical texts, focusing on *Confessions*,[70] *The Trinity*,[71] the Cassiciacum dialogues,[72] and the sermons and letters.[73] These scholars have shown convincingly that Augustine appropriates classical therapies to educate his Christian audiences, but they do not usually attend to political passages in Augustine's texts.[74] Part of my purpose in this chapter and the next is to extend this rhetorical reading to show how Augustine's pedagogical purposes shape the meaning of his more political texts.

We have already seen these pedagogical purposes at work in chapter 3, where we considered the genre and purposes of the *Enchiridion*. Attending to the text's implicit form and function revealed that the *Enchiridion* is more than an exposition of theological or moral doctrines meant to instruct readers about what to hope for; it is also a set of implicit moral and spiritual practices intended to teach readers how to hope. The *Enchiridion* itself is a kind of spiritual exercise, a protreptic aimed at not only explicating the theological virtues but exhorting readers to exercise them. Since Augustine suggests practicing the Lord's Prayer can facilitate a relationship with God in the here and now, we can even say that the *Enchiridion* is a *proleptic protreptic*, a text where the very practice of reading helps to inaugurate participation in the City of God.

The same pedagogical purposes are even more apparent in Augustine's sermons, his most rhetorical texts. In what follows, I apply recent scholarship on Augustine's rhetorical and homiletical practices to his sermons on hope, highlighting how the distinctive characteristics of the genre alter our understanding of his counsels and encouragements.[75] When situated within their ecclesial, social, and pedagogical contexts, Augustine's homilies of hope do not appear as otherworldly or antipolitical as many critics claim.

II. Contextualizing Augustine's Homilies of Hope

Content and Form: Pedagogical Purposes and Rhetorical Constraints

To understand the context of Augustine's homilies, it is helpful to begin with the genre itself, which places constraints on the kinds of arguments that Augustine can advance. Consider, for example, a sermon's typical length. Although many of Augustine's sermons are longer than our contemporary counterparts, the need to offer concise interpretations and keep audiences engaged would have prevented the bishop from giving detailed or lengthy expositions, especially in a context where the congregation remained standing throughout the service.[76] As a skilled rhetorician, Augustine knew the difficulty of communicating concisely and holding audiences' attention over a long period of time. At a meeting of bishops, he voices worries that his two-hour sermon was "too laborious" for his audience.[77] In other places, he observes that the sermon is not the place to give lengthy or precise expositions of philosophical concepts.[78]

Nor would philosophical expositions have been his primary purpose. His aim in a sermon was not to provide an abstract analysis of a concept or even to identify the purely propositional content of the Christian faith.[79] Although he frequently explicates scriptural texts and discusses theological doctrines, his work as a pastor takes priority over his work as a scholar. "If I have some ability in this area," he writes to Jerome, himself a noted biblical scholar and translator, "I use it completely for the people of God. But on account of my work for the Church I cannot at all have the leisure for training scholars in more details than the people will listen to."[80] In his sermons in particular, Augustine goes beyond giving his congregation detailed or readymade knowledge about scripture or the good life. He also attempts to exhort, entreat, and inspire them to live it.[81] His purpose is both to instruct and encourage.

These pedagogical purposes shape both the content and form of Augustine's sermons. As Paul Kolbet argues, Augustine "recognized that persuasion was exceedingly difficult because successful persuasion requires an active change in the life of the hearer rather than passive assent. Much of the challenge of preaching, then, becomes employing a form that inculcates the content of the homily, that is, a form that educates the mind and trains the soul. It is for this reason that explicit propositions, even if they are true, do not cultivate the necessary *habitus* involved in reforming the self."[82] As Peter Brown affirms, Augustine's sermons enact the "inseparable wedding of form and content."[83]

Performing Hope: A Dialectic of Presumption and Despair

Augustine's efforts to shape a *habitus* of hope are evident in his sermons.[84] As we saw in earlier chapters, Augustine often exhorts audiences to develop the virtue of hope, ordering their hopes in a way that avoids the vices of presumption and despair. Here, we can see how the very form of his sermons encouraged this reordering. Augustine not only describes the dialectic of presumption and despair but leads his listeners through it, alerting them to the dangers of these two sirens. His homilies function as exercises of hope.

Consider Sermon 157, where Augustine distinguishes between "temporal" and "eternal" hopes and applies his distinction between use and enjoyment. He opens with one of his favorites passages of scripture, Romans 8:24: "It is by hope that we have been saved. But hope, [Paul] says, that can be seen is not hope; for why should anyone hope for what he can see? But if we are hoping for what we cannot see, we wait for it in patience."[85] "On this point," Augustine preaches,

> I am reminded I must offer you words of encouragement and consolation by the Lord our God himself, to whom it says in the psalm, *My hope are you, my portion in the land of the living* (Ps 142:5). He himself, I am telling you, who is our hope in the land of the living, is bidding me address you in this land of the dying; to urge you not to be too concerned about the things that can be seen, but about the things that cannot be seen. *For the things that can be seen are temporal; but the things that cannot be seen are eternal* (2 Cor 4:18).[86]

With the contrast in view, Augustine takes listeners through the oppositions between "temporal" and "eternal" things, "the land of the living" and the "land of the dying," warning them of the dangers of hoping only for worldly goods or despairing that there is no hope amidst life's "troubles and trials."[87] Citing Paul's admonition that *Bad talk corrupts good habits* (1 Corinthians 15:32–34), Augustine encourages his listeners not to have their "habits" corrupted by the "bad talk" of those who encourage them to turn their hopes from God to "temporal delights": "So take care, brothers and sisters, that your habits aren't corrupted by that kind of talk, your hope undermined, your patience discouraged, and you yourselves turned aside into crooked ways."[88] He then cites Christ as the "example" of proper hope, narrating Christ's suffering and resurrection in a way that encourages listeners to emulate Christ's patient and enduring hope.[89] He continues by repeating the oppositions between hope for temporal and eternal goods, admonishing the presumption of those who "hope in man" while citing Abraham's example of "hope against hope" to console those tempted to "despair."[90] Importantly, he concludes not with a counsel of condemnation but with a note of encouragement: "Walk along the narrow but sure way that leads to the wide open spaces of the heavenly Jerusalem, which is our eternal mother; hope with unshakeable conviction for what you cannot yet see, wait patiently for what you do not yet possess; because you can be assured with absolute confidence that in Christ you have one whose promises are true."[91]

Augustine uses a similar structure in Sermon 352A, encouraging listeners to put off vice and put on hope: "'Change your way of life, in case you lose your life. Condemn past sins, fear the evil things that are going to come, hope for the good things.' The bad man should begin by not contradicting himself in hoping for good things, while not being good himself. You're hoping for the good; be what you hope for."[92] In other words, Augustine suggests, by "putting on hope," listeners can habituate the virtue.

To aid this process, Augustine takes listeners through a dialectic of presumption and despair, alerting them to the "two sirens" that the "storm-tossed" must avoid to have virtuous hope:

> Which of them shall I put in the dock first: perverse hope or unbelieving despair? Why perish for hoping, why perish for despairing? Let those who want to perish for hoping listen to a thing or two: *Go back, transgressors to your heart* (Is 46:8). . . . I'm speaking to you, there, getting ready to be converted to the Lord, but putting it off; I'm speaking to you, on whose account I'm afraid of hope being your undoing; listen not to me, but to the one from whom you hope so much, and from whom your hoping too much may be your undoing.[93]

After chastening the presumption of those who hope "too much" in Christ without recognizing their limits or changing their character, Augustine proceeds to dispel the "despair" of those who believe they "have already committed so much evil that [they] cannot hope for forgiveness":

> Now let those who were likely to perish by despairing listen . . . to the voice of God, not your own. "Desperate soul, start hoping again. Listen to what Paul has to say: *For this reason I obtained mercy—I who persecuted the Church of God—that Christ Jesus might display in me all his long-suffering, to show the form to the very ones who were going to trust him for eternal life* (1 Tm 1:16). So there you have the form; don't despair; listen to the bond which was quoted a short while ago by a person who was hoping in a bad way, and let those who are despairing put themselves right by that.[94]

Here again, Augustine alerts listeners to the dangers of evil to chasten presumption but follows with encouragement to chasten despair, elevating both Paul and Christ as exemplars of virtuous hope.[95] He concludes by noting that "God hasn't abandoned either sort, neither those who hope in the wrong way nor those who despair in the wrong way. For the sake of those who despair in the wrong way he has provided the haven of forgiveness; for those who hope in the wrong way, he has left the day of death uncertain."[96] "There is nothing to be said," he adds, "but there is something to be done."[97] Here, Augustine not only tells listeners *what* hope is, but teaches them *how* to hope in both attitude and action, leading them through a dialectic of presumption and despair intended to help them resist both vices. In this pedagogical context,

Augustine's performance of properly ordered hope is as important as his proclamation.[98]

Augustine's advocacy of rhetoric to cultivate virtuous hope is evident in *The Gift of Perseverance*, an anti-Pelagian text written around 427–429, just after Augustine had completed *City of God*. Responding to a group of monks from Provence who had sought advice on how to teach the doctrine of grace and predestination,[99] Augustine acknowledges that placing a strong emphasis on the necessity of grace and the truth of God's providence might breed either reckless presumption or debilitating despair: presumption among those who assume they have already received the promise of salvation or despair among those who think they are condemned no matter what they do.[100] Both postures license premature rest and discourage any effort to realize the future good. How, then, are pastors to speak truthfully about salvation without encouraging the fatalism of either presumption or despair?

Augustine insists on preaching the truth while being sensitive to one's audience.[101] Too much emphasis on the certainty of predestination can discourage human striving and encourage "laziness" in those who presume their fates are sealed, or it can generate "despair" in those who hope only in themselves or believe they are destined for damnation. A good preacher should offer "hope" to all listeners rather than suggesting only a few will be saved.[102] To this end, the bishop recommends using particular rhetorical practices to encourage hope and the intentional effort it requires. For example, he encourages preachers to make conditional statements rather than condemnatory ones, to use third-person language rather than second-person language to avoid direct accusation, and to offer more inclusive promises of salvation so that specific doctrines are not "stated more harshly than they need be" and listeners do not despair of salvation.[103] Even if a statement is "surely true," it is "most brutal, most inopportune, and most inappropriate" if it is "not applied in a salutary manner to the frailty of human weakness."[104] Indeed, "it is an act of a deceitful or inexperienced physician to apply even a useful medicine in such a way that it either does no good or does harm."[105] Despite Nussbaum's suggestion to the contrary, Augustine recommends a "therapy of desire" that attends to content and form, helping pastors and their flocks avoid both presumption and despair.[106]

Augustine advocates a similar approach in *On Reprimand and Grace*, one of two treatises addressed to monks seeking guidance on how to properly reprimand erring Christians. The monks wanted to know whether they should reprimand their erring brothers (which would imply the free will to reform) or pray to God (which would imply grace's ultimate role in effecting transformation). Emphasizing God's grace too much, the monks worried, might cause Christians to think they have no free will and therefore remain either too lax or licentious when they err, assuming they could do nothing to affect their future salvation. Augustine responds by affirming the ultimate role of God's grace and the importance of prayer while advocating instruction and encouragement as ways of reforming the character of wayward brothers.[107] The monks should reprimand sin and acknowledge grace to deflate the "pride of human presumption" while recognizing the power of God's mercy to dispel "despair."[108] The hiddenness of God's judgment serves to chasten both vices, preventing the presumptuous from assuming they will receive salvation without reform and discouraging the despairing from giving up on the possibility that good works will elicit or reflect God's mercy.[109] As Conrad Leyser argues, "Augustine's message to the monks of Hadrumetum was that they should be neither encouraged to the point of presumption nor discouraged to the point of despair."[110] While Leyser does not mention Augustine's virtue of hope here, it is clear that the content and form of On Reprimand and Grace aims to help the monks exercise and encourage it.

Here and elsewhere, Augustine shows a pastor's sensitivity to the needs and temptations of his audience. Since Augustine identifies distorted vision and false self-estimation as causes of presumption and despair, he frequently recommends reforming one's perception to reorder hope. "There is hardly anyone who has a true opinion of himself," he writes in The Advantage of Believing. "Those who underestimate themselves need to be encouraged, those who overestimate themselves need to be repressed, so that the former will not break with despair and the latter will not crash through overconfidence."[111]

Throughout his sermons, Augustine often employs the default and challenge structure of discursive reasoning analyzed in chapters 4 and 5 to address listeners' temptations toward presumption and despair. Acknowledging these temptations and providing counterarguments to defeat or undermine them, Augustine appeals to reason and authority—including the authority of scripture and example of Christ—to bolster a default hope and enable listeners to persevere in faith and hope on their pilgrimage toward the heavenly city. His rhetorical strategy reflects a rational strategy to provide evidence that grounds hope and resists potential challenges or defeaters that might threaten it. Even his legal metaphors reinforce this strategy. By putting "perverse hope" and "unbelieving despair" "in the dock," he prosecutes a case against them, showing that they are guilty of disordering hope.[112]

Augustine enacts this dialectic of presumption and despair throughout his sermons, deploying the same rhetorical methods he commends in his treatises. In particular, he uses the restrained, moderate, and grand styles to instruct, delight, and encourage listeners in ways that cast new light on his contrasts between temporal and eternal hopes. Like Paul who uses the grand style to encourage audiences to develop an "assured hope in the assistance of God" amidst the "persecutions of the world,"[113] Augustine employs the grand style and stark contrasts between temporal and eternal hopes to diagnose disordered hope and exhort listeners to turn their hopes to God in the face of present evils.[114] In light of his pedagogical purposes, his stark contrast between this-worldly and otherworldly hopes emerges less as a precise, philosophical statement about the value of temporal or eternal goods than an emotionally weighted opposition intended to reorder audiences' desire, chastening the presumption that the world is the ultimate source of goodness.

The pedagogical purposes of these contrasts are especially apparent when we consider another of his favorite exhortatory devices, "antitheses" or "oppositions," the pairing of contrary ideas to draw a contrast between the two.[115] In Book 11 of *City of God*, Augustine endorses "antitheses" as one of the "most elegant figures of speech."[116] Although they are "not a usual feature of our vocabulary," he observes, "Latin speech, and, indeed, the languages of all nations, make use of the same ornaments of style."[117] The former professor of rhetoric then invokes the authority of the Old and New Testaments, highlighting an explanation of the practice in the Book of Ecclesiasticus and Paul's "graceful display of antithesis" in 2 Corinthians.[118] He even suggests God employs this kind of divine rhetoric when opposing good and evil, "adorning the course of the ages like a most beautiful poem set off with antitheses."[119]

Augustine's use of antitheses contextualizes the dueling contrasts he sometimes draws between hopes for temporal and eternal goods. Strikingly, he almost always presents these hopes in paired oppositions, using excessive rhetoric to exhort listeners to forfeit their worldly hopes and turn their hopes to the heavenly city.[120] While modern readers may interpret such oppositions as zero-sum expressions of Augustine's metaphysical dualism or otherworldly longing, attention to his use of antitheses complicates this view.[121] His excessive rhetoric does not necessarily express a literal devaluation of the world but instead reflects an attempt to change audiences' attitudes toward it.[122] In the next chapter, I argue that recognizing Augustine's use of such antitheses in *City of God* challenges the "pessimism" often attributed to him.

Proclaiming Hope: Aurality, Repetition, and Rhyme

In addition to their exhortatory effects, antitheses offered Augustine other rhetorical advantages, including a symmetry that is pleasing to the ear and a formula that is easy to remember.[123] These rhetorical features were especially useful in Augustine's context where homilies were heard rather than read. The aural aspect of performance is a significant feature of ancient sermons that modern interpreters may overlook. When many of us approach Augustine's homilies, we encounter them primarily as written texts. With the words at our fingertips, we have the ability to analyze the text slowly, pausing over sentences, attending to their structure, and rereading the sermon multiple times to understand its message.[124] Most in Augustine's congregation would not have had this ability. They would have heard the sermon only once and would not have been able to take home a copy for further reflection. Presenting ideas orally required Augustine to devote special attention to clarity and accessibility.[125]

He was particularly sensitive to differences between presenting ideas in sermons and in books. As he explains in *On Christian Teaching*,

> There are some things which are not understood, or barely understood, in themselves, no matter how carefully they are expressed or how many times they are repeated by even the plainest of speakers. These things should seldom be put to a popular audience, and then only if there is a pressing need, or arguably never at all. But in the case of books, which because they are in writing somehow grip the reader when they are understood, and do not annoy people when they are not understood, if they really want to read them, . . . we should not shirk the duty of making plain to the minds of others the truths which we have ourselves perceived, however hard they may be to comprehend, with as much effort and argument as may be necessary.[126]

Whereas books can be read and reread, pored over by educated audiences, sermons are heard by the literate and illiterate alike, requiring constant auditory attention and prohibiting pauses to reflect on a point or ask a question. The oral performance requires speakers to pursue the "aim of being intelligible," which, Augustine argues, "should be strenuously pursued not only in debates, whether with one person or several, but also, and this is even more important, in public gatherings when a sermon is delivered. In debates everyone has an opportunity to ask questions, but when all hush their voices to listen to one speaker, and turn their attentive faces towards him, it is not usual or acceptable for someone to ask questions about something he has not understood. So the speaker's sensitivity must come to the aid of the silent listener."[127]

Augustine's emphasis on simplicity and intelligibility may frustrate contemporary interpreters seeking precise philosophical formulations of hope in his homilies. The aural nature of these performances involved looser, more dynamic language, including brief and pithy formulas to please the audience, hold their attention, and facilitate retention, leaving listeners with phrases they could remember when they left the sanctuary. Attending to aural aspects of Augustine's homilies can perhaps illuminate another reason why his contrasts between temporal and eternal hopes are so stark: antitheses are easy to remember when heard. In one of his most important sermons on hope, Augustine notes explicitly that he is offering a "brief formula" to aid listeners: "I will say it again so you can all fix it in your minds in a brief formula: don't presume on your virtue to win the kingdom, don't presume on God's mercy and think you can get away with sinning."[128] Here, Augustine calls attention to the pedagogical function of antitheses, providing listeners with a regulative ideal, a "brief formula," they can recall and rehearse.

As we saw in chapter 3, the importance of providing memorable messages is one reason Augustine ties his discussion of hope to the Lord's Prayer. Along with its brevity, the prayer's frequent repetition in religious services makes it easier to remember and repeat. It is no surprise, then, that repetition is also a hallmark of Augustine's homilies and early Christian preaching more generally, where teaching "was carried out as much by the regular repetition and affirmation of familiar themes as by actual argument."[129] Such repetition is especially important when inculcating virtues that require repeated practice. As Kolbet argues, by tying theological reflections and interpretations to brief formulas and regular practices, Augustine "articulates the message in a form that facilitates its internalization in the souls of his hearers. . . . The form of the homily cultivates a *habitus* that fosters the life described in its content."[130] Repetition aids the habituation of hope.

Along with brief formulas and repetitive phrases, Augustine utilizes other rhetorical devices—rhymes, puns, and word-play—to aid retention, produce pleasure, and encourage attentive listening.[131] These rhymes and puns are often hard to recognize in English translations. Consider Augustine's frequent contrast between "hope" (*spes*) and "reality" (*res*), which the translator Edmund Hill describes as a "favorite jingle" of Augustine's.[132] In Sermon 313F, for example, Augustine says that "[w]hen the reality [*res*] comes, there will be no more hope [*spes*]."[133] Elsewhere, he argues that God will "give us the reality [*res*] in exchange for the hope [*spes*]."¹³⁴ In these formulations, Augustine uses "reality" to refer to eternal life and "hope" to refer to a posture in the present life, but sometimes, he reverses their meaning, using *res* to describe the present condition and *spes* to orient listeners to God's future kingdom. In a sermon on Psalm 42, he uses the rhymes to consider whether the "voice" of the church "is rejoicing in hope or sighing in the present condition [*uel laetantem in spe, uel suspirantem in re*]."¹³⁵ Or, as he preaches in Sermon 345, "[I]f you are faltering now under the harsh realities [*re*] of the present, be strong in your hopes [*spe*] for the future."¹³⁶ Note how the rhyming parallelisms in Latin—*Si titubas in re, esto fortis in spe*—make the line more memorable and pleasing to the Roman ear.

Augustine uses this rhyme between *res* and *spes* throughout his sermons and most influential books, including *On Christian Teaching* and *City of God*.¹³⁷ As he writes in Book 19 of *City of God*, "[I]f any man uses this life in such a way that he directs it toward that end which he so ardently loves and for which he so faithfully hopes, he may without absurdity be called happy even now, though rather by future hope than in present reality [*spe illa potius quam re ista*]."¹³⁸ Interpreters who read these passages in translation may assume Augustine is positing a strict opposition between "hope" and "reality," which may, in turn, reinforce impressions that Augustine maintains an otherworldly dualism and futurist eschatology that locates hope and reality in two different metaphysical or temporal realms. But if Augustine is using a rhyme between *res* and *spes* to delight his listeners and help them remember how to order their hopes, it may be inappropriate to assume the opposition marks a strict metaphysical dualism. Augustine may simply be using the expression more loosely to delight and exhort his listeners.

Augustine's discussion of how one can "groan over present reality [*re*]" and still "rejoice in hope [*spe*]" also illuminates an aspect of his account worth highlighting: hope is not incompatible with lament.¹³⁹ Hoping for a future good that is not yet possessed requires waiting and working for it, knowing that its attainment is not imminent or certain.¹⁴⁰ Such waiting and working can be "wearying," but as Sarah Stewart-Kroeker argues, "world-weariness itself is not a symptom of disorder": "Rightly ordered weariness and lament are necessary components of a virtuously perceptive—and therefore loving—response to the world."¹⁴¹ Analyzing Augustine's exposition of Psalm 36, Stewart-Kroeker shows how Augustine's emphasis on the suffering, labor, and toil that cause lament in this life only helps to direct hope to the heavenly city, reordering loves toward eternal goods rather than the incomplete temporal goods of this life.¹⁴² Such eschatological reordering does not license pessimism about earthly existence, as many critics assume. On the contrary, Augustine repeat-edly encourages audiences "to do good: to feed the hungry and help the needy, to do good work, to take action, to live well," all as enactments of "neighborly love" that participates in the heavenly city here and now.[143] "In this way," Stewart-Kroeker concludes, "Augustine's world-weary vision of earthly life that drives the gaze heavenward complements his exhortations to work in the world to love and serve others."[144]

This analysis of hope and lament is relevant for the account of hope offered here for three reasons. First, it shows that the Augustinian virtue of hope, un-like the optimism that often passes for "hope" in contemporary discourse, does not necessarily crowd out negative emotions or require a Pollyannaish form of positive thinking, as critics sometimes assume.[145] By necessity, the virtue of hope requires an accurate assessment of reality, including the risks, challenges, and tribulations that threaten the realization of its objects. Other-wise, the posture would reflect the vice of presumption rather than the virtue of hope. The compatibility of hopeful longing with groaning lament distin-guishes Augustine's virtue from shallower semblances.

Second, if hope is compatible with lament, then lament can implicitly re-flect a form of hope. When we lament current realities, we implicitly long for a better alternative, hoping for a way out of or beyond the current reality of suffering, injustice, or tribulation. Recognizing implicit hope alongside rigor-ous critique can provide a way forward in the face of present difficulties and prevent lament from hardening into despair.

Finally, joining longing with lament highlights why, both theologically and politically, a cheerful rhetoric is not necessarily the most effective means of facilitating virtuous hope, particularly if an audience is tempted toward pre-sumption. Sometimes, chastening presumption and cultivating proper hope requires a rhetoric calibrated to the particular needs of an audience, applying a pedagogy of desire to reorder their hopes and loves, depending on which vices they find most tempting. In his context, Augustine's excessive rhetoric and stark contrasts between hope and reality, *spes* and *res*, help to effect this reordering.

Social Context and Ecclesial Practice: Rhetorical Excess and Scriptural Exegesis

At other times, Augustine uses antitheses and parallelisms to address a partic-ular political and social event in his community. In these cases, recognizing a sermon's broader historical, political, and social context can shed light on his strong language. Consider Augustine's sermons on feast days of martyrs, where he made strong contrasts between temporal and eternal hopes: "The fact that today is both a feast of the martyrs and the Lord's day constrains me to speak to your graces about what concerns indifference or contempt for the present age and hopes for the age to come."[146] Christian feast days were not the only occasions for such contrasts. Consider Sermon 198, where Augustine contrasts pagans who "hope for the vanities of this age" and Christians who "hope for eternal life."[147] Abstracting this passage from its context may reinforce Augustine's dualism or exclusivism, but situating the sermon in its social context presents a more complex picture. Consider the date: January 1, the pagan celebration of the New Year, a day in which many members of his congregation would have been tempted to indulge in what, by Augustine's lights, involved licentious debauchery. Augustine criticizes these festivities in the first lines of the sermon, describing the pagan new year as a "false feast day."[148] As a pastor all too aware of peer pressure,[149] he suspects congregants might be tempted to attend these pagan celebrations.[150] His stark contrast between "hope in the vanities of the age" and "hope for eternal life" is intended to dissuade them, employing rhetorical excess to discourage moral excess.

Augustine's occasionally polemical contrasts take on more meaning in light of his recognition that "both pagan and Christian worship," as Jennifer Herdt suggests, can be "construed as spectacle, as the authoritative public presentation of attractive exemplars before the eyes of a collected assembly."[151] As Michael McCarthy affirms, Augustine sought to present a "spectacle" (*spectaculum*) in his sermons that contrasts with pagan spectacles and thereby sets the church apart, bringing an ecclesial community into being.[152] In Sermon 198, for example, he observes that those in his church have gathered as "if it were a feast" and then sets Christian worship against "the festival of the Gentiles which is taking place today in the joys of the world and the flesh, with the din of silly and disgraceful songs, with disgraceful junketing and dances, with the celebration of this false feast day."[153] He suggests that faithful Christians will be "set apart" by "the soundness of faith, the soundness of hope, the soundness of the most genuine charity, a spiritual soundness, the utterly reliable soundness of the promises of God."[154] He goes on to proclaim that "[n]obody in fact can live any style of life without those three sentiments of the soul; of believing, hoping, loving," but that "you must prove it by your life, demonstrate it by your actions."[155] Here, the stark contrast between pagan and Christian, temporal and eternal, contributes to the spectacle intended to attract Christians and exhort them to resist temptations that await them beyond the basilica, bringing them into a community that can help them persevere in faith, hope, and love.[156] This social context helps to illuminate the rhetorical and pedagogical purposes of this homily of hope.

The nature of spectacle points to another relevant feature of Augustine's homilies: they are *occasional* texts, real-time responses to specific occasions in his community conditioned by distinctive political, social, and theological contexts. Consider Sermon 313F, preached after a local bishop requested a homily on hope following Augustine's morning sermon on charity. Augustine likely would not have known he would be preaching on hope later that night. At the least, he would have had little time to prepare. He would have had to preach extemporaneously and may have felt the need to satisfy the bishop while trying to remain consistent with what he had said about "restless" charity earlier in the day.[157] In such improvisational situations, philosophical consistency might not have been at the forefront of Augustine's mind, nor even expected the way it is now. Unlike contemporary scholars, Carol Harrison argues, Augustine "writes within a tradition of rhetoric which was not at all constrained by matters of general consistency."[158]

Spontaneous sermons were not unusual in Augustine's time. Possidius observes that many of Augustine's sermons were extemporaneous.[159] Although the bishop often prepared a mental plan for expounding the scripture set for the day, he did not use written notes when he preached, and he occasionally digressed from the topic at hand.[160] Sometimes, he even preached on scriptural passages that were unplanned. "Whenever the lector inadvertently read a different text," Kolbet notes, "Augustine was known to delight his hearers by accepting the challenge presented by providence by preaching on whatever was read."[161] Such spontaneous, ad hoc remarks highlight a crucial difference with contemporary homiletical practice. Contemporary pastors usually preach from written remarks and typically give only one sermon per week, which affords time to prepare and reflect on what they will say. Augustine, by contrast, sometimes preached once or twice a day and, given other pastoral, ecclesial, and political responsibilities, did not have the luxury of extensive preparation. Extemporaneous sermons would have been a practical necessity. As a result, what Augustine says off-the-cuff in one homily on hope might not always be consistent with what he says in another.

One feature of his sermons that did encourage consistency was his deep reliance on scripture.[162] Scripture gave structure and content to Augustine's sermons, enabling him to draw on biblical authority to educate audiences and affirm their membership in a shared community, an aspect on display in his

Expositions of the Psalms and *Homilies on First John.*[163] Yet, while scripture offered authority and inspiration, it also placed linguistic and conceptual constraints on expositors.[164] In *City of God*, Augustine notes that adherence to scriptural vocabulary limits theologians in a way that it does not constrain philosophers: "For the philosophers use words in whatever way they like, and they do not bother to avoid offending the ears of religious men even in the most difficult matters. But we are obliged by religious duty to speak according to a fixed rule, lest verbal license beget impious opinions concerning the matters which our words signify."[165]

The constraints of his inherited vocabulary are important to remember when analyzing Augustine's sermons on hope. As his discussion of Paul's "antitheses" suggests, some passages included either/or formulations that would have required Augustine's comment. At the least, he may have felt the need to be faithful to scriptural vocabulary even as he tried to extend its meaning. In one sermon, for example, he goes to great lengths to explain why faith is like a "fish," hope is like an "egg," and love is like "bread," using the concrete metaphors Paul supplies to offer a theological exposition.[166] Elsewhere, he tries to reconcile Paul's early triad of "faith, hope, and charity" (1 Corinthians 13:13) with the later triad of "single-hearted charity, a good conscience, and unfeigned faith" (1 Timothy 1:5), offering reflections to make the two consistent. In these places, Augustine improvises and stretches his inherited vocabulary to bear the weight of his theological and philosophical expositions.

An Egalitarian Education: Accessibility, Openness, and Dialogue

While fidelity to scripture might have constrained the vocabulary available for explaining a concept like hope, it also had powerful enabling effects in Augustine's social milieu. Augustine often preached to mixed audiences that included people who were rich and poor, schooled and unschooled, free and enslaved.[167] A large majority of people—about 90 percent in one estimate—would have been illiterate.[168] Yet many were familiar with scripture because it was read frequently in church.[169] In this context, Augustine's efforts to tie theological reflections on hope to scriptural texts would have provided a way to ground them in religious authority while engaging texts familiar to largely illiterate audiences.

For Augustine, accessibility remains a consistent concern. As a practiced pastor and skilled rhetorician, he emphasizes the importance of making messages accessible to diverse audiences.[170] Like a doctor treating different patients, Augustine urges preachers to attend to the needs of diverse listeners: "[T]he same medicine is not to be administered to all."[171] Augustine emphasizes clarity and intelligibility over elegance, ornament, and even grammatical correctness: "What is the use of correct speech if it does not meet with the listener's understanding? There is no point in speaking at all if our words are not understood by the people to whose understanding our words are directed."[172] In *On Christian Teaching*, he admonishes preachers to avoid obscure, pretentious, or ambiguous Latin words that mixed audiences would not understand, going so far as to encourage the use of colloquialisms even if they violate proper grammar.[173] Similarly, in *On the Catechising of the Uninstructed*, he advises bishops, priests, and deacons to be sensitive to the differing educational levels of their audiences, making sure their messages are appropriately suited to those who had studied the liberal arts, for example, and those who had not.[174] In these texts, Augustine counsels a pastoral prudence that is more sensitive to audience and context than his more systematic treatises might suggest.

Augustine was especially concerned to make his "sermons for the people" accessible to less educated audiences.[175] In countless homilies, including some on hope, he adjusts his message to engage his audience and facilitate understanding. As John Cavadini argues, Augustine "developed a homiletic style that was intentionally simple, shorn of rhetorical intricacy, plain and vivid, specially created to reach just such a heterogeneous group."[176] While this style creates difficulties for contemporary philosophical interpreters seeking to extract precise formulations from Augustine's sermons, it highlights an egalitarian impulse and public purpose that captures a distinctive feature of Augustine's homiletic practice: the very form of his sermons challenges the social stratification and cultural elitism he saw in the Roman Empire. As Cavadini argues, Augustine's homiletic practice was intentionally countercultural: his "renunciation of the intricate, jeweled rhetorical style meant forgoing a traditional, identifying characteristic of the elite, so that such a rhetorical posturing was itself a kind of social statement."[177]

Averil Cameron describes this more egalitarian, inclusive style as a distinctive characteristic of early Christian rhetoric: "[I]t was indeed a mark of Christian discourse, and thus of Christian ideas, to be able to work horizontally in a society where few channels of horizontal communication existed."[178] Trained in classical rhetoric and philosophy, the educated Roman elite "had no interest in sharing its privileges with society at large, not even when the needs of imperial government might have suggested that it was in its interests to develop a larger literate class."[179] Christians, by contrast, deliberately sought to reach as wide of an audience as possible. While their "'language of fishermen'" often offended the tastes of rhetorically trained elites, "as Augustine knew best of all, it was also one of the greatest strengths of Christian discourse that it could in some sense reach all levels of society and all levels of education—that is, it could form horizontal as well as vertical links in society."[180] Because sermons could reach the educated and uneducated alike, Cameron concludes, they "cut across the barriers of class and genre in a way not open to classical writers."[181] Augustine was one of the most persuasive practitioners of this more egalitarian art.

Augustine's commitment to reaching a wide audience helps to explain his frequent appeal to scripture in his sermons. He celebrates the "humble" and "lowly" style of scripture, which is accessible to diverse audiences, not just the educated elite:

> [H]ow accessible to all is the very style in which scripture is composed, though very few can enter deeply into it. Like a close friend, it speaks without pretense those clear ideas it contains to the heart of the unlearned and of the learned. It does not exalt those things that it conceals in mysteries with a proud language to which the sluggish and untrained mind dares not approach, as a poor man dares not approach a rich one, but invites all with its lowly language.[182]

Challenging Roman critics who saw scriptural rhetoric as crude and unornamented, Augustine commends the humility that scripture teaches and embraces its style as a kind of training meant to disrupt intellectual presumption.[183] "We know of no other books," he writes in *Confessions*, "with the like power to lay pride low."[184]

This humbling language had significant educational import in Augustine's social and political context, offering access to moral wisdom in ways that elite education did not.[185] In Sermon 133, for example, Augustine assures those "educated in the scriptures of the Lord" that they "aren't uneducated persons, not country bumpkins, not ignorant simpletons": "Sure, there are among you highly educated and learned men, widely and deeply read in all kinds of literature. But those of you also who have not been schooled in what they call the liberal arts, well of much more value is the fact that you have been brought up on the word of God."[186]

Augustine's educational metaphors are significant. As scholars note, here and elsewhere, Augustine casts the church as a kind of "school" (*schola*) free and open to all.[187] In one sermon, he emphasizes how this school offers "hope" not just to the rich but to the poor.[188] In another, he describes the church as a "school" that "demands good students . . . *unflagging in keenness, fervent in spirit, rejoicing in hope* (Rom 12:11–12)." "[I]n this school," he continues, "we learn something every day. We learn something from commandments, something from examples, something from sacraments. These things are remedies for our wounds, material for our studies."[189] As Kolbet observes, Augustine's references to commandments or precepts, examples, and remedies echo the central components of classical education in the Neoplatonic and Stoic schools.[190] Augustine implies that the church is a school open to those who have been denied access to the elite schools typically seen as the site of intellectual and moral formation in the Roman Empire. As Augustine writes to Nectarius, the virtues that Cicero celebrated are now "being taught and learnt in the churches that are springing up all over the globe, like sacred lecture halls for the peoples of the world."[191] Augustine reiterates this sentiment in a letter to Marcellinus, suggesting that the "command not to *return evil for evil* . . . echoes from our pulpits around our congregations, as if they were at public lectures, open to both sexes and to every age-group or rank."[192] Of course, the ecclesial context of these sermons would not have been made them as open to religious outsiders who did not share Augustine's Christian commitments, but by emphasizing the church as an egalitarian institution where many people can conceivably be students, no matter their age, office, gender, or class, Augustine is offering increased access to moral education in his Roman context, supplying ordinary people with opportunities to pursue wisdom and cultivate virtue that they had previously been denied.[193] In this sense, his sermons are strikingly egalitarian pedagogies of hope.[194]

Augustine's egalitarian emphasis is apparent in the homilies on the Lord's Prayer, his quintessential practice of hope. These sermons often have a political valence that challenges forms of the social hierarchy and political domination that pervade the Roman Empire. In one sermon, for example, he asks listeners to consider the first words of the Lord's Prayer, "Our Father who art in heaven":

> Now we say *Our Father* all together; what all-embracing generosity! The emperor says it, the beggar says it; the slave says it, his master says it. They all say together, *Our Father who art in heaven.* So they must realize that they are brothers, since they all have one Father. The master must not scorn to have as a brother the slave of his whom the Lord Christ was willing to have as a brother.[195]

In another sermon, Augustine acknowledges that some forms of social stratification and domination that define hierarchies in Rome do not hold in the
church: "You have begun to belong to a huge family. Under this Father rich
and poor are brothers; under this Father master and slave are brothers; under
this Father emperor and private soldier are brothers. Christian believers all
have different fathers on earth, some aristocrats, some commoners. But they
all call upon one Father who is in heaven."[196] He emphasizes that the church
offers a kind of acceptance that the Roman Empire cannot: "[Y]ou are going
to be children of God, not of some great man or other. I mean does your governor prepare to adopt any of you? But divine grace has made everyone into
sons and daughters."[197] These passages show that, for Augustine, the Lord's
Prayer is not only a practice intended to cultivate the virtue of hope but also
an exercise that seeks to make the virtue accessible to people from diverse
social, political, and cultural classes.

In addition to expressing more egalitarian content, Augustine's sermons
also have a more egalitarian form. While Augustine plays the role of teacher
in the "school of Christ" when preaching to catechumens, he insists elsewhere
that he is also a student, framing his sermons as shared inquiries into the mysteries of faith: "What after all am I, but someone needing to be set free with
you, cured with you?"[198] Augustine notes that "bishops are called teachers
[doctores], but in many matters we seek a teacher ourselves, and we certainly
don't want to be regarded as masters [magistros]. That is dangerous, and for-
bidden by the Lord himself, who says 'Do not wish to be called masters; you
have one master, the Christ' (Mt 23:10)."[199] Repeatedly, Augustine emphasizes
that it is God, not himself, who is the master teacher.[200] While critics may
interpret this as "mere rhetorical posturing," Kolbet suggests that Augustine
"purposefully constructed sermons as exercises in which both he and his congregation participate in order to develop for themselves habitual skills of reading and living."[201] Cavadini concurs, arguing that Augustine is "above all a
listener."[202] As Augustine suggests in one sermon, "[I]t's a futile preacher out-
wardly of God's word, who isn't also inwardly a listener."[203]

Most of the time, Augustine listens for the meaning of scripture. He frequently reframes sermons as expositions where he and the audience seek
scripture's meaning, attempting to discern the truth as the text unfolds.[204]
Augustine does not simply share the "*results*" of an inquiry he had conducted
prior to his exposition; rather, Cavadini concludes, he "recontextualizes inquiry itself *for* the people. In his homilies such inquiry is no longer the exclusive province of the liberally educated elites."[205]

This seeking posture means that Augustine's sermons are more like *essays* or *attempts* than definitive or demonstrable conclusions.[206] His homilies have an open-ended, often digressive quality that resists premature closure. Frequently, he poses questions before offering a response, giving voice to doubts and confusions he imagines his audience might have, and he expresses an openness to uncertainty, ambiguity, and possibility, practicing what Jeffrey Bullock describes as a "dialectical combination of exploration and exegesis."[207] According to Bullock, Augustine's sermons "were experientially open rather than propositionally closed. Rather than the transmission of information, Augustine's innovative homiletic practice helped to facilitate an experience of the word where both speaker and audience were co-participants in an event of understanding."[208]

For the purposes of assessing Augustine's homilies of hope, this more provisional, participatory, and dialogical form of exposition and inquiry is significant for two reasons. First, it reinforces the insight that Augustine is less interested in offering precise definitions of philosophical concepts than testing out ideas and interpretations. Like his dynamic and fluid formulations of "use" and "enjoyment," his loose, rhetorical oppositions of temporal and eternal hopes do not always bear the philosophical weight that many contemporary interpreters place on them. They are intended to shape how readers hope, not simply what they hope for.

Second, Augustine's openness to his audience reflects a more dialogical and discursive style of inquiry that opens itself to the interpretations—and corrections—of his audience. Augustine frequently implores his audience to hold him accountable: "For although to all appearances I am standing in a higher place than you, this is merely for the convenience of carrying my voice better, and in fact it is you who are in the higher place to pass judgment, and I who am being judged."[209] Elsewhere, he enlists his audience to ensure he does not dissolve difficult doctrinal problems through hasty or mistaken formulations: "You are listening as judges; the case has been stated, let the witnesses step forward."[210] These moments, often dramatized as part of a legal trial, suggest Augustine's insistence on practices of shared inquiry and accountability. They also highlight the default and challenge structure of discursive reasoning discussed in chapter 4. With the humility required of Christian faith and hope, Augustine opens himself to challenges from others and seeks a dialogue to ensure that faith properly seeks understanding.

This discursive mode of engagement fits Augustine's context, where the sermon was a more dialogical form than is typically recognized. This is evident in the sermon's etymological roots: the Greek word *homilia* initially meant "conversation,"[211] a point Augustine emphasizes. When introducing a particularly difficult psalm to exposit, he tells his congregation that he has "decided to tackle it in public sermons, which the Greeks call homilies," which "is the fairest way, because then church congregations will not be denied comprehension of this psalm."[212]

The conversational mode of many of Augustine's sermons reflects the distinctive features of his ecclesial context. As Peter Brown notes, the preacher of late antique sermons "interacted with his audience in the most face-to-face manner possible":

> There was no raised pulpit. There were no confining pews. The congregation stood on the spacious floor of the basilica. They were free to move around. They would surge up to the edge of the slightly raised area in front of the apse in order to listen to the preacher. The preacher would come forward toward them from his seat in the middle of the semicircular bench on which he and his clergy sat with their backs to the circular wall of the apse. Or he would step down from the apse into the center of the church so as to preach beside the altar that stood near the middle of the basilica, set apart by low railings of wood or carved marble. A mobile lectern of light wood was all that the preacher needed, to hold the copy of the Bible from which he sowed his words.[213]

According to Brown, this face-to-face setting meant that Augustine's sermons would have been intimate, personal affairs with congregants, who themselves constituted a kind of "grassroots" *populus*.[214] Augustine's sermons could be rightly considered "dialogues with the crowd."[215]

Of course, these more dialogical and egalitarian features of Augustine's homilies of hope do not make the bishop a radical democrat, but they do suggest points of convergence and overlap with more egalitarian forms of political theory. At the least, this more contextualized account of Augustine's homiletic practice complicates criticisms from political theorists such as Romand Coles and William Connolly, who dismiss Augustine because of his "monological" and "imperative" style.[216] Contextualized readings of the sermons present a more egalitarian, discursive, and dialogical form of teaching than most political theorists typically recognize.

Yet aspects of his sermons that might have signaled an egalitarian impulse in Augustine's context also reveal how troubling his thought can be to contemporary citizens. Consider, for example, Augustine's frequent mention of "slaves" in his sermons. Slavery was widespread in Roman North Africa.[217] Augustine grew up in a household that included enslaved persons, and in one sermon he notes how he and his congregants encountered slavery "every day," witnessing it in "[n]early all households."[218] In alignment with his interpretation of passages from the New Testament, Augustine uses slavery as a metaphor to describe human beings' relationship to God. Because human beings are ultimately and utterly dependent on God's being and power, Augustine believes that *all* human beings are "slaves" to God, and many also remain "slaves to sin."[219] In this sense, all human beings share the status of slaves equally; the question for Augustine is whether they are good slaves or bad slaves, faithful slaves or fugitive slaves, and whether the relationships support the slave's participation in eternal goods.[220] The idea that humans are "slaves of God" is disturbing to many contemporary audiences and might have been disturbing to some of Augustine's, especially enslaved persons whose viewpoint and agency are not often considered in contemporary appraisals of his thought.[221]

In a comprehensive, contextualized, and philosophically sophisticated account of Augustine's views on slavery, Olaoluwatoni Alimi has traced his complex arguments, texts, and examples to analyze the "varieties of slavery" in his thought and examine their implications for his conceptions of religion, law, and citizenship.[222] Seeking to understand how central slavery was in Augustine's theological and political imagination, Alimi rightly describes Augustine's views on chattel slavery as "horribly wrong" and "abhorrent" while suggesting that Augustine introduces normative constraints that many of his contemporaries would not have recognized, including, for example, that "masters" (including God) are accountable to "slaves" to provide for their wellbeing and that "slaves of God" can also be "citizens" in the heavenly city, thereby challenging a distinction between "slavery" and "citizenship" that was common to the Roman republican tradition.[223] Despite these normative constraints, Augustine draws on this metaphor in significant and sometimes troubling ways, providing conceptual linkages that he uses to encourage Christians to be obedient to God, admonish Donatists to join the unity of the Catholic Church, and defend the role of bishops in exercising authority over congregants.[224]

Moreover, as Alimi and other scholars emphasize, slavery was not simply a metaphor for Augustine and should not be minimized as such.[225] While Augustine viewed slavery as "wretched," argued that slavery is not caused "by nature" but by "sin," recognized the dignity of enslaved persons because of their humanity, saw the "plague" of slave-trading as a "wicked form of commerce," and worked to liberate some enslaved persons and prevent some free citizens from being enslaved, he also accepted and sometimes justified the institution as "ordained" by God as a "punishment" for sin.[226] He encouraged enslaved persons to be obedient to their "masters," and he admonished Christian masters to punish enslaved persons in their households to correct their sins for the benefit of their souls. He believed that slavery to sin was worse than slavery to human masters since slavery to sin has eternal consequences. Therefore, he held that slavery to Christian masters could help to convert enslaved persons to Christianity and thereby save their souls.[227] Many of Augustine's predecessors and peers held similar (and sometimes worse) views. But as Alimi emphasizes, others—such as Lactantius—believed the human institution of slavery to be unjust, even as he, like Augustine, considered human beings to be "slaves" of God. This means we cannot simply dismiss Augustine's acceptance of slavery as the only option he could imagine in his context. Since Augustine drew on Lactantius in *City of God*, he would have been familiar with Lactantius's critique of the institution.[228]

As more work on Augustine's account of slavery emerges, it will require significant consideration of how his concepts and commitments are implicated in other aspects of his thought. We must keep these views in mind when we consider Augustine's pedagogies of hope and how they might have been heard by different members of his audiences. Although they are, in some ways, more egalitarian than some other pedagogies on offer in his late antique Roman context, they fall far short of contemporary ideals of justice and equality and at times even those of his predecessors. Nonetheless, these sermons show that Augustine's rhetoric of hope is more complex and nuanced than interpreters typically recognize.

Conclusion

By situating Augustine with the ancient philosophical tradition and showing how he uses rhetoric to both instruct and encourage his audiences, I have tried to offer a suitably complex account of Augustine's homilies of hope. While Augustine uses stark contrasts between "temporal" and "eternal" hopes to exhort audiences to pursue the heavenly city, his antitheses are not necessarily intended as precise formulations or literal valuations of the world. Rather, these rhetorical devices serve pedagogical functions, helping to diagnose the dangers of presumption while discouraging listeners from sliding into despair. When viewed in light of passages where Augustine counsels properly ordered hope for temporal goods, his sermons themselves emerge as spiritual exercises, pedagogies of hope that lead listeners through a dialectic of presumption and despair intended to train their desires and defeat any challenges that might threaten their perseverance in faith and hope. Since this pedagogy is free, public, and open to all, including those traditionally excluded from private institutions of elite education, it is also a more egalitarian form of moral education that challenges some of the cultural, social, and political hierarchies of Augustine's time. An interpretation attentive to Augustine's implicit homiletic practices thus reveals a more complex portrait than we find in common caricatures.

Lest readers think these rhetorical practices are confined to Augustine's theological sermons and expositions, his more "systematic" and "political" texts also make extensive use of rhetoric. A pedagogically sensitive approach to *City of God* in particular can further challenge the "pessimism" that Augustine's most infamous passages seem to commend.

7

Into Hell and Out Again

A STRUCTURE OF ENCOURAGEMENT
IN THE *CITY OF GOD*

Suppose that, gnarled as I am, I did not consider it enough simply to seek payment for my gnarledness, the establishment of communion through evils held in common? Suppose I would also erect a structure of encouragement, for all of us? How should I go about it, in the sequence of imagery, not merely to bring us most poignantly into hell, but also out again?

—KENNETH BURKE, "SEMANTIC AND POETIC MEANING"[1]

CITY OF GOD is a difficult text to interpret. Comprising twenty-two books and over one thousand pages, Augustine's magnum opus is, as Peter Brown argues, a "loose, baggy monster."[2] Its sprawling expanse makes it difficult to analyze Augustine's diffuse claims, much less to assess their coherence and consistency. These interpretative difficulties are magnified by the duration of its composition. *City of God* was written over a period of thirteen or fourteen years in which Augustine was constantly interrupted by political and ecclesial responsibilities and drawn into theological controversies that demanded his attention.[3] "Barbarian" armies surrounded the edges of the empire while religious critics hammered away at the orthodoxy of the Catholic Church, leaving both institutions embattled in a fight for survival. Augustine's shifting arguments and tone in *City of God* reflect his diverse audiences and the changing temper of his times.[4] Over thirteen years, a book that began as a polemic against critics who blamed Christianity for the sack of Rome becomes a

broader reflection on a range of theological and political topics, from the nature of virtue to the glories of the heavenly city.[5]

Given these changing circumstances, we should not be surprised that Augustine uses different rhetorical styles for distinct pedagogical purposes, applying the three styles mentioned in Book 4 of *On Christian Teaching*, which—
importantly—was completed around the time he was finishing *City of God*.[6]
Since *City of God* grapples with many complex theoretical and textual issues,
Augustine writes much of it in the restrained style, which affords more analytical precision and is "easier to tolerate over a long period than the grand style."[7]
Yet *City of God* does not employ only one style, as most interpreters assume.
In *On Christian Teaching*, Augustine explicitly warns against using a single
style, suggesting it can become "less absorbing for the listener."[8] Keeping audiences engaged requires varying styles so that "the intensity of our speech ebbs
and flows like the tides of the sea."[9]

In particular, Augustine suggests combining the mixed and grand styles
when the aim is not simply to "delight" an audience through eloquence but to
motivate an "audience's assent and action."[10] Beginning with the ornament of
the mixed style can secure an audience's attention, while concluding with vivid
description in the grand style can inspire action, which can be particularly
useful when exhorting an audience to develop an "assured hope in the assistance of God" amidst the "persecutions of this world" and "the evils of the
present time."[11] This, I believe, is how Augustine proceeds in *City of God*,
where he combines the mixed and grand styles in the final book to reorder
readers' hopes toward the eternal city.[12]

Augustine suggests as much in a recently discovered letter to Firmus, who
had written to him after reading and listening to several books of *City of God*.[13]
The "whole fruit of so many books that you love," Augustine writes, "does not
consist in delighting the reader or in making someone know many facts that
he does not know but in persuading a person either to enter into the City of
God without hesitation or to remain there with perseverance."[14] Augustine's
most influential political text, in other words, aims not simply to instruct but
to encourage. Only when we recognize how Augustine employs various rhetorical styles to effect this purpose can we begin to discern the intended meaning of the text.

That Augustine employed the art of rhetoric not only in sermons but in
treatises like *City of God* would not have surprised his contemporaries. As we
saw in the previous chapter, Augustine belonged to a rhetorical culture where

using different styles of rhetoric was a common feature of even the most systematic texts. This is especially true of *City of God*, whose composition and reception have more in common with spoken rhetoric than most interpreters realize.[15] Many contemporary readers—like the medieval artists who painted Augustine alone in his study—assume the bishop wrote his books in solitude, using a stylus to record his innermost thoughts.[16] But composition in Augustine's age was often a more oral, social, and rhetorical affair. Like many of his predecessors and contemporaries, Augustine composed many of his longer works, including parts of *City of God*, by dictating thoughts to scribes, who then drafted the text on wax tablets. Once they were combined into a coherent draft, Augustine reviewed and revised the text, making edits before the codex was complete.[17] The initial composition, however, was often an oral performance, which allowed Augustine to build on his extensive training as a rhetorician.

If the composition of *City of God* was largely rhetorical, so was its reception. Today, most people assume that reading is a private, silent, and solitary act of an individual alone with a text, but in late antiquity, reading was often communal, public, and performative.[18] Because of the cost and labor involved in producing scrolls and codices, access to written texts was limited, which meant many late antique citizens would only encounter texts through oral readings.[19] Although those with access could read silently, as Augustine observes of Ambrose in *Confessions*,[20] many philosophical and theological texts were recited aloud rather than read in solitude.[21] Augustine's letter to Firmus provides a striking example: while Firmus read the first ten books of *City of God* on his own, Augustine notes that the Catholic layman "listened attentively along with us when [Book 18] was read on three consecutive afternoons" and was "set afire a blazing desire to have all the books."[22] This reference highlights the pedagogical effect that such rhetorical performances could have on audiences. Knowing that *City of God* would frequently be received aurally likely shaped Augustine's intentions, allowing him to use various rhetorical styles to instruct and encourage.[23]

Few political theorists, however, read *City of God* rhetorically, though a handful of interpreters have been more sensitive. Andrew Murphy analyzes Augustine's use of the "rhetoric of Roman decline" in *City of God*, while Thomas W. Smith highlights the book's "pedagogical and hortatory dimension," showing how Augustine seeks to redirect readers' love away from human glory toward the glory of God.[24] John von Heyking suggests that Augustine employs a "dialectic of excess over excess" to "form the inordinate passions into ordinate love,"[25] and Veronica Roberts Ogle argues that Augustine applies "psychagogic" rhetoric to "liberate his readers from an excessive attachment to Rome so that they might express a proper allegiance to the city of God."[26] These interpreters helpfully illuminate how Augustine's rhetorical and pedagogical purposes shape his political thought.

In what follows, I extend this approach to illuminate key passages in *City of God*. I focus on an influential passage from Book 22 frequently cited as evidence of Augustine's "pessimism." By situating this passage within its larger context, I argue that Augustine's vivid description of earthly evils in 22.22–23 should not be taken as a literal expression of "pessimism" written in the restrained style, but rather as an excessive use of rhetoric offered in the grand style intended to transform readers' vision, reorder their loves, and redirect their hopes. Instead of affirming Augustine's pessimism, Book 22.22–23 functions as a moral and spiritual exercise of hope that helps readers find a way between presumption and despair. Ultimately, I conclude, Augustine's triad of presumption, hope, and despair exposes "pessimism" as an anachronistic and conceptually confining description of his thought and offers a more nuanced vision of the posture he recommends.

I. A Spiritual Exercise in Book 22

Augustine's rhetorical purposes become clear in a close reading of *City of God* 22.22–24, a set of chapters situated within his final book on "the eternal blessedness of the City of God."[27] In Book 22, he explains God's creation, will, and promises of blessedness for the saints (22.1–3), defends the bodily resurrection, Christ's resurrection, and the possibility of miracles (22.4–11, 26–28), addresses questions about what kinds of bodies and bodily features will be resurrected (22.12–21), and presents a vision of the felicity of the heavenly city (22.29–30). Within this context, Augustine's account of earthly goods and evils in 22.22–24 serves to contrast the miseries of earthly existence with the peace of the heavenly city and point readers to signs of God's goodness and grace.[28]

A quick glance at 22.22–23 reveals why interpreters frequently cite this passage as evidence of Augustine's "pessimism."[29] In Book 22, as in Book 19, Augustine provides a lengthy list of what he sees as the "many and grave evils" that accompany "life under condemnation":

> gnawing cares, disturbances, griefs, fears, insane joys, discords, litigation, wars, treasons, angers, hatreds, falsehood, flattery, fraud, theft, rapine,

perfidy, pride, ambition, envy, homicides, parricides, cruelty, ferocity, wickedness, luxury, insolence, immodesty, unchastity, fornications, adulteries, incests, and so many other impure and unnatural acts of both sexes of which it is shameful even to speak: sacrileges, heresies, blasphemies, perjuries, oppression of the innocent, slanders, plots, prevarications, false witness, unrighteous judgments, acts of violence, robberies, and other such evils which do not immediately come to mind, but which are never far away from men in this life.[30]

Augustine goes on to lament the "fear and distress [that] accompany widowhood and mourning, injury and condemnation, the deceptions and lies of men, false accusations, and all the violent crimes and wicked deeds of others."[31] In addition to moral evils, he bemoans the "innumerable other evils" that "threaten our bodies from without," from "tempest, rain and flood" to the "opening up of chasms in the earth," from the "poisons" in plants and attacks of "wild creatures" to diseases "so numerous that all the books of the physicians cannot contain them."[32] If this was not enough to capture the "condition of misery common to us all," he extends his inventory of evils into the next chapter, describing the darkness, suspicion, and sin that reign even among the most righteous.[33] Ultimately, his verdict seems clear: "This is a state of life so miserable that it is like a hell on earth."[34] Taken in isolation, it is hard to find a more powerful expression of Augustine's pessimism.

This is how many political realists interpret the passage.[35] Deane alludes to Augustine's description of life as a "hell upon earth" four times, invoking it to compare Augustine's view of human nature with that of Hobbes.[36] Deane's most extensive use appears in his chapter, "The Psychology of Fallen Man," where he repeatedly cites Book 22.22 to sketch "Augustine's grimly pessimistic picture of the evils and sufferings that inevitably mark the lives of men as they live, work, struggle, and die in the world."[37] Alternating between Books 19 and 22, Deane sees both as evidence of Augustine's singular focus on sin: "His picture of man's life on earth is a somber one; life is indeed a hell on earth, filled with suffering, sorrow, disappointment, strife, and bitterness, and ended by death."[38] "Pessimistic realism," Deane concludes, is the attitude that Augustine endorses.[39]

A decontextualized, disproportionate emphasis on evil in 22.22–23, however, ignores important contextual and structural features of this passage. Consider its relation to the next chapter. After cataloging earthly evils in 22.22–23, Augustine offers a lengthy litany of earthly *goods* in 22.24, celebrating how God has "filled the whole of His creation with many good things of all kinds."[40] He points to the "visible forms of beauty which we behold" and praises the "wondrous nature" of human beings, who possess "a certain spark of that reason in respect of which [they were] made in the image of God," which even in their miserable condition "has not been wholly quenched."[41] He extols God's many gifts to humanity, from "reason" and "intelligence" to the "virtues" and "arts," from the delights of music and poetry to the "wonderful spectacles" of the theater, from the "colour and fragrance of the flowers" to the "manifold and varied beauty of the sky and earth and sea."[42] Even the body receives Augustine's lavish praise: "[H]ow clearly does the providence of our great Creator appear even in the body itself!"[43] For Augustine, goodness is so abundant that it surpasses our ability to describe it: "Who could give a complete account of all these things? . . . If I had chosen to deal with each one of them in turn—to unfold each of them, as it were, and discuss it in detail what I have indicated only broadly—what a time it would take!"[44] Rather than simply indicting earthly evil, the final book of *City of God* offers a soaring testament to creation's goodness. It is, as Garry Wills concludes, "a long series of 'ooh's and 'ah's at creation's surprises, hints of the great surprise to come in heaven."[45]

Some political interpreters do not acknowledge this overflowing affirmation of goodness.[46] Others are more careful, acknowledging Augustine's affirmation in 22.24 but only in passing, as if it were window-dressing for a more fundamental account of evil. Deane cites Augustine's description of the "rich and countless blessings" in 22.24 to suggest that "even in the depths of the misery of human life in this world, God has not completely abandoned the fallen human race."[47] Eventually, he declares that "Augustine's pessimism and despair are not ultimate": "[T]he sorrow and pain of earthly life, when seen in their proper context, are the means by which the ultimate triumph of good is being accomplished."[48] Given these claims, one cannot accuse Deane of neglecting Augustine's theological superstructure, but in other places, Deane seems to excise 22.22–23 from its context to support his emphasis on Augustine's "grim realism."[49] Since Deane's account has been so influential in political theory, a closer look at his reconstruction can illuminate assumptions that frequently plague realist accounts of Augustine.

First, consider Deane's emphasis. In "The Psychology of Fallen Man," he includes a few paragraphs that affirm God's goodness or providence, but the majority of the chapter, as its title indicates, focuses on Augustine's portrait of "fallen man."[50] Most tellingly, his concluding chapter attends exclusively to Augustine's "pessimistic realism" and "one-eyed" vision of "man in his fallen condition, as completely vitiated by sin."[51] Given this emphasis, it is no surprise that Deane focuses on one piece of a more complex mosaic. Like other realists, Deane assumes that the description of life as a "hell on earth" reflects Augustine's fundamental judgment of earthly matters and hence political ones.

Realists are right to recognize Augustine's awareness of evil. This is one of the advantages of his political thought: he punctures the illusions that disguise the ignorance, weakness, and self-interest that often arise in human affairs. But focusing exclusively or disproportionately on evil downplays Augustine's consistent attempts to contextualize evil within a larger frame of goodness.[52] In particular, it puts too much weight on the "sin" side of the love/sin dialectic and fails to register how sin is ontologically and psychologically dependent on love.[53] By fixating on the realities of earthly evil, realists risk obscuring the realities of earthly goodness, making pessimism the filter through which they interpret the rest of Augustine's thought. We must resist this temptation. While we can join realists in invoking Augustine to "give injustice its due,"[54] we should also follow Augustine in insisting that "both good and evil are given their due."[55] A more capacious realism recognizes, as Augustine does in 22.24, that "in this river or torrent of the human race . . . both elements run side by side."[56]

The problem with Augustinian pessimism, however, is not simply its disproportionate emphasis. Augustine's claim that good and evil exist "side by side" also points to a *rhetorical* feature of Book 22 often missed by interpreters who focus solely on Augustine's explicit utterances. His juxtaposition of good and evil reflects pedagogical purposes.[57]

Augustine suggests as much in Book 11, where he endorses the use of "antitheses" or "oppositions," which Cicero describes as a device where "things inconsistent are placed side by side, and things contrasted are paired."[58] As we saw in the previous chapter, Augustine celebrates this "most elegant" figure of speech and describes how God uses evil to reveal the good, "adorning the course of the ages like a most beautiful poem set off with antitheses."[59] Ultimately, Augustine suggests these oppositions can be employed rhetorically to illuminate the goodness in the world: "Just as the opposition of contraries bestows beauty upon language, then, so is the beauty of this world enhanced by the opposition of contraries, composed, as it were, by an eloquence not of words, but of things."[60]

Augustine's appropriation of this rhetorical device casts new light on Book 22. By putting good and evil "side by side," Augustine *performs* the rhetorical technique he endorses in Book 11. In both content and form, Augustine offers "a most beautiful poem set off with antitheses." Rather than simply cataloguing sins to emphasize the prevalence of evil, he also accentuates evil to enhance an awareness of goodness. As he writes in *On Order*, "This clashing of contraries, which we love so much in rhetoric, gives body to the overall beauty of the universe."[61]

Why do many political theorists miss this aspect of Book 22? Focusing primarily on Book 19 and other "political" passages, most do not consider the entirety of *City of God*, particularly Book 11, a more "theological" book that focuses on God's work of creation. As a result, they miss clues that hint at Augustine's later rhetorical purposes.

But textual selectivity is not the only explanation. Deane, whose textual breadth is unmatched, explicitly cites 11.18 to illuminate Augustine's "aesthetic argument" about why God allows evil in the world.[62] Yet Deane does not recognize that Augustine himself may be employing the same technique in 22.22–24. Focusing on Augustine's explicit political ideas rather than his implicit rhetorical practices, Deane takes Augustine's claims at face-value and neglects the possibility that Augustine is using excessive rhetoric for moral purposes. Deane assumes Augustine's descriptions in 22.22–24 are offered in the "restrained style" of instruction, not in the "grand style" of encouragement.

Many political interpreters share this methodological habit. Reading *City of God* as a systematic treatise written in the restrained style, they tend to take Augustine's declarations as neutral descriptions of reality. If Augustine devotes two chapters to the "grave evils" of our "miserable" condition, that must mean he has a bleak picture of earthly affairs. The assumption that such statements are literal representations of Augustine's views licenses interpreters to abstract passages from their literary context and assemble them into an overarching political "theory." If each statement is a "restrained" description of reality, its relation to other passages is less relevant; its propositional content can be extracted without losing its meaning.[63] Such an approach enables interpreters to take Augustine's description of the world as a "hell on earth" and present it as evidence of his "grim realism."[64]

If, however, Augustine is practicing philosophy as a way of life and using rhetoric to delight and move his audience, it is a mistake to interpret *City of God* solely in the restrained style. While certain passages reflect more analytical aims, the aim of Book 22 is not merely to inform readers but to transform them, to redirect their loves and hopes toward the heavenly city. Rather than offering a neutral description of good and evil simply to instruct, Augustine employs emotionally weighted rhetoric in the mixed and grand styles to convey the significance of good and evil and motivate readers to pursue the good.[65] By leading his audience through these oppositions, he thrusts his readers into the drama, helping them become agents capable of recognizing—and enduring—good and evil. In this way, the experience of moving through the text itself becomes a "spiritual exercise,"[66] a moral itinerary that functions not to promote pessimism but to cultivate the virtue of hope.

II. Faith, Hope, and Love in *City of God*

As in the *Enchiridion*, Augustine's first aim involves transforming his readers' faith, which he identifies in Book 22 with a kind of vision.[67] While a complete vision of God will be the faithful's possession in eternity, he quotes 1 Corinthians 13:12 to acknowledge that human beings can experience partial vision in this life: "Now we see through a glass, darkly; but then face to face."[68] To redirect readers' hopes, Augustine must correct their vision, helping them see traces of the divine, even if through a glass darkly.[69] The problem is that our vision remains distorted, our beliefs disordered, our faith unsteady and incomplete. In particular, Augustine believes that human beings are tempted to see earthly goods as the ultimate source of happiness, casting them under false descriptions and thereby failing to recognize their dependence on God or their tendencies toward pride and domination.[70] Acting under false perceptions, they grasp at temporal goods for selfish purposes, loving and hoping for finite goods too much or in the wrong ways. Their loves and hopes become disordered, and vice ensues. For Augustine, then, the first step in reordering love and hope is redirecting faith, changing how they see the world and thus helping them to act under more truthful descriptions.[71] For this purpose, Augustine uses vivid and excessive rhetoric, offering negative descriptions of earthly goods to pierce illusions that the world is an unadulterated source of goodness. By highlighting how cherished earthly goods and relationships are fleeting and flawed, he enables readers to see these goods in new ways and develop more realistic views of their social and political world.

This is an aspect of Augustine's thought that political realists find attractive. They admire Augustine's recognition of the realities of sin and self-interest in politics, but they neglect how he uses the "oppositions" of good and evil to *enhance* our vision of goodness in the world. Paradoxically, Augustine's emphasis on evil in 22.22–23 serves a preparatory function, illuminating the abundant goodness that follows in 22.24. Conceived as a whole, 22.22–24 is a spiritual exercise intended to clarify readers' vision, reorder their beliefs, and expand their imaginations, helping them see the realities of goodness where they previously saw only the depths of evil.

The way Augustine approaches this exercise may reflect the "Stoic-Platonic synthesis" discussed in chapter 6. As Sarah Catherine Byers argues, Platonists argued that one ascends the "ladder" of love from the earthly to the heavenly through a shift in vision: by seeing higher goods as beautiful and necessary to one's happiness, one is drawn upward toward the Highest Good.[72] This Platonic ideal of ascent fits with Augustine's emphasis on "beauty" in 22.24: he repeatedly invokes the "beauty" of earthly goods as signs of God's goodness. Indeed, his "beautiful poem" highlights one way to participate in the heavenly city, encouraging what a contemporary poet might describe as a "deeper level of looking and working, of seeing through the heavenly visibles to the heavenly invisibles."[73]

Yet, if Augustine incorporates Platonic themes in 22.22–24, it is not the rationalistic or deductive Platonism that Arendt and Nussbaum attribute to him.[74] Augustine does not believe human beings participate in goodness only through *rational* contemplation of the good. In 22.24, he locates goodness in *sensible* qualities of the world and highlights the "beauty," "utility," and "variety" of the world's goods. Importantly, he does not limit aesthetic perception to sight alone. He also celebrates our "fastidious tastes" and the "great variety of seasonings which have been devised to whet the appetite and please the palate." He extols the sweet "fragrance of flowers," the "soothing coolness of breezes," and the delight that "the ears find in musical instruments and the various kinds of melody which have been devised."[75] Rather than reducing ethics to reason alone, he ties spiritual and moral insight to aesthetic sensibility and conceives vision as a conduit to the divine.

If Augustine's emphasis on vision challenges the "rationalistic" Platonism that critics impute to him, it also challenges their assumption that his theology can be "deduced" from its Platonic foundations. In Book 22, Augustine applies the "indirect" methods that Nussbaum celebrates in Hellenistic philosophers but fails to identify in his work.[76] Augustine's aim is not necessarily to provide a *foundationalist metaphysics* from which to "deduce" the principles of morality. Rather, to borrow a distinction that Melissa Lane applies to other varieties of Platonism, he offers an *aspirational ethic* intended to reorder readers' desires and loves.[77] Augustine's account of good and evil is a moral and spiritual practice aimed at transforming his reader's faith, hope, and love. By presenting aspirational visions of heaven and earth in the grand style, Augustine exhorts readers to *desire* the good, not simply to understand it.

This connection between vision, desire, and exhortation connects to Augustine's Stoic sources. Stoics held that emotion and motivation are based on visions or perceptions (*visa*) of objects, especially objects perceived as conducive to a person's emotional, physical, or spiritual well-being.[78] Byers argues that Augustine integrates a Platonic emphasis on love with a Stoic emphasis on perception: love for an object explains "why" we are motivated to pursue it, while the perception of an object as "fitting," "beautiful," "useful," or "good" explains "how" we come to love it.[79] Proper loves reflect accurate perceptions of reality, whereas improper loves reflect improper perceptions of an object's value, particularly the "false judgment that a temporal good has the value of the eternal goods."[80] In Book 22, Augustine uses vivid language to change the readers' perception of the world and encourage an "ascent" to the heavenly city, which, as he says elsewhere, "must be made in the heart, by a good intention, in faith and hope and charity, in a desire for eternity and everlasting life."[81]

To effect this shift in virtue and vision, Augustine employs another rhetorical device common in ancient Rome, *vivid description*. Encompassing a variety of techniques (including what Cicero described as *illustratio* and *evidentia* and Quintilian called *enargeia*), vivid description involves using words to create clear, visual images in the minds of audiences, helping them visualize a scene and thereby stirring emotion and action in response to it.[82] The technique is especially useful for calling to mind things that are absent or uncertain and, by the clarity and vivacity of the visual signs, making them seem more present and plausible and thereby more persuasive.[83] Far from encouraging passive acceptance, vivid description has an activating effect on audiences. As Joy Connolly notes, it "engages the reader actively in the scene," preparing them to perceive the world more clearly and respond accordingly.[84]

Recognizing Augustine's use of this technique further illuminates the rhetorical effect of Book 22.22–24. Using clear, vivid language to describe earthly evils and point to earthly goods as visible signs of the invisible goodness yet to come in heaven, the passage attempts to reorder the vision of its audience, making them more aware of the goods and evils around them and thereby reordering their desires for them. As we saw earlier, one function of faith is to provide hope and love with the evidence needed to warrant a belief that an object is possible to attain.[85] Faith does this, in part, by supplying a partial vision of an object, helping to determine what one is "aiming" at when loving or hoping for a particular good.[86] As a result, changing how one sees an object affects how one loves or hopes for it.

Augustine recognizes that changing beliefs about good and evil is not enough to transform the character of his readers. Instruction alone is insufficient; readers also need encouragement. This points to a second purpose of Book 22: Augustine uses excessive rhetoric to reorder readers' loves.[87] Since human beings are tempted to love earthly goods too much or grasp at them for their own purposes,[88] part of his purpose in *City of God* is to diagnose the effects of excessive self-love and highlight how pride fuels a "lust for domination."[89] As we saw in chapter 2, Augustine's "order of love" is intended to chasten and correct inordinate desires, providing a regulative ideal that discourages domination and disordered love.[90] In Book 22, Augustine uses antitheses and vivid description to facilitate this reordering. By vividly describing the "evils" of this "hell on earth," he attempts to change readers' vision of earthly goods and disrupt their excessive love of them, and by extolling the abundant goodness of the heavenly city, he attempts to expand their vision and reorder their loves to God. His "pessimistic" descriptions are not necessarily indicative of a metaphysical belief that earthly goods have no value, but of a psychological recognition that human beings are tempted to give earthly goods too much value or love them in the wrong ways.[91] Augustine's rhetorical undervaluation attempts to chasten moral overvaluation, encouraging readers to loosen their grip on worldly goods and hold fast to the heavenly city.[92]

Some critics may worry that ordering one's loves to God only affirms the otherworldly dualism they find so troubling. But Augustine does not conceive of the City of God as an entirely transcendent realm, as many critics assume. He constantly notes how pilgrims participate in the heavenly city "even now, albeit in a far different and far inferior way."[93] In chapter 8, I consider the political implications of this inaugurated eschatology, but here it is helpful to note its presence in Book 22, where Augustine locates goodness not only in heaven but on earth, within creation. He celebrates the "visible forms of beauty which we behold" and the "manifold and varied beauty of sky and earth and sea," and, significantly, he does not limit these goods either to nature or God's original creation.[94] While he emphasizes God's grace, he also describes the goodness mediated through human agency. He praises the "many arts invented and exercised by human ingenuity," the "achievements of human industry in devising clothing and shelter," and "achievements in pottery, painting, and sculpture."[95] While he does not mention political goods explicitly in 22.24—his account of civic peace and the goods of the commonwealth appears in Book 19—many of the goods he catalogues are, as Todd Breyfogle notes, "the work not of single individuals but of persons in *societas*."[96]

Moreover, many of these communal achievements—progress in "agriculture and navigation," the "wonderful spectacles" in the theater, and the "ornaments of oratory"—originated as distinctively *pagan* contributions.[97] Augustine even goes so far as to praise "the great ingenuity displayed by philosophers and heretics in defending even errors and false doctrines."[98] Rather than encouraging otherworldliness, Augustine alerts readers to the goods that exist as part of God's order.[99]

Augustine's celebration of goodness in Book 22 points to a third pedagogical purpose most relevant for us: by reorienting faith and love, Augustine attempts to reorder readers' hope and help them resist temptations toward presumption and despair. By vividly describing the evils that afflict earthly life, his account in 22.22–23 helps his audience develop the prudence needed to recognize possible pitfalls and discourages them from placing their hopes only in temporal goods.[100] Augustine's catalogue of evils serves to chasten perverse hope, warning readers against presuming earthly life will provide ultimate satisfaction. Yet he also recognizes that chastening presumption risks leaving readers in a debilitating despair, causing them to dwell only upon the evils they see. His expansive catalogue of goods in 22.24 seeks to dispel this despair by unfolding the abundant goodness in the world. By placing the readers in this scene, the experience of reading the text sets them on a journey through the oppositions of presumption and despair that helps to cultivate the virtue of hope.

The rhetorical structure of 22.22–24 reinforces this pedagogical effect. Trained in rhetorical technique of "arrangement" (*dispositio*),[101] Augustine is sensitive to how ordering an argument can shape readers' attitudes and emotions. He explicitly offers reasons for his arrangement of Books 21 and 22: given what readers are likely to find most "credible" or "incredible" about heaven or hell, he structures the discussion in a way that is sensitive to their current level of belief while attempting to take them beyond it.[102] This same pedagogical sensitivity emerges in 22.22–24.[103] Knowing that readers may be tempted to despair, he offers a spiritual exercise that acknowledges these temptations while supplying grounds for hope. In this way, 22.22–24 enacts what Kenneth Burke describes in a different context as a "structure of encouragement":

> Suppose that, gnarled as I am, I did not consider it enough simply to seek payment for my gnarledness, the establishment of communion through evils held in common? Suppose I would also erect a structure of encouragement, for all of us? How should I go about it, in the sequence of imagery, not merely to bring us most poignantly *into* hell, but also *out* again?[104]

In 22.22–24, Augustine supplies a similar "structure of encouragement." By taking his readers into a "hell on earth," he alerts them to the presence of evils and thus deflates their presumptuous fantasies about the world and their own self-sufficiency. Yet he does not establish communion with readers simply by emphasizing the evils they hold in common. While he takes readers into hell in 22.22–23, he brings them out again in 22.24, helping them see the abundant goodness in the world as a ground for hope.[105] Through this sequence of imagery—into hell and out again—Augustine offers an itinerary meant both to instruct and encourage.

Importantly, the combined effect of this structure of encouragement is not merely rhetorical. As we saw in previous chapters, Augustine insists on an essential connection between rhetoric and reasoning, requiring that rhetorical proofs are aimed not at emotional manipulation but at rational persuasion. He often employs a default and challenge structure of reasoning to effect such persuasion, seeking to defeat any defeaters that might challenge a default hope. A default and challenge structure is implicit in 22.22–24. Augustine recognizes that the widespread evils of the world might tempt despair and thereby threaten to defeat one's hope. He does not deny these challenges—to do so would be irresponsible and even presumptuous—but he seeks to rebut them in 22.24 by providing evidence of God's goodness in the world as a ground for hope. This evidence does not provide definitive knowledge or proof of the possibility of realizing this hope, but it gives further grounds for persevering in hope in the face of doubts and difficulties that might otherwise defeat it.

This analysis of Augustine's structure of encouragement highlights a new reading of 22.22–24 and points to the dangers of abstracting other books of City of God from their literary and rhetorical contexts. Consider Book 19, another text frequently cited as evidence of Augustine's pessimism. There, Augustine identifies the "great mass of evils" that accompany social and political life (19.5–9), laments the realities of war and limits of peace (19.11–13), and concludes with a vivid description of the "everlasting misery" that the wicked will experience in hell (19.28). If interpreters focus exclusively on Book 19, as many political theorists do, they are likely to see Augustine as a dour pessimist: both its substance and structure might tempt despair. But if Book 19 is interpreted within its larger context in City of God, it becomes clear that Augustine takes his readers through hell in Book 19 but out into the "felicity" of heaven in Book 22.[106]

This reading is supported by Augustine's own description of City of God's structure, which reflects his awareness of arrangement.[107] In Retractions and a letter to Firmus, Augustine divides his "huge work" into two volumes with five parts.[108] The first volume—Books 1–10—consists of two parts: Books 1–5 argue "against those who claim that the worship clearly not of gods but of demons contributes to the happiness of this life," while Books 6–10 challenge "those who think that either such gods or many gods of any sort whatever should be worshiped by sacred rites and sacrifices on account of the life that will exist after death."[109] While the first ten books "refute the vanities of non-believers," the last twelve books constitute Augustine's constructive attempt to "demonstrate and defend our religion."[110] He divides this second volume symmetrically into three equal parts: Books 11–14 focus on the "origin of the two cities," Books 15–18 describe their "growth or progress," and Books 19–22 analyze their "destined ends."[111] Strikingly, then, although Book 19 appears near the end of *City of God*, it constitutes the first book of the section dealing with the "proper ends of these two cities."[112] Augustine begins with a vivid description of the evils of the earthly city in Book 19 before concluding with a soaring account of earthly and heavenly goods in Book 22. As a whole, *City of God* enacts the structure of encouragement we find in microcosm in 22.22–24.

Political theorists who fixate on Augustine's "pessimism" neglect this structure of encouragement. Some even invert the order altogether. When Deane briefly acknowledges Augustine's affirmation of goodness in 22.24, he immediately returns to the realities of evil, reversing the order found in Augustine.[113] Deane ultimately concludes his book by highlighting the advantages of Augustine's pessimism.[114] Similarly, both Niebuhr and Shklar stress how Augustine's realism deflates political optimism, concluding their accounts in a way that chastens presumption but risks tempting despair.[115] Rather than being faithful to Augustine's structure of encouragement, these realists tend to plug bits of Augustine into their own structure of discouragement.[116] The result is a hardened picture of Augustine's pessimism.

The tendency to exaggerate Augustine's pessimism reflects the limitations of the simple binary between "optimism" and "pessimism" so influential in Augustinian studies and political theory.[117] By emphasizing Augustine's diagnosis of evil, realists rightly argue that Augustine is no optimist. But because they equate hope with optimism and limit their options to either optimism or pessimism, they see no alternative but to describe him as a "pessimist." This description obscures Augustine's complex account of hope as the virtue between presumption and despair.

Some scholars recognize the limits of the binary.[118] A few attempt to categorize modern Augustinians either as "pessimistic optimists" or "optimistic pessimists,"[119] while others distinguish Augustine's position with some sort of qualifier, describing his thought, for example, as "courageous optimism."[120] Deane tries to escape the binary by arguing that Augustine's "realistic, pessimistic analysis of human nature" is qualified by an "ultimate optimism" in God's providence.[121] Yet even this attribution of otherworldly "optimism" does not accord with Augustine's warnings against presumption.[122] Augustine explicitly cautions individuals not to presume they will necessarily become members of the heavenly city; to deny their sin and assume certain salvation is itself an expression of prideful presumption.

Ultimately, the opposition between optimism and pessimism is anachronistic and conceptually confining. "Pessimism" and "optimism" are modern concepts, originating with Leibniz and Voltaire in the eighteenth century.[123] Their application to Augustine emerges largely in the work of Niebuhr and Deane, who ascribe "pessimism" to capture Augustine's diagnosis of sin and evil. While their emphasis on "pessimism" may have been an appropriate response to the utopian ideologies advanced amidst the horrors of the mid-twentieth century, it neither exhausts the conceptual possibilities nor accurately reflects Augustine's own views.[124] A more accurate and expansive rendering would abandon this binary and adopt the more capacious triad of presumption, hope, and despair, which offers conceptual resources for recognizing a posture that avoids both extremes.

Presumption is the vice that most concerns Augustinian realists. In preferring "pessimism," they seek to chasten the "optimism" they see as presumption and advance a more realistic account of politics that attends to evil, injustice, and self-interest. Undoubtedly, when optimism becomes a universal disposition or attitude applied in every circumstance—the expectation or certainty that something good will always come about—realists are right: optimism can morph into presumption, assuming more certainty than the facts warrant. Yet pessimism has the tendency to collapse in the opposite direction, sliding into a habitual despair that assumes no good can come. Paradoxically, this vice of despair also reflects a kind of presumption: by presuming that something bad will inevitably happen, pessimists assume a certainty about the future not warranted by reality. By neglecting or minimizing the realities of goodness, pessimists foreclose the possibility that goodness can emerge when possibilities seem dim.

By registering temptations that surround hope on both sides, the Augustine I have brought into view exposes the binary between optimism and pessimism as too simplistic. Unlike optimism, Augustine's virtue of hope does not gloss

over dark and unpleasant realities. To do so would encourage the vice of presumption, not the virtue of hope. But neither does Augustine's account license
a debilitating despair. Although we may see through a glass darkly, darkness
does not overwhelm our vision. As 22.22–24 affirms, we can see grounds for
hope even when we experience our condition as a "hell on earth."

Conclusion

By reading influential passages of *City of God* within their rhetorical and pedagogical context, I have offered an interpretation of 22.22–24 as an exercise of
hope. When situated within an ancient view of philosophy as a "way of life,"
Augustine's vivid description of earthly evils in Book 22 emerges not as a
straightforward expression of pessimism in the restrained style, but as an excessive use of rhetoric in the mixed and grand styles that reorients readers'
faith, love, and hope. By putting good and evil "side by side," this "beautiful
poem" forms a protreptic intended not simply to instruct readers about the
City of God but to encourage them to pursue it.

Book 22.22–24, of course, is only one selection in Augustine's massive corpus, and it does not explicitly address how distinctly political goods can be
proper objects of hope. That is the task of the next chapter. With Augustine's
virtue and rhetoric of hope in view, we are now in position to evaluate his tale
of two cities.

PART III

The Politics of Hope

8

Hope for the Commonwealth

ESCHATOLOGY, ECCLESIOLOGY, AND POLITICS

> Both cities alike make use of the good things, or are afflicted with the evils,
> of this temporal state; but they do so with a different faith, a different hope,
> a different love.
>
> —AUGUSTINE, *CITY OF GOD*, 18.54

AUGUSTINE'S MOST distinctive contribution to political thought is his account
of the "two cities," the earthly and heavenly. The "two cities," he argues, "have
been created by two loves: that is, the earthly by love of self extending even
to contempt of God, and the heavenly by love of God extending to contempt
of self."[1] In *City of God*, Augustine traces the history of these two cities, encouraging readers to become "pilgrims" on the way to the "most glorious"
City of God.[2]

What interpreters fail to notice is that Augustine also distinguishes the two
cities by their hopes. In his famous account of politics in Book 19, he distinguishes
the "proper ends of these two cities" by pointing to the "difference between
their vain beliefs and the hope which God gives us."[3] In Book 15, he suggests the
biblical record offers a "fitting way" of differentiating the two cities: "the one
trusting in the things of this world, and the other in the hope of God."[4]

That Augustine distinguishes the two cities by their hopes may feed suspicions that his political thought is both otherworldly and antipolitical, encouraging a withdrawal from politics or a refusal to engage with diverse citizens in
public life. As we have seen, Augustine's friends and foes give voice to both

positions. In this chapter, I offer a more hopeful, pluralistic account that recovers Augustine's complex vision of the goods that diverse citizens can share in the commonwealth.

Since many critics assume Augustine's "futurist eschatology" precludes "political hope," part I begins by considering his view of "last things." Against democratic critics and Augustinian realists who believe Augustine defers the eschaton into an "absolute future," I show how his inaugurated or partially realized eschatology enables participation in the heavenly city here and now. Against Augustinian communitarians, I argue that Augustine does not confine that participation to the institutional church. Challenging narrow conceptions of both the "secular" and the "political," I argue that Augustine's distinctive vision of the *saeculum*, or "secular age," encourages more openness toward plurality than many interpreters recognize.

Part II applies this understanding of the *saeculum* to Augustine's distinctive vision of the "commonwealth." By analyzing Augustine's definition of the commonwealth, advancing a more positive understanding of "civic peace," and putting Augustine in conversation with contemporary political theorists, I explore the kind of civic friendship and provisional convergence he recommends.

Part III considers the resources that this account makes available for political deliberation in the face of disagreement. Examining Augustine's use of immanent critique and drawing on insights from earlier chapters, I highlight how his conceptual grammar of hope, default and challenge structure of reasoning, and implicit continuum of virtue and vice might facilitate conversation and cooperation across difference and alert citizens to the temptations that accompany the pursuit of shared political goods. Against those who see Augustine as a paragon of pessimism, I argue that he commends a legitimate hope for the commonwealth.

I. Eschatology, Ecclesiology, and Politics in the *Saeculum*

Eschatology was a matter of intense dispute in the early Christian church.[5] Many of Augustine's predecessors and contemporaries were "millenarians" who believed that the apocalypse was imminent.[6] Millenarianism became especially popular at the end of the fourth century and beginning of the fifth as increasing numbers of Christians interpreted recent events—religious persecution by the Romans, the sack of Rome by the Visigoths, encroaching attacks by the Vandals—as confirmation that apocalyptic prophecies were coming true and that Christ would soon come again.

This sense of eschatological immediacy had implications for politics. If the end was near, Christians had no reason to engage in politics, especially in an empire that had executed their savior and persecuted his followers. Rather than colluding in this imperial project or attempting to reform it, millenarians sought to escape the evil influences of the sin-soaked world by retreating into the purity of the Church, where they could pursue holiness, keep the commandments, and await Christ's triumphant return. Many millenarians were Donatists who focused on the purity of the "true" Church and persecuted those whom they saw as impure.[7]

Augustine rejects millenarianism and the worldly withdrawal it licenses.[8] Although he accepts the Church's traditional teaching on the Second Coming and once held millenarian views himself,[9] in *City of God* he prosecutes what Robert Markus describes as a "frontal attack" on millenarianism, refusing to calculate the time of the apocalypse or interpret contemporary events as signs of its immediacy.[10] Drawing on Scripture, Augustine argues that we should not take earthly blessings or misfortunes to signify anything about God's judgment: there are "good men who suffer evils and evil men who enjoy good things," just as "there are bad men who come to a bad end, and good men who arrive at a good one."[11] This suggests that "the judgments of God are all the more inscrutable, and His ways past finding out."[12]

The "hiddenness" of God's judgment and limits of human knowledge are persistent themes in Augustine's work.[13] Although "nothing is hidden" from God, "[a] man . . . sees a man only as he is at this present time—if, indeed, he can be said to see one whose heart he does not see. He does not see even himself clearly enough to know what kind of person he will be in the future."[14] Augustine knows firsthand that we can become an "enigma" to ourselves.[15] His *Confessions* is a testament to the limits of human knowledge, a theme that he takes up in *City of God*, where he recites a chorus of things we do not know:

We do not know why the ungodly man lives in the best of health, while the pious man wastes away in sickness. We do not know why young men who are robbers enjoy excellent health, while infants who could not hurt anyone, even with a word, are afflicted by all manner of dreadful diseases. We do not know why one who plays a beneficial part in human affairs is snatched away by premature death, whereas one who, as it seems to us, ought never to have been born at all lives on long beyond the normal span. We do not know why one whose life is full of crimes is crowned with honours, whereas the man who is without reproach lies buried in the darkness of unrecognition. Who could collect or enumerate all the other examples of this kind?[16]

Given the extent of human ignorance, Augustine recommends that we resist millenarian predictions about the imminent end of the world. Such presumption displaces God's knowledge and power with our own. To press the point, Augustine repeatedly invokes Acts 1:7: "It is not yours to know the times that the Father has established by his own authority," and Matthew 24:36: "No one knows the day or the hour."[17] Like Socrates, he insists the wisest person is one who does not claim to know what he does not know: "[A] person does not seem to me to be in error when he knows that he does not know something, but when he thinks that he knows what he does not know."[18] Augustine's focus on the inevitability of human ignorance and hiddenness of God's purposes encourages a virtue of humility that chastens apocalyptic presumption.

Now and Not Yet: Augustine's Inaugurated Eschatology

With this rejection of eschatological immediacy in view, some interpreters assume Augustine goes to the opposite extreme, assuming a completely *futurist eschatology* that holds the Kingdom of God will appear only at the end of time, in some indefinite future. This assumption underwrites many textbook interpretations and critiques of Augustine's political pessimism.[19] Arendt, for instance, argues that Augustine makes a "desert out of this world" because he defers the Kingdom of God indefinitely into an "absolute future."[20] Rather than conceiving the world as a realm of action and meaning, Augustine portrays the temporal realm as a crowded waiting room of sinful souls, patiently awaiting the eschaton and directing their hopes solely toward the City of God. For Arendt, Augustine's futurist eschatology encourages a "worldlessness" that precludes political action and requires us to stand "against the world, not simply without it."[21]

Nussbaum agrees, charging that Augustine's otherworldly longing precludes any striving for justice in the "here and now."[22] Citing Nietzsche's vigorous critique of Christianity, Nussbaum argues that "[l]onging for the other world puts people to sleep in this world": "The virtues of a merely provisional social world are 'soporific virtues,' because the focus on the beyond discourages risk taking and enterprise here and now."[23] For Nussbaum, Augustine's futurist eschatology authorizes political passivity.

Billings makes the connection between eschatology and politics central to his critique of Augustinian hope. Focusing on the dangers of Augustine's "futurist eschatology," Billings endorses Arendt's view that Augustine's hope is so trained on the heavenly city that it excludes any "hope that can sustain and enrich political action."[24] For Billings, Augustine's futurist eschatology licenses political pessimism and otherworldly escape.

Interestingly, these democratic critics are not alone in emphasizing Augustine's futurist eschatology. Many Augustinian realists also assume Augustine defers the eschaton indefinitely. Whereas democratic critics see such eschatological deferral as encouraging retreat from the world, realists believe it authorizes a more active engagement in combatting cruelty and injustice here and now. If true and perfect justice is continually deferred until the end of time, human beings must do whatever is necessary *now* to eliminate injustice; "necessity" requires it.[25] Thus, some realists have invoked Augustinian authority to encourage a kind of this-worldly consequentialism, going so far as to justify war, torture, and violence to prevent more dangerous evils.[26] On this view, this-worldly politics can achieve only a kind of "relative" or "imperfect" justice; true justice will not be realized until the end of time. Realists like Niebuhr, Deane, and Elshtain are most known for such a view, but traces of a futurist eschatology also appear in Judith Shklar's interpretation of Augustine. According to Shklar, Augustine holds that the "eventual redemption of Christ" has "nothing to do with justice" in the "here and now."[27] Since Christ will not establish true justice until the end of time, it is up to us to restrain cruelty and domination now.

When situated within its larger theological, political, and ecclesial contexts, Augustine's complex eschatology cannot be adequately captured by this futurist focus. As we saw in chapter 2, a strict separation between heaven and earth, time and eternity, denies the ways in which Augustine encourages *participation* in the City of God here and now. For Augustine, the heavenly city is not simply a matter of otherworldly expectation; it is also a matter of this-worldly experience.[28] Rather than assuming a deferred, futurist eschatology, Augustine offers what scholars have described in other contexts as an "inaugurated," or partially realized, eschatology, a view that recognizes that, though the City of God will not be *ultimately* fulfilled until the end of time, human beings can participate *proleptically*, if only partially, in that kingdom here and now.[29] On this account, human beings are not simply passive observers waiting for the coming of Christ, but active citizens participating in the City of God during this passing age.

Augustine develops this inaugurated eschatology most explicitly in *City of God*. Although he sometimes suggests the two cities will be separated only at the end of time,[30] he insists that some citizens have already begun to be citizens of the heavenly city even while they sojourn on earth. Instead of existing solely in some transcendent realm, the eternal city "has been coming down out of heaven since its beginning" and continues even in this "present age."[31] As citizens of the heavenly city, "the saints of Christ are reigning with Him even now, albeit in a far different and far inferior way."[32] Indeed, although the ultimate "City of the Saints is on high," it "produces citizens here below."[33] As "God's fellow-workers," these citizens can participate in the Kingdom of God here on earth.[34] The City of God is both "now" and "not yet."[35]

This inaugurated eschatology comports with Augustine's participationist ontology and implicit order of hope. If all temporal goods participate in God's goodness, loving and hoping for temporal goods properly can be a way of participating in God's goodness here and now, and hoping in the visible neighbor can be a way of hoping in the invisible God. Moreover, as the *Enchiridion* suggests, eternal goods are not simply relegated to a transcendent realm: "[T]hey begin here and as we progress they grow in us."[36] By hoping properly for eternal goods in God, human beings can begin to possess and participate in them here and now.[37]

Between Church and World: Religion, Politics, and the Secular

Augustine often ties his eschatology to his ecclesiology, suggesting that the eternal City of God is already being realized by the "true" church. The "'coming' of the Saviour," he writes, is already "going on throughout this present age in His Church: that is, in His members. In this sense, He comes part by part and little by little, since the whole Church is His body."[38] Since the "Second Coming" has already begun, the first fruits of God's kingdom can be realized daily through the *ecclesia*, the body of Christ in the world. The church helps Christians cultivate the virtues, keep the commandments, and sustain the faith. For Augustine, the *ecclesia* is the eschaton's earthen vessel.[39]

The role of the church is important for an Augustinian account of eschatology and politics. As discussed earlier, many of the practices Augustine identifies as necessary for forming hope—saying the Lord's Prayer or imitating virtuous exemplars—are embedded within the rituals and practices of the church, as are the sermons identified as exercises of hope in chapter 6. For Augustine, the church shapes both the content and form of Christian hope, helping Christians recognize the proper objects of hope and how to properly order it to God. The formative role of the church in fostering the virtue of hope is important, not least because, as some critics argue, the role of the church is sometimes downplayed in contemporary reconstructions of Augustine's political thought.[40] The account offered here seeks to avoid this limitation by recognizing Augustine's emphasis on the *ecclesia* as a context for embodying and educating eschatological hope.

Ultimately, this account of eschatology-as-ecclesiology challenges Augustinian realists and democratic critics who claim that Augustine postpones the eschaton indefinitely into an "absolute future." Instead of offering a purely futurist eschatology, Augustine offers an inaugurated eschatology that recognizes how citizens can experience the first fruits of the Kingdom here and now. But if such an account defuses concerns that Augustinian hope is too otherworldly, it may seem to buttress Augustinian critiques of democracy that emphasize the church as the exclusive site for moral formation and divine participation. Communitarians such as John Milbank and Stanley Hauerwas explicitly build on Augustine's ecclesiology to elevate the church as the proper "counter-kingdom" to secular democracy.[41] In their more oppositional moments, Milbank and Hauerwas can be read as counseling Christians to withdraw from the diseased body politic and retreat into the purifying body of Christ.[42] As members of the church, Christians should be *in* the world but not *of* it, assuming a status as "resident aliens" in a strange land while they sojourn toward their true home in heaven.[43] Instead of engaging in secular politics, Christian pilgrims should focus on *being the church*, effecting God's justice through the body of Christ.[44] Both Milbank and Hauerwas cite Augustinian authority to suggest a sometimes rigid distinction between church and world.[45]

At times, Augustine seems to provide support for this appropriation. In Book 19, he resists the view that the church should simply be accommodated to the state, recognizing it is sometimes necessary for the heavenly city "to dissent from the earthly city" and "become a burden to those who think differently."[46] In Book 20, his language is even stronger. There, he describes the church in the present time as a "kingdom militant" at war with sin and the "enemies" of God.[47]

Communitarians draw on such passages to elevate the church as a "contrast" society or "peaceable kingdom" that exposes the "ontology of violence" they find in an entirely immanent political liberalism.[48] In one sense, communitarians are right to resist the futurist eschatology of Augustinian realists and the violence it too often commends in the name of necessity. They are also right to question any political project that attempts to merely accommodate or subsume the church under the political community.[49] Augustine refuses simplistic accommodation or subordination. Yet Augustinian communitarians often take this claim further, implying that the church is not only distinct from the world but *hostile* to it, setting itself against the world to unmask its apparent virtues as vices.[50] Such an impulse challenges an Augustinian openness to pluralism and oversimplifies Augustine's ecclesiology, which is more complex than a rigid church-world distinction suggests.

While Augustine's rhetoric can sometimes license oppositional postures,[51] in his less polemical moments, even in Book 20, he is careful to distinguish between the *institutional church* and the *true church*, between the "Church as she now is" and the "Church as she will be."[52] Augustine acknowledges that the institutional church—the church in this world—is the City of God "in one sense" since it provides a community where members can cultivate bonds of affection and sustain spiritual fellowship. But in another sense, the church in this world is not the true "kingdom of heaven" since many of its members do not live a holy life or order their loves to God.[53] Some churchgoers may proclaim the faith, Augustine argues, but they do not practice it. Only those who love God and neighbor properly are members of the "true Church," the "wheat" who will be taken up into heaven in the final harvest. The wicked are the "tares" who "do not reign with Him, even though they are growing in the Church alongside the wheat."[54]

If realists and critics fail to recognize Augustine's partially realized eschatology, then Augustinian communitarians assume an "overly realized" eschatology that too fully identifies the heavenly city with the institutional church.[55] For Augustine, the heavenly city is not constituted by any particular empirical institution, including the church, but by its *members*—"they reign with Him who are in His kingdom in such a way that they themselves *are* His kingdom."[56] Those who love God and neighbor are citizens in that kingdom even now. Citizenship is determined by the order of their loves.[57]

That "citizens" are defined by their loyalties and loves, not necessarily by their affiliations with particular institutions (whether "church" or "state"), has significant implications for Augustine's understanding of religion and politics.[58] If the two cities coexist in this present time and cannot be distinguished by their institutional affiliations, it follows that the political community is not necessarily the "earthly city," even if, as Veronica Roberts Ogle argues, the earthly city seeks to usurp the political community for its own purposes.[59] Moreover, the institutional church is not the "true Church" in the most

complete sense, even as it remains the "sign" of the heavenly city.[60] The institutional church is also a mixed body, a *corpus permixtum*, that includes members of both the earthly and heavenly cities.[61] In the *saeculum*, members of the
two cities are "entangled and mingled with one another; and they will remain
so until the last judgment shall separate them."[62] In "this passing age," we cannot know who belongs to each city.[63] Everything remains hidden: like wheat
and tares, the citizens of the two cities are now mixed together in the *saeculum*,
only to be separated in the final harvest.[64] Some who appear to be "enemies"
of the church may be future "citizens" of God's kingdom, while some who are
"bound to [the church] by the communion of the sacraments" will not join
the saints in heaven.[65] Vice permeates the church, even as some non-Christians
exemplify a genuine form of virtue.[66] During the secular age, the two cities
remain "mingled together."[67]

This Augustinian conception of the *saeculum* contrasts with conceptions of
the "secular" current in contemporary political theory. Unlike those who
sometimes equate the "secular" with the "world" (Billings) or identify the
"secular" with "sin" and the "earthly city" (Milbank),[68] Robert Markus suggests
that, for Augustine, the "secular" refers not simply to a *spatial* or *institutional*
reality but to a *sphere of time*.[69] As Eric Gregory puts it, the *saeculum* "refers
simply to that mixed time when no single religious vision can presume to
command comprehensive, confessional, and visible authority."[70] Secularity is
"interdefined by its relation to eschatology."[71] The *saeculum* is the age before
the eschaton, where the two cities coexist in time and remain intertwined.[72]
In this way, the "secular" contrasts not with the "sacred" but with the "eternal":
it is primarily a *temporal* term.[73]

This conception of the secular as an ambiguous time has implications for
Augustinian politics. For one, it challenges the churchly triumphalism and
sectarian withdrawal that has often come to be associated with Augustine's
name. Contrary to what many interpreters assume, the church is not the exclusive site for virtue or participation in the City of God.[74] Although the
church in this world constitutes a community that helps pilgrims keep the
commandments and cultivate the virtues, having a name on the church roll or
showing up for a religious service does not guarantee either holiness or salvation.[75] God's goodness exceeds the boundaries of any institutional form.

If Augustine's vision of the *saeculum* challenges churchly triumphalism,
however, it also undermines any form of political idolatry that deifies the
"state" or encourages totalizing domination in the name of political community. Part of Augustine's purpose in *City of God* is to unmask what he saw as

the idolatry of pagan Rome. As Markus argues, by situating the history of Rome within the history of God's dominion and attributing imperial success not to human achievement but to divine providence, Augustine attempts to *debunk* and *desacralize* Rome's claim to ultimate and supreme authority, stripping the state of eschatological significance and reminding Romans that their emperors are not gods.[76] If "citizens" of the two cities are defined by their loyalties and loves rather than institutional or political affiliations, the heavenly city, not Rome, becomes the proper "eternal city."[77] For Augustine, the City of God is the "true" commonwealth that sets the standard for earthly politics and models what a true political community should be.[78]

That Augustine elevates the City of God as a political community and desacralizes the institutions of government authorizes a more expansive view of politics. For Augustine, politics is not confined to what we might describe as the "state," "government," or "electoral politics."[79] It involves not only formal laws, institutions, and procedures but also more informal customs, practices, and institutions of civil society, including the church. Ultimately, Augustine, like his Greek and Roman predecessors, imagines politics as the broader realm of life where people pursue temporal goods in common and work together to ensure a temporal peace.[80] The institutions of government can facilitate that temporal peace, but politics is not reduced to its institutions or procedures. As Ogle argues, Augustine follows Cicero in conceiving politics more in terms of "communities" than "institutions," with a focus on the "members" of a commonwealth instead of its "institutional branches."[81] This relational conception of the commonwealth is one reason why many Augustinians describe the politics more inclusively, casting it in terms of "political society,"[82] "public life,"[83] "a space for multiple publics,"[84] and a "way of life" rather than a set of institutions or procedures.[85] As one influential Augustinian suggests, "'public life' includes everything concerned with the 'public good.'"[86]

This more expansive view of politics is significant for the Augustinian account I have offered for several reasons. First, it challenges realists who, as we will see below, reduce politics to a negative, remedial view of the "state" as a coercive order intended only to correct sin.[87] Because they assume politics consists only in the coercive and legal institutions of government,[88] they cast Augustine as a pessimist about "politics" and neglect how citizens can seek common goods that support the political community but are not necessarily tied to the formal offices or institutions of government. A more expansive vision recognizes objects and grounds of political hope that go beyond, and perhaps even challenge, formal institutions of government, which unsettles

accounts of Augustine's pessimism that focus only on the negative functions
of the "state."

Second, by challenging any rigid distinction between church and world, this
expansive conception of politics in the *saeculum* undermines political and theological ideologies that tie virtue too closely to any particular institution and
encourages a more humble posture toward diversity and plurality.[89] Instead of
hardening divisions based on institutional loyalties, either to "church" or "state,"
it commends an ethic of humility and an openness toward plurality.[90] If virtue
is not confined to any one institution and God's purposes remain largely "hidden," then citizens must be open to others with different beliefs and commitments, for they too may be hidden members of the City of God.[91] During the
secular age, humility remains an essential Augustinian virtue.[92]

Finally, this Augustinian vision of the *saeculum* shifts the focus of political
life away from entrenched disputes about metaphysical doctrines or ultimate
ends toward deliberation about the common goods that diverse citizens can
share. It highlights the "secular" not purely as a "realm of sin,"[93] but as a passing
age in which members of both cities—earthly and heavenly—share proximate
goods and build a common life together. It is this aspect of the *saeculum*, I
believe, that informs Augustine's hope for the commonwealth.

II. A Commonwealth of Hope

In Book 2 of *City of God*, Augustine explicates Cicero's definition of the "commonwealth" as the "property of a people" (*res populi*)—literally, their "public
thing" (*res publica*).[94] For Cicero, what distinguishes a "people" from other
multitudes is that its members are "united in fellowship by common agreement as to what is right and by a community of interest."[95] After explaining
Cicero's definition, Augustine promises to "show that no such commonwealth
ever existed, because true justice was never present."[96] Seventeen books and
several years later, Augustine fulfills his promise, offering a more sustained
critique of Cicero's definition in Book 19. If a commonwealth is "the property
of a people" and a people is a multitude united by "common agreement as to
what is right," Augustine argues, the Roman republic was "never truly 'the
property of a people'" and thus never a true commonwealth because "common
agreement as to what is right" requires "true justice," and the Romans did not
achieve it. As a result, the Roman republic failed to secure "common agreement as to what is right."[97] Thus, "where there is not this justice," Augustine
concludes, "there is no commonwealth."[98]

Augustine's criticism puts him in position to offer a "more practicable definition" that recognizes a "commonwealth" even if a "people" has not achieved true justice. A "people," he argues, is better conceived as an "assembled multitude of rational creatures bound together by a common agreement as to the objects of their love." A "commonwealth" (*res publica*) is simply the "property," or "public thing," of this people.[99] "In this case," he concludes, "if we are to discover the character of any people, we have only to examine what it loves . . . no matter what the objects of its love may be."[100]

Common Objects of Love

To understand the significance of Augustine's definition, it is helpful to consider the several features of a *populus* and *res publica*. For Augustine, what distinguishes a "people" from any other "assembled multitude" is that, first, it consists of *rational creatures*, human beings with the capacity for reason.[101] Modern interpreters must be careful not to read too much into Augustine's use of "rational" here, particularly when considering the "agreement" that members of a *populus* share. Augustine simply uses "rational" to distinguish human persons from "animals," to identify the kind of beings they are and the kinds of capacities they have.[102]

For my purposes, two rational capacities are most relevant. First, Augustine holds that human beings, unlike animals, have the ability not only to move toward certain objects of desire but to regard those objects as *ends*, as goods to be *willed* and *pursued* intentionally as ends.[103] This is why human beings can "sin" or do "evil," but animals cannot; irrational animals cannot voluntarily will certain goods as ends.[104] Human beings, by contrast, can will these goods as ends and therefore supply reasons for pursuing them. The rationality of these actions makes them subject to moral praise or blame in a way that animal behavior is not. This distinction is important for specifying the kind of "common agreement" required for a commonwealth. The rationality of the agreement means that it is not merely a reflection of animal instinct or natural desire, but the result of a complex process of reflection where rational creatures make determinations about what they regard as *good*, what they love and hope for as ends.

To reach "common agreement" about these ends, the capacity for intentional action is not sufficient. Agreement requires, second, the capacity for *communication*, the ability to use intelligible signs to communicate intentionally with other rational creatures about what they regard as proper ends: "For when men cannot communicate their thoughts to each other, they are completely unable to associate with one another despite the similarity of their natures."[105] For Augustine, the linguistic capacity for using signs and regarding them *as* signs, as expressions intended to communicate meaning, distinguishes rational creatures from irrational animals.[106] The capacity to communicate through words, actions, and signs is what enables human beings to come to a "common agreement," even if it is only implicit in their shared way of life.[107]

These capacities for rational reflection and communication are fairly minimal conditions of rationality. Yet, given the influence of the modern liberal tradition, some political theorists interpret an "assembled multitude of rational creatures bound together by a common agreement" in a *contractualist* way, assuming that rational agreement implies some abstract consensus to associate or contract for a particular purpose. Michael Hollerich, for example, points to contractualist overtones in Markus's neutralist vision of the Augustinian commonwealth: "[H]is actual account of the secular state seems cast in terms drawn entirely from modern individualist liberalism, in which the state is founded on contract and consent, not on our nature as social beings, and which lacks any transcendental legitimation or attachment."[108] A similar reading is implicit in George Klosko's interpretation of the Augustinian commonwealth as a "community of interest."[109] Klosko focuses in particular on common interests in earthly peace, suggesting that individual people consent to form a commonwealth for the sake of security. "Whatever their particular desires," Klosko writes, "a people requires peace in order to pursue them. Because there is no man who does not wish for peace, people enter into a kind of agreement to limit pursuit of their interests for the sake of harmony."[110] Such a liberal reading might suggest that Augustine is a proto-Hobbesian who assumes people leave the state of nature to join a social contract for the sake of peace.

We must be careful not to import modern conceptions of liberal legitimacy into interpretations of Augustine's late antique account of the commonwealth.[111] As a premodern eudaimonist, Augustine does not have a social contract theory in mind, nor does he think that complete consensus about what is truly just will ever be possible in this life. This is one upshot of his critique of Cicero's definition of the commonwealth, which assumes the possibility of common agreement about what is "truly just." In specifying agreement instead around "common objects of love," Augustine looks to identify general aims, ends, and goods that various individuals pursue and share in their daily lives, whether or not the individuals themselves are subjectively aware that they share these goods. Augustine does not suggest that isolated individuals come together to form a society or contract to protect their rational interests. Rather, he endorses the ancient idea that human beings are, by nature, social beings. "[T]he life of the wise man," he writes, "is a social one."[112]

Augustine points to biblical authority to emphasize natural human sociality. Explicating Genesis to explain why God chose to create Eve and the rest of humanity from Adam, Augustine argues that God "chose to create the human race from one single man" for a reason: "His purpose in doing this was not only that the human race should be united in fellowship by a natural likeness, but also that men should be bound together by kinship in unity of concord, linked by the bond of peace."[113] As a result, "there is nothing so social by nature as this race, no matter how discordant it has become through its fault."[114]

Augustine's emphasis on natural human sociality becomes even more evident in his original Latin. The phrase *concordi communione sociatus*, which is usually translated as "common agreement," can suggest a kind of rational consensus, but as John von Heyking notes, Augustine's invocation of coming together (*coetus*) in concord (*concordi*) has social and affective connotations that are often downplayed in modern accounts of Augustine's political thought.[115] The difference is especially clear when contrasting Augustine's definition with Cicero's: in place of a people joined by common agreement on justice and law (*iuris consensu*) and the sharing of interests or benefits (*utilitas communione sociatus*), Augustine emphasizes agreement and harmony (*concordi communione sociatus*) around common objects of love (*rerum quas diligit*).[116] Many interpreters assume that common objects of love refers to something closer to what modern philosophers mean by *common interests*, which can connote a rationalist or contractualist approach to politics.[117] While common interests are certainly among common objects of love, the modern language of interests can also suggest "rational" or "economic" interests that do not necessarily map onto the affective and social complexity of Augustine's account. "Common goods," "values," or "concerns" are better analogies since they capture the ways in which these objects engage affections along with reason.[118] Augustine's conception of a commonwealth united around common objects of love carves out a political role for virtues and affections—such as love and hope—that are sometimes elided in contemporary political theories that emphasize epistemic justification and abstract rationality.[119] Moreover, as James K. A. Smith argues, this conception highlights the *formative* aspects of politics as a set of practices that express and shape the "character" of a people, not simply their cognitive attitudes or professed beliefs.[120] The affective, dispositional, and formative aspects of Augustine's political thought are central to the account offered here.

Civic Peace in a Secular Age

For Augustine, citizens form a "people," and thus a "commonwealth," by sharing and deliberating about common objects of love, the ends they pursue together as rational creatures committed to particular goods that conduce to the
"health of the commonwealth."[121] What are these proper objects, and in what
sense do citizens share them in common?

Importantly, Augustine does not cast these "common objects" simply as
ultimate or otherworldly ends. Rather, these common objects include proximate, this-worldly goods, the "good things appropriate to this life."[122] Among
the most important are "temporal peace, in proportion to the short span of a
mortal life, consisting in bodily health and soundness, and the society of one's
own kind; and all things necessary for the preservation and recovery of this
peace," including "those things which are appropriate and accessible to our
senses, such as light, speech, breathable air, drinkable water, and whatever the
body requires to feed, clothe, shelter, heal or adorn it."[123] These are similar to
the goods of health, friendship, and "temporal well-being" Augustine identifies
in Letter 130 to Proba.[124] In both texts, Augustine stresses that these goods are
proper as long as citizens observe the right "use" and "order."[125]

For Augustine, the supreme good is not temporal peace but eternal peace,
which consists in "a perfectly ordered and perfectly harmonious fellowship in
the enjoyment of God, and of one another in God."[126] Although this peace is
"our Final Good," temporal peace remains a genuine good: "For peace is so
great a good that, even in the sphere of earthly and mortal affairs, we hear no
word more thankfully, and nothing is desired with greater longing: in short, it
is not possible to find anything better."[127] Augustine's emphasis on temporal
peace reflects his view of human beings as inherently social beings who desire
peace with their fellows: "[J]ust as there is no one who does not wish to be
joyful, so there is no one who does not wish to have peace."[128]

"Civic peace" (*concordiam ciuium*) constitutes one species of this temporal
peace.[129] It consists in the "ordered concord, with respect to command and
obedience, of the citizens."[130] Many Augustinian realists, particularly those
with liberal tendencies, interpret civic peace in a minimalist way, identifying
peace negatively as the mere absence of violence or harm in a "realm infected
with sin."[131] Markus, for example, argues that the purpose of politics consists
solely in protecting and promoting "a lowly form of 'peace': the public order
and security which human sin has made unstable in society."[132] "The greater
goods," he argues, are "beyond the scope of politics," which simply aims to

secure "a living space for society in the midst of strife and conflict."[133] Herbert Deane shares this tragic vision of politics as a *modus vivendi* whose remedial function is negative rather than positive: "[T]he state, for Augustine, is an external order; the peace that it maintains is external peace—the absence, or at least the diminution, of overt violence."[134] For these Augustinian realists, the primary purpose of politics is not to promote good but to prevent evil, not to foster virtue but to restrain violence.[135]

Augustine certainly believes civic peace requires such remedies and restraints. When he explains what constitutes the "well-ordered concord" of "peace among men," he identifies a duty not to harm as the first principle.[136] Yet he also specifies more positive responsibilities of justice and civic friendship alongside these negative duties: "[T]he order of this concord is, first, that a man should harm no one, and, second, that he should do good to all, so far as he can."[137] This second, more positive form of concord challenges those who cast politics simply as a negative remedy for constraining the effects of sin.[138]

In emphasizing positive forms of concord and obligations of justice, Augustine may be appropriating insights from Cicero's republican political theory. Linking justice and human sociability, Cicero argues that "common agreement about justice or law" (*iuris consensu*) contributes to "bonding men together" (*ad hominum consociationem*) in the commonwealth, partly by serving to reduce and prevent domination.[139] But for Cicero, the justice required for a commonwealth goes beyond the mere absence of injustice; it also entails a positive obligation to treat other citizens justly and contribute to the good of the entire commonwealth.[140] In *On Duties*, Cicero identifies two fundamental duties of justice: "first that one should harm no one; and secondly that one serve the common advantage," a formula that Augustine echoes.[141] Importantly, in explaining this second duty, Cicero employs the distinction between the "common" and the "private," advising citizens to "treat common goods as common and private ones as one's own."[142] He goes on to argue that citizens have a duty not only to respect individuals but "to contribute to the common stock the things that benefit everyone together, and, by the exchange of dutiful services, by giving and receiving expertise and effort and means, to bind fast the fellowship of men with each other."[143]

In appropriating Cicero's twofold formula, Augustine advocates a more positive form of concord and relates it to his conception of sociality, justice, and civic peace. Although Augustine emphasizes social and moral "order," his conception of order is more akin to justice in giving others what they are due:

"[O]rder is the disposition of equal and unequal things in such a way as to give to each its proper place."[144] Moreover, Augustine suggests that the pursuit of common goods requires and often elicits "peaceful association" among citizens: the "society of one's own kind" remains a necessary precondition for peace.[145] In this way, the commonwealth he advocates, like Cicero's, is not simply a set of minimal government structures, laws, or institutions, but also a set of *ordered relationships*, a kind of concord or civic friendship between members of the *populus*.[146] To borrow Nigel Biggar's phrase, Augustine's vision of politics is less a *modus vivendi* than a *modus convivendi*.[147] The "city's life," Augustine concludes, "is inevitably a social one."[148]

This emphasis on civic peace as a form of civic friendship aligns with Augustine's more expansive vision of politics. If civic peace consists partly in civic friendship, then the coercive forms of law and government that realists emphasize in their remedial accounts of the "state" are not the only instruments or sites of "politics." Citizens can also participate in politics when they serve their communities within and beyond government and form civic friendships with other citizens to advance common goods. When combined with an expansive view of politics, this emphasis on civic friendship challenges interpreters who attribute Augustine's "pessimism" about politics to a narrow, remedial, and largely coercive vision of the commonwealth and do not recognize how other forms of politics beyond the formal laws, institutions, and procedures of government can become the objects and sites of political hope.

That many critics and realists downplay these more associational and affective aspects of Augustine's thought may reflect their futurist eschatology. If one assumes a strict separation between heaven and earth, the "relative" peace of the *saeculum* can seem detached from participation in the City of God. But if one recognizes Augustine's inaugurated eschatology and participationist ontology, temporal or civic peace is no longer simply an absence of violence, but a kind of *participation* in the peace of the Heavenly City.

Augustine suggests as much in *City of God*. When he identifies the various forms of peace—the peace of the body, irrational and rational souls, the household, the city, and the heavenly city—he identifies them in ascending order, suggesting that each participates in the larger whole.[149] He makes this part-whole structure explicit in 19.16, where he describes how "domestic peace has reference to civic peace": "A man's household, then, ought to be the beginning, or a little part, of the city; and every beginning has reference to some end proper to itself, and every part has reference to the integrity of the whole of which it is a part."[150] Even the "peace of the unjust" ultimately participates in the peace of the heavenly city: "Even that which is perverse . . . must of necessity be in, or derived from, or associated with, and to that extent at peace with, some part of the order of things among which it has its being or of which it consists. Otherwise, it would not exist at all."[151] In the *saeculum*, this peace remains proximate and imperfect, but the properly ordered friendships that constitute the peace of the just are genuine goods, friendships that participate in friendship with God. Given the part-whole structure of human society, Augustine's civic peace is not merely a "lowly form of 'peace'"[152] but constitutes a more positive form of civic friendship that participates in friendship with God.

Yet, even if temporal peace participates in eternal peace, Augustine recognizes that the commonwealth includes citizens of both the heavenly and earthly cities, diverse citizens with different ways of ordering their hopes and loves.[153] Importantly, Augustine does not require complete agreement on ultimate objects of love to ensure civic peace, but neither does he preclude the possibility of imperfect convergence. Rather, he encourages citizens to unite around proximate objects of love in the *saeculum*, especially those goods that preserve civic peace:

> [B]oth kinds of men and both kinds of household make common use of those things which are necessary to this mortal life; but each has its own very different end in using them. So also, the earthly city, which does not live by faith, desires an earthly peace, and it establishes an ordered concord of civic obedience and rule in order to secure a kind of co-operation of men's wills for the sake of attaining the things which belong to this mortal life. But the Heavenly City—or, rather, that part of it which is a pilgrim in this condition of mortality, and which lives by faith—must of necessity make use of this peace also, until this mortal state, for which such peace is necessary, shall have passed away. Thus, it lives like a captive and a pilgrim, even though it has already received the promise of redemption, and the gift of the Spirit as a kind of pledge of it. But, for as long as it does so, it does not hesitate to obey the laws of the earthly city, whereby the things necessary for the support of this mortal life are administered.[154]

Ultimately, Augustine concludes, "since this mortal condition is common to both cities, a harmony [*concordia*] is preserved between them with respect to the things which belong to this condition."[155]

Here Augustine's emphasis on civic "harmony" or "concord" (*concordia*) is illuminating. Augustine takes the term from Cicero, who invoked the musical harmony of "even the most dissimilar voices" as an analogy for the concord of the commonwealth: "What musicians call harmony in singing is concord in the city, which is the most artful and best bond of security in the commonwealth, and which, without justice, cannot be secured at all."[156] In appropriating Cicero's analogy, Augustine acknowledges how dissimilar voices can join together in concord to secure the common goods of the commonwealth.

That Augustine promotes concord as a proximate object common to diverse citizens, and that he encourages members of the heavenly city to "obey the laws of the earthly city," challenges the assumption that Augustine endorses a "theocratic" conception of the state.[157] Although he maintains that the City of God sets the standard of perfect peace, he does not require all citizens to share the same ultimate religious, philosophical, and moral commitments to be part of the earthly commonwealth.[158] He allows for a diversity of beliefs, values, and comprehensive doctrines as long as the political community maintains a common agreement on the proximate goods of civic peace.

But if common agreement on proximate ends need not entail complete agreement on ultimate ends, neither does it entail complete "neutrality," as some Augustinian liberals assume.[159] Most pointedly, Robert Markus declares that Augustine's "'secularisation' of the realm of politics implies a pluralistic, religiously neutral civil community."[160] According to Markus, "[W]e may not unreasonably apply the anachronistic epithet 'pluralist'" since Augustine's political order remains "neutral in respect of ultimate beliefs and values."[161] Yet, while Markus rightly casts the *saeculum* as the "sphere in which different individuals with different beliefs and loyalties pursue their common objectives in so far as they coincide," his attribution of "religious neutrality" goes too far.[162] In *Christianity and the Secular*, Markus concedes the point, recognizing that, for Augustine, "people cannot act intentionally without reference to ultimate ends."[163] Nonetheless, Markus still occasionally slips into a language of "autonomy" and "neutrality" and even compares Augustine's position to Rawls's liberal conception of "overlapping consensus," in which citizens with diverse "comprehensive doctrines" arrive at a shared political consensus based on "public reason."[164] Augustine does not commend such neutrality.[165] He frequently states his preference for Christian rulers, counsels those in office to care for the souls of citizens, and explicitly encourages citizens to bring their religious and moral values into public life.[166] He clearly believes that civic peace participates in eternal peace and that some ways of life are more conducive to happiness than others, both for the citizen and the city: "The happiness of a city and of man do not, after all, arise from different sources."[167]

And even if citizens are able to secure agreement on common objects of love, he insists the quality of their love matters: "[T]he better the objects of this agreement, the better the people; and the worse the objects, the worse the people."[168]

Yet, if Augustine does not endorse neutrality, he does not endorse totalizing uniformity either. As Kristen Deede Johnson observes, Augustine suggests that God "chose to create one individual for the propagation of many, so that men should be admonished to preserve unity among their whole multitude," to achieve a kind of "unity in plurality" (*in multis concors unitas*).[169] Rather than requiring homogeneity, Augustine welcomes plurality as part of God's creation and encourages a robust form of concord and convergence of diverse citizens around common goods.[170]

Recent work in political theory can help to bring Augustine's recommended posture into view. In particular, the "common agreement" that Augustine endorses is similar to what Cass Sunstein describes as "incompletely theorized agreement," a practical and provisional convergence around common goods that seeks to promote coordination and stability in the face of disagreement without requiring strict neutrality or comprehensive agreement on ultimate ends.[171] By engaging in a "conceptual descent" from abstract theories of the good or the right to more proximate and particular goods, incompletely theorized agreement enables diverse citizens to secure practical agreements on concrete aims needed to ensure social stability, promote mutual respect and reciprocity, and encourage humility and openness in the face of diversity and difference.[172] This reasoning process can also work in the opposite direction, involving a conceptual ascent that enables citizens to work up from disagreements about particular objects to agreements about more distant ends. In either form, the possibility of incompletely theorized agreement enables citizens to converge around common goods and maintain civic friendships in the face of potential conflict. Sunstein does not cite Augustine in specifying his account, but his insights helpfully illuminate assumptions implicit in Augustine's. In recognizing that members of both the earthly and heavenly cities make use of civic peace in the *saeculum*, Augustine endorses a kind of incompletely theorized agreement in the face of diversity and disagreement, encouraging diverse citizens to converge around the common good of civic peace, regardless of "any differences in the customs, laws, and institutions by which earthly peace is achieved or maintained."[173] "For whatever differences there are the among various nations," Augustine argues, "these all tend towards the same end of earthly peace."[174] As long as they are allowed to worship God, pursue truth, and enact the virtues, Christians should largely obey the political authorities that preserve peace, whatever institutional form they take.[175]

Importantly, this Augustinian posture resists the "freestanding," "overlapping consensus" that characterizes John Rawls's influential idea of "public reason."[176] The common agreement that Augustine endorses does not require an abstract consensus that citizens must justify from the perspective of neutral public reason. Rather, he implies that a commonwealth obtains when diverse citizens with different fundamental reasons and ultimate ends converge around shared conclusions about proximate ends and common goods, especially the good of civic peace. Such a posture allows Christians to speak in their own terms without having to abide the strict constraints of Rawlsian public reason.

This approach fits with the default and challenge structure of reasoning analyzed in chapter 4. Augustine does not require foundational or freestanding reasons to justify our beliefs before we can accept them. He allows instead that we may hold many default beliefs until we have good reason to abandon, adapt, or revise them. Such beliefs are often "innocent until proven guilty."[177] But, if and when such beliefs are challenged, we must "be ready to respond to everyone who asks us for an account of our faith and hope."[178] For Augustine, this process of exchanging reasons and responding to potential challenges and defeaters is diachronic, social, and dialogical. Its iterative process involves being sensitive to different sources of evidence and entitlement at different times, recognizing how beliefs are socially embedded within shared communities of inquiry, and exchanging reasons with others, often through forms of rhetorical persuasion and immanent critique that honor the authorities that others accept on their own terms.

This Augustinian model of reasoning aligns with approaches to political deliberation defended by Jeffrey Stout, Nicholas Wolterstorff, and Nigel Biggar, among others.[179] This approach entails that citizens need not be required to justify their theological or political positions on the basis of foundational or freestanding public reasons before they can accept or advocate them. Rather, they may hold their default political positions on the basis of trustworthy authorities, including moral and religious authorities. Yet they must also be willing to exchange reasons for those default positions, standing ready to respond to any challenges that opponents press against them and to affirm, adapt, or abandon their positions accordingly. This process of political justification is dynamic rather than static, iterative rather than isolated, social rather than solitary. Instead of requiring citizens to forfeit their religious convictions to offer neutral public reasons, it encourages forms of immanent critique and rhetorical persuasion in which interlocutors engage each other on their own terms, either to show that their default position is inconsistent with collateral commitments or to find a way that their divergent default views can support a convergence around a particular position without requiring a shared justification in freestanding public reasons.[180] Such a position allows candid and robust political expression and contestation while protecting freedom of religion and recognizing that citizens with diverse beliefs, commitments, and ultimate ends may be able to arrive at incompletely theorized agreement without abandoning their religious commitments or appealing to strict neutrality.[181] Not only does such an approach show respect to the moral and religious sources of authority that diverse citizens are entitled to accept, but it provides a more effective means of engaging citizens on their own terms and finding instances of convergence that enable diverse citizens to share common objects of love in light of their differences.[182]

Augustine recognizes, of course, that such provisional and incompletely theorized agreement will not always be stable, nor will it displace political conflict, contestation, or resistance.[183] Citizens with different visions of the good will not always agree on what "civic peace" or "justice" requires in a particular situation.[184] The Ciceronian ideal of concord that Augustine invokes does not eliminate disagreement. As Joy Connolly notes, Cicero's vision of "concord" among "dissimilar voices" is more agonistic than liberal consensus models of politics often assume.[185] Concord is not permanent, static, or stable but involves ongoing contestation and resistance as citizens of different political and economic classes negotiate a shared but temporary peace.[186] That Augustine inherits this more agonistic conception helps to explain why he can elevate civic peace as a common good while advancing a vigorous critique of Roman political life, using rhetoric to persuade interlocutors and acknowledging that members of the heavenly city should sometimes "dissent from the earthly city" and be "a burden to those who think differently."[187]

Ultimately, the convergence that Augustine assumes is similar to what Nigel Biggar describes as "tense consensus"—agreement that is provisional, incomplete, and, at times, tense.[188] While both Christians and non-Christians can converge around common goods, Biggar cites Augustine's conception of the *saeculum* to suggest that any "overlapping consensus" will not be "Rawlsian, but Augustinian."[189] Because diverse citizens have divergent views of justice and different ultimate ends, any consensus on temporal goods they share will not be "whole and stable, but partial and provisional."[190] "What this implies,"

Biggar concludes, "is that, insofar as Christians agree with non-Christians, they should regard it as an imperfect compromise, subject to criticism and yearning for perfection. So, yes, consensus—but tense."[191]

Echoing Sunstein's "incompletely theorized agreement," Biggar's preference for "tense consensus" points to an Augustinian vision different from most contemporary versions of either liberalism or communitarianism. Like Markus, Biggar affirms the importance of humility and openness toward fellow citizens in the *saeculum* and encourages Christians to find a practical consensus with non-Christians around common goods, but he does not believe public space can be as neutral as Markus supposes. Like Hauerwas and Milbank, Biggar affirms a central role for the church in cultivating the virtues of citizens and informing public discourse around moral and political questions, but he holds that Christian love and humility require more openness toward non-Christian citizens than a rigid opposition between church and world allows.

Yet, while Biggar's Augustinian pluralism highlights an aspect of the "common agreement" implicit in Augustine's vision of the commonwealth, his emphasis on "consensus" might be seen to support a more liberal rendering that downplays the relational role of affections and the importance of civic friendship. Given Augustine's emphasis on "concord" and "communion" (*concordi communione sociatus*) more than "consensus" (*consensu*), Joshua Hordern's version of "tense communion" may offer a helpful complement to this Augustinian posture.[192] Emphasizing more dialectical and affective dimensions of political reasoning, Hordern describes "tense communion" as a description of "how people, subscribing to multiple eschatological visions or none, live together in a way whereby common, created social loyalties and obligations are discerned without occluding eschatological ones."[193] Such a vision, Hordern acknowledges, is "similar in Augustinian spirit to Nigel Biggar's 'tense consensus'" but "differs by suggesting a political life of both closer *relational* proximity and greater *eschatological* distance between believers and unbelievers than 'consensus' denotes."[194] Disagreement about eschatological horizons makes the communion "tense," while the relational and affective dimension of civic friendship makes it "communion." Both allow for critical participation in political life and the kind of "mutual learning and critique" that emerge from "dialectical democratic conversation" about the common good.[195] Although Hordern develops his account in conversation with Jonathan Edwards, Martha Nussbaum, and Jeffrey Stout, it captures the kind of concord that Augustine believes diverse citizens can share in the secular age.

An emphasis on "communion" also helps to distinguish Augustine's form of civic concord from agonistic conceptions of politics that make conflict the aim of political life rather than a temporary condition. As Charles Mathewes and Kristen Deede Johnson argue, while Augustine welcomes plurality as a part of God's creation and recognizes conflict as an inevitable part of political life in the *saeculum*, he does not assume an ontology of conflict or see agonism as the fundamental condition of human being.[196] Rather, he presents communion with God and neighbor in the eschaton as the ultimate aim of human life and therefore the ultimate model for politics. And given his participationist ontology in which the concord of the commonwealth participates in the peace of the heavenly city, he assumes an ontology of peace and communion rather than conflict.[197] While agonistic contestation over common goods is inevitable in the *saeculum*, concord rather conflict remains the animating aim, enabling citizens to see each other not merely as rivals or adversaries but as neighbors and friends, even in the face of disagreement.

III. Common Objects of Hope

If any convergence around common goods remains incomplete, fraught, and at times tense, the temporal peace and civic friendship that unites a commonwealth will remain fragile and uncertain. As a bishop involved in the affairs of church and empire, Augustine knew this firsthand. If "there is no security even in the home from the common evils which befall the human race," he asks, "what of the city? The larger the city, the more is its forum filled with civil law-suits and criminal trials. Even when the city is at peace and free from actual sedition and civil war, it is never free from the danger of such disturbance or, more often, bloodshed."[198] Augustine has no illusions about the difficulty of stable agreement, but neither does he believe tragic conflict is desirable or inevitable. He provides several moral and political resources to facilitate convergence around common objects of love.

Political Conversation and Immanent Critique

First, the fact that citizens with different ultimate ends can share genuine political goods means that diverse citizens can join a shared conversation about those goods. Shared ends, even if incompletely specified, can get the conversation up and running and provide alternative routes in the face of deliberative roadblocks. As a result, disagreements over ultimate ends need not become "conversation-stoppers."[199] If citizens can recognize the goods they share in common, even if only abstractly, they can at least begin to discuss what "civic peace" means in a particular context and what it might require in diverse circumstances. Because they share a common referent, they do not talk past each other, and because they recognize the other as capable of rationally pursuing a genuine good, they are not tempted to attribute irrationality to their opponent.[200] Recognizing each other as rational enables them to begin exchanging reasons, giving each other reasons why a particular specification of civic peace or justice is necessary in a particular context. In this way, acknowledging common objects keeps the conversation alive, even when disagreement threatens to stifle it.[201] Augustine, after all, would not have been able to engage pagan interlocutors in a meaningful conversation about the meaning of happiness if they had not at least agreed on what they were discussing and shared a commitment to happiness as their final end.[202]

Second, for Augustine, common objects of love do not simply identify shared attitudes, feelings, or mental states. Rather, as argued in chapter 2, love achieves its completion in action: it is enacted and expressed through specific activities and pursuits. Since every act is motivated by some underlying love, by some desire for an object perceived as good, the connection between love and action entails that a person's common objects of love can be discerned by looking at their actions, by inquiring into why they act in certain ways or inferring what goods they take themselves to be pursuing when they act in particular cases.[203]

The possibility of inferring objects of love from action is politically significant in at least two ways. First, it allows citizens to identify possible common objects with other citizens whose verbal professions or collateral commitments diverge but whose actions and aims overlap. Consider an example from Augustine's own correspondence with Nectarius, a pagan civil servant who wrote asking Augustine to intercede on behalf of pagans accused of breaking the law and committing violence against Christians in Calama.[204] Judging by their diverse backgrounds and beliefs, Nectarius and Augustine seem to have few shared values or common objects. As their exchange reveals, they certainly do not share the same ultimate ends.[205] Nevertheless, Nectarius's plea for clemency on behalf of fellow pagans converges with Augustine's Christian understanding of mercy. In this case, Nectarius's act of pleading for clemency provides evidence of a common object that may not have been obvious by simply inquiring into their verbal professions or ultimate commitments. This act expresses a common objective that enables Nectarius and Augustine to engage in a larger dialogue about the value of mercy and the nature of civic virtue. While Augustine goes on to exhort Nectarius to serve a "much finer city"—the City of God—what is striking about his reply is that he argues on Nectarius's own terms.[206] In addition to praising Nectarius's virtue and commitment to serving his city, Augustine quotes Virgil, the "most famous poet in your literary tradition," before making an appeal to Cicero's On the Commonwealth, which Nectarius had quoted.[207] "Please think about [Cicero's volumes]; notice how they proclaim as praiseworthy simplicity and restraint, along with faithfulness to the marriage bond, and behavior that is chaste and honourable and upright. When a city is strong in such virtues as these, then it can truly said to be 'flourishing.'"[208] Here, Augustine appeals to the authorities and virtues of pagans that Nectarius could accept on his own terms to explain his position and urge the reform of those in Calama. Such immanent critique would not have been possible without an initial convergence around a common referent, a common object of love.

Second, inferring loves from actions can enable citizens to hold others accountable when their actions do not match their verbal expressions. Imagine a political leader who professes a love of liberty but then enacts policies that arbitrarily exploit and dominate citizens. These actions suggest a love for some other good—glory, power, or wealth—that contradicts the leader's expressed love of liberty. That these contradictory loves can be inferred from the leader's actions can enable a social critic to point to inconsistencies between professed and enacted commitments, supplying powerful leverage for dialogue and potentially reform.

Augustine frequently employs this kind of immanent critique in City of God, drawing on authorities that Romans purport to admire to show how their actions fail to measure up to their professed commitments.[209] When criticizing Greek and Roman conceptions of virtue in Book 19, he begins by appealing to their sources of authority, telling readers that he will proceed "not only by calling upon divine authority, but also, for the sake of unbelievers, by making as much use of reason as possible."[210] A similar appeal to shared authorities is evident in his opening polemic against paganism.[211] In building his case against the Roman Empire, Augustine draws extensively on the philosophers, historians, and poets that Romans regard as authoritative.[212] He cites Sallust to highlight the "moral collapse" of the republic,[213] Horace to condemn love of praise as a vice,[214] and Cicero to argue that the Roman commonwealth is not actually the "property of a people."[215] That all of these citations appear in the first five books of City of God is rhetorically significant: their location in the opening books shows how Augustine begins his critique by engaging pagan critics on their own terms, enacting a "procedure of working through the familiar, by appealing from the known to the unknown."[216] In these passages, Augustine attempts to show that the loves that actually motivate Roman leaders—the love of glory and dominion—do not square with their professed love of virtue, justice, and liberty, the goods celebrated by their beloved authorities. Here, Augustine uses inferences from actions to identify implicit objects of love that he then subjects to immanent critique. This procedure aligns with the default and challenge structure of reasoning analyzed in chapter 4. In employing immanent critique, Augustine recognizes the default authorities that his pagan interlocutors accept and then proceeds to offer defeaters that undercut or rebut views based on those authorities.

Identifying common objects of love, however, is not always easy, even when making inferences from action. In such cases, Augustine's account offers an additional resource. As Oliver O'Donovan explains, he recognizes that "every determination of love implies a corresponding hatred."[217] A "lover of the good," Augustine writes, "must hate what is evil."[218] This connection between love and hatred has implications for agreement around common objects of love. According to O'Donovan, "For a community to focus its love on *this* constellation of goods is to withdraw its love from *that*. Every concrete community, then, is defined equally by the things it does *not* love together, the objects it refuses to accept as a ground of its association."[219] For O'Donovan, this conceptual connection illuminates a neglected aspect of Augustine's definition of the "two cities," which are "determined not only by ultimate objects of love, but by ultimate objects of refusal: 'love of God to the point of contempt of self, love of self to the point of contempt of God.'"[220]

For our purposes, this insight is significant for two reasons. First, it provides another resource for securing incompletely theorized agreement among diverse citizens when conversation comes to a standstill. If citizens cannot agree on what they love or value, they may at least be able to agree on what they *hate*, on what they despise or find horrendous. This approach fits with research that suggests it is often easier to build political coalitions and social movements by identifying what citizens fear, resent, or detest rather than what they desire, hope, or love.[221] "When equality became, with liberty and fraternity, one of the three great slogans of the French Revolution," Kwame Anthony Appiah writes, "it was not because people had a clear idea what it was they wanted equality of. What they knew for sure was what they were *against*: treating people badly merely because they were not born into the nobility, looking down your nose at the common people. The ideal of equality in modern times begins, in short, with the thought that there are certain things that are *not* a proper basis for treating people unequally, and only gradually moves on to identify some things that *are*."[222] Amartya Sen makes a similar point about the abolitionist movement: "It was the diagnosis of an intolerable injustice in slavery that made abolition an overwhelming priority, and this did not require the search for a consensus on what a perfectly just society would look like."[223] In such cases, imperfect convergence around common objects of refusal, not perfect consensus around common objects of love, enabled collaboration and cooperation.

We can imagine this dynamic at work among Augustine's audiences. Consider a passage from *City of God* where he argues that a lust for glory and domination entails a hatred of "just peace": "[P]ride hates a fellowship of equality under God, and wishes to impose its own dominion upon its equals, in place of God's rule."[224] Now imagine a Roman reader who stumbles upon this passage and, like many educated elites in Augustine's audience, admires Cicero, a devoted civic republican. This Ciceronian republican does not share Augustine's Christian commitments or even his particular vision of what "just peace" requires, but like Augustine and Cicero, he hates imperial domination, despising the way in which imperial power is wielded arbitrarily over citizens.[225] This shared hatred about a proximate object might enable an Augustinian Christian and Ciceronian republican to begin a conversation about specific instances of imperial domination they have witnessed and deliberate about how to address them. Their shared hatred of domination may even enable them to identify a common object of love they did not know they shared—a love of liberty. In this way, recognizing corresponding objects of love and hate, approval and refusal, can facilitate cooperation and provide additional resources for dialogue in the face of disagreement.

A Continuum of Virtue and Vice

That an Augustinian Christian and Ciceronian republican might share common objects of love or refusal reflects another advantage of this account: it complicates an either/or account of love's objects. Recall the ultimate objects of love that Augustine assigns to the "two cities": "love of self extending even to the contempt of God" and "love of God extending to the contempt of self."[226] Typically, this distinction is read in an either/or way: one *either* loves God *or* self—the ultimate objects of love determine one's membership in the two cities. But the fact that citizens from both cities can share proximate objects of love suggests that love of God and love of self do not constitute an *either-or dichotomy* but are poles on a *continuum* of virtue, a gradation of good and bad loves. Notice Augustine's way of phrasing the antithesis: it is not *either* love of God *or* love of self, but rather, love of self *extending even to the contempt of God* and love of God *extending to contempt of self*. Augustine's conjunction (*usque*)—"extending to" or "to the point of"—implies that some loves fall between these two poles. As Augustine observes, in the present life, no one will achieve a complete love of God to the point of complete contempt of self: "We cannot manage to achieve this in our present life, no matter how much we may wish to."[227] Even the most virtuous are tempted by vice.[228] This means that all loves—including those of both "pilgrims" and "pagans"—are located somewhere on the continuum.[229] Describing a person either as perfectly virtuous or perfectly vicious fails to acknowledge the gradations of imperfect or incomplete virtue between these two poles.[230]

Recognizing these gradations is particularly important for Augustinian hope. For one, a continuum chastens the pride of those who presume their virtue is perfect and complete: placing oneself on the continuum—and thus acknowledging one falls short of perfect "love of God extending to contempt of self"—disrupts temptations toward presumption and prevents one from acting complacently toward important political goods. Recognizing the continuum can also dispel despair among those who assume more perfect virtue is impossible, either for themselves or for their fellow citizens. If they see "love of God extending to contempt of self" as the only way to achieve "virtue," their failure to realize this seemingly impossible standard in this life might tempt despair. In this context, recognizing gradations of goodness can discourage citizens from either abandoning hope for more perfect virtue or seeing the political realm simply as a seedbed of vice.

Furthermore, acknowledging that everyone falls on the continuum encourages an openness to citizens who maintain different standards of goodness. These citizens may not have perfect virtue according to one's own lights, but that does not necessarily entail that they are fully vicious. The continuum of ordered love marks a space between perfect virtue and perfect vice that allows a movement toward either pole, which means that citizens can be good, even if imperfectly or incompletely so. Such a recognition encourages the humble acknowledgment that diverse citizens may share common goods in the *saeculum*, even if they order them to different ultimate ends.[231] For this reason, Christians need not give up their political coalitions with citizens who, from their perspective, do not possess "true virtue."[232]

One of Augustine's earliest formulations of the "two cities" provides pur-chase on which goods diverse citizens can share in common. In *Literal Mean-ing of Genesis*, Augustine defines the two cities again by their "two loves,"

> of which one is holy, the other unclean, one social, the other private, one taking thought for the common good because of the companionship in the upper regions, the other putting even what is common at its own personal disposal because of its lordly arrogance; one of them God's subject, the other his rival, one of them calm, the other turbulent, one peaceable, the other re-bellious; one of them setting more store by the truth than by the praises of those who stray from it, the other greedy for praise by whatever means, one friendly, the other jealous, one of them wanting for its neighbor what it wants for itself, the other wanting to subject its neighbor to itself; one of them exercising authority over its neighbor for its neighbor's good, the other for its own—these two loves were first manifested in the angels, one in the good, the other in the bad, and then distinguished the two cities, one of the just, the other of the wicked.[233]

What is striking about this formulation is that it opposes "common" goods to "private" goods, much like Cicero did. As we saw in chapter 2, Augustine envi-sions God as the most common and public good and the self as the most private.[234] From Augustine's point of view, what distinguishes the earthly city is that its members reject this most common good and aim instead at merely private goods, which lead ultimately to pride and domination. The distinction between "common" and "private" goods thus provides a way to recast the dis-tinction between the two cities, one seeking the ultimate common good to the point of contempt for a purely private good, the other seeking a private good to the point of contempt for the ultimate common good.[235] This redescription makes it easier to identify how a citizen may take thought for the "common good" without fully loving it while also refusing to put "what is common at [their] own personal disposal because of [their] lordly arrogance."[236] A citizen can order their virtues to common goods without fully loving the most com-mon good (God) but also without ordering those ends entirely to the most private good (self).

Augustine acknowledges such citizens in his account of Romans who "held their own private interests in low esteem for the sake of the common good, that is, for the commonwealth. For the sake of its treasury they resisted avarice, and they took counsel for the good of their fatherland with unfettered minds; nor were they guilty of any offence against its laws, or of any unwholesome desires."[237] By Augustine's lights, such citizens may not order all of their loves to God to the point of contempt of self, but they order their loves to genuine common goods. If they love common goods more than their purely private good, they might be "on the way" to more perfect virtue, "not . . . yet holy" but "less vile."[238]

In chapter 10, I will argue that acknowledging gradations of virtue opens a way for a more inclusive Augustinian account of non-Christian virtue that recognizes genuine if incomplete virtues in those who do not, according to Augustine, have "true godliness." But if everyone falls somewhere on the continuum, *no one* has true and perfect godliness in this life; both pilgrims and pagans are on the way.[239] This humble recognition can facilitate more inclusive understandings of common objects of love and hope.

A Political Grammar of Hope

My aim thus far has been to show how Augustine recognizes genuine political goods that diverse citizens can share in the *saeculum* as essential for maintaining the civic peace and concord of the commonwealth.[240] Since Augustine describes these goods as objects of love, I have followed his lead, explicating the commonwealth in terms of citizens' loves and showing how members of the earthly and heavenly cities can share proximate objects of love, even as they order them to different ultimate ends. The same insights, however, also apply to common objects of hope. Because hope is ordered to love and because love for certain goods propels hope's pursuit, the same temporal goods that Augustine identifies as common objects of love—civic peace, health, friendship, and all the necessary things required to preserve peace and concord—are also common objects of hope. This means a political community is also a commonwealth of hope, a multitude of rational agents united by a common agreement as to the objects of their hope.

As noted in previous chapters, a key distinction between hope and love is that hope regards goods under a certain description, goods believed to be possible, future, unseen, and not fully possessed. When goods are desired under this description, they are properly characterized as objects of hope. Importantly, many of the civic goods Augustine identifies as common objects of love fit this description: they are possible future goods that are not fully possessed. This is one implication of Book 19's description of the "evils" that abound in the commonwealth. In the *saeculum*, civic friendship is fraught with difficulty. Even peace remains an "uncertain good, since we do not know the hearts of those with whom we wish to maintain peace," and "even if we could know them today, we should not know what they might be like in the future."[241] In this life, temporal peace is never fully possessed, and even when we realize instantiations of it, its protection and preservation remains an uncertain future good, an object that is unseen. In the *saeculum*, peace and all of the goods necessary to achieve it can be properly described as objects of hope.

Recognizing these goods as objects of hope rather than simply of love offers several advantages. First, it affords additional conceptual and discursive resources for finding common ground during political deliberation, particularly when citizens' objects of faith and love seem to conflict or diverge. Recall the reciprocal relations between faith, hope, and love analyzed in chapter 1. Augustine identifies hope as the "middle term" between faith and love: since hope presupposes both belief and desire, "from this middle term, hope, we can work backward to the beginning, that is, to faith; and forward to the end, which is charity."[242] If hope is the "middle term," it is possible to infer what one *believes* and *loves* from what one *hopes*. This is a significant resource for an Augustinian account of politics. For one, it gives citizens an additional vocabulary to identify goods they share in common. In cases where asking or inferring what other citizens believe or love leads to abstractions or disagreements, asking or inferring what citizens hope may elicit unexpected sources of common ground. In particular, working backward from hope to identify implicit objects of faith or belief, and working forward to identify implicit objects of love or desire, may help when there is deep disagreement about what citizens profess to believe or love. Asking what diverse citizens hope—appealing to hope as a "middle term"—can provide insight into how diverse citizens with different professed faiths and loves might be able to identify common objects and engage in a conversation about the proximate hopes they share.

A focus on proximate objects of hope points to another distinctive feature of an Augustinian account: even if citizens order their proximate political hopes to different ultimate objects, all citizens can order their hopes to the proximate goods of civic peace and the ordered concord of the political community.[243] Diverse citizens, in other words, can share *spes publica* for the *res publica*—common hope for the commonwealth. Although Augustine does not use the term *spes publica*, it was common on Roman coins in the early empire and fits with the Roman emphasis on hope for the republic.[244] The phrase usefully captures the kind of common hope that Augustine commends. Contrary to what many interpreters suggest, Augustinian hope is not necessarily otherworldly, exclusivist, or antipolitical. Augustine recognizes the possibility of proper hope for the commonwealth.

Moreover, an Augustinian hope for the commonwealth not only coheres with Sunstein's conception of "incompletely theorized agreement" but also identifies the *affective* and *motivational* posture needed to seek or sustain it. If incompletely theorized agreement on civic peace remains provisional, fragile, and uncertain, an Augustinian account of hope adds the recognition that citizens must neither *presume* their agreement is either complete or stable, nor *despair* when realizing it seems impossible. Hope for the commonwealth must avoid both vices.

This points to the most important benefit of identifying political goods as common objects of hope: it enables us to take advantage of Augustine's grammar of hope, which offers the conceptual and political vocabulary needed to identify the virtue required to patiently endure difficulties that hinder the pursuit of difficult goods and resist temptations that endanger that pursuit. Describing uncertain political goods as objects of hope highlights temptations toward presumption and despair in ways that focusing more generally on love or faith might not. For example, since hope is grounded in faith, a grammar of hope captures the *epistemic* dimension of pursuing these difficult future goods in a way that is obscured by focusing only on love. One can desire or love a particular good without either considering whether it is possible to attain or developing the constancy and resolve required to realize it in the face of difficulties. An account of hope, by contrast, highlights the difficulty, uncertainty, and futurity of these goods as essential aspects of their pursuit and thereby furnishes conceptual resources for responding properly to them. Given the importance of faith, some might think, with Vincent Lloyd, that an account of "faith" would be sufficient to address these epistemic uncertainties and volitional difficulties.[245] Yet, as I argued in previous chapters, casting objects of hope simply as objects of faith obscures the affective and volitional movements of the will required to *motivate* the pursuit of particular goods and *persevere* in the face of difficulties or delays. By capturing both epistemic and motivational dimensions, Augustine's grammar of hope calls attention to the myriad ways in which our pursuits can be threatened by presumption and despair and identifies the virtue needed to resist these vices.

Moreover, by providing a conceptual and normative account of how we hope not only *for* objects but *in* agents of assistance, Augustine's grammar of hope alerts us to the dangers of pridefully presuming on our own self-sufficiency and thereby neglecting to seek the assistance of fellow citizens in achieving difficult goods. Hoping in others is especially important in a political context where difficult future goods are subject to contingencies outside of citizens' control and where realizing collective goods is beyond the capacity of any isolated individual. In such cases, citizens need to hope and trust in their fellow citizens to avoid the despair that might arise from the difficulty and uncertainty of attaining particular political goods. At the same time, they must consider who can be helpful agents of assistance and how they can hope in them without presuming too much about either their motives or capacities. An Augustinian virtue of hope that disposes citizens to hope properly in others highlights the complex social, motivational, and epistemic dimensions of these political dynamics and enables them to recognize and resist the temptations that characterize an uncertain social and political life.

Finally, if a properly ordered hope involves not only objects of desire and approval but objects of hate and refusal, then identifying forms of presumption and despair can offer additional resources for finding common ground. Even if citizens cannot easily identify what they hope for or whom they hope in, they may be able to identify forms of presumption and despair they want to resist. In such cases, they may be able to find common ground in resisting these vices, even if their common hopes remain inarticulate or incomplete.

As we saw in the previous two chapters, Augustine often leads audiences through a dialectic of presumption and despair. We are now in a position to apply this dialectic to politics. As Kristen Deede Johnson argues, Augustine understands that "political society cannot be the site of the fulfillment of utopian dreams of harmony in the midst of diversity. This side of the fall, even with the far-reaching consequences of the cross and the ever-important role of hope in sustaining the society known as the Church, we dare not look for too much in the earthly city."[246] Yet, unlike many realists, Johnson recognizes that Augustine does not authorize a politics of despair. Although he believes the perfect realization of God's peace lies in the future, citizens can already begin to experience the "first fruits" of God's kingdom here and now.[247] As a result, Augustine's political vision "lies somewhere in between the two extremes of completely abandoning the earthly city and looking to the earthly city to achieve utopian-like harmony and peace."[248] Luke Bretherton agrees: "For Augustine, politics in the *saeculum* is about enabling a limited peace that is on the one hand shorn of messianic pretensions but on the other not given over to demonic despair."[249]

The vocabulary I have brought into view provides a way to identify this Augustinian posture. Augustine counsels citizens to develop a *virtue of hope* that finds a middle way between the vices of presumption and despair, one that enables citizens to resist temptations toward despair that accompany political difficulties and delays without thereby licensing the complacency, recklessness, and cruelty that often follow from prideful presumption. By disposing citizens to hope properly *for* political goods and *in* others to assist, this virtue alerts them to the epistemic and motivational difficulties that accompany uncertain future goods and discourages them from placing too much, or too little, hope in politics and fellow citizens.

Conclusion

Augustine's political hope was not superficial or banal. He did not ignore the realities of evil in politics, but neither did he encourage political passivity or pessimism. Although he recognizes that politics is fraught with dangers, toils, and snares, he acknowledges that seeking the peace of the commonwealth can be a way to participate in the eternal city. Rather than deferring the eschaton indefinitely or confining God's kingdom to the institutional church, he recognizes the value of developing civic friendship with citizens who hold different ultimate ends. In the *saeculum*, citizens of both cities make use of civic peace and all the goods appropriate to this life. By recognizing these goods as proper objects of hope, Augustine provides conceptual and discursive resources that can help make political cooperation possible and elevates a virtue that equips diverse citizens to share common hopes for the commonwealth. To find an example of this hope, we need to look no further than Augustine himself.

9

An Example of Hope

AUGUSTINE'S POLITICAL LIFE IN LETTERS

[I]f you believe something else, hope for something else, love something else,
you must prove it by your life, demonstrate it by your actions.

—AUGUSTINE, SERMON 198.2

Augustine seems to have been the last to know at least what it once meant
to be a citizen.

—HANNAH ARENDT, *THE HUMAN CONDITION*, 14.

EVEN ACROSS sixteen centuries, Augustine's life comes to us with surprising
familiarity. We may know more about Augustine than any other thinker from
late antiquity.[1] Not only do we have a biography by his friend and contemporary, Possidius, but we also have access to Augustine's personal narrative
in the *Confessions*, a book often hailed as the West's first autobiography. In
Confessions, Augustine paints a rich and textured portrait of his relationships
with family and friends, his early career as a professor of rhetoric, his shifting
philosophical and theological loyalties, and his ultimate conversion to Christianity, offering a vivid and poetic account of his spiritual awakening. When
many political theorists consider how Augustine's life shapes his thought, *Confessions* is often their first and only port of call.

Yet we must be careful not to let *Confessions* bear all the historical weight
in interpreting Augustine's life and work. As we saw in chapter 5, *Confessions*
is as much of an "anti-autobiography" as an autobiography, a narrative that
casts God as the ultimate author of Augustine's story.[2] Throughout *Confessions*,

Augustine repeatedly warns readers against presuming too much, either about others or themselves. His claim to be an "enigma" to himself highlights the limits of self-knowledge.[3]

Even if we set these considerations aside, there is another reason to go beyond *Confessions*: the narrative was written in 396–397 during his early years as Bishop of Hippo, more than thirty years before his death in 430 at age 76 and before his most active period of engagement as a bishop and citizen in the Roman empire. The early narrative of *Confessions* reveals nothing about the last half of his life, the time of his most controversial disputes with Roman officials, Catholic bishops, and religious critics. As one commentator puts it, "The man in his forties who wrote the *Confessions* is [so] well-known to us . . . that we are sometimes in danger of making the older Augustine merely ancillary to his younger self."[4]

Luckily, Augustine supplies rich historical evidence of his later life and work in extensive correspondence with Roman officials, Christian bishops, and friends soliciting spiritual or political advice. These letters—numbering in the hundreds—are a treasure trove for scholars interested in Augustine's civic engagement and the social and political conditions that shaped his moral and theological vision. Surprisingly, however, many standard accounts of Augustine's political thought, especially those that focus on his "pessimism," hardly engage these epistles at all, focusing instead on *Confessions* or *City of God*.[5]

Recently, scholars in history, theology, and religious studies have highlighted the significance of Augustine's letters as distinctly political writings.[6] His letters not only illuminate and amplify Augustine's political concepts and commitments, but they also show him applying his theological and political ideas to practical contexts and lived experiences in ways that complicate received understandings of his thought, belying his occasionally polemical rhetoric and the doctrinal conclusions they tend to license. For our purposes in particular, his letters challenge the view of Augustine as an otherworldly escapist encouraging retreat into the church. Instead, they present him as an example of political hope who actively participates in Roman political life and seeks common objects of hope with diverse citizens.

This attention to Augustine's life is particularly important given the account of rhetoric I brought into view in earlier chapters. A central claim of this book is that Augustine's rhetorical context significantly shapes his pedagogical and political purposes. A prominent strand of the ancient rhetorical tradition that Augustine inherited focuses on the *life* and *character* of a speaker as important means of persuasion. Aristotle included *ethos*, or character, as one of three available forms of rhetorical proof, alongside rational arguments (*logos*) and emotional appeals (*pathos*),[7] while later Roman rhetoricians emphasized the importance of presenting examples (*exempla*) as an effective form of persuasion. Yet, as George Kennedy argues, the Roman emphasis on rhetorical style and technique sometimes minimized the role of *ethos*.[8] One of Augustine's contributions, Kennedy suggests, is that he "revives ethos as a major factor in rhetoric, though not ethos as projected in a speech, which is what Aristotle discussed," but as a form of character and "moral authority" exhibited in "the life of the teacher."[9]

Augustine emphasizes exemplarity in *On Christian Teaching*: "More important than any amount of grandeur of style . . . is the life of the speaker."[10] While Augustine acknowledges that "eloquent but evil" speakers can "benefit many people by preaching what they do not practice," "they would benefit far more people if they practiced what they preached."[11] Augustine thus urges the teacher "to live in such a way that he not only gains a reward for himself but also gives an example to others, so that his way of life becomes, in a sense, an abundant source of eloquence."[12] "In a brief but bold affirmation that itself is a masterpiece of rhetorical understatement," Thomas Martin comments, "Augustine proposes that the way one lives (*forma uiuendi*) can have the same discursive potential as the very heights of rhetorical mastery (*copia dicendi*)."[13] The best teachers are those whose life is a form of persuasion.

Noting how Augustine's attention to the persuasive power of a "way of living" has been neglected by most commentators, Martin shows how Augustine's "rhetorically based vision" of exemplarity sheds new light on his understanding of the monastic community, highlighting how Christian priests and monks are called to be "persuasive" public examples to those within and beyond the ecclesia.[14] I want to extend Martin's rightful emphasis on the rhetoric of lived example beyond the bounds of the church into the realm of public life.

While Augustine's primary aim in *On Christian Teaching* is to instruct Christian preachers and lay people, he also emphasizes the rhetorical importance of examples in correspondence with political leaders. In encouraging Roman officials to show mercy in their punishments, for instance, he suggests Christian bishops are pleading for leniency partly to set "an example of gentleness in order to win love for the word of truth."[15] In a letter to Marcellinus, he exhorts the Roman tribune to do the same: "[S]often the harshness of your judgements and do not forget to set an example of your faith (for you are sons of the Church) and of the gentleness that belongs to your mother herself."[16]

Augustine's appeal to examples is not confined to correspondence with Christians. He also highlights positive and negative examples of Roman leaders in a letter to Nectarius and appeals to Nectarius's own "example" to discourage him from having a negative impact across the region.[17] In resisting Nectarius's plea for leniency for pagan rioters in Calama who had stoned the church, killed a monk, and hunted the bishop, Augustine emphasizes the importance of their "example" and the need to deter others from following it.[18] While he affirms the need for "Christian gentleness," "mercy," and "moderation" to avoid excessive punishment, he does not believe the accused should go unpunished, lest they leave "destructive examples in the city for others to imitate."[19]

Augustine's emphasis on examples as a rhetorical form highlights an aspect of his political thought often submerged by an exclusive focus on his explicit utterances: Augustine sees his life itself as a potential means of teaching and persuasion. In this chapter, I apply this lesson to Augustine's own example of citizenship. As Ambrose, Victorinus, and Monica served as exemplars of hope for Augustine, so, I argue, Augustine is an example of hope for his congregants and citizens. A closer look at Augustine's political life in letters reveals how he attempted, albeit imperfectly, to practice what he preached.

Part I considers Augustine's explicit claim that Christianity is not incompatible with the "practices of the commonwealth," a claim he embodies in his political advocacy in the Roman Empire. I consider how he counsels others engaged in public life and examine episodes where he uses his rhetorical skill, political influence, and ecclesial connections to free enslaved persons, advocate for people who were poor, and oppose torture and capital punishment. I also consider Augustine's views on the duties and burdens of public service and respond to one prominent interpreter who draws on Augustine's correspondence as evidence of his "pessimism." Part II extends this argument by considering how Augustine's example commends a "liturgy of citizenship,"[20] suggesting ways the political community can provide citizens with opportunities to train their virtues and participate in the City of God.

I. Augustine and the Ethics of Citizenship

As we saw in the previous chapter, some Augustinian communitarians invoke the Bishop of Hippo to encourage Christians to focus first on *being the Church*. For John Milbank, Augustine's vision of the church as a "counter-kingdom" exposes the ontology of violence at the heart of contemporary politics and shows how citizens should enact love, peace, and hope in this world.[21]

According to Stanley Hauerwas, Augustine insists that "the church is the only true political society, because only in the church are we directed to worship the one true God. Only through the church do we have the resources necessary for our desires to be rightly ordered, for the virtues to be rightly formed."[22] Communitarians are right to claim that Augustine saw the church as the foundational community for Christian citizens, one that challenged the imperial order.[23] Nevertheless, the bishop does not consider the institutional church to be the only site of participation in the heavenly city. As the previous chapter suggested, his account of eschatology, ecclesiology, and politics in the *saeculum* challenges a strict opposition between church and world. Here, I want to extend that argument by highlighting how Augustine's civic engagement in the Roman Empire challenges claims about his political passivity and ecclesial isolationism.

Throughout his correspondence with Roman officials and Christian bishops, Augustine encourages and enacts a robust ethic of citizenship. Rather than simply counseling hostility toward politics, he rejects the accusation that Christianity is incompatible with the "ethics of citizenship" or "practices of the commonwealth" (*rei publicae moribus*).[24] As Joseph Clair highlights, Augustine makes the compatibility clear in letters to Marcellinus and Volusian, where he refutes the charge that the Christian religion is an "enemy of the state" (*inimica republicae*).[25] Surveying the writings of Cicero, Augustine argues the Christian religion "would establish, consecrate, strengthen, and increase the state far better than Romulus, Numa, Brutus, and those other illustrious men of the Roman nation have." After all, "what is the state but something belonging to the people? It is, therefore, something common, something, of course, belonging to the city. But what is a city but a multitude of human beings brought into some bond of harmonious unity [*concordia*]?"[26] Christians, he continues, can contribute to this concord, for "even someone apart from that religion" can recognize the spirit behind Christianity's "great commandments of harmonious unity," all of which encourage acts of love, mercy, and sacrifice that facilitate peace among citizens.[27] For Augustine, "there is nothing more useful for the city" than this peaceful concord.[28]

As a Christian bishop, Augustine might have preferred that the Christian religion serve as the bond that unites all citizens, but against Eusebius's insistence on Christian theocracy, Augustine does not require religious uniformity as a condition of a commonwealth.[29] Instead, as we saw in the previous chapter, he recognizes the need for diverse societies to maintain political forms appropriate to their cultural conditions.[30] Rather than encouraging the overthrow of secular government or instituting a theocracy, Augustine follows Paul's admonition in Romans 13 to respect the "governing authorities," even if they do not perfectly reflect the heavenly city.[31] Given contingent cultural, political, and historical traditions, political communities will comprise a wide and diverse array of "customs, laws, and institutions" that "tend towards the same end of earthly peace."[32] Augustine thus encourages Christians "to obey the laws of the earthly city, whereby the things necessary for the support of this mortal life are administered," so long as these laws and customs "do not impede the religion by which we are taught that the one supreme and true God is to be worshipped."[33] Here, it might seem that Augustine identifies the violation of religious liberty (rather than other forms of domination or injustice) as the only legitimate reason for civil disobedience. Yet, as I will suggest below, Augustine holds that "worship" (*latreia*) involves not only participating in religious sacraments but also enacting forms of justice, service, and sacrifice that reflect love of God and neighbor.[34] Accordingly, his caveat about worship above implies that other forms of earthly injustice or domination may also require criticism, resistance, or refusal. Thus, even in encouraging Christians to obey the law to secure civic peace, Augustine situates temporal citizenship within the context of heavenly citizenship, suggesting that God's standards of justice and love place some limits on obedience to earthly laws and commonwealths.[35] This is why Augustine can suggest, as Martin Luther King Jr. famously notes, that "[a]n unjust law is no law at all."[36]

Augustine's own political engagement reflected his views of service and citizenship in light of love of God and neighbor. As a pastor and bishop, he occupied an important office in the Roman Empire, advocating on behalf of moral causes and organizing bishops, congregants, and citizens to address specific political and legal challenges.[37] It is perhaps no surprise that some contemporary scholars have noted Augustinian affinities in activists such as King[38] and community organizers such as Saul Alinsky.[39] Augustine's example of practical involvement in politics provides another challenge to Augustinian pessimism: his virtue of hope finds expression in political engagement, not otherworldly escape.[40]

Augustine's Political Engagement

After Christianity became the official religion of the Roman Empire in the fourth century, Christian priests and bishops began to wield significant power on matters both theological and political.[41] By the time Augustine became a priest in 391 and a bishop in 395, the political power of ecclesiastical leaders had increased significantly. Under Augustine's leadership, it would grow even more. As Robert Dodaro argues, Augustine did not hesitate to use the power of his office to engage in a kind of "political activism."[42]

Drawing on neglected sermons and letters, Dodaro traces the multiple modes of Augustine's political engagement, noting his frequent efforts on behalf of those subject to imperial power. Like a tribune in the Roman republic, Augustine saw intercession with magistrates on behalf of citizens as a responsibility of his ecclesial and political office.[43] As Bishop of Hippo, he frequently pleaded with Roman officials to grant clemency to criminals, particularly those sentenced to death, describing such intervention as an imperative of his faith.[44] In Letter 153 to Macedonius, he cites Jesus's example of saving a woman from a stoning to justify his "duty of intercession" and discourage cruelty and retribution among those who wield power.[45] While Macedonius's "strictness" can inspire fear that encourages criminals to do good, Augustine argues his intercession is also "beneficial" since it tempers Macedonius's strictness. No punishment should be given "out of a desire to inflict harm, but everything out of love of serving others." For Augustine, "both chastisement and pardon have a place in the successful reform of human life."[46]

Augustine's emphasis on "successful reform" highlights one of his key objections to capital punishment: the finality of the death penalty forecloses any possibility for human beings to repent and reform. As he writes to Macedonius, "[T]here is no space to reform character except in this life. After that, each person will have whatever he has won for himself here. That is why we are forced to intercede for the guilty, out of love for the human race. For otherwise punishment will end this life for them, and once it is ended, they will not be able to bring their punishment to an end."[47] Augustine makes a similar claim in a letter to Donatus:

> We do not ask for vengeance on our enemies on this earth. . . . We love our enemies and we pray for them. . . . That is why we desire their reform and not their deaths, through the intervention of judges and laws that inspire fear, so that they will not meet with the punishment of everlasting judgement. We do not want you to neglect their correction; but neither do we want you to impose the punishments they deserve. Restrain their sins, therefore, in such a way that they will live to repent of having sinned.[48]

Throughout his letters, Augustine recommends reforming criminals' characters rather than taking their lives, urging "humanity" and "gentleness" even against Donatists who had killed one of his fellow priests in the Catholic church.[49]

Augustine also voiced strong opposition to torture at a time when it was widely accepted.[50] In a letter to Nectarius, he affirms the need to reform rioters who attacked Christians in Calama but rejects the use of physical torture, describing it as "abhorrent to our way of thinking."[51] In other letters, he pleaded with Roman officials to avoid using torture as a form of interrogation or punishment, encouraging them to exercise "mercy" and "humanity" and "set an example of Catholic gentleness."[52] While he recognized the need for punishment, deterrence, and "public peace," he opposed torture and extreme punishment as inhumane.[53] In one sermon, he explains that he refused a major bequest of ships to the church because he was afraid of implicating the church in torture if the sailors lost a vessel.[54]

Augustine's opposition to torture in his letters provides a stark contrast to the common interpretation of *City of God* 19.6, where he seems to suggest the "wise judge" may be required to torture out of "necessity" in the face of "unavoidable ignorance" and "unavoidable duty."[55] Most interpreters, like Peter Iver Kaufman, take this passage as a "grudging endorsement of torture."[56] Citing 19.6 as evidence of Augustine's "utilitarian" and "non-ideal theory of justice," Terrance McConnell suggests that Augustine "approved of the practice of torture because he believed it was necessary for maintaining peace and order."[57] Herbert Deane cites 19.6 as evidence that Augustine views torture as a "grim necessity of criminal justice" that shows the state cannot "be truly just," while Robert Markus suggests torture by the "conscientious judge" reflects "the mature complexity of Augustine's attitude to social institutions."[58]

Yet, as Veronica Roberts Ogle has compellingly argued, the larger context of this passage in *City of God* resists such a reading.[59] 19.6 is part of Augustine's extended critique of Stoic accounts of happiness and virtue, which rely, in part, on "equanimity" (*apatheia*), the quality of being unmoved by passions. Stoics maintain the wise person will be "happy" insofar as their equanimity enables them to be undisturbed by the passions and pain that accompany life in this world. On Ogle's close reading, Augustine's analysis in 19.6 shows that even the "wise judge"—a paradigm of Stoic wisdom and justice—cannot avoid suffering, and that, because of his commitment to equanimity, he cannot recognize or feel the suffering of others, including innocent people who are tortured. In this context, Augustine's account is a critique of the Stoic judge's lack of compassion (*misercordia*) and humanity (*humanitas*) rather than an endorsement of torture.[60] As Ogle concludes, 19.6 is not "an apology for the politics of necessity. If anything, it calls predominant views on judicial necessity into question."[61] Ogle bolsters this interpretation by drawing extensively on Augustine's letters to political officials, which show "a remarkably consistent emphasis on *humanitas*" in his efforts to discourage torture and temper excessive punishment.[62] While Augustine could not envision changing the entire Roman system of law and punishment,[63] his example of compassion and humanity challenges those who invoke Augustinian authority to justify torture or "coercive interrogation" in our own time.[64]

That Augustine opposed torture and excessive punishment, of course, does not mean he rejected all forms of coercion. In fact, Augustine defended coercing Christian schismatics to rejoin the Catholic communion, a position that, according to John von Heyking, "may be the most vexing problem in all of Augustine's political thought."[65] It is one that generates strong criticism from defenders and detractors alike.[66]

In recent decades, scholars have considered how Augustine's political, religious, and rhetorical contexts might illuminate his defense of coercing Donatists to rejoin the Catholic communion. Elsewhere, I survey four approaches to contextualizing Augustine's position on the coercion of Donatists.[67] First, von Heyking and Deane take what I call a "developmental approach" that traces Augustine's evolution on the issue. They emphasize that Augustine only gradually accepted the coercion of Donatists after witnessing increased violence from Circumcellions and seeing coercion's effectiveness in reforming Donatists.[68] Second, Peter Brown and John Bowlin advance a "justificatory approach," emphasizing Augustine's efforts to provide justifications for coercing Donatists (and limiting its use) at a time when it was widely accepted and often violent.[69] For Bowlin, "[I]t is this reason-giving enterprise, this attempt to make sense of a practice that most of his contemporaries consider morally unproblematic, that distinguishes Augustine, not his participation in this or that persecution. Without his persistent efforts he would have been just another thoughtlessly intolerant North African bishop."[70] Third, Brown, von Heyking, and Jill Harries take a "rhetorical approach" that examines Augustine's use of excessive rhetoric to construct authority, educate opponents, and persuade Roman officials to enforce the law.[71] Although potentially troubling to contemporary readers, Augustine's sharp and aggressive tone may have been used to challenge recalcitrant Roman officials who were more inclined toward physical violence than Augustine wished them to be.[72] Finally, I supplement these accounts with a "republican" approach that shows how Augustine's justifications for coercing Donatists reflect Roman commitments to "1) liberty as non-domination, 2) legitimate authority and the rule of law as constraints on arbitrary power, and 3) contestability, publicity, and immanent critique as means of preventing domination and holding power accountable."[73] When combined, these approaches show that Augustine was more sensitive to liberty, justice, and accountability than most interpreters allow, challenging an imperial order that simply took violent coercion for granted.[74] Yet the fact that he ultimately defended coercion for religious purposes reminds us of how far Augustine's context is from that of many contemporary democracies.

Beyond his engagement with the Donatists, Augustine occasionally had to enforce Roman law as a member of the "bishop's tribunal" or "episcopal court," where he arbitrated civil disputes over property, debts, and contracts among claimants who sought to have their cases heard by the bishop.[75] As John Lamoreaux notes, the episcopal court was "immensely popular" among Romans in Augustine's time.[76] Since episcopal courts did not require bribes to be paid to the magistrates, they were less corrupt than secular courts and often less violent.[77] Unlike secular judges who frequently resorted to extreme forms of interrogation or punishment, Christian bishops refrained from using torture, meted out less severe punishments, and often sought compromise between opposing parties, allowing disputants to save face.[78] And because there was no right to appeal a decision of the bishop, the episcopal court led to swifter resolutions and were less costly to poor defendants who could not afford the multiple appeals that would advantage the wealthy, who could use the time and cost of appeals to encourage poorer defendants to abandon their suit.[79] As Ogle argues, these features made the episcopal courts "an alternative justice system that strove to operate on the principle of *humanitas*."[80] Although Augustine sometimes complained about his judicial duties, he nonetheless encouraged Christians to take their cases to the episcopal courts, and he dedicated many mornings to fulfilling his judicial duties, sometimes fasting all day in order to hear cases.[81] He provided mediation, delivered judgments, imposed fines, and handed down sentences, all with the binding authority of law.[82] And since he had no professional legal training, he spent additional time studying Roman law and solicited legal advice from a professional expert named Eustochius, investing a significant amount of time, money, and energy to become a more discerning judge and advocate.[83] Rather than disengaging from the system, Dodaro argues, Augustine tried to learn its laws and institutions to be more effective within it.[84]

Augustine frequently parlayed his legal and political knowledge to address social injustices and advocate for the most vulnerable. As Dodaro observes,

Augustine's extensive legal activism on behalf of criminal defendants reflects "how easy it was in Augustine's day for poorer members of society to be criminalized on account of inequities introduced and maintained through political structures, such as the unjust and oppressive distribution of the tax burden."[85] But tax burdens were not the only forms of inequity that Augustine challenged. He also sought to combat other forms of economic, social, and political domination. In 428, for example, he petitioned his friend and fellow bishop, Alypius, to intervene with the emperor in Italy to stop slave traders from kidnapping free citizens and selling them overseas. Augustine drafted a detailed memorandum outlining this "wicked form of commerce" and enclosed a copy of the law that the Emperor Honorius had decreed to prohibit the practice.[86] In this instance, the rule of law became a means of exposing domination and safeguarding the liberty, health, and well-being of citizens. Yet, as discussed in chapter 6, the fact that he upheld the rule of law in relation to those who were not free citizens but considered "slaves" in Roman law shows the limits of his activism, even as he sought to encourage accountability among masters and reduce some of slavery's worst effects.[87]

In another case, Augustine appealed to the rule of law to protect a tenant farmer whose affluent landowner had accused him of a crime. After being arrested, the farmer was sent to await trial in another jurisdiction in violation of Roman law. Recognizing how economic power could be parlayed into political influence, Augustine feared the landowner might exploit his "great wealth" to exert political power and persuade the military governor either to convict the farmer or use torture to elicit a confession.[88] So that "money may not prevail before the court," Augustine wrote to imperial officials requesting that the farmer be granted the requisite thirty-day period to prepare his defense and that the trial be moved back to the municipal court in Hippo, as law required.[89] Augustine enclosed a copy of the edict to remind officials of the law and enlisted a local bishop to present his case to the governor in the province where the farmer had been sent.[90] This episode reveals the great lengths to which Augustine went to use his legal knowledge, personal connections, and ecclesial authority to defend "the civil rights of the poor" against the arbitrary power exercised by economic and political elites.[91] It also reveals how Augustine frequently coordinated his political activity with other bishops, priests, and laypeople in the church. As Dodaro argues, Augustine's letters leave "the clear impression of an African church capable, against almost all odds, of undertaking an extremely limited level of coordinated political activity in support of social justice."[92]

Augustine's political coordination with bishops went beyond the local level. As a member of larger church councils, he met regularly with other African bishops to articulate stated positions on doctrinal issues, develop ecclesial rules and regulations, and respond to heretical or imperial challenges. While many of these councils focused on matters of church doctrine, bishops also used their regular meetings and unified authority to "apply delicate, diplomatic pressure to the imperial court in order to redress social and political injustices occurring within Roman Africa."[93] Dodaro catalogues numerous examples of church councils seeking political reform on behalf of people who were enslaved, indebted, or poor.[94] Peter Brown suggests the bishops' "capacity for collective action made them the most formidable pressure group in Latin Christianity."[95]

Augustine was an active leader in this group and continued his leadership back in Hippo.[96] In letters, sermons, and treatises, he exhorted audiences to give alms and practice other "works of mercy" as expressions of Christian love, a way for pilgrims to invest their "hope" in heaven.[97] One letter reveals Augustine taking up a collection at church to help a member of his congregation repay a debt,[98] and Possidius reports that Augustine melted some of his church's chalices to help the needy and purchase the freedom of people who were enslaved.[99] In *City of God*, he celebrates the Christian practice of maintaining a common fund and distributing it to those in need,[100] and as bishop, he attempted to alleviate the worst effects of poverty and domination. His desire to serve the city even influenced his decision of where to locate his monastery. Unlike early church fathers who founded monasteries in the desert to escape the corrupting influences of the world, Robert Markus notes, Augustine chose to locate his in the city to make it more public, offering yet another way to engage the world.[101] These actions suggest that Augustine's leadership and citizenship is animated by a hope to improve public life in ways that were meaningful for many who were vulnerable to its worst effects.

Augustine's Political Counsel

In addition to his advocacy and activism, Augustine praised public officials for their service. He opens a letter to Macedonius, a fellow Christian, by commending his service to the commonwealth: "You are a man extremely busy with your involvement in public life and very attentive to the interests of others rather than your own. I congratulate you, and human affairs, too, on this."[102] In addition to praising Christian public officials and celebrating Roman leaders from Regulus to Cato,[103] he commends the pagan public official Nectarius for being willing to serve his "home-town" (*patria*) in his old age.[104] "I am not reluctant, but rather delighted," Augustine writes, "to see you not only recalling accurately, but also showing by your life and your behaviour, that 'a good man's service of his home-town has no limit or terminus.'"[105] Although Augustine encourages Nectarius to serve a "much finer city"—the City of God— the bishop nonetheless commends Nectarius's civil service.

Most strikingly, rather than discouraging Christians from being involved in politics, he actively encourages them to govern and serve. Augustine's exchange with Boniface, a Roman military official, is perhaps most instructive.[106] When Boniface was considering abandoning his office and all "worldly activities" to join a monastery, Augustine made a long and difficult journey with his friend Alypius to encourage Boniface to remain in public life.[107] While Augustine commends Boniface's "hope in Christ Jesus our Lord" and affirms that a monastic life of renunciation holds a "higher place" with God, he encourages Boniface to stay in office to fulfill his vocation, protect the commonwealth, and practice Christian virtue.[108] According to Augustine, Boniface's political and military service is not only compatible with love of God and neighbor but necessary to preserve peace and defend the province against enemy invaders.[109] Augustine's counsel to Boniface highlights his emphasis on temporal peace and subverts any simple suggestion that Augustinian hope entails political passivity or ecclesial escape.[110]

Yet the case of Boniface also reveals that Augustine's endorsement of civic engagement is not unconditional. After Boniface and Augustine exchanged letters in 417, Boniface gradually ascended the ranks of the Roman army to become a special commander. After a series of events in 427, Boniface joined a conspiracy against rival generals and took up arms against Roman soldiers. While Boniface remained embattled in the rebellion, Augustine wrote a letter in 428 admonishing him to lay down his sword against the Roman Empire and either return to his post protecting the province against Vandals or give up his command entirely.[111] Augustine chastises Boniface for neglecting his role-specific responsibilities for the people he was commissioned to protect: "The barbarians of Africa are succeeding here without meeting any resistance so long as you are in your present state, preoccupied with your own needs, and are organising nothing to prevent this disaster."[112] As Clair highlights, Augustine attributes Boniface's dereliction of duty to disordered loves.[113] When Augustine had previously encouraged Boniface to remain in office, he assumed Boniface would use his power virtuously to secure the peace of the commonwealth, but over the next decade, Boniface had ignored Augustine's admonitions, seeking temporal goods of power and wealth for private purposes rather than using them to serve the common good. His perverse loves fueled a lust for domination. Augustine thus encourages Boniface to reorder his love and hope, in part, by following Christ, who taught the need to "disdain rather than love the goods of the world, and to love and hope from him for the future that he revealed in his own resurrection."[114] "[D]on't love the goods of this earth, however plentiful you may possess them," Augustine writes. "Make use of them in this way: do much with them, but no evil for their sake."[115]

If we focused only on this second letter, it might seem that Augustine denies the legitimacy of hoping for political goods and encourages Boniface to train his hope solely on the heavenly city. But we have already seen that Augustine advised Boniface to remain in his post a decade earlier. Even in his later letter, Augustine affirms that political power, influence, strength, and wealth are "good things."[116] He simply insists that Boniface ought "to make use of this world as if you were not using it; to do good with its good things, rather than to become bad."[117] Here, Augustine uses strong rhetoric and scriptural antitheses between love of the world and love of God to reorder Boniface's loves and hopes. He concludes by exhorting the general to renounce his position and seek the spiritual life: "I should also add something that we forbade you to do then: that now, in so far as you might without jeopardizing peace in human affairs, you should withdraw from the affairs of war and give yourself leisure for a life in the fellowship of the holy."[118]

As Clair observes, Augustine's advice to Boniface—both in 417 and 428—aligns with his understanding of virtue as rightly ordered love.[119] Power is not bad in itself; it is only the perverse use of power that is problematic.[120] Augustine allows and even encourages Boniface's pursuit and use of political power when they are properly ordered to common goods such as civic peace and eternal goods such as spiritual wellbeing, but when Boniface's loves become disordered, Augustine exhorts him to renounce public affairs and seek fellowship with those whose character will shape his. In both cases, Augustine's advice reflects a concern about Boniface's fulfillment of his role-related responsibilities. Rightly ordered love and hope requires the virtue of prudence to attend to particular circumstances, contexts, and duties that accompany one's role, a virtue that Boniface lacks when he seeks his own private goods rather than the goods of both the eternal and temporal commonwealth.[121] Here, Augustine's advice about political engagement parallels his advice about other temporal goods: he does not suggest that leaders should have no love or hope for political goods; he simply wants that love and hope to be rightly ordered.

The Duties and Burdens of Public Service

In defining the "two cities" by their "loves," Augustine contrasts each city's approach to rule: members of the earthly city rule with the "lust for mastery," while members of the heavenly city "serve one another in charity."[122] Augustine's correspondence with Roman officials and extensive engagement in the Roman Empire show that he believes politics can be one way to "serve one another in charity." This may be why Arendt, in discussing the "disappearance of the ancient city-state," suggests that "Augustine seems to have been the last to know at least what it once meant to be a citizen."[123]

Yet Arendt also notes that Augustine considered the "active life" a "burden," which points to a prominent feature of Augustine's view of civic engagement.[124] While Augustine encouraged Christian citizens and leaders to be involved in politics to secure the justice, peace, and health of the commonwealth, he did not believe they should "enjoy" rule for its own sake, resting in it as their final end or ultimate source of satisfaction. Expressing his characteristic concern about pride, Augustine argues that those who live an "active life" ought "not to love the honour or power which this kind of life affords, since 'all things under the sun are vanity.' Rather . . . we should seek to use that same honour or power righteously and beneficially, for the wellbeing of those under us, according to the will of God."[125]

The same applies for leaders of the church. The word "episcopate" in Greek, he explains, implies that someone "who is set over others 'oversees' them, that is, bears a responsibility for them."[126] Alluding to 1 Timothy 3:1 and emphasizing accountability and care, he argues that the episcopate "is the name of a duty, not an honour," and if the "burden" of service is "imposed on us," we should undertake it only "under the impetus of love": "[A] bishop who takes delight in ruling rather than in doing good is no true bishop."[127] As Kaufman emphasizes, Augustine's worry is that Christian bishops and Roman officials who become "local celebrities" will become entranced by their own glory and lust for domination.[128] Taking delight in ruling will lead them to care more about power than peace, a tendency that Augustine's experience with Boniface only affirmed.

Augustine's attitude toward office-holding characterizes his ambivalent relationship to power in the Catholic Church and Roman Empire, which is marked more by groaning under duty than delighting in rule. As Possidius tells us, Augustine wept profusely when he was conscripted to become a priest in Hippo in 391, "bemoaning the many great dangers to his way of life that he anticipated would come crowding on him if he had to govern and direct the church."[129] Augustine explains his tears in a letter to the bishop who ordained him and begs Valerius for a leave to study the scriptures before starting "such work as now torments and crushes me."[130] Augustine opens with a reflection on the burdens of ecclesial service:

[I]n this life, and especially at this time, nothing is easier, more pleasant, and more attractive for men than the office of bishop, priest, or deacon, if the task is carried out perfunctorily or in a self-serving manner, but that before God nothing is more miserable, more sad, and more worthy of condemnation. Likewise, nothing in this life, and especially at this time, is more difficult, more laborious, and more dangerous than the office of a bishop, priest, or deacon. But before God nothing is more blessed if one soldiers as our emperor commands![131]

Twenty years later at the ordination of another bishop, he provides advice he might have needed at his own ordination: "The man, you see, who presides over the people ought first of all to understand that he is the servant of many masters. And let him not disdain this role; let him not, I repeat, disdain to be the servant of many people, because the Lord of lords did not disdain to serve us."[132] He acknowledges his sermon is meant to give "encouragement" to himself as much as offer "sound advice" to the bishop and "sound doctrine" to the congregation.[133] Citing scriptural passages where Christ humbled himself to be a servant, Augustine elevates Christ's "example" of "service" and "humility" to exhort the bishop and congregation to emulate it.[134] Taken as a whole, the sermon is a striking meditation on Augustine's vision of servant leadership.[135]

Although he eventually embraced the duties of service, Augustine occasionally lamented its burdens. This is especially clear in one of his most important homilies of hope.[136] On the thirtieth anniversary of his ordination, he explains the "burden" and "danger" of being a bishop who is ultimately held accountable for his flock:

Even if I have to think about the weight of it day and night, still this anniversary somehow or other thrusts it on my consciousness in such a way that I am absolutely unable to avoid reflecting on it. And the more the years increase, or rather decrease, and bring me nearer to my last day, which of course is undoubtedly going to come some time or other, the sharper my thoughts become, and ever more full of needles, about what sort of account I can give for you to the Lord our God. This, you see, is the difference between each one of you and me, that you, practically speaking, are only going to render an account for yourselves alone, while I shall be giving one both for myself and for you. That's why the burden is so much greater; but carried well it wins greater glory, while if it is handled unfaithfully, it hurls one down into the most appalling punishment.[137]

Augustine worries he will rest in others' praise and, in his pride, fail to challenge congregants to live better, which will make him culpable both to his church and to God, with potentially damning consequences.[138] Augustine admits he would forfeit this burden if he did not consider it his divine duty: "There's nothing better, nothing more pleasant than to search through the divine treasure chest with nobody making a commotion. . . . But to preach, to refute, to rebuke, to build up, to manage for everybody, that's a great burden, a great weight, a great labor. Who wouldn't run away from this labor?"[139] "But," he concludes, "the gospel terrifies me."[140]

Augustine held a similar attitude toward the duties and burdens that accompany bishops' political and legal offices. In a letter to an abbot named Eudoxius, Augustine describes the "difficult labors" that accompany his political role and asks the abbot and his monks to pray for him.[141] Elsewhere, he laments to his parishioners that their needs "compel me to go where I would much rather not":

[T]o stand outside the door, to wait while the worthy and the unworthy go in, to be announced, to be scarcely admitted sometimes, to put up with little humiliations, to beg, sometimes to obtain a favor, sometimes to depart in sadness. Who would want to endure such things, unless I was forced to? Let me be, let me not have to endure all that, don't let anybody force me to. Look, as a little concession to me, give me a holiday from this business. I beg you, I beseech you, don't let anybody force me to it; I don't want to have to deal with the authorities. He knows, I'm forced to do so.[142]

As Possidius writes, Augustine spent significant time writing "letters to various people about their temporal affairs. But this he regarded as forced labor that took him away from better things. What he really enjoyed was addressing or conversing with the brethren about the things of God in the intimacy of the home circle."[143] For this reason, Kaufman writes, Augustine occasionally saw "political practice as a set of snares."[144] Nevertheless, he remained an effective advocate and adjudicator, earning praise for his fairness and service from Christian bishops and Roman officials alike.[145]

Reconsidering Augustine's "Pessimism"

Augustine's personal ambivalence toward his political responsibilities might suggest his ethic of engagement precludes any hope for politics. Defending a "politically pessimistic Augustine," Peter Iver Kaufman offers the most sophisticated interpretation of Augustine's pessimism, arguing that Augustine's reflections on the burdens of service and correspondence with public officials confirm he saw politics merely as a form of "damage control."[146] Considering Kaufman's account can help to illuminate how some interpreters take Augustine's political engagement to exemplify pessimism rather than hope.

Channeling Arendt and echoing Milbank, Kaufman suggests that Augustine counsels "strategic withdrawal" and "temperamental disengagement" from politics, advocating a "communitarian alternative" that involved participating in "alternative communities"—such as the church, monastery, or communities he gathered at Cassiciacum and Thagaste—that were free of the corrupting influence of politics.[147] In explicating Augustine's "predominantly pessimistic outlook," Kaufman offers a series of rhetorically powerful antitheses to press his case.[148] He argues, for example, that, according to Augustine, Christians should "transcend rather than transform the social and political order," be "helpful" rather than "hopeful," and practice "patience, not politics."[149] In using these antitheses, Kaufman is Augustine's faithful follower and notes how the bishop uses antitheses to "mark the contrast" between the earthly and heavenly cities.[150] Yet, as we saw in chapters 6 and 7, while antitheses can serve important rhetorical purposes, they do not always capture the nuance of a particular position or relationship. In places, Kaufman is careful to note that, despite his purported pessimism, Augustine believes that Christians must serve in politics if asked or appointed and that law, public policy, and "positive political results" are not "meaningless."[151]

But Kaufman's potent antitheses can at times obscure the nuance he offers here and elsewhere. One example is his claim that, for Augustine, government could be "used but not improved," a phrase that Kaufman makes the title of one of his chapters.[152] It is clear from Augustine's extensive correspondence with public officials, however, that he did actually hope to improve the lives and character of specific political leaders and the ways they enacted their commitments within the political community. Because of the influential role that officeholders held in making, moderating, and enforcing law in the Roman Empire, Augustine believed that changing their conduct and character could in turn improve the political community. Kaufman therefore qualifies his claim in several places, suggesting that government could be used but not "meaningfully," "tellingly," or "appreciably" improved.[153] Similarly, he acknowledges that Augustine did not expect "significant political improvement" or "meaningful rehabilitations of political relations."[154] Kaufman does not specify precisely what "significant" or "meaningful" improvement entails, but he implies it is a matter of scope, sometimes equating significant political improvement with the "extensive, redemptive changes" or "progressive political reform" assumed by "optimists."[155]

In this sense, Kaufman is right—Augustine did not necessarily "expect" political society or laws to change dramatically or systematically.[156] Augustine recognized the limits of politics and the provisional nature of civic peace. But as we saw in chapter 1, hope is not the same as expectation. Hope involves possibility, not necessarily likelihood. One can hope for an outcome without necessarily expecting it.[157] Expectation can even be a form of presumption if it assumes more than the facts warrant. Moreover, "meaningful" or "significant" change need not involve systematic reform or "regime change."[158] One can hope for more localized changes in laws, practices, and officeholders without necessarily expecting a wholescale reform of political institutions or structures.

This is the kind of political hope that seems to characterize Augustine's own life. As Kaufman rightly notes, Augustine was not a radical revolutionary. While he frequently advocated on behalf of the poor and vulnerable and used his political, legal, and ecclesial power to resist some forms of injustice and domination, his personal engagement did not coalesce into anything as coherent or comprehensive as a systematic attempt at government reform, even though he did sometimes appeal to the emperor for changes in laws.[159] His politics was directed at a much more local level.[160] Most often, as Kaufman emphasizes elsewhere, Augustine sought to exercise influence on particular imperial or ecclesial officials rather than pursue wholesale reform, using a "personalist platform" of "admonitions, injunctions, and exhortations" to secure civic peace.[161] Such a personalist approach to soulcraft fits with his sense of pastoral responsibility as a shepherd of souls and preserver of peace, but it may also reflect a realistic assessment that the vast machinery of empire was nearly impossible to reform on his own.[162] By Augustine's lights, localized and "ad hoc" efforts to constrain behavior and shape character may have been the most effective forms of political engagement given the realities of his age.[163] This does not mean that Augustine was a pessimist; he simply knew the difference between presumption and hope.

In resisting ascriptions of political "hope" to Augustine, Kaufman seems to make several assumptions analyzed in previous chapters. For example, though he acknowledges Augustine's "more nuanced, ambiguous, realistic views about the possibilities of public life," he sometimes implies a futurist eschatology that separates "this world" from "the next" and overemphasizes the "not yet" nature of Augustine's hope, downplaying the ways that Augustine's inaugurated eschatology allows citizens to begin participating in the heavenly city here and now.[164] Moreover, his account sometimes implies a narrower, negative view of civic peace as the absence of violence and equates "politics" with "government," presupposing a remedial view of politics that primarily involves using coercive power to restrain sin rather than a more expansive, classical view that also includes the pursuit and promotion of common goods.[165]

In a similar vein, Veronica Roberts Ogle has questioned Kaufman's description of politics as a form of "damage control," arguing that "the duty with which Augustine charges leaders is better described as healing the damage from the root, rather than plugging holes in a faulty dam."[166] Citing Augustine's praise of Theodosius for seeking peace with his enemies and allowing them to retain their property, Ogle notes that Theodosius "not only controlled the negative effects of strife, but created a set of conditions that allowed for the reconciliation of former enemies."[167] "For Augustine," she argues, "the ability to bring about the restoration of peace is a positive power, and even a way of participating in God's healing work."[168] Ogle finds further evidence for this view in Augustine's intercession on behalf of those accused of crimes, where he commends not "leniency" but "mercy" that seeks to lovingly correct the wrongdoer and heal the relationships that have been sundered.[169] Ultimately, Ogle affirms that Augustine sees political engagement not simply as a potentially corrupting source of sin, but as "an opportunity for service," a chance to promote the well-being of neighbors and citizens.[170]

This emphasis on service fits with Augustine's conception of *latreia*, which he defines as "that service which pertains to the worship of God."[171] While Augustine emphasizes that worship involves the practice of the sacraments and sacrifices to God, he also quotes Micah 6:8 to suggest that "to do justly, love mercy, and walk humbly with thy God" are worthy sacrifices since they instantiate and encourage "love of God and neighbour."[172] "True sacrifices," he argues, "are works of mercy shown to ourselves or to our neighbors, and done with reference to God."[173] For this reason, several scholars have suggested that public service and political engagement—when rightly ordered— can be a proper form of sacrifice, a way to worship God by serving the neighbor with justice, mercy, and love.[174] Although Augustine celebrates the contemplative life and occasionally laments his lack of holy leisure, he recognizes the active life as an expression of "love": "For no one ought to live a life of leisure in such a way that he takes no thought in that leisure for the welfare of his neighbour."[175] Colleen E. Mitchell and Mary Keys draw on these and related passages to argue that "Augustine's best life is a mixture of contemplation and work, one founded in and held together by love, propelling one freely to undertake even arduous tasks of public service."[176] Ogle similarly suggests that Augustine's account of *latreia* challenges interpretations of his pessimism: "What makes Christianity hopeful is that every action incorporated into *latreia* is allowed to participate in God's work of healing the world."[177]

In more recent work, Kaufman has come closer to such a view, acknowledging that "damage control," "when narrowly conceived, connotes reaction rather than proactive efforts to control damage," but when "more broadly conceived— as it was intended," encompasses the "healing" and "promotion of conditions conducive to reconciliation" that Ogle affirms.[178] Here, Kaufman inches closer to the positions that Ogle and I defend, particularly given that a more expansive view of politics entails that the alternative communities he finds Augustine advocating can constitute proper objects of political hope. Nonetheless, Kaufman still characterizes the "distances" between our positions and his as "considerable."[179] Much of the distance reflects our differing views about the nature of hope and the status of politics in Augustine's thought.[180]

Throughout this essay, Kaufman largely avoids using the label "pessimism" to describe Augustine's political thought, which sidesteps concerns I have about earlier work where he frames debates about Augustine's political thought in terms of "optimism" and "pessimism."[181] Many other interpreters still embrace this binary.[182] Because they often identify hope with optimism—a form of positive thinking that requires a cheerful feeling or expectation about political possibilities—they argue that Augustine cannot be optimist and must be a pessimist. Yet, as I argued in chapter 7, this binary does not fit with Augustine's complex conception of hope as a mean between presumption and despair. Augustine's virtue of hope requires a careful and realistic appraisal of political difficulties and duties; otherwise, it would risk the vice of presumption rather than reflect rightly ordered hope.

Moreover, contrary to modern assumptions, hope is not necessarily tied to optimistic notions of "progress" or "change." As Jeffrey Stout argues in another context, "The question of hope is whether a difference can be made, not whether progress is being made or whether human beings will work it all out in the end. You are still making a difference when you are engaged in a success-ful holding action against forces that are conspiring to make things worse than they are. You are even making a difference when your actions simply keep things from worsening to the extent they would have worsened if you had not acted."[183] In this sense, even if some of Augustine's so-called "damage control" aims not at "an end to misery but . . . an avoidance of its 'increase,'" as Kaufman argues in an earlier essay,[184] the avoidance of worse suffering, injustice, and domination—as well as the continuation of institutions, relationships, and practices that prevent such worsening—can be legitimate objects of hope. The fact that political leaders "could only hope to make bad situations and corrupt systems a little less dreadful" still implies hope.[185] Hope need not always be directed toward positive change. The preservation and protection of civic peace and other uncertain political goods in the face of current and future threats can also be worthy objects of the virtue.[186]

As we saw in chapter 6, the fact that Augustine's virtue of hope does not necessarily require a cheerful mood or positive psychological profile makes hope compatible with "groaning" or "lament."[187] Lament can even be an expres-sion of hope, an indication that what one hopes for is not yet possessed and worth pursuing.[188] Indeed, Augustine often pairs "hope" with "groaning": "[T]he people making progress are the people groaning with longing for the Heavenly City . . . who by desiring that country cast their hope ahead like an an-chor."[189] While such groaning often "implies sadness," "there is a kind of groaning that also has room for joy."[190] This is why Augustine believes those who love God properly can be "happy in the hope of the world to come": "[I]f any man uses this life in such a way that he directs it toward that end which he so ardently loves and for which he so faithfully hopes, he may without absurdity be called happy even now, though by future hope than in present reality."[191] While Augustine ties happiness to hope for the heavenly city, that hope need not exclude hope for specific political goods as long as one refers such hope to God.

II. A Liturgy of Citizenship

If acts of public service and sacrifice can be a way to worship God and express rightly ordered love and hope, then this account challenges Augustinian com-munitarians who imply that worship requires avoiding politics to focus on being the church.[192] Politics can also be a labor and liturgy of love.[193]

Augustine's example of public engagement demonstrates this possibility, which is why prominent interpreters have invoked his authority to cast service to the political community not simply as a matter of duty but as a form of training for eternal life, a kind of partially proleptic participation in the City of God.[194] An Augustinian ethic of citizenship counsels neither a politics of limits focused solely on restraining sin, nor a sectarian vision of the church as the sole site of virtue. Rather, as Charles Mathewes argues, it envisions the political community as a training ground for virtue, a limited site of moral formation that offers citizens opportunities to seek peace and exercise the virtues of faith, hope, and love in response to fellow citizens.[195]

Several passages in Augustine's treatises and letters support this reading. In *City of God*, Augustine proclaims that citizens of the heavenly city "have a life in this age which is not in the least to be regretted: a life which is the school of eternity, in which they make use of earthly goods like pilgrims, without grasping after them, and are proved and corrected by evils."[196] He urges a similar training in his letter to Boniface when he was considering leaving the military for the monastery: "[I]t is necessary in this age for the citizens of the kingdom of heaven, surrounded as they are by the lost and the impious, to be vexed by temptations, so that they can be trained and tested *like gold in a furnace* [Wisd 3.5–6]. We oughtn't therefore before the time is right to wish to live only with the holy and the just; then we might deserve to be granted that in its proper time."[197] For Augustine, participation in the body politic can be an exercise of desire, a way to "train" hopes, loves, and longings in such a way that human beings are able to begin participating in the City of God.[198]

Developing this Augustinian insight, Mathewes argues that engagement in "public life" can even constitute a kind of "liturgy" (*leitourgia*)—literally, in Greek, a "work of the people"—aimed at facilitating civic and theological virtues.[199] Within the Christian tradition, liturgy refers to a set of religious and social practices that orient people of faith to God and encourage them to extend peace and love to neighbors, pointing them beyond time to eternity.[200] At the time same, liturgy creates and constitutes a temporal community oriented toward a common good here and now. It brings diverse people together in shared communal rituals to cultivate virtues, cement bonds of affection, and enact the community they seek. In this way, liturgy directs hopes toward two horizons—the temporal and the eternal, the "now" and the "not yet."[201] By considering the practice of political citizenship as a form of liturgy, Christian citizens can discover new ways to participate in God and enact peace on earth, participating in a form of shared community that challenges the sin, domination, and despair of the earthly city while simultaneously constituting a community able to imagine and partially embody an alternative future.[202]

Importantly, for Mathewes, the political practices that constitute this "liturgy of citizenship" need not focus simply on voting, running for office, or writing letters to elected representatives.[203] On an expansive Augustinian view of politics, this liturgy can involve the kind of activities that Augustine himself pursued: working on behalf of the poor, advocating for society's most vulnerable, preserving the rule of law, diagnosing the lust for domination, talking with neighbors, building coalitions with local leaders, and participating in activities that unite citizens around common hopes.[204] This liturgy of citizenship need not require citizens to sacrifice their faith but can instead encourage a faithful form of sacrifice, helping to promote the health of the commonwealth and the peace of the pilgrim city. For Mathewes, this liturgy can supply the practical conditions for "hopeful citizenship."[205]

James K. A. Smith offers a similar "liturgical lens on the political" that takes inspiration from Augustine.[206] Recognizing human beings as "liturgical creatures" who are "always being shaped by *some* liturgies," Smith elevates the church as the liturgical "body politic" that forms Christians in the habits, dispositions, and virtues needed to participate faithfully in public life.[207] While Smith puts the church at the center of his Augustinian public theology, however, he does not cast the church as an "'alternative' *polis*" simply to indict the world or encourage Christians to "huddle into an enclave," as some Augustinian communitarians recommend.[208] Smith recognizes that simply participating in the liturgies of the institutional church does not necessarily ensure holiness and that the institutional church can sometimes form vice as well as virtue.[209] The same, of course, also applies to politics, which also consists in a set of rituals, norms, and practices that can form citizens in either virtue or vice.[210] Citing Augustine's vigorous critique of the "rites" of "civil theology" to caution Christians against the potentially deforming effects of public life, Smith argues that politics can tempt citizens to "absolutize the penultimate" and thereby derail their pilgrimage toward the heavenly city.[211] Yet, in warning against political idolatry, Smith does not counsel retreat or withdrawal.[212] He also cites Augustine's emphasis on the common good of "earthly peace" and his correspondence with Boniface to encourage Christians to participate in public life, and he offers four "Augustinian principles for public participation" to guide Christians in seeking "selective" and "ad hoc" collaborations with diverse citizens.[213]

In many ways, Smith's Augustinian account aligns with the one offered here, particularly in its emphasis on seeking a "penultimate convergence" around common goods, its acknowledgment of the possibilities and limits of political engagement, and its focus on how liturgical practices can form virtues such as hope, which fits with Augustine's discussion of the Lord's Prayer discussed in chapters 1 and 3.[214] Smith also rightly emphasizes the potentially deformative effects of politics and affirms the church as the primary locus of moral formation in Augustine's thought, identifying the church as a "re-centering community of practice" that Christians are "sent *from*" to serve the world.[215] Yet, as Molly Farneth has suggested (and Smith has acknowledged), an exclusive emphasis on being "sent" from the church can imply that the movement between church and world is only "outward" and one-way, that Christians are sent into the world without potentially being formed positively by engagement in public life.[216] In reply to Farneth, Smith has recognized the need for a more "*positive*" account of this "dialectic."[217] As before, he might find resources in Augustine, who at key points cites Roman exemplars to exhort Christians to cultivate the virtues and appeals to Jeremiah 29—a passage that Smith cites approvingly—to highlight how Christians can engage non-Christian citizens in mutually formative ways.[218]

Writing after the Israelites were exiled from Jerusalem into Babylon, the prophet Jeremiah counsels his people not to abandon hope but to embrace their new city and seek its peace with other citizens in that common place:

> Thus says the Lord of hosts, the God of Israel, to all the exiles whom I have sent into exile from Jerusalem to Babylon: Build houses and live in them; plant gardens and eat what they produce. Take wives and have sons and daughters; take wives for your sons, and give your daughters in marriage, that they may bear sons and daughters; multiply there, and do not decrease. But seek the welfare of the city where I have sent you into exile, and pray to the Lord on its behalf, for in its welfare you will find your welfare.[219]

Just as Jeremiah encourages Israelites exiled in Babylon, so, too, Augustine invokes Jeremiah to encourage "pilgrims" exiled in the "Babylon" of Rome:

> [F]or, while the two cities are intermingled, we also make use of the peace of Babylon. We do so even though the people of God is delivered from Babylon by faith, so that it is only for a while that we are pilgrims in her midst. . . . Again, when the prophet Jeremiah foretold the captivity which was to befall the ancient People of God, he bade them, by divine command, to go obediently into Babylon, thereby serving God even by their patient endurance; and he himself admonished them to pray for Babylon, saying "In the peace thereof shall ye have peace": the temporal peace which is for the time being shared by the good and the wicked alike.[220]

Notice how Augustine has glossed "welfare" as "peace." Like Jeremiah proph-esying to Israelites to seek peace in the midst of Babylon, Augustine calls Christians to seek the peace of the commonwealth in the midst of plurality.[221] Smith cites this passage (and Augustine's reference to it) to encourage "'pil-grims' of the city of God to seek the welfare of Babylon."[222] Here, Augustine seems to encourage Christians not simply to be "sent" from the church into Babylon but to remain there, forming and being formed by relationships with fellow citizens in a city they now share.

For similar reasons, Luke Bretherton points to Augustine's engagement with Jeremiah 29 as a parable of Christian citizenship in a secular age. "For Augustine," Bretherton writes, "Jeremiah 29 is an allegory of what it means to be a Christian in the earthly city while we wait, not for a return of Jerusalem, but the coming of the New Jerusalem."[223] Ultimately, Bretherton argues, "What Jeremiah 29 alerts us to is how the place of exile is now the place where justice and faithfulness can be pursued and how Jerusalem—i.e., where we were most at home—has become a place of faithlessness, oppression, and corruption. . . . Instead of seeing suffering, dislocation, and domination as a reason to despair, the Israelites were invited by Jeremiah to see it as the context where God is most powerfully at work bringing new vision and being present in new ways."[224] In invoking Jeremiah, then, Augustine encourages not hasty withdrawal but hard work, the work of seeking peace in a strange land where one encounters domination, difference, and despair. In Augustine's hands, Jeremiah 29 is a counsel of encouragement, an exhortation for citizens to find a way between presumption and despair.

Conclusion

Throughout his life, Augustine often sought the welfare of his city, conversing and collaborating with diverse citizens and leaders—both Christian and non-Christian—to challenge injustice, combat domination, and pursue hopes they shared in common. Although he spent much of his life tending to members of his church, he devoted significant time and energy to political engagement. In fulfilling his duties and embodying active citizenship, he did not make an idol of politics or see it as the ultimate source of salvation. He did, however, recog-nize that the commonwealth could serve as a potential seedbed of virtue, a site of moral and spiritual formation that can supply opportunities for citizens to train their longings during their pilgrimage toward the heavenly city, even as they recognize the burdens of duty. And if a person's life is the most important means of persuasion, the bishop sought to exemplify the hope he professed. According to Possidius, "[T]his priest ... lived rightly and sanely in the faith and hope and charity of the Catholic Church; and no one can read what he wrote on theology without profit. But those were able to profit still more who ... had some knowledge of him as he lived among his fellow men."[225] For many of his contemporaries, Augustine's example was a testament to political engagement, not escape.

Of course, as Jeffrey Stout reminds us, whenever we engage examples like Augustine's, we must consider what they are examples *of* and whom they are examples *for*.[226] We must also recognize that examples are often characterized by the "problem of excess," the fact that real-life examples often exceed the boundaries of our generalizations.[227] The more we know about the details and complexity of their lives, the harder it is to say that they are fully (or only) examples of one specific thing. That means that we must critically engage our examples rather than imitate them uncritically, lest we ignore more disturbing aspects that might not be worthy of admiration or emulation.[228]

Augustine recognizes the need to engage examples critically. When he offers political examples for consideration—from Regulus to Theodosius—he presents them as examples of specific qualities for specific audiences and purposes, and he does not shy away from highlighting their faults along with their virtues.[229] He adopts the same approach when openly confessing his sins in the *Confessions*.[230] He even recognizes that, for finite and fallen human beings, humble and imperfect examples can sometimes offer more motivation and instruction than exemplars of perfect virtue who might seem unattainable or out of reach, especially early in the progression toward virtue.[231] That is one reason why, as Dodaro shows, Augustine sometimes encourages political leaders to emulate the saints rather than Christ. While Christ is the "only perfect exemplar of justice," Christ's perfect virtue means that he never had to experience or confess sin, which contrasts with the saints who had to struggle against sin and seek pardon for it.[232] For fallen human beings who need to repent, the saints' specific examples of penitence and persistence might provide a model that is more accessible than Christ's example of seemingly "unreachable perfection."[233]

In presenting Augustine as an example of hope, I am not elevating or endorsing Augustine as a perfect exemplar of virtuous citizenship for all citizens for all times. Not only is his context dramatically different from ours, but as I have suggested here and in previous chapters, his example suffers from an "excess" that contemporary citizens rightly resist, from his acceptance of slavery and the coercion of Donatists to his patriarchal views of women and occasionally polemical views of "pagans," "heretics," and religious outsiders. Rather than embracing Augustine's example in its entirety, I have focused more narrowly on Augustine as an example *of* someone whose civic engagement was animated by a hope for political goods that he saw as part of his ultimate hope for the heavenly city, and as an example *for* those who take him to be an authority, particularly those who see his life as evidence of his "pessimism." By examining his political correspondence and showing how he actively worked to serve his fellow citizens in localized and ad hoc ways, I have inferred Augustine's hope for political goods from his actions—actions that, however limited, would not have been adequately motivated without hope for the preservation, protection, and promotion of temporal and eternal goods. Along with the analyses of virtue, rhetoric, and politics offered in previous chapters, this account undercuts claims that Augustine was a pessimist about politics. When we examine Augustine's political life in letters, we see how he seeks to "prove" his hope by his "life" and "demonstrate it by [his] actions."[234]

Augustine's example provides scholars and citizens who take him to be an authority with compelling, if defeasible, reasons to engage in public life and seek common objects of hope with diverse citizens. But if this account challenges those who encourage a retreat into the church, it also raises a final set of questions: is "true virtue" only available to Christian citizens who order their hopes ultimately to God, or can non-Christian citizens also cultivate a civic virtue of hope? What can an Augustinian account of politics say to citizens who do not share a belief in Augustine's Christian God? Can these citizens possess genuine virtue, or are their virtues simply vices parading in virtue's glittering guise? To address these questions, we must turn to Augustine's contested discussion of "pagan virtue."

10

Hope among the Civic Virtues

GENUINE VIRTUES OR SPLENDID VICES?

God revealed in the wealth and fame of the Roman empire how powerful are civic virtues even without true religion.

—AUGUSTINE, LETTER 138.17, IN *POLITICAL WRITINGS*, 41.

IN BOOK 5 OF *CITY OF GOD*, Augustine makes a bracing claim: "[N]o one who is without true godliness—that is, without the worship of the true God—can have true virtue."[1] In Book 19, he repeats the charge, arguing that the apparent virtues of those who aren't members of the heavenly city "are really themselves vices, and not virtues at all, if they do not have reference to God."[2] While some may "suppose that the virtues are true and honorable even when they have reference only to themselves and are sought for no other end," these virtues "are puffed up and proud, and so are to be adjudged vices rather than virtues."[3] These statements constitute what is often described as Augustine's critique of the "splendid vices," semblances that appear to be virtues but are actually vices.[4]

This critique of "pagan virtue" presents a special challenge for my Augustinian account of political hope. Augustine seems not only to denounce the "true virtue" of non-Christian citizens but also to deny them any "true" hope. Amidst "all the great evils of this world," he writes in Book 19, only those with "true virtues" can be "happy in the hope of the world to come, and in the hope of salvation."[5] Only those with "true virtue" can be "saved by hope"; those without "true godliness" seem doomed to despair.[6] For political interpreters who focus narrowly on Book 19, these passages might confirm an interpretation of Augustine as an antipolitical, otherworldly exclusivist who denies any hope for pluralist politics.[7]

In this chapter, I advance an alternative Augustinian account that recognizes non-Christians as capable of virtue, even the virtue of hope. Part I sketches the "legacy of the splendid vices" and briefly identifies competing appropriations of Augustine's infamous critique.[8] Part II complicates these interpretations by moving beyond Book 19 and retrieving other passages that suggest a more ambivalent and inclusive attitude toward non-Christian virtue. Part III evaluates a prominent proposal to reconstruct these insights into a workable Augustinian view, while part IV develops an alternative account that solves a remaining interpretative puzzle by recovering Augustinian virtues of piety and humility. Recognizing the role of these interconnected virtues, I argue, provides an innovative way for Augustinians to acknowledge non-Christian virtue while responding to the concerns about pride and presumption that motivate Augustine's critique. Finally, part V highlights the relevance of this account for the Augustinian virtue of hope, illuminating ways in which virtues of humility and piety enable citizens to resist presumption and despair. When these interconnected virtues cooperate, hope can be a genuine civic virtue that diverse citizens can cultivate and sustain in the *saeculum*.

I. The Legacy of the Splendid Vices

In her elegant and incisive analysis of modern moral philosophy, Jennifer Herdt argues that many of the disputes that prompted modern philosophers and theologians to reject eudaimonism can be traced to "hyper-Augustinian" anxieties about the insufficiency of "pagan" virtue—in short, the "legacy of the splendid vices."[9] Importantly, Herdt notes, Augustine never used the phrase "splendid vices" (*splendida vitia*).[10] Like "pessimism," the label was applied by subsequent interpreters. But what Augustine says in certain passages might authorize the attribution.[11] In Books 5 and 19 of *City of God* in particular, he seems to insist that "true virtue" requires "true godliness," the ordering or referring of all virtuous acts and attitudes ultimately to God.[12] Any interpreter of Augustine's political thought must grapple with this complex legacy.

Many already have. Augustine's critique of pagan virtue has led many to dismiss him as a religious exclusivist with no interest in pluralism and a disdain for competing visions of the good. Leibniz, for example, argues that the notion of "splendid vices" is "a sally of St Augustine's which has no foundation in holy Scripture, and which offends reason."[13] Others consider Augustine's critique among the most attractive aspects of his thought. Martin Luther, for example, appropriated Augustinian anxieties about acquired virtue to indict any presumption of self-sufficient virtue as an expression of pride and radical denial of dependence on God's grace. According to Luther, "[S]ince love of himself remains, it is utterly impossible for man to love, speak, or do righteousness, even though he can feign all this. The result is that the virtues of all the philosophers, yes, of all men, be they jurists or theologians, are virtues in outward appearance but vices in reality."[14] Luther's "hyper-Augustinian" preoccupations with pride, hypocrisy, and self-sufficiency have had an enduring influence on modern theology and philosophy, leading later thinkers—such as Rousseau, Hume, and Kant—to develop secular philosophies to resist these anxieties, even while preserving crucial aspects of their Augustinian inheritance. As Herdt deftly shows, these tensions persist in contemporary debates in Christian ethics over the role of virtue, the distinctiveness of the church, and the relationship between authenticity and hypocrisy.[15]

Anxieties about Augustine's critique of pagans also persist in contemporary political theory. Highlighting Augustine's frequent resort to labels such as "pagan," "heretic," and "schismatic" to renounce opponents, William Connolly argues that Augustine exploits a rhetoric of excess to consolidate his community and demoralize outsiders.[16] Connolly rejects what he calls the "Augustinian Temptation," the "temptation to translate a series of alternative faiths that deviate from the intrinsic order you confess into instances of blasphemy, heresy, evil, infidelism, or nihilism."[17] Following Connolly, Romand Coles declares that Augustine's "monological" and "totalizing" style precludes the kind of the generous and dialogical engagement required in the context of deep pluralism.[18] Similarly, Martha Nussbaum suggests Augustine authorizes "a politics of anger and retribution based on the dominance of the one true doctrine," and, as a result, "is no friend to such a pluralist politics."[19] According to these critics, Augustine's polemic against pagans and other non-Christians only solidifies his reputation as a rabid culture warrior and political provocateur.[20]

Rather than defending Augustine against these attacks, many Augustinian communitarians exploit his critique of pagan virtue for their own purposes, invoking it to impugn liberal democracy and displace any hope from the political realm. Although one can find traces of this view in the writings of Stanley Hauerwas and Alasdair MacIntyre,[21] John Milbank provides the most illustrative example. A founder of Radical Orthodoxy, Milbank marshals Augustine's "counter-history" and "deconstruction of antique political society" to furnish a "counter-ethics," "counter-ontology," and "counter-kingdom" that challenges any form of civic virtue not "referred" to the transcendent God.[22] At his most polemical, Milbank argues that "European and American liberal democracy" has "engendered a continuous horror almost as grave as the Holocaust."[23] In particular, Milbank argues that liberalism produces a "secular immanence" that is "totalizing and terroristic because it acknowledges no supra-human power beyond itself by which it might be measured and limited."[24] Because the "secular" city fails to refer its virtues to God, it strips the political realm of any transcendent standard of justice that might forestall economic, social, and political domination. Unlike those who attack Augustine for being too otherworldly, Milbank argues the problem with "pagan" politics is its "*lack* of 'otherworldliness.'"[25] Without a transcendent referent, "the goods sought by the *civitas terrena* are not merely limited, finite goods, they are those finite goods regarded without 'referral' to the infinite good, and, in consequence, they are unconditionally *bad* ends."[26] "The realm of the practical, cut off from the ecclesial," Milbank concludes, "is quite simply a realm of sin."[27]

Milbank appropriates Augustine's critique of pagan virtue to advance his counter-ethics.[28] According to Milbank, Augustine "tries to show that, by its own standards, its virtue is not virtue, its community not community, its justice not justice."[29] In particular, "Augustine contends that the Roman notion of virtue itself reduced to the pursuit of glory and pre-eminence that is involved in an attainment of self-control and victory over one's passions."[30] The "main gist" of *City of God* "is that these [pagan] virtues were hopelessly contaminated by a celebration of violence."[31] This is "the fundamental truth of Augustine's claim about pagan virtue."[32] For Augustine, Milbank concludes, "there can be no true fulfilment of natural justice and natural peace without reference to the Church and the workings of grace."[33] Since Augustine is the hero of Milbank's counternarrative, it is easy to see why many contemporary political theorists dismiss the Bishop of Hippo for his seemingly domineering style. In the hands of one of his most influential interpreters, Augustine appears to be an otherworldly exclusivist who refuses any purported virtue outside the church.

Milbank's critique of non-Christian civic virtue provides a challenge to my Augustinian effort to unite diverse citizens around common objects of hope in the *saeculum*. If Augustinians must deny non-Christian citizens any true virtue, as Milbank assumes, it is hard to see how diverse citizens will be able to build successful and sustainable political coalitions to realize the proximate hopes they share in common. Unmasking the apparent virtue of other citizens as vice endangers the civic friendship needed to foster social cooperation and political hope.

While some passages from *City of God* might seem to justify such a position, Augustine is not always so polemical, and neither are his interpreters. Robert Dodaro, who presents a more textually sensitive and contextually sophisticated interpretation of Augustine's claim that "true virtue" requires "true piety,"[34] does not parlay Augustine's critique for the polemical purposes that Milbank does. Nonetheless, Augustine's complex thoughts on "pagan virtue" authorize multiple interpretations. Sometimes, Herdt argues, his "attitude toward pagan virtue was more ambivalent and ambiguous than definitive."[35] In what follows, I tend to that ambiguity to offer one interpretation of Augustine's account of non-Christian virtue that is more inclusive than the prevailing interpretation in political theory. Looking beyond Book 19 and examining other neglected passages of *City of God*, along with several sermons and letters, can reveal an Augustine who is more willing to acknowledge certain forms of "pagan virtue" than many interpreters allow.

II. Civic Virtue as Genuine Virtue

Consider Book 5 of *City of God*. In the same book where Augustine offers one of his strongest statements about "true virtue" and "true godliness," he also lifts up specific Roman leaders as exemplars of virtue. He describes Marcus Cato and Gaius Caesar, for example, as "two Romans of great virtue," "outstanding in virtue even though different in character."[36] Similarly, in Book 1's opening attack on pagan critics of Christianity, Augustine elevates Regulus as a "most noble example": "Among all their praiseworthy and illustrious men of outstanding virtue, the Romans offer no one better than this man. He was neither corrupted by good fortune, for he remained entirely poor even after his great victories, nor defeated by adversity, for he went back unmoved to so grim an end."[37] For Augustine, these Roman leaders—Caesar, Cato, and Regulus—are so admirable that even Christians should emulate aspects of their character:

> It is thanks to that empire, so broad and enduring, so famous and glorious for the virtues of its great men, that those men received the rewards that they sought by their striving, and that we have before us such examples for our necessary admonition. If, for the sake of the most glorious City of God,

we do not hold fast to the same virtues [*uirtutes . . . similes*] that they held fast to for the sake of glory of an earthly city, let us be pierced with shame. And if we do hold fast to them, let us not be lifted up with pride.[38]

According to Robert Markus, Augustine's tone here is "often unmistakably and authentically Roman, and full of legitimate pride in the stock *exempla* of Roman virtue. . . . Few Roman writers can rival Augustine's praise of the self-denial and discipline that went into the making of Roman greatness."[39]

But we must be careful not to make too much of these passages. Part of Augustine's aim is to exhort Christians to pursue the virtues of the eternal city: if Romans act virtuously for the mere sake of human glory, why shouldn't Christians be willing to do the same for even greater rewards?[40] Yet, although Augustine considers Roman virtues inferior to Christian virtues, it is nonetheless significant that he praises these virtues as a way of encouraging the virtuous behavior they embody. As Herdt notes, the affirmation of Roman virtue here "stands in striking contrast to Augustine's treatment of pagan theater, where his counsel to Christians is *not* to look, *not* to become spectators, because to look is to become open to having one's loves contaminated and reoriented."[41] By contrast, Augustine encourages Christians to look at these "pagan examples" who "become a legitimate object of spectation and emulation even if not a perfect exemplar."[42] Given the role of esteem in human affairs, Augustine recognizes that praising someone's virtues, even if they are not fully perfect, is one way to reinforce good behavior and encourage others to repeat that behavior, to "put on" virtue even if initially the aim is to win esteem. Implicitly, by holding up Romans as instructive exemplars, Augustine's own practice of virtue-attribution highlights the pedagogical role that virtue-talk plays in identifying and exhorting virtuous attitudes and actions. Even more strikingly, he suggests that Christians should cultivate the "same" or "similar virtues" (*uirtutes . . . similes*), even if they refer them to different ultimate ends.[43] Here, Augustine implies that a virtue can be genuine if it is directed toward genuine *proximate* goods, even if not toward the *ultimate* good of God.

Augustine makes this suggestion more explicit in other passages. In 5.13, he argues that God granted the success of the empire to "men who, for the sake of honour and praise and glory, so devoted themselves to their fatherland that they did not hesitate to place its safety before their own, even though they sought glory for themselves through it."[44] Although Augustine suggests it is better to acknowledge that "even the love of praise is a vice," he recognizes that "[i]t may be that, in this life, it cannot be completely eradicated from the heart."[45] He goes on to acknowledge the value of those citizens "who bridle their baser desires by means of the desire for human praise and glory, and not with the faith of godliness and the love of intelligible beauty given by the Holy Spirit."[46] These citizens "are not, therefore, yet holy," but they are "less vile."[47] Though they have not achieved "true" or "perfect" virtue, their incomplete virtue has enabled them to resist "baser desires."[48]

Augustine suggests these incomplete virtues also enabled Roman leaders to achieve genuine goods for their political community: "Romans held their own private interests in low esteem for the sake of the common good, that is, for the commonwealth. For the sake of its treasury they resisted avarice, and they took counsel for the good of their fatherland with unfettered minds; nor were they guilty of any offence against its laws, or of any unwholesome desires."[49] Here is another example of the continuum of virtue I described in chapter 8. The goods that Augustine acknowledges are *common* goods, not the *private* goods that preoccupy those who are fully vicious. Romans who seek these common goods and resist their private vices practice a genuine form of virtue that falls short of complete virtue but does not collapse into complete vice. As Augustine suggests, echoing Sallust, these Romans seek these goods "as by a true way."[50]

While Roman leaders pursued these goods out of love of human glory (a typical target of Augustine's scorn), he concedes that a proper love of glory does not necessarily lead to domination:

> Although he who delights excessively in human glory will also be much inclined ardently to desire mastery, those who aspire to the true glory even of human praise will nonetheless take care not to displease men of good judgment. For there are many good aspects of character, and many persons are competent judges of such aspects even though not many have them. And it is by means of such good qualities of character that those men ascend to glory and authority and lordship of whom Sallust says that they strive after these things "by the true way."[51]

Notice the suggestion here: the "true glory even of human praise" is a genuine good, even if it is not directly or consciously ordered to the glory of God. Love for this good must simply be rightly ordered. This view fits with Augustine's suggestions in *City of God* 19.19 that "honour and power" should be used "righteously and beneficially, for the wellbeing of those under us," and with his claim in Letter 130 to Proba that "honors and positions of power" may be proper objects of love and hope if they are sought for the wellbeing of the community.[52]

Another aspect of the above passage is also significant: those who seek the esteem of people "of good judgment" will be more likely to achieve virtue when they act as "'by the true way.'"[53] Augustine seems to suggest that subjecting themselves to the praise or blame of virtuous people, even if initially to win esteem, helps them act in virtuous ways. As a result, they become less vicious and more virtuous as they repeat those actions. By making them accountable to an "economy of esteem," a love of glory provides a check on more dangerous vices and helps citizens "put on" virtue, encouraging them to repeat virtuous behaviors in a way that causes them to gradually seek virtue for its own sake rather than for the sake of glory.[54] At the least, accountability to persons of "good judgment" discourages cruelty and the lust for domination: "[O]ne who desires to rule and command but who lacks that love of glory which will deter him from displeasing men of good judgment will very often seek to obtain what he loves even by the most blatant acts of wickedness."[55] In Book 5, then, Augustine implicitly accepts that a certain kind of civic virtue, even if pursued for love of glory, can be a way to make progress toward more perfect virtue. Though this civic virtue remains incomplete without a full reference to the ultimate end, it is on the way toward more complete virtue.[56]

To be sure, Augustine still deems it more praiseworthy to eradicate the lust for glory altogether: "[H]owever much we may praise and proclaim the virtue which serves the glory of men without true godliness, it is not for one moment to be compared even with the first and least virtue of the saints who have placed their hope in the grace and mercy of the true God."[57] Hope for the heavenly commonwealth remains greater than any hope for earthly goods.

Yet, even while repeating the claim that "true virtue" requires "true godliness," Augustine makes two important concessions. First, he confesses that he cannot know God's "hidden" causes and that God may have enabled the Romans to exercise virtues not just to provide an example for Christians but because God wanted to recognize their goodness and acknowledge "the diverse merits of the human race."[58] By calling attention to this possibility, Augustine cautions readers against making hasty judgments about other people's virtues and vices, lest they deny the potential that God may be working in hidden ways. A humble openness to plurality and awareness of fallibility is an appropriate Augustinian posture when engaging difference.

Second, Augustine seems to acknowledge the account of genuine but incomplete virtue suggested above. Though he argues that "no one who is without true godliness—that is, without the worship of the true God—can have true virtue, and that virtue is not truly such when it serves human glory," he concedes that, "[n]onetheless, those who are not citizens of that eternal City which is called the City of God in our sacred writings are more useful to the earthly city when they have even that imperfect kind of virtue than they would be if they did not have it [*quando habent uirtutem uel ipsam, quam si nec ipsam*]."[59] In the most widely accepted translation of *City of God*, R. W. Dyson glosses the crucial phrase—*uirtutem uel ipsam*—as "even that imperfect kind of virtue," but we must be careful here. The Latin is more ambiguous. The word for "imperfect" or "incomplete" (*imperfecta*) is missing from the original text. This may explain why earlier translators, such as Henry Bettenson, leave the statement more open and ambiguous: "[S]till, those who are not citizens of the Eternal City . . . are of more service to the earthly city when they possess *even that sort of virtue* than if they are without it."[60] Regardless of which translation we accept, the implication is similar: Augustine seems to acknowledge some form of genuine, if incomplete, virtue in those who do not consciously refer their actions to God.

This interpretation comports with what Augustine writes in Letter 138 to Marcellinus, a Catholic who serves as a high-ranking official in the Roman Empire. Two aspects of Letter 138 are most significant for us. First, while Augustine praises God for giving Christians "splendid and powerful virtues"— including the "true piety" and "[f]aith, hope, and charity" that make Christians "adopted citizens" of the "heavenly and divine commonwealth"—he warns against trying to exact vengeance or punishment on other citizens who seem to exhibit vice.[61] Rather than resorting to violence and vengeance, Christians should use "goodness" to overcome "evil."[62] While Christians can legitimately use persuasion to reform "evil characters," "if we are unable to reform them, we should tolerate those who want the commonwealth to remain with its vices unpunished."[63] The previous paragraphs of the letter suggest why Augustine calls for "toleration" or "endurance": these citizens are also members of the commonwealth, part of a people "united by a specific bond of peace."[64] Because of this shared membership, they must patiently endure difference, even objectionable difference, for the sake of the commonwealth and the civic friendship they share in common.[65] Augustine recognizes this act of patient endurance will require sacrifice:

> In overcoming an evil person through goodness, then, we patiently accept the loss of temporary benefits in order to show him how worthless we should consider them by comparison with faith and justice; after all, excessive love of such benefits makes him evil. In this way the wrongdoer might

learn from the very person he's wronged what the things are really like that tempted him to do wrong. Then too he might repent and be won back to peace—the most beneficial thing there is for a city—not defeated by force and violence, but by patient goodwill.[66]

Here, as we saw in chapter 9, Augustine suggests that being a virtuous example can be one of the most effective forms of persuasion. Of course, he knows that such sacrifice will be difficult, which is why he elevates examples of "holy martyrs" who practiced tolerance before invoking the model of Christ, "our outstanding example of forbearance," who did not return an eye for an eye in pursuit of vengeance but instead turned the other cheek as an act of love.[67] For Augustine, Christ exemplifies the kind of forbearance and tolerance Christians should bear toward others in the *saeculum*.

To modern ears, Augustine's call here for "tolerance" or "endurance" may seem half-hearted, a mere concession to a world ravaged by sin. But John Bowlin argues that Augustine's call for tolerance marks a significant contribution, not only to ancient political thought but to modern political thought as well. What distinguishes Augustine's account, Bowlin suggests, is that tolerance and forbearance are not simply acts of self-control or self-restraint, a negative pulling-away from a tolerated citizen, but rather a more positive expression of sacrificial love. It is an act that incarnates the love of Christ in the willingness to patiently endure difference, disagreement, and even "vice" out of the love for the other person and the common good they share, namely, the bond of peace.[68] For Bowlin, this sort of tolerance, this positive act of love, can be a basis for civic friendship and political cooperation in the *saeculum*, where citizens can achieve only incompletely theorized agreement about the common good and must patiently endure differences and disagreements about ultimate ends.[69] In considering Augustine's account of non-Christian virtue, we should not underestimate the importance of his call for such tolerance, not only of pagan virtues but, in this case, even of pagan vices.

What Augustine says next in Letter 138 is equally important for our purposes. He writes,

> The first Romans indeed used their virtues to establish and enlarge the commonwealth, even if they failed to show the sort of true piety for the true God that could, through its saving religion, also lead them to the eternal city. However, they still protected their *own sort of integrity*, which was adequate for establishing, enlarging and preserving their earthly city. For God revealed in the wealth and fame of the Roman empire *how powerful are civic*

virtues even without true religion; to make it clear with the addition of this human beings become citizens of the other city, whose king is truth, whose law is love, and whose limit is eternity.[70]

Augustine again invokes the example of Roman virtue to exhort Christians to practice true virtue. If Romans perform great deeds of virtue and make noble sacrifices for the sake of merely human glory, Christians should be even more willing to exercise those same virtues and make similar sacrifices for the promise of eternal glory. Yet, while Augustine appeals to Roman virtue for exhortatory purposes, it is striking that he still describes their "civic virtues" as genuine virtues, "even without true religion."[71]

These passages complicate simplistic renderings of Augustine's critique of pagan virtue. Standing back and looking at the larger Augustinian mosaic reveals more ambiguity, ambivalence, and sensitivity than historical interpreters and contemporary political theorists often assume. When we juxtapose these passages, consistent themes emerge: a call for "humility" and "tolerance" when making judgments about others whose situation may be fully comprehensible only with knowledge of God's "hidden causes" and the "diverse merits of the human race"; an acknowledgment of the power of "civic virtues" in promoting temporal well-being and preserving civic peace; a suggestion that non-Christians may possess incomplete virtue "on the way" to fuller and more complete virtue; and a recognition that Christians and non-Christians may share the "same" or "similar virtues" even if they are ordered to different ultimate ends. Implicit in these claims is a distinction between proximate and ultimate objects and an affirmation of the importance of sharing common goods in the *saeculum*.

If these passages suggest a more nuanced approach to "pagan virtue," how are we to square these implicit suggestions with Augustine's more explicit admonitions about "true virtue" and "true godliness"? Should we simply chalk these claims up to excessive rhetoric or philosophical inconsistency, or is there a way to dissolve these interpretative difficulties? In what follows, I want to consider one proposal to alleviate these tensions.

III. A Proposal, a Puzzle, and Three Replies

Drawing on some of the passages analyzed above, T. H. Irwin offers a carefully crafted reconstruction of Augustine's account of non-Christian virtue that attempts to rescue him from the pernicious legacy of the splendid vices.[72]

Irwin notes the ambiguity of Augustine's criteria for "true virtue" and acknowledges two possible formulations.[73] According to an *extremely strict criterion*, genuine virtue requires "a wholly correct conception of the ultimate end."[74] This strong version precludes any non-Christian virtue that is not directed explicitly to the Christian God since any virtue without reference to God would lack a wholly correct conception of the ultimate end. A *moderately strict criterion*, by contrast, requires "a morally correct conception of the ultimate end" but allows that the conception may be not be wholly correct or complete.[75] A moderate version of "true virtue" makes room for virtues that have a "morally correct" conception of an end, even if it is only "partly correct."[76] This would constitute genuine, if incomplete, virtue.[77]

Irwin acknowledges that Augustine's ambiguity can support both readings, but he argues the moderate version better captures his complex attitudes toward non-Christian virtue. Rather than rejecting pagan accounts of virtue wholesale, Augustine affirms central aspects of Greek and Roman conceptions: their eudaimonist vision of virtue as a noninstrumental good, the idea that virtue surpasses all external goods, and the notion that virtue requires not just an act directed to a genuine good but the proper use or enjoyment of that good in relation to other ends.[78] Because Augustine accepts that virtue can be pursued at least partly for its own sake, it follows that some non-Christians act for the sake of a *partly correct*, though *incomplete*, conception of their ultimate end.[79] Although they do not consciously acknowledge dependence on God or act for God's sake, "these errors do not remove the goodness of [their] actions or [their] character."[80] According to Irwin, "Pagan virtues are genuine virtues because they aim at some particular praiseworthy end."[81]

What motivates Irwin's account is the idea that an ultimate end is not necessarily in competition with other ends but encompasses many of these ends as more intermediate or proximate parts.[82] This conception fits with the participationist ontology and order of love advanced in chapter 2. On Irwin's picture, the "absence of the higher end" in a conception of an end "does not imply the absence of the lower, and hence it does not imply the absence of the goodness appropriate to the lower end."[83] If a civic virtue is properly ordered toward a proximate good that is a compatible with the ultimate end, then it assumes a morally correct, if incomplete, conception of the ultimate end and can be counted as a genuine, if incomplete, virtue.

Irwin acknowledges that Augustine does not make this distinction between "perfect" and "imperfect" virtue explicit, so he enlists another Augustinian who does.[84] Thomas Aquinas cites Augustine to argue that, if a particular proximate end is not a "true good" but only an "apparent good," then any virtue ordered to that apparent good is "not a true virtue" but "a counterfeit virtue."[85] While Aquinas affirms Augustine's critique of pagan virtue, he goes on to suggest the possibility of true but imperfect virtue: if "this particular good be a true good, for instance the welfare of the state, or the like, it will be indeed be a true virtue, imperfect, however, unless it be referred to the final and perfect good."[86] True but imperfect virtues are ordered to genuine goods, even if their possessors do not consciously order those goods to God. Aquinas does not quote Augustine when making these latter claims, but both in the main article and in the response to the first objection, Aquinas cites Augustine's critique of pagan virtue and implies his account is compatible with it.[87] For Irwin, Aquinas's more nuanced account "does justice to Augustine's position as a whole."[88]

I am sympathetic with Irwin's reconstruction and the distinctions between perfect and imperfect virtue that underwrite it. He captures Augustine's more nuanced attitude toward the virtues of Roman *exempla* who sought genuine goods, including the "welfare" of the commonwealth, without referring them explicitly to God. Yet, while I share Irwin's sense that Augustine is closer to Aquinas than many interpreters allow, we must tread with caution lest we read Augustine too much through Aquinas, particularly through a more simplistic "two-tiered" Thomism that assumes theological ends can simply be "added" onto more natural ends.[89] At times, Irwin's language suggests this two-tiered reading. He argues, for example, that Augustine "implicitly recognizes" the two types of happiness—perfect and imperfect—that Aquinas identifies,[90] and he sometimes writes as if faith if merely additive: "Faith adds to the civil virtues, but does not reject them. Augustine does not suggest that Christian morality turns away from these civil virtues, but that it turns these same virtues in a different direction."[91] Irwin's claim here can be read in two ways, depending on which sentence is emphasized. The first sentence—"faith adds to the civil virtues"—suggests that theological ends simply supplement those we possess by nature. Admittedly, Augustine's loose language can sometimes support this interpretation. In Letter 138, for example, Augustine suggests that God enabled the Romans to possess the civic virtues without true religion "to make it clear that with the *addition* of [true religion] human beings become citizens of the other city,"[92] implying that reference to God is additive. But this view does not seem to capture Augustine's emphasis on the continuity between divine and human loves canvassed in chapter 2, nor does it acknowledge his suggestion in *Confessions* that ordering one's ends ultimately to

God transforms one's hopes and loves. Irwin's second sentence—"Christian morality . . . turns these same virtues in a different direction"—better captures this transformation. It acknowledges that virtues ordered to God do not simply *add* to natural ends but, in some ways, *re-form* or *re-create* human hopes and loves.[93]

This transformative account more accurately conveys Augustine's praise of "true virtue," but it also raises a difficult question: how much is this end reformed or recreated when cast under a new description, when reference to God is made explicit? Augustinians such as Milbank often imply that the transformation is so radical that it vitiates any goodness or value in a virtue not explicitly referred to God. Recall Milbank's categorical claim: "[F]inite goods regarded without 'referral' to the infinite good . . . are unconditionally *bad* ends."[94] On this view, proximate ends, no matter how genuine or praiseworthy, lose all of their value when they are not consciously ordered to God. As such, any virtues ordered to these ends may look like virtues but are really only vices in virtue's guise.

While Milbank is right to resist simplistic two-tiered accounts of Augustine, he goes too far in stressing the discontinuity between proximate and ultimate objects.[95] I believe Augustine would acknowledge that ordering virtues to God helps to redirect or recreate these virtues, but it does not entirely replace these virtues. Augustine's suggestion that pagans and pilgrims can share the same or similar virtues supports more continuity than Milbank assumes.[96]

What specific difference, then, does explicitly ordering one's loves to God make? What are we to make of the passages where he states that true virtue requires true godliness? *City of God* 19.25 provides the most acute challenge: "Some, indeed, suppose that the virtues are true and honourable even when they have reference only to themselves and are sought for no other end. Then, however, they are puffed up and proud, and so are to be adjudged vices rather than virtues," for virtues "are really themselves vices, and not virtues at all, if they do not have reference to God."[97] How are we to address the tension between Augustine's explicit statements and implicit suggestions?

There are at least three possible ways to address this interpretative puzzle. The first is simply to acknowledge that, unlike analytic philosophers and medieval scholastics, Augustine does not aspire to build a perfectly coherent theological or philosophical system. Given the improvisational style and pedagogical purposes analyzed in chapters 6 and 7, he might have been using these formulations for rhetorical effect, using antitheses between Roman vice and Christian virtue to exhort Christian readers and would-be converts to turn away from the seductions of human glory toward the City of God. On this view, Augustine's rhetorical excess might be intended to chasten moral and political excess rather than furnish a strict and rigid dichotomy between Christian and non-Christian virtue. This is a plausible suggestion, particularly in light of Augustine's changing historical, rhetorical, and political circumstances. Augustine's most explicit discussions of pagan virtue and vice appear in Books 5 and 19 of the *City of God*, which were separated by a span of fourteen books and up to fourteen years during which his political, pedagogical, and rhetorical purposes shifted. Attending to the social, literary, and rhetorical contexts of these passages may complicate attempts to make Augustine completely consistent.

Yet, given the troubling legacy of the splendid vices, we must resist the temptation to prematurely close inquiry without exploring other ways to alleviate the tensions. Recalling the alternative accounts of the orders of love and hope from chapters 2 and 3 can bring a second alternative into view. One of Augustine's central claims in *City of God* 19.25 is that true virtues must be "referred" or "related" to God. Unfortunately, Augustine does not spend much time explaining what "referral" requires. In light of his silence, most interpreters assume this "reference" must involve an explicit, conscious, or occurrent awareness of ordering a specific action or attitude toward God as a final end. On this view, a truly virtuous person must have God subjectively "in mind" when they act, actively directing their proximate aims and objectives to God as their ultimate end in each moment. But as I argued in chapter 2, subjectively conscious referral may not be required for every properly ordered act of virtue. We can often act for a reason—act out of a love for an ultimate end—without necessarily having that end subjectively "in mind" when we act.[98] In one sermon, for example, Augustine argues that all action is motivated by a kind of love for an end, which means that we can discern a person's "loves" or "ends" in part by looking at their actions: "After all, what is it in any one of us that prompts action, if not some kind of love? Show me even the basest love that does not prove itself in action. Shameful deeds, adulteries, villainies, murders, all kinds of lust—aren't they all the work of some sort of love?"[99] The same can be said about rightly ordered love: we can infer one's ends by looking to one's actions rather than simply inquiring into their explicit beliefs and professions. As Augustine suggests in the *Faith in the Unseen*, the trust required for friendship *requires* these kinds of inferences: since we cannot know the mind of a friend, the hiddenness of their interior thoughts and motives makes inferences from action necessary.[100]

Augustine affirms the centrality of enacted love in other contexts. In Letter 155, he argues that "our character is usually judged not from what we *know*, but from what we *love*. It is good and bad loves that make good and bad characters."[101] In *City of God*, he claims that "it is not he who *knows* what is good who is justly called a good man, but he who *loves* it."[102] And in the *Enchiridion*, he suggests that "when we ask whether somebody is a good person, we are not asking what he believes or hopes for but what he loves."[103] In these passages, Augustine suggests a twofold claim: (1) that we can determine the quality of others' character by looking at their "loves" rather than simply at the conscious content of their knowledge,[104] and (2) that we can infer what they love in part by examining their actions.

In light of this twofold claim, it is helpful to recall Augustine's frequent appeal to Matthew 25, which suggests those who love the "least of these" will receive eternal salvation, even if they do not consciously know they are loving God.[105] Augustine's extensive use of Matthew 25 implies that what makes people virtuous is not necessarily that they subjectively know they are loving God, but that they are objectively loving God by loving the neighbor in the same way that God loves.[106] The quality of love is not reducible to conscious mental awareness. Read one way, this suggests that nonbelievers who love genuine goods, even without consciously referring their love to God, may be able to possess ordered loves. And if virtue is nothing but "rightly ordered love,"[107] they can possess genuine, if incomplete, virtue.

But caveats are required. For this account of "referral" to remain faithful to Augustine, not just any temporal good will suffice. For implicit loves or hopes to be properly ordered to God, these temporal goods must be *genuine goods*, goods that, for Augustine, enable participation in the goodness of God. Objects or actions that directly violate, contradict, or diminish participation in God—such as domination or exploitation—are automatically ruled out as improper.[108] With Eric Gregory, then, we might say that properly ordered loves must be "*referable* to God, even if they are not *referred* to God in each instance."[109] Distinguishing between *referable* and *referred* goods offers a useful way to square Augustine's claim that true virtues require "reference" to God with his implicit suggestions that non-Christians can exercise a genuine, if incomplete, kind of virtue.[110] Non-Christians can be characterized as possessing a properly ordered love or hope if, objectively, the objects of their love or hope are referable to the goodness of God. As Gregory argues, acknowledging the possibility of implicit reference can itself be an expression of Augustinian humility, a recognition of the pervasive hiddenness of the human heart:

"Dogmatic emphasis on explicit reference to God can be a prideful rejection of the limits of our self-interpretations."[111] A focus on referability rather than explicit reference can encourage a posture of humility toward other citizens in the *saeculum*.

Yet the distinction between referable and referred goods, though helpful, is not sufficient. For Augustine, it is not enough simply to love genuine goods, for, as we saw in chapter 2, the quality of love is not determined simply by the metaphysical nature of its objects. Rather, for love to be properly ordered, human beings must also *use* these goods in proper ways, ordering them properly to God in the right ways at the right times and not loving them as if they were their final or supreme end. Any Augustinian account of genuine non-Christian virtue must attend not only to the metaphysical status of its proximate objects but the moral psychology of their use.

Attention to the moral psychology of love and sin illuminates a third possible way to acknowledge Augustine's explicit concerns about pagan virtue while preserving a more inclusive account. Viewing his critique of pagan virtue through the lens of his moral psychology reveals a striking feature: Augustine's primary concern seems to reflect the dangers of pride and domination.[112] In particular, he worries that virtues which refer "only to themselves and are sought for no other end" tend to make their possessors "puffed up and proud" and thus fuel a lust for glory and domination.[113] If ordering one's virtues to God chastens pride and presumption, then anyone who does not perform this act of referral will either pursue virtue solely for the sake of glory and self-promotion or attribute all of their virtue to their own efforts.[114] Either way, they refer their virtues back to love of self, which, Augustine suggests, engenders prideful presumption and the domination that often follows.[115]

Irwin offers a helpful diagnosis of these concerns. He identifies two failures that Augustine attributes to the prideful person: "(1) He attributes to himself what in fact he achieves only in dependence on God. (2) He fails to recognize the shortcomings in his own achievements."[116] Those with "true virtue," by contrast, attribute their virtue to God and recognize they lack the "perfection of righteousness."[117] The truly virtuous acknowledge both their dependency and their limitations, which prevents them from becoming puffed up with pride.

To present a faithfully Augustinian account of genuine but incomplete virtue, Irwin must address these two failures. He does so by resisting Augustine's assumption that pagan virtues necessarily lead to pride or arrogance: Augustine "has no good reason to maintain that the pagan virtues, as opposed to other aspects of the pagan outlook, are a special source or manifestation of arrogance."[118] Instead, Augustine should have distinguished the "arrogance" of those who possess the "conceptions of virtue" from the "conceptions of virtue" themselves: "Although they are virtues of arrogant people, they do not themselves aim at the distinctive ends of arrogant people; they aim at praiseworthy ends that are equally appropriate ends for anyone who lacks arrogance."[119] According to Irwin, "It is consistent to claim that pagan virtues are virtues and that they are vices; some features of them make them virtues and other features make them vices. The two claims are consistent because virtues are good states or conditions or actualizations of some capacity or tendency; pagan virtues are good states of one capacity, but bad states of another."[120]

While I agree with Irwin's diagnosis of the two failures and appreciate his attempt to a recover a more inclusive Augustinian stance, his reconstruction is not properly attentive to Augustine's concerns about pride and domination for three reasons.[121] First, Irwin seems to assume that the "arrogance" and "pride" of pagans can be separated from their "praiseworthy ends." This is what makes it "consistent" to claim that pagan virtues are both "virtues" and "vices": they are virtues when directed toward good ends and vices when directed toward bad ends. Yet Irwin neglects the part-whole structure of proximate and ultimate ends. As I argued in chapter 2, for Augustine, proximate ends (such as political goods) cannot be separated easily from the ultimate ends to which they are directed (such as human glory or the love of God). The relationship between proximate and ultimate ends matters to the moral quality of an act, capacity, or intention. In particular, the ultimate end to which more proximate ends are ordered affects the moral quality of the act or capacity.[122] In suggesting an easy separation between different ends, Irwin denies the part-whole relationship between proximate and ultimate ends.

Second, if, as Augustine assumes, a virtue is not simply an attitude, affection, or feeling but "a capacity to live well," an excellence or perfection of a particular human capacity, it is difficult to see how a *perfected* capacity, even one that is only partially perfected, can be both a virtue and a vice at the same time.[123] It may be an *unstable* virtue, or a capacity *on the way* to more complete virtue, but "a capacity to live well" is hard to style as a "vice" without denying its character as "virtue." Irwin's compartmentalization seems alien to Augustine's moral psychology.

Part of Augustine's concern about pagan virtue, I take it, is that pride or disordered love actually *infects* one's ability to properly pursue and achieve praiseworthy ends. We cannot judge a virtue based on its particular praiseworthy ends apart from assessing the affections and dispositions that motivate, inspire, and sustain pursuit of those ends, which is why praiseworthy ends must be *used* properly in relation to other goods and ends. In focusing on praiseworthy ends and separating assessment of these ends from one's internal dispositions, Irwin seems to minimize the importance of Augustine's psychology of use and enjoyment and downplays his efforts to provide a regulative ideal that discourages pride, glory, and the lust for domination.[124]

This limitation points to a third concern: Irwin's proposed solution seems to deny Augustine's commitment to the interconnectedness of the virtues. In a footnote, Irwin notes that Augustine accepts the "reciprocity of the virtues," the "claim that anyone who has one of the virtues has them all."[125] Given the virtues' interconnectedness, one cannot have perfect justice, for example, without possessing prudence to determine what justice requires, or without courage to act justly when doing so is dangerous or difficult. Irwin rightly acknowledges Augustine's appropriation of the interconnectedness of virtues, but his proposed solution seems to neglect its implications. Recall the two failures of the prideful person that Irwin identifies: (1) a failure to recognize one's dependency and (2) a failure to recognize one's shortcomings. Since, for Augustine, these failures, like other moral failures, are privations or perversions of goodness, one way to redescribe them is to cast them as the absence of, or resistance to, particular virtues—specifically, the virtues of *piety*, which involves proper acknowledgment of dependency, and *humility*, which involves proper acknowledgment of limitation.[126] This redescription provides another way to frame Augustine's criterion for "true virtue": "true virtue" requires the virtues of both piety and humility, which cooperate with every virtue to avoid failures to recognize dependency or limitation. This redescription reveals why Irwin's solution is insufficient: in assuming that "arrogance" or "pride" can be separated from a virtue's "praiseworthy ends," he ignores how Augustine requires virtues of piety and humility for the possession of any true virtue.[127]

If Irwin's solution for reconciling genuine but imperfect virtue with Augustine's explicit critique is inadequate, the limits of his account point to an alternative possibility: rather than isolating "arrogance" or "pride" from the possession of genuine virtue, we can instead argue that any genuine but incomplete virtue must be also accompanied by genuine, if incomplete, virtues of piety and humility.[128] Conceiving piety and humility as genuine civic virtues can provide a way to reconcile Augustine's seeming openness to certain forms of non-Christian virtue with his anxieties about the pride and domination that follow when human beings lack a transcendent end. This alternative account comports with Irwin's attempts to rescue a faithfully Augustinian position, but it does so by drawing resources from Augustine himself rather than turning to Aquinas. Careful attention to Augustine's less familiar texts and implicit practices uncovers conceptual resources for reconstructing piety, humility, and hope as genuine civic virtues.

IV. The Virtues of Piety and Humility

Throughout *City of God*, Augustine distinguishes persons with "true virtue" by their piety and humility: "[N]o matter how great the virtues that they are able to possess in this life, [they] attribute them only to the grace of God, Who has given these things to them according to their good will, their belief and their prayers [piety]. At the same time, they understand how much they lack that perfection of righteousness which exists only in the fellowship of the holy angels, of which they strive to be worthy [humility]."[129] Sometimes, he even mentions the two virtues in the same breath, describing "humble piety" (*humili pietate*) as a distinguishing feature of Christian teaching.[130] He applies this teaching in his advice to Boniface on how to make progress in virtue: "Give thanks also for what you do possess to God, as the source of the goodness you have, and in every good deed that you do, *give* him the *glory* [cf. Ps 115(113b).1], and yourself the humility. . . . However much you advance . . . in the love of God or of your neighbour and in true piety, however long you are involved in this life, do not believe that you are sinless."[131] As we saw in chapter 3, piety and humility are mutually reinforcing virtues.

Augustine's most systematic discussion of piety (*pietas*) appears in Book 10 of *City of God*, where he employs a kind of ordinary language analysis to explicate its meaning. Augustine notes that *pietas*, "which the Greeks call *eusebeia*, is usually understood in the strict sense to mean the worship of God; yet," he adds, "this word is also used to denote the duties which we owe to parents," the sources of our natural existence and our moral, spiritual, and intellectual progress.[132] Augustine goes on to note that, "in common speech," *pietas* also "frequently refers to works of mercy," a usage that has come about, he supposes, "because God especially commands the performance of such works, and declares that He is pleased with them instead of, or in preference to, sacrifices"—in this case, animal sacrifices.[133] According to Augustine, acts of gratitude, worship, and service are proper ways to acknowledge one's dependence on others, especially God.

Augustine's analysis of piety reflects his Roman context. Roman philosophers had long considered *pietas* a central part of justice, the virtue that disposes one to give others their due. Piety is the virtue that disposes one to give proper due to those on whom they are dependent. This connection between piety and justice is present in Augustine's most influential Roman source, Cicero. Throughout his political treatises, Cicero links piety and justice to identify those to whom one owes grateful acknowledgment and service, including one's family and country: "[C]ultivating justice and piety . . . is important in relation to your parents and family, but most important in relation to your fatherland. That way of life is the way to the heavens and to this gathering of those who have ceased to live and after having been released from the body now inhabit the place you see."[134] Cicero counts piety as one of "those praiseworthy qualities on account of which ascent into heaven is granted to humans" and celebrates the fact that Romans have dedicated a public temple to Piety to encourage citizens to cultivate the virtue.[135]

Augustine is aware of Cicero's account of piety. He even quotes Cicero's definition from *On Invention*: "Piety is that by which kindly concern and loving honor are shown to blood relations and to one's fatherland."[136] Augustine adopts the general structure of this traditional Roman virtue but fills it with Christian content, directing it ultimately to God. After presenting his ordinary language analysis of *pietas* in Book 10, Augustine argues that God is the ultimate and true object of *pietas*, the object of true "worship" and "true religion."[137] Yet, while God is the ultimate object of piety, Augustine does not thereby exclude acts of gratitude, piety, or mercy toward one's country or the human neighbors on whom one depends. In Letter 220, he emphasizes Boniface's duty to acknowledge and return gratitude to Rome for what it has done for him: "[I]f the Roman empire provides you with good things, even if they are ephemeral and earthly (for it is an earthly, not a heavenly, institution and can only provide what is in its power); if then it has bestowed good things on you, do not return evil for good."[138] Elsewhere, he recognizes our dependence on neighbors, suggesting that we "ought to be led to [God] by those who love us, and we ought to lead those whom we love to [God]."[139] Implicitly, Augustine acknowledges that gratitude and piety toward those on whom one depends is appropriate, as long as it is properly ordered to God.

Again, Augustine's own implicit practice in *Confessions* makes the point. Although Augustine is determined to show that God is the author of his story and the source of his hope, he does not assume that virtue comes down like manna from heaven. As we saw in chapter 5, grace works through ordinary means, especially the imitation of virtuous exemplars and participation in communal practices.[140] These earthly, temporal means are the *proximate sources* of Augustine's moral and spiritual progress and thus the *proximate objects* of his piety. In *Confessions*, he expresses piety toward those on whom he relies for assistance, praising exemplars like Ambrose,[141] Antony,[142] Victorinus,[143] and Monica[144] and acknowledging the importance of practices such as reading,[145] confession,[146] and conversation.[147] While Augustine recognizes God as the ultimate object of piety and ultimate source of his virtue, he does not hesitate to offer just and grateful acknowledgment to these more proximate objects of piety, the temporal sources of his virtue and progress through life.

By confessing these exemplars, communities, and practices as proper objects of piety, Augustine implicitly performs a kind of piety compatible with an account of piety as a civic virtue. Whether or not citizens follow Augustine in recognizing God as the ultimate source of virtue, they can at least follow him in acknowledging the proximate sources of their moral existence. Although oriented toward different ultimate ends, Christians and non-Christians can converge on the need to acknowledge their dependence on shared exemplars, communities, and traditions. They can express piety toward the same proximate referents, even if they order those referents to different ultimate ends. *Confessions* affirms that the virtue of piety can have proximate objects of assistance among its proper objects.

But can those who do not order their piety ultimately to God have any form of genuine virtue, or is pagan piety merely a splendid vice? At times, Augustine's rhetoric seems to suggest the latter. He repeatedly claims that anyone without "true piety" cannot possess "true virtue." But other passages complicate this view, supplying resources to reconstruct a genuine, if incomplete, virtue of piety that can be shared by Christians and non-Christians alike.

First, consider Augustine's procedure for explaining the meaning of *pietas* in *City of God*. As in the case of hope in the *Enchiridion*, he adopts an ordinary language analysis that draws on both Christian and Roman practices to capture the meaning of the concept, and he resists reducing either *pietas* or *religio* to purely Christian or theological meanings. He makes this explicit for *religio*: "[W]e cannot strictly speaking say that *religio* means nothing other than the worship of God, since we should then be unjustifiably disregarding the sense in which the word applies to the observance of duties in human relationships."[148] In the next paragraph, he implies the same holds for *pietas*, which is "usually understood in the strict sense to mean the worship of God," but is "also used to denote the duties which we owe to parents."[149] Since he is explaining the proper uses of the word in his larger social and political context, he suggests that *pietas* can be properly applied to good actions and excellences of character in those who are not Christians but who faithfully fulfill duties of piety toward their parents and teachers, whether or not they direct that piety ultimately to God.

This broader conception of piety fits with what Augustine says about natural or human charity. Augustine argues that "human" love toward friends, spouses, and citizens is "lawful," not only "in the sense that it's permitted; but also lawful in the sense that if it's lacking, you are very much at fault. It's absolutely right for you to love your wives, to love your children, to love your friends, to love your fellow citizens with human charity. All these names, you see, imply a bond of relationship, and the glue, so to say, of charity."[150] Augustine goes on to acknowledge that "this sort of charity can be found also among the godless, that is, among pagans, Jews, heretics": "Which of them, after all, does not naturally love wife, children, brothers, neighbors, relations, friends, etc.? So this kind of charity is human. So if anyone is affected by such hardness of heart that he loses even the human feeling of love, and doesn't love his children, doesn't love his wife, he isn't fit even to be counted among human beings." Since this sentiment is "natural," a person "who loves his children is not thereby particularly praiseworthy," but Augustine insists that "one who does not love his children is certainly blameworthy."[151] Here, natural charity seems like a genuine virtue that diverse human beings can exercise regardless of their ultimate ends. Although natural love is not as perfect or praiseworthy as full Christian love, it at least enables its possessors to achieve genuine goods of human friendship and resist "blameworthy" vices of cruelty, disregard, or domination. A similar claim can be made for piety. Presumably, part of maintaining the "glue" of natural love is expressing piety toward one's family and friends, gratefully acknowledging their gifts and assistance. Without piety, the bond of love will falter. Thus, if both pilgrims and pagans alike can exercise this kind of natural piety as part of natural love, this account offers Augustinian resources for recognizing a genuine, if incomplete, virtue of piety.

As we saw in chapter 4, such natural piety is on display in *Faith in the Unseen*. There, Augustine celebrates the value of social trust for friendship and explicitly declares that being a virtuous friend entails reciprocating a gift with gratitude and piety, even if we cannot know the giver's motives or intentions. A "kindness" that goes "unreciprocated" is "not clever but despicable."[152] Augustine implies that friendship not only permits piety but requires it; otherwise, human friendships—and the reciprocity that sustains them—would no longer be secure. Augustine's discussion implies that friends can express piety toward both Christians and non-Christians who do them a kindness and that non-Christians can express a genuine, if incomplete, virtue of piety in return. Indeed, they would be "blameworthy" or "despicable" if they did not.

On an Augustinian account, this incomplete or partially correct virtue of piety would not be as praiseworthy as a virtue consciously or directly ordered to God, but it might nonetheless reflect a kind of incomplete virtue, where citizens acknowledge their dependence on family, friends, teachers, and fellow citizens in a way that checks and restrains the worst vices.[153] Those who gratefully acknowledge their dependence on others will be more likely to form relations of love, trust, and friendship with family, friends, and strangers. They will also be less likely to use, manipulate, or dominate them for their own purposes.

This virtue of piety is supported by another Augustinian virtue: humility (*humilitas*), the virtue that involves the proper recognition of one's own limitations and weaknesses. If piety addresses the failure to recognize one's dependence, humility addresses the failure to recognize how one falls away from the good. Humility chastens the human temptation to rely only on ourselves and presume that we are the ultimate and final source of our being and goodness, which allows us to see ourselves, others, and the world as they really are. In this way, the virtue of humility reinforces the virtue of piety: those who humbly recognize their weaknesses are more likely to recognize that they are not the source of their being and goodness and thus more likely to express proper piety toward those who are. Similarly, those who piously recognize their dependence on others are more likely to recognize they did not achieve their virtues on their own. Piety and humility are mutually reinforcing.[154]

As we saw in chapter 3, humility is an essential Augustinian virtue, one needed to resist temptations toward prideful presumption and the domination it often fuels. Given its role in chastening pride and domination, Augustine deems humility especially important for politics. In the opening words of *City of God*, he explains that part of his purpose is to "persuade the proud how great is that virtue of humility."[155] He contrasts the "swollen fancy of the proud-spirited" in those who are "dominated by the lust for domination" with those who accept the "maxim of the divine law": "God resisteth the proud but giveth grace to the humble."[156] The rest of *City of God* expands on this theme, attempting to turn the pursuit of this-worldly glory toward the City of God to chasten the lust for domination and the injustice it breeds.[157] According to Mary Keys, "Humility counters false divinization of self and society and so strengthens commitment to moderation and justice among human beings. It opens one to a love of rightful equality among humans, to recognition of true merits in others, to willing personal and public service on behalf of others, and to extension of one's natural familial affection and care to include the poor and abandoned of society."[158] Ultimately, Keys concludes, *City of God* is an "*apologia* for the virtue of humility."[159]

Importantly, Augustine's commitment to humility is not abstract or sentimental. He believes the virtue of humility, like piety, must be enacted daily, even in political life. One of his favorite exemplars is Theodosius, the emperor whose "marvellous" exercise of "humility" led him to repent publicly after exacting vengeance on an opposing army.[160] After seeing this act of humility, Augustine writes, the people "were more ready to weep when they saw the imperial majesty thus brought low than they were to fear it when it was angered by their sin."[161] By concluding his series of *exempla* in Book 5 of *City of God* with Theodosius, Augustine elevates the emperor as a paradigmatic exemplar of humility.

Although Theodosius exemplifies the importance of humility as a distinctly civic virtue, Theodosius was also a Christian, which raises the question: can non-Christians exercise a genuine virtue of humility? Augustine's account of the *saeculum* suggests that possibility. He warns both Christians and non-Christians against rashly judging others during the present age where members of both cities are mingled together and where God's causes remain radically "hidden."[162] Such humility requires acknowledging the limits of human knowledge and recognizing, as Augustine writes in another context, that the "conjecture of the human mind . . . sometimes achieves the truth, but sometimes fails to do so."[163] God may be working in ways that escape conscious knowledge or interpretation. For Augustine, it would be better to focus on the log in our own eye than the speck in our neighbor's.[164]

While Augustine never explicitly develops an account of humility as a genuine if incomplete virtue, less familiar texts supply resources for a reconstruction.[165] In a recently discovered sermon, Augustine seems to acknowledge that some non-Christians—including some Jews and Platonist philosophers—may receive eternal salvation, even if they do not hold or express an explicit belief in Christ or the Triune God.[166] While he criticizes theurgical rites popular among pagans, he acknowledges that Christians need not deny the possibility that some non-Christians may be saved: "[O]ne must not say anything rashly about those who have not worshipped any idols, nor bound themselves over to Chaldean or magical rituals, in case perhaps it has escaped our notice how the savior, without whom nobody can be saved, has revealed himself to them in some manner or other."[167] Robert Dodaro calls attention to the implication: though salvation comes through Christ, "Christ may still choose to reveal himself to individuals in some form other than in the Christian dispensation."[168] "Taken in its full context," Dodaro concludes, "Augustine's statement allows for a new revelation in which Christ manifests himself as the savior to individuals who are following a pathway to purification of the soul that does not explicitly involve Christian teachings or sacraments."[169] Importantly, Dodaro argues, what distinguishes non-Christians who might be saved is that they practice the virtue of humility: they at least acknowledge that their virtue is not simply the result of their own goodness or effort but remains largely a gift, even a mystery.[170] This sermon suggests that humility can be a genuine virtue in non-Christian citizens, one that helps to restrain the vices of pride and presumption.

This Augustinian reconstruction of piety and humility fits with Irwin's emphasis on partly correct, but incomplete, conceptions of ultimate ends and Bowlin's notion of truthful description surveyed in chapter 2. Non-Christians who have correct but incomplete conceptions of praiseworthy ends—and who regard those proximate goods under a truthful but incomplete description—can properly love or hope for genuine temporal goods, even if they do not explicitly or consciously refer them to God. Virtues of piety and humility aid right perception and truthful description.[171] If "truthful description" requires attending to everything about other people, ourselves, and temporal goods that is "true and relevant" about them, as Bowlin suggests, humility and piety can help citizens recognize that their human neighbors "cannot be a substitute for God, that they are mortal, that they are not extensions of ourselves or instruments of our aims, that they are both creatures of a certain kind and individuals with specific quirks, characteristics, and defining features."[172] Implicit in such truthful description is the recognition of one's mortality and limits (humility) and the acknowledgment of one's dependency on others (piety). These virtues cooperate to discourage the presumption that virtue is solely a matter of personal achievement and to encourage the grateful acknowledgment of dependence on family, friends, and fellow citizens. Though the incomplete forms of these virtues would not be ultimately ordered to God, they could still be ordered to genuine goods and therefore help "bridle baser desires," preventing their possessors from being "puffed up and proud." Indeed, these virtues would address the two failures that Irwin identifies in Augustine's critique of "pagan virtue." Avoiding these failures may not make citizens fully virtuous, but their incomplete virtue would at least put them on the path to more perfect virtue. Citizens who exercise piety and humility could thus act "as by a true way," possessing a genuine form of virtue "even without true religion."

Even if this reconstruction of piety and humility goes beyond what Augustine explicitly argues, it offers several advantages for an Augustinian account. First, it helps to dissolve the tension between Augustine's explicit critique and implicit affirmation of non-Christian virtue without ignoring one or the other. By highlighting a more inclusive posture that humbly affirms that Christians and non-Christians can share genuine goods in the *saeculum*, this account avoids the exclusivism often associated with Augustine's critique of pagan virtue, and it does so by finding resources within Augustine's texts themselves, showing how humble openness to plurality is a faithfully Augustinian position. Moreover, unlike approaches that attempt to rescue Augustine by severing pride from the ends of virtue or classifying capacities as both "virtues" and "vices," this account takes seriously Augustine's concerns about pride and presumption by requiring any genuine virtue to be accompanied by piety and humility, the virtues needed to prevent failures to acknowledge dependency or limitation. Citizens who possess these two reciprocal virtues can order their virtues to genuine goods without, by necessity, ordering those goods simply to the private love of self. Although these proximate goods must still be potentially referable to God, they need not be explicitly or consciously referred to God in each action or attitude.

Along with these interpretative and conceptual advantages, this reconstruction also has significant implications for contemporary politics. By recovering resources from Augustine's own texts, it engages Augustinian communitarians on their own terms, showing why a faithfully Augustinian account does not necessarily require indicting the genuine virtues of non-Christian citizens or limiting genuine virtue to the institutional church. Citizens can possess genuine virtues even if they do not share the same ultimate theological commitments or ecclesial communities. Moreover, exemplars, institutions, and traditions outside of the institutional church may be possible sites of moral formation, a recognition that blurs the church-world distinction. This account shifts the focus of politics away from securing completely theorized agreement on ultimate ends toward incompletely theorized agreements on proximate ends, highlighting how more localized, provisional, and fluid convergences can enable diverse citizens to sustain the practices and traditions they share in common.

Augustinian communitarians may worry that the absence of a transcendent horizon or regulative ideal will cause non-Christian citizens to slide into presumption or idolatry, precluding any acknowledgment of limitation or dependency that would chasten cruelty, domination, and violence. The above account takes this concern seriously, acknowledging that, for Augustinians, piety and humility remain necessary, not optional, virtues—virtues that citizens require to preserve their commonwealth and chasten temptations toward presumption, idolatry, and domination. Piety and humility dispose citizens to acknowledge their sources of progress and existence throughout life as well as their own weaknesses and shortcomings, providing the psychological and moral postures that make practices of conversation and mutual accountability possible. Because these citizens do not view themselves as the sole source of their own virtue or goodness, they are willing to subject themselves to persons of "good judgment" and thus remain accountable to others in their social and political community. And because they recognize their dependence on fellow citizens, they are willing to perform "sacrifices" and "works of mercy" to help maintain relationships of mutual trust and civic friendship. The virtues of piety and humility discourage relations of domination while preparing the way for the kinds of political coalitions and communities needed to combat injustice and exploitation.

Democratic theorists may worry that civic piety and humility are not compatible with a democratic culture that promotes self-reliance, preserves religious liberty, and allows for reasonable pluralism. From Machiavelli, Hume, and Nietzsche to more contemporary scholars, many political theorists have reckoned humility more as a civic vice than a virtue, one that leads to servility, subjection, and complacency in the face of injustice rather than resistance to domination.[173] Recently, however, Mark Button has elevated humility as "one of the most important qualities for late-modern societies marked by ethical and political pluralism."[174] Drawing explicitly on an Augustinian notion of humility reflected in the work of St. Bernard of Clairvaux, among others, Button casts humility as "a cultivated sensitivity toward the limitations, incompleteness, and contingency of both one's personal moral powers and commitments, and of the particular forms, laws, and institutions that structure one's political and social life with others."[175] Importantly, this definition includes Bernard's emphasis on humility as both an epistemic and relational concept, as both "a virtue of self-knowledge" and "a precondition for fraternity or neighborliness with others."[176] Button goes on to show how this virtue supports key aims of both post-Nietzschean radical democrats and Rawlsian political liberals, helping to "facilitate a critical attentiveness toward those differences that may have only been tolerated before."[177] This virtue of humility is critical for achieving "democratic ideals of mutual attentiveness, political inclusion, reciprocal learning, and moral growth," particularly in a society marked by deep difference and ethical pluralism.[178] Ultimately, Button concludes, "Instead of marking individual pride or vanity as our essential vice, a democratic ethos of humility would put us on guard against the ethical and political dangers of complacency, premature closures, and dogmatism—especially those forms of political dogmatism that foster the illusion of moral completeness and that express a will to mastery or domination."[179] In this sense, Button's civic virtue of humility resonates with the Augustinian virtue of humility and critique of domination advanced here.[180]

Piety may be a more difficult virtue for democratic theorists, encouraging deference to a unifying authority that vitiates commitment to democratic pluralism and individualism. Jeffrey Stout has recently shown that such worries are misplaced.[181] Drawing on Emerson, Whitman, and Dewey, Stout has advanced an account of piety as a civic virtue that diverse citizens need to preserve the political, social, and cultural conditions for democracy. Taking piety as the "virtuous acknowledgment of dependence on the sources of one's existence and progress through life," Stout argues that critical but genuine piety toward the democratic tradition—including its exemplars, institutions, and practices—is necessary for the preservation of democratic institutions and the culture of mutual recognition, accountability, and conversation that enables democratic life.[182] Without a proper acknowledgment of the sources of their existence and progress, citizens are likely to neglect the institutions, norms, people, and practices that have enabled them to develop and sustain the virtues, capacities, and skills needed to preserve democratic institutions and challenge leaders who exploit economic or political power for their own advantage. To prevent domination and preserve democracy, Stout argues, piety is necessary.[183]

In advocating piety as a civic virtue, Stout does not require religious citizens to forfeit their religious piety. Unlike many secularists, he allows citizens to acknowledge different ultimate ends and sources of authority, recognizing that their epistemic and social context might entitle them to these commitments.[184] Rather than "squinting at one another suspiciously and uncomprehendingly," Stout recommends that citizens adopt a posture of interpretative charity and epistemic humility, the appropriate counterparts of democratic piety.[185] When working together, these interconnected virtues encourage citizens to take each other seriously on their own terms while focusing on what they share in common, shifting conversation away from intractable debates about ultimate ends toward more fluid and dynamic dialogue about proximate ends and the proximate communities, practices, and traditions that preserve their common life together. Citizens can direct their piety toward common referents, even if they order those referents to different ultimate ends.

By highlighting the centrality of civic virtue, recognizing the value of tradition, and encouraging religious citizens to draw from their own traditions and commitments, Stout identifies common ground on which Emersonian democrats and Augustinians can converge. Stout pursues this convergence by appealing to authority within the democratic tradition, showing why Emersonian democrats can embrace this account of civic piety. My account seeks convergence from the other side, appealing to authority within the Augustinian tradition to show why Augustinians have internal reasons to engage in the kind of democratic conversation and community Stout commends. Augustinian Christians do not need to bracket their religious faith or theological virtue to participate in public life. They can continue to recognize God as their ultimate object of piety while also acknowledging proximate objects of piety among fellow citizens. Christians and non-Christians can share common objects of piety, just as they can share common objects of hope and love.[186]

To be sure, on strictly Augustinian terms, the virtues of piety and humility would not be perfect or complete virtues, but they can restrain the worst vices, chastening the Pelagian pursuits of perfection that worry Augustinian realists while recognizing the importance of tradition in the ways that matter to Augustinian communitarians. The virtues of piety and humility can even encourage a kind of openness to diversity and plurality, recognizing that the two cities remain intertwined in the *saeculum* and that God's grace is often mediated through human exemplars, practices, and institutions, including political ones. By cultivating piety and humility, citizens can acknowledge that God's "hidden" causes may be working through citizens who do not share their explicit professions of faith, and they can accept that tolerance and forbearance require patiently enduring those differences for the sake of their common life together. Indeed, as Herdt suggests, Augustinian humility can even encourage citizens to recognize that no one can achieve perfect virtue in this life: for Augustine, all citizens—both Christian and non-Christian—are, at best, "on the way."[187] In this sense, incomplete virtue remains the lot of all human beings in the *saeculum*. East of Eden and on this side of the eschaton, genuine if incomplete virtue is the best anyone can do.

V. Piety, Humility, and Hope

The purpose of this chapter so far has been to defend a faithfully Augustinian account of non-Christian virtue by emphasizing the need for interconnected virtues of piety and humility. With this account in view, we can now return at last to the virtue of hope. Importantly, calling attention to the interconnected virtues of piety and humility illuminates a central feature of Augustinian hope analyzed briefly in chapter 3: to find the mean between presumption and despair, hope requires the reciprocal support of humility and piety. By disposing us to recognize our ignorance and weakness, humility chastens the presumption that might cause our hopes to become disordered or perverse. Piety functions similarly, reminding us that achieving our objects of hope will require the assistance of others. We cannot presume to attain our objects of hope on our own. This acknowledgment of dependence can also help to defy despair. If we have successfully relied on others in the past to achieve what we hope for, we may be able to rely on them again. In this way, piety provides potentially isolated individuals with a sense of belonging and a shared history that can supply grounds for hope. By calling attention to these social and political relations of dependence, piety can help citizens resist despair.

This relationship among hope, humility, and piety brings us at last to the relation between "true virtue" and "true hope." As mentioned above, Augustine at times seems to suggest that anyone who lacks true virtue—including piety and humility—lacks true hope. The account I have brought into view, however, provides Augustinian resources to reconstruct hope as a genuine, if incomplete, virtue that non-Christians can also possess in the *saeculum*. While Christians may refer their hope ultimately to God, virtuous non-Christians may also share the "same virtue" if they direct their hope toward more proximate goods that are potentially referable to God and "use" these goods in ways that avoid both presumption and despair. Avoiding these vices, of course, will require genuine, if incomplete, virtues of piety and humility to chasten utopian presumptions about a perfect political society and prevent citizens from seeing the realities of evil as reasons to despair. But if citizens can cultivate these virtues in the face of both temptations, a civic virtue of hope can direct them toward common goods and foster the relationships of social trust and civic friendship needed to realize them. Achieving these goods and maintaining these friendships will not be easy, particularly given the realities of self-interest and the uncertainty of civic peace, but these difficulties are what give the virtue of hope its purpose. The virtue of hope functions to guide and sustain citizens

HOPE AMONG THE CIVIC VIRTUES 261

in their pursuit of difficult political goods. Without it, citizens would lack the motivation and resolve to do the hard work of citizenship in the face of difficulties that tempt presumption and despair.

Some Augustinians may object that citizens who lack hope for eternal life cannot have any hope at all since any true hope necessarily requires a transcendent ordering to God. Without hope for eternal life, they might say, there would be no way to resist despair. A final passage from *City of God* suggests that this is not necessarily Augustine's view. In 21.15, Augustine returns to his claim that virtue is consistently at "war" with vice. In this "miserable condition," he argues, the saving grace of Christ has given humanity the ability to "wage war in the hope of eternal peace."[188] Here, it might seem that hope for eternal peace is necessary to enable any citizens to have any hope in the *saeculum*. Yet consider what Augustine says next: "But even if—which God forbid—there were no hope of this great good, we ought nonetheless to prefer to endure the distress of this conflict [with vice], rather than permitting our vices to have dominion over us by ceasing to resist them."[189] Notice the implication: Augustine acknowledges the functional value of a virtue that lacks any completion in the heavenly city or any hope of its ultimate realization. Like other forms of incomplete virtue, its value lies in its ability to help citizens resist the worst vices here and now. Presumably, as the "two evils" that "kill souls," Augustine would include presumption and despair among these vices.[190] If so, Augustine counsels readers to resist presumption and despair and to maintain a struggle against these vices even when there is no hope for eternal peace.

Conclusion

Augustine's views of non-Christian virtue would offend many contemporary citizens. His framing of "true virtue" only in terms of faith in a Christian God and his occasionally polemical critiques of those with different views fall short of the more respectful posture toward religious difference that characterizes much contemporary political theory and interfaith dialogue, including the Augustinian account of imperfect convergence outlined in chapter 8. In explicating Augustine's view of non-Christian virtue here, I am not defending it. But I am suggesting that his views of non-Christian virtue are more ambiguous, nuanced, and inclusive than many friends and foes assume. By retrieving passages that imply a tacit affirmation of non-Christian virtue and exploring how they might cohere with Augustinian anxieties about pride and presumption, I have attempted to reconstruct a faithfully Augustinian account that recognizes piety, humility, and hope as genuine virtues that can be shared by diverse citizens, including those who do not belong to the institutional church. Challenging communitarians who summon Augustine's critique to denounce the *saeculum* as a realm of sin or deny the virtue of those outside the church, this account offers Augustinian reasons to approach fellow citizens with humility, tolerance, and forbearance, recognizing that diverse citizens can possess genuine virtue although they share different ultimate ends. This account prepares the way for the recognition, conversation, and collaboration that enables diverse citizens to identify and pursue common hopes for the commonwealth. It also challenges democratic critics who worry that political Augustinianism entails a totalizing rejection of diversity, difference, or pluralism. Rather, the Augustinian account I have presented supports a humble openness to diversity and an aspiration for unity in plurality, supplying citizens with reasons to endure difference, resist domination, and unite around the hopes they share in common.

CONCLUSION

Augustine and the Politics of Hope

Bad times, hard times—this is what people keep saying; but let us live well, and times shall be good. We are the times: such as we are, such are the times.

—AUGUSTINE, SERMON 80.8[1]

You are hoping for the good; be what you hope for.

—AUGUSTINE, SERMON 352A.5

AUGUSTINE IS NOT A PESSIMIST. He is a subtle and sophisticated teacher of hope. That is the central claim of this book. When we explore his neglected texts, situate him in his historical, rhetorical, religious, and political contexts, and recognize the complex connections among relevant concepts, the Augustinian mosaic appears more complex, interesting, and hopeful than most political interpreters recognize. Rather than counseling pessimism, Augustine commends hope—not the false hope that assumes politics is the ultimate source of happiness, nor the shallow optimism that presumes positive thinking will solve all of our problems, but the virtue of hope that supplies the motivation and resolve to hope properly for difficult political goods and in fellow citizens in ways that avoid presumption and despair. While Augustine suggests hope must be ordered ultimately to God, he does not train his hope solely on heaven. He believes the heavenly city is being inaugurated here and now and not simply in the institutional church. In the secular age, earthly commonwealths play an essential role in securing common goods for members of both the "heavenly" and "earthly" cities. While the City of God is the standard by which all earthly commonwealths are judged, the common objects that unite a commonwealth need not necessarily be theological, even if Augustine may

263

have preferred them to be. Rather, he encourages citizens of different religions, cultures, and creeds to unite around common objects of love and hope, especially the good of civic peace. And in his life and work as a bishop, theologian, and citizen, he enacts the political hope he commends.

In recovering this Augustinian vision of hope, my aim has been not only to correct historical and interpretative inaccuracies but to challenge the normative stances toward politics these interpretations have authorized, making it more difficult for contemporary interpreters to either appropriate or attack Augustine's "pessimism." In particular, I have engaged three groups of interpreters: Augustinian realists, Augustinian communitarians, and democratic critics of Augustine. All three assume Augustine licenses despair toward politics, but each relates to that despair in different ways.

Realists typically draw on Augustine's emphasis on sin and domination to chasten political hope or justify violent or coercive action to resist evil in the name of "necessity." By extracting Augustine's more pessimistic passages from their rhetorical contexts, assuming a futurist eschatology that locates the heavenly city beyond history, and emphasizing the prevalence of sin and self-interest, realists neglect Augustine's view that human beings can participate partially in the heavenly city here and now and miss how the former professor uses rhetoric to "instruct" and "encourage" audiences.[2] By highlighting his rhetorical purposes, uncovering his participationist ontology, and emphasizing his inaugurated eschatology, my account offers a more expansive view of politics and a more positive view of civic peace. It challenges the purely negative, remedial views of the commonwealth that realists use to justify the use of force and highlights the genuine political goods that Augustine affirms in this life.

Augustinian communitarians also authorize despair toward politics but from a different angle. They rightly recognize Augustine's inaugurated eschatology, but they too quickly identify the heavenly city with the institutional church. Assuming an ecclesiology that draws a rigid boundary between church and world, they obscure the value of seeking common goods across difference and cast the purported virtues of non-Christians as vices that perpetuate conflict. To avoid being corrupted by this realm of sin, they often encourage Christians to withdraw from the body politic into the body of Christ, which they see as the only true political community. My account acknowledges the role of the church in Augustine's political thought but distinguishes the institutional church from the true church that comprises the heavenly city. As Augustine emphasizes, earthly institutions, including the church, include members of both cities. Christians should seek common goods in cooperation with diverse citizens, including non-Christians, who, on Augustine's view, may potentially be members of the heavenly city and possess genuine virtue. By emphasizing this possibility, my account offers a more inclusive and pluralistic account of Augustinian politics that resists the ecclesial isolationism or worldly withdrawal that often follows from communitarian commitments.

Encouraged, in part, by the pessimism of Augustinian realists and communitarians, many democratic critics tend to dismiss Augustine as otherworldly, antipolitical, and exclusivist, seeing his despair about earthly politics as a reason to reject his thought altogether. Assuming, with realists, that Augustine locates the heavenly city beyond time and, with communitarians, that he dismisses any virtue beyond the Christian church, they argue that Augustine's order of love instrumentalizes the neighbor, abandons the world, and denies the possibility of pluralist politics. Their critique discounts the potential contributions of Augustine's thought to contemporary politics and exacerbates the alienation and resentment that many religious citizens feel toward forms of politics that do not take their religious commitments seriously. In many cases, this resentment only makes Augustinian communitarianism more appealing. My account disrupts this dynamic by questioning the assumptions that underwrite it. Challenging criticisms that Augustine's order of love is otherworldly or instrumentalizing, I show instead that he allows love and hope for political goods and that his political thought is more open to pluralism than most interpreters assume. Because he encourages citizens to seek common goods in the *saeculum* with those who do not share his Christian commitments, he offers a common hope for concord that resists the politics of despair.

In highlighting these neglected pieces of the Augustinian mosaic, my aim has been to engage interlocutors on their own Augustinian terms and identify common ground that can be shared across competing visions of both Augustine and politics. To this end, I have followed Augustine's example of immanent criticism and cultural bridge-building, which, as Justo L. González argues, is central to his background and vocation as a "mestizo," a person embedded in multiple cultures who serves as a living "bridge" between them.[3] My goal has been to offer an account of Augustine that can provide a bridge for diverse citizens wishing to unite the commonwealth around common hopes.

Strikingly, this historically contextualized account makes Augustine more, not less, relevant for contemporary accounts of hope in politics, even for scholars and citizens who do not share Augustine's moral or theological commitments or endorse the ultimate objects of his hope.[4] Given some of Augustine's problematic views, assumptions, and entanglements, my aim in this concluding chapter is not to offer or defend a comprehensive or systematic Augustinian political theory for contemporary politics. Rather, I seek to identify resources in his account of hope, rhetoric, and politics that might enrich our contemporary political imaginations and potentially even challenge some of Augustine's views on their own terms. When we situate Augustine within his late antique Roman context, we uncover not only Augustine's complicities in some forms of injustice but also valuable conceptual resources that are often rendered invisible in the selective and decontextualized interpretations of his "pessimism" currently on offer in political theory.[5]

First, Augustine's spectrum of presumption, hope, and despair provides a useful conceptual vocabulary for contemporary politics. Although a rhetoric of hope has recently pervaded political discourse, politicians, scholars, and citizens often equate "hope" with "optimism" or "positive thinking" and set it in opposition to "pessimism."[6] While this binary may be appropriate in some contexts, it can be confining in others, causing defenders to ignore how the affection of hope can swell into presumption and leaving critics with no other option but to embrace pessimism or despair. Like presumption, such despair can also license apathy or fatalism, encouraging citizens to withdraw from politics rather than stretch toward difficult political goods. When despair becomes a habit—a vice—it can further entrench the social and political problems that prompted pessimism in the first place. To avoid temptations on both sides, citizens need a way to resist despair without thereby licensing presumption or false hope.

Augustine's conception of hope as a virtue supplies this alternative. By seeing hope as an *affection* that can be rightly ordered or disordered, Augustine acknowledges that hope is not always an appropriate attitude and that it can be directed toward the wrong objects in the wrong ways. But by elevating a *virtue* that properly orders the affection toward the right objects in the right ways and resists the vices of presumption and despair, Augustine supplies critical leverage for distinguishing cases when hope is appropriate from cases when it is excessive or deficient. He provides a way to affirm, with hope's defenders, the necessity of the virtue and acknowledge, with hope's critics, how the affection can go wrong.[7]

This vocabulary is especially relevant for contemporary democratic politics, which, in many ways, can be characterized by presumption and despair. Each vice typically tempts different groups.[8] Many political elites are tempted toward presumption, assuming they have the power to speak or act in the name of the people without consulting or considering their concerns. If they possess a lust for glory and a prideful presumption about their own ability, they may seek more power for themselves and their allies without a concern for the common good, or with the presumption that they know what the common good is without needing to ask others if they share it. Their followers may begin to place all their hopes in them, presuming that electing or supporting a single person or party will solve all their problems. Failing to recognize the limits of politics and imperfect political leaders, these citizens could potentially make idols of particular leaders, parties, or causes and neglect the goods they share in common with other citizens. Such presumption, in turn, may generate despair among citizens who feel they have no ability to address overwhelming and persistent political challenges. As a result, many citizens may be tempted to give up or withdraw from the political process, which allows elites to fill the vacuum since they presume citizens cannot—or will not—rule. This vicious cycle further entrenches the problems that generated the temptations in the first place.

Leaders and citizens need a virtue to break this cycle, to provide the motivation and resolve to hope properly for political goods and in each other in ways that avoid both presumption and despair. Unfortunately, contemporary political theory does not offer much guidance on how to conceptualize and cultivate such a virtue. Most political theorists proffer institutional and procedural approaches to politics and neglect the formative character of political life along with the dispositions, motivations, and virtues that motivate and sustain citizens. In recent years, some political theorists have helpfully elevated the civic virtues as a necessary complement to institutional reform and policy change, but they do not usually include hope on their lists.[9] As we saw in chapter 1, Vincent Lloyd even rejects the idea that hope is a virtue, casting it aside as a mere "rhetorical technique."[10] An Augustinian account of hope makes a useful contribution to political theory and practice by identifying hope as a virtue that can motivate citizens to pursue difficult goods wisely in light of political risks and realities and thereby resist the politics of presumption and despair.

This Augustinian account also encourages diverse citizens to share a common hope for the commonwealth. Although Augustine believes that God is the ultimate object and ground of hope, his vision of the commonwealth does not necessarily require citizens to order their hopes toward the same ultimate ends. Members of both the "earthly" and "heavenly" cities can "make common use of those things which are necessary to this mortal life," even if they do so with a "different faith, a different hope, a different love."[11]

Augustine focuses especially on the common good of civic peace. While he recognizes that laws, norms, and institutions are necessary to secure civic peace, he does not see peace negatively as the mere absence of violence, as most interpreters assume. Rather, he affirms what another Augustinian, Martin Luther King Jr., calls a "positive peace," the peace of civic friendship born of justice and mutual affection.[12] Moreover, Augustine recognizes that sustaining this peace requires securing "all things necessary for [its] preservation and recovery," including "breathable air, drinkable water, and whatever the body requires to feed, clothe, shelter, heal or adorn it."[13] In the face of political, social, economic, and ecological crises that threaten the lives and livelihoods of citizens, Augustine's focus on tangible goods—food, housing, health care, and clean air and water—highlights some of what is needed to sustain a healthy body politic.

In a democratic context, this Augustinian account might align with a Tocquevillian ideal of democracy as "the art of pursuing in common the objects of common desires."[14] Recently, Bonnie Honig has drawn on this Tocquevillian ideal to reassert the importance of "public things," objects of common concern that "press us into relations with other," encourage us to "act in concert," and "provide a basis around which to organize, contest, mobilize, defend, or reimagine various modes of collective being together in a democracy."[15] Honig suggests that a "common love for shared objects" can even supply objects of "hope" that enable citizens to resist temptations toward "messianism" and "despair" that accompany social change and cultural loss.[16] While Honig draws on Jonathan Lear rather than Augustine to articulate her account, her conception of hope as a way between "messianism" and "despair" coheres with the structure of Augustine's virtue, and her account of "common love for shared objects," including the "*res* of *res publica*," aligns with Augustine's vision of a commonwealth.[17] Some of the public things that Honig seeks to preserve—"air, water, earth," "climate, the planet, health care"—echo the temporal goods that Augustine identifies as preconditions of temporal peace.[18] Such common objects can help to inspire political action and unite diverse citizens at a time of deep political and religious polarization.

While Augustine's account might be most relevant for Christians who regard him as an authority, an Augustinian vision of "incompletely theorized agreement" invites other citizens to draw on their own authorities to support convergence around common goods.[19] In recent years, many religious leaders have done just that, offering reasons from within their traditions to encourage collaboration across difference. Within the Jewish tradition, for example, Jonathan Sacks, former Chief Rabbi of the United Hebrew Congregations of the

Commonwealth in the United Kingdom, has endorsed Jacques Maritain's call for "practical points of convergence" among citizens with "quite different, even opposite, metaphysical or religious outlooks."[20] For Sacks, having "different points of departure—even different systems of justification—does not imply that we cannot arrive at something like consensus": "We can agree on much that is fundamental to our moral life without necessarily agreeing on why."[21]

Muslim leaders have commended a similar form of incompletely theorized agreement. In "A New Covenant of Virtue: Islam and Community Organizing," Muslim leaders in the United Kingdom have offered a distinctively Islamic rationale for involvement in broad-based coalitions.[22] Appealing to "examples in the life of the Prophet Muhammed," they show how the Prophet's leadership involved building "relationships with others in the community over a common agenda" and "working alongside his neighbours and fellow citizens in order to create a more just and tolerant society at a time when Muslims were a persecuted minority."[23] Gathering examples from the Prophet, passages from the Koran, and stories from the history of Islam, these leaders appeal to Islamic authorities to encourage Muslim citizens to "build a stronger, more cohesive society."[24] As Luke Bretherton has suggested, this posture can make common cause with a broadly Augustinian "politics of a common life."[25]

Such convergence need not apply only to general attitudes toward politics. It can also inspire collective action on concrete political projects. Climate change provides an urgent example. From Pope Francis's encyclical *Laudato Si'*, the Islamic Declaration on Global Climate Change, and the Hindu Declaration on Climate Change to the Lambeth Declaration, Evangelical Climate Initiative, Jewish Climate Action Network, and the Alliance for Religions and Conservation, religious leaders and communities have invoked authorities within their own traditions to encourage their communities to act.[26] Even scientists who do not profess religious belief have sought common ground with people of faith. Writing to an imagined Southern Baptist minister, the naturalist E. O. Wilson has encouraged scientists and religious leaders to find "common ground" "on the near side of metaphysics," finding convergence around proximate ends to "save the Creation."[27] Such incompletely theorized agreement fits with an Augustinian vision of the commonwealth.

In encouraging such convergence, Augustine requires neither strict neutrality nor totalizing exclusion. Contrary to what some liberal interpreters suggest, an Augustinian commonwealth is not "autonomous" or "neutral" with respect to the good.[28] Rather than licensing a Rawlsian liberalism that requires citizens to give "freestanding" public reasons for their political positions,[29]

Augustine encourages citizens to engage each other on their own terms, based on authorities they can accept. Informed by a default and challenge structure of reasoning, this approach aligns with forms of political dialogue that encourage convergence around common goods without assuming neutrality or requiring citizens to deny their religious commitments.[30] This approach shows respect for citizens by honoring their values and commitments rather than requiring them to withhold, hide, or abandon them, and it discourages domination by engaging diverse citizens on terms that are not arbitrary from their point of view.[31] It is also highly effective. Research affirms that engaging others according to their own values is typically more persuasive than trying to convince them based on one's own.[32] Augustine knew that immanent critique is, as social scientists suggest, "the key to political persuasion."[33]

But Augustine was not naïve or sentimental. He recognized that civic peace is fragile and that civic friendship cannot guarantee complete agreement on every moral or political issue. Even when citizens can unite around common objects in theory, they often disagree about how best to realize them in practice. Conflict and contestation are part of the political condition and often necessary to challenge injustice and hold power accountable. In this way, an Augustinian approach fits with more agonistic conceptions of politics that recognize the inevitability of conflict and affirm the value of contestation and accountability. Yet Augustine does not lionize conflict as part of his political ontology or present it as the aim of politics.[34] Even if conflict is unavoidable in this life, he believes citizens should forge unity in plurality and seek concord around common goods.

Moreover, Augustine does not confine his view of politics to the institutions of government. He offers a more expansive view of politics than many contemporary scholars and citizens assume. Today, most citizens equate "politics" with the laws, institutions, or procedures of "government" and thus despair about politics' lack of responsiveness to citizens. But rather than seeing the commonwealth simply as a "state" or set of formal institutions, processes, or procedures, Augustine imagines the commonwealth as the broader realm in which citizens pursue temporal goods in common, which means that diverse citizens can seek political goods and build civic friendships in ways that do not directly relate to political institutions or electoral processes.[35] This has salutary implications for political hope. When citizens despair about particular elections, institutions, or instantiations of power, they can direct their action and attention to other objects of hope that might serve their communities beyond the boundaries of formal political institutions.

This expansive vision of politics, in turn, recognizes the role that politics plays in forming (and deforming) citizens as well as the vital importance of other institutions in educating citizens and promoting common goods.[36] For Augustine, the most significant of these formative institutions is the Christian church, which, he argues, is the place where Christians can worship God, serve their neighbor, and form the virtues needed on their pilgrimage to the heavenly city. Yet, as Augustine's own example of citizenship shows, he does not believe that participating in the institutional church is the only way to worship God or love the neighbor. He also advocates acts of mercy and humanity to those in need, and he sees serving in office, whether in the church or the commonwealth, as a way to enact love and promote the wellbeing of citizens. His example challenges leaders whose ambition to rule reflects a lust for power rather than a desire to serve. It also affirms an insight supported by religious studies and political science: religious leaders play important political roles in shaping the beliefs, conduct, and character of those in their communities, elevating the importance of particular issues, values, and virtues, organizing their communities to advocate for a policy change, and encouraging engagement with (or withdrawal from) the larger political community.[37]

Augustine's example of political activism and civic engagement, including with Roman leaders who did not identify as Christians, is especially instructive given that many Christian leaders have endorsed antagonism toward, or disengagement from, contemporary politics. The most prominent example is Rod Dreher's "Benedict Option," which despairs so much about the world that it encourages Christians to follow St. Benedict's monastic model and escape the world's corrupting influences by huddling together within the church.[38] Though Dreher draws inspiration from Benedict, he also recruits Augustine to inform his theological vision.[39] My account of Augustinian hope provides a direct counterargument and counterexample to the worldly withdrawal that Dreher and his followers commend.[40]

While Augustine enacts a "liturgy of citizenship," he does not encourage easy accommodation to the state.[41] He joins "political activism" with "political criticism."[42] He recognizes that religious leaders must sometimes "dissent" from the domination of the "earthly city" and provide rigorous criticism of injustice.[43] In his letters, sermons, and treatises, he does not hesitate to apply his immense rhetorical powers to practice robust social criticism, which is why many interpreters assume he must be a pessimist about politics. Yet Augustine recognizes what Jeffrey Stout articulates in another context: "The delicate task of the social critic is to adopt a perspective that makes the dangers of our situation visible without simultaneously disabling the hope of reforming it."[44] While Augustine frequently diagnoses the evils that afflict political life, he also acknowledges his responsibility to offer hope, adopting a "structure of encouragement" that emphasizes the world's evils to chasten presumption while highlighting its goods to dispel despair.[45]

This Augustinian structure of encouragement offers a helpful model for contemporary social critics. Much contemporary social criticism rightly offers rigorous analyses of political systems and structures to diagnose, deconstruct, and disrupt domination. The virtue of hope depends on such criticism to register and resist presumption. Yet this criticism can breed cynicism, resignation, and despair if it does not also empower leaders and citizens to address the problems it diagnoses.[46] This may explain why many contemporary scholars and social critics are "relatively pessimistic" about politics.[47] As Jennifer Hochschild suggests in her 2015 presidential address to the American Political Science Association, social science that focuses only on persistent structural problems without attending to positive examples of human agency can leave citizens feeling despairing and disempowered, unmotivated to address the problems that social science has helpfully identified.[48]

bell hooks finds a similar dynamic at work in much contemporary social criticism. Calling critics to "continue rigorous critique" of domination while "also fully and deeply articulating what we do that works to address and resolve issues," hooks argues that "[b]oth exercises in recognition . . . are needed to generate anew and inspire a spirit of ongoing resistance."[49] "When we only name the problem, when we state complaint without a constructive focus on resolution," hooks writes, "we take away hope. In this way critique can become merely an expression of profound cynicism, which then works to sustain dominator culture."[50] hooks's call for rigorous yet empowering critique aligns with an Augustinian structure of encouragement that sustains a realistic hope while resisting the presumption and despair that often fuels domination.

An Augustinian model of social criticism could be especially useful for responding to urgent issues such as climate change. Despite the widespread consensus that human-induced climate change is occurring, most citizens are not motivated to address it, presuming either that its future effects will not be that bad or that new technology will emerge to mitigate it.[51] To challenge such presumption and the complacency it licenses, environmental activists have emphasized the dangers of ecological destruction to spur audiences to action.[52] While "fear appeals" can raise awareness of the threat and increase attention to it, research shows they can sometimes have a disabling effect, causing audiences to feel resignation and despair in the face of potential catas-trophe.[53] This effect has led many climate communicators to use "hope ap-peals" instead, yet research also suggests that hope appeals can encourage complacency if they are unrealistic and downplay the dangers that climate change poses to people and the planet.[54] Augustine's virtue and rhetoric of hope could offer a valuable framework for communicating this threat. Rather than seeing hope simply as an attitude or emotion, as is common in climate communication, he recognizes hope as a virtue that must avoid both presump-tion and despair, and he structures his rhetoric and reasoning to help audi-ences recognize and resist both temptations, modeling a structure of encour-agement that emphasizes the real dangers to avoid presumption while concluding with legitimate reasons for hope to prevent despair.[55] Empirical research on climate communication affirms that such "emotional sequencing" is effective, particularly if one begins with reasons for fear but concludes with grounds for hope, as Augustine often does.[56]

Augustine, of course, might have had difficulty envisioning many of our con-temporary challenges or what we know today as liberal democracy. Although he resists theocracy and recognizes the value of diverse citizens uniting around common goods, he does not endorse a strict separation of church and state. He is more comfortable with certain forms of coercion and paternalism than we are, and he is complicit in some forms of injustice that we find morally hor-rendous, even as he often sought to limit their worst abuses. And although he practiced a kind of "political activism" in ancient Rome,[57] his focus on forming the character of leaders and citizens sometimes obscures the more systematic reforms needed to resist domination and reform unjust institutions.

Yet, at a time of deep division, when political challenges seem intractable and politics is plagued by both presumption and despair, Augustine reminds us that a commonwealth cannot be reduced to its institutions. We the people form the institutions that form us. As leaders and citizens, we have opportuni-ties and responsibilities to serve our local communities, reform our civic in-stitutions, and cultivate our character in ways that seek the welfare of the city. Augustine's political thought is a call to active citizenship, not only in the heav-enly city but in the earthly commonwealths where citizens seek civic peace in the secular age.

The work of citizenship is not easy, particularly when the lust for domina-tion remains a persistent threat. Sustaining hope will require accurately diag-nosing and resisting domination, maintaining resolve in the face of difficulty, and relying on others to realize common goods that are not possible on our own. Augustine identifies the virtue of hope needed to persevere in this work and offers conceptual, political, and rhetorical resources to enlist others in the effort. Ultimately, he knows the most powerful form of persuasion is our example: "We are the times: such as we are, such are the times."[58]

In this passing age, as we stand on the edge of the now and not yet, many of Augustine's questions are ours: What objects of hope will unite our commonwealth? Will we, like Rome, lust for glory and domination, or will we embody the love that does justice and secures unity amid plurality? Will we sustain civic peace in the midst of deep difference, or will we allow our disagreements, real as they are, to sever our bonds of affection? Will we, in the face of political challenges, swell with presumption, surrender to despair, or sustain virtuous hope? As Augustine reminds us, how we answer depends not only on what we say but on how we live.[59]

ACKNOWLEDGMENTS

TO FIND the mean between presumption and despair, the virtue of hope requires the cooperation of other virtues, especially humility and piety. Humility encourages us to recognize our limitations, reminding us that we are not the sole source of our progress through life. Piety, in turn, encourages us to gratefully acknowledge those who are.

As I mark the completion of this book, I begin with confessions of humility and piety. This book, imperfect though it remains, was made possible and better because of the family, friends, and teachers who supported, taught, and inspired me along the way. Augustine would likely acknowledge that such gifts exceed our capacity to repay thanks, but I would like to express my gratitude.

My interest in politics, ethics, and religion was nurtured as an undergraduate at Rhodes College. Courses and conversations with Daniel Cullen, Timothy Huebner, Michael McLain, Michael Nelson, Patrick Shade, and Stephen Wirls, among others, fueled my passion for history, hope, and political theory. They taught me what it means to be a committed teacher and scholar. Jessica Anschutz, Marie Lindquist, Billy Newton, Mel Richey, Bill Troutt, and others provided opportunities to connect my liberal arts education with service and citizenship.

Two years studying at the University of Oxford deepened my understanding of politics at home and abroad and furthered my work at the intersection of philosophy, politics, and religion. I am grateful to the Rhodes Trust and Trinity College for making those transformative years possible and to my tutors and friends for making them so meaningful.

This book began at Princeton University, which was the ideal place to study politics, ethics, and religion. My deep appreciation goes to the Graduate School, Department of Politics, Program in Political Philosophy, and University Center for Human Values for their intellectual and financial support, and to the Josephine De Karman Fellowship Trust for funding my final year of dissertation research and writing.

My graduate education was transformative, in large part, because of faculty whose support has remained unflagging, even years after graduation. I am especially grateful to my dissertation committee whose instruction and example has made me a better teacher, scholar, and citizen. John Bowlin has contributed his expansive knowledge of moral philosophy and theology, along with his distinctive ability to combine historical sensitivity with philosophical precision. In the process, he has taught me much, not only about Augustine and hope but also about tolerance, charity, and friendship. Eric Gregory's teaching and scholarship introduced me to the more complex vision of Augustine that pervades these pages. Eric's work exemplifies how to integrate careful and holistic interpretations of Augustine with serious engagement with theology, religious studies, and political theory. My attempts to extend his insights testify to both his influence and example. Melissa Lane brought her wide-ranging intellect and characteristic energy to this project, combining her deep knowledge of ancient texts and contexts with her commitment to making ancient political thought relevant for contemporary politics. She exemplifies how to work carefully and constructively across academic disciplines and historical epochs. Steve Macedo has also been a wise and encouraging mentor. I especially appreciated his support as this project shifted away from contemporary democratic theory toward more historical work on Augustine. He engaged that work eagerly and shared his broad knowledge to help me make critical connections to contemporary democratic theory. Jeffrey Stout has been a constant support from this project's conception to its completion. His generous and perceptive feedback has wed philosophical rigor, rhetorical sensitivity, and historical nuance with an abiding commitment to democratic theory and practice. Devoted to training scholars and forming citizens, he has been an exemplar of civic, scholarly, and pedagogical excellence. His influence informs every page.

Other faculty at Princeton also offered thoughtful instruction and support. I am particularly grateful to Kwame Anthony Appiah, Charles Beitz, John Cooper, Eddie Glaude, George Kateb, Nannerl Keohane, Victoria McGeer, David Miller, Jan-Werner Müller, Alan Patten, Philip Pettit, Alan Ryan, Anna Stilz, and Cornel West.

When I applied to graduate school, mentors told me I would learn as much from peers as from professors. They were right. During my time at Princeton, friends challenged, encouraged, and taught me. I am especially grateful to Alexis Andres, Samuel Arnold, Alda Balthrop-Lewis, Paul Baumgardner, Anna Bialek, Alison Boden, Mimi Bowlin, Brookes Brown, Emilee Booth Chapman,

Joseph Clair, Sarah Cotterill, Tom Dannenbaum, Ryan Davis, Charles De la Cruz, David Decosimo, C. J. Dickson, John DiIulio, Emily Dumler-Winckler, Will Durbin, Adam Eitel, Yiftah Elazar, Loubna El Amine, Benjamin Ewing, Molly Farneth, Sandra Field, Jessica Flanagan, James Foster, Daniel Frost, Katie Gallagher, Sarah Goff, Clifton Granby, Phil Hannam, Drew Harmon, Lynn Casteel Harper, Ryan Harper, David Henreckson, Javier Hidalgo, Benjamin Hofmann, Amy Hondo, Leah Hunt-Hendrix, Trevor Latimer, Ted Lechterman, Daniel Lee, Alex Levitov, Isabella Litke, James Linville, John Lombardini, Nate Klemp, Barry Maguire, Daniel Mark, Daniel May, Gustavo Maya, Matt McCoy, Benjamin McKean, Hartley Miller, Melissa Moschella, Herschel Nachlis, Joseph Naron, Evan Oxman, Elizabeth Phillips, Russell Powell, Lucia Rafianelli, Leslie Ribovich, Christopher Ro, Julie Rose, Geneviève Rousselière, Elias Sacks, Geoffrey Sigalet, Gabrielle Speech, Sarah Stewart-Kroeker, Sally Stout, Michael Sullivan, Kelly Swartz, Nathaniel Van Yperen, Josh Vandiver, Ian Ward, Mel Webb, Jim Wilson, Joe Winters, Derek Woodard-Lehman, Kevin Wolfe, Jake Zuehl, and David Zuluaga.

After my second year of graduate school, I served as chief of staff on Roy Herron's campaigns for governor and US Congress in my home state of Tennessee. My experience on the campaign fostered practical wisdom, alerted me to threats that endanger democracy, and helped me think more concretely about virtue, citizenship, and the relationship between religion and politics. This political education deepened my appreciation for the insights that Augustine could offer. I am grateful to Roy Herron and Nancy Miller-Herron for their wisdom, integrity, and example, and to Jake Dunavant, Rob James, Martha Stutts, Byron Trauger, and others whose support, counsel, and commitment supplied grounds for hope.

A two-year postdoctoral fellowship with the Oxford Character Project and McDonald Centre for Theology, Ethics, and Public Life at the University of Oxford provided a particularly congenial and generative environment to continue my research on Augustine and expand my understanding of virtue. The Templeton World Charity Foundation generously funded the fellowship, the Faculty of Theology and Religion provided a wonderful academic home, and Harris Manchester College offered a warm and welcoming college community. I am particularly grateful to Nigel Biggar for his wise mentorship, steadfast support, and valuable feedback, and to Jonathan Brant and Ed Brooks who have remained faithful friends and creative collaborators on all matters related to character. Conversations with Ed about Augustine's account of hope, as well as his excellent work on the topic and thoughtful feedback on my manuscript, continue to inform my work. I also benefited from helpful feedback at the Christian Ethics Research Seminar (2014), History of Political Thought Seminar (2014), Postgraduate Diploma in Theology Seminar (2015), and Augustine and Politics Graduate Reading Group (2018), as well as from students in my lectures on Augustine's Political Thought (2015). I am grateful to those who invited me to present on these occasions and the many colleagues, students, and friends who offered feedback and support during my time in Oxford and beyond, including Matthew Anderson, Hannah Baylor, Teresa Bejan, Paul Billingham, David Carel, Josh Carpenter, JanaLee Cherneski, Benedict Coleridge, Charles Conn, Edward David, Ian Desai, Ginny Dunn, Mary Eaton, Steven Firmin, Jack Fuller, Carol Harrison, Donald Hay, Robert Heimburger, Carl Hildebrand, Emily Holman, Joshua Hordern, Sarah Kleinman, Elizabeth Li, Matthew Longo, Joseph McCrave, Alister McGrath, David Miller, Sarah Mortimer, Emilie Noteboom, Jim O'Connell, James Orr, Stuart Ramsey, Diana Saverin, Mubeen Shakir, Matthew Simpkins, Tom Simpson, Sophie Smith, Will Tant, Bronwyn Tarr, Jim Van Dyke, Ashwini Vasanthakumar, Luna Wang, Graham Ward, Ralph Waller, Ben Wilcox, Brian Williams, Bethan Willis, Bill Wood, Brian Young, Johannes Zachhuber, and Simeon Zahl.

For the last six years, Wake Forest University has provided an ideal community to pursue my vocation as a teacher, scholar, and citizen. I am especially grateful to Nathan Hatch for envisioning the program that brought me to Wake Forest and for offering wise counsel and steadfast support throughout my time here. Michele Gillespie, Rogan Kersh, and Reid Morgan have provided invaluable guidance and support on my research, and the Interdisciplinary Humanities Program has offered an especially collegial environment to pursue my interdisciplinary teaching and research. I am grateful to students and colleagues in the Program, particularly Ashley Hairston, David Phillips, Corey Walker, and José Luis Venegas, whose leadership and support as program director has been particularly meaningful. Other Wake Forest colleagues who have shared their friendship and support are too many to name here, but I especially want to thank those whose discussions of Augustine, hope, and virtue have informed this book: Emily Austin, Michaelle Browers, Dylan Brown, Andrius Galisanka, Rebecca Gill, Adrian Greene, Eranda Jayawickreme, Kevin Jung, Adam Kadlac, Christian Miller, John Oksanish, Michael Pisapia, Michael Sloan, Erica Still, and Jonathan Lee Walton.

I am particularly indebted to the incredible team of Wake Forest's Program for Leadership and Character, whose partnership and friendship has made this work so meaningful and enjoyable, and to the generous donors who have supported the program and the foundations who have supported my research, including the F. M. Kirby Foundation, John Templeton Foundation, Kern Family Foundation, and Lilly Endowment, Inc. The opinions expressed within this book are my own and do not reflect the views of any of the institutions or individuals listed here.

A central aim of this book is to lift recent scholarship on Augustine in religious studies and theology into political theory. I have attempted to acknowledge my debts to particular scholars on specific matters in the notes, but after a decade of working on Augustine, their influence extends beyond anything that can be captured by citations. I especially want to acknowledge John Bowlin, Luke Bretherton, Joseph Clair, Robert Dodaro, Eric Gregory, Jennifer Herdt, Kristen Deede Johnson, Peter Iver Kaufman, Paul Kolbet, Charles Mathewes, Veronica Roberts Ogle, Sarah Stewart-Kroeker, Jeffrey Stout, John von Heyking, and James Wetzel, whose scholarship and conversation have expanded and enriched my understanding of Augustine and politics.

In addition to those mentioned above, many other colleagues and friends have shared helpful feedback and thoughtful conversation on topics relevant to this book. I am particularly grateful to Robert Audi, Richard Avramenko, Nancy Bedford, Susan Bickford, Todd Breyfogle, Winter Brown, Peter Busch, Peter Buttigieg, Paul Camacho, John Cavadini, Andrew Chignell, Ian Clausen, Aaron Cobb, Susan Collins, Kody Cooper, Alexandra Conliffe, Clay Cooke, Jesse Couenhaven, Andreas Coutsoudis, Kendall Cox, Prithviraj Datta, Giulia Delogu, Matthew Dickinson, Rob Dove, Matthew Drever, Robert Edgecombe, Ashleigh Elser, Nita Farahany, Allan Fitzgerald, Paul Gleason, Seth Gilpin, Paul Griffiths, Scott Grinsell, Adam Grogg, Tim Hartman, Stanley Hauerwas, Benjamin Hertzberg, Miles Hollingworth, Susan James, Jakatae Jessup, Stuart Johnston, Mark Jordan, Bolek Kabala, Elizabeth Kistin Keller, Chandran Kukathas, Kristy Kummerow, Sean Larsen, Joseph Lenow, Thomas A. Lewis, Philip Lorish, Robin Lovin, Luke Mayville, Brett McCarty, Alison McQueen, Christina McRorie, David Meconi, Ashleen Menchaca-Bagnulo, Andrew Murphy, Justin Mutter, Samuel Newlands, David Newheiser, Shifa Amina Noor, Kristopher Norris, Anne Norton, Joshua Nunziato, Stephen Ogden, Travis Pickell, Nathan Pinkoski, Adam Potkay, Matthew Puffer, Sabeel Rahman, Rubén Rosario Rodríguez, Eugene Rogers, Melvin Rogers, Andrew Sabl, Robert Schiff, Joel Schlosser, Molly Scudder, Joseph Sherrard, Ganesh Sitaraman, Ted Smith, Nancy Snow, Allison Stanger, Mark Storslee, Daniel Strand, Adam Thomas, Gregory Thompson, David Thunder, William Umphres, Daniel Weeks, Mara Willard, Jonathan Yates, and Alex Zakaras.

In September of 386, after retiring as the emperor's professor of rhetoric in Milan, Augustine retreated with a small circle of family, friends, and students to a friend's villa in Cassiciacum where he engaged in a series of philosophical dialogues and wrote his first book that still survives. During the decade of writing my first book, generous friends provided my own personal Cassiciacum by lending their homes for focused writing retreats. These retreats were enormously helpful in supplying the solitude and space needed to finish this book. I am grateful to Alison Boden and Jarrett Kerbel, Brenda and Frank Cox, Jennifer Geddes and Charles Mathewes, Nannerl and Robert Keohane, Matt and Llew Ann King, Jim and Pat Marino, Gerald and Stephanie Roach, and Margaret and Scott Wray.

Three research fellows from Wake Forest provided valuable assistance on the manuscript. Hannah Lafferrandre helped to format the bibliography. Cameron Silverglate carefully edited and checked citations for several chapters, while William Morgan meticulously reviewed and edited the entire manuscript, checked citations, and offered substantive suggestions. Their careful attention strengthened the book and saved me from numerous errors.

Over the past decade, I have presented my work on Augustine at a number of conferences, workshops, and institutions, including annual meetings of the American Academy of Religion (2014, 2016, 2018); American Political Science Association (2014, 2015, 2017); Association for Political Theory (2014), and Northeast Political Science Association (2011); the University of Virginia Graduate Colloquium in Theology, Ethics, and Culture (2012); Middlebury College (2012); The Politics of Spirit: Augustine and Hegel in Dialogue Conference at Princeton University (2014); International Conference on Patristic Studies at the University of Oxford (2015); London School of Economics Legal and Political Theory Forum (2016); Reconsiderations V at Villanova University (2016); L'Arca delle Virtù Conference at the University of Pavia (2017); Hope and Optimism Working Group at Cornell University (2017); Molly Farneth's Ethics and Good Life course at Haverford College (2017); Kevin Jung's Theological Ethics course and Michael Sloan's Seminar in Classical Studies at Wake Forest University (2017); Augustine and Political Theory: Dialogue or Dialectic? at Princeton University (2018); and the Institute for the Study of Human Flourishing at the University of Oklahoma (2021). Generous feedback and discussion at a manuscript workshop organized by Sean Larsen and Charles Mathewes at High Point University (2015) was especially helpful in refining the manuscript. I am grateful to colleagues across multiple fields who organized and attended these events, served as respondents, and provided valuable comments and criticism.

Portions of this book draw from material previously published in "Augustine and Contemporary Theory," in *Augustine in a Time of Crisis: Politics and Religion Contested*, edited by Boleslaw Z. Kabala, Ashleen Menchaca-Bagnulo, and Nathan Pinkoski (New York: Palgrave Macmillan, 2021), 261–282; "Augustine and Political Theory," in *T&T Clark Handbook of Political Theology*, edited by Rubén Rosario Rodríguez (London: T&T Clark, 2020), 89–116; "Between Presumption and Despair: Augustine's Hope for the Commonwealth," *American Political Science Review* 112, no. 4 (2018): 1036–1049; "Beyond Pessimism: A Structure of Encouragement in Augustine's *City of God*," *Review of Politics* 80, no. 4 (2018): 591–624; and "Biden's Augustinian Call for Concord," in *Breaking Ground: Charting Our Future in a Pandemic Year*, edited by Anne Snyder and Susannah Black (New York: Plough Publishing House, 2022), 267–269. I am grateful to the editors and reviewers for their feedback and to the publishers for their kind permission to adapt this material here.

Princeton University Press has been an ideal publisher for this book. I am especially grateful to my editor, Rob Tempio, for believing in this project and embodying the steadfast support, patience, and good humor needed to see it to completion. Matt Rohal, Chloe Coy, and Kathleen Cioffi provided timely feedback and helped to shepherd the book through publication. Elliot Linzer provided helpful assistance with the index, and Hank Southgate improved the book with his careful and conscientious copyediting. Mary Keys and James Wetzel served as external reviewers and offered insightful comments that helped to increase the book's clarity and concision.

In the final year of writing, several friends offered invaluable support that helped to take this book across the finish line. Bradley Burroughs and Colleen Mitchell read the entire manuscript and offered extensive and perceptive feedback, while other friends offered thoughtful guidance on new and revised sections. I am grateful to Toni Alimi, John Bowlin, Edward Brooks, Eric Gregory, Julie Hatch, Nathan Hatch, Ryan Juskus, Brooks Lamb, Elizabeth Morgan, Reid Morgan, Ann Phelps, Anne Snyder, Jeffrey Stout, Kenneth Townsend, and especially Tiffany Thompson, whose faithful presence, joyful hope, and spirited cocreation provided the ideal support for finishing a decade's work. These and other friends prove what Augustine avers in *City of God*, 19.8: "the unfeigned faith and mutual delight of true and good friends" is one of life's great joys and consolations.

Finally, I would like to thank my family for their unwavering love and support. My grandparents John and Brenda Bradford nurtured my love of words and passion for inquiry, while Horace and Glenda Lamb taught me the importance of commitment and hard work. Patrick and Brooks Lamb have been not only loyal brothers but faithful friends, and my parents, Ken and Angela Lamb, have been exemplars of love. My mother taught me how to read and how to serve. My father taught me how to work and how to sacrifice. Together, they taught me how to hope. This book is dedicated to them.

NOTES

Preface: Why Augustine? Why Hope?

1. On Augustine as a "bridge," see González, *Mestizo Augustine*, 13–19, 167–171. "In the West," González argues, "there is no theologian who can compare with Augustine" (13). On Augustine as a "transitional figure" who presents "a synthesis of classical and Christian philosophy," see Klosko, *History of Political Theory*, 257, 223. See also Deane, *Political and Social Ideas*, 2–3.

2. Wolin, *Politics and Vision*, 110. See also Fortin, "St. Augustine," 176.

3. Ryan, *On Politics*, 149. Charles Taylor locates the origin of the Western focus on interiority in Augustine (*Sources of the Self*, 127–142, esp. 131), while Jennifer Herdt suggests the rise of modern moral philosophy can be traced, in part, to the Augustinian "legacy of the splendid vices" (*Putting on Virtue*, 1–19).

4. E.g., Russell, *History of Western Philosophy*, 334–335.

5. For a comprehensive account of Augustine's influence, see Pollmann and Otten, eds., *Oxford Guide to the Historical Reception of Augustine*; and Fitzgerald et al., eds., *Augustine through the Ages*. Larry Siedentop claims that "Augustine became the greatest single influence on Western theology for the next thousand years" (*Inventing the Individual*, 110). "Throughout history," Henri Marrou argues, "[Augustine's] influence is constantly present in the most widely different spheres of thought, education and religious life. It is hard to imagine, without actually verifying it, how much the example and teaching of St. Augustine have moulded the Latin tradition: with more justice even than Virgil he deserves the title of 'Father of the West'" (*Saint Augustine*, 151).

6. Noting Augustine's influence on Christian theology, Velde suggests that "[a]ll medieval theologians are more or less 'Augustinians'" ("Thomas Aquinas," 1799).

7. McGrath, *Iustitia Dei*, 38, as cited by Bok, "Peter Lombard," 1527. See also Kent, "Reinventing Augustine's Ethics," 231–232.

8. See, e.g., Torrell, *Saint Thomas Aquinas*, 39–45; Velde, "Thomas Aquinas"; Gregory and Clair, "Augustinianisms and Thomisms"; Dauphinais, David, and Levering, eds. *Aquinas the Augustinian*; Decosimo, *Ethics as a Work of Charity*.

9. Reinhold Niebuhr describes Augustine as "both the father of Catholicism and of the Reformation" ("How Faith and Reason Are Related," as cited by Brown, *Niebuhr and His Age*, 157).

10. Saak, "Luther," 1341. See also Krey, "Luther."

11. Luther, *D. Martin Luthers Werke*, Weimarer Ausgabe (WA) 9:29, ll. 5–6, as cited by Saak, "Luther," 1343.

12. Smits, *St. Augustin dans l'oeuvre de Jean Calvin*, 6, as cited by Marshall, "Calvin," 117.

13. Calvin, *Aeterna Dei praedestinatione*, 266, as cited and translated by Marshall, "Calvin," 116.

14. For a thematic overview, see Vanderjagt, "Political Thought."

15. Wetherbee, "Dante Alighieri." For a more extensive account, see Marchesi, *Dante and Augustine.*

16. Savoie, "Milton, John," 1397, alluding to Milton, *Complete Prose Works,* 4.419. Savoie suggests Augustine's "pervasive influence" on Milton "cannot be overstated" (1397–1398). On *Paradise Lost,* see Sloan, "*De civitate Dei,*" 259.

17. Christine de Pizan, *Body Politic,* 1.2; *City of Ladies,* 1.2.2, 1.10.4. Christine cites the fact that "Saint Augustine, the glorious Doctor of the Church, [was] converted to the Faith by his mother's tears" to answer critics who attack "women for their habit of weeping" (*City of Ladies,* 1.10.3–4). On Christine's engagement with Augustine, see Forhan, "Christine de Pizan."

18. For overviews of Rousseau's Augustinian influences, see Brooke, "Rousseau's Political Philosophy"; and Qvortrup, "Rousseau." On Rousseau's *Confessions,* see Qvortrup, "Rousseau," 1675–1676; and Hartle, *Modern Self in Rousseau's Confessions.* Scholars also suggest that Rousseau's accounts of the "general will" and *amour propre* bear Augustinian imprints. On Augustinian sources for the general will, see Riley, *General Will before Rousseau.* On Augustinian sources for *amour propre,* see Brooke, "Rousseau's Political Philosophy"; and Qvortrup, "Rousseau," 1675–1676. While Rousseau's thinking is "diametrically different" from Augustine's in many ways, Qvortrup argues, Rousseau "was at every level deeply influenced, inspired by, and indebted to the writings of Augustine" ("Rousseau," 1675).

19. Miller, *New England Mind,* 4. In identifying the "Augustinian strain of piety" in Puritan thought, Miller refers to an Augustinian "frame of mind" more than direct textual influence.

20. See Hairston, *Ebony Column,* 16, 82.

21. For analyses of recent varieties of political Augustinianism, see Bruno, *Political Augustinianism*; Scott, "Political Thought"; and Lamb, "Augustine and Political Theory."

22. Martha Nussbaum has praised Augustine for elevating the emotions, even as she rejects his "otherworldly" account of love (*Upheavals of Thought,* 551–553). John Rawls cites Augustine extensively throughout his senior thesis but presents his own account as an alternative to Augustine's "egoistic" account of love (*Brief Inquiry,* 209; see also 161–162, 174–175, 182–183, 216–217, 220). Later, Rawls identifies Augustine among thinkers whose "comprehensive doctrines" oppose a distinctly "political" liberalism (*Political Liberalism,* 134–135; "Justice as Fairness," 248). Paul Weithman has defended a vision of Augustinian liberalism that aligns with Rawlsian accounts ("Toward an Augustinian Liberalism"). Eric Gregory suggests that "the continuing debate over modern liberalism has to a large extent consisted in variations on Augustinian themes and antiphonal responses to them" (*Politics,* 1).

23. Michael Oakeshott "read all that St. Augustine wrote," describing him and Montaigne as "the two most remarkable men who have ever lived" (see letter from Michael Oakeshott to Patrick Riley [1988], cited in Riley, "Michael Oakeshott," 664). Oakeshott's lecture on Augustine is included in *Lectures in the History of Political Thought,* 323–340. On similarities between Augustine and Oakeshott, see Coats, *Oakeshott and His Contemporaries,* 28–38; Worthington, "Michael Oakeshott and the City of God"; and Corey, *Michael Oakeshott,* 20–45.

24. Alasdair MacIntyre begins his history of the Catholic philosophical tradition with a chapter on Augustine (*God, Philosophy, Universities,* 21–32) and draws on an "Augustinian alternative" to challenge liberal accounts of justice (*Whose Justice?,* 147–163). I use the term

"communitarianism" given its wide acceptance in the field, though some typically included in this group resist the label.

25. Reinhold Niebuhr, Judith Shklar, and Jean Bethke Elshtain have invoked Augustine's trenchant diagnosis of sin and self-interest to resist utopianism and emphasize the limits of politics. See Niebuhr, "Augustine's Political Realism"; Shklar, "Giving Injustice Its Due"; Elshtain, *Augustine*.

26. Hannah Arendt wrote her dissertation on *Love and Saint Augustine* and drew on Augustinian insights throughout her works. On Arendt's engagement with Augustine, see Gregory, *Politics*, 197–240; Elshtain, *Augustine*, 71–87; Mathewes, *Evil*, 149–197; Scott, "Hannah Arendt's Secular Augustinianism"; and Scott and Stark, "Rediscovering Hannah Arendt."

27. Michael Hardt and Antonio Negri have enlisted Augustine's critique of empire to bolster their own (*Empire*, 205–208, 393), while William Connolly and Romand Coles have argued instead that Augustine's "imperative" and "totalizing" vision embodies the dominating tendencies he otherwise resists (Connolly, *Augustinian Imperative*, xviii–xxxiv, 63–90; Coles, *Self/Power/Other*, 51–52, 173–174, 179). For Augustinian responses to criticisms from radical democrats, see Skerrett, "Sovereignty and Sadness"; Skerrett, "Indispensable Rival"; Johnson, *Theology*, 82–260; Mathewes, *Theology of Public Life*, 105–142, 266–307; and Dodaro, "Augustine's Secular City."

28. Pollmann, "Proteanism of Authority."

29. O'Donnell, "Authority of Augustine," 7, 23; Lane, "Calvin," 739.

30. See, for example, Brooks, "How Movements Recover," and *Road to Character*, 186–212; Dionne, *Souled Out*, 31, 185–186, 194, and "Kinder Mix"; Meacham, "End of Christian America"; Montás, *Rescuing Socrates*, 8–10, 20–65; West, "Called Far and Wide," and "Power Is Everywhere"; Worthen, "Is There a Way to Dial Down the Political Hatred?"

31. See Elshtain, *Just War against Terror*, and "But Was It Just?"; Thistlethwaite, "'Just War,' or Is It Just a War?" and "Iraq War." For analyses, see Lee, "Selective Memory."

32. See Pelosi, interview on *Meet the Press*; Kengor, "Pelosi v. Augustine"; Duin, "Catholics Rap Pelosi's Abortion Remarks." For an academic analysis, Jones, "Thomas Aquinas, Augustine, and Aristotle on 'Delayed Animation.'"

33. Luban, "What Would Augustine Do?"

34. Biden, "Inaugural Address"; Pecknold, "Joe Biden Misreads Augustine." For one analysis, see Lamb, "Biden's Augustinian Call for Concord."

35. See Ratzinger, *Volk und Haus Gottes*; Bruno, *Political Augustinianism*, 121–127; George, "Benedict XVI"; Glatz, "Holy, Holy, Holy"; Povoledo, "Pope Visits Assisi."

36. For his collected essays, see Williams, *On Augustine*. For an overview of Williams's interpretation, see Bruno, *Political Augustinianism*, 148–153.

37. Doody, Hughes, and Paffenroth, eds., *Augustine and Politics*; Dixon, Doody, and Paffenroth, eds., *Augustine and Psychology*; Cary, Doody, and Paffenroth, eds., *Augustine and Philosophy*; Kennedy, Paffenroth, and Doody, eds., *Augustine and Literature*; Daly, Doody, and Paffenroth, eds., *Augustine and History*; Doody, Goldstein, and Paffenroth, eds., *Augustine and Science*; Paffenroth and Hughes, eds., *Augustine and Liberal Education*; Doody, Paffenroth, and Smillie, eds., *Augustine and the Environment*.

38. Longfellow, "Ladder of St. Augustine"; Oliver, "Don't Worry"; Dylan, "I Dreamed I Saw St. Augustine"; Sting, "Saint Augustine in Hell."

39. Gregory, "Modern Politics in the Shadow of Augustine."

40. For Augustine's narrative of his life, see *Confessions*. For the first biography written by a fellow bishop and friend, see Possidius, "Life." For contemporary biographies, see Brown, *Augustine of Hippo*; González, *Mestizo Augustine*; Hollingworth, *Saint Augustine of Hippo*; and O'Donnell, *Augustine*. For more concise accounts, see Marrou, *Saint Augustine*; and Wills, *Saint Augustine*.

41. See González, *Mestizo Augustine*, 21–32.

42. *Confessions*, 2.3.5–6.

43. Brown, *Augustine of Hippo*, 9–10; O'Donnell, *Augustine*, 10.

44. *Confessions*, 3.3.6.

45. Clair, *On Education*, 13. See also *Confessions*, 5.13.23; Brown, *Augustine of Hippo*, 54–61; Kolbet, *Cure of Souls*, 65–66.

46. *Confessions*, 3.3.6, 6.11.19, 6.6.9, 9.2.2–4, 9.5.13; Possidius, "Life," §2; Kolbet, *Cure of Souls*, 65–67.

47. See *Confessions*, 9.2.2–9.6.14; *Happy Life*; *On Order*; Brown, *Augustine of Hippo*, 102–120.

48. *Confessions*, 9.6.14; Possidius, "Life," §3; Brown, *Augustine of Hippo*, 117–130.

49. *Catechising of the Uninstructed*, 12.17, as translated and cited by Wills, *Saint Augustine*, 72.

Introduction: Beyond Pessimism

1. Also cited by Quinn, "Disputing the Augustinian Legacy," 233.

2. On Augustine's interest in mosaics, see Wills, *Saint Augustine*, 3; Harmless, introduction to *Augustine in His Own Words*, xvii–xviii; and *Augustine and the Catechumenate*, 39. Harmless also uses the mosaic as a metaphor for constructing a portrait of Augustine. On mosaics in Roman North Africa, including Augustine's basilica in Hippo, see Dunbabin, *Mosaics*, 188–195, 238–239. On archaeological evidence from the basilica at Hippo, see Phelan, "St. Augustine."

3. *On Order*, 1.2. See also *City of God*, 12.4.

4. *On Order*, 1.2.

5. Rawls, *Lectures on the History of Political Philosophy*, 302. Dostoyevsky is the other "dark mind."

6. Baier, "Unsafe Loves," 36.

7. Russell, *History of Western Philosophy*, 345–346, 355, 365.

8. See Niebuhr, "Augustine's Political Realism," 140–141, 128. See also Niebuhr, *Faith and History*, 221, where he argues that "St. Augustine's Christian realism errs in its too consistent emphasis upon the sinful corruptions of the world's peace," and *Man's Nature*, where he describes Augustine's realism as "too consistent" and "too excessive" (46, 97). In *Moral Man and Immoral Society*, Niebuhr identifies Augustine's thought as authorizing a "defeatism" that can tempt one "to despair of society" (69–70).

9. *City of God*, 1.Pref., 5.19, 14.28. For an insightful account of Rome's lust for domination and its relation to the earthly city, see Ogle, *Politics and the Earthly City*.

10. Ibid., 19.8, 19.5.

11. Ibid., 22.22–23.

12. Wills, *Saint Augustine*, 129.

13. For overviews, see Krey, "Luther"; Saak, "Luther"; Marshall, "Calvin"; Lane, "Calvin"; and Marsden, "Jonathan Edwards, American Augustine."

14. Whether Luther, Calvin, and Edwards are as "pessimistic" as often assumed is also a matter of dispute.

15. Arendt, *Love*, 18–22, at 19; see also 93–97. In *The Human Condition*, Arendt suggests that Augustine's Christian vision assumes its "main political task" is to "find a bond between people strong enough to replace the world" (53). For Arendt, such "worldlessness" makes Augustinian Christianity "non-political and even antipolitical" (53–54).

16. Nussbaum, *Upheavals*, 551–552.

17. Billings, "Natality," 135–136, endorsing the view he finds in Arendt's *Love*.

18. Ibid., 136.

19. Elshtain, *Augustine*, 19; see also "Augustine," 36. Rosemary Radford Ruether argues that "Augustine ultimately fails to give us . . . a sufficiently hopeful basis for conducting a moral struggle toward the political order" ("Augustine and Christian Political Theology," 263). Terrance C. McConnell argues that "Augustine is pessimistic about what man can attain on earth" ("Torturing and Punishing," 487). Janet Coleman highlights Augustine's "pessimism" in her overview of his political thought ("St Augustine," 334; see also 315, 330).

20. Gregory, "Sympathy and Domination," 34.

21. There are notable exceptions, though some of these treatments remain condensed or focus on a limited number of texts. See Deneen, *Democratic Faith*, 243; Jackson, "Faith, Hope and Charity"; Markus, *Saeculum*, 166–186; Mathewes, *Theology of Public Life*, 215–260; Mittleman, *Hope in a Democratic Age*, 151–156; Studer, "Pauline Theme of Hope." For an insightful Augustinian account of hope in relation to modernity, see Brooks, "What May I Hope For?"

22. Fitzgerald et al., *Augustine through the Ages*.

23. Cartwright, "Aquinas to Zwelethemba."

24. Markus, *Saeculum*, 154–186; Mathewes, *Theology of Public Life*, 214–260. Pieper, "On Hope," draws from Augustine's sermons and treatises to develop a conception of theological hope, but he seems to use Augustine primarily to explicate Aquinas.

25. Niebuhr, "Augustine's Political Realism."

26. Deane, *Political and Social Ideas*, esp. 56–66, 241–243. Deane equates Augustinian "realism" with "pessimism" (56–57, 66, 242–243).

27. Shklar, "Giving Injustice Its Due," 1136–1140. Other scholars affirm this emphasis. Discussing Augustine's view of "humankind's sinful nature," W. M. Spellman argues that "Augustine concentrated his greatest energies on how to make sense of a world that was filled with an inordinate share of cruelty and danger" (*History of Western Political Thought*, 29–31).

28. Elshtain, *Augustine*, esp. 89–112; *Just War*; Deneen, *Democratic Faith*, 243, 271–272; Galston, "Augustine or Emerson?," 24–25; Kaufman, *On Agamben*, ix; see also *Incorrectly Political*, 1, 227–232. In a later essay, Elshtain offers a qualified assessment of Augustine's realism, suggesting that "one must rescue Augustine from those who would appropriate him to a version of political limits or 'realism' that downplays his insistence on the great virtue of hope and the call to enact projects of *caritas*" ("Augustine," 47). Galston invokes Niebuhr's (Augustinian) authority in "When in Doubt." Bruno generally affirms Kaufman's interpretation of Augustine's "strong pessimism" but acknowledges he is not "completely pessimistic" (*Political Augustinianism*,

235–237; see also 257, 268). Schall equates Augustine's "realism" with "pessimism" ("'Realism,'," 193–197, 205).

29. MacIntyre, *Whose Justice?*, 146–163.

30. Milbank, *Theology and Social Theory*, 382–442.

31. Hauerwas, *After Christendom?*, 13–44, esp. 40, 19; *Community of Character*, esp. 72–86, 108–110, 260n40. See also Hauerwas, *Peaceable Kingdom*. On Hauerwas's conception of the church as an alternative "place of hope," see Mittleman, *Hope in a Democratic Age*, 238–245.

32. See Hauerwas, *Community of Character*, 1–3, 9–12, 73–74, 83–86, 108–110; Hauerwas and Willimon, *Resident Aliens*.

33. Isaiah Berlin, quoted in Schlesinger Jr., "Forgetting Reinhold Niebuhr," and Hobsbawn, *Age of Extremes*, 1. On the influence of this context on interpretations of Augustine, see also Kaufman, *Incorrectly Political*, 118–123; and Bruno, *Political Augustinianism*, 7–9, 15–17, 63–64, 70–78, 116–117.

34. Rawls, *Brief Inquiry*, 200, 195–198.

35. See Scott, "Hannah Arendt's Secular Augustinianism," 294.

36. George Kateb observes that Shklar's personal experience kept her "mindful of the way ideologically inflamed people, possessed by hope for a radically changed world, can make a hell on earth" (foreword to Shklar, *Political Thought and Political Thinkers*, viii).

37. On the "banality of evil," see Arendt, *Eichmann in Jerusalem*. While Arendt does not cite Augustine explicitly in *Eichmann*, several scholars have connected her conception of evil's banality to her earlier engagement with Augustinian ideas. See Mathewes, *Evil*, 66–67, 149–197; Elshtain, *Augustine*, 72–87; Grummett, "Arendt, Augustine, and Evil." Daniel Strand argues more cautiously that "Arendt's banality . . . may carry some Augustinian insights or traces or fragments," but "the echo is faint and diverges significantly with the substance of Augustine's account" ("Augustine's Privation," 423). On Shklar's engagement with Augustine, see "Giving Injustice Its Due," 1136–1140.

38. Arendt, "Understanding and Politics," 321.

39. Niebuhr, "Augustine's Political Realism." On Niebuhr's earlier engagement with Augustine, see Brown, *Niebuhr and His Age*, 32, 59, 153–157. According to Brown, the "legacy of Saint Augustine remained a pervasive influence on Niebuhr's thought" (73).

40. Niebuhr, "Augustine's Political Realism," 124–126. Elsewhere, Niebuhr argues that "the Augustinian *Civitas Terrena* was the first and most rigorous expression of Christian realism" (*Man's Nature*, 43).

41. Niebuhr, "Augustine's Political Realism," 133, 141. On the influence of "a world depression and two world wars," see Niebuhr, *Man's Nature*, 16, 21–23. As Brown notes, the "tragic experience of two world wars and the possibility of worse to come" sparked "renewed interest in the thought of Saint Augustine, who had faced such questions during the crisis of the late Roman Empire" (*Niebuhr and His Age*, 153). See also Bruno, *Political Augustinianism*, 64–78.

42. As an illustrative example, David Miller identifies Deane as "Augustine's main interpreter" ("Tale of Two Cities," 238). For a summary of Deane's view, including how it was shaped by Deane's historical context, see Bruno, *Political Augustinianism*, 90–105.

43. "As a result of our own experiences," Deane continues, "we are much more prepared than our fathers were to give a hearing to the doctrine of original sin and to the view that ceaseless application of coercive power is necessary in order to hold in check human pride and the fruits

of pride—aggression, avarice, and lust—and to preserve the fabric of civilization which is constantly imperiled by these forces" (*Political and Social Ideas*, 241–242).

44. Ibid., 242–243.

45. Bonnie Kent notes that "there is nothing new about scholars' extracting only those parts of an author's works that they like or can use while ignoring the rest. From the outset Augustine was one of the authors most subject to such treatment" ("Augustine's Ethics," 228).

46. Ryan, *On Politics*, 149; O'Donnell, *Augustine*, 135–136.

47. Possidius, "Life," §18, also cited by O'Donnell, *Augustine*, 135; and Kent, "Augustine's Ethics," 228.

48. "Menditur, qui te totum legisse fatetur / An quis cuncta tua lector habere potest?" (Isidore, *Opera Appendices*, Appendix III, column 1109). Kent translates the passage as "He lies who claims that he has read all of you. What reader can even have all of your works?" ("Reinventing Augustine's Ethics," 228). Brown, "Political Society," 311, 330n1; and O'Donnell, *Augustine*, 135, also cite this passage. Kent argues that, for Isidore, "the problem lay less in finding time to read Augustine's works than in getting copies of them" ("Reinventing Augustine's Ethics," 228). Joseph Kelly agrees that Isidore's remark "referred not to the number of the saint's works but to their accessibility in the early Middle Ages" ("Carolingian Era, Late," 129). As I read Isidore's quote, number and accessibility need not be mutually exclusive.

49. Arendt, *Past and Future*, 165.

50. Elshtain, *Augustine*, 19–20; "Augustine," 36.

51. Gregory, *Politics*, 47. See also Elshtain, *Augustine*, 19.

52. *City of God*, 19.5–13.

53. O'Donovan, "Political Thought of *City of God* 19," 72, also cited in Gregory, *Politics*, 47.

54. Gregory and Clair, "Augustinianism and Thomisms," 183. As Kaufman notes, "Sourcebooks for political theory compress it for student use as if Augustine's tale of two cities . . . were easier to abridge than Dickens's" (*Redeeming Politics*, 130).

55. Schofield, "Epilogue," 667, notes that parts of Book 19 make for "grim reading."

56. On the relevance of Augustine's sermons and letters to his political thought, see Atkins and Dodaro, introduction to *Political Writings*, xi–xxvii; Dodaro, *Christ and the Just Society*; Clair, *Discerning the Good*; and Bruno, *Political Augustinianism*, 268.

57. See Atkins and Dodaro, introduction to *Political Writings*, xii; Clair, *Discerning the Good*.

58. Several scholars note that Augustine did not offer a systematic or comprehensive "political theory" separate from his theological reflections. See, e.g., Deane, *Political and Social Ideas*, vii–ix; Dodaro, *Christ and the Just Society*, 1; "Church and State," 181–182; Dyson, introduction to *City of God*, xv, xxviii–xxix; Fortin, "St. Augustine," 176, 178; Hollingworth, *Pilgrim City*, 6–7, 64; Markus, *Saeculum*, 63–64, 73; Vanderjagt, "Political Thought," 1562–1563; Weithman, "Augustine's Political Philosophy," 234, 248–249.

59. Bruno, *Political Augustinianism*, 6, 267–270, 307, makes a similar point.

60. E.g., Bathory, *Political Theory as Public Confession*; Elshtain, *Augustine*; von Heyking, *Augustine*; Connolly, *Augustinian Imperative*; and more recently, Dougherty, ed., *Augustine's Political Thought*; Ogle, *Politics and the Earthly City*; and Kabala, Menchaca-Bagnulo, and Pinkoksi, eds., *Augustine in a Time of Crisis*.

61. Almost sixty years after the publication of their work, Niebuhr and Deane remain the main—and sometimes only—secondary sources on Augustine included on recommended

reading lists for PhD programs in political theory. In a respected textbook, Klosko cites Deane more than any other source in his account of Augustine (*History of Political Theory*, 221–257).

62. See Saak, "Luther," 1344.

63. Brooks, "What May I Hope For?," 62–67, identifies Lutheran theologian Adolf von Harnack as one source of "the pessimistic Augustine." Harnack argued that Augustine "first perfected Christian pessimism" (*History of Dogma*, 65, as cited by Brooks, "What May I Hope For?," 59).

64. Rist, *Augustine Deformed*, 173–208. Sometimes, Rist refers to this view as "ultra-Augustinian" (192, 208).

65. See Taylor, *Sources of the Self*, 246–248, 334, 400–401, 412–413, 440–443; Herdt, *Putting on Virtue*; Gregory, *Politics*, 39–40; Decosimo, *Ethics as a Work of Charity*, 5–7, 253–255, 263–264.

66. Although I do not analyze Elshtain below, she opens *Augustine and the Limits of Politics* by acknowledging her Lutheran background (xi).

67. Arendt, "Augustine and Protestantism," 24–27.

68. Ibid., 24.

69. Ibid., 24–25. Arendt suggests that "neither the Protestant conscience, Protestant individuality, nor Protestant biblical exegesis, which began with young Luther's commentaries on the letters to the Galatians and the Romans, would be conceivable without Augustine's *Confessions*, on the one hand, or, on the other, without his great commentaries on the Gospel and letters of St. John, on Genesis, and on the Psalms" (24–25). She credits Augustine's conception of confession to "God alone, not to other human beings," as an origin of Luther's conception of individual conscience and rejection of the meditating authority of the Catholic Church (27).

70. See Bluhm, "Nietzsche's Final View," and "Nietzsche's Religious Development."

71. See Sommer, "Nietzsche, Friedrich," 1451, citing Nietzsche, *Sämtliche Werke*, 5:70, 11:242; 12:12; 12:24; 13:156. Nietzsche describes Augustine as one of the "monsters of morality" who wage "revenge against spirit," a "Christian agitator" who lacks the "cleanly instincts" that distinguished the Greeks and Romans, and a thinker whose mindset of an "undeserved slave who has been pardoned or promoted" is "offensively lacking any nobility of demeanor and desire." See, respectively, Nietzsche, *Gay Science*, §359; *Anti-Christ*, §59; *Beyond Good and Evil*, §50. On Augustine's "*vulgarized* Platonism," see Nietzsche, "To Franz Overbeck," 239–240. See also Sommer, "Nietzsche, Friedrich," 1451, citing *Sämtliche Werke*, 12:340, 13:156, 13:161.

72. Nussbaum, *Therapy*, 17–19, citing Nietzsche, *Twilight of the Idols*, 485–486. See also Nussbaum's reference to Nietzsche in her response to Charles Taylor's Augustinian account in Nussbaum, *Love's Knowledge*, 370.

73. Nussbaum, *Upheavals*, 553, citing Nietzsche's *Thus Spoke Zarathustra*, in *Portable Nietzsche*, part I: "On the Virtuous" (though I believe it should be part I: "On the Teachers of Virtue"). Nussbaum does not cite any of the passages where Nietzsche engages directly with Augustine. She acknowledges that Nietzsche is "hasty . . . when he indicts the entirety of the Christian tradition for this failing," but suggests his critique aptly applies to Augustine (*Upheavals*, 553).

74. See Brown, *Niebuhr and His Age*, 9–11; Fox, *Reinhold Niebuhr*, 4–5. Brown suggests "the Lutheran element predominat[ed] because of its German roots" (*Niebuhr and His Age*, 10), while Fox notes that Niebuhr's "formative tradition" was "more Lutheran than Calvinist" (*Reinhold Niebuhr*, 140). Such Lutheran influence, however, was likely more creedal and theological than liturgical and political. I am grateful to Robin Lovin for an insightful discussion of Niebuhr's background.

75. Fox, *Reinhold Niebuhr*, 3–5, 8–9. Brown notes that Niebuhr inherited a copy of Luther's *Werke* from his father, whose views reflected Lutheran commitments, and that students at El-mhurst College studied Luther (*Niebuhr and His Age*, 11–14). "Niebuhr's family heritage and his studies at the preparatory school and seminary of his denomination were formative . . . in his appreciation—mingled with criticism—of Luther" (6). After taking over his father's German-speaking congregation for a few months after his unexpected death, Niebuhr attended Yale Divinity School before returning to a Synod church in Detroit (Fox, *Reinhold Niebuhr*, 19–20; Brown, *Niebuhr and His Age*, 16).

76. Although Niebuhr reported he "was first influenced not so much by the Reformers as by the study of St. Augustine" (Niebuhr, "Reply to Interpretation and Criticism," 437, quoted by Brown, *Niebuhr and His Age*, 60), he gained a deeper appreciation of both as he prepared his Gifford Lectures in the late 1930s when he began a more rigorous study of Augustine, Luther, Calvin, Kierkegaard, and Emil Brunner, all of whom formed part of the "Augustinian Protestant tradition" that Niebuhr inhabited (Brown, *Niebuhr and His Age*, 69–70).

77. On critiques of Luther's politics, see, e.g., Niebuhr, *Man's Nature*, 25, 34–35. On Niebuhr's engagement with Luther and Augustine on politics, see Lovin, *Reinhold Niebuhr*, 158–190; and Bruno, *Political Augustinianism*, 75–78.

78. Niebuhr, *Man's Nature*, 43–46; see also 63–64; Niebuhr, *Moral Man*, 69–71, 76–77n21. See also "Augustine's Political Realism," 140, 128, where he describes Luther's approach to politics as "too pessimistic" and Augustine's realism as "excessive," and *Faith and History*, 199–200, where he discusses Luther's "defeatism." For discussion, see Lovin, *Reinhold Niebuhr*, 159–160.

79. Niebuhr, *Man's Nature*, 43–46, 97–98; see also "Augustine's Political Realism," 135–136; *Moral Man*, 69–71. On Niebuhr's concern about Luther's "dualist" tendencies, see Crouter, *Reinhold Niebuhr*, 49.

80. Niebuhr, "Augustine's Political Realism," 136–138. Niebuhr is later more critical of Nygren (and Luther) in "Love and Law," 151–154.

81. Lovin, *Reinhold Niebuhr*, 176; see also 160–170, 187. On Niebuhr's analysis of politics, including the "Augustinian-Lutheran understanding of politics," see ibid., 158–190. Crouter lists Augustine and Luther as among Niebuhr's most important influences (*Reinhold Niebuhr*, 4, 123, 128; see also 42–46 on Augustine; 69–70, 111, on Luther).

82. Rawls, "On My Religion," 261.

83. For insightful accounts of Rawls's neoorthodox theological influences, see Gregory, "Before the Original Position"; Cohen and Nagel, introduction to Rawls, *Brief Inquiry*; and Adams, "Theological Ethics." Galisanka, *John Rawls*, 17–44, emphasizes the influence of liberal Protes-tantism on the young Rawls.

84. Rawls, *Brief Inquiry*, 254.

85. Ibid., 162, 169, 170–174, 229–230, 241, 244. Adams, "Theological Ethics," 32, notes that Rawls shares Luther's view of sin as "primarily a state of mind, a complex of attitudes and mo-tives, rather than a straightforwardly voluntary act or a pattern of action." Rawls's view of justi-fication by faith (244) and conception of faith primarily as an "inner state of a person" (113) also reflect his Lutheran inheritance, as does his critique of Catholicism and Calvinism (197–198). Nelson, *Theology of Liberalism*, 49–72, emphasizes Rawls's anti-Pelagianism but attributes it more to the influence of Marx than Luther.

86. See Rawls, *Brief Inquiry*, 108, 174, 174n37, 177–178, 182–183, 189. For discussion, see Adams, "Theological Ethics," 34n12.

87. Deane, *Political and Social Ideas*, 56.

88. Ibid., 234.

89. Ibid.

90. Ibid., 56. In *History of Political Theory*, Klosko, who relies heavily on Deane, compares Luther with Augustine more than any other figure, noting similarities in their views on the sinfulness of human nature (326, 329–330), the necessity of grace for virtue and salvation (331–332), the doctrine of justification by faith alone (328–329), the priority of faith over reason (329), the division of humankind into two cities (339), and the negative role of the state in constraining sin (339). "Parallels with the views of St. Augustine are apparent," Klosko argues, and "Luther draws strikingly similar theological—and political—conclusions" (326). Yet, though Klosko believes "Luther's political theory is immediately similar to that of St. Augustine" (339), he never explicitly acknowledges Augustine's intellectual or theological influence on Luther. Rhetorically at least, it can seem that Klosko presents the two theologians as arriving at similar but independent conclusions. He uses phrases such as "like Augustine," "as is also true of St. Augustine," or "similar to that of Augustine" to note similarities without indicating influence. While this may seem like a semantic squabble, the suggestion that Augustine and Luther arrive at similar conclusions independently tends to reify a Lutheran reading of Augustine without making the influence explicit. Because Klosko's language does not explicitly acknowledge how Luther is interpreting and appropriating Augustine for his own constructive purposes, readers might not recognize the possibility that Luther's interpretation of Augustine is selective and often polemical. As it stands, Klosko's account gives the impression that Augustine's political thought is essentially the same as Luther's, which may help to explain why Klosko interprets Augustine as a pessimist.

91. I was inspired to consider this methodological influence by Melissa Lane's analysis of Lutheran influences on interpretations of Platonism in *Plato's Progeny*, 8.

92. Garsten, *Saving Persuasion*; Brandom, *Tales of the Mighty Dead*, 91–92.

93. My interpretation is especially indebted to Bretherton, *Christianity*; Clair, *Discerning the Good*; Dodaro, "Between the Two Cities"; Gregory, *Politics*; Herdt, *Putting on Virtue*; Johnson, *Theology*; Mathewes, *Republic of Grace*; and *Theology of Public Life*.

94. As Coleman affirms, Augustine's "wide-ranging views cannot be fully appreciated if they are removed from the soil in which they grew" ("St Augustine," 313).

95. See Lamb, "Augustine and Political Theory," 100.

96. While "citizen" was a significant legal status in Rome that conferred specific political rights, responsibilities, and protections on individuals (and, by extension, excluded others from those same rights and privileges), I typically use "citizen" more broadly to refer to a member of a political community under the aspect of that membership, whether or not they have a recognized legal status. For an insightful account of Augustine's support for expanding access to citizenship in Rome, see Keys and Mitchell, "Augustine's Constitutionalism."

97. For a skeptical view of Augustine's relevance for contemporary politics, see Kaufman, "Patience and/or Politics."

98. Several scholars make this observation: Elshtain, *Augustine*, 5; Gregory, *Politics*, 1; Brown, *Augustine of Hippo*, 229–230.

99. See Breyfogle, "Augustinian Understanding," 218–222; Gregory, *Politics*, 54.

100. For an excellent discussion, see Keys and Mitchell, "Augustine's Constitutionalism."

101. Markus, *Saeculum*, 149–150. Kaufman notes that Augustine "was more concerned to improve magistrates' dispositions than change the policies and structures over which they presided" (*Incorrectly Political*, 108; see also 126, 131). For late antique citizens shaped by a rhetorical education, Brown argues, "how individuals acted mattered far more than did the structures within which they acted" (*Through the Eye*, 56).

102. Ogle, *Politics and the Earthly City*, 169–170.

103. For one set of analyses, see Stark, *Feminist Interpretations*.

104. See, e.g., Letters 91, 103, 104, 153, and 155, in *Political Writings*.

105. See, e.g., *City of God*, 19.15; *Expositions of the Psalms*, 124.7–8; *Homilies on the Gospel of John*, 41.4–10.

106. On Augustine's views of women, see, e.g., Stark, *Feminist Interpretations*; Conybeare, "Augustine's *The City of God*"; Webb, "'On Lucretia Who Slew Herself'"; and Grosse, "Love and the Patriarch," along with forthcoming work by Mel Webb and Colleen Mitchell, among others. On Augustine's views of coercion, see, e.g., Bowlin, "Augustine on Justifying Coercion"; Brown, "Religious Coercion"; and Lamb, "Augustine and Republican Liberty." On Augustine's views of slavery, see, e.g., Alimi, "Slaves of God"; Elia, "Ethics in the Afterlife of Slavery"; "Slave Christologies"; Elm, "Sold to Sin"; and forthcoming books by all three.

107. Here I am referring not to historical interpreters who simply read Augustine as a "pessimist," but rather to political theorists who attribute "pessimism" to Augustine and then draw on his authority to support normative conclusions he might not have endorsed.

108. See Dodaro, "Between the Two Cities." I engage these examples in chapter 9.

109. *Enchiridion*, 1.4.

110. Hebrews 11:1, cited in Sermon 126.3. See also Sermon 359A.3; *Enchiridion*, 2.8.

111. For example, in Sermon 334.3, Augustine encourages listeners to "hope in God for God."

112. Hadot, *Philosophy as a Way of Life*.

113. When Augustine discusses non-Christian virtue, he tends to focus on those whom he describes as "pagans," an expansive group that often includes anyone who did not share his Christian commitments. When discussing his views directly or engaging scholars who analyze his position on "pagan virtue," I employ Augustine's categories. When discussing my own views, I use the term "non-Christian virtue" since "pagan" can sometimes be used as a derogatory term and has a much narrower denotation now than it did in Augustine's time.

114. This mode of interpretation is what Robert Brandom describes as *de dicto* interpretation (*Tales of the Mighty Dead*, 94–99). In a *de dicto* interpretation, "[o]ne seeks to know so thoroughly what an author actually said, how his thought developed over his lifetime, what the rhetorical strategy of each work is and how it was understood by its author as fitting into the oeuvre, what his extraphilosophical concerns, attitudes, and experiences were that one can answer questions on his behalf in something like his own voice. One wants to be able to say what the author *would in fact have said* in response to various questions of clarification and extension" (98–99).

115. This mode of interpretation aligns with Brandom's account of *de re* interpretation (ibid., 99–107). *De re* interpretations attempt to specify the conceptual content of an author's claims in light of collateral commitments that the interpreter takes to be true. They "attempt to say what *really* follows from the claims made, what *really* is evidence for or against them, and so what the

author has *really* committed herself to, regardless of her opinion about the matter" (102). As Brandom argues, "*de dicto* and *de re* readings can both be assessed as to their correctness in specifying conceptual content relative to a context" (104). In *de dicto* readings, the author's context is privileged, while, in *de re* readings, the interpreter's context is privileged. Gregory, *Politics*, 5, applies this distinction to Augustine and advances his own interpretation primarily in the *de re* mode.

116. For a defense of political theory that combines historical analysis with normative theorizing, see Green, "Political Theory as Both Philosophy and History."

117. *Gift of Perseverance*, 21.55.

118. See, e.g., *Retractions*, Prologue.1; *Trinity*, 1.3.5, 1.8.17; and chapter 4 below.

119. *Confessions*, 12.26.36. Here, Augustine is considering biblical interpretation and wondering how he would want readers to respond if he had authored Genesis.

Chapter 1. A Conceptual Grammar: On Faith, Hope, and Love

1. *Enchiridion*, 1.4; Ramsey, introduction to *Augustine Catechism*, 9.

2. *Enchiridion*, 1.4.

3. Augustine sometimes calls the treatise by this second name (ibid., 33.122; *Retractions*, 2.90), but since scholars typically refer to it as the *Enchiridion*, I maintain that usage here.

4. *Enchiridion*, 1.4.

5. Ibid., 2.8, 30.114–116.

6. Aquinas, *Summa Theologica*, II–II.17.3, 18.3. As Brooks, "What May I Hope For?," 117n60, notes, Aquinas draws on Augustine's *Enchiridion* to structure his *Compendium of Theology*, including his discussion of hope, which, like Augustine, is tied to the Lord's Prayer (Aquinas, *Compendium*, 1.1, 2.1–10).

7. Deneen, *Democratic Faith*, 243; Mittleman, *Hope in a Democratic Age*, 151–156.

8. Lloyd, *Problem with Grace*, 70–88.

9. Ramsey, introduction to *Augustine Catechism*, 12. The count excludes the fifteen articles devoted to introducing or concluding the exposition, some of which include references to all three virtues.

10. Augustine, *Quaestiones in Heptateuchum*, 1.Preface, as cited and translated by Auerbach, *Literary Language*, 24.

11. O'Donnell, *Augustine*, 309. See also Brown, "Political Society," 311–312.

12. Wills, *Saint Augustine*, 98.

13. Breyfogle, "Augustinian Understanding," 218.

14. *City of God*, 11.19. Here, Augustine is discussing passages of scripture, but the hermeneutical principle applies.

15. Augustine may have adopted this ordinary language procedure from Cicero, Quintilian, and Varro. For an interesting account of Cicero, Quintilian, and Varro and their similarities with later Wittgensteinian analyses of linguistic change, see Arena, *Libertas and the Practice of Politics*, 258–276.

16. *Enchiridion*, 2.8.

17. Ibid.

18. Ibid.

19. Elshtain notes that "Augustine performs many such 'Wittgensteinian' operations on central words" (*Augustine*, 30). Wittgenstein himself opens part I of *Philosophical Investigations* (§1.1–3) by engaging Augustine's conception of language acquisition from *Confessions*, 1.8.13. For interesting analyses of the connection, see Burnyeat, "Wittgenstein and Augustine *De Magistro*," 1–24; Bearsley, "Augustine and Wittgenstein on Language," 229–236; and Wetzel, "Wittgenstein's Augustine," 225–247.

20. *City of God*, 10.1.

21. *Enchiridion*, 2.8. In chapter 4, I show how Augustine describes faith (*fides*) in terms of "trust" as well as "belief." Both are possible translations of *fides*. The verb, *credere*, also can be translated as "to believe" or "to trust." See Lewis, *Elementary Latin Dictionary*, 325, 195.

22. Hebrews 11:1. Augustine only cites the second half of this Pauline definition in *Enchiridion*, 2.8, but the first half would have been familiar to readers. Elsewhere, he cites both parts of Hebrews 11:1 to explain hope's relation to faith (e.g., Sermon 359A.3). For more on Paul's influence, see Studer, "Pauline Theme of Hope."

23. Romans 8:24–25, cited in *Enchiridion*, 2.8. Marrou identifies the number of citations of Romans 8:23–25 (*Saint Augustine*, 84).

24. *Enchiridion*, 2.8. The connection between faith and hope may help to solve a puzzle that has long plagued interpreters. One of the *Enchiridion*'s most striking features is its disproportionate emphasis on faith. Boniface Ramsey suggests two possible reasons for this imbalance. "The first is that he did not feel that he could give a shorter account of faith . . . than he actually did, and that, as a result, he had to compress his treatment of hope and charity if he wanted to stay within the bounds of a handbook or *enchiridion*, of which he seems to have been quite conscious" (introduction to *Augustine Catechism*, 12). The practical constraints of Augustine's genre, in other words, prevented a more complete explication of hope and love. A second option is that faith was "discussed at greatest length because it is the most 'teachable' of the three virtues, the most susceptible to being written about in a systematic way" (12). Hope, by contrast, "is the most elusive of the three and could hardly but receive short shrift," while "charity could be appropriately handled with brevity if it were clear that, as the last of the three, it was also the greatest of them and their *raison d'etre*" (12). Deneen makes a similar suggestion, arguing that while "hope 'occupies' a central place in the thought of Augustine's work, it is in fact little discussed, perhaps reflecting its ultimate mystery" (*Democratic Faith*, 347n11). The suggestion that hope is elusive or mysterious risks obscuring the virtue's importance in Augustine's larger moral vision. My account brings other potential reasons into view. Augustine, for example, may focus most on faith because it is the "beginning" of progress toward the good life, a beginning that is necessary for hope and love, since neither can exist without faith (*Enchiridion*, 1.5, 2.8). If faith in the unseen supplies the necessary belief about what to hope or love, it makes sense for Augustine to focus first on faith, particularly if Laurentius is new to Christianity, as his questions suggest. Faith is the "beginning," or precondition, of the other virtues. For a thoughtful account of hope in the *Enchiridion*, see Brooks, "What May I Hope For?," 117–152.

25. 1 Corinthians 13:12, cited in *City of God*, 22.29; Letter 120.2.11; *Enchiridion*, 16.63.

26. For example, one of the most influential categorizations of virtues in positive psychology equates "hope" with "optimism" and defines it as "[e]xpecting the best in the future and working to achieve it; believing that a good future is something that can be brought about" (Peterson and Seligman, *Character Strengths and Virtues*, 30, cited by Brooks, "What May I Hope For?," 20).

27. *Enchiridion*, 2.8.

28. Ibid.

29. Ibid.

30. See also Letter 120.9.

31. *Enchiridion*, 2.8.

32. Ibid., 33.122.

33. E.g., Letter 26.1.

34. Aquinas cites this passage from *Enchiridion*, 2.8 as his *sed contra* when addressing whether one may properly hope for another's happiness (*Summa Theologica*, II–II.17.3).

35. Ibid.

36. Ibid.

37. *Enchiridion*, 2.8.

38. For helpful discussions of Augustine's eudaimonism, see Herdt, *Putting on Virtue*, 50–56; Kent, "Augustine's Ethics"; and Clair, *Discerning the Good*, 1–38. Wolterstorff, *Justice*, 180–206, argues that Augustine makes a "break with eudaimonism." For a compelling critique, see Clair, "Wolterstorff on Love and Justice."

39. *Enchiridion*, 2.8.

40. James 2:19, as cited in *Enchiridion*, 2.8.

41. *Enchiridion*, 2.8.

42. See, e.g., *City of God*, 14.6. On aversion and attraction in Augustine's account of emotions, see Wetzel, "Prodigal Heart," 82–83.

43. Deneen, *Democratic Faith*, 243. According to Deneen, Augustinian "hope cannot be extended to inappropriate objects. Hope is directed toward the eternal: as the aspiration for good things beyond sensory evidence, hope, by Augustine's estimation, cannot be accorded purely to human attempts to achieve the object of hope. . . . Augustine's immediate and stern reminder of the simultaneous infinite extent of hope and yet its limitations to human endeavors appears as a consistent rebuke to the overweening ambitions of a humanity longing for mastery" (243). While Deneen stresses the transcendent, otherworldly horizon of hope to impugn "democratic faith," I argue in chapters 2 and 3 that the implied dualism between temporal and eternal goods does not accurately capture Augustine's participationist ontology.

44. Ibid.

45. Ibid.

46. Lloyd, *Problem with Grace*, 71.

47. Ibid., 70–75.

48. Ibid., 75.

49. Ibid., 71.

50. Ibid.

51. Deneen, *Democratic Faith*, 243; Lloyd, *Problem with Grace*, 71, citing *Enchiridion*, 2.8; see also 84–85.

52. Deneen, *Democratic Faith*, 243.

53. When introducing the *Enchiridion*, Deneen writes that "many commentators have been forced to acknowledge that faith and hope themselves seem to resemble each other extensively" (ibid., 242–243).

54. We can also find support for the distinction between hope and faith in Augustine's passing remark that "faith believes, hope and charity pray" (*Enchiridion*, 2.7). The difference between

"belief" and "prayer" is that prayer enacts either a *desire* for some good or an *affective movement* toward the one to whom the prayer is directed. Belief does not necessarily involve desire or affection in this way. In the next sentence, Augustine says that "hope and charity cannot be without faith, and so faith prays as well" (2.7). Even here the implication is that faith only "prays" when it "works through" hope and charity. Without hope and charity, faith would only "believe," not "pray." As Augustine writes elsewhere, "[P]ious faith does not want to be without hope and love. A believer, therefore, ought to believe what he does not yet see in such a way that he both hopes for and loves that vision" (Letter 120.8). For a compatible analysis of these concepts and their connection to prayer, see Jackson, "Faith, Hope and Charity."

55. Sermon 359A.4.

56. Sermon 359A.3–4.

57. Sermon 359A.4. Augustine presses the point in Sermon 158.7–8. During this present life, the faith "which works through love cannot exist without hope": "Certainly hope is very necessary for us in our exile, it's what consoles us on the journey. When the traveler, after all, finds it wearisome walking along, he puts up with the fatigue precisely because he hopes to arrive. Rob him of any hope of arriving, and straightaway his strength is broken for walking."

58. *Expositions of the Psalms*, 31(2).4.

59. Ibid., 31(2).3.

60. Ibid., 31(2).5. "If you loved nothing," Augustine writes, "you would be sluggish, dead, loathsome and unhappy" (ibid.). See also Letter 120.8.

61. *Expositions of the Psalms*, 31(2).5.

62. A similar role for hope as a "middle term" is implied in Augustine's explanation of why Noah's Ark had three levels: "God wished the Ark to contain dwelling-places not only on the lowest level but also on the next higher level (which He called the second storey), and again on the level above that (which He called the third storey), so that there should be a habitation rising up in three stages from the bottom; and this could be taken to signify the three virtues extolled by the apostle: faith, hope and charity" (*City of God*, 15.26). Augustine does not elaborate the meaning here, but considering hope as a "stage" above faith and on the way to love suggests that (1) hope rests on faith, (2) hope necessarily connects faith and love, and (3) hope is perfected by love.

63. Gregory, *Politics*, 22–23.

64. Aquinas makes this explicit in his account of "lifeless faith" (*fides informata*), which requires acts of the will, including acts of hope and love, to become "living faith." Without these motivating, in-forming acts, faith remains "lifeless" (*Summa Theologica*, II–II.4.4).

65. Augustine explicitly identifies the will with love: "A righteous will, then, is a good love; and a perverted will is an evil love" (*City of God*, 14.7; see also 14.6). "For Augustine," Carol Harrison writes, "the will is synonymous with love; to will is not just to rationally deliberate and choose to act, rather it is to love something and to be moved to act on the basis of that love" (*Augustine*, 94–95).

66. Sermon 359A.4.

67. *City of God*, 11.28; see also *Confessions*, 13.9.10. James K. A. Smith captures this Augustinian insight in the title of his book, *You Are What You Love* (see esp. 7–14). Similarly, Janet Coleman suggests that, for Augustine, "we are what we love" ("St Augustine," 318; see also 321–322).

68. *City of God*, 14.6; see also 14.7.

69. *Enchiridion*, 2.8.

70. Ibid., 31.117. See also Sermon 126.15.

71. Sermon 359A.4.

72. In Sermon 158, Augustine suggests that faith and hope are "part and parcel" of the pilgrimage toward the heavenly city: "When we get there, we will possess it; and now it will be vision, not faith. When we get there, we will possess it, and now it will be the thing itself, not hope. What about love? It's surely not the case, is it, that love too has its place now, and won't have it then? If we love while we believe and don't see, how much more will we love when we see and possess! So there will be love there, but it will be perfect. As the apostle says, *Faith, hope, love, these three; but the greatest of these is love* (1 Cor 13:13)" (Sermon 158.7, 9).

73. *Expositions of the Psalms*, 91.1. See also Sermon 158.9; *On Christian Teaching*, 1.38.42–1.39.43; Meconi, "Heaven," 253–254.

74. Sermon 105.5; *Enchiridion*, 2.8.

75. Sermon 359A.2.

76. "Between the extremes of the beginning of faith and the perfection of perseverance, there are those in-between virtues by which we live correctly" (*Gift of Perseverance*, 21.56). In *Expositions of the Psalms*, 83.7, Augustine identifies faith, hope, and love as "virtues proper to this present life" to help on the way "home" (see also Brooks, "What May I Hope For?," 110).

77. See Bowlin, "Augustine Counting Virtues," 282.

78. Sermon 359A.3–4.

79. *City of God*, 19.4. "Here we have the practice of the virtues, there their result; here their labours, there their reward; here their duties, there their goal. In this way all those who are good and holy can indeed be called blessed while suffering any torture you like, provided they rely on divine assistance in the hope of that end which will make them blessed" (Letter 155.16, in *Political Writings*, 98).

80. In discussing the "patience" required for hope, Augustine says, "Patience doesn't seem to be needed when things are going well, but when they are going badly. Nobody patiently tolerates what is enjoyable. But anything we tolerate, anything we bear with patiently, is harsh and bitter; and thus patience is not needed when you're happy, but when you're unhappy. However, as I started to say, any who are on fire with a yearning for eternal life, in whatever country they may be happily living, must of necessity live patiently, because they have reluctantly to tolerate the fact of their being strangers and exiles, until they reach the desired home country after loving it so long" (Sermon 359A.2).

81. Sermon 105.5–7. See also Sermon 21.1; *Confessions*, 13.13.14; and Letter 147.23.53 on "stretching ourselves out to what is ahead."

82. Markus, *Saeculum*, 83.

83. Ibid., 154–186.

84. Taking Markus as a paradigmatic Augustinian realist, Gregory argues that Markus is not properly attentive to love. While Markus "does link hope to love," it is a "weak" link: he provides "no explicit treatment of love's relation to political engagement or hope" and "no explicit treatment of the dangers of love" (Gregory, *Politics*, 95). My account in chapters 2 and 3 avoids this danger by making the relationship between hope and love central and identifying the vices that accompany their disorder.

85. Ibid., 80.

86. Ibid. In analyzing different emphases, Gregory suggests it "may be the case that any given moment in political history requires preference for one type over another" (80). Gregory's own

political moment may help to explain why he focuses on the connection between love and justice rather than love and hope. Since the publication of Rawls's *Theory of Justice* in 1971, political theory that has been dominated by disputes over theories of justice. Because Gregory is engaging this tradition and adding an Augustinian voice to it, his focus on love and justice may reflect his intellectual and political context.

87. Ibid., 178–179.

88. *Enchiridion*, 1.3.

Chapter 2. Against Otherworldliness: The Order of Love

1. Sermon 198.2.

2. Billings, "Natality," 135–136.

3. Ibid.

4. Ibid., 136.

5. *On Christian Teaching*, 1.26.27.

6. Ibid., 1.27.28.

7. Ibid., 1.3.3. For an excellent analysis of Augustine's distinction between "use" and "enjoyment" in light of his pilgrimage motif, see Stewart-Kroeker, "Resisting Idolatry," and *Pilgrimage*, 204–244.

8. *On Christian Teaching*, 1.4.4.

9. Ibid.

10. Ibid., 1.5.5–1.6.6, 1.22.20.

11. Ibid., 1.3.3–1.4.4, 1.22.20–21. See also Sermon 335C.13, in *Political Writings*, 58–59.

12. *On Christian Teaching*, 1.22.20.

13. Ibid., 1.22.21.

14. Ibid., 1.23.22.

15. *Confessions*, 4.12.18. *City of God*, 19.13; Gregory, *Politics*, 42, describes this as Augustine's "mature formulation" of *ordo amoris*.

16. Wolterstorff, *Justice*, 205, suggests, for example, that "Augustine's employment of the language of utility here is offensive to us" since "we have ringing in our ear Kant's dictum about never treating a human being merely as a means."

17. Arendt, *Love*, 14. For an insightful analysis of Arendt's interpretation, see Gregory, *Politics*, 197–240.

18. Arendt, *Love*, 9–44, 106.

19. See ibid., 37–44.

20. Ibid., 105–106. For discussion, see Gregory, *Politics*, 235–237.

21. Arendt, *Love*, 96–97.

22. Ibid.

23. Nussbaum, *Upheavals*, 551, 528–529, 552–555. According to Nussbaum, the Augustinian "ascent of love and desire from the earthly to the heavenly . . . strips away and leaves behind the merely human in love" (529).

24. Ibid., 528–529. Nussbaum adds a qualifying footnote: "Not all Christian love is love of God: there may be human loves that are distinctively Christian. But these other loves are suffused by the love of God, and, as we shall see, their real object always is, in a way, God" (528n1).

25. Ibid., 552.

26. Ibid., 549–550, endorsing Arendt, *Love*, 96. As Nussbaum acknowledges, the love of God helps to "solve the problem of unevenness or partiality" since all human beings are treated as equals, and it promises a safety that human beings cannot offer: whereas finite and needy humans can disappoint, hurt, and betray us, an infinite and eternal God is an object of love that "can never fail" us (548). But for Nussbaum, the assurance comes at too high a price, undercutting any genuine compassion for the suffering of other human beings (551–553). For a more detailed version of this argument, see Baier, "Unsafe Loves."

27. Nussbaum, *Upheavals*, 549–556, quoted at 553.

28. Ibid., 556. See also Coleman, "St Augustine," 333: "Political life . . . must serve as a waiting station. Salvation is an escape from history and politics."

29. Niebuhr, "Augustine's Political Realism," 130. Marrou expresses a similar critique. For Marrou, Augustine's distinction between "enjoying" and "using" entails that "in God alone, the Supreme Being and our End, is it lawful to rest and to have joy; all the rest we should only use, as *instruments*, as *means* subordinate to this end" (*Saint Augustine*, 79, emphasis added). Marrou goes on to argue that Augustine's "'eudemonism' involves a strict utilitarianism": "Always in a hurry to pass over the intermediate stages, he will allow no delay to define the subordinate ends: he will only call them means." According to Marrou, "[W]e cannot disguise the often ruthless and sometimes excessive rigour with which he deduces the practical consequences of this great principle" (79).

30. Niebuhr, "Augustine's Political Realism," 136.

31. Ibid., 137.

32. Ibid., 137–138.

33. Ibid., 137. Niebuhr offers a similar critique in "Love and Law," 147: "Augustine makes the mistake of never being concerned whether, in a relation of love, we rise to the point of loving the other person for his own sake or only for our sake. His concern is always whether we love the person for his own sake or for God's sake. This is to say, he is afraid that love of the other may degenerate into idolatry. He compounds this error by insisting that the love of the neighbor must express itself not so much in meeting his needs as in leading him to God."

34. Niebuhr, "Augustine's Political Realism," 137. See also Arendt, *Love*, 30–34; Nussbaum, *Upheavals*, 542–543. For analysis, see Gregory, *Politics*, 40–47, 197–240, 337n28.

35. Arendt, *Love*, 96; Nussbaum, *Upheavals*, 548. See also Baier, "Unsafe Loves."

36. Billings, "Natality," 135–136.

37. Niebuhr, "Augustine's Political Realism," 136–137; "Love and Law," 147; Arendt, *Love*, 30; Nussbaum, *Upheavals*, 528–529. For discussion, see Gregory, *Politics*, 3–5, 35–47, 221, 319–350.

38. Nussbaum, *Upheavals*, 528–529.

39. Gregory, *Politics*, 330; see also 36, 221, 260, 323.

40. Arendt, *Love*, 32–34, 37, 40. See also Chadwick, *Augustine*, 64; Marrou, *Saint Augustine*, 79.

41. Gregory, *Politics*, 197–240; Mathewes, *Theology of Public Life*, 74–94; Stewart-Kroeker, "Resisting Idolatry"; *Pilgrimage*, 204–244; Williams, "Language, Reality and Desire."

42. Arendt, *Love*, 48–50, 36–44. See also Nussbaum, *Upheavals*, 549–556; *Therapy*, 18–22. Standard accounts of Augustine in political theory share this emphasis on transcendence. Sophie Lunn-Rockliffe suggests that, for Augustine, "the truly important community is not this-worldly,

but transcendent" and argues that Augustine's primary critique against classical philosophers targeted their "inappropriately earthly focus" ("Early Christian Political Philosophy," 150–151).

43. *Confessions*, 9.4.11; *On Christian Teaching*, 1.10.10. See also *City of God*, 8.6, 12.2.

44. *City of God*, 14.13; see also 12.5, 11.28. Coles argues that, for Augustine, "God is the ground and origin of all being" (*Self/Power/Other*, 17).

45. *True Religion*, 10.19; *Retractions*, 1.12.2; *Confessions*, 10.6.8–9.

46. For discussion of Augustine's ontology of participation, see Gregory, *Politics*, 41–47; Mathewes, *Theology of Public Life*, 74–94; Jenson, *Gravity of Sin*, 8–15; Johnson, *Theology*, 150–161, 252; Smith, *Awaiting the King*, 217; and Ogle, *Politics and the Earthly City*, 4–5, 92, 145.

47. *On Christian Teaching*, 1.32.35; see also *City of God*, 11.28, 12.1. As Augustine argues, "The supreme and true God, then, . . . is the one almighty God, the Creator and Maker of every soul and every body. It is by participation in Him that all are happy who are happy in truth and not in emptiness" (*City of God*, 5.11).

48. *True Religion*, 18.35; see also 11.21.

49. *Confessions*, 7.12.18. See also *City of God*, 11.21, 12.1, 12.5; Sermon 21.3.

50. See *City of God*, 9.15, 9.17, 10.6, 10.20, 10.24, 21.15; *Confessions*, 10.42.67–43.68; *Trinity*, 1.7.14–1.10.21, 4.7.11–4.9.12; Letter 147.22.51.

51. *City of God*, 9.17; see also 10.6, 21.15; *Confessions*, 10.42.67–43.68.

52. An increased attention to Christology is central to several recent interpretations of Augustine's political thought. See Gregory, *Politics*; Dodaro, *Christ and the Just Society*; Herdt, *Putting on Virtue*; Johnson, *Theology*; Mathewes, *Theology of Public Life*; *Republic of Grace*; Bowlin, "Augustine Counting Virtues"; Bruno, *Political Augustinianism*, 254–258; Stewart-Kroeker, "Resisting Idolatry," and *Pilgrimage*.

53. Gregory, *Politics*, 40–41, 221, 337n28; Stewart-Kroeker, "Resisting Idolatry," 211; *Pilgrimage*, 227.

54. "For, though earthly things were not intended to be coequal with heavenly things, it would still not be fitting for the universe to lack these things altogether, even though heavenly things are better" (*City of God*, 12.4).

55. Sermon 21.3.

56. *City of God*, 15.4. "But," he adds, "if the higher goods are neglected . . . and those other goods desired so much that they are thought to be the only goods, or loved more than the goods which are believed to be higher, then misery will of necessity follow, and present misery be increased by it" (15.4). I address this point below.

57. See, e.g., *Homilies on the First Epistle of John*, 9.10; Sermon 21.2–3; *City of God*, 11.28. For discussion, see Gregory, *Politics*, 44–45, 221–222, 322–350; Mathewes, *Theology of Public Life*, 82–84, 91–92; Jenson, *Gravity of Sin*, 28; Smith, "Glory and Tragedy," 201. Aquinas makes this point, alluding to Augustine's Platonic influences: "The Divine Essence Itself is charity, even as it is wisdom and goodness. Wherefore just as we are said to be good with the goodness which is God, and wise with the wisdom which is God (since the goodness whereby we are formally good is a participation of Divine goodness, and the wisdom whereby we are formally wise, is a share of Divine wisdom), so too, the charity whereby formally we love our neighbor is a participation of Divine charity. For this manner of speaking is common among the platonists, with whose doctrines Augustine was imbued; and the lack of averting to this has been to some an occasion of error" (*Summa Theologica*, II–II.23.2.1).

58. As Gregory argues, "Augustine's God does not compete with the neighbor for the self's attention, as if God were simply the biggest of those rival objects considered worthy of love. In short, his God is not a *particular* thing" (*Politics*, 41). James Wetzel agrees: "For Augustine, God is not a supreme person among other lesser persons, but a wholly other kind of reality" ("Snares of Truth," 134). Another Augustinian, Martin Luther King Jr., affirms that God is not "an object among other objects" ("Pilgrimage to Nonviolence," 40).

59. Herdt, *Putting on Virtue*, 53–55, 69.

60. Gregory, *Politics*, 39, 221, 256–263; Mathewes, *Theology of Public Life*, 78, 83; Bowlin, "Augustine Counting Virtues," 297. As Augustine preaches, "It is by loving irregularly something created or loving it out of turn, by loving created things against honest and lawful use, against the law and will of the creator himself, that you sin. . . . Now attend closely, observe carefully, reflect and see that *every creation of God is good* (1 Tm 4:4). And there is no sin there, apart from your bad use of things. . . . How is that you sin, after all, but by treating the things you have received for your use in a disordered way, or out of turn? Be a good user of lower things, and you will be an upright enjoyer of the higher good" (Sermon 21.3).

61. *City of God*, 15.22. See also Sermon 21.3; *True Religion*, 20.38.

62. *City of God*, 15.22. For Augustine, virtue and vice depend less on the nature of the goods loved than on the "quality" of a person's will: "For if the will is perverse, the emotions will be perverse; but if it is righteous, the emotions will not only be blameless, but praiseworthy" (14.6).

63. See ibid., 12.3–4, 12.6–9, 14.6–7, 19.13. According to Charles Mathewes, "Augustine understood evil's challenge in terms of two distinct conceptual mechanisms, one ontological and the other anthropological. Ontologically he defines the concept of evil as simply the *privation* of being and goodness. Anthropologically he defines human wickedness in terms of original sin, and sin as fundamentally the *perversion* of the human's good nature—created in the *imago Dei*—into a distorted and false imitation of what it should be. *Privation* and *perversion*: together these summarize the Augustinian tradition's interpretation of the problem of evil, and delineate the conceptual contours within which the tradition proposes its practical response to it" (*Evil*, 59–103, at 75).

64. *City of God*, 11.22, 12.5–9; *Confessions*, 7.12.18–7.16.22.

65. *City of God*, 12.9, 19.13; *True Religion*, 13.26.

66. *City of God*, 11.9, 11.22, 12.7–9, 19.3. For discussion, see Elshtain, *Augustine*, 76–85; Mathewes, *Evil*, 75–81; Jenson, *Gravity of Sin*, 15–32; Burroughs, *Christianity, Politics, and the Predicament of Evil*, 37–50.

67. See *City of God*, 12.3, 12.9, 14.6; Sermon 23A.1; *Free Choice of the Will*, 2.19.194–3.3.13.

68. Gregory, *Politics*, 14–15, 20–22, 35–36.

69. *City of God*, 14.6–7; Sermon 352A.6; Gregory, *Politics*, 14–15, 20–22, 35–36; Mathewes, *Theology of Public Life*, 82–85.

70. *City of God*, 19.4. Augustine offers one of his most explicit descriptions of the dialectic between virtue and vice in *True Religion*, 19.37: "Vice and death do no damage to anything except by depriving it of soundness, and vice would not be vice if it did no damage. If vice is the opposite of wholeness no doubt wholeness is good. All things are good which have vice opposed to them, and vice vitiates them. Things which are vitiated are therefore good, but are vitiated because they are not supremely good. Because they are good they are of God. Because they are

not supremely good they are not God. The good which cannot be vitiated is God. All other good things are of him. They can themselves be vitiated because by themselves they are nothing. God keeps them from being wholly vitiated, or, if vitiated, makes them whole."

71. *City of God*, 19.4.

72. Ibid., 1.Preface, 1.30–31, 12.6, 12.8, 14.13, 15.5, 19.12, 19.15, translation altered.

73. Ibid., 1.Preface, 12.1, 14.13–14, 19.12. See also Elshtain, *Augustine*, 16–18, 49–51; Jenson, *Gravity of Sin*, 25–28.

74. *City of God*, 14.13.

75. Ibid.

76. See ibid., 1.Preface, 1.30–31, 12.1, 15.5, 19.12; Jenson, *Gravity of Sin*, 25–32; Gregory, *Politics*, 42–44, 329–331, 343–347; Clair, *Discerning the Good*, 60–61n48.

77. *Literal Meaning of Genesis*, 11.20. For an insightful discussion, see Johnson, *Theology*, 161–162.

78. See *City of God*, 12.1, where Augustine describes good angels as those who sought God as "the common good of them all" and bad angels as those who, "delighting in their own power, and supposing that they could be their own good, fell from that higher and blessed good which was common to them all and embraced a private good of their own."

79. Ibid., 1.Preface, 14.28.

80. Ibid., 19.12.

81. Ibid., 5.12, 5.17.

82. Ibid., 1.Preface, Bettenson translation. For discussion, see Johnson, *Theology*, 142–143, 162–163.

83. Gregory, *Politics*, 221; see also 40–42. For Augustine, morality and metaphysics can never be ontologically separated. Because he affirms the convertibility of God's being and goodness and argues that human beings must participate in both, he assumes moral psychology must, in part, reflect a participationist ontology as a proper response to the goods God has created. In emphasizing moral psychology, then, I am not denying this connection but simply correcting an exclusive emphasis on metaphysics that has distorted views of Augustinian love in political theory. This is why I emphasize that Augustine is concerned about moral psychology "as much as" metaphysics instead of saying he is concerned about moral psychology "rather than" or "more than" metaphysics.

84. Mathewes, *Theology of Public Life*, 89–90. See also Williams, "Language, Reality and Desire"; Bowlin, "Augustine Counting Virtues," 297–299.

85. Sermon 335C.13. See also Sermon 34.2.

86. Williams, "Language, Reality, and Desire," 140; Mathewes, *Theology of Public Life*, 78–93; Gregory, *Politics*, 41–44, 329–331, 343–347; Bowlin, "Augustine Counting Virtues," 297–299; Stewart-Kroeker, "Resisting Idolatry," 205, 218–221; *Pilgrimage*, 239–244. My account of the order of love as a regulative ideal benefited from Jennifer Herdt's application of the concept to Aquinas's order of charity in her Warfield Lectures, entitled "*Reditus* Reformed."

87. Williams, "Language, Reality and Desire," 140.

88. *On Christian Teaching*, 1.22.20. Augustine's reflections on the death of an unnamed friend in *Confessions* 4.7.8–12 highlights this danger.

89. Gregory, *Politics*, 42; see also 221, 329–331, 346–347.

90. As Gregory argues, "The self that is ordered toward God is released to love rather than grasp or possess the neighbor" (*Politics*, 329). See also Kent, "Augustine's Ethics," 214.

91. Bowlin, "Augustine Counting Virtues," 298.

92. Ibid., 297.

93. Ibid., 298. Ogle, *Politics and the Earthly City*, 122–123, makes a similar point in relation to created goods as "signs" of God that must be "read" properly as pointing to the Creator.

94. As Herdt explains, "It is not, then, that all things other than God are to be used as a means, are to be instrumentalized, for the purpose of my own aim of enjoying God. Rather, I cannot love properly anything in creation unless I have grasped its nature as created being, utterly dependent on God and lovable as God's beloved creation" (*Putting on Virtue*, 54; see also Gregory, *Politics*, 42–43; Mathewes, *Theology of Public Life*, 74–94).

95. Gregory, *Politics*, 39; Meilaender, *Friendship*, 31.

96. See Gregory, *Politics*, 243, 318, 322–324; Herdt, *Putting on Virtue*, 55–56.

97. Gregory, *Politics*, 44.

98. *City of God*, 15.5. See also *True Religion*, 55.112–113.

99. *Confessions*, 4.12.18; *On Christian Teaching*, 3.10.16. Both Gregory *Politics*, 43, 46, and Herdt, *Putting on Virtue*, 54–56, allude to these formulations. As Herdt writes elsewhere, "[T]o be turned toward God is not to be turned away from the world or away from other people. Rather, we learn to love the world as God's beloved creation; loving God, we love as God loves, in the self-emptying love that we witness in the incarnation" ("Theater of the Virtues," 127).

100. *Trinity*, 8.9.12, as quoted by Gregory, *Politics*, 43.

101. Wolterstorff, *Justice*, 205, notes how, for Augustine, loving one's neighbor "in" God can be "a component within, a constituent of, one's love for God."

102. My view of "reinforcement" relations is informed by a lecture by Akeel Bilgrami, "Why Does Liberalism Find It So Hard to Cope with Religious Identity?," which presents a conception of moral psychology in which two preferences or reasons for an action may be conceptually consistent and motivationally reinforcing but not in a simple means-end way.

103. The following account is indebted to Gregory, *Politics*, 335–350.

104. Baer, "Fruit of Charity," 49, also cited by Gregory, *Politics*, 340.

105. *Trinity*, 10.11.17; O'Connor, "*Uti/Frui* Distinction," 45–62, at 57, also cited by Gregory, *Politics*, 342.

106. O'Connor, "*Uti/Frui* Distinction," 57, also cited by Gregory, *Politics*, 342.

107. *On Christian Teaching*, 1.31.34–1.32.35. See O'Connor, "*Uti/Frui* Distinction," 54.

108. *Trinity*, 6.10.11; O'Connor, "*Uti/Frui* Distinction," 58.

109. O'Connor, "*Uti/Frui* Distinction," 57–58. See also Kent, "Augustine's Ethics," 214–215.

110. Augustine, for example, uses the language of "proximate" (*proximis*) or "ultimate" (*superioram*) to describe "causes" (*Trinity*, 3.2.7–3.2.8). He often identifies God or happiness as the "ultimate" or "supreme" good (*summum bonum*) (*Expositions of the Psalms* 70[2].6; 102.8; *City of God*, 19.1) and uses *proximum* to identify the "neighbor" (*On Christian Teaching*, 1.22.21, 1.26.27, 1.30.31–33). In this sense, love of God and neighbor can easily be cast in terms of "ultimate" and "proximate" goods. See von Heyking, *Augustine*, 224–225, 232; Mittleman, *Hope in a Democratic Age*, 155.

111. *Excellence of Marriage*, 9.9. See O'Connor, "*Uti/Frui* Distinction," 55–59; O'Donovan, *Common Objects of Love*, 16.

112. This equation of "use" and "enjoyment" with "means" and "ends" is common in introductions to Augustine's thought. For example, Henry Chadwick argues that the "distinction

between means and ends seemed to him of cardinal importance": "To seek only goods in time and to neglect eternal good, worse still to treat the eternal good as a tool for obtaining a this-worldly end, is to act unethically. Even one's fellow men may become mere tools for one's self-advancement if they are not respected as deserving to be 'loved in God.' The supreme end of man is to enjoy God for ever. Accordingly Augustine translated the distinction between ends and means into 'enjoyment and use'" (*Augustine*, 64; see also Marrou, *Saint Augustine*, 79; Arendt, *Love*, 32–34, 37, 40).

113. See *City of God*, 11.31, 19.13, 19.16; *Sermon* 57.7; *Confessions*, 3.8.15: "a part which fails to harmonize with the whole is a source of mischief." See also Elshtain, *Augustine*, 35; von Heyking, *Augustine*, 194–195; Mathewes, *Theology of Public Life*, 89–90; Johnson, *Theology*, 219–220.

114. Billings, "Natality," 135–136.

115. *City of God*, 21.27. See also Letter 155.14–15, in *Political Writings*, 97–98.

116. *Homilies on the First Epistle of John*, 9.10. For discussion, see Gregory, *Politics*, 44–45; Mathewes, *Theology of Public Life*, 81–88.

117. *Homilies on the First Epistle of John*, 9.10. See also Sermon 21.2–3; *City of God*, 11.28.

118. Mays, "Love of God and Love of Man—Inseparable," 16, 23, also alluding to 1 John. I am grateful to Jonathan L. Walton for this reference.

119. Canning, *Love for God and Neighbor*, 342 and 342n33, as cited by Gregory, *Politics*, 348. Marrou puts the number of Augustine's citations of Matthew 25 at 360 (*Saint Augustine*, 83).

120. Matthew 25:31–46.

121. Sermon 25.8. This passage is cited by Canning, *Love for God and Neighbor*, 369; and Gregory, *Politics*, 349, though with a slightly different translation.

122. *Trinity*, 8.5.12, as cited by Gregory, *Politics*, 45.

123. Sermon 198.2.

124. *Expositions of the Psalms*, 31(2).7.

125. Sermon 23A.1. See also Sermon 87.2.

126. Sermon 23A.1.

127. See, e.g., *City of God*, 21.27.

128. As Herdt writes, "The perfect life is something objective, not a subjective state" (*Putting on Virtue*, 55).

129. Letter 155.13, in *Political Writings*, 97, emphasis added.

130. *City of God*, 11.28, emphasis added.

Chapter 3. Between Presumption and Despair: The Order of Hope

1. *Enchiridion*, 2.8.

2. *City of God*, 14.7, 14.9, 15.22; *Catholic Way of Life*, 1.15.25; 1.25.46. See Bowlin, "Augustine Counting Virtues"; Langan, "Interconnection of the Virtues"; Kent, "Augustine's Ethics," 228–229; Dodaro, *Christ and the Just Society*, 211.

3. *City of God*, 14.7; see also 14.6.

4. Aquinas, *Summa Theologica*, II–II.17.4, 17.6.3.

5. Sermon 56.2. See also *Expositions of the Psalms*, 31(2).6.

6. *Expositions of the Psalms*, 129.11.

7. *Enchiridion*, 1.3, 30.114–116. For a compatible account, see Studer, "Pauline Theme of Hope," 217.

8. *Enchiridion*, 30.115, citing Matthew 6:9–10.

9. Ibid.

10. I analyze Augustine's inaugurated eschatology in chapter 8.

11. Drawing on the *Enchiridion*, Mittleman is one of the few interpreters to note the permissibility of Augustinian hope for temporal goods (*Hope in a Democratic Age*, 155). See also Studer, "Pauline Theme of Hope," 211.

12. *Enchiridion*, 30.115, citing Matthew 6:11–13.

13. Ibid.

14. Ibid.

15. See also Mittleman, *Hope in a Democratic Age*, 155–156.

16. See Deneen, *Democratic Faith*, 243.

17. *Expositions of the Psalms*, 129.11, emphasis added.

18. As Augustine writes, "If you run through all the words of holy petitions, you will not find, in my opinion, anything that this prayer of our Lord does not contain and include. . . . Therefore, faith, hope, and love lead one who prays to God, that is, one who believes, hopes, desires, and considers what he asks of God in the Lord's Prayer" (Letter 130.12.22–13.24). In particular, the Lord's Prayer offers an exercise of desire that fosters a "greater capacity" to receive God's gifts during pilgrimage toward the heavenly city, enabling pilgrims to "believe it with more fidelity, and hope for it more firmly, and love it more ardently" (130.8.17). By repeating the Lord's Prayer, "we stir up our desire for that kingdom that it may come for us and that we may merit to reign in it" (130.11.21).

19. Letter 130.6.13. For an illuminating discussion, see Clair, *Discerning the Good*, 52–65. Augustine makes a similar claim in *The Excellence of Marriage*, 9.9: "Undoubtedly we should take note that God gives us some benefits that are to be sought after for their own sake, such as wisdom, health and friendship, and others are necessary for the sake of something else, such as learning, food, drink, marriage, and sleeping together." He goes on to emphasize the importance of proper "use" (9.9).

20. Letter 130.6.13.

21. Letter 130.6.12.

22. Ibid.

23. Ibid. See *City of God*, 12.8: "Nor is pride the fault of him who gives power, or of power itself, but of the soul which perversely loves its own power, and despises a more righteous higher Power. Hence, he who perversely loves the good of any nature whatsoever is made evil through this very good even as he attains it, and is made wretched because deprived of a greater good."

24. Letter 130.6.12.

25. Letter 130.5.11–130.7.14, 130.12.22–130.13.24. See also Studer, "Pauline Theme of Hope," 211.

26. Sermon 157.5.

27. Ibid.

28. Ibid. See also Letter 130.12.

29. Sermon 157.5, emphasis added.

30. Letter 130.6.12–13.

31. Letter 130.7.14.

32. Sermon 87.10, translation altered. I translate *peruersa* as "perverse" rather than "wrong-headed," as Hill does. In Sermon 352A.7, Augustine also describes "perverse hope" (*spem peruersam*) and "unbelieving despair" (*infidelem desperationem*) as the two vices related to hope.

33. *Expositions of the Psalms*, 129.10.

34. Ibid.

35. Sermon 105.7.

36. Sermon 157.4; *City of God*, 19.4.

37. *On Christian Teaching*, 1.18.17.

38. Sermon 87.10. See also Sermon 352A.6–8; *Advantage of Believing*, 10.24.

39. Sermon 87.10. See also Sermon 352A.6–9.

40. Sermon 352A.6.

41. Sermon 87.10.

42. Sermon 352A.7–9. Augustine sometimes uses "presumption" (*praesumptio*) to describe inordinate hope; at other times, he uses "perverse hope" (*peruersa spes*). Here, I use them interchangeably.

43. Sermon 87.11. See also 352A.6.

44. Sermon 352A.7–9.

45. Sermon 56.2.

46. *Expositions of the Psalms*, 31(2).6.

47. Sermon 56.2–3.

48. The death of one's enemies is, we might say, "against honest and lawful use, against the law and will of the creator" (Sermon 21.3).

49. *On Christian Teaching*, 3.30.43.

50. *Expositions of the Psalms*, 31(2).1; Sermon 87.11; Sermon 352A.7–9.

51. *Expositions of the Psalms*, 31(2).1.

52. Sermon 87.10–11; Sermon 352A.6.

53. Sermon 87.10. See also *Commentary on the Gospel of John*, 33.8, in *Political Writings*, 106–107.

54. See *Confessions*, 4.16.28.

55. Cicero, *On Duties*, 1.89, 2.59–60.

56. Ibid., 1.73.

57. Aquinas makes this structure explicit in his account of magnanimity, which he describes as the moral virtue that perfects the passion of hope and finds a mean between vices of presumption and pusillanimity, which is akin to despair. For an analysis, see Lamb, "Passion and Its Virtue."

58. *Commentary on the Gospel of John*, 33.8, in *Political Writings*, 106–107.

59. See chapter 2. The "human mind," Augustine writes, "dithers between opposite dangers, wavering between confession of its weakness and rash presumption, and for the most part it is tossed between these two and battered on either side, and whichever way it is driven there is a ruinous fall awaiting it" (*Expositions of the Psalms*, 31[2].1). Here, Augustine is speaking of two kinds of presumption, the presumption of those who confess "weakness" but believe God will offer salvation no matter what, and the "rash presumption" of others who assume that they can achieve salvation by their own efforts. Both forms of presumption reflect excessive and inordinate hope. What distinguishes the "presumption" of someone who confesses weakness from the "despair" of another who professes weakness is that the presumptuous person still has a

hope of salvation whereas the despairing person has abandoned this hope, deeming salvation impossible.

60. Sermon 352A.6.

61. Sermon 87.10.

62. Jenson, *Gravity of Sin*, 4–46, identifies Augustine as a source of the idea of sin as being "curved in on oneself" (*incurvatus in se*).

63. Sermon 87.10.

64. In *Confessions*, 1.13.22–1.14.23, Augustine describes reading Homer and Virgil as part of his early education, which suggests it was a common practice across much of the Roman Empire. On Homer's place in Roman education, see Marrou, *Education in Antiquity*, 262.

65. E.g., Sermon 56.19. For discussion of this motif, see Stewart-Kroeker, *Pilgrimage*.

66. In an early dialogue on *The Happy Life*, Augustine argues that the way to "the happy life" is through the "harbor" or "port of philosophy" (1.1). On the ancient connection between travel and *theoria*, see Wolin, *Tocqueville*, 5, 34–36.

67. Wills notes that Augustine's voyage to Rome in 383 was his "first harrowing experience of the sea. He would sail only one more time in his life—to get back to Africa, and to stay there. The sea, despite its beauty, was a terror to anyone venturing on it" (*Saint Augustine*, 36, citing *City of God*, 22.24; and Perler, *Les voyages de Saint Augustin*, 57–81). In Letter 149.3.34, Augustine notes Paulinus's recent experience of a "very violent storm" at sea and, in a sermon on faith, hope, and love, tells his congregation to "[f]ear the sea, even when it is a flat calm" (Sermon 105.11). He frequently describes vices or bad behaviors as "shipwrecks" (Sermon 56.11; *Expositions of the Psalms*, 31(2).4, 91.8, 99.7; Letter 55.7.13).

68. Sermon 359A.1, citing Hebrews 6:19.

69. *City of God*, 19.4. See also *Free Choice of the Will*, 1.13.27.89–90; Letter 155.12–13.

70. *Trinity*, 14.9.12.

71. See, e.g., *Catholic Way of Life*, 1.15.25; 1.25.46; Letter 155.12–13; Letter 167; *City of God*, 15.22, 22.24. For insightful discussions, see Bowlin, "Augustine Counting Virtues"; Langan, "Interconnection of the Virtues"; and Kent, "Augustine's Ethics," 228–229.

72. *Catholic Way of Life*, 1.15.25.

73. Ibid.

74. Ibid.

75. On the relationship between hope, courage, prudence, and justice, among other virtues, see Stout, *Democracy and Tradition*, 59.

76. Clair, *Discerning the Good*, 167.

77. Ibid., 167–172.

78. *On Christian Teaching*, 1.27.28.

79. See Clair, *Discerning the Good*, 135–143. Although Clair does not emphasize the virtue of prudence, it is compatible with the "way of discernment" he commends (167).

80. *City of God*, 19.4; *Trinity*, 14.9.12.

81. E.g., *City of God*, 1.31; 5.19; Letter 189.8, in *Political Writings*, 218.

82. Keys describes "Augustinian humility" as "the foundational virtue of human beings according to their finite, social, and especially created natures" ("Augustinian Humility," 110). Clair notes "Augustine's trademark emphasis on the virtue of humility as the necessary groundwork for the practice of the other virtues" (*Discerning the Good*, 141). Dodaro elevates "humility" as

the Augustinian virtue needed to overcome "weakness" and the "foundation of statesmanship and political discourse in a truly just society" (*Christ and the Just Society*, 27–71, 183).

83. *City of God*, 14.13. "If pride is the root of sin," Deane argues, "sin can be overcome only by complete humility and by attributing to God any good that man does" (*Political and Social Ideas*, 20). Gregory characterizes humility as the "preeminent virtue that attaches to proper love" and quotes *The Trinity*, 8.5.12: "The more we are cured of the tumor of pride, the fuller we are of love" (*Politics*, 324). Rist identifies Augustine's virtue of humility as "the companion of love for God just as pride is the companion of love of self." It involves "two sorts of reference: to a recognition that man is not God but that he depends on God for his existence, and to a recognition that in his fallen state he needs the help of God's 'humility,' God's being willing to serve others, as shown above all in the Incarnation. At bottom, humility is honesty about the human condition, and it is on the basis of that honesty, that willingness to face the facts, that man's moral and spiritual regeneration has to be founded" (*Augustine*, 190). Ogle argues that "Augustine's main goal in *City of God* is to persuade the proud of the *virtus* (power or excellence) of humility" (*Politics and the Earthly City*, 96).

84. *City of God*, 14.13.

85. Brown, "Political Society," 320. For a useful discussion of this insight in the context of humility, see Johnson, *Theology*, 162.

86. *City of God*, 14.13; see also 10.28. On humility, see also Kaufman, *On Agamben*, 85–87.

87. *City of God*, 14.13.

88. Ibid., 16.4.

89. My account is indebted to Jeffrey Stout's discussion of piety as the "virtuous acknowledgment of dependence on the sources of one's existence and progress through life" (*Democracy and Tradition*, 30). I engage Stout's account in chapter 10.

90. Ibid. For a paradigmatic account of Roman piety and its relation to justice, see Cicero, *On the Commonwealth*, Pref.1–2, 1.8, 6.16; *On the Laws*, 1.43, 2.19–20, 2.26–28.

91. See *City of God*, 10.1. For discussion, see chapter 10.

92. E.g., Letter 189.8. It is striking that in the *Enchiridion*, which was written in the context of Augustine's anti-Pelagian disputes, he describes the eternal and temporal goods that we hope for as "gifts" (30.115).

93. For a distinction between piety as virtue and feeling, see Stout, *Democracy and Tradition*, 20.

94. *City of God*, 10.1; *Enchiridion*, 1.2.

95. *City of God*, 19.4.

96. Ibid. See also *Expositions of the Psalms*, 60.3: "During this earthly pilgrimage our life cannot be free from temptation, for none of us comes to know ourselves except through the experience of temptation, nor can we be crowned until we have come through victorious, nor be victorious until we have been in battle, nor fight our battles unless we have an enemy and temptations to overcome."

97. All three descriptions are included in Bogan's editor's notes in *Retractions*, 264.

98. *Enchiridion*, 1.4, 1.6.

99. See, e.g., ibid., 1.3–4, 2.7, 8.23, 33.122.

100. Ibid., 1.3. See also *Retractions*, 2.89. Augustine also emphasizes the value of repeated reading in Letters 212A and 1A*.3 to Firmus when sending copies of *City of God*.

101. The New City Press translation of the *Enchiridion* is entitled *The Augustine Catechism*.

102. *Enchiridion*, 1.3.

103. Ibid., 2.7.

104. On literacy, see Gamble, *Books and Readers*, 5, 141. For more on how drawing on biblical passages aided accessibility in a context where most people were illiterate, see chapter 6.

105. See Sermon 56.13; Sermon 58.12.

106. My description is indebted to the helpful account provided by Hill in Sermon 56n1. For Hill's speculations on the dates of the sermons, see ibid. and Sermon 57.6n8.

107. See Hill's summary in Sermon 56n1.

108. Sermon 58.1.

109. I borrow this phrase from Brennan and Pettit, *Economy of Esteem*.

110. Sermon 59.1. See also *Faith and the Creed*, 1.1; Sermon 58.1, where he describes the Creed as a "brief summary of the faith."

111. Sermon 57.1. See also Sermon 56.1.

112. Sermon 58.13. For another use of the "clothing" metaphor, see Letter 120.2.8.

113. Herdt, *Putting on Virtue*, 2, 45–71, esp. 61–71.

114. *Confessions*, 8.12.29, as cited by Herdt, *Putting on Virtue*, 69.

115. Sermon 58.1.

116. Sermon 58.12.

117. Sermon 56.13. See also Sermon 58.12.

118. Sermon 59.8.

119. Sermon 58.1: "As you heard when the gospel was read, the Son himself taught this prayer to his disciples and his faithful followers. We have a real hope of winning our suit, when a lawyer of that class has dictated the petition for us." See also Sermon 57.2; 59.1.

120. See, e.g., Sermon 56.4, 57.12, 58.2, 58.6, 59.3. For an excellent exposition of how Augustine casts Christ and the saints as exemplars of virtue, see Dodaro, *Christ and the Just Society*.

121. Sermon 59.5.

122. Sermon 56.4. Hill translates *forma* as "framework," but it can also mean "pattern," "model," "form," or "figure." See Lewis, *Elementary Latin Dictionary*, 334.

123. Christ's role as exemplar, teacher, and source of hope is evident in *Expositions of the Psalms*, 60.4: "Only inasmuch as he has become our hope does he guide us. As our leader he guides us; he leads us along in himself because he is our way, and he leads us finally to himself because he is our homeland. He is our guide, then; but how? Because he has become our hope. But how has he become our hope? Precisely in the way I have just been pointing out to you: by being tempted, by suffering, by rising again. That is how he has become our hope. . . . In him you see mirrored both your labors and your reward: your labors in his passion, and your reward in his resurrection. That is how he has become our hope, for we have two lives, one in which we find ourselves now, and another for which we hope. . . . Christ has made himself a pattern for the life you live now by his labors, his temptations, his sufferings, and his death; and in his resurrection he is the pattern for the life you will live later." See also Sermon 157.1–3 and Letter 155.4, in *Political Writings*, 92: "It is in the hope of gaining [eternal life] that we lead this temporary and mortal life, with endurance rather than with delight. We face its evils bravely, relying on sound purpose together with divine assistance; while we rejoice in God's faithful promise of, and our faithful hope for, goods that will last for ever. The apostle encourages us with the words:

rejoicing in hope, patient in trials [Rom 12:12]. He shows why he says *patient in trials* by putting *rejoicing in hope* first. I encourage you in this hope through Jesus Christ our Lord. God himself, our master, taught us this, when the majesty of his divinity was hidden but the weakness of his flesh manifest. He did this not only by his spoken word, but also by the example of his passion and resurrection. He revealed in the one what we ought to endure, and in the other what we ought to hope for." On the Christological aspect of Augustinian hope, see also Brooks, "What May I Hope For?," 136–140. On "Christ's entire life on earth" as "a splendid education in morals" for Augustine, see Kent, "Augustine's Ethics," 217.

Chapter 4. Faith in the Unseen: Trusting in Another

1. Hebrews 11:1, cited in Sermon 126.3; *Homilies on the Gospel of John*, 79.1, 95.2, 111.3; see also *Enchiridion*, 2.8. The Latin is *fides est sperantium substantia, conuictio rerum quae non uidentur*. In Sermon 359A.3, Hill translates *substantia* as "ground."

2. A notable exception is Rawls, *Brief Inquiry*.

3. For an insightful account of Augustine's concept of faith, see TeSelle, "Faith," 347–350. On meanings of *fides*, see Lewis, *Elementary Latin Dictionary*, 325; Morgan, *Roman Faith*, 7; McKaughan, "Value of Faith."

4. *Enchiridion*, 2.7; TeSelle, "Faith," 347. See also Letter 147.4.9: "faith by which he believes." On "believing that," see Peters, *Logic of the Heart*, 65.

5. Here and below, I am informed by Robert Audi's categorization of varieties of faith in "Belief, Faith, Acceptance, and Hope," 54–65.

6. For examples, see *Enchiridion*, 2.8 (on the faith of demons); Sermon 144.2; Sermon 168.3; Letter 149.3.32.

7. On differences between premodern and modern conceptions of faith, see Wolterstorff, *Practices of Belief*, 173–216.

8. *Enchiridion*, 1.6; *Trinity*, 13.2.5, translation altered.

9. Audi, "Belief, Faith, Acceptance, and Hope," 57.

10. E.g., Sermon 214.12; *Faith and the Creed*, 1.1; Sermon 4.33; Sermon 7.4; Sermon 9.4; Letter 11.2; *Advantage of Believing*, 7.18; *True Religion*, 9.17; *Predestination of the Saints*, 14.28–29; *Answer to Faustus*, 23.10.

11. *Enchiridion*, 2.7, 30.114.

12. Sermon 58.1. See also Sermon 214.1; *Faith and the Creed*, 1.1: "[T]he Catholic Faith is made known to the faithful in the Creed, and is committed to memory, in as short a form as so great a matter permits."

13. See McKaughan, "Value of Faith." Audi describes this variety as a kind of "attitudinal faith" ("Belief, Faith, Acceptance, and Hope," 55–56; see also 71–72).

14. Albert Camus suggests that, for Augustine, "One must believe, not *that* God exists, but *in* God" (*Christian Metaphysics and Neoplatonism*, 128). Morgan recognizes how "trust" and "belief" are intertwined in ancient discussions of *pistis* in Greek and *fides* in Latin (*Roman Faith*, 18, 22, 30, 44, 75, 124n2, 143). For an example of how propositional faith depends on relational faith in an authority of a witness, see Letter 147.4.10. The relationship may also be inverted: trusting in someone may require believing that they exist or that they are trustworthy (Audi, "Belief, Faith, Acceptance, and Hope," 63–65).

15. See Morgan, *Roman Faith*; McKaughan, "Value of Faith," 8–12; Treggiari, *Roman Marriage*, 237–238.

16. Cicero, *On Duties*, 1.23, 2.33, 2.84. For Cicero and other Romans, Margaret Atkins argues, "*fides*, mutual trust and trustworthiness, is the cement of civic society," supplying the social and political conditions that unite citizens: "[I]t is because we can trust men to do what they have said they will do, or to carry out public duties, that we can exchange the duties that bind us" ("'Domina et Regina Virtutum,'" 268). See also Morgan, *Roman Faith*, 57–60, 77–122.

17. Cicero, *How to Be a Friend*, §65. I have altered Freeman's translation of *fides* from "loyalty" to "faith." See also Morgan, *Roman Faith*, 57.

18. Morgan, *Roman Faith*, 14.

19. *Trinity*, 13.2.5; Morgan, *Roman Faith*, 11. Later, she more cautiously suggests this neglect emerges "*probably* under the influence of Augustine" (14, emphasis added).

20. Morgan, *Roman Faith*, 11–12.

21. Ibid., 28. Morgan finds this binarism problematic since it "divides *fides* into subject and object, excluding the shared ground of their relationship," and "focuses attention on the interiority of the subject and the content of the object" (28). According to Morgan, Augustine's account of faith remains "oddly limited" because it excludes the intersubjective faith that defines a relationship between fellow human beings or between human beings and God: "Augustine's model fits very poorly with the way *pistis* and *fides* are presented in any body of late Hellenistic or early imperial, Graeco-Roman, Jewish, or Christian material," sources that "have very little interest in the interiority of *pistis/fides*" and instead "focus constantly on its relationality" (29). While she acknowledges "signs" that Augustine "also understands *fides* as a relationship"—when, for example, he describes "*fides* working through love"—she concludes that "relationality remains rather submerged in his, and hence in much later Christian, thinking about faith" (29).

22. Part of the issue may relate to translation. Whereas the noun and verbs forms of *pistis* are similar in Greek (*pistis/pisteuien*), the verb most often used in relation to the noun *fides* in Latin is not *fidere* (which, Morgan notes, is "rare and largely poetic"), but *credere*, which can also mean "to trust," though it is frequently translated as "to believe" in Augustine's works (Morgan, "Response to My Commentators," 604n1). Those who approach Augustine in English may not discern the subtleties of different Latin meanings, thereby making it seem as if he emphasizes "belief" more than "trust."

23. Morgan, *Roman Faith*, 29.

24. *Excellence of Marriage*, 4.4, 24.32.

25. *Excellence of Widowhood*, 3.4–4.5.

26. *Faith in the Unseen*, 2.4.

27. *Advantage of Believing*, 10.23–24.

28. Sermon 21.5.

29. *Faith in the Unseen*, 2.4.

30. Morgan, *Roman Faith*, 28. As best as I can tell, Morgan only cites one passage from Augustine (*Trinity*, 13.2.5, in *Roman Faith*, 11). Uncharacteristically, she does not cite any additional primary sources from Augustine, and most of her secondary sources are drawn from scholars in biblical studies rather than Augustinian studies.

31. TeSelle, "Faith," 347; Peters, *Logic of the Heart*, 69.

32. Audi describes this as "allegiant faith" ("Belief, Faith, Acceptance, and Hope," 62).

33. This is one of the meanings of faith implicit in Cicero's account in *On Duties*, 1.23, 2.84. Relational faith relies on the fidelity involved in keeping faith.

34. See TeSelle, "Faith," 347; Morgan, *Roman Faith*, 108–116.

35. *Excellence of Marriage*, 24.32; TeSelle, "Faith," 347. On the Roman context of *fides* in the marital bond, see Treggiari, *Roman Marriage*, 237–238; and Morgan, *Roman Faith*, 47–51.

36. "When one makes a promise," Augustine advises Boniface, "one must keep faith [*fides*], even with an enemy with whom one is waging war. How much more so with a friend, for whose sake one is fighting" (*Letter* 189.6; see also Sermon 21.5).

37. *City of God*, 22.1. As he writes elsewhere, "God, therefore, who is able to do what he promised, produces the faith of the nations" (*Predestination of the Saints*, 2.6).

38. Ibid., 2.5. See also *Enchiridion*, 7.8: "[I]f assent is taken away, faith is taken away, since nothing can be believed without assent." For an insightful discussion of how Augustine transforms the Stoic conception of "assent," see Rist, "Faith and Reason," 32–37.

39. As Rist writes, "Assent is not only a determining judgment, but a determining love" (ibid., 36). See also Peters, *Logic of the Heart*, 60–74, 80.

40. *Enchiridion*, 2.8; Sermon 144.2.

41. *Enchiridion*, 2.8; Sermon 144.2: "[I]t makes a great deal of difference whether someone believes that Jesus is the Christ, or whether he believes in Christ. That he is the Christ, after all, even the demons believed, but all the same the demons didn't believe in Christ. You believe in Christ, you see, when you both hope in Christ and love Christ. Because if you have faith without hope and without love, you believe that he is the Christ, but you don't believe in Christ. So when you believe in Christ, by your believing in Christ, Christ comes into you, and you are somehow or other united to him and made into a member of his body. And this cannot happen unless both hope and charity come along too."

42. E.g., Letter 171A.2; *Enchiridion*, 1.3; Sermon 4.1; Sermon 105.5–6; Letter 130.9.18, 13.24; Letter 138.3.17; *Answer to Faustus*, 20.23.

43. *Expositions of the Psalms*, 91.1; Letter 147.17.43.

44. Letter 147.14.34–35. See also *Enchiridion*, 2.8, alluding to Galatians 5:6 and 7.20, alluding to Habakkuk 2:4; Romans 1:17; Galatians 3:11; and Hebrews 10:38.

45. *Faith and the Creed*, 2.3–3.3.

46. Early in the *Enchiridion*, Augustine seems to conceive faith primarily as propositional faith, a *belief that* God exists or that a particular outcome is possible. This is why demons can be said to possess faith in one sense: they *believe that* God exists (2.8). But they lack the virtue of faith since they do not possess the "faith that works through love" (2.8, citing Galatians 5:6). After this early exposition, Augustine goes on to align the contents of faith with the creed (2.7, 30.114), so all three forms of faith are operative.

47. See, e.g., Letter 55.14.26; Letter 147.1.6–4.11, 14.35; *Enchiridion*, 1.5; *City of God*, 22.29; *Expositions of the Psalms*, 91.1, 97.3, 120.6; Sermon 88.4; Sermon 159.1.

48. E.g., *Teacher*, 11.36–12.40. For Augustine's evolution, see Siebert, "Augustine's Development."

49. See Letter 147.1.4–147.4.11. See also *Enchiridion*, 16.63. Kinneavy affirms that Augustine "placed the level of certainty of faith below that of science" (*Greek Rhetorical Origins*, 31).

50. See Letter 147.1.3, 147.2.7, 147.17.41.

51. See, e.g., *City of God*, 22.29; Letter 147.14.35, 147.22.51; *Enchiridion*, 16.63.

52. 1 Corinthians 13:12, cited, e.g., in *City of God*, 22.29; Letter 120.2.11; *Enchiridion*, 16.63.

53. Letter 147.2.7.

54. Letter 147.3.8.

55. See Siebert, "Augustine's Development," 223–225.

56. Ibid., 230, citing *Trinity*, 13.3.6.

57. *City of God*, 19.18, as cited and discussed in Siebert, "Augustine's Development," 232–233.

58. *Advantage of Believing*, 9.21–11.25.

59. Ibid., 9.22, 11.25. See also *Enchiridion*, 6.19, 7.21, on related epistemic "errors."

60. For Augustine's most explicit discussions, see *True Religion*, 24.45; *Against the Academicians*, 3.20.43; *Catholic Way of Life*, 1.2.3; *On Order*, 2.9.26–2.11.34; Letter 120; Letter 147; *Confessions*, 6.5.7–8; *Advantage of Believing*, 9.21–17.35.

61. For an insightful account of the development of Augustine's views, see van Fleteren, "Authority and Reason," 33–71. For an overview of Augustine's views of belief, trust, and authority in the context of his political thought, see Coleman, "St Augustine," 315–319. My account is also indebted to Rist, "Faith and Reason"; Ramirez, "Priority of Reason"; von Jess, "Reason as Propaedeutic"; and Peters, *Logic of the Heart*, 60–83.

62. *Confessions*, 3.6.10–4.1.1, 5.6.10, 5.10.18; *Catholic Way of Life*, 1.18.34, 2.19.68; *Advantage of Believing*, 1.2.

63. *Retractions*, 1.13. See also *Advantage of Believing*, 1.2.

64. *Advantage of Believing*, 1.2.

65. Ibid.; *Confessions*, 5.3.6; see also 4.3.6, 6.5.7. For discussion, see Ramirez, "Priority of Reason," 128; and van Fleteren, "Authority and Reason," 36.

66. *On Order*, 2.9.26. See also *Against the Academicians*, 3.20.43.

67. *Confessions*, 6.5.7. See also *Advantage of Believing*, 13.29; *Trinity*, 4.16.21.

68. *True Religion*, 24.45. For discussion, see Peters, *Logic of the Heart*, 74–76. As Augustine writes, "[T]he minds of human beings obscured by their familiarity with the darkness, by which they are veiled in the night of sins and vices, cannot direct a suitable gaze toward the clarity and purity of reason" (*Catholic Way of Life*, 1.2.3; see also Letter 118.5.32).

69. *Catholic Way of Life*, 1.2.3; *Advantage of Believing*, 10.24, 14.31, 15.33–17.35; Letter 120.1.3; Letter 147.17.44. On occasion, Augustine seems to suggest that a few people can use reason to see divine truths, but even then, it is not clear whether he is affirming this view or simply granting it for the sake of his imagined argument with Honoratus (*Advantage of Believing*, 10.24). In any case, he suggests that even those capable of reasoning to divine truths ought not to do so since "their example would be harmful to others," particularly those who need to accept authority in order to understand. Even if the few do not need authority to "prepare and predispose the mind" to God, it is better to "circle for a while where the approach is safest rather than to be a cause of danger to yourself and an example of recklessness to others" (10.24).

70. Ibid., 9.21. As Augustine affirms later, "[W]hen you do not have the ability to appreciate the arguments, it is very healthy to believe without knowing the reasons and by that belief to cultivate the mind and allow the seeds of truth to be sown" (14.31; see also *True Religion*, 8.14).

71. *Advantage of Believing*, 17.35; see also Letter 120.1.6.

72. *On Order*, 2.9.26; *Catholic Way of Life*, 1.2.3; *Trinity*, 15.12.21. On the "necessary" and "non-optional character of belief," see Ramirez, "Priority of Reason," 125. See also van Fleteren, "Authority and Reason," 37–38; Peters, *Logic of the Heart*, 61–63.

73. *Advantage of Believing*, 7.17.

74. *Faith in the Unseen*, 2.4. See also *Confessions*, 6.5.7; *Advantage of Believing*, 12.26.

75. *Advantage of Believing*, 12.26.; see also 14.31.

76. *Faith in the Unseen*, 2.3. See also *Advantage of Believing*, 10.23. "Even friendship cannot exist unless we believe some things that cannot be proved for certain" (10.24).

77. *Faith in the Unseen*, 2.4. See also *Advantage of Believing*, 12.26.

78. *Faith in the Unseen*, 2.4.

79. *Advantage of Believing*, 12.26.

80. *Faith in the Unseen*, 2.4; Letter 120.2.10.

81. *Confessions*, 6.5.7. See also *Faith in the Unseen*, 2.4.

82. For a lengthy list of other ordinary things we believe "on the testimony of others," see *Trinity*, 15.11.21. For discussion, see King, "Augustine on Knowledge," 158, 160.

83. E.g., Letter 147; *City of God*, 11.3. For analysis of Augustine's views on testimony, see King and Ballantyne, "Augustine on Testimony"; and Siebert, "Augustine's Development."

84. *City of God*, 11.3.

85. Letter 147.1.4–5, 147.3.8. See also *Faith in the Unseen*, 2.4; *Advantage of Believing*, 12.26.

86. E.g., *Faith in the Unseen*, 4.7.

87. Ibid., 2.4; *Advantage of Believing*, 12.26.

88. *Advantage of Believing*, 7.15, 7.17, 14.31.

89. *Advantage of Believing*, 14.31. For an insightful account of the church's authority, see Eno, "Authority," 80–82.

90. *Faith in the Unseen*, 3.5, 4.7. See also *Advantage of Believing*, 16.34. Augustine suggests, questionably, that "[t]here are now more Christians than even pagans and Jews combined," which, he argues, lends support to the church's testimony (7.19).

91. *Advantage of Believing*, 17.35.

92. Ibid., 14.31. See also *Faith in the Unseen*, 7.10.

93. See also *Advantage of Believing*, 11.25.

94. *City of God*, 11.3. For discussion, see Eno, "Authority," 80.

95. *On Christian Teaching*, 4.26.55; *Faith in the Unseen*, 4.7; *Advantage of Believing*, 14.32–17.35. See Dodaro, *Christ and the Just Society*, 115–146. Strikingly, Augustine defines a "miracle" as "any event that is so difficult or extraordinary as to be beyond the expectation or power of those it astonishes" (*Advantage of Believing*, 16.34). On this view, miracles need not be supernatural. Indeed, he goes on to explain how nature itself provokes the "wonder" associated with miracles (16.34).

96. Letter 147.1.3; *Literal Meaning of Genesis*, 2.5.9, as cited by Eno, "Authority," 80.

97. Letter 147.1.3, emphasis added.

98. See *City of God*, 15.23; see also 11.3.

99. Letter 147.1.4. See also Letter 147.5.14: "[I]t is in no way possible that this authority of the scriptures is not truthful."

100. Letter 147.1.4.

101. Sermon 43.3–4. See also *City of God*, 22.24.

102. Letter 119.1; Letter 120.1.2–3.

103. Letter 120.1.6. As Rist notes, such a view helps to explain why Augustine "is prepared to endure the long circuitous paths which reason demands, urging that reason not be abandoned because of its frequent abuse" ("Faith and Reason," 27).

104. Letter 120.1.2.

105. *On Order*, 2.9.26. In *True Religion*, 24.45, Augustine suggests that authority "has priority by the order, not of nature or its inherent excellence, but of time." See also *Against the Academicians*, 3.20.43. For helpful discussions, see Ramirez, "Priority of Reason"; and van Fleteren, "Authority and Reason."

106. *True Religion*, 24.45.

107. Letter 120.1.4.

108. *True Religion*, 24.45. See also Letter 147.16.39–40.

109. Letter 147.16.39–40.

110. Ibid.

111. *On Order*, 2.10.28.

112. *Predestination of the Saints*, 2.5. Contrary to what some interpreters assume, this passage affirms that Augustine is an intellectualist rather than a voluntarist, one who holds that an act of the intellect precedes the free choice of the will.

113. Ibid., quoting 2 Corinthians 3:5.

114. Ibid.

115. Isaiah 7:9. Since this verse does not appear in the Latin Vulgate, Hill suggests Augustine may have taken it from a Latin translation of the Septuagint or a "mistranslation" of the verse (Hill, "Unless You Believe," and Hill's note at *Trinity*, 7.6.12, p. 236n51). In *On Christian Teaching*, 2.12.17, Augustine acknowledges two different translations of Isaiah 7:9: "[O]ne version has 'if you do not believe, you will not understand,' another has 'if you do not believe, you will not stand fast.'" As Augustine writes, "It is not clear which of these represents the truth unless the versions in the original language are consulted. Yet both convey something important to those who read intelligently." He defends the use of the translation focused on "understanding" even if is not as accurate to the original language.

116. E.g., Letter 120.1.3; *Trinity*, 7.6.12, 15.2.2; *Free Choice of the Will*, 1.2, 2.2.4–6; *Homilies on the Gospel of John*, 29.6. For discussion, see Peters, *Logic of the Heart*, 60–83.

117. Sermon 43.9.

118. Ibid., emphasis added.

119. Letter 120.4.20. In his letter to Paulina, Augustine stresses the importance of "diligent inquiry" and suggests that the view of Ambrose "has now been confirmed not by his authority but by the truth itself" (147.22.51–23.52).

120. *City of God*, 19.1; *Catholic Way of Life*, 1.2.3.

121. Van Fleteren, "Authority and Reason," 34.

122. Augustine's own intellectual and spiritual development in *Confessions* provides an example of this dialectic between authority and reason. See Rist, "Faith and Reason," 27–28.

123. One notable exception is King and Ballantyne, "Augustine on Testimony," 212–213, who gesture toward ways that Augustine's account of testimony parallels forms of "*defaultism, credulism*, or *Reidianism*," which assumes we have reasons to trust testimony until there are sufficient reasons to doubt or abandon it. King affirms this position in "Augustine on Knowledge," 157–161. I seek to fill out a compatible position with philosophical and interpretative detail in connection to Augustine's views on reason and authority, his implicit use of defeaters and immanent critique, and his understanding of the relations among faith, virtue, perseverance, rhetoric, dialogue, trust, and hope. I also draw on different sources in contemporary epistemology to

explicate what is implicit in Augustine's account. For the "default and challenge" accounts of discursive reasoning that inform what follows, see Brandom, *Making It Explicit*, esp. 176–178; and Williams, *Problems of Knowledge*, esp. 146–158. For other accounts with a similar argumentative structure, see Pollock, *Knowledge and Justification*, 23–49; Wolterstorff, *Practices of Belief*, 86–117, 217–264; and Stout, *Democracy and Tradition*, 209–213, 270–283. I am grateful to Jeffrey Stout for suggesting this connection.

124. For a helpful overview of Augustine's account of knowledge and the differences between what can be known directly and nondiscursively versus discursively on testimony, see King, "Augustine on Knowledge," 152–161, citing, e.g., *Trinity*, 10.9.12. For an account that emphasizes the inferential basis of testimonial knowledge, see Siebert, "Augustine's Development." Siebert challenges King's suggestion that Augustine adopts a "defaultist" view of testimonial knowledge. But Siebert's critique seems to rely on a particularly strong view of what a defaultist position requires. It seems strong in three ways. First, Siebert seems to assume that a defaultist view requires accepting *all* testimony by default, including testimony from those who might be less trustworthy, rather than a subset of beliefs based on trustworthy authorities. Second, his view depends on a particularly strong account of what a belief entails. On his view, defaultism entails "an entitlement to a flat-out belief that *p*, not just an entitlement to believe *p* to some degree less than 1" (228n56). I do not believe defaultism requires a "flat-out belief." Third, Siebert assumes defaultism is only a doxastic account that implies provisional assent rather than certainty and thus is incompatible with the nonprovisional assent that Augustine seems to defend in his later account of testimonial knowledge. But Siebert does not consider this alternative Latin meaning of certain (*certa*) in his primarily doxastic rendering of Augustine's view of faith and testimony. I believe alternative translations of *certa* allow Augustine to say that faith in the unseen can be held "firmly" or "resolutely" without necessarily having the same epistemic status as knowledge of what is "seen." Thus, while Siebert is right to highlight the historical shifts in Augustine's account of testimony and the possibility of inferential testimonial knowledge, his critique does not necessarily undermine the claim that *some* examples of Augustine's discursive reasoning assume a default and challenge structure, particularly in relation to human testimony about temporal matters rather than testimony about divine matters or from divine authorities. Siebert suggests his case against defaultism and in favor of an inferentialist view shifts the "burden of proof . . . to the defaultist" (230). In what follows, I attempt to show how Augustine, both explicitly and implicitly, affirms a default and challenge structure for *some* beliefs toward *some* forms of authority and testimony, but this is a weaker and more permissive view of defaultism than the one Siebert rejects.

125. Peters attributes a similar dialectical model to Augustine but describes it as his "Socratic" view: "The purpose of rational inquiry in this context is not to determine a set of indubitable starting points from which to conduct one's life, but to clarify first of all just what one really believes and then test whether one's fundamental beliefs can function coherently in the context of one's other beliefs as well as in one's life" (*Logic of the Heart*, 82).

126. Brandom, *Making It Explicit*, 177. See also Stout, *Democracy and Tradition*, 212; Wolterstorff, *Practices of Belief*, 247. To be clear, not all default beliefs are "innocent" in this way. Some beliefs have causal origins—for example, in self-deception, wishful thinking, or unjust bias— that generate suspicion from the start and prevent others in the discursive community from conferring entitlement to, or acknowledging the authority of, that belief (see Brandom, *Making*

It Explicit, 179–180). But many of our beliefs do not, prima facie, have such suspicious causal histories and are thus a trustworthy, if defeasible, basis from which to start an inquiry, conversation, debate, or joint action. In such cases, deference to the authority of some beliefs is often the only way to get an inquiry, conversation, debate, or joint action off the ground. I am grateful for John Bowlin for this point.

127. The following account of "defeaters," including the terms "rebutting" and "undercutting" defeaters, is indebted to Pollock, "Self-Defeating Arguments"; *Knowledge and Justification*, 41–46; Plantinga, *Warranted Christian Belief*, 357–373; and Wolterstorff, *Practices of Belief*, 311.

128. I am grateful to Jeffrey Stout for this formulation.

129. See Wolterstorff, *Practices of Belief*, 310–311; Plantinga, *Warranted Christian Belief*, 357–373.

130. Wolterstorff, *Practices of Belief*, 219.

131. Williams, *Problems of Knowledge*, 157n2.

132. See *Confessions*, 5.10.19, 5.14.25; *Advantage of Believing*, 8.20; *Happy Life*, 1.4; *Enchiridion*, 7.20. He shows awareness of these doctrines in *Against the Academicians*.

133. In *The Advantage of Believing*, which is directed against skepticism, he acknowledges a similar way of relating to his past involvement with Manicheanism: "I retain the truth that I learned when I was with them, but I repudiate the false opinions I held" (18.36). He may take a similar approach to Academic skepticism.

134. See, e.g., *Against the Academicians*, 3.4.9–3.5.12; *Enchiridion*, 7.20.

135. See, e.g., Letter 147.21.49.

136. Ibid.

137. Ibid.

138. Letter 147.21.50.

139. Letter 147.3.9.

140. Letter 147.21.50–147.23.54.

141. Letter 147.23.54.

142. *True Religion*, 10.20.

143. Letter 120.1.4.

144. *Enchiridion*, 7.21.

145. See Deane, *Political and Social Ideas*, vii–ix; Dodaro, "Church and State," 181–182; Dyson, introduction to *City of God*, xv, xxviii–xxix; Fortin, "St. Augustine," 176; Hollingworth, *Pilgrim City*, 64; Vanderjagt, "Political Thought," 1562–1563.

146. *Retractions*, 1.13. See also Letter 147.3.8.

147. Letter 147.1.4; see also 147.1.3, 5.12. Coleman, "St Augustine," 317, suggests that, for Augustine, all "sources and evidence," including those based on "scriptural authorities," are evaluated "according to plausibility rather than demonstrated certitude" (see also 318–319).

148. See, e.g., *Advantage of Believing*, 10.24.

149. *Predestination of the Saints*, 11.21.

150. Ibid.

151. Letter 147.16.40. Comparing the authority of Ambrose and himself to that of the canonical scriptures, he suggests to Paulina that "if you are truly wise in drawing distinctions, you see that we are far below that authority and that I am indeed farther below it" (147.16.39).

152. This is how Aquinas addresses the puzzle around the "certitude of faith" (*Summa Theologica*, II–II.4.8). Although he does not invoke Augustine in this passage, he draws on Augustine

extensively when defining an "act of faith" and "belief" (II–II.2.1–2), which means Aquinas likely sees his views on certitude as Augustinian, if not necessarily Augustine's.

153. Smith, *Believing*, 41; McKaughan, "Cognitive Opacity," 579.

154. Siebert, "Augustine's Development," tends to downplay these aspects in his analysis of Augustine's views of testimonial knowledge and his critique of defaultism.

155. Lewis, *Elementary Latin Dictionary*, 123.

156. Wolterstorff, *Practices of Belief*, 307.

157. Ibid.

158. Ibid.

159. See, e.g., Lane, "Calvin."

160. Letter 147.14.35.

161. *On Christian Teaching*, 2.12.17, emphasis added.

162. See, e.g., *Gift of Perseverance*, 1.1–3.6, 14.36, 17.43–47; Letter 77.1; and Letter 147.14.34, where he joins faith and perseverance in his interpretation of Ephesians 3:18–19.

163. See *Gift of Perseverance*; TeSelle, "Faith," 349.

164. 2 Corinthians 5:7, in, e.g., *On Christian Teaching*, 2.12.17. See also Sermon 359A.4; Sermon 158.7–8. For an insightful account of "walking with faith" in relation to contemporary philosophy of religion, see McKaughan, "Action-Centered Faith," 78.

165. See McKaughan, "Action-Centered Faith," 78–79.

166. See, e.g., *Gift of Perseverance*, 1.1–2.2; Sermon 115.1.

167. *Advantage of Believing*, 1.1; *Gift of Perseverance*, 14.36.

168. Sermon 115.1. See also Letter 77.1, where Augustine argues faith requires perseverance when it is "exercised and tested."

169. Sermon 115.1. As he writes, "[I]n order to pray, let us believe; and in order that the very faith by which we pray may not fail, let us pray."

170. Although he does not use the term "persevere," the idea is implicit in how Augustine interprets the prayer, "*I believe, Lord; help my unbelief*" (Mark 9:24): "Think of the apostles themselves: they wouldn't have left everything they had, trampled on their worldly hopes and followed the Lord, unless they had had great faith; and yet if they had had complete faith, they wouldn't have said to the Lord, *Increase our faith* (Lk 17:5). Look also at that man who admitted both things about himself (look at his faith, and his incomplete faith), who brought his son to the Lord to be cured of an evil demon, and on being questioned whether he believed, answered and said, *I believe, Lord; help my unbelief* (Mk 9:24). *I believe*, he said, *I believe, Lord*; so there's faith there. But, *help my unbelief*; so faith is not complete" (Sermon 115.1). See also *Predestination of the Saints*, 2.3–5, 4.8, 11.22, 20.40; *Gift of Perseverance*, 2.3–7.15, on the Lord's Prayer.

171. Sermon 115.1.

172. McKaughan, "Value of Faith."

173. Ibid., 20–21; McKaughan, "Action-Centered Faith," 76–77; "Cognitive Opacity," 578–579.

174. McKaughan, "Action-Centered Faith," 89, emphasis in original; see also "Value of Faith," 21–22.

175. McKaughan, "Value of Faith," 8; see also 18–19, 28. See also McKaughan, "Action-Centered Faith"; Howard-Snyder, "Propositional Faith," 368, on "resilience."

176. See McKaughan, "Value of Faith," 9–17; "Cognitive Opacity."

177. See McKaughan, "Value of Faith," 28.

178. *Confessions*, 8.12.29.

179. I am grateful to Jeffrey Stout for discussion of this point.

180. See, e.g., *Predestination of the Saints*, 2.3–6.

181. See, e.g., ibid., 11.22; *Gift of Perseverance*, 3.6.

182. Wolterstorff, *Practices of Belief*, 86.

183. Ibid., 86–98. See also Brandom, *Making It Explicit*, 141–198; Stout, *Democracy and Tradition*, 209–213, 270–283.

184. Wolterstorff, *Practices of Belief*, 93–96.

185. *Confessions*, 6.3.3–6.5.8.

186. Ibid., 5.14.24, 6.3.3–6.5.8.

187. Ibid., 8.12.29.

188. Ibid.

189. Ibid., 8.12.30.

190. On inheritance of entitlement, see Brandom, *Making It Explicit*, 173–178.

191. Ibid.; Stout, *Democracy and Tradition*, 209–213.

192. *Advantage of Believing*, 14.31.

193. Ibid.

194. Ibid., 14.31, 7.19. See also *True Religion*, 3.5.

195. *Advantage of Believing*, 14.31, 7.19. Augustine makes a similar argument about the authority of miracles. Arguing that Christ performed miracles to "bring people to believe in him," he explains how this authority is passed down to give others entitlement to their beliefs: "[H]e who brought the remedy that would heal corrupted morals established authority with miracles, won belief with authority, held the masses with belief, endured through the masses, and made religion strong by enduring" (14.32). He goes on to suggest that this faith has endured in the face of various attempts to defeat it: "The crude novelties of the heretics have failed to dislodge it in any way with their deceits, any more than did the violent opposition of the ancient errors of the pagans" (14.32). For Augustine, the fact that the Christian faith has survived and secured wide acceptance in the face of potential defeaters lends weight to its authority. See Fiedrowicz, introduction to *Advantage of Believing*, 91.

196. Brandom, *Making It Explicit*, 157–168, 176–198; Stout, *Democracy and Tradition*, 209–213.

197. Williams notes that a default and challenge structure requires one to be entitled to *challenges or defeaters*, not simply to default beliefs, which is why it can avoid global skepticism. Because global skepticism assumes every belief must be justified before being accepted (what Williams calls the "Prior Grounding Requirement"), global skepticism relies on the ability to issue "naked challenges" without any need to justify those demands or requests for evidence (*Problems of Knowledge*, 150–152). If beliefs are seen as "guilty until proven innocent" (Brandom, *Making It Explicit*, 177), then the skeptic can always reasonably ask for evidence to prove a belief's innocence. A default and challenge structure, however, rejects this Prior Grounding Requirement and thus blocks any "naked challenges" from global skeptics. If beliefs instead are "innocent until proven guilty," the skeptic cannot simply pose a naked challenge or ask for justification without also having a reason for doing so; the skeptic must also be entitled to enter a challenge (177). This means that the believer need not always answer a skeptic's challenge but

can reasonably respond by asking for specific reasons for the challenge. If the challenger lacks a good answer or is not targeting a belief that the believer actually holds, the believer need not give further justification since there is no actual challenge. As such, requests for justification cannot continue indefinitely; they must eventually come to a halt by appeal to some default entitlement. A default and challenge structure blocks the infinite regress that global skeptics target and thus fends off skepticism's most persistent challenge (Williams, *Problems of Knowledge*, 150–152; Brandom, *Making It Explicit*, 177). It is striking that Augustine, in defending his own beliefs against skeptics, asks potential challengers for specific reasons for their challenges and then sometimes answers that they cannot meet them, which ends the challenge and preserves his default position. In responding to potential worries about three "errors" that might accompany reading and interpreting an authority, for example, he explains why opponents cannot rightfully impugn the Catholic Church: "If it is the first [error], then it is a very serious allegation but not one that requires an extended defense. It is enough to say that we do not understand it in the way they ascribe to us in their attack. If it is the second kind of error, it is no less serious, but they are refuted with the same statement. If it is the third, there is nothing to answer [since it is not actually an error]" (*Advantage of Believing*, 5.12). This passage shows Augustine fending off a potential challenge by demanding specific reasons from challengers and then offering defeaters to rebut them.

198. *Retractions*, Prologue.1. Of course, Augustine's retrospective reflections in the *Retractions* are not simply responses to errors or inconsistencies. In some cases, they are subtle attempts to make his earlier thought seem consistent with his later views, not least to avoid giving succor to Pelagian opponents. I am grateful to John Bowlin for discussion of this point.

199. *Confessions*, 5.6.10–5.7.13. See also *Advantage of Believing*, 8.20.

200. *Confessions*, 6.4.5–6.5.8, 7.20.26. See also *Advantage of Believing*, 8.20.

201. *Trinity*, 1.3.5, as translated and cited by Wills, *Saint Augustine*, xiv. See also *Advantage of Believing*, 7.14.

202. *Trinity*, 1.8.17. For discussions of his openness to correction during sermons, see chapter 6.

203. *Letter* 93.5.17. For discussion, see Lamb, "Augustine and Republican Liberty," 140–141.

204. *On Christian Teaching*, Preface. *City of God*, Books 1–10, are focused on "refuting the objections of the ungodly" (10.32). As he writes in the Preface of Book 7, he is "endeavouring most diligently to uproot and extirpate depraved and ancient opinions which the long-continued error of the human race has implanted deeply and tenaciously in the dark places of the soul."

205. For example, in Letter 220 to Boniface, Augustine recalls Boniface's previous visit to Hippo and urges him to "please listen to me, my son, now that I'm at least conversing with you by letter" (Letter 220.2, in *Political Writings*, 219).

206. See *Against the Academicians*. Wills suggests that these early dialogues reflect "his view that all thought is an effort best pursued with others" (*Saint Augustine*, 28).

207. See *Soliloquies*, 1.1.

208. In *On Christian Teaching*, for example, Augustine begins his preface by anticipating objections and replying "to those who are likely to criticize this undertaking, or who would be minded to do so if not placated in advance" (Pref.1).

209. For a helpful summary, see Fiedrowicz, introduction to *Faith in the Unseen*.

210. See *Advantage of Believing*, 1.1–3, 10.23–24.

211. As Augustine tells him, "My object then is to prove to you, if I can, that, when the Manicheans attack those who, before they are capable of gazing on that truth which is perceived by a pure mind, accept the authority of the Catholic faith and by believing are strengthened and prepared for the God who will bestow light, they are acting irrationally and sacrilegiously" (ibid., 1.2).

212. Ibid., 18.36.

213. *Catholic Way of Life*, 1.2.3. Strikingly, Augustine even appeals to authority to defend his decision to start with reason, suggesting that he is "imitating, as much as I can, the gentleness of my Lord Jesus Christ, who clothed himself even with the evil of the death of which he wanted to strip us." Augustine takes himself to be doing something similar, clothing himself in the defective method of reason to strip Manicheans of their obedience to it. Similarly, in *The Advantage of Believing* (14.31), he challenges Manicheans by "speaking their language," raising questions meant to show that their own reasoning is snared in "self-contradiction."

214. *City of God*, 19.1.

215. Lamb, "Augustine and Republican Liberty," 154–155.

216. Morgan, *Roman Faith*, 7.

217. Ibid. See also Kennedy, *Classical Rhetoric*, 146.

218. Hay, "Pistis," 461–476. See also Morgan, *Roman Faith*, 6.

219. Plato, *Phaedo* 70b, *Laws* 966c, as cited by Hay, "Pistis," 462. See also Kinneavy, *Greek Rhetorical Origins*, 18.

220. Aristotle, *Rhetoric*, 1354a, 1355b, 1375a–1377b, as cited by Hay, "Pistis," 462.

221. Kennedy, *Classical Rhetoric*, 146; Morgan, *Roman Faith*, 7. Etymologically, the Greek verb for "to believe" (*pisteuein*) shares the same root as the verb "to persuade" (*peithein*), and the noun forms of both verbs take the form of the same word, *pistis*, meaning that belief is "semantically related" to persuasion in Greek (Kinneavy, *Greek Rhetorical Origins*, 48, citing Bultmann, "Pisteūo," 175).

222. Kinneavy, *Greek Rhetorical Origins*.

223. Ibid., 20, 36–37, 57–91. Kinneavy cites Marrou, *Education in Antiquity*, 194, 285. Kennedy describes rhetoric as "the core subject of formal education" in the Greek-speaking world of early Christians. "Rhetoric was a systematic academic discipline taught throughout the Roman empire. It represented approximately the level of high school education today and was, indeed, the exclusive subject of secondary education" (*New Testament Interpretation*, 5, 9).

224. Kinneavy, *Greek Rhetorical Origins*, 50. Kennedy also describes the Bible as "rhetorical" (*New Testament Interpretation*, 158).

225. Kennedy, *New Testament Interpretation*, 5–6.

226. Romans 10:11, cited by Kinneavy, *Greek Rhetorical Origins*, 125.

227. John 1:1–14. See also Burke, *Rhetoric of Religion*, 11–14.

228. Kinneavy, *Greek Rhetorical Origins*, 56–57, 79, 146.

229. Ibid., 144; see also 133–134.

230. Ibid., 147.

231. Kennedy, *New Testament Interpretation*, 7, 154. See also Kinneavy, *Greek Rhetorical Origins*, 127–129.

232. Morgan, *Roman Faith*, 243–246, at 243.

233. Ibid., 260–261.

234. Sermon 126.3. See also Sermon 359A.3; *Enchiridion*, 2.8.

235. On Augustine's education in Greek language and literature, see *Confessions*, 1.13.20, 1.14.23. For examples of Augustine engaging the Greek version of the New Testament, see *Gift of Perseverance*, 6.12; and *Retractions*, 1.6.2–3.

236. Kinneavy, *Greek Rhetorical Origins*, 127.

237. Ibid., 127–128.

238. Ibid., 128.

239. Ibid.

240. Ibid., 127–129. Morgan prefers "foundation" to "substance" as the best translation of the Greek *hypostatis* and "proof" as the best translation of *elegkos* (*Roman Faith*, 338–340). She also notes that "things not seen" in the Greek more likely refers to an unseen "future" rather than unseen "metaphysical" realities (340), which fits with Augustine's sense of hope as being ordered toward unseen future goods.

241. See Morgan, *Roman Faith*, 5–15; Kinneavy, *Greek Rhetorical Origins*, 160n119.

242. Kinneavy, *Greek Rhetorical Origins*, 160n119; Freyburger, *Fides*, 33, as cited by Morgan, *Roman Faith*, 5n10.

243. Kennedy, *Classical Rhetoric*, 146.

244. *Confessions*, 1.17.27, 3.3.6.

245. Kolbet, *Cure of Souls*, 65–66.

246. *Confessions*, 9.5.13; Wills, *Augustine's "Confessions,"* 45. See also Kaufman, *Incorrectly Political*, 24–34. As Wills suggests, even Augustine's rejection of rhetoric in *Confessions* serves rhetorical purposes, putting Augustine's early life of academic ambition and intellectual vanity in stark contrast with the humble, God-centered ethic he tries to embody after his conversion. For this reason, Wills describes Augustine as the "antirhetorical rhetorician," a "great rhetorician rhetorically dismissing rhetoric" (*Augustine's "Confessions,"* 144–145, 27–28). Cameron notes similar tensions in Paul, Antony, and Augustine, arguing that the opening chapters of Book 4 of Augustine's *On Christian Teaching* "could only have been written by a supreme practitioner of the art" (*Christianity*, 34–35n65; see also 66–68, 85–87).

247. Augustine's defense of rhetoric is evident in *On Order*, a text written just after he retired his post. There, he defends the use of rhetoric, arguing that it supplements reasoned reflection and helps teach the crowd what is "right, useful, and good" by "arousing" the emotions and performing the "necessary but by no means simple task of scattering charms and delight among the crowd, with the intent of turning it towards what is good for it" (*On Order*, 2.38). For discussion, see Cipriani, "Rhetoric"; van Deusen, "*Rhetorica, De*"; and Martin, "'Abundant Supply of Discourse,'" 15–16.

248. Dodaro, *Christ and the Just Society*, 66.

249. For overviews, see Green, introduction to *On Christian Teaching*; O'Donnell, "*Doctrina Christiana, De*," 278–280; Harrison, "Rhetoric of Scripture and Preaching"; and Kennedy, *Classical Rhetoric*, 174–182. For *On Christian Teaching*'s influence on the subsequent rhetorical tradition, see Ward, "Roman Rhetoric."

250. *On Christian Teaching*, 4.2.3, 4.4.6; Cameron, *Christianity*, 35.

251. Ibid., 4.7.21–4.26.57. I engage these three styles in more depth in chapter 6.

252. Ibid., 4.7.12.

253. Dodaro, *Christ and the Just Society*, 115–146, at 121, 115.

254. See, e.g., *On Christian Teaching*, 3.10.14, 3.29.40, 4.5.8–4.6.9; *Letter* 82.5. For Dodaro's analysis, see *Christ and the Just Society*, 115–122.

255. See *City of God*, 18.41. For Augustine, that this belief is "rightly held" by "great numbers of people, in the country and in the towns, learned and unlearned alike" adds further weight to its authority (18.41).

256. *Answer to Faustus*, 11.6, as cited by Dodaro, *Christ and the Just Society*, 120.

257. See, e.g., *City of God*, 11.18.

258. *City of God*, 18.41.

259. Dodaro, *Christ and the Just Society*, 121.

260. Ibid., 122. Of course, not all uses of rhetoric are justified. Like other goods, it, too, can be abused. As Dodaro highlights (82, 67–69), Augustine attributes the Fall to Satan's "malicious persuasion" in the Garden, when he convinced Adam and Eve through his "deceitful converse" that they, too, could be "as gods" (*Free Choice of the Will*, 3.20.57; *City of God*, 14.11, 14.13).

261. See Aristotle, *Rhetoric*, 1.2, 2.1; Quintilian, *Orator's Education*, 6.2. For discussion, see Kennedy, *Classical Rhetoric*, 82, 179–181; and Morgan, *Roman Faith*, 72–74.

262. *On Christian Teaching*, 4.27.59; *Letter* 2*.13. For a more detailed discussion, see chapter 9.

263. *City of God*, 22.1. See also *Predestination of the Saints*, 2.6.

264. *City of God*, 9.15, 9.17, 10.6, 10.20, 10.24, 21.16; *Trinity*, 1.7.14–10.21, 4.7.11–9.12; *Confessions*, 10.42.67–43.68; *Letter* 147.22.51.

265. Morgan, *Roman Faith*, 99, 101, 292.

266. See ibid., 274, 293–294, 318, 333, 345–346, 403, 507–508.

267. *City of God*, 9.15, 9.17, 10.6, 10.20, 10.24, 11.2, 21.16; *Confessions*, 10.42.67–43.68; *Trinity*, 1.7.14–10.21, 4.7.11–9.12.

268. *City of God*, 11.2; see also 9.15, 10.6.

269. Dodaro, *Christ and the Just Society*, 105–107; see also 115–116, 216–218.

270. Augustine's invocation of the relational metaphor of Christ as a "Mediator" provides another challenge to Morgan's reading of Augustinian faith as interior and propositional rather than relational.

271. *Letter* 120.1.4, quoting 1 Peter 3:15.

272. We must not let contemporary understandings of "objects" influence our understanding of Augustine's use of the term. Augustine did not perceive God or human beings as mere "objects" in the objectifying way that modern readers might understood the term. As we saw in chapter 2, describing God or human beings as "objects" of faith, hope, or love does not objectify them or reduce them to a mere instrument of our will. Rather, Augustine's premodern participationist ontology suggests an intersubjective ethic that resists modern dichotomies between "subjects" and "objects."

273. E.g., *Advantage of Believing*, 13.28; Sermon 234.3; Sermon 229H.3, as cited by O'Collins, "St. Augustine as Apologist," 326.

274. James 2:19, as cited in *Enchiridion*, 2.8. See also *Homilies on the First Epistle of John*, 10.1–2.

275. *Enchiridion*, 2.8. See also *Letter* 194.3.11; *Homilies on Gospel of John*, 6.21; *Homilies on the First Epistle of John*, 10.1: "[A] Christian's faith is with love, whereas a demon's is without love."

276. TeSelle, "Faith," 349.

277. *Expositions of the Psalms*, 77.8.

278. Ibid.

279. TeSelle, "Faith," 349.

280. This is one place where Augustine may break from the Christian scriptures. As Morgan emphasizes, New Testament writers tend to use *pistis/fides* to refer to divine-human relationships rather than intra-human relationships, "which marks a radical departure from both Jewish and Graeco-Roman tradition" (*Roman Faith*, 259). When Augustine discusses placing *fides* in other human beings, he may be drawing on the larger cultural understanding of "trust" common in Roman politics, philosophy, rhetoric, and law.

281. Sermon 21.5.

282. For discussion of this treatise's date, see Fiedrowicz, introduction to *Faith in the Unseen*, 57–58.

283. *Faith in the Unseen*, 1.1.

284. Ibid., 1.2.

285. Ibid.

286. Ibid., 2.3.

287. Ibid., 2.4.

288. Ibid.

289. Ibid.

290. Ibid.

291. *Trinity*, 13.1.3.

292. E.g. *Enchiridion*, 2.8, quoting Galatians 5:6; *On Grace and Free Choice*, 7.18. See also Letter 189.2, *City of God*, 21.25; *Trinity*, 13.2.5.

293. *Against the Academicians*, 2.3.8. See also *Advantage of Believing*, 10.24, where he opposes "despair" and "overconfidence."

294. *Retractions*, 1.1.1.

295. *Enchiridion*, 7.20. See also *Against the Academicians*, 2.5.11–13.

296. *Against the Academicians*, 2.1.1; *Retractions*, 1.1.1; *Enchiridion*, 7.20.

297. *Against the Academicians*, 2.9.23; see also 2.1.1.

298. *Advantage of Believing*, 11.25.

299. *Enchiridion*, 7.21. Although Augustine does not explicitly mention "overconfidence" here, it is implicit in his account of faith.

300. See *Against the Academicians*, 2.12.27, 3.11.24–25, 3.15.34; *Advantage of Believing*, 10.24–11.25.

301. *Advantage of Believing*, 11.25.

302. *Against the Academicians*, 2.1.1.

303. *Advantage of Believing*, 11.25.

304. Ibid.

Chapter 5. Hope in the Unseen: Hoping in Another

1. Hebrews 11:1. Hill translates *substantia* as "ground" in Sermon 359A.3.

2. *Advantage of Believing*, 9.22.

3. See, e.g., *Expositions of the Psalms*, 48(2).5, 85.23, 134.2; Sermon 260C.3; Sermon 280.4; *Trinity*, 2.17.29, 14.18.24; *Answer to Faustus*, 11.8; *Free Choice of Will*, 2.20.54, where *certa* is

translated by King as "resolute." Augustine quotes Cicero, *On Invention*, 2.163, on courage as rely-
ing on a "certain confident hope" (*certa cum spe*) in *Miscellany of Eighty-Three Questions*, 31.1.
Augustine also implies that hope can increase and be held "more firmly" (*speramus firmius*)
(Letter 130.8.17).

4. Sermon 359A.1, citing Hebrews 6:19. He offers a similar image of faithful Christians in
Expositions of the Psalms, 41.2. "These are the people who groan with longing for the heavenly
city, who know they are on pilgrimage, who hold steadily to their road, and who by their desire
for that abiding country have cast their hope ahead like an anchor."

5. Sermon 359A.1.

6. *On Christian Teaching*, 4.20.43.

7. Ibid. ("assured hope in the assistance of God"); *Free Choice of Will*, 2.20.54 ("resolute
hope"); *Answer to Faustus*, 11.7 ("unwavering hope").

8. Sermon 337.1. See also Sermon 159A.12.

9. Wolterstorff, *Practices of Belief*, 93–96. For discussion, see chapter 4.

10. *Advantage of Believing*, 7.15, 14.31, 7.19.

11. I am grateful to Jeffrey Stout for suggesting this structure.

12. See, e.g., *On Christian Teaching*, 1.22.20; *Expositions of the Psalms*, 129.6–12; *Enchiridion*,
30.114; *Homilies on the First Epistle of John*, 4.5.

13. *Enchiridion*, 30.114. This is one passage Deneen quotes and commends. In suggesting that
"hope cannot be extended to inappropriate objects," Deneen argues that Augustine's hope "is
directed toward the eternal: as the aspiration for good things beyond sensory evidence, hope,
by Augustine's estimation, cannot be accorded purely to human attempts to achieve the object
of hope" (*Democratic Faith*, 243). He cites Augustine's warning against trusting in mere mortals:
"Of the few things Augustine writes about hope in the *Enchiridion*, worth noting is this immediate emphasis on the *limitations* of the object of hope—hope is oriented ultimately toward the
divine, not the secular. There is a suggestion that a danger accompanies the pious belief in hope,
namely, a form of confidence in the human potential for the realization of hope within the
earthly sphere. Augustine's immediate and stern reminder of the simultaneous infinite extent
of hope and yet its limitations to human endeavors appears as a consistent rebuke to the overweening ambitions of a humanity longing for mastery" (243). While I agree with Deneen's
emphasis on Augustine's anxiety about pride and mastery, Augustine commends more continuity between divine and human, eternal and temporal, hopes than Deneen's dualism suggests, as
I argue in chapters 2 and 3.

14. *Expositions of the Psalms*, 129.11.

15. Sermon 334.3. I am grateful to Brooks, "What May I Hope For?," 115, for pointing me to
this passage.

16. Letter 130.13.27, referring to hope for "the fountain of life."

17. See, e.g., *Enchiridion*, 30.114; *Expositions of the Psalms*, 129.12; Sermon 352A.8; Letter 218;
Letter 155.8–9, in *Political Writings*, 94.

18. Letter 218.3, emphasis added.

19. See, e.g., *Predestination of the Saints*, 1.2.

20. *City of God*, 17.4. For discussion, see Dodaro, *Christ and the Just Society*, 107–110.

21. *On Christian Teaching*, 1.22.20.

22. Brown, *Through the Eye*, 360, citing Hanoune, "Le paganisme philosophique," 63–75, at 71.

23. *Predestination of the Saints*, 1.2, citing Virgil's *Aeneid*, 11.309.

24. See, e.g., *Expositions of the Psalms*, 129.6.

25. *On Christian Teaching*, 1.32.36–1.33.37.

26. Ibid., 1.32.36.

27. *Faith in the Unseen*, 2.3.

28. *Enchiridion*, 2.8.

29. *Faith in the Unseen*, 2.3–4.

30. See *Confessions*, 8.7.17, translation altered. Boulding translates this sentence as "Grant me chastity and self-control, but please not yet," but I have maintained the popular translation that accompanies caricatures of Augustine's obsessive focus on sin. For more on the "Great Sinner Myth" in *Confessions*, see Wills, *Augustine's "Confessions,"* 137–140; see also Wills, *Saint Augustine*, xiv–xvii.

31. *On Christian Teaching*, 1.10.10; Mathewes, *Theology of Public Life*, 87; Brooks, "What May I Hope For?," 181, citing *Exposition of the Psalms*, 117.2: "The divine writings customarily use the word 'confession' to mean not only the avowal of sins but also the praises of God."

32. Mathewes, "Book One," 8.

33. Ibid., 23. Mathewes notes three senses in which the first line relies on others: "First, it begins not with its own words, but with a citation of another work, the Psalms (specifically Ps. 48:1). Second, it begins not in Augustine's own voice, but in that of another—namely, David. Third and finally, it is not speaking of the self, but of someone else—namely, God" (10).

34. Brooks, "What May I Hope For?," 180.

35. *Confessions*, 1.17.27, 8.1.2, 8.12.30, 9.10.26, 6.11.18, 3.4.7.

36. Ibid., 3.8.16.

37. Ibid., 1.19.30. Augustine's disordered hopes were driven by "the damnably proud desire to gratify my human vanity" (3.4.7).

38. Ibid., 2.3.8. Later, however, Monica did arrange a marriage for Augustine (see 6.13.23).

39. Ibid., 8.10.22–24, 9.4.11, citing Psalm 4:10.

40. Ibid., 11.22.28. As he prays later, "Our hope is that we may cease to be miserable in ourselves and may find our beatitude in you" (11.1.1; see also 9.13.34).

41. Ibid., 7.7.11, 7.10.16, 10.3.4; see also 10.1.1.

42. Ibid., 4.5.10: "[H]ope and joy surged up within me at your mercy, Father."

43. Ibid., 10.35.57, 9.4.9; see also 10.32.48. Augustine describes God as his "hope" (4.6.11; 11.18.23) and implies that we should "hope in you for the world to come" (2.3.8).

44. Herdt, *Putting on Virtue*, 67–71, emphasizes the role of virtuous exemplars in *Confessions*.

45. *Confessions*, 5.13.23.

46. Ibid.; cf. 6.3.3–4.

47. Ibid., 5.13.23, 5.14.24.

48. Ibid., 5.13.23, 5.14.24.

49. Ibid., 6.3.3. On the "scaffolding" of hope generally, see McGeer, "Art of Good Hope."

50. *Confessions*, 8.2.3–4. See also Herdt, *Putting on Virtue*, 68–69.

51. *Confessions*, 8.5.10.

52. Ibid., 8.2.4.

53. Ibid., 3.11.20, 9.12.29.

54. Ibid., 9.10.23.

55. Ibid., 9.10.23–24.

56. I am grateful to John Bowlin and Eric Gregory for discussion of these passages.

57. According to Nussbaum, Augustine's "rejection of ordinary human passion is nowhere more vividly expressed than in the *Confessions*, where Augustine movingly recalls his own intense delight in earthly love, portraying this delight, with contrition, as a deviation from the true love and the true passion" (*Upheavals*, 529).

58. Gregory, *Politics*, 280.

59. Ibid., 283–287.

60. Ibid., 286. See also Bowlin, "Augustine Counting Virtues," 296–297; Meilaender, *Friendship*, 16–19.

61. *Confessions*, 4.8.13, includes one of Augustine's most powerful odes to friends: "There were other joys to be found in their company which still more powerfully captivated my mind— the charms of talking and laughing together and kindly giving way to each other's wishes, reading elegantly written books together, sharing jokes and delighting to honor one another, disagreeing occasionally but without rancor, as a person might disagree with himself, and lending piquancy by that rare disagreement to our much more frequent accord. We would teach and learn from each other, sadly missing any who were absent and blithely welcoming them when they returned. Such signs of friendship sprang from the hearts of friends who loved and knew their love returned, signs to be read in smiles, words, glances and a thousand gracious gestures. So were sparks kindled and our minds were fused inseparably, out of many becoming one."

62. Meilaender, *Friendship*, 18.

63. *On Christian Teaching*, Pref.6.

64. Ibid., Pref.4. Augustine's concern here is with pride, with the "arrogant and dangerous temptations" of those who "boast" of their special gift or assume these gifts reflect some special feature of their virtue or favor rather than God's grace (Pref.4–7).

65. He cites Paul, Moses, and Cornelius the centurion (ibid., Pref.5–6).

66. Ibid., Pref.6.

67. Ibid.

68. Sermon 87.10.

69. Sermon 159A.12. Augustine does not mention despair explicitly in this passage, but he is describing a case of it.

70. Sermon 87.10.

71. Sermon 352A.6–8; *Advantage of Believing*, 10.24.

72. Sermon 352A.7.

73. *On Christian Teaching*, 3.30.43.

74. *Expositions of the Psalms*, 31(2).6.

75. Ibid. See also Sermon 56.2: "From the devil, from idols, from demons you mustn't ask for anything that is properly asked for. From the Lord our God, from the Lord Jesus Christ, from God the Father of the prophets, apostles, and martyrs, from the Father of our Lord Jesus Christ, from the God who made heaven and earth and the sea and all that is in them, it's from him that you must ask for anything that it is right to ask for. But you must take care not to ask for anything, even from him, that we ought not to ask for."

76. *Enchiridion*, 16.60.

77. *Expositions of the Psalms*, 31(2).1.

78. Ibid.; Sermon 87.11.

79. I develop the connection between the virtues of hope, humility, and piety in chapter 10.

Chapter 6. Pedagogies of Hope: Augustine and the Art of Rhetoric

1. For an insightful account, see Brown, *Augustine of Hippo*, 240–255, and *Through the Eye*, 339–341.

2. On invitations for Augustine to preach, see Possidius, "Life," §9.

3. Kolbet, *Cure of Souls*, 168, 292n12, citing Sermon 301A.9, which Augustine gave when traveling through Bulla Regia: "So it was God's will, my brothers and sisters, that I should pass this way. My brother detained me, ordered me, begged me, forced me to preach to you." See also Sermon 360B. For an example of Augustine giving multiple sermons as a visiting preacher, see Sermon 313F.

4. Possidius, "Life," §31. Kolbet, *Cure of Souls*, 4, also cites this passage.

5. Augustine was ordained as a priest in 391 and died in 430. Possidius writes that "up to his last illness he had preached God's Word in the church unceasingly, vigorously, and powerfully, with sound mind and sound judgment" ("Life," §31, also cited by Kolbet, *Cure of Souls*, 3–4). On scholarly estimates of the number of sermons Augustine preached, see Doyle, "Bishop as Teacher," 85. Brown estimates the number of sermons at over six thousand (*Through the Eye*, 72, 339, citing Mandouze, *Saint Augustin*, 624–625).

6. O'Donnell, *Augustine*, 137; Kolbet, *Cure of Souls*, 4, 209, and 213n21 for a description of the count. See also Harmless, introduction to *Augustine in His Own Words*, xiii. Brown notes that many of the sermons that were passed down were slightly redacted by medieval copyists who edited the sermons to focus on the theological content and therefore eliminated some of the concrete details that expressed the cultural context of North Africa (*Through the Eye*, 339).

7. For a useful analysis of why these homilies have received little scholarly attention, see Kolbet, *Cure of Souls*, 4–5.

8. Sermon 313F.2–3.

9. Sermon 198.2–3.

10. Sermon 157.5.

11. Coles, *Self/Power/Other*, 11, 52, 170–180, esp. 173–174. See also Connolly, *Augustinian Imperative*, xvii–xxxiv, 34–55, 63–90.

12. Hadot, *Philosophy as a Way of Life*; *What Is Ancient Philosophy?*; Nussbaum, *Therapy*; Cooper, *Pursuits of Wisdom*. For a critical survey, see Antonaccio, "Contemporary Forms of Askesis," 69–92.

13. Hadot, *Philosophy as a Way of Life*, 83, 264–276. For a helpful overview, see Davidson, "Introduction."

14. Hadot, *Philosophy as a Way of Life*, 265. Similarly, Averil Cameron notes that scholarship on the exchange between early Christian discourse and Greek philosophy "has in most cases focused on content rather than on mode of expression" (*Christianity*, 9).

15. Hadot, *Philosophy as a Way of Life*, 59–60, 81–82; *What Is Ancient Philosophy?*, 6. For a critical analysis, see Cooper, *Pursuits of Wisdom*, 1–23, who argues that Hadot tends to

"spiritualize" these practices in ways that do not always accord with the rational exercises many Greek and Roman philosophers promoted. Cooper also argues that Hadot justifies his generalizations about the role of "spiritual exercises" by citing selected passages from *later* Hellenistic philosophers and thereby reading *earlier* philosophers through the lens of thinkers from the second century CE and beyond (19–22, 402n4). I agree with Cooper that Hadot's occasionally anachronistic and overly spiritualized account can distort our understanding of early Greek and Roman philosophy, but Cooper's complaints do not apply as readily to Hadot's understanding of Augustine, a Christian thinker who appropriates later Stoic and Neoplatonic philosophical practices, as Cooper recognizes (22, 387).

16. Hadot, *Philosophy as a Way of Life*, 59.

17. See Schenkeveld, "Philosophical Prose," 204–213.

18. Hadot notes that *askēsis* is one of the Greek terms for "exercise" or "training." Though it is the basis for the term "asceticism," ancient *askēsis* did not have the extreme self-abnegating sense that often accompanies modern uses (*Philosophy as a Way of Life*, 128).

19. See ibid., 61; Nussbaum, *Therapy*, 6–8. For an analysis of how the "rhetorical situation" affects understandings of early Christian texts in the Roman Empire, see Kennedy, *New Testament Interpretation*, 3–38, esp. 34–35, where he cites Bitzer, "Rhetorical Situation."

20. Hadot, *What Is Ancient Philosophy?*, 274, emphasis in original. Cameron notes how Christian authors—including Augustine—appropriated rhetoric as a formative pedagogical practice: "[R]hetoric—the strategies of discourse—was itself one of the many technologies by which early Christianity implanted 'habits of the heart' more powerful than institutions and more lasting than social welfare" (*Christianity*, 28, quoting Bellah et al., *Habits of the Heart*). See also Charry, *Renewing of Your Minds*, 120–149.

21. This neglect is sometimes avoided when texts appear in genres, such as poems or dialogues, that are out of place in contemporary philosophy. In such cases, the genre's unfamiliarity can encourage interpreters to attend to how its literary structure informs the philosophical argument.

22. Hadot, *Philosophy as a Way of Life*, 64. Even when presenting ideas systematically, Hadot argues that many ancient philosophers did not aspire to "a total, systematic explanation of the whole of reality," but rather made their philosophy "systematic in order that it might provide the mind with a small number of principles, tightly linked together, which derived greater persuasive force and mnemonic effectiveness precisely from such systematization. Short sayings summed up, sometimes in striking form, the essential dogmas, so that the student might easily relocate himself within the fundamental disposition in which he was to live" (267–268). One of Hadot's favorite examples is Marcus Aurelius's *Meditations* (59–60, 179–205). Against modern readers who interpret *Meditations* as a repository of pessimism, Hadot argues that "Marcus' seemingly pessimistic declarations are not expressions of his disgust or disillusion at the spectacle of life; rather, they are a *means* he employs in order to change his way of evaluating the events and objects which go to make up human existence" (186). In other words, Marcus's clinical statements attempt to objectify, and thereby sterilize, the pleasures he finds so tempting (186). The "consciously willed application of rhetoric" constitutes a "discipline of desire" aimed at reorienting Marcus's vision and thereby reforming his desire (59–60, 187, 197). Considering *Meditations* within its rhetorical context casts new light on Marcus's "pessimism" and illustrates the importance of a text's rhetorical form. The same insight, I believe, applies to many passages typically seen as evidence of Augustine's "pessimism."

23. For an insightful analysis of Augustine's appropriation of the classical rhetorical tradition, see Kolbet, *Cure of Souls*.

24. *Confessions*, 6.11.18, 3.4.7–8, 8.7.17; *Happy Life*, 1.4.

25. *Confessions*, 7.9.13–15; see also 8.2.3. Augustine frequently praises Plotinus while appropriating important aspects of his metaphysics and ethics (e.g., *Happy Life*, 1.1–4).

26. *City of God*, 8.5; see also 8.5–8.9, 8.11. See Hadot, *What Is Ancient Philosophy?*, 250–252. For Augustine's later assessment of his early Platonism, see *Retractions*, 1.1.4, 1.3.2. On Augustine's disputes with Platonists on the body and death, see Jones, "Not Good for Anyone."

27. *City of God*, 19.1. In ibid., 4.21, Augustine notes that his predecessors described "virtue" as "the art of living well and rightly. Hence, they considered that it was from the Greek word *arete*, which means 'virtue,' that the Latin-speaking peoples derived the word 'art.'" For discussion of Augustine's "more practical" mode of philosophy, see Kent, "Augustine's Ethics," 205–206. See also MacIntyre, *God, Philosophy, Universities*, 21–22.

28. On Neoplatonism as a way of life, see Hadot, *What Is Ancient Philosophy?*, 146–171; and Cooper, *Pursuits of Wisdom*, 305–387. On Neoplatonic practices of commentary and "books as guides to living," particularly in relation to Augustine, see Clark, "City of Books," 134–138.

29. See, e.g., Brown, *Augustine of Hippo*, 241–242. Nussbaum traces Augustine's appropriation of Platonic "ascent" in *Upheavals*, 527–556, but ignores the more rhetorical and indirect aspects of Augustine's account.

30. For possible reasons for this neglect, see Byers, *Perception*, 56.

31. Ibid., esp. 23–99.

32. For details, see ibid., 45–54. Byers does not suggest that Stoicism is more important than Platonism for Augustine; both "are equally important" (53).

33. Ibid., 1–22, 55–69, 151–171.

34. Ibid., 27–28.

35. *Expositions of the Psalms*, 118.1.1, as cited by Byers, *Perception*, 28; ibid., 21. Byers cites numerous examples: *Expositions of the Psalms*, 30.2.3.11, 33.1.1, 33.2.6, 33.2.10, 36.3.8, 38.12, 48.1.12, 64.3, 66.1, 67.5, 67.40, 70.2.6, 100.1, 102.1, 145.2, 145.5, and 148.3, among others.

36. The importance of rhetoric may also reflect Augustine's Christian inheritance. "Of the major Latin Fathers of the Church," Kennedy notes, "five were teachers of rhetoric before their conversion to Christianity: Tertullian in the second century, Cyprian in the third, and Arnobius, Lactantius, and Augustine in the fourth" ("Christianity and Classical Rhetoric," 264).

37. *Confessions*, 3.3.6–3.4.7; *Happy Life*, 1.4.

38. See Cameron, *Christianity*, 47–88, 139–140; Brown, *Through the Eye*, 56–57.

39. *On Christian Teaching*, 4.5.8, using Cipriani's translation in "Rhetoric," 725. For a historical analysis of Augustine's defense of rhetoric in relation to his Christian predecessors and contemporaries, see Murphy, "Christian Rhetoric," 400–410.

40. Augustine emphasizes these two defects in *Enchiridion*, 22.81: "[T]here are two reasons why we sin, either because we do not see what we ought to do or because we do not do what we know ought to be done: the first of these evils comes from ignorance, the second from weakness. We should fight against both of them." For discussion, see Dodaro, *Christ and the Just Society*, 27–32, 66–67; and Clair, *Discerning the Good*, 54–55. Sometimes, Augustine describes weakness of the will as "difficulty" (*difficultas*). See Rist, "Faith and Reason," 28.

41. *Excellence of Widowhood*, 1.2. I am grateful to Clair, *Discerning the Good*, 54, for bringing this passage to my attention.

42. For overviews, see Green, introduction to *On Christian Teaching*, vii–xxiii; O'Donnell, "*Doctrina Christiana, De*," 278–280; Harrison, "Rhetoric"; and Kennedy, *Classical Rhetoric*, 174–182. For *On Christian Teaching*'s influence on the subsequent rhetorical tradition, see Ward, "Roman Rhetoric."

43. According to Frederick van Fleteren, "Augustine knew Cicero's *De Oratore* and *Orator ad Brutum* well," but "did not follow them slavishly" ("Augustine and Philosophy," 267n67). Similarly, Green argues that "Book 4 shows the extent of what he owed to classical rhetorical theory" and agrees that the "Ciceronian framework is clear" (introduction to *On Christian Teaching*, xiv, xviii). But he acknowledges that "Augustine is far from accepting Ciceronian theory unreservedly" (xviii). See also O'Donnell, "*Doctrina Christiana, De*," 278–280; Harrison, "Rhetoric," 219–229; and Kennedy, *Classical Rhetoric*, 114, 174–182. Augustine praises Cicero for his rhetorical skill at *City of God*, 6.2.

44. *On Christian Teaching*, 4.12.27. See Cicero, *Orator*, 21.69. See also Cicero, *Best Kind of Orator*, 1.3–4, 5.16; *On the Ideal Orator*, 2.114–116, 2.121, 2.128–129, 2.176, 2.310–312; Kennedy, *Classical Rhetoric*, 114, 179.

45. *On Christian Teaching*, 4.12.27–28, 4.13.29. See Harrison, "Rhetoric," 220.

46. *On Christian Teaching*, 4.12.27. See also *On Order*, 2.38; and *On Christian Teaching*, 4.13.29: "[W]hen advocating something to be acted on the Christian orator should not only teach his listeners so as to impart instruction, and delight them so as to hold their attention, but also move them so as to conquer their minds."

47. *On Christian Teaching*, 4.25.55: "The general function of eloquence, in any of these three styles, is to speak in a manner fitted to persuade, and the aim is to persuade people, by speaking, of what you are trying to put over. . . . In the restrained style he persuades people that what he says is true; in the grand style he persuades them to do what they knew to be necessary but were not doing; in the mixed style he persuades people that he is speaking attractively or elaborately."

48. Ibid., 4.17.34; cf. Cicero, *Orator*, 29.101. Auerbach suggests that Augustine's emphasis on "context and purpose" is a departure from the classical tradition, which distinguished styles by the "subject matter" being discussed (*Literary Language*, 34–39). See also von Heyking, "Disarming," 170–172.

49. *On Christian Teaching*, 4.18.35–4.19.38.

50. Ibid., 4.4.6, 4.19.38–4.20.39, 4.21.46.

51. Ibid., 4.4.6.

52. Ibid., 4.19.38, 4.22.51.

53. Ibid., 4.25.55.

54. Kennedy suggests that *On Christian Teaching* "exemplifies" the principle that "interpretation should be based not only on an understanding of the context in which a word or passage occurs but also on the overall meaning or structure of the work in which it occurs" (*Classical Rhetoric*, 182).

55. As Kennedy argues, "[I]t is remarkable how small a part . . . theological 'doctrines' play in *De Doctrina Christiana*" ("Christianity and Classical Rhetoric," 270). In this sense, the Latin title can mislead. Whereas some tend to translate *De doctrina Christiana* narrowly as *On*

Christian Doctrine, other scholars recommend *On Christian Teaching* to capture the text's capacious function and scope. According to O'Donnell, "The proper sense [of the Latin title] is less specifically religious and might be better expressed as *On the Form of Teaching Suitable for Christians*" ("*Doctrina Christiana, De*," 278).

56. See, e.g., Skinner, *Foundations*.

57. Ibid., xiiii–xiv, 88–89, referencing Petrarch who, notably, took inspiration from Augustine. On Skinner's distinction between "saying" and "doing," see Hamilton-Bleakley, "Linguistic Philosophy."

58. See, e.g., Lane, *Method and Politics*; Viroli, *Machiavelli*; and Skinner, *Reason and Rhetoric*.

59. Exceptions, e.g., include von Heyking, *Augustine*, 17–50; "Disarming"; Murphy, "Rhetoric of Roman Decline"; and Smith, "Glory and Tragedy."

60. Arendt, *Love*, 4–6. In his formal assessment of Arendt's dissertation, Karl Jaspers notes that Arendt's "method does some violence to the text. The foreword and the execution of the whole make clear that no attention is given to the great transformations in Augustinian thought that came about in the course of his life. Neither historical nor philosophical interests are primary here" (Arendt and Jaspers, *Correspondence, 1926–1969*, 689–690n1). To her credit, Arendt is not unaware of these difficulties (*Love*, 3). She concedes that "it may seem completely irresponsible" to neglect Augustine's intellectual "evolution," but she justifies her detached and systematic approach by appealing to Augustine's philosophical influences: "[N]one of the philosophical ideas of antiquity and late antiquity that Augustine absorbed in various periods of his life, from Cicero's *Hortensius* to Victorinus's translation of Plotinus, were ever radically excised from his thinking. . . . However faithful and convinced a Christian he became, and however deeply he penetrated Christianity's intrinsic problems by studying Saint Paul's epistles, the Psalms, the Gospels, and the epistles of Saint John, he never wholly lost the impulse of philosophical questioning" (6). "What this means to interpretation," Arendt concludes, "is the possibility of tracing various fundamental intentions independently of the evolutions that bring them to various points" (6). This coherence authorizes her to take what she describes as "a systematic approach that, far from seeking to yoke Augustine to a consistency unknown to him, merely attempts to interpret even seemingly heterogeneous statements and trains of thought in the direction of a substantially common base" (4). Arendt acknowledges that this "analytical" approach requires "making explicit what Augustine himself has merely implied" (4), but her explication is focused solely on Augustine's philosophical ideas. She neglects to consider that philosophical and rhetorical practices may be implicit, too.

61. Niebuhr, "Augustine's Political Realism." Niebuhr is not always inattentive to rhetorical style. In journal entries from his early years as a pastor, he reflects on the preacher's "pedagogical art," describing how pastors can "begin to change the viewpoints and perspectives of their people" and "move the audience" through emotional appeals (*Leaves*, 128–129, 56–58). In one entry, he describes hearing a sermon on Augustine by Dr. Lynn Harold Hough (Brown, *Niebuhr and His Age*, 32) and notes how preaching about the "City of God" can inspire audiences out of "aspiration" rather than "duty" (113). Though Niebuhr recognizes this Augustinian impulse in Hough's sermon, he does not consider that Augustine may be using the same aspirational rhetoric when Niebuhr later advances his interpretation of Augustine's realism.

62. Rawls, *Brief Inquiry*.

63. Ibid., 171.

64. In *Political and Social Ideas*, Deane rightly recognizes that Augustine was not a systematic theorist: "Genius he had in full measure, but system-building and architectonic skill were not his forte; he is the master of the phrase or the sentence that embodies a penetrating insight, a flash of lightning that illuminates the entire sky; he is the rhetorician, the epigrammist, the polemicist, but not the patient, logical, systematic philosopher" (viii). Yet, despite this lack of systematicity, Deane argues that Augustine's insights "fall into coherent and consistent patterns" (ix). Part of Deane's purpose is "to organize the material from Augustine's writings and to elucidate the general point of view that permeates his reflections about social and political life" (ix). To his credit, Deane recognizes "the temptation to make his thought more systematic than it really is," suggesting that interpreters "have sometimes been drawn into this temptation by the striking manner in which he expresses his ideas" and therefore "have allowed themselves to reduce his complex insights to a simple, consistent theory" (ix). Deane resists such reduction, consistently noting tensions and situating Augustine's ideas within their social and political context (e.g., 216–219). His contextualized account of Augustine's shifting views on coercion is especially illuminating (172–220). Elsewhere, however, Deane seems to succumb to the systematizing temptations he hopes to avoid. Describing Augustine's political pessimism as his key political insight, Deane weaves together passages from various periods of Augustine's career without considering their distinctive genre or how Augustine's concern during a particular period or dispute might shape the meaning of the passage.

65. Deane, *Political and Social Ideas*.

66. To understand Hellenistic philosophy, Nussbaum argues, readers must be sensitive to the role of "therapeutic" methods that attempt "not simply to deal with the patient's invalid inferences and false premises, but to grapple, as well, with her irrational fears and anxieties, her excessive loves and crippling angers" (*Therapy*, 37). Because deductive arguments do not always accomplish these therapeutic purposes, Hellenistic philosophers often relied on more "indirect" and "psychologically engaging" literary forms—such as poems, dialogues, and letters—that "are hard to teach in the usual analytic manner" (35; see also x–xi). Because "[t]herapeutic arguments have their own rhetoric and their own literary style," they "cannot be decoded by someone who simply ignores those aspects of the argument, as much teaching of philosophy is apt to do. Only if one reads these arguments with sensitivity to their therapeutic purpose will one be able, after quite a lot of work, to see how good, as arguments, they really are" (xi). Such sensitivity is especially important for texts whose rhetorical form and structure constitute important aspects of the argument (6–8, 35–36, 47). Attending to a philosopher's literary, rhetorical, and historical contexts is "the only way in which we can get a full idea of what these philosophical teachings have to offer—for central in what they offer is their rich responsiveness to the concrete," which "will be obscured if we characterize their enterprise too timelessly and abstractly" (44). For Nussbaum, "Hellenistic therapeutic argument is, by design, so context-dependent that it can be fully understood in no other way" (7).

67. Nussbaum acknowledges the difficulty of analyzing a period that spans "six centuries and two different societies" (ibid., 6).

68. Ibid., 18–19, 32–36. According to Nussbaum's Augustine, "God has set up certain ethical standards; it is our job to do what God wants. But we may or may not be endowed with the capability of seeing, or wanting, what God wants. Truth and God's grace are out there; but the ability to see ethical truth or to reach for grace is not something we can control" (18). Because

Augustine emphasizes the need for God's grace, there is "no reliable method by which we can construct an ethical norm from the scrutiny of our deepest needs and responses and desires," which, Nussbaum argues, puts us in an even "more helpless position" than scientific or Platonist visions of ethics (18–19). Nussbaum does not say much more about this Augustinian picture; throughout the rest of the chapter, she simply lumps Augustine into her general discussion of Platonism. But both accounts share the same "central structural idea"—"the idea of the radical independence of the true good from human need and desire"—and thus both proceed from the same deductive methods and use logical reasoning to apply transcendent truths to this-worldly realities (19). Nussbaum sets her "medical" model against this metaphysical deductivism, arguing that therapeutic philosophy uses "techniques that are more complicated and indirect, more psychologically engaging, than those of conventional deductive or dialectical argument" (35). Ultimately, she implies that Augustine's Platonism transforms his theology into a rational deductivism that eschews these more indirect rhetorical techniques.

69. Augustine makes "medical" and "therapeutic" analogies to moral and spiritual healing throughout his works. For one prominent example, see *On Christian Teaching*, 1.13.12–1.15.14. For discussion, see Kolbet, *Cure of Souls*.

70. Burke, *Rhetoric of Religion*, 1–171; Hadot, *Philosophy as a Way of Life*, 52, 68; Martin, "Augustine's *Confessions* as Pedagogy."

71. Hadot, *Philosophy as a Way of Life*, 107; Charry, *Renewing of Your Minds*, 120–149; Stalnaker, "Spiritual Exercises," 138–140.

72. Stock, "Ethical Values," analyzes Augustine's rhetorical innovations in the *Confessions* and early Cassiciacum dialogues. Stock explicitly endorses Hadot's conception of philosophy as a way of life and its application to Augustine (4–5, 10–11).

73. See, e.g., Stalnaker, "Spiritual Exercises"; Kolbet, *Cure of Souls*; Byers, *Perception*; Dodaro, *Christ and the Just Society*; Clair, *Discerning the Good*; Cavadini, "Simplifying Augustine"; Bullock, "Augustinian Innovation." Atkins and Dodaro's edition of Augustine's *Political Writings* has helped to reorient scholars' attention to the political relevance of Augustine's sermons and letters.

74. In contrast to Augustine's theological works, von Heyking notes, "comparatively little has been done on his political rhetoric in the *City of God* beyond demonstrating Augustine's antipolitical rhetoric" (*Augustine*, 17).

75. My exposition is particularly indebted to the insightful accounts offered by Brown, *Augustine of Hippo*, 240–255; Cameron, *Christianity*; Cavadini, "Simplifying Augustine"; and Kolbet, *Cure of Souls*.

76. See Sermon 355.2; Brown, *Augustine of Hippo*, 248.

77. *Expositions of the Psalms*, 93.30, cited by McCarthy, "Ecclesiology of Groaning," 38.

78. In introducing a sermon on Psalm 4, for example, Augustine references disputes about which songs count as "psalms" and alludes to various "historical books," but ultimately suggests that a sermon "is not the place to examine this question, because it requires a protracted investigation and a lengthy discussion" (*Expositions of the Psalms*, 4.1).

79. "Augustine's sermons," Brown affirms, "were never abstract lubrications on his part" (*Through the Eye*, 353).

80. Letter 73.5, as discussed by Brown, *Augustine of Hippo*, 249. Brown offers a somewhat different translation, but the differences are not of consequence. See also O'Donnell, "Bible,"

100, on Augustine's impatience with the "scholarly preoccupations" of scholars such as Jerome.

81. See Kolbet, *Cure of Souls*, 183–184.

82. Ibid.

83. Brown, *Augustine of Hippo*, 253.

84. Typically, Augustine is interpreted as offering a negative view of habits, particularly when describing *consuetudo* in *Confessions*. There, he likens habits to forms of "bondage" and constraint, describing how he suffers under the "tyranny of habit," particularly the "weight of carnal habit" (*Confessions*, 7.17.23, 8.9.21, 9.12.32.). By associating habits primarily with *bad* habits, Augustine suggests that habits entrench vice instead of virtue. For a discussion of this negative view, see, e.g., Brown, *Augustine of Hippo*, 143, 166–167.

Contrary to these accounts, I believe Augustine has a more positive view of habits than many interpreters acknowledge. In some of his letters, he describes the importance of "chaste and pious habits" (Letter 91.6, in *Political Writings*, 5) and suggests that the role of the church is to provide "good rules and good habits" so that wayward members (e.g., Donatists) can "be healed" (Letter 185.13, in *Political Writings*, 181). In *On Christian Teaching*, he argues that the Spirit works to break the "stranglehold" of "evil habits" and "establish the peace brought by good habits" (1.24.25). Even the *Confessions* assumes a more positive view of habits, for it was Victorinus's good "habit of reading holy scripture and intensely studying all the Christian writings" that contributed to his conversion and "hope" in God (*Confessions*, 8.2.4).

Even if we grant the interpretative point that Augustine tends to use the *term* "habit" negatively, he frequently employs the *concept* more positively, implicitly referring to good dispositions of character that are more stable and habitual than a simple affection. For example, he frequently discusses the necessity of the "virtues" and attributes virtues to his friends and Roman political leaders, praising them not simply for momentary affections but for particular excellences of character (e.g., *City of God*, 19.1–4, 5.13, 5.19; *Confessions*, 3.11.20, 9.12.29). Furthermore, he describes loves as "weights," an image that suggests that a person's whole self, not just a temporary emotion, is carried toward a particular good (*Confessions*, 13.9.10; *City of God*, 11.28). And when Augustine declares that people become members of the eternal city because of their "loves," he is presumably referring to a more stable love or virtue of character, not a fleeting or momentary feeling of love toward God (*City of God*, 14.28; see also Weithman, "Augustine's Political Philosophy," 236). In addition, Augustine offers several accounts of development, progress, or growth in virtue, implicitly suggesting the possibility that virtues are more perfected capacities of character, even if they are not fully perfect and complete in this life (*On Christian Teaching*, 2.7.9–2.7.11; *Confessions*, 13.12.13–13.38.53; *Enchiridion*, 31.118–119; Herdt, *Putting on Virtue*, 47, 66–71). Given his anxieties about pride and temptation, of course, these virtues will not be as stable as those commended by Aristotle or Aquinas, but implicitly, Augustine seems to suggest a more positive view of habit and virtue than some interpreters assume.

85. Sermon 157.1. Augustine appeals to this passage in multiple sermons, including Sermon 96.9, 105.7; *Expositions of the Psalms*, 31(2).20, 4.9, 91.1.

86. Sermon 157.1.

87. Sermon 157.1–2.

88. Ibid.

89. "The truth is, without patience amid the troubles and trials of this life hope in the future life cannot be kept alive; and you cannot maintain unflagging patience unless you are meek and mild, never resisting God's will, because his *yoke is easy and his burden light* (Mt 11:30)—but for those who believe in God, and hope in him and love him. . . . That's how you must act, that's how you must walk. You are, after all, walking in Christ, who said *I am the way* (Jn 14:6). Learn how you should walk in him not only from his words but also from his example. . . . So he was handed over, the Most High through whom all things were made, handed over thanks to the form of a servant, to be abused by men, cast aside by the people, to be ridiculed, to be scourged, to die on the cross; in this way he taught us by the example of his sufferings with what patience we must walk in him; and by the example of his resurrection he assured us of what we should be patiently hoping for from him. *For if we are hoping for what we cannot see, we wait for it in patience* (Rom 8:24). Yes, we are hoping for what we cannot see; but we are the body of that head in whom what we are hoping for has already been achieved. . . . But if we are hoping for what we cannot see, we wait for it in patience, with nothing to worry about; because the one who has risen is our head, he is keeping our hope warm for us" (Sermon 157.2–3). This last reference is likely an allusion to other sermons where Augustine compares hope to an "egg," which Christ, like an "evangelical hen," keeps warm until human beings are born into new life (Sermon 105.7–11).

90. Sermon 157.5–6.

91. Sermon 157.6.

92. Sermon 352A.5. The quotation is Augustine's imagined response to Christians "living bad lives." See also Sermon 345.6: "Love what you are about, imitate what you are celebrating, do what you admire."

93. Sermon 352A.7.

94. Sermon 352A.8.

95. Ibid.

96. Sermon 352A.9.

97. Ibid.

98. On "showing" and "telling" in the early Christian church, see Cameron, *Christianity,* 47–88, esp. 59–61, 66–68, 79–80.

99. See Letter 225, 226.

100. *Gift of Perseverance,* 22.57–62. See also Sermon 87.10–11.

101. According to Cameron, "Augustine's long career in the intimate relationship of a bishop to his congregation developed in him an exceptional sensitivity to both the practical and the theoretical aspects of Christian language. His debt to Platonism combined with his early practice of Latin rhetoric and his own experience with audiences at all intellectual levels to make him vividly aware of the power and the limits of language" (*Christianity,* 157).

102. *Gift of Perseverance,* 22.57–62.

103. Ibid., 22.57–61.

104. Ibid., 22.61.

105. Ibid., 22.57.

106. Here I borrow Nussbaum's phrase from *Therapy.*

107. See *On Reprimand and Grace,* 2.3–3.5, where Augustine cites the apostles as exemplars of this method.

108. Ibid., 12.37–16.49.

109. Ibid., 13.40–42, 15.46. See also Letter 2*7–8.

110. Leyser, "Problem of Authority," 27.

111. *Advantage of Believing*, 10.24.

112. Sermon 352A.7.

113. *On Christian Teaching*, 4.20.43, referencing Romans 8:28–39.

114. See, e.g., Sermon 157.5, 198.2–3, 313F.2–2.

115. Markus suggests that although the "exploitation of dramatic contrasts has always been one of the favoured devices of rhetoric," Augustine shared a particular "liking for it" that fits his distinctive "cast of mind," "which made dramatic contrasts a more than normally apt means of expressing his ideas" (*Saeculum*, 45).

116. *City of God*, 11.18.

117. Ibid.

118. Ibid., citing 2 Corinthians 6:7–10 and Ecclesiasticus 33:14–15.

119. Ibid. For a general discussion of Augustine's understanding of good and evil, including this passage, see Bussanich, "Goodness," 390–391.

120. See, e.g., Sermon 105.7, 157.1–6, 198.2–3, 313F.

121. Brown notes the tendencies of scholars to see Augustine's oppositional rhetoric as licensing assumptions about "zero-sum competition" between pagan festivals and Christian almsgiving (*Through the Eye*, 356).

122. Cameron observes that "a long series of preachers" in the early Church used antitheses "as a means of hinting at what was essentially inexpressible" (*Christianity*, 160).

123. See Bullock, "Augustinian Innovation," 9–12, for examples of Augustine's use of "antithesis" and "parallelism in sound and structure" to captivate listeners. See also Auerbach, *Literary Language*, 31–34.

124. Augustine notes the value of rereading in Letter 212A to Firmus: "[Y]ou, as an educated man, are well aware of how much a repetition of the reading helps for coming to know what one is reading. For there is either no difficulty or only a slight one in understanding where it is easy to read a text, and it is easier to read the more often the reading is repeated. In that way what remained unclear due to inattentiveness may become clear by repeated reading" (see also 1A*.3)

125. We see this emphasis on accessibility in the introduction of a sermon on hope: "Dearly beloved, this psalm that we have undertaken to study with you is a short one, and we hope that the Lord will help us speak about it in a way that is concise, yet still does it justice. Insofar as I have the assistance of him who commands me to speak, I will not shirk my full duty to those who are eager to hear, but will try not to make things difficult for others of slower understanding. I will neither be long winded to please a few, nor burdensome to those who have business to attend to" (*Expositions of the Psalms*, 60.1).

126. *On Christian Teaching*, 4.9.23. Augustine counsels communicators to assume "that our listener or disputant has the will to learn and does not lack the mental capacity to absorb such things, in whatever way they are presented by a teacher concerned not for the eloquence of his teaching but its clarity" (4.9.23). I am indebted to Cavadini, "Simplifying Augustine," 67n15, for pointing me to this passage.

127. *On Christian Teaching*, 4.10.25.

128. *Expositions of the Psalms*, 31(2).1.

129. Cameron, *Christianity*, 79–80. Cameron suggests that "the weekly or at times daily homilies reinforced [listeners'] consciousness of the familiar texts and fixed the mysteries of the faith in their minds" (160).

130. Kolbet, *Cure of Souls*, 186. See also Harrison, "Rhetoric," 228; McCarthy, "Ecclesiology of Groaning," 40–43.

131. Wills, *Saint Augustine*, 70–72; Brown, *Augustine of Hippo*, 248; Bullock, "Augustinian Innovation," 8–9; Harrison, "Rhetoric," 226; Auerbach, *Literary Language*, 31–32. For discussion of Augustine's use of "prose rhythms" and other rhetorical devices, see Oberhelman, *Rhetoric and Homiletics*, 89–91, 117–120.

132. See Hill's notes in Sermon 313F.1n3, 345.1n3, 21.1n3, 359A.1n3. Studer describes the "tension between *spes* and *res*" as indicative of Augustine's "basic theme of expectation and fulfillment" ("Pauline Theme of Hope," 202). See also Meconi, "Heaven," 268–270.

133. Sermon 313F.1, adapting Hill's translation. See also Sermon 21.1: "[J]oy will be full, when it is no longer hope [*spes*] suckling us with milk, but the real thing [*res*] providing us with solid food."

134. Sermon 359A.1; see Hill's note in Sermon 359A.1n3. See also Sermon 360B.16: "Your health, your salvation, lies in hope, not yet in reality" (*Salus uestra in spe est, nondum in re*).

135. *Expositions of the Psalms*, 42.1, cited by McCarthy, "Ecclesiology of Groaning," 44.

136. Sermon 345.1.

137. *On Christian Teaching*, 1.22.20; *City of God*, 19.20.

138. *City of God*, 19.20.

139. *Expositions of the Psalms*, 31(2).20. For discussion, see McCarthy, "Ecclesiology of Groaning," 45.

140. Such a view is clear in *Expositions of the Psalms*, 31(2).20: "If you hope, you rejoice; if you are waiting with patience, you still groan; for there is no need for patience when you have no evil to put up with. What we call endurance, what we call patience, what we call bearing up, what we call steadfastness, has no place except amid misfortunes. Where you are hard pressed, there you feel the pinch. If we are still waiting in patience, we still have reason to say, *Save me from those that hem me in*; but because we are saved in hope, we can say both these things simultaneously: *you make me dance with happiness*, and *save me*."

141. Stewart-Kroeker, "World-Weariness," 205–206.

142. Ibid., 204, 213–221. McCarthy draws on Augustine's exposition of Psalm 93 to note that, in positioning God as one who suffers, grieves, and laments with human beings, Augustine offers an "interpretative framework [that] places such tribulation in the context of hope grounded in the Word's own Incarnation, death, and Resurrection" ("Ecclesiology of Groaning," 38–39). McCarthy cites a passage from *Expositions of the Psalms*, 101(1).2, that accentuates the point: "How does the Word experience toil? How does it groan, the Word through whom all things were made? If he has thought fit to share in our death, will he not give to us his life? He has raised us up in great hope, when we groan in great hope. Groaning includes sadness, but there is a groaning which includes joy too" (47).

143. Stewart-Kroeker, "World-Weariness," 225, citing *Expositions of the Psalms*, 36(1).2, 36(1).4, 36(1).8, 36(1).6, 36(1).1.

144. Ibid.

145. See my engagement with Lloyd in chapter 1.

146. Sermon 345.1.

147. Sermon 198.2.

148. Sermon 198.1.

149. See Augustine's infamous theft of pears in *Confessions*, 2.8.16–2.9.17.

150. "At times," Kolbet writes, "the surrounding cultural events were so attractive to his hearers that the bishop felt compelled to comment on them in his homilies" (*Cure of Souls*, 180). Kolbet cites Sermon 51.2, *Expositions of the Psalms*, 30(4).11, 32(2).1, but this insight also applies to Sermon 198.

151. Herdt, "Theater of the Virtues," 111.

152. McCarthy, "Ecclesiology of Groaning," 25. "Pay attention to this great spectacle [*spectaculum*]," Augustine preaches in an exposition of Psalm 80. "For God does not fail to provide for us something to look at with great joy. Can the crazy fascination of the circus be compared to this spectacle? Those shows are like to the dregs; this to the oil" (*Exposition of the Psalms*, 80.1, as cited by McCarthy, "Ecclesiology of Groaning," 36). Augustine concludes by noting that "God has put on for you in Christ's name entertainments [*spectacula*] that have gripped your imagination and held you spellbound, not only kindling your desire for certain things but warning you to avoid others" (*Exposition of the Psalms*, 80.23; McCarthy, "Ecclesiology of Groaning," 36). On Augustine's critique of spectacles, see also Kaufman, *On Agamben*, 76–79.

153. Sermon 198.1.

154. Sermon 198.2.

155. Ibid.

156. Ibid.: "If you don't believe what the Gentiles believe, don't hope what the Gentiles hope, don't love what the Gentiles love; then you are gathered from among the Gentiles, you are segregated, set apart that is, from the Gentiles."

157. Sermon 313F.1.

158. Harrison, *Augustine*, 216.

159. Possidius, "Life," §7. Oberhelman describes Augustine's sermons as "deliberately informal," "simple improvisations on the meaning of biblical passages read to the laity in church," "spontaneous creations that entered unplanned territory as the bishop extemporized" (*Rhetoric and Homiletics*, 89). See also Kolbet, *Cure of Souls*, 181; Brown, *Augustine of Hippo*, 248, *Through the Eye*, 340–342.

160. Kolbet, *Cure of Souls*, 180. See also Oberhelman, *Rhetoric and Homiletics*, 91. See Sermon 225.3 for one example of such preparation and Possidius, "Life," §15, for an instance of digression.

161. Kolbet, *Cure of Souls*, 181, citing, e.g., Sermon 114B.1; Sermon 352.1; *Expositions of the Psalms*, 138.1.

162. O'Donnell notes that this reliance on scriptural interpretation also informs many of Augustine's treatises, which often take their structure and substance from meditation on scriptural texts rather than abstract speculation ("Bible," 102–103).

163. Through their sermons, "the hidden iceberg of Christian discourse," Christian preachers "not only sought to teach but, through regular repetition and by continually drawing on and reinterpreting an increasingly familiar body of texts, also constantly reaffirmed the essence of the faith and the constituents of membership of the Christian community. The regular homily, like the episcopal letter, might use the arguments of apologetic, but it also confirmed the structure of the Christian groups and continually reminded the faithful of the essentials of the system

to which they now belonged. Preaching therefore became for most Christians the medium through which they heard and were regularly reminded of the interpretation of the Scriptures, the relation of the Old Testament to the life of Jesus, and of both to the overall divine providence" (Cameron, *Christianity*, 79).

164. According to Kennedy, "Early Christians had new thoughts to express, and their verbal resources were often taxed," not least by the different languages and styles they had inherited (*New Testament Interpretation*, 26).

165. *City of God*, 10.23, also cited by von Heyking, *Augustine*, 35.

166. See, e.g., Sermon 105.5–11.

167. Brown, *Augustine of Hippo*, 246–248; Cavadini, "Simplifying Augustine," 67–68; Kolbet, *Cure of Souls*, 174.

168. According to Harry Gamble, "[T]he ability to read, criticize, and interpret [Christian literature] belonged to a small number of Christians in the first several centuries, ordinarily not more than about 10 percent in any given setting, and perhaps fewer in the many small provincial congregations that were characteristic of early Christianity" (*Books and Readers*, 5). I am grateful to Cavadini, "Simplifying Augustine," 66n12, for pointing me to this work. See also O'Donnell, "Bible," 100, and *Augustine*, 143.

169. Gamble, *Books and Readers*, 141, cited in Cavadini, "Simplifying Augustine," 66n12.

170. The expositors of scripture "should not speak in such a way that they set themselves up as similar authorities, themselves in need of exposition, but should endeavor first and foremost in all their sermons to make themselves understood and to ensure, by means of the greatest possible clarity, that only the very slow fail to understand, and that the reason why anything that we say is not easily or quickly understood lies in the difficulty and complexity of the matters that we wish to explain and clarify, and not in our mode of expression" (*On Christian Teaching*, 4.8.22). Cameron describes Augustine's concern for the audience as "amazingly modern": "[T]here was no one more conscious than Augustine of the need to reach all sections of the populace or of the appropriate methods by which this could be done" (*Christianity*, 35).

171. *Catechising of the Uninstructed*, 15.23. For discussion, see Kolbet, *Cure of Souls*, 154.

172. *On Christian Teaching*, 4.10.24: "The teacher, then, will avoid all words that do not communicate; if, in their place, he can use other words which are intelligible in their correct forms, he will choose to do that, but if he cannot—either because they do not exist or because they do not occur to him at the time—he will use words that are less correct, provided that the subject-matter itself is communicated and learnt correctly."

173. Ibid.

174. See *Catechising of the Uninstructed*, 8.12–9.13. See also 15.23: "It will likewise make a considerable difference, even when we are discoursing in that style, whether there are few present or many, whether they are learned or unlearned, or made up of both classes combined; whether they are city-bred or rustics, or both the one and the other together; or whether, again, they are a people composed of all orders of men in due proportion. For it is impossible but that they will affect in different ways the person who has to speak to them and discourse with them, and that the address which is delivered will both bear certain features, as it were, expressive of the feelings of the mind from which it proceeds, and also influence the hearers in different ways, in accordance with that same difference (in the speaker's disposition), while at the same time the hearers themselves will influence one another in different ways by the simple force of their presence

with each other. But as we are dealing at present with the matter of the instruction of the un-learned, I am a witness to you, as regards my own experience, that I find myself variously moved, according as I see before me, for the purposes of catechetical instruction, a highly educated man, a dull fellow, a citizen, a foreigner, a rich man, a poor man, a private individual, a man of honors, a person occupying some position of authority, an individual of this or the other nation, of this or the other age or sex, one proceeding from this or the other sect, from this or the other common error." For discussion, see Kolbet, *Cure of Souls*, 154; Cavadini, "Simplifying Augustine," 65n8.

175. Cavadini, "Simplifying Augustine," 66–69.

176. Ibid., 67–68.

177. Ibid., 68–69. See also Herdt, "Theater of the Virtues," 120.

178. Cameron, *Christianity*, 202.

179. Ibid., 110. According to Cameron, pagan literature "for the most part was directed at the perpetuation of the elite" (186).

180. Ibid., 185–186; see also 147.

181. Ibid., 112. According to Cameron, "the homiletic tradition . . . was the real conveyor of Christianity to the population at large" (180).

182. Letter 137.18. See also *Confessions*, 12.27.37, on "scripture's humble mode of discourse." For more on Augustine's engagement with the "lowly" style, see especially Auerbach, *Literary Language*, 27–66 (Auerbach cites a different translation of the passage from Letter 137.18 on p. 50). Von Heyking also notes how "scripture provides a simple down-to-earth model of rhe-toric that is not generally available to classical rhetoric because scripture is intelligible both to philosophical elites and to the uneducated, which creates an egalitarian basis for communicating moral truths in a democratic culture" ("Disarming," 175).

183. "The authority of the sacred writings seemed to me all the more deserving of reverence and divine faith in that scripture was easily accessible to every reader, while yet guarding a mysterious dignity in its deeper sense. In plain words and very humble modes of speech it of-fered itself to everyone, yet stretched the understanding of those who were *not shallow-minded*. It welcomed all comers to its hospitable embrace, yet through narrow openings attracted a few to you—a few, perhaps, but far more than it would have done had it not spoken with such noble authority and drawn the crowds to its embrace by its holy humility" (*Confessions*, 6.5.8). For discussion of Augustine's defense of the scripture's lowly style, see Auerbach, *Literary Language*, 45–54; Kolbet, *Cure of Souls*, 204–205; and Harrison, "Rhetoric."

184. *Confessions*, 13.15.17. For discussion of this passage in its larger context, see Clark, "City of Books," 131–133.

185. Analyzing Augustine's Christian appropriation of Roman rhetoric in *On Christian Teach-ing*, Thomas Martin argues that "the exclusive world of a select and highly trained elite, the rhetori-cal world of Augustine's day, has abruptly been thrown open to all. Ciceronian ideals, the preserve of the privileged few of traditional Roman aristocracy—these values suddenly find themselves supplanted if not shattered by the radical universality of gospel living: *all* are capable of *forma ui-uendi*. This kind of 'discourse' excludes no one!" ("'Abundant Supply of Discourse,'" 8).

186. Sermon 133.4. See also Cavadini, "Simplifying Augustine," 73.

187. Cavadini, "Simplifying Augustine," 72–73; Kolbet, *Cure of Souls*, 175–176, and 295n62, where Kolbet cites several sermons where Augustine describes the church as a "school": Sermon 2.5, 32.2, 33A.4, 52.13, 74.1, 122.3, 177.2, 261.2; *Expositions of the Psalms*, 90(2).1, 98.1.

188. Sermon 33A.4.

189. Sermon 16A.1; Kolbet, *Cure of Souls*, 175–176, 295n62.

190. Kolbet, *Cure of Souls*, 295n62.

191. Letter 91.3, in *Political Writings*, 3.

192. Letter 138.10, in *Political Writings*, 35.

193. Gregory notes how "Augustine both *democratizes* and *publicizes* love through a theological (and so political) populism" (*Politics*, 355). Clark contrasts Augustine's practice of explicating scripture aloud in church with the practices of Roman experts explicating authoritative texts from law and philosophy. In contrast to the Roman courtroom and lecture hall, Augustine emphasizes "a classroom for all ages, both genders, and all levels of education" ("City of Books," 137).

194. The phrase "pedagogies of hope" is an allusion to the work of Freire, *Pedagogy of Hope*; and hooks, *Teaching Community*.

195. Sermon 58.2.

196. Sermon 59.2. Importantly, these sermons were likely preached between 410 and 412, just after the fall of Rome, when Augustine and his listeners would have been all too aware of the fleeting nature of political power. Of course, the fact that the Christian community is more open does not mean it was just, as the troubling acceptance of slavery makes clear.

197. Sermon 59.7.

198. Sermon 9.10; Kolbet, *Cure of Souls*, 167.

199. Sermon 23.1, as cited by Cavadini, "Simplifying Augustine," 74.

200. Sermon 134.1: "Your graces know that all of us have one Teacher, and that under him we are fellow disciples, fellow pupils. And the fact that we bishops speak to you from a higher place does make us your teachers; but it's the one who dwells in all of us that is the Teacher of us all." See also Sermon 399.15: "After all, who is the master that is doing the teaching? Not any sort of man, but the apostle. Clearly the apostle, and yet not the apostle. *Or do you wish*, he says, *to get proof of the one who is speaking in me, Christ?* (2 Cor 13:3). It is Christ who is doing the teaching; he has his chair in heaven, as I said a short while ago. His school is on earth, and his school is his own body. The head is teaching his members, the tongue talking to his feet. It is Christ who is doing the teaching; we hear; let us fear, let us act."

201. See Kolbet, *Cure of Souls*, 186.

202. Cavadini, "Simplifying Augustine," 74.

203. Sermon 179.1, as cited by Cavadini, "Simplifying Augustine," 74.

204. E.g., "Let's be companions in believing. What am I saying? Let's be companions in seeking" (Sermon 53.13, cited by Cavadini, "Simplifying Augustine," 77). See also Kolbet, *Cure of Souls*, 184–186, 202.

205. Cavadini, "Simplifying Augustine," 71–72, emphasis added.

206. Bullock, "Augustinian Innovation," 5–8. Charles Mathewes recognizes both the egalitarian and open-ended aspects of Augustine's view of exegesis in the final books of *Confessions*: "This is a radically open, nonelitest account of exegesis, in which the newfound understanding of human life as fundamentally exegetical enables all people, in their daily life and work, to serve as hermeneuts, legitimate participants—as both explorers and exponents—in the community's inquiry, its ongoing ingoing, into God's mysterious providence" ("Liberation of Questioning," 555).

207. Bullock, "Augustinian Innovation," 7.

208. Ibid., 5. According to Bullock, "Augustine's homiletic practice demonstrated that he was more interested in what a sermon may do or even undo in the experience of the receiving audience, than pointedly conveying content" (12).

209. Sermon 23.1; see Cavadini, "Simplifying Augustine," 74–75; and *Trinity*, 1.3.5. Here, Augustine implies that he is "standing above" the audience, but we need to be careful not to imagine Augustine as if he were in the pulpit of a contemporary cathedral. As Brown notes, "Augustine would not even have been physically isolated from his audience, as a modern preacher would be, who stands in a pulpit above a seated congregation. The congregation of Hippo stood throughout the sermon, while Augustine usually sat back in his *cathedra*. The first row, therefore, would have met their bishop roughly at eye level, at only some 5 yards' distance. Augustine would have spoken directly to them, quite extempore: the natural flow of vivid, pure Latin would occasionally lapse, with charming self-consciousness, into an unclassical term, or it would run into a jingle of rhymed phrases and puns, to delight the ear of an illiterate audience" (*Augustine of Hippo*, 248, citing van der Meer, *Augustine the Bishop*, 405–467).

210. Sermon 52.8.

211. Kennedy, "Christianity and Classical Rhetoric," 258.

212. *Expositions of the Psalms*, 118.Prologue.

213. Brown, *Through the Eye*, 340.

214. Ibid., 336–341, 344–345.

215. Ibid., 340, citing and endorsing Mandouze, *Saint Augustin*, 591–663.

216. Coles, *Self/Power/Other*, esp. 11, 52, 170–180, esp. 173–174; Connolly, *Augustinian Imperative*, xvii–xxxiv, 39–42, 62–90.

217. For discussion, see Alimi, "Slaves of God," 29–33; and Garnsey, *Ideas of Slavery*, 206.

218. *Confessions*, 9.20; *Expositions of the Psalms*, 124.7. For discussion, see Alimi, "Slaves of God," 29, 32; and Garnsey, *Ideas of Slavery*, 206.

219. See, e.g., *City of God*, 19.15, *Expositions of the Psalms*, 124.7–8; *Homilies on the Gospel of John*, 41.4–10. For discussion, see Alimi, "Slaves of God," esp. 261; Garnsey, *Ideas of Slavery*, 220–235; and Elia, "Slave Christologies," 22–29.

220. See Alimi, "Slaves of God"; Elia, "Ethics in the Afterlife of Slavery," 101–106; and Garnsey, *Ideas of Slavery*, 210–211, citing *Expositions of the Psalms*, 124.7–8.

221. Elia, "Ethics in the Afterlife of Slavery," 100, 105–106; Alimi, "Slaves of God," 24–25.

222. I am grateful to Olaoluwatoni Alimi for sharing a version of his insightful book manuscript, "Slaves of God: Augustine and Other Romans on Religion and Politics."

223. Alimi, "Slaves of God," 13, 26, 217–238.

224. See, e.g., *Homilies on the Gospel of John*, 41.4–10; *Expositions of the Psalms*, 124.7; Letter 185.21; Sermon 359B.1, 7–10. For discussion, see Alimi, "Slaves of God"; Elia, "Ethics in the Afterlife," 102–103; "Slave Christologies," 22–29; and Garnsey, *Ideas of Slavery*, 220–221, 231–234.

225. Alimi, "Slaves of God," 4–5; Elia, "Ethics in the Afterlife," 101, 103; "Slave Christologies," 20–21, 24–25; Elm, "Sold to Sin," 15; Garnsey, *Ideas of Slavery*, 206–221, 242.

226. *Homilies on the Gospel of John*, 41.4; *City of God*, 19.14–19.15; Letter 10*; Letter 24*; Possidius, "Life," §24. For discussion, see Alimi, "Slaves of God," esp. 33–34, 55–70; and Elia, "Ethics in the Afterlife," 101–104.

227. *City of God*, 19.6; *Homilies on the Gospel of John*, 41.4. For discussion, see Alimi, "Slaves of God," 57–69. Elia argues that "Augustine, while genuinely troubled over the question of

slavery, seeks not to challenge the institution but to Christianize it . . . and thus, to stabilize it" ("Ethics in the Afterlife of Slavery," 104).

228. See, e.g., *City of God*, 18.23; Alimi, "Slaves of God," 8, 12n31; 15–16, 24–25, 33, 46–55, 68–69.

Chapter 7. Into Hell and Out Again:
A Structure of Encouragement in the *City of God*

1. Burke, "Semantic and Poetic Meaning," 160.

2. In the Preface to *City of God*, Augustine describes the "work" as "great and arduous" (*magnum opus et arduum*). Brown takes his phrase from Henry James's description of nineteenth-century Russian novels ("Political Society," 311). According to Gillian Clark, *City of God* is "the biggest book Augustine ever wrote, and in extant patristic writing there is no obvious competitor" ("City of Books," 118). Markus describes it as a "long and rambling book" (*Saeculum*, 47). See also Kent, "Reinventing Augustine's Ethics," 227–231.

3. As Augustine writes in *Retractions*, "This work kept me busy for some years because many other things, which should not be deferred, interfered and their solution had first claim on me" (2.69). Similarly, in a letter from 419 when composing *City of God*, he complains that he "find[s] it annoying that the things that people from one side or another unexpectedly call upon us to dictate interfere with the projects that we have under way and that they neither cease nor can be put off" (Letter 23A*.4). For discussion, see Clark, "City of Books," 117–118.

4. See Dyson, introduction to *City of God*, xi–xiv; Markus, *Saeculum*, 70–71; Harrison, *Augustine*, 197–199. Brown describes *City of God* as "a book of controversy" that "should never be treated as though it were a static, complete photograph of Augustine's thought": "It reads like a film of a professional boxing championship: it is all movement, ducking and weaving. Augustine is a really stylish professional: he rarely relies on the knockout; he is out to win the fight on points. It is a fight carried on in twenty-two books against nothing less than the whole of the pagan literary culture available to him. Thus he is reluctant to follow an argument through to its conclusion in one move: instead, he twists a definition here, demolishes another there, proposes one to annoy an opponent, ignores it in the next few chapters, then takes it up again no less than seventeen books further on, that is, ten whole years later. To try to extract from this infinitely flexible book a rigidly coherent system of political ideas is like trying to square the circle: it is a problem that has fascinated many great minds, and baffled all of them" ("Political Society," 311–312; see also Dyson, introduction to *City of God*, xv; Harmless, introduction to *Augustine in His Words*, xiv).

5. O'Daly, *Augustine's "City of God,"* esp. 27–38, 272. Eventually, Augustine came to see *City of God* as an opportunity to articulate a more positive vision to sustain the Christian community in an uncertain century. Although he offers nothing like a modern-day introduction, he supplies a brief summary in *Retractions*, 2.69; Letter 212A, and Letter 1A*.1 (cf. *City of God*, 2.2, 11.1).

6. Harrison, "Rhetoric," 215.

7. *On Christian Teaching*, 4.22.51.

8. Ibid. "Nobody should think that it is against the rule of the art to combine these styles. On the contrary, our discourse should be varied by all three [styles], as far as is possible without impropriety" (ibid.). Sometimes, Augustine suggests his three aims—instructing, delighting,

and moving—"should not be understood in the sense that a single aim is assigned to each style (so that to be listened to with understanding would be the business of the restrained style, to be listened to with pleasure that of the mixed style, and to be listened to with obedience that of the grand style), but rather in the sense that a speaker should always have these three aims and pursue them to the best of his ability even when operating within one particular style" (4.26.56).

9. Ibid., 4.22.51.

10. Ibid., 4.22.51–4.25.55.

11. Ibid., 4.23.52, 4.20.42–43. In the latter passage, Augustine is describing Paul's exemplary use of the grand style in Romans 8:28–39 and 2 Corinthians 6:2–11.

12. Von Heyking highlights Augustine's use of the three styles in *City of God* (*Augustine*, 36; "Disarming," 172n16, 176–177).

13. Augustine describes his purpose in sending *City of God* in Letter 212A and offers a reply to Firmus in Letter 2*. For discussion, see O'Daly, *Augustine's "City of God,"* 36–37.

14. Letter 2*.3.

15. Clark describes *City of God* as Augustine's "most consciously and consistently Ciceronian work, both in content and in style" ("City of Books," 126).

16. See Harmless, introduction to *Augustine in His Own Words*, ix–xi, on how artists often misportray Augustine, including by presenting him as alone in his study rather than dictating to stenographers.

17. For evidence of Augustine's dictation, see Letter 23A*.3; Possidius, "Life," §28. On Augustine's process of composing and revising texts, see Stock, *Augustine the Reader*, 288n79; and O'Donnell, *Augustine*, 136–137. For a history of *City of God* as a book, see Clark, "City of Books"; and Vessey, "History of the Book," 27–32.

18. Stock, *Augustine the Reader*, 5–6; Hampl, preface to *Confessions*, xiii–xxvi, esp. xvii. Scholars in classics have long debated the extent of reading aloud in ancient Greek and Roman culture, and some have cited Augustine's reaction to Ambrose in *Confessions* 6.3.3 as evidence of its rarity. In recent years, scholars have refuted this idea and shown convincingly that while reading aloud was common in late antiquity, reading silently was also a common practice, especially among educated elites. See Gavrilov, "Techniques of Reading"; and Burnyeat, "Silent Reading."

19. In Letter 212A and Letter 1A*.2, for example, Augustine encourages Firmus to share *City of God* with those in Carthage who lack access. Possidius, "Life," §18, describes how many of Augustine's texts were copied and shared. "Even for the small part of the population that was literate," O'Donnell writes, "books were scarce and expensive and the spoken word was still the most effective way of achieving wide distribution" ("Bible," 100; see also *Augustine*, 143). On the "economic" aspects of reading aloud and sharing books, see Burnyeat, "Silent Reading," 75n6.

20. *Confessions*, 6.3.3.

21. Stock, *Augustine the Reader*, 5; Hollingworth, *Pilgrim City*, 64.

22. Letter 2*.3.

23. The prevalence of oral reading does not mean Augustine failed to see *City of God* as a treatise to be read. As Clark argues, "Augustine was particularly aware of *City of God* as a book, a physical object used by readers," which is apparent in various references, summaries, and notes he supplies to readers ("City of Books," 120; see also O'Daly, *Augustine's "City of God,"* 277–278). Augustine's correspondence with Firmus provides relevant evidence: Augustine explains how

to divide the twenty-two books of *City of God* into two or five volumes, based on the size and content of its sections (see Letter 212A; Letter 1A*.1; Clark, "City of Books," 120).

24. Murphy, "Rhetoric of Roman Decline"; Smith, "Glory and Tragedy," 202. On *City of God*'s "hortatory" dimension, see also O'Daly, *Augustine's "City of God,"* 36–37. On Augustine's attempt to redirect the love of glory, see Roberts, "Augustine's Ciceronian Response."

25. Von Heyking, *Augustine,* 17–50, at 20. See also "Disarming," 176–177. As von Heyking notes, *City of God*'s "use of the grand style can be understood in light of the fact that the work's purpose is in part pastoral and in part poetic in the sense that he intended it to be a monument for future generations set against an old civilization" (172n16).

26. See Ogle, *Politics and the Earthly City,* 3–4, 12, 19. Ogle also reads Augustine rhetorically to challenge common assumptions about his "pessimism" (3–6, 96–97, 182–183).

27. *City of God,* 22.1.

28. For a summary of Book 22, see O'Daly, *Augustine's "City of God,"* 225–233.

29. See, e.g., Vanderjagt, "Political Thought," 1563, who cites the "chilling summary of miseries" in *City of God* 22.22 as evidence of Augustine's "deep pessimism with regard to worldly life."

30. *City of God,* 22.22–23.

31. Ibid., 22.22.

32. Ibid.

33. Ibid., 22.22–23.

34. Ibid., 22.22.

35. See, e.g., Deane, *Political and Social Ideas,* 61, 66, 92–93, 236; Markus, *Saeculum,* 95; *Christianity and the Secular,* 56. While acknowledging the goods listed in 22.24, O'Daly describes 22.22–23 as "an uncompromisingly grim picture of the human condition" (*Augustine's "City of God,"* 230–231). Klosko does not cite *City of God* 22.22–23, but he relies on Deane's interpretation and alludes to Book 22 when contrasting the heavenly city with "the hell of this life" (*History of Political Theory,* 242–243). Kaufman cites *City of God* 22.22 and 22.24 in one paragraph to suggest that, for Augustine, "[l]ife in time was a Gulag or—in current coin—a Gitmo, a detention camp. Christians were fortunate to be passing through to a better place, yet their here and now would always be a dreadfully sad place and time." However, he goes on to suggest that Augustine held that "this world was loaded with 'consolations'" ("Augustine's Dystopia," 56). Elsewhere, Kaufman endorses the suggestion that the "final books" of *City of God* "betoken Augustinian pessimism" (*Redeeming Politics,* 147) and describes 22.22 as the *City of God*'s "most scalding rationale for detachment" (*Incorrectly Political,* 106). Augustine's "grim" conclusion about this "hell on earth" notwithstanding, Kaufman concedes that "calamity" is not his "last word" (106).

36. Deane, *Political and Social Ideas,* 61, 66, 92–93, 236.

37. Ibid., 59–60.

38. Ibid., 66; see also 60–62, 234–243. For Deane, "Any thinker who, like Augustine, sees man as essentially selfish, avaricious, ambitious for power and glory, and lustful, cannot possibly be a cheerful optimist when he surveys the world and the human activities that go on in it" (59).

39. Ibid., xiii, 230, 241.

40. *City of God,* 22.24. Kent also cites this passage to suggest that "Augustine never reduces the present life to some miserable waystation on the train route to heaven. *De civitate Dei*'s notorious, often-reprinted catalogue of all the troubles of mortal life—a staple of late twentieth-century anthologies—comes followed by a much less noticed catalogue of all the *goods* of the

present life" ("Augustine's Ethics," 211). Kaufman also notes the "blessings" and "consolations" evident in *City of God* 22.24, which, he suggests, makes Augustine's view "only mildly dystopian" ("Augustine's Dystopia," 56, 58; see also *On Agamben*, 9).

41. *City of God*, 22.24.

42. Ibid.

43. Ibid.

44. Ibid.

45. Wills, *Saint Augustine*, 138. Brown describes 22.24 in passing as an "argument for hope" but does not elaborate on its specific relation to the virtue or how it is cultivated (*Augustine of Hippo*, 328).

46. See, e.g., Billings, "Natality," 132–136.

47. Deane, *Political and Social Ideas*, 64. Deane acknowledges that "Augustine does not advocate a completely negative, ascetic attitude toward the world; nor does he encourage the view that possessions and other earthly goods are *per se* evil. He frankly recognizes that, in addition to eternal blessings, there are temporal blessings, such as health, material possessions, honor, friends, a home, wife and children, and peace and quiet" (43).

48. Ibid., 66–67.

49. Ibid., 60–62, 66, 243.

50. A crude count of the tone and substance of each paragraph in this chapter illustrates this distinctive emphasis: roughly thirty paragraphs focus primarily on sin or evil, while only nine paragraphs attend predominantly to ascriptions of goodness or divine providence. Twenty-two paragraphs are more balanced or neutral.

51. Ibid., 230, 241, 237–239.

52. Mathewes, *Evil*, 75–103. Niebuhr wonders whether "a realistic interpretation may not err in obscuring the residual capacity for justice and devotion to the larger good, even when it is dealing with a dimension of collective behavior in which the realistic assumptions about human nature are most justified" (*Man's Nature*, 71). Though Niebuhr does not explicitly mention Augustine here, he criticizes Augustine's influential strand of Christian realism for being "too consistent to give a true picture of either human nature or the human community" and "too excessive to do justice to the Roman and Stoic genius for universal community or, rather, for the quasi-universal imperial community" (46, 97; see also 44, 71). I agree with Ernest Fortin that "Augustine was neither the starry-eyed idealist for which he has been taken by some, nor the hard-nosed realist for which he has been taken by others," and that to see him as such is to take his "long series of hyperbolic statements" "out of context" ("Problem of Modernity," 142, 146).

53. Gregory, *Politics*, 20–21.

54. Shklar, "Giving Injustice Its Due," 1139–1140.

55. *On Order*, 1.19. Augustine may take his rhetorical cue here from Cicero, who argues that "in making accusations it isn't fair to pass over the good things and select and enumerate only the bad and the faulty" (*On the Laws*, 3.23).

56. *City of God*, 22.24.

57. Unlike other realists, Elshtain challenges the disproportionate emphasis on Augustine's account of evil and insists on his affirmation of goodness: "Only someone caught up in a love affair with the world would describe so deliciously its many delectations and articulate so

artfully its temptations. Peace and hope are twin possibilities that emerge from all our yearnings and longings, holy and otherwise. But peace in its true form as harmony and righteousness is not attainable on this earth, although the hope that keeps alive our longing for it is what stands between us and that emptiness of the abyss, that flatness of being Augustine credited as the work of sin and the fruit of deformed willing" (*Augustine*, 89; see also 117). Yet Elshtain does not attend adequately to the *rhetorical* and *pedagogical* features of Book 22. My account elevates these features as an important aspect of Augustine's argument in *City of God*.

58. *City of God*, 11.18; Cicero, *Orator*, 12.38. See also Cicero, *On the Ideal Orator*, 2.263, 3.207.

59. *City of God*, 11.18. See Bussanich, "Goodness," 390–391.

60. *City of God*, 11.18. Note that the "course of the ages" (*ordinem saeculorum*) and "the beauty of this world" (*saeculi pulchritudo*) refer to the *saeculum*, which will be a major theme of the next chapter.

61. *On Order*, 1.18.

62. Deane, *Political and Social Ideas*, 70–71.

63. For discussion, see Brandom, *Tales of the Mighty Dead*, 91–92.

64. *City of God*, 22.24; Deane, *Political and Social Ideas*, 243; see also 60–62, 66.

65. My analysis is indebted to Burke, "Semantic and Poetic Meaning." Though Burke does not discuss Augustine here, his analysis of the "semantic" and "poetic" styles helps to illuminate the functions of Augustine's "restrained" and "grand" styles. Burke discusses Augustine's rhetoric in *Rhetoric of Religion*, 1–171.

66. See Smith, "Glory and Tragedy," 189.

67. *City of God*, 22.29; *Enchiridion*, 1.5.

68. 1 Corinthians 13:12, cited in *City of God*, 22.29.

69. Meconi highlights the importance of "seeing" in Augustine's works ("Heaven," 255–262), while Smith emphasizes "vision" and Augustine's aim to "give his readers new eyes" ("Glory and Tragedy," 190).

70. See Bowlin, "Augustine Counting Virtues."

71. This insight is developed by Byers, *Perception*; and Bowlin, "Augustine Counting Virtues." Ogle suggests that, in *City of God*, "Augustine's goal is to help us see the world, even the political world, anew: as part of a created order that is *good*, but that points beyond itself all the same" (*Politics and the Earthly City*, 4; see also 68–69, 183). Ogle affirms how, for Augustine, "distorted vision" can lead to "distorted love" (101).

72. Byers, *Perception*, 46. According to Byers (50), Augustine may have appropriated these insights from Plotinus, particularly since Plotinus's account of perception in *Ennead* 5.3.3 is similar to Augustine's account of perception.

73. *City of God*, 11.18; Oliver, in Cook and Oliver, *Our World*, 72. Ogle emphasizes the "sacramental" character of Augustine's vision: "[T]he visible bears witness to the invisible; it points toward it by its very existence" (*Politics and the Earthly City*, 14, 16).

74. In *Plato's Progeny*, Lane diagnoses Nussbaum's Nietzschean interpretation of Platonism as dualistic and foundationalist (53–61, 79–80). My analysis of Augustine's Platonism reflects Lane's recovery of a more "immanent" and "aspirational" Platonism in ibid., esp. 53–96. See also Kerr, *Immortal Longings*.

75. *City of God*, 22.24.

76. Nussbaum, *Therapy*, esp. ch. 1.

77. Lane develops this distinction in *Plato's Progeny*, 53–96. Given the more "immanent" character of the Neoplatonism that Augustine inherited, I believe he is offering a more "aspirational" account in Book 22.

78. Byers, *Perception*, 24–26, 37–39.

79. See ibid., 46–54.

80. Ibid., 59–60, 64–68, 72–73.

81. *City of God*, 22.24; *Expositions of the Psalms*, 120.3 cited by Brooks, "What May I Hope For?," 118.

82. Vasaly, *Representations*, 89–104; Innocenti, "Towards a Theory"; Connolly, *Life of Roman Republicanism*, 73–74.

83. Vasaly, *Representations*, 93–97; Innocenti, "Towards a Theory," 358–363.

84. Connolly, *Life of Roman Republicanism*, 74.

85. *Enchiridion*, 2.8.

86. *Expositions of the Psalms*, 31(2).4.

87. My analysis here is compatible with, and complementary to, von Heyking's account of Augustine's "dialectic of excess over excess" to "form the inordinate passions into ordinate love" (*Augustine*, 20; "Disarming," 176–177), Smith's emphasis on Augustine's "pedagogical and pastoral" attempt to reorder our loves away from human to divine glory ("Glory and Tragedy," 189), and Fortin's analysis of Augustine's "hyperbolic" statements to persuade the Roman elite to moderate their devotion to the empire and accept the Christian faith ("Problem of Modernity," 146–147).

88. See Gregory, *Politics*, 39–42.

89. *City of God*, 1.Pref., translation altered; see also 14.28, 19.12.

90. See ibid., 19.25; 15.22; *On Christian Teaching*, 1.3.3–1.5.5; 1.22.20–1.24.25.

91. Gregory, *Politics*, 39–41, 221.

92. Though he does not mention 22.22–24, von Heyking makes a similar argument regarding the use of rhetorical styles in *City of God*: "Augustine's rhetoric in that treatise is meant, through all three types of rhetoric, to tame the political ambitions of his readers and to harness them to virtue. His rhetoric appears immoderately antipolitical because he considered most of his audience's passion for political glory as inordinate and deformed, and his rhetoric is meant to illuminate goods that transcend politics and to demonstrate how political glory is insufficient to secure the complete happiness that Roman statesmen implicitly sought by way of their ambitions" ("Disarming," 176; see also *Augustine*, 20, 32, 50).

93. *City of God*, 20.9.

94. Ibid., 22.24.

95. Ibid.

96. Breyfogle, "Citizenship and Signs," 508.

97. *City of God*, 22.24.

98. Ibid.

99. Moreover, Augustine does not confine goodness to any particular human institution or the achievements of "great" leaders. He praises the work not only of doctors, scientists, mathematicians, inventors, philosophers, poets, and orators, but also of farmers, sailors, artists, dressmakers, homebuilders, potters, painters, musicians, sculptors, actors, hunters, soldiers, nurses, and cooks. His description of the diverse products of human labor reflects his egalitarian impulse. In the final book of *City of God*, he implicitly challenges the aristocratic assumptions of

an empire that identifies political and military leaders as the primary paradigms of virtue and goodness.

100. In *City of God*, 22.24, Augustine lists "prudence" as one of the "virtues . . . by which a man is equipped to resist errors and the other vices implanted in him, and to conquer them by fixing his desires upon nothing but the Supreme and Immutable Good."

101. Cicero argues that *dispositio* is "so powerful in oratory that nothing contributes more to winning a case" (*On the Ideal Orator*, 2.179–181; see also 2.307–349). Skinner describes the functions of *dispositio* in *Reason and Rhetoric*, 46–47. For more on "arrangement," see Kennedy, *New Testament Interpretation*, 23–25.

102. See *City of God*, 21.1. Cameron highlights the early Christian practice of "working through the familiar, by appealing from the known to the unknown" (*Christianity*, 25). See also Murphy, "Rhetoric of Roman Decline," 597; Smith, "Glory and Tragedy," 190–191; and Keys, "Augustinian Humility."

103. Critics might wonder why Augustine does not explicitly mention this ordering in *City of God*, 22.22–24, as he did in 21.1. The reason may relate to his pedagogical purposes. In *City of God*, 21.1, Augustine is explicitly attempting to *instruct* his readers and shape their *beliefs* about heaven and hell by appealing to their intellect. In Book 22.22–24, he is attempting to *transform* their *will*, to *encourage* them to aspire for the City of God. To alert his readers of his intention would diminish the indirect effect of 22.22–24 and cause them to engage the text with their intellect rather than their will. Augustine may also keep his purposes hidden to "exercise" the mind of his readers. In *On Christian Teaching*, 4.8.22, he describes how some passages of scripture maintain a "helpful and healthful obscurity in order to exercise and somehow refine their readers' minds or to overcome the reluctance and whet the enthusiasm of those seeking to learn, or even in order to cloud the minds of the wicked." Elsewhere, he appeals to such exercises to justify why "the scriptures need to be examined carefully": "[W]e ought not to be content with their surface meaning, since they were composed to exercise our minds and hence demand to be penetrated more deeply" (Letter 199.11.42; see also 11.45; *City of God*, 11.19). Dodaro notes that "indirection" was a common aspect of Ciceronian rhetoric used to persuade through emotion rather than reason and suggests that even God uses "indirection" and "figurative language" to provide "conceptual stepping stones connecting visible, temporal reality with invisible, eternal reality" (*Christ and the Just Society*, 62–63, 133–135).

104. Burke, "Semantic and Poetic Meaning," 160, emphasis in original. For the introduction to Burke, I am grateful to Stout, *Democracy and Tradition*, 55, and "Transformation of Genius," 6n12.

105. This fits with Murphy's analysis of Augustine's "sequential" rhetorical strategy against pagan critics early in *City of God*, where "first, he destabilizes, then he substitutes" ("Rhetoric of Roman Decline," 597, citing Conybeare, "*Terrarum Orbi Documentum*," 63).

106. *City of God*, 22.30.

107. I am grateful to Charles Mathewes for discussion of this connection. Kennedy notes that analyzing the "arrangement" (*dispositio*) of a text involves considering "what subdivisions it falls into, what the persuasive effect of these parts seems to be, and how they work together—or fail to do so—to some unified purpose in meeting the rhetorical situation" (*New Testament Interpretation*, 37).

108. *City of God*, 22.30; Letter 212A; Letter 1A*. Several scholars emphasize that this division in Letter 212A and Letter 1A* reflects both the substantive content of *City of God* and the

practical necessity of publishing such a massive work in more manageable codices. See Clark, "City of Books," 120–121; Vessey, "History of the Book," 29–30; O'Daly, Augustine's "City of God," 69–73.

109. Letter 212A and Letter 1A*.1; *Retractions*, 2.69.1.

110. Letter 212A. See also Letter 1A*.1; *Retractions*, 2.69.1–2.

111. *Retractions*, 2.69.2. See also Letter 212A; Letter 1A*.1.

112. *City of God*, 19.1.

113. Deane, *Political and Social Ideas*, 60–62, 92–93.

114. Ibid., 221–243.

115. Niebuhr, "Augustine's Political Realism," 140–141; Shklar, "Giving Injustice Its Due," 1139–1140.

116. Two notable exceptions are Jean Bethke Elshtain and Peter Iver Kaufman. Elshtain cites 22.22 early in *Augustine and the Limits of Politics* but later cites 22.24 to suggest that, for Augustine, "[t]he world is an overflowing abundance, a consolation to *all* humankind" (37–38, 61–62; see also 117–118). Similarly, Kaufman cites *City of God*, 22.24, to suggest that Augustine's text is "loaded" with "consolations" and "blessings" ("Augustine's Dystopia," 56). While Kaufman emphasizes Augustine's "dystopia," he concludes by acknowledging the "bad news" that Augustine offers is not "the final word": "marking the differences" between the faith, hope, and love of the two cities "has the effect of making *City of God* a comfort and consolation" (74). "'Evils of this temporal state' invariably stain every attempt to politicize or institutionalize what the virtues of good pilgrims inspire. But their different faith, hope, and love are portals through which Augustine permits another reality to make itself known" (74).

117. See Niebuhr, "Augustine's Political Realism," 128, 140; Deane, *Political and Social Ideas*, 60, 68, 242. As Donald Burt argues, "Whether St. Augustine was an optimist or pessimist continues to be a matter of debate, and reasonably so. The Bishop of Hippo seems to go through violent mood swings on the issue, saying of the world at one time that it is a 'smiling place' and at another that it is like an old man groaning in his bed, saying of human beings that they are the 'best of creation' and at another that they are 'cracked pots'" ("Courageous Optimism," 55). Henry Paolucci opens his introduction to Augustine's political writings by asking whether Augustine was a "political pessimist" or "prophetic utopian" (*Political Writings*, vii). Miles Hollingworth cites Paolucci's poles to frame his discussion in *Pilgrim City*, 16, 85–87; see 204 on "optimism" and "pessimism." As Ogle, *Politics and the Earthly City*, 10, notes, Bruno analyzes recent varieties of political Augustinianism through the lens of "optimism" and "pessimism" (*Political Augustinianism*, 230–244). Kaufman likewise frames differing interpretations of Augustine's political thought in these terms, arguing that "[r]eaders must choose whether the optimism or pessimism of interpreters corresponds with Augustine's views, passage by prickly passage" (*Incorrectly Political*, 230; see also 1–9, 121–127, 227–232). Coleman also notes shifts between Augustine's "early optimism" and later "pessimism" ("St Augustine," 311, 313, 315, 330, 334).

118. See Gregory, *Politics*, 363–384; Mathewes, *Evil*, 56–103; Avramenko, "Time," 784–785, 810–811; Brooks, "What May I Hope For?," 59–62, 73–76.

119. Brown, introduction to *Essential Reinhold Niebuhr*, xi–xiii, describing Niebuhr. Crouter suggests that the "standard labels of 'optimist' and 'pessimist' are inadequate for Niebuhr, who combines both elements as a self-described 'tamed cynic'" (*Reinhold Niebuhr*, 4; see also Brown, *Niebuhr and His Age*, 3). Niebuhr himself argued that neither pessimism or optimism are

appropriate political options for his own time: "[A] free society prospers best in a cultural, religious, and moral atmosphere which encourages neither a too pessimistic nor too optimistic view of human nature" (*Children of Light*, viii).

120. Burt, "Courageous Optimism," 55. See also Schall, "'Realism,'" 202, on Augustine's "streak of optimism midst his pessimism." Similarly, Bruno argues that, "while Augustine's vision is certainly marked by a strong pessimism, it is not and cannot be completely pessimistic precisely because of the prospect of grace's work within the human soul" (*Political Augustinianism*, 237; see also 257, 268).

121. Deane, *Political and Social Ideas*, 68.

122. See, e.g., Sermon 87.10; *Gift of Perseverance*, 22.57–62.

123. For a history of "pessimism" in modern political thought, see Dienstag, *Pessimism*, esp. 9n7.

124. Note how Burt anachronistically organizes his discussion around a distinctly Leibnizian question, asking if Augustine believed if "this is the best possible world" ("Courageous Optimism," 61–64).

Chapter 8. Hope for the Commonwealth: Eschatology, Ecclesiology, and Politics

1. *City of God*, 14.28.

2. Ibid., 1.Pref., 5.14, 5.18. On the importance of "glory" for Augustine, see Brown, *Augustine of Hippo*, 310; von Heyking, *Augustine*, 150–171; and Kaufman, *On Agamben*, 49–97.

3. *City of God*, 19.1.

4. Ibid., 15.21.

5. For more on the variety of early eschatological accounts, see Daley, *Hope of the Early Church*.

6. For discussion, see ibid., 124.

7. Ibid., 127–131.

8. See Markus, *Saeculum*, 20.

9. See *City of God*, 20.7.

10. Markus, *Saeculum*, 20. See also Daley, *Hope of the Early Church*, 134; Mommsen, "Christian Idea of Progress."

11. *City of God*, 20.2.

12. Ibid., paraphrasing Romans 11:33, which he cites earlier at 20.1.

13. For an illuminating exposition of this theme in *City of God*, see O'Donovan, "*City of God* 19," 70–72. See also Fortin, "St. Augustine," 196; Markus, *Saeculum*, 23; and Murphy, "Rhetoric of Roman Decline," 600–601.

14. *City of God*, 20.7.

15. *Confessions*, 4.4.9; see also 10.33.50.

16. *City of God*, 20.2.

17. Letter 199.1.1, 3.7, 3.10, 4.13, 6.16, 6.18, 8.22, 8.24, 9.33, 10.35.

18. Letter 199.13.52.

19. Textbook treatments of Augustine in political thought assume this futurist eschatology. Sophie Lunn-Rockliffe, for example, traces Augustine's "idea that the truly important community is not this-worldly, but transcendent" to Neoplatonic influences and suggests that

Augustine's "two cities" are "transcendent and invisible" and "take shape only eschatologically."
Citing *City of God*, 19.4, Lunn-Rockliffe argues that Augustine's primary critique against classical
philosophers targeted their "inappropriately earthly focus" ("Early Christian Political Philosophy,"
151). Similarly, in his classic article, Mommsen suggests that "[t]he fact that only one book of *The
City of God* (b. XVIII) treats historical developments proper, shows clearly that Augustine regarded the purely secular aspects of the drama of mankind as relatively insignificant" ("Christian
Idea of Progress," 370). Markus emphasizes that the earthly and heavenly cities are "eschatological
entities" that will only be visible "at the end of time," "beyond temporal history" (*Saeculum*, 62).

20. Arendt, *Love*, 19.

21. Ibid., 106. For Arendt's discussion of Christian "worldlessness," see *Human Condition*,
5–58.

22. Nussbaum, *Upheavals*, 556; see also 553, 543.

23. Ibid., 553.

24. Billings, "Natality," 135–136.

25. Realists often cite Augustine's discussion of the "necessity" of the judge in *City of God*,
19.6, to support this view.

26. See, e.g., Elshtain, *Just War*, and "Problem of 'Dirty Hands.'" McConnell, "Torturing and
Punishing," 486–490, offers a "utilitarian" reading of Augustine's views of human punishment.
See also Coleman, "St Augustine," 334–336, on his "consequentialist position." For insightful
analyses of Augustine's opposition to torture, see Ogle, "Sheathing the Sword"; and Kolbet,
"Freedom from Grim Necessity."

27. Shklar, "Giving Injustice Its Due," 1139.

28. The contrast between "expectation" and "experience" comes from the classic text on realized eschatology: Dodd, *Parables of the Kingdom*, 50, as found in Clark, "Realized Eschatology."
The concept of realized eschatology was introduced by Dodd.

29. For a brief overview of eschatology in Christian theology, see McGrath, "Last Things."
On "participation," see *City of God*, 20.3. By emphasizing partial participation, I hope to avoid
Burroughs's worries about prolepsis indicating the complete presence of the City of God (see
Christianity, Politics, and the Predicament of Evil, 67).

30. Ibid., 20.5, citing Matthew 13:37.

31. Ibid., 20.17.

32. Ibid., 20.9.

33. Ibid., 15.1.

34. See ibid., 16.5.

35. See, e.g., 1 John 3:1–3; *City of God*, 20.6.

36. *Enchiridion*, 30.115.

37. Augustine emphasizes temporal participation in the heavenly city when commenting on
the final verse of Psalm 4 ("*Because you, Lord, through hope have established me in unity*"), a passage he quotes in *Confessions* to describe his own hope. In explicating the passage, Augustine
notes that the psalmist "did not say, 'You will establish me,' but, *You have established me*, for in
him this hope is already grounded, and in him most certainly this hope will be fulfilled" (*Expositions of the Psalms*, 4.10; see also Letter 218.3).

38. *City of God*, 20.5. Augustine makes a similar point in Letter 199.11.45, suggesting that
Christ "comes daily in his body, which is the Church."

39. As Griffiths argues, "[T]he Church shows itself to be, in its politics—the practices that order its common life as a polity, a city—the fullest possible participant in the city of God" ("Secularity," 47).

40. Michael Hollerich, for example, argues that the church "threatens to disappear from view" in Markus's account of Augustine ("John Milbank," 321). More recently, Jonathan Tran has suggested that many contemporary Augustinian democrats, including those whose work informs my account, "minimize the role of the church" ("Augustinian Democrats," 533). While they offer a compelling "speculative" vision of Christian political participation in relation to the ontology of creation, they leave incomplete the "practical task" of connecting Christian political participation with the church, "presuming church without much talking about it" (531–538). Tran does not deny the valuable contribution that Augustinian democrats have made, particularly in showing alignment with contemporary democratic theory and resisting communitarian accounts that encourage a rigid opposition between church and world. But in "[w]anting to avoid crowding out the world," he argues, "the Augustinian democrats overcompensate and crowd out the church" (533). For our purposes, it is striking that Tran identifies debates over hope as the context where this divergence becomes evident (524–525, 532–538).

41. See Milbank, *Theology and Social Theory*, 2, 382–442; and Hauerwas, *After Christendom?*, 19–22, 39–44. "There is no doubt that Augustine's account of the worldly city invites a Niebuhr-like interpretation," Hauerwas writes. "Yet missing from Niebuhr's account is Augustine's equally strong insistence that the church is the only true political society, because only in the church are we directed to worship the one true God. Only through the church do we have the resources necessary for our desires to be rightly ordered, for the virtues to be rightly formed" (40). For a helpful overview of Milbank's core argument, see Hollerich, "John Milbank." For an insightful analysis of Hauerwas's, see Burroughs, *Christianity, Politics, and the Predicament of Evil*, 129–178.

42. Hauerwas and Milbank are not always so oppositional, and they sometimes resist characterizations of their thought as licensing sectarian withdrawal. Milbank occasionally acknowledges the blurry boundaries of the church and even concedes that the institutional church can sometimes "mimic the procedures of political sovereignty" through its "bureaucratic management of believers": "Better, then, that the bounds between Church and State be extremely hazy, so that a social existence of many complex and interlocking powers may emerge, and forestall either a sovereign state, or a statically hierarchical Church" (*Theology and Social Theory*, 413). For his part, Hauerwas denies criticisms that he encourages exclusivism or sectarian withdrawal, claiming that he is "not asking the church to withdraw, but rather to give up the presumptions of Constantinian power, particularly when those take the form of liberal universalism" (Hauerwas, *After Christendom?*, 18; see also *Community of Character*, 85; "Where Would I Be," 318–320). For helpful discussions of tensions produced by Hauerwas and Milbank's rhetoric and their occasional attempts to blur the line between church and world, see Stout, *Democracy and Tradition*, 92–179; Gregory, *Politics*, 125–148; Herdt, *Putting on Virtue*, 346–352; Biggar, *Behaving in Public*, 79–105; "Is Stanley Hauerwas Sectarian?," 141–160; and Burroughs, *Christianity, Politics, and the Predicament of Evil*, 130–134, 153–157, 161–169.

Defenders of Hauerwas and Milbank may object that my brief summary ignores their rhetorical and pedagogical purposes. In the same way that Augustine uses rhetoric to shape readers, they employ excessive rhetoric to reorient their readers. Hauerwas makes this explicit in response to critics, suggesting that he uses these slogans to unsettle standard assumptions about ethics and politics: "Epigrams like the 'the Church's first task is not to make the world more just, but to make the world the world' are meant to invite thought" ("Where Would I Be," 318). In using such antitheses, Hauerwas and Milbank might be simply exercising another aspect of their Augustinian inheritance.

I appreciate the force of this suggestion and acknowledge that their thought should be read in light of its rhetorical purposes. But this recognition does not entirely blunt my worries. Augustine's rhetorical context and theirs are different in important ways. For one, Augustine's context was shaped by a culture where rhetorical training was part of the educational curriculum. Our contemporary context, by contrast, lacks a similar rhetorical culture, which means contemporary readers might be less alert to the pedagogical use of rhetoric than those in Augustine's time. This is especially important since both Hauerwas and Milbank write partly for academics, including theologians and philosophers whose discourse is shaped by norms that value clarity and precision over rhetorical excess. In this discursive community, excessive rhetoric and loose formulations can lead to misunderstanding, as Hauerwas acknowledges (318). That both continue to use excessive rhetoric even after it has led to misunderstanding means they bear some of the responsibility for how audiences perceive their claims. Even setting these considerations aside, there is another reason why Hauerwas and Milbank's polemical rhetoric can potentially distort interpretations of Augustine. Although they both occasionally acknowledge their own position is more complex than their rhetoric suggests, they do not make the same claims for their interpretation of Augustine. Rather, they present Augustine's position at face value and do not acknowledge how he uses rhetoric to shape readers, which has the potential to mislead scholars and students who rely on their interpretations of Augustine's thought.

43. Hauerwas and Willimon, *Resident Aliens*.

44. Rather than seeking to do justice and solve practical political issues, Hauerwas counsels Christians to focus first on *being the church*, creating an alternative polis to embody truth, justice, peace, and love: "Christians must again understand that their first task is not to make the world better or more just, but to recognize what the world is and why it is that it understands the political task as it does. The first social task of the church is to provide the space and time necessary for developing skills of interpretation and discrimination sufficient to help us recognize the possibilities and limits of our society. *In developing such skills, the church and Christians must be uninvolved in the politics of our society and involved in the polity that is the church.* . . . For the Christian, therefore, the church is always the primary polity through which we gain the experience to negotiate and make positive contributions to whatever society in which we may find ourselves" (*Community of Character*, 74, emphasis added; see also 1–3, 9–12, 83–84; *After Christendom?*, 44). In *Theology and Social Theory*, Milbank uses similar language about the need for the church "to be the Church" (428).

45. See, e.g., Milbank, *Theology and Social Theory*, 382–442; Hauerwas, *After Christendom?*, 19–22.

46. *City of God*, 19.17. Here, he is referring to resistance to the earthly city's "laws of religion."

47. Ibid., 20.9.

48. See Milbank, *Theology and Social Theory*, 2, 383, 414–416; Hauerwas, *Peaceable Kingdom*; *Community of Character*, 72–86; Hauerwas and Willimon, *Resident Aliens*, 19–22, 35–44.

49. See, e.g., Hauerwas, *After Christendom?*, 16–21; Hauerwas and Willimon, *Resident Aliens*, 19–44; Bretherton, *Christianity*, 72; and Smith, *Awaiting the King*, 179, 205, on the dangers of "liturgical capture."

50. I take up Milbank's critique of "pagan virtue" in chapter 10.

51. See, e.g., *City of God*, 8.24, 13.16, 16.2, where Augustine identifies the City of God with the "Church." Burroughs cites these passages in *Christianity, Politics, and the Predicament of Evil*, xv.

52. *City of God*, 20.9. See also Griffiths, "Secularity," 52; Johnson, *Theology*, 159–160.

53. "In one sense, then, we are to understand the kingdom of heaven as a kingdom in which both are included: that is, the man who breaks what he teaches, and he who performs it; though one is the least and the other is great in the kingdom. In another sense, however, it is a kingdom into which only he who performs what he teaches will enter. In the first sense, then, where persons of both kinds are present, the 'kingdom of heaven' is the Church as she now is. But in the second, where only persons of the second kind will be present, it is the Church as she will be when no wicked man shall be within her. Therefore, the Church even now is the kingdom of Christ and the kingdom of heaven. Thus, even now the saints of Christ reign with Him, though not in the same way as they will reign hereafter. But the tares do not reign with Him, even though they are growing in the Church alongside the wheat" (*City of God*, 20.9).

54. Ibid.

55. Burroughs analyzes Hauerwas's "overly realized" eschatology (*Christianity, Politics, and the Predicament of Evil*, 153), while Bruno notes Milbank's problematic tendency to identify "the Church as the *civitas dei* on earth without qualification" (*Political Augustinianism*, 252). In *Theology and Social Theory*, for example, Milbank describes the "Church itself" as "the realized heavenly city" (407).

56. *City of God*, 20.9, emphasis added.

57. Ibid., 14.28.

58. See Markus, *Saeculum*, 60–61; Weithman, "Augustine's Political Philosophy," 236–237.

59. See Ogle, *Politics and the Earthly City*, 144–159, 180–183. For a comparable analysis, see Smith, *Awaiting the King*, 15, 18–31.

60. Ibid., 140.

61. For helpful discussion, see Dodaro, "Augustine on the Statesman," 386–397; Griffiths, "Secularity," 42–44; Markus, *Saeculum*, 122, 179–181; Kaufman, *Incorrectly Political*, 128–129; and Smith, *Awaiting the King*, 165–208.

62. *City of God*, 1.35. Markus, *Saeculum*, 58–71, makes much of this passage.

63. *City of God*, 1.Pref., 1.35. See also Griffiths, "Secularity," 42.

64. *City of God*, 19.6; see also 20.5 and 20.9, where Augustine explicitly engages the parable of the "wheat" and the "tares" from Matthew 13:37ff.

65. Ibid., 1.35.

66. Ibid., 5.19. I address this argument in chapter 10.

67. Ibid., 15.22, 18.54. See also *Literal Meaning of Genesis*, 11.15.20.

68. Billings, "Natality," 135–136; Milbank, *Theology and Social Theory*, 411.

69. For the classic statement, see Markus, *Saeculum*, 133, which describes the *saeculum* as that "sphere of human living, history, society and its institutions, characterised by the fact that in it the ultimate eschatological oppositions, though present, are not discernible." Markus rejects what he describes as Milbank's "radical equation of the secular with sin" (*Christianity and the*

Secular, 41; see also Biggar, *Behaving in Public*, 97–99). For another insightful account, see Griffiths, "Secularity." For an overview of Markus, see Bruno, *Political Augustinianism*, 127–134. For modern understandings of the secular, see Taylor, *Secular Age*. In describing the "secular" as a *temporal* reality, I have deliberately avoided describing it in spatial terms for fear of perpetuating confusion about the "secular" as a spatial common ground that might be classified as "neutral." Yet the temporal term also implies a certain spatial reality, for we exist in both time and space. On the dangers of "spatializing the political," see Smith, *Awaiting the King*, 8–12, 19–20.

70. Gregory, *Politics*, 79.

71. Ibid. As O'Donovan writes, "Secularity is a stance of patience in the face of plurality, made sense of by eschatological hope" (*Common Objects of Love*, 68–69).

72. *City of God*, 1.Pref., 1.35.

73. Gregory, *Politics*, 11; Markus, *Christianity and the Secular*, 5–6; Griffiths, "Secularity," 33–34; Wetzel, "Splendid Vices," 272–275.

74. Burroughs, *Christianity, Politics, and the Predicament of Evil*, 64–72, makes a similar claim.

75. Smith, *Awaiting the King*, 168, 204, makes a comparable point.

76. Markus, *Saeculum*, 150–151; *City of God*, 1.36. As Markus writes, "No identification of either of the two cities with any institution or with any empirically definable body of people can be reconciled with this radical dichotomy. Membership of the two cities is mutually exclusive, and there can be no possible overlap; but membership of either is compatible both with belonging to the Roman—or some other—state and with belonging to the Church. This entails a logical loosening of the equation of Rome with the earthly city. Rome can only be called the earthly city in a secondary or derivative sense, in so far as the Empire is a society organised around loyalties with no positive relation to God" (*Saeculum*, 60–61). For discussion, see Gregory, *Politics*, 78–79; and Milbank, *Theology and Social Theory*, 394–395.

77. See Markus, *Saeculum*, 58–62; Mommsen, "Christian Idea of Progress," 349–350.

78. *City of God*, 2.21, 19.21. See Burroughs, *Christianity, Politics, and the Predicament of Evil*, 3–8; Weithman, "Augustine's Political Philosophy," 248.

79. In his Augustinian political theology, Smith also resists reducing "the political" to the "government," "state," or "electoral politics" (*Awaiting the King*, 8–12, 35). As Breyfogle writes, "Augustine does not, of course, speak of 'politics' and has no theory of the 'state.' The insistence on the use of modern political terminology with respect to Augustine, even with caveats, has done much to obscure the contours of Augustine's thought" ("Augustinian Understanding," 218). Griffiths rejects the translation of *res publica* as "state" since "it is a quintessentially modern term and conjures, for most contemporary users of English, the apparatus of government (legislatures, judiciaries) and their documentary and institutional affines (constitutions, courts, prisons), all of which is, again, more specific than what Augustine intends by *res publica*." Instead, *res publica* "approaches what we mean by culture" and "is certainly broader than what we mean by politics or the state" ("Secularity," 41).

80. See also Ogle, *Politics and the Earthly City*, 146–148, 159, 170.

81. Ibid. See also Markus, *Saeculum*, 149–150.

82. As Brown notes, "[W]e tend to treat the state in isolation. But this is something which Augustine never did, at any time. The object of his contemplation, the aspect of human activity that he sought to make intelligible and meaningful, is not the state: it is something far, far wider. For him, it is the *saeculum*. And we should translate this vital word, not by 'the world,' so much

as by 'existence'—the sum total of human existence as we experience it in the present, as we know it has been since the fall of Adam, and as we know it will continue until the Last Judgement" ("Political Society," 321).

83. See Mathewes, *Theology of Public Life*, 1–2, 160–166; Bretherton, *Christianity*, 3–6, 16–21, 71–125.

84. See Johnson, *Theology*, 220–225. See also Bretherton's argument for various "levels" of political action and "genuinely public spaces of shared responsibility and cooperation" (*Christianity*, 93).

85. Smith, *Awaiting the King*, 8–12, 53.

86. Mathewes, *Theology of Public Life*, 1. According to Mathewes, "public life" includes "everything from patently political actions such as voting, campaigning for a candidate, or running for office, to less directly political activities such as serving on a school board or planning commission, volunteering in a soup kitchen, and speaking in a civic forum, and to arguably non-political behaviors, such as simply talking to one's family, friends, co-workers, or strangers about public matters of common concern" (1).

87. E.g., Markus, *Saeculum*, xii, xviii, 86–101, 174; Deane, *Political and Social Ideas*, 117. Ogle, *Politics and the Earthly City*, 147, offers a similar critique of scholars who apply modern conceptions of politics to Augustine's premodern view.

88. Burroughs, *Christianity, Politics, and the Predicament of Evil*, 88–89, notes this pattern in Niebuhr.

89. As Griffiths notes, "[B]ecause final political allegiance in this sense is not knowable, Augustine's talk about it in the *City* serves principally as a check on facile identifications of the members of one or the other particular visible city (Rome, Babylon, the Church, the United States) with the members of one or another of the two fundamental and eternal cities, the *civitas terrena* and the *civitas Dei*" ("Secularity," 43).

90. Markus, *Saeculum*, 161–167, has stressed the importance of Augustinian "ambivalence" to the earthly city, and others have echoed this Augustinian theme. See Gregory, *Politics*, 384; Herdt, *Putting on Virtue*, 45–46; Mathewes, *Theology of Public Life*, 200; Smith, *Awaiting the King*, 212–213; Wetzel, "Splendid Vices," 299. On the importance of humility and openness, see Johnson, *Theology*, 244–246.

91. *City of God*, 1.35.

92. Gregory, *Politics*, 138. I develop this argument at length in chapter 10.

93. Milbank, *Theology and Social Theory*, 411.

94. *City of God*, 2.21. I follow Atkins and Dodaro in translating *res publica* as "commonwealth" (translator's notes in *Political Writings*, ed. Atkins and Dodaro, xxviii–xxix). For an insightful exposition of Cicero's understanding of *res publica*, see Schofield, "Cicero's Definition of *Res Publica*," 63–83. Griffiths, "Secularity," 40–41, prefers "public thing" as the translation of *res publica*.

95. *City of God*, 2.21.

96. Ibid.

97. Ibid.; 19.21–19.24.

98. Ibid., 19.23. Augustine's critique of Cicero's definition is complex, and therefore, its interpretation is contested. Scholars offer multiple interpretations of why, by Augustine's lights, the Roman republic failed to exhibit "true justice." For one original account that addresses and avoids limitations of other interpretations, see Alimi, "Slaves of God," 239–270.

99. *City of God*, 19.24, emphasis added.

100. Ibid.

101. The distinctively human aspect of the commonwealth is more evident in other formulations, for example, when he describes a "city" as "a concordant multitude of men" (*concors hominum multitudo*) (ibid., 1.15), or "a multitude of men bound together by some tie of fellowship" (*hominum multitudo aliquo societatis vinculo conligata*) (15.8).

102. Ibid., 19.24, 12.1, 12.3–4, 12.16, 11.27. As Augustine notes, "non-rational animals" have a capacity for sensory perception that "resembles knowledge," but only human beings have the capacity for rational judgment about these sensory perceptions, for "we perceive these things by our bodily senses in such a way that we do not judge them by means of those senses. For we have another, and far nobler, sense, belonging to the inner man, by which we perceive what things are just and what unjust: just by virtue of an intelligible idea, unjust by the lack of it" (11.27).

103. For a philosophical discussion of this difference, see Foot, *Natural Goodness*, 52–56.

104. "For no one suffers punishment for faults of nature, but for vices of the will; for even the vice which has come to be seems natural because strengthened by habit or because it has taken an undue hold derives its origin from the will. For we are here speaking of the vices of a natural creature whose mind is capable of possessing the light of reason by which the righteous is distinguished from the unrighteous. . . . It is, however, ridiculous to condemn as vices the faults of beasts and trees and other mutable and mortal things which entirely lack intellect or sensation or life, even if those faults should corrupt their perishable nature. For these creatures, at their Creator's will, have received a mode of existence which fits them" (*City of God*, 12.3–4).

105. Ibid., 19.7.

106. Augustine devotes Book 2 of *On Christian Teaching* to developing a distinctive account of "signs," suggesting that "attention should not be paid to the fact that they exist, but rather to the fact that they are signs or, in other words, that they signify. For a sign is a thing which of itself makes some other thing come to mind, besides the impression that it presents to the senses" (2.1.1). Signs "are those which living things give to each other, in order to show, to the best of their ability, the emotions of their minds, or anything that they have felt or learnt. There is no reason for us to signify something (that is, to give a sign) except to express and transmit to another's mind what is in the mind of the person who gives the sign" (2.2.3).

107. For insightful discussions of the importance of communication for sharing common goods, see O'Donovan, *Common Objects of Love*, 26–44; and von Heyking, "Disarming," 166–170. For the best analysis of Augustine's account of signs, see Markus, *Signs and Meanings*. For its political relevance, see Ogle, *Politics and the Earthly City*, 118–143.

108. Hollerich, "John Milbank," 320.

109. Klosko, *History of Political Theory*, 247. According to Klosko, "Augustine's new definition strips political life of its exalted trappings. A group of people does not comprise a state because of the values they seek. A state is simply their union. Human beings have wants and desires. In order to fulfill them they band together, united by common interests. The state, then, is simply an agency people erect to help get what they want—regardless of precisely what this is" (233).

110. Ibid., 247.

111. As Keys and Mitchell emphasize, Augustine believes it is better for political communities to founded by mutual "agreement" and "free consent of the people" than by force and

conquest (*City of God*, 5.17), but "it would be a mistake to read him as having the same understanding of consent (*concordia*) as modern social contract theorists" ("Augustine's Constitutionalism").

112. *City of God*, 19.5. On human sociality and relationality in Augustine's thought, see also Elshtain, "Augustine," 38–41.

113. Ibid., 14.1. As he writes, God bound human beings together "not only by similarity of nature, but by the affection of kinship" (12.22). See also Elshtain, "Augustine," 39.

114. Ibid., 12.28.

115. Von Heyking, *Augustine*, 85–88; "Disarming," 182–184.

116. To be clear, I am not suggesting Cicero is a contractualist. He explicitly rejects contractualism at *On the Commonwealth*, 1.39a, and *On Duties*, 1.158. In highlighting the contrast, I am simply calling attention to Augustine's focus on the affective components of common agreement that modern interpreters may neglect.

117. Contractualist connotations, for example, seem implicit in Klosko's identification of "common objects of love" with "common interests" (*History of Political Theory*, 247).

118. See Gregory, *Politics*, 66–69, 167–175; Stout, *Blessed Are the Organized*, 216–218.

119. Ibid., 23, 38, 66–74, 99–107, 149–175, 241–256, 366–367; Weithman, "Augustine's Political Philosophy," 249. For an insightful Augustinian account of the affections and its implications for contemporary political theory, see Hordern, *Political Affections*.

120. See Smith, *Awaiting the King*, 48–52, citing *City of God*, 19.24; 8–14, 214–215.

121. *City of God*, 19.24; Letter 137.5.17. I follow Clair's translation of *salus* as "health" in *Discerning the Good*, 82. For a discussion of the "health of the commonwealth" (*res publicae salus*), see ibid., 80–86.

122. *City of God*, 19.13.

123. Ibid. On peace as "first and foremost" among "worthy" temporal goods, see also Elshtain, "Augustine," 40.

124. Letter 130.6.12–7.14.

125. *City of God*, 19.13.

126. Ibid.; see also 19.11, 19.20.

127. Ibid., 19.11.

128. Ibid., 19.12.

129. Ibid., 19.13, 19.16.

130. Ibid., 19.13.

131. Markus, *Saeculum*, 173; Coleman, "St Augustine," 339. Although Griffiths acknowledges "earthly peace is a good," he also casts it as the mere absence of violence, "a breathing-space, a short pause in the shedding of blood" ("Secularity," 53).

132. Markus, *Saeculum*, 174.

133. Ibid. Noting this Augustinian "sense of the precariousness of human order secured and maintained in the teeth of chaos and perpetually threatened by deep human forces poised delicately between civilisation and savagery," Markus compares Augustine's vision to the bleak vision offered in *Lord of the Flies* and contrasts it with the Aristotelian tradition, which afforded a more positive vision of political community. The Augustinian account of civic friendship I advance below moves Augustine closer to Aristotle and Aquinas. For a helpful discussion and compatible account, see Gregory, *Politics*, 89–91.

134. Deane, *Political and Social Ideas*, 117. According to Deane, "This external, coercive, repressive, remedial order—and its main virtue is that it *is* an order—is clearly distinguished by
Augustine from the order or hierarchy found among the angels and in the whole City of God;
the latter is a spontaneous order of love and not an order of coercion or domination" (117;
see also 133–134, 138–143). Fortin advances a similar interpretation: "The whole of political society becomes punitive and remedial in nature and purpose. Its role is essentially a negative one,
that of castigating wrongdoers and of restraining evil among men by the use of force.... At best,
civil society can by its repressive action maintain relative peace among men and in this fashion
insure the minimal conditions under which the church is able to exercise its teaching and saving
ministry. Of itself it is incapable of leading to virtue" ("St. Augustine," 183–184). See also Schall,
"'Realism,'" 205, on the "state" as a "remedy" and a "necessary evil."

135. Standard interpretations reinforce this view. Citing Book 19, Lunn-Rockliffe, for example, suggests the "bleak assessment of the pragmatic necessity of political institutions was
eventually developed by Augustine to accompany his articulation of the centrality of sin to
man's post-fall political and social life" ("Early Christian Political Philosophy," 147). McConnell
advances a similar view when discussing Augustine's theory of punishment: "The best the state
can do is to keep people's worse desires in check. But even if the state is successful in the endeavor, it will not have created truly virtuous people.... At best, the state can see to it that the
external behavior of most of its citizens is as it should be; but its motivating force is fear of
punishment, and so most its citizens will not be truly virtuous" ("Torturing and Punishing,"
488). Similarly, Coleman interprets Augustine's view of politics as a "*modus vivendi*, not some
setting for the achievement of man's true needs, nor the setting for the performance of the morally good act.... Politics is a tragic necessity whose foundation is not justice but domination
by force or the threat of its use" ("St Augustine," 322). Assuming a negative view of "peace," she
argues that Augustine's "state" can offer "no more and no less than a shaky peace. The 'state'
cannot improve us. It contains and constrains us" (318; see also 332–336).

136. *City of God*, 19.14.

137. Ibid. See also Elshtain, "Augustine," 43.

138. For Augustine, Elshtain affirms, "human civic life is not simply a remedy for sin—with
order and coercion to constrain our wickedness—but an expression of our sociality; our desire
for fellowship; our capacity for a diffuse *caritas*" ("Augustine," 40). Weithman agrees that "claims
that Augustine has a 'negative' view of politics or that he thinks politics is 'morally neutral'
are ... overstated" ("Augustine's Political Philosophy," 244).

139. As Asmis notes, Cicero highlights this opposition through the use of a rhetorical antithesis between *ius* (law, justice) and *vis* (violence) ("State as a Partnership," 578).

140. Ibid., 595.

141. Cicero, *On Duties*, 1.31; see also 1.20.

142. Ibid.

143. Ibid., 1.22. In describing types of injustice, Cicero criticizes not only those who actively
harm others but those who, out of selfishness, "abandon those whom they ought to protect" or
contribute "nothing" to the common good (1.28). Justice, Cicero argues, is "the virtue which
beyond all others is completely devoted to and concerned with the interests of others," the
virtue without which the "commonwealth cannot possibly function" (*On the Commonwealth*,
2.69–2.70).

144. *City of God*, 19.12. See also Burroughs, *Christianity, Politics, and the Predicament of Evil,* 9–12, 18–20.

145. Ibid., 19.12–13.

146. See, e.g., ibid., 19.14, 19.17. For a helpful discussion of how civic friendship can contribute to Augustine's understanding of *oikeosis*, see Clair, *Discerning the Good,* 78–80. For a more positive account of civic friendship in Augustine's commonwealth, see von Heyking, *Augustine,* 77–89; "Disarming," 182–184; Elshtain, *Augustine,* 38–39, 96–97; "Augustine," 39–40; Gregory, *Politics,* 350–362; Alimi, "Slaves of God," 262–268.

147. Biggar, *Behaving in Public,* 61.

148. *City of God,* 19.16–17.

149. Ibid., 19.13. See also Elshtain, *Augustine,* 34–35; *Public Man, Private Woman,* 70, as cited by Johnson, *Theology,* 219–220.

150. *City of God,* 19.16.

151. Ibid., 19.12. Citing this passage, Klosko recognizes that earthly peace "partakes to some extent of the heavenly peace," but he does not draw the same implications for his understanding of Augustine's commonwealth. Instead, he follows Deane in seeing the purposes of the "state" as primarily "negative" (*History of Political Theory,* 246–249).

152. Markus, *Saeculum,* 174.

153. *City of God,* 18.54, 19.17.

154. Ibid., 19.17. For a helpful discussion of how the earthly city "limits" the kind of "compromise" achieved to temporal goods, see Ogle, *Politics and the Earthly City,* 154–155.

155. Ibid.

156. Cicero, *On the Commonwealth,* 2.42.69, as cited in *City of God,* 2.21.

157. Russell, for example, attributes a "theocratic" doctrine to Augustine (*History of Western Philosophy,* 363).

158. As Ogle argues, if the earthly city refuses the perfect peace of the heavenly city and confines what can be shared only to temporal goods, any peace that characterizes the earthly commonwealth remains imperfect when measured against the peace of the heavenly city (*Politics and the Earthly City,* 153–158).

159. Gregory, *Politics,* 82–107, provides a useful analysis of varieties of Augustinian liberalism.

160. Markus, *Saeculum,* 173. Coleman follows Markus in suggesting that "politics" is "neutral" for Augustine ("St Augustine," 332, 339).

161. Markus, *Saeculum,* 151.

162. Ibid., 173.

163. Markus, *Christianity and the Secular,* 44; see also 1–6, 44–48, 50–51, 63–64.

164. Ibid., 5–7, 40, 44, 63, 66–69. See also Bruno, *Political Augustinianism,* 53–54, 260–265.

165. See also Griffiths, "Secularity," 36–37, 54; Johnson, *Theology,* 214–215; and Kaufman, *Incorrectly Political,* 121–127.

166. See *Letter* 138, 155, 189.

167. *City of God,* 1.15. See also *Letter* 155.9, in *Political Writings,* 94: "The source of blessedness is not one thing for a human being and another for a city: a city is indeed nothing other than a like-minded mass of human beings."

168. *City of God,* 19.24.

169. Ibid., 12.28, comparing translations between Dyson and Bettenson. On Augustine's emphasis on "unity in plurality," see Johnson, *Theology*, 154–155. According to Elshtain, "The importance of plurality, of the many emerging from a unique one—for God began with the singular—cannot be overestimated in Augustine's work" ("Augustine," 39; see also *Augustine*, 43–44, 101–105).

170. This convergence around conclusions of reasoning about proximate goods rather than the *premises, final ends*, or *motivating reasons* that generate those conclusions is similar to the political and religious convergence endorsed by Stout, *Democracy and Tradition*, 63–91; Wolterstorff, "Role of Religion"; and Biggar, *Behaving in Public*, 45–78.

171. Sunstein, "Practical Reason," 268–269. See also Johnson, *Theology*, 233–249. Smith offers a similar Augustinian emphasis on the importance of finding "penultimate convergence even where there is ultimate divergence" (*Awaiting the King*, 218, emphasis removed). Markus at times seems to suggest something like incompletely theorized agreement around "intermediate principles" and values "which need not—indeed must not—be specified," but he tends to cast it too readily in terms of a "neutral" public sphere (*Saeculum*, 69, 101, 151, 173).

172. Ibid., 268–272, 276–280. I am grateful to Melissa Lane and Stephen Macedo for helpful discussions of Sunstein's account.

173. *City of God*, 19.17.

174. Ibid.

175. Ibid.

176. Rawls, *Political Liberalism*, 9–11, 211–254, 435–490.

177. Brandom, *Making It Explicit*, 177. See also Stout, *Democracy and Tradition*, 212; Wolterstorff, *Practices of Belief*, 247.

178. Letter 120.1.4, quoting 1 Peter 3:15.

179. Stout, *Democracy and Tradition*, 63–91; Wolterstorff, "Role of Religion"; Biggar, *Behaving in Public*, 45–78.

180. On immanent critique, see Stout, *Democracy and Tradition*, 69.

181. Lamb, "Augustine and Republican Theory," 101–102.

182. See Stout, *Democracy and Tradition*, 63–91.

183. The importance of disagreement and deliberation may itself be an object of incompletely theorized agreement: people with a wide range of moral, theological, and political commitments may agree on the need to debate and decide issues in particular ways, even if they disagree about the ultimate outcomes of that deliberative process. Even here, incompletely theorized agreement provides a practical means to encourage convergence and conversation in the face of deep disagreement. See Biggar, *Behaving in Public*, 60–61.

184. See *City of God*, 19.4.

185. Cicero, *On the Commonwealth*, 2.69, as cited in *City of God*, 2.21; Connolly, *Life of Roman Republicanism*, 38–39. For discussion of Cicero's more agonistic conception of concord, see Connolly, *Life of Roman Republicanism*, 23–64.

186. Ibid.

187. *City of God*, 19.17.

188. Biggar, *Behaving in Public*, 25–61.

189. Ibid., 43.

190. Ibid.

191. Ibid.

192. Hordern, "Loyalty, Conscience and Tense Communion," 167–184.

193. Ibid., 181.

194. Ibid., 182.

195. Ibid., 181, 184.

196. See Mathewes, *Theology of Public Life*, 261–307; Johnson, *Theology*, 82–173.

197. See *City of God*, 19.12–13. For discussion, see Mathewes, *Theology of Public Life*, 274–282; Johnson, *Theology*, 22, 140–173, 176–185; Burroughs, *Christianity, Politics, and the Predicament of Evil*, 8–12, 28n8. Milbank rightly emphasizes the "ontological priority of peace over conflict" in Augustine's thought but locates that vision of peace in an overly realized eschatological account of the institutional church and ignores how politics can also contribute to a positive peace in the *saeculum* (*Theology and Social Theory*, 392).

198. *City of God*, 19.5. Ogle, "Sheathing the Sword," 725–726, helpfully situates this passage within Augustine's critique of Stoic accounts of happiness in *City of God*, 19.1–7.

199. Rorty, "Religion as a Conversation-Stopper," 168–174. For a compelling response to Rorty, see Stout, *Democracy and Tradition*, 85–91. My Augustinian account of the conversation made possible by shared practices and expressive acts is indebted to Stout's account of democratic conversation, accountability, and reason-giving in *Democracy and Tradition*. It is also compatible with the Augustinian "theology of public life" that Mathewes develops in *Theology of Public Life* and the Augustinian "theology of public conversation" that Johnson advances in *Theology*, 233–249, esp. 241.

200. This approach is informed by Donald Davidson's "Radical Interpretation" and "Idea of a Conceptual Scheme." For other accounts of how common objects can facilitate conversation, contestation, and joint action, see also Honig, *Public Things*; and Bretherton, *Resurrecting Democracy*, 95.

201. Stout, *Democracy and Tradition*, 87–91.

202. See *City of God*, 19.1–3.

203. See, e.g., *Expositions of the Psalms*, 31(2).3–7; Sermon 198.2, 23A.1. For a philosophical account of the relation between intention and action, see Anscombe, *Intention*. For a useful analysis, see Moran and Stone, "Expression of Intention." I have benefited from conversations with Jeffrey Stout on Anscombe's philosophy of action and intention.

204. See Letter 90.

205. Ibid.

206. Letter 91.1, in *Political Writings*, 2.

207. Letter 91.1–3, in *Political Writings*, 2–3.

208. Letter 91.3, in *Political Writings*, 3.

209. For discussions of Augustine's invocation of Roman *exempla* and use of immanent critique in *City of God*, see Milbank, *Theology and Social Theory*, 391–393; von Heyking, "Disarming," 177; and Murphy, "Rhetoric of Roman Decline," 595–597.

210. *City of God*, 19.1, emphasis added.

211. Ibid., 4.1: "It was necessary, therefore, to demonstrate from the books in which their own authors have recorded and published the history of times gone by, that matters are far other than the ignorant suppose." According to Clark, one reason Augustine focused on deconstructing Roman literary and philosophical authorities was that Rome—especially after its sack in

410—was primarily a "city of books" since "books are the collective memory, the 'societal archive'" of Roman religion, history, and culture ("City of Books," 125–126, 130–131, citing Stock, *Augustine the Reader*, 13).

212. As Ogle argues, part of Augustine's purpose is to deconstruct and renarrate the history of Rome to disrupt readers' disordered love of Rome and reorder it to the City of God (*Politics and the Earthly City*, 90–118).

213. *City of God*, 2.18.

214. Ibid., 5.13.

215. Ibid., 2.21.

216. Cameron, *Christianity*, 25; see also 121. Murphy endorses Cameron's claim: "By establishing Augustine's *bona fides* as one versed in Roman literature and history, by using familiar figures and arguments to prepare the ground for more controversial ones, Augustine has opened his work with a significant gesture to his classically-trained audience" ("Rhetoric of Roman Decline," 597).

217. See O'Donovan, *Common Objects of Love*, 22.

218. *City of God*, 14.6.

219. O'Donovan, *Common Objects of Love*, 22.

220. Ibid., 22–23.

221. See Stout, *Blessed Are the Organized*, 53–69, on the way in which anger, grief, and hatred of domination can mobilize citizens to form grassroots coalitions and facilitate mutual recognition and democratic accountability.

222. Appiah, *Honor Code*, 127.

223. Sen, *Idea of Justice*, 21. According to Sen, "It is fair to assume that Parisians would not have stormed the Bastille, Gandhi would not have challenged the empire on which the sun used not to set, Martin Luther King would not have fought white supremacy in 'the land of the free and the home of the brave,' without their sense of manifest injustices that could be overcome. They were not trying to achieve a perfectly just world (even if there were any agreement on what that would be like), but they did want to remove clear injustices to the extent they could" (vii). In other words, incompletely theorized agreement on injustice—an object of refusal—made common hope and cooperation possible, even while they had "a continuing divergence of views on other matters" (26).

224. *City of God*, 19.12.

225. On a republican understanding of liberty as "security from domination," "[l]ove of liberty and hatred of domination are two sides of the same coin" (Stout, *Blessed Are the Organized*, 59).

226. *City of God*, 14.28.

227. Ibid., 19.4.

228. Ibid., 19.5, 22.23. See also Letter 153.12–15, in *Political Writings*, 77–80.

229. *City of God*, 19.4. "It is not simply pagans, then, whose virtue is corrupted by the love of praise," Herdt argues. For Augustine, "the imperfect virtue of Christians is often corrupted by the same ordering to self that rendered pagan virtue merely counterfeit virtue. We cannot simply say that Christian virtue is true but imperfect while pagan virtue is not virtue at all. Just as in this world the city of God and the city of man are inextricably mixed, so the splendid vices are found among Christians as well as pagans" (*Putting on Virtue*, 60). Biggar makes a similar point

from the perspective of soteriology: "[I]f Christians consider themselves to have been saved from sin, they consider themselves at the same time to be in the *process* of being saved from it. . . . They remain not only imperfect, but corrupt. . . . What this means is that, even if all who profess themselves Christians were 'saved,' they would nevertheless share with the 'unsaved' non-Christians a common need for the enlightenment and correction of moral understanding—and for the growth of moral character. Therefore, Christians should certainly not presume that they have nothing to learn. And since they have reason to suppose that the church is not the only place where true moral words are spoken, they should bend a humble and docile ear to what is said outside of it" (*Behaving in Public*, 27–28). See also Wetzel, "Splendid Vices," 276; Ogle, *Politics and the Earthly City*, 57–58; Kent, "Augustine's Ethics," 228–229.

230. As Markus argues, "Being imperfectly just is not the same thing as being unjust" (*Christianity and the Secular*, 44). "Augustine's polemic against the virtues of pagans should not induce us to believe that all acts of virtue, to be virtuous, need to be perfectly virtuous, that justice can be real only when perfect" (43). Markus's claim challenges Fleischacker's assumption that "[t]here is, and can be, no justice in people who are not subject to God" (*Short History of Distributive Justice*, 11). For accounts of Augustine on "imperfect" virtue, see Markus, *Christianity and the Secular*, 44; and Irwin, "Splendid Vices?" I engage this issue in chapter 10. For another Augustinian account affirming the need to recognize "degrees" of virtue and vice while evaluating the end toward which each is directed, see Smith, *Awaiting the King*, 217–218.

231. Markus, *Christianity and the Secular*, 45.

232. See chapter 10.

233. *Literal Meaning of Genesis*, 11.15.20. For an insightful discussion, see Johnson, *Theology*, 161–162.

234. See, e.g., *City of God*, 15.3. In Letter 137.5.17, Augustine argues that "the best city is established and protected only by the foundation and bond of faith and solid harmony when the common good is loved, namely, God, who is the highest and truest good." As John Burnaby argues, "If the *Summum Bonum* is by its very nature the *bonum commune*, a good which can be possessed only by being shared, then the desire and pursuit of it can never be the desire and pursuit of a *bonum privatem*" (*Amor Dei*, 127). Herdt, *Putting on Virtue*, 56, discusses Burnaby's insight to suggest continuity between love of God and neighbor, while Johnson, *Theology*, 159, affirms this claim to emphasize how "citizens of the Heavenly City are no longer merely individuals, turned in on themselves and their lower, private goods, but are together united around the common good of God in the Body of Christ, the Church of Christ, by the Holy Spirit."

235. Johnson, *Theology*, 153–163, offers a particularly useful discussion of "common" and "private" goods. See also Markus, *Saeculum*, xvii–xviii; Griffiths, "Secularity," 39–40; Ogle, *Politics and the Earthly City*, 75–76; and Kent, "Augustine's Ethics," 218.

236. *Literal Meaning of Genesis*, 11.15.20.

237. *City of God*, 5.15; see also 5.18.

238. Ibid., 5.13.

239. See Herdt, *Putting on Virtue*, 60–61.

240. Challenging those who focus only on the evils of the earthly city, Augustine insists that "it is not rightly said that the goods which this city desires are not goods; for, in its own human fashion, even that city is better when it possesses them than when it does not" (*City of God*, 15.4; see Gregory, *Politics*, 53).

241. *City of God*, 19.5.

242. *Expositions of the Psalms*, 31(2).5.

243. *City of God*, 19.17.

244. Stevenson, Smith, and Madden, *Roman Coins*, 757; Clark, "Spes."

245. Lloyd, *Problem of Grace*, 70–88. See my discussion of Lloyd in chapter 1.

246. Johnson, *Theology*, 177.

247. Ibid., 176–177, 253.

248. Ibid., 169. Johnson sometimes equates the "earthly city" with the earthly commonwealth in ways I seek to avoid.

249. Bretherton, *Christianity*, 83. Elsewhere, Bretherton describes Augustine's posture as a kind of "hopeful realism" (85). See also Mathewes's chapter on "hopeful citizenship" in *Theology of Public Life*, 214–260.

Chapter 9. An Example of Hope: Augustine's Political Life in Letters

1. As Marrou writes, "[W]e know many facts about him, facts more numerous and more profound than about any man of the ancient world, with the sole possible exception of Cicero" (*Saint Augustine*, 59).

2. Mathewes, "Book One," 8. MacIntyre makes a similar point when describing *Confessions* as "a prayer of narrative acknowledgment": "It is only as Augustine puts himself into the hands of God that he can write truly and truthfully about himself, ridding himself of those distortions that are the expression of pride" (*God, Philosophy, Universities*, 28).

3. *Confessions*, 10.33.50.

4. Leyser, "Problem of Authority," 19.

5. One notable exception is the work of Peter Iver Kaufman, who bases his account of Augustine's "pessimism" in a deep and expansive knowledge of Augustine's letters to public officials. See Kaufman, *On Agamben*, and *Incorrectly Political*.

6. See, e.g., Dodaro and Atkins, "Introduction," in *Political Writings*; Dodaro, *Christ and the Just Society*; Clair, *Discerning the Good*.

7. Aristotle, *On Rhetoric*, 1.2.3–6. For a historical overview, see Kennedy, *Classical Rhetoric*, 74–93.

8. Kennedy suggests the Romans downplayed the role of ethos as a primary means of persuasion (ibid., 178–180). While Cicero made room for *logos* and *pathos* in his emphasis on instructing and motivating audiences, he cast the orator's second duty as delighting audiences rather than projecting character, thereby minimizing the traditional role of *ethos* in Greek rhetoric. In this context, Kennedy argues, Augustine's emphasis on the life of the speaker marks an innovative recovery in the tradition (179–180). John O. Ward agrees. Tracing the "Augustinian 'revolution,'" Ward argues that Augustine's discussion of rhetoric in *On Christian Teaching* "is in some senses a revolutionary work as it attempted to divert rhetorical attention away from Greco-Roman technical precepts, toward *imitatio* based on persuasive and exemplary biblical models" ("Roman Rhetoric," 356).

While I agree with this renewed emphasis on the value that Augustine places on imitation and character, I am not convinced he sees this emphasis as a departure from his Roman sources. When we move beyond *On Christian Teaching* (which is Kennedy's and Ward's focus) and look at a letter Augustine wrote to Firmus, who had shared the progress his son had been making in his "rhetorical exercises" (Letter 2*.12), we see Augustine affirming his view that Firmus's son should develop good character and aim "to please good people . . . not only in his words and speeches but also in his life and actions" (Letter 2*.13). Importantly, Augustine suggests he is following Cicero in offering this counsel: "For what the most prolific and most elegant teacher of this skill said is absolutely true: 'Eloquence along with wisdom is most beneficial to cities, but eloquence without wisdom generally does much harm but is never beneficial'" (Letter 2*.12, citing Cicero, *On Invention*, 1.1). According to Augustine, "[T]he ancients thought that they should define not the man of eloquence—for eloquence can exist without wisdom—but an orator in such a way as to say that he was 'a good man skilled in speaking'" (ibid.). Here, Augustine seems to suggest that Cicero and "the ancients" *assume* the importance of character in their rhetorical writings, even if they do not make it one of the three explicit duties of the orator. See also Martin, "'Abundant Supply of Discourse,'" 19–20n19.

9. Kennedy, *Classical Rhetoric*, 179–180.

10. *On Christian Teaching*, 4.27.59.

11. See ibid., 4.27.59–4.30.63. Augustine's claim that those who are evil can still teach something beneficial stands in tension with his endorsement of Cicero's view that "eloquence without wisdom generally does much harm but is never beneficial" (Letter 2*.12, discussed in n7 above).

12. *On Christian Teaching*, 4.28.61–4.29.61. See Martin, "Abundant Supply of Discourse,'" 7. Notice the rhyme in the original Latin couplet: *quasi copia dicendi forma uiuendi*. For more on *copia dicendi* as a "thoroughly classical expression" used twenty-two times in Cicero's rhetorical works, see ibid., 8, 17n5.

13. Ibid., 7.

14. See ibid., esp. 8–15.

15. Letter 153.18, in *Political Writings*, 82.

16. Letter 133.3, in *Political Writings*, 63. See also Letter 139.2.

17. Letter 91.3–6, 10, in *Political Writings*, 3–5, 8.

18. Letter 91.10, in *Political Writings*, 7.

19. Letter 91.6, 10, in *Political Writings*, 5, 7.

20. Mathewes, *Theology of Public Life*, 143; *Republic of Grace*, 231–233. I engage his account below.

21. Milbank, *Theology and Social Theory*, 392, 440–442; "'Postmodern Critical Augustinianism,'" 229–233.

22. Hauerwas, *After Christendom?*, 40.

23. Mathewes, who does as much as any contemporary Augustinian to encourage Christian participation in political life, acknowledges that Augustine's "first and primary polis is the church, the republic of grace, and the fundamental political task for this polis lies in the evangelical extension and ascetical preparation of its citizens to be fit to bear the joy that is humanity's eschatological destiny." Far from authorizing a "sectarian" theology, Mathewes argues that recognizing Augustine as a "fundamentally Christian thinker speaking primarily to Christians" attends to his "particularities" in a way that generic attempts to apply Augustine in "public discussion" do not ("Augustinian Look at Empire," 293).

24. See Augustine's exchanges with Marcellinus in Letter 136 and 138 and Volusian in Letter 137.5.20. Atkins and Dodaro translate *rei publicae moribus* as "ethics of citizenship" in Letter 136,

in *Political Writings*, 29. I adopt "practices of the commonwealth" from Clair, *Discerning the Good*, 81. See also Fortin, "St. Augustine," 201.

25. Letter 138.2.9–10. See also Letter 137.5.20. For an illuminating discussion, see Clair, *Discerning the Good*, 80–86.

26. Letter 138.2.10. In Letter 137.5.17, Augustine highlights the political value of the double-love commandments. "In these commandments there is also found the praiseworthy safety of the state, for the best city is established and protected only by the foundation and bond of faith and solid harmony when the common good is loved, namely, God, who is the highest and truest good, and when human beings love one another in complete sincerity in him by loving one another on account of him from whom they cannot hide the disposition with which they love."

27. Letter 138.2.11.

28. Ibid.

29. On Augustine's rejection of Eusebius's views, see Markus, *Saeculum*, 52–55.

30. Breyfogle suggests that "Augustine recognized that reflection on political things is always the prudential consideration of contingent circumstances largely dependent on a people's self-understanding of their age" ("Augustinian Understanding," 219).

31. See Romans 13:1–7.

32. *City of God*, 19.17.

33. Ibid.

34. *City of God*, 10.1, 10.5.

35. For an insightful discussion, see Alimi, "Slaves of God," 264–265.

36. King, "Letter from Birmingham City Jail," 293, citing *Free Choice of the Will*, 1.5.11, which Peter King translates as "a law that is not just does not seem to me to be a law." See also Alimi, "Slaves of God," 265n135.

37. We might say that Augustine's roles accord with what Andrew Sabl, *Ruling Passions*, has described as the political "offices" of activist and organizer.

38. Gregory, *Politics*, 192–196.

39. Bretherton, *Christianity*, 71–125; *Resurrecting Democracy*, 39–40.

40. Mathewes marks the contrast between "engagement" and "escape," suggesting that "Augustine is the ultimate theorist and therapist of escapism." In its place, Augustine advances a "theology of engagement" (*Theology of Public Life*, 22–23, 31–35).

41. For an account of priests and bishops in Augustine's time, see Brown, *Power and Persuasion*; *Augustine of Hippo*, 183–197; Dodaro, "Church and State," 176–184; Cameron, *Christianity*, 120–154.

42. For an excellent overview to which I am indebted, see Dodaro, "Between the Two Cities"; see also "Church and State." Brian A. Williams also draws on Augustine's letters and sermons to highlight his role as a "social activist, legal reformer, and mentoring pastor" (*Potter's Rib*, 191–208, at 194).

43. On the role of the tribune in the Roman republic, see, e.g., Connolly, *Life of Roman Republicanism*, 52–55.

44. Dodaro, "Between the Two Cities," 102, 112n8, citing Letter 100, 133, 134, 139, 151, 153, 155.11; *Expositions of the Psalms*, 50; Possidius, "Life," §20. See also Kolbet, "Freedom from Grim Necessity," 144, who notes Augustine's "consistent" opposition to the death penalty.

45. Letter 153.9–11, 15–16, in *Political Writings*, 76–77, 79–81.

46. Letter 153.19, in *Political Writings*, 82–83.

47. Letter 153.3, in *Political Writings*, 73.

48. Letter 100.1, in *Political Writings*, 135. Kolbet, "Freedom from Grim Necessity," 144, notes that Augustine gave similar advice in Sermon 13.8 to an audience in Carthage that likely included judges: "[D]o not condemn people to death, or while you are attacking the sin you will destroy the man. Do not condemn to death, and there will be someone there who can repent. . . . Do not have a person put to death, and you will have someone who can be reformed."

49. See Letter 133, 134, 139, 153.2; Dodaro, "Between the Two Cities," 102. Augustine's call for "gentleness" is especially striking in a letter to Apringius, who is responsible for administering punishment to the Circumcellions and Donatists who had brutally attacked and killed Augustine's fellow Catholics (Letter 134.4, in *Political Writings*, 65–66).

50. On the use of violence and torture in the empire, see, e.g., Brown, "Religious Coercion," 107–116, at 115; Harries, *Law and Empire*, 118–134; MacMullen, "Judicial Savagery." For thoughtful accounts of Augustine's opposition to torture, see Ogle, "Sheathing the Sword"; and Kolbet, "Freedom from Grim Necessity." Other scholars also note Augustine's critique of torture. See, e.g., Clair, *Discerning the Good*, 90n42, and Dodaro, "Between the Two Cities," 102–103.

51. Letter 104.17, in *Political Writings*, 21.

52. Letter 91.9, 104.17, 133.2, 134, 139.2, 153, in *Political Writings*, 6–7, 21–22, 62, 63–66, 67, 71–88; Dodaro, "Between the Two Cities," 102–103. On the importance of "humanity," see Ogle, "Sheathing the Sword."

53. See, e.g., Letter 133, 153, 91.9, 104.17, in *Political Writings*, 61–63, 71–88, 6–7, 21–22. See also Sermon 277A.1.

54. Sermon 355.5, also cited by Kolbet, "Freedom from Grim Necessity," 144n30.

55. *City of God*, 19.6.

56. Kaufman, "Augustine's Dystopia," 66.

57. McConnell, "Torturing and Punishing," 481–482, 490.

58. Deane, *Political and Social Ideas*, 301–302n61, 135–137; Markus, *Saeculum*, 99–100.

59. Ogle, "Sheathing the Sword."

60. Ibid., 720–721, 723–732.

61. Ibid., 726.

62. Ibid., 732–741, at 732.

63. Ibid., 741.

64. See, e.g., Elshtain, "Problem of 'Dirty Hands.'" Though Elshtain does not cite Augustine explicitly in "Problem of 'Dirty Hands,'" her defense of "coercive interrogation" or "torture lite" aligns with her Augustinian (and Nieburhian) argument for "just war against terror" in *Just War*. On Elshtain's "applied Augustinianism" in relation to torture, see Gregory, "Taking Love Seriously." On Augustine's views of torture in relation to contemporary debates, see also Kolbet, "Freedom from Grim Necessity," 139, who argues that "no appeal can be made to Augustine's life or thought to authorize torture under any circumstances."

65. Von Heyking, *Augustine*, 2.

66. For a summary, see Lamb, "Augustine and Republican Liberty," 119–121.

67. Ibid.

68. Von Heyking, *Augustine*, 222–257; Deane, *Political and Social Ideas*, 172–220. For an overview, see Lamb, "Augustine and Republican Liberty," 121–129.

69. Brown, "Religious Coercion"; Bowlin, "Augustine Justifying Coercion."

70. Bowlin, "Augustine Justifying Coercion," 53.

71. Brown, *Authority and the Sacred*, 44–45; von Heyking, *Augustine*, 240–248; Harries, *Law and Empire*, 92–96. For an overview, see Lamb, "Augustine and Republican Liberty," 137–141.

72. Lamb, "Augustine and Republican Liberty," 137–141.

73. Ibid., 121, 141–159.

74. Ibid., 156.

75. See Possidius, "Life," §19; Dodaro, "Between the Two Cities," 99; Brown, *Augustine of Hippo*, 190–192, 222. For a helpful historical overview, see Dodaro, "Church and State," 176–178; and Lamoreaux, "Episcopal Courts." For an excellent account of Roman law and adjudication in late antiquity, including Augustine's involvement, see Harries, *Law and Empire*, esp. 172–211.

76. Lamoreaux, "Episcopal Courts," 143.

77. Ibid., 151–152.

78. E.g., Letter 133.2; Lamoreaux, "Episcopal Courts," 161–164, 156, 167.

79. Lamoreaux, "Episcopal Courts," 149, 152–153, 167.

80. Ogle, "Sheathing the Sword," 742.

81. *Expositions of the Psalms*, 80.21, 118.24.3, as cited by Lamoreaux, "Episcopal Courts," 153; Possidius, "Life," §19.

82. Dodaro, "Church and State," 177; Lamoreaux, "Episcopal Courts," 148–149.

83. See, e.g., Letter 24*; Dodaro, "Between the Two Cities," 105–106; Lamoreaux, "Episcopal Courts," 159.

84. Dodaro, "Between the Two Cities," 105–107. See also Markus, *Saeculum*, 57.

85. Dodaro, "Between the Two Cities," 106.

86. Letter 10*, in *Political Writings*, 43–47; Dodaro, "Between the Two Cities," 104–105.

87. On how Augustine and fellow African bishops "sought to institute reforms to the practice of slavery in order to limit its growth and mitigate its harmful effects," see Dodaro, "Between the Two Cities," 104. On Augustine's emphasis on the accountability of masters for the wellbeing of enslaved persons, see Alimi, "Slaves of God," 228–237. For more on Augustine on slavery, see also Elia, "Ethics in the Afterlife of Slavery"; "Slave Christologies"; Elm, "Sold to Sin"; and Garnsey, *Ideas of Slavery*, 220–235.

88. Letter 115. For discussion, see Dodaro, "Between the Two Cities," 106–107; and Harries, *Law and Empire*, 92–93.

89. Letter 115. See also Letter 113, 114, and 116.

90. Letter 115; Dodaro, "Between the Two Cities," 107.

91. Dodaro, "Between the Two Cities," 107.

92. Ibid., 108.

93. Ibid.

94. Ibid., 109–110. The bishops, for example, petitioned the imperial court to allow their churches to support the ecclesiastical manumission of enslaved persons, a practice where slave-owners appeared in church to emancipate those who were enslaved who, in turn, gained citizenship in the Roman Empire.

95. Brown, *Through the Eye*, 326.

96. As Williams highlights, one of Augustine's most important forms of service was his "practice of mentoring for pastoral formation" (see *Potter's Rib*, 200–208).

97. See, e.g., Letter 157.35–36, 220.11; *Expositions of the Psalms*, 38.12, 102.12–13, 136.13–14; Sermon 9.20, 25.7–8, 56.12, 350b, 390; see also *Enchiridion*, 19.70, 19.72, 20.76. For a comprehensive account of Augustine's preaching on poverty and wealth, see Brown, *Through the Eye*, 322–384. See also Brown, "Crisis of Wealth," 5–30; Lepelley, "Facing Wealth and Poverty"; Clair, *Discerning the Good*, 107–129.

98. Letter 268; Dodaro, "Between the Two Cities," 106.

99. Possidius, "Life," §24.

100. *City of God*, 5.19. For discussion, see Keys and Mitchell, "Augustine's Constitutionalism."

101. Markus, "City or Desert?," esp. 158–160. See also Martin, "Politics of Monasticism," 165–186; and "'Abundant Supply of Discourse.'"

102. Letter 153.1, in *Political Writings*, 71. See also Letter 155.17.

103. *City of God*, 1.15, 1.24, 5.12, 5.18. For further discussion, see chapter 10.

104. Letter 91.1, in *Political Writings*, 2.

105. Ibid., citing Cicero's *On the Commonwealth*. See also Letter 91.3.

106. See Letter 189, in *Political Writings*, 214–218. For insightful analyses, see Clair, *Discerning the Good*, 87–93; Smith, *Awaiting the King*, 198–201; and "The Benediction Option or the Augustinian Call?"

107. Letter 189.5, in *Political Writings*, 216. Augustine refers to earlier conversation with Boniface in Letter 220.3, 12, where Augustine and Alypius encouraged him to stay in office. O'Donnell discusses this incident in *Augustine*, 225–226.

108. Letter 189.1, 189.5–8, in *Political Writings*, 215–218.

109. Letter 189.6, in *Political Writings*, 217. On "necessity" in the letter, see Clair, *Discerning the Good*, 89–93.

110. "In these letters," Smith affirms, "we hear something of Augustine's hopes for Boniface and those like him: the hope for faithful agents of the coming kingdom who answer the call to public life, who administer the common good in this *saeculum* of our waiting" (*Awaiting the King*, 200).

111. Letter 220, in *Political Writings*, 218–225.

112. Letter 220.7, in *Political Writings*, 221.

113. Clair, *Discerning the Good*, 92, 131–134.

114. Letter 220.1, in *Political Writings*, 218–219.

115. Letter 220.11, in *Political Writings*, 224.

116. Letter 220.10–11, in *Political Writings*, 223–224.

117. Letter 220.10, in *Political Writings*, 223–224.

118. Letter 220.6, 9, citing 1 John 2:15–17; Letter 220.12, in *Political Writings*, 221, 223–224.

119. Clair, *Discerning the Good*, 87–93, 130–135.

120. *City of God*, 12.8. On the implications of this passage for Augustine's understanding of political community, see Ogle, *Politics and the Earthly City*, 152–153.

121. Clair, *Discerning the Good*, 87–93.

122. *City of God*, 14.28. See also Griffiths, "Secularity," 49.

123. Arendt, *Human Condition*, 14.

124. Ibid., 16n14, citing *City of God*, 19.19.

125. *City of God*, 19.19.

126. Ibid. "For *epi*," he adds, "means 'over' and *skopein* is 'to see.' If we so wish, therefore, we can translate *episcopein* into Latin as 'to oversee'" (19.19). See also Sermon 340A.4 on the ordination of a bishop where he alludes to the same etymology to emphasize a bishop's responsibility to serve.

127. *City of God*, 19.19.

128. Kaufman, "Augustine's Dystopia," 73.

129. Possidius, "Life," §4.

130. Letter 21.3.

131. Letter 21.1. Here we see Augustine's excessive rhetoric again. Surely there were things in Augustine's context that were "more difficult, more laborious, and more dangerous" than being a bishop, priest, or deacon. Being enslaved, for example, would be one. I am grateful to Colleen E. Mitchell for this point.

132. Sermon 340A.1. On the responsibility of bishops, Augustine adds, "[T]o put it in a nutshell, we are your servants; your servants, but also your fellow servants. We are your servants, but all of us here have one Lord and master" (340A.3). For discussion, see Williams, *Potter's Rib*, 206.

133. Sermon 340A.1.

134. Sermon 340A.3–5.

135. For the classic text on servant leadership, see Greenleaf, *Servant Leadership*.

136. Sermon 339.2–3.

137. Sermon 339.1. See also *Catechising the Uninstructed*, 1.1.2; Williams, *Potter's Rib*, 200–201.

138. On Augustine's personal tensions with accepting praise, see Sermon 339.1.

139. Sermon 339.4.

140. Ibid.

141. Letter 48.1: "The dark tumult of worldly courtroom procedures, after all, often wounds and weakens our prayers. Even if we do not have such cases of our own, those who force us to go one mile, and with whom we are commanded to go another two, impose upon us such great burdens that we can scarcely catch our breath."

142. Sermon 302.17.

143. Possidius, "Life," §19; see also §24. Augustine offers an example of his duties of ministry in Letter 110.5.

144. Kaufman, "Augustine's Dystopia," 60.

145. See, e.g., Possidius, "Life," §§19–20; Letter 154.

146. Kaufman, *On Agamben*, ix; "Augustine's Dystopia," 66, 69.

147. See Kaufman, *On Agamben*, esp. 95–96, 146, 13–28.

148. Kaufman, *Incorrectly Political*, 230.

149. Ibid., 104, 230, 126.

150. Ibid., 120, citing *City of God*, 18.1 (Bettenson translation).

151. See e.g., Kaufman, *Incorrectly Political*, 110–113, 228.

152. Ibid., 99, 118.

153. Ibid., 8, 126, 230.

154. Ibid., 8, 126, 228.

155. Ibid., 228, 230.

156. On what Augustine "expected," see ibid., 126; on "expectations," see 229.

157. Ogle makes a similar distinction between hope and expectation in relation to Kaufman in "Healing Hope," 49.

158. See, e.g., Kaufman, *Incorrectly Political*, 126.

159. Kaufman, "Augustine's Dystopia," 61–63. On Augustine's appeals to the emperor, see, e.g., Letter 10*. Dodaro affirms that Augustine's "political activism" was "not programmatic": "[H]e does not seek to implement a particular political plan. His activity responds to particular social ills as they arise among people for whose pastoral care he feels responsible" ("Between the Two Cities," 111)

160. On the importance of the local, see especially Bretherton, *Christianity*, 71–125.

161. Kaufman, *Redeeming Politics*, 146. See also Kaufman, "Augustine's Dystopia," 66–69; Markus, *Saeculum*, 149–150. In *Incorrectly Political*, Kaufman regrets his earlier claim that Augustine "offered a personalist platform for the renewal of political culture" (231), but I believe the earlier claim remains accurate.

162. Kaufman, "Augustine's Dystopia," 66–69; *Incorrectly Political*, 126.

163. Markus emphasizes the "fragmentary, piecemeal, and *ad hoc* character" of political engagement inspired by eschatological hope (*Saeculum*, 171). Similarly, Smith identifies four "Augustinian principles" that support "ad hoc" and "selective collaborations for the common good" (*Awaiting the King*, xiv, 209, 216–221).

164. See, e.g., Kaufman, *Incorrectly Political*, 35, 45, 108, 110, 112, 125, 130–131.

165. See, e.g., ibid., 118, 125, 130–132.

166. Ogle, *Politics and the Earthly City*, 166.

167. Ibid., citing *City of God*, 5.20.

168. Ibid.

169. Ibid., 167–168, citing Letter 153.17–19.

170. Ibid., 168, citing *City of God*, 19.19.

171. *City of God*, 10.1.

172. Ibid., 10.5. Augustine emphasizes in particular the "sacrifice of a contrite heart."

173. Ibid., 10.6. See also Menchaca-Bagnulo, "Deeds and Words," 75, 82–88.

174. Ogle, *Politics and the Earthly City*, 171–180; "*Latreia* and Its Parodies"; Menchaca-Bagnulo, "Deeds and Words"; von Heyking, *Augustine*, 175–180; Gregory, *Politics*, 269–270, 379.

175. *City of God*, 19.19.

176. Mitchell and Keys, "Love's Labor Leisured," 320. See also Elshtain, "Augustine," 43.

177. Ogle, *Politics and the Earthly City*, 180.

178. Kaufman, "Hopefully, Augustine," 19.

179. Ibid., 24.

180. For replies to Kaufman, see Lamb, "Augustine on Hope and Politics"; and Ogle, "Healing Hope."

181. See, e.g., Kaufman, *Incorrectly Political*, 1–9, 121–127, 227–232.

182. See, e.g., Deane, *Political and Social Ideas*, 60, 68, 242; Burt, "Courageous Optimism," 55; Paolucci, introduction to Augustine's *Political Writings*, vii; Hollingworth, *Pilgrim City*, 16, 85–87, 204; Bruno, *Political Augustinianism*, 230–244.

183. Stout, *Democracy and Tradition*, 58. As Stout argues, "If you make hope depend on the thought that things are going to keep getting better, or on the thought that things will all work

out in the end, then you are bound to be demoralized before long. There is no persuasive evidence for members of our generation that things are getting better on the whole or that everything will work out in historical time. If, however, you set your sights on making a difference, you can give hope a foothold in the life of the people itself" (59).

184. Kaufman, "Augustine's Dystopia," 69–70.

185. Kaufman, *Incorrectly Political*, 229.

186. Mittleman, *Hope in a Democratic Age*, 14–15, makes a similar point about the need for both "emancipatory" and "conserving" hope.

187. See chapter 6.

188. Griffiths, "Secularity," 51–53, rightly notes that Augustine offers a politics of both "longing" and "lament," though I resist his suggestion that Augustine advocates a form of "political quietism" in regard to positive political outcomes.

189. *Expositions of the Psalms*, 42.2; see also 54.3, 85.23, 100.3, 101.1.2, 139.2.2, 148.1. I am grateful to Sarah Stewart-Kroeker for pointing me to several of these passages.

190. *Expositions of the Psalms*, 101(1)2.

191. *City of God*, 19.4, 19.20. On the relation between joy and hope for God, see also *Expositions of the Psalms*, 54.3, 85.23, 100.3, 148.1.1; *Confessions*, 10.1.1.

192. See, e.g., Hauerwas, *After Christendom?*, 40, 44, 108; *Peaceable Kingdom*, 108. For an analysis and critique, see Burroughs, *Christianity, Politics, and the Predicament of Evil*, 136–138, 160–161; and Stout, *Democracy and Tradition*, 147–161.

193. Mitchell and Keys, "Love's Labor Leisured." See also Smith's "*liturgical* political theology" in *Awaiting the King*, 151.

194. Mathewes, *Theology of Public Life*, 11–14, 26–27, 87; Johnson, *Theology*, 220–224, 252–253.

195. Mathewes, *Theology of Public Life*, 11–14, 26–27, 87. For a similar view, see Burroughs, *Christianity, Politics, and the Predicament of Evil*, 67–69, 192–233.

196. *City of God*, 1.29.

197. Letter 189.5, in *Political Writings*, 216–217. Smith, *Awaiting the King*, 198–201, also cites this exchange with Boniface to defend his Augustinian account of political engagement.

198. See Mathewes, "Augustinian Look at Empire," 303; *Republic of Grace*, 11; *Theology of Public Life*, 26–27.

199. Mathewes, *Republic of Grace*, 230–233; *Theology of Public Life*, 26–27, 261. Finley acknowledges non-ecclesial meanings of *leitourgia* in Greek and translates it as "public service" (*Politics in the Ancient World*, 36–38).

200. My description of "liturgy" draws on Mathewes, *Republic of Grace*, 230–233. See also Johnson, *Theology*, 220–221.

201. Mathewes, *Republic of Grace*, 231, 233.

202. Ibid., 11, 230–233.

203. Mathewes, *Theology of Public Life*, 261, 1–2, 143.

204. Ibid., 1.

205. Ibid., 214–260; Mathewes, *Republic of Grace*, 218–243.

206. Smith, *Awaiting the King*, 13.

207. Ibid., 169, 16, 54–60.

208. See ibid., 54–58, 96–97, 192.

209. See ibid., 54–58, 96, 192, 168, 201–204.

210. Embracing an expansive view of the "political" that resists reducing it to "government" or "state" or seeing it merely as a "space" or "sphere" where citizens simply express their reasons, beliefs, or values, Smith emphasizes politics as comprising a set of formative practices that shape citizens' habits and loves in their common life (ibid., 8–12, 35, 194–195).

211. *City of God*, 6.6–7; Smith, *Awaiting the King*, 23, 27–31, 18.

212. Smith, *Awaiting the King*, 52, 94–97, 192, 197.

213. See ibid. 132–133, 198–201, 209–221, xiv.

214. Ibid., 218–221, emphasis removed. One key difference is that, whereas I seek to show more compatibility between aspects of Augustine's political thought and aspects of contemporary liberal democracy, Smith seems overly critical of "liberal democracy," casting it as an "*insidious* tradition" (39), even while encouraging Christians to be politically engaged within it (17, 94–95, 215). For discussion, see Gregory, "What Hippo and Grand Rapids Have to Say to Each Other," 121.

215. Ibid., 96, emphasis in original. According to Smith, "Christian worship constitutes the 'civics' of the city of God, forming a people who are sent out for the sake of the common good, sent to love not only their neighbors but even their enemies" (221; see also 151, 153).

216. Farneth, "A Politics of Tending and Transformation," 115–116; Smith, "A Response to Critics," 131. Smith's emphasis on positive "spillover" or "ripple" effects implies a similar unidirectional movement outward (*Awaiting the King*, 58, 151), but his attention to ethnography as a way to "affirm positive interplay between 'public' and 'ecclesial' liturgies, attuned to listen and look for the work of the Spirit beyond the church" implies a more dynamic, bidirectional relationship (191).

217. Smith, "A Response to Critics," 131–132.

218. *City of God*, 5.18, 19.26; Smith, *Awaiting the King*, 35, 47, 219.

219. Jeremiah 29:4–7, cited by Bretherton, *Christianity*, 4.

220. *City of God*, 19.26. See Bretherton, *Christianity*, 4–5.

221. See Bretherton, *Christianity*, 5. For a similar invocation of Jeremiah 29 to encourage Christians to serve those beyond the bounds of the church, see Burroughs, *Christianity, Politics, and the Predicament of Evil*, 99–101.

222. Smith, *Awaiting the King*, 219, citing *City of God*, 19.26.

223. Bretherton, *Christianity*, 4.

224. Ibid., 5.

225. According to Possidius, Augustine was "one of those in whom is fulfilled the text 'So speak and so act' (see Jas 2.12) and of whom the Savior said: 'he who does them and teaches them shall be called great in the kingdom of heaven' (Mt 5.19)" ("Life," §31).

226. Stout, *Democracy and Tradition*, 168–173.

227. Ibid., citing Lyons, *Exemplum*, 34.

228. Stout, *Democracy and Tradition*, 168–173, 324n7.

229. See, e.g., *City of God*, 1.15, 1.24, 2.23, 3.18, 3.20, 5.18, 5.26. I explore the examples of Regulus and Theodosius further in chapter 10.

230. For an insightful discussion, see Brown, *Augustine of Hippo*, 151–175.

231. On the importance of examples early in the process of moral progress, see *True Religion*, 49, where Augustine identifies being "taught by the rich stores of history which nourish by

examples" as the first of seven stages of inner transformation. For discussion, see Dodaro, *Christ and the Just Society*, 150–151.

232. Dodaro, *Christ and the Just Society*, 78, 182–183.

233. Ibid., 182–183; see also 4, 89–94.

234. He encourages others to do this in Sermon 198.2.

Chapter 10. Hope among the Civic Virtues: Genuine Virtues or Splendid Vices?

1. *City of God*, 5.19.

2. Ibid., 19.25.

3. Ibid.

4. Fortin, for example, argues that, according to Augustine, the Romans' "reputedly heroic virtues were in fact little more than resplendent vices" ("St. Augustine," 189–190). Rosemary Radford Ruether suggests that the "virtues of those who know only this [secular] realm are only 'noble vices,' and their destiny is death on the temporal plane and hell on the eternal plane if they should imagine such virtues to be self-sufficient" ("Christian Political Theology," 261). For a comprehensive discussion of the "legacy of the splendid vices," see Herdt, *Putting on Virtue*.

5. *City of God*, 19.4; see also 5.19.

6. Ibid., 19.4.

7. Citing a passage from Book 19, Samuel Fleischacker argues that, for Augustine, "nobody can be truly just without being a faithful Christian": "There is, and can be, no justice in people who are not subject to God, Augustine maintains. There are and can be, therefore, just republics only where faithful Christians rule. This may mean that there never have been and never will be any truly just republics. Augustine is skeptical about the likelihood that truly faithful Christians will ever have much political power. His point is that faithful Christians should put their trust in God rather than in political rulers, that the City of God is radically different from, and more worthy of obedience than, the city of man." For Fleischacker, this makes Augustine "an apolitical, even an antipolitical thinker" (*Short History of Distributive Justice*, 11).

8. This phrase is from the subtitle of Herdt, *Putting on Virtue*.

9. For a helpful overview, see ibid., 1–19.

10. Ibid., 45. Wetzel also notes that the phrase "*vitia splendida* is nowhere to be found in his description of paganism in *City of God*—his compendium and critique of polytheistic myth, ritual, and philosophy—or, for that matter, anywhere else in his writings" ("Splendid Vices," 271). See also Irwin, "Splendid Vices?," 106.

11. Irwin, "Splendid Vices?," 106, cites Kent, *Virtues of the Will*, 25: "Hence the famous claim that all the virtues of pagan Rome, because they were not directed to the Christian God, were merely 'splendid vices'—an expression Augustine himself never used but that does express his viewpoint with reasonable accuracy."

12. *City of God*, 5.19, 19.4. See also 19.10: "[V]irtue is true virtue only when it directs all the good things of which it makes good use, and all that it does in making good use of good and evil things, and itself also, towards that end where our peace will be so perfect and so great that it can be neither better nor greater."

13. Leibniz, *Theodicy*, §259, as quoted by Irwin, "Splendid Vices?," 105–106.

14. Luther, *Lectures on Hebrews*, 1.9, also cited by Irwin, "Splendid Vices?," 111n23, with a slightly different translation. For an illuminating discussion of Luther's "hyper-Augustinianism," see Herdt, *Putting on Virtue*, 173–196.

15. See Herdt, *Putting on Virtue*, 1–11, 341–352.

16. See Connolly, *Augustinian Imperative*, esp. 63–90.

17. Ibid., xviii–xix.

18. Coles, *Self/Power/Other*, 11, 52, 170–180, esp. 173–174. See also Connolly, *Augustinian Imperative*, xvii–xxiv, 39–42, 63–90.

19. Nussbaum, *Upheavals*, 549. According to Nussbaum, "So much of Augustine's literary output expresses anger—against heretics, pagans, unbelievers, Jews. Anger and hatred based on the mere fact that someone follows a different religious conception, or even none at all" (548).

20. See also O'Donnell, *Augustine*, 217.

21. See, e.g., Hauerwas, *After Christendom?*, 39–44; Hauerwas and Pinches, *Christians among the Virtues*, 27; MacIntyre, *Whose Justice?*, 204–205. For discussion, see Decosimo, *Ethics as a Work of Charity*, 5–6, 254–255.

22. Milbank, *Theology and Social Theory*, 383–384, 392–395, 410–417, 429–434, 439–442.

23. Milbank, "Evil," 5. Despite his appropriation of Augustine, Milbank even targets *Augustinian* forms of liberalism, including Reinhold Niebuhr's, for being insufficiently theological. See "Poverty of Niebuhrianism."

24. Milbank, "Evil," 5. Applying an Augustinian hermeneutic of suspicion to liberal democracy, Milbank contends that liberalism only disguises a "troublingly sustainable mode of nihilism," which permits "deliberate terror" against ordinary citizens and vulnerable victims (5).

25. Milbank, *Theology and Social Theory*, 414, emphasis in original.

26. Ibid., 411, emphasis in original.

27. Ibid.

28. For an analysis of Milbank's "hyper-Augustinian" account of pagan virtue, see Decosimo, *Ethics as a Work of Charity*, 5–6, 252–253, 262–264.

29. Milbank, *Theology and Social Theory*, 392; see also 414–417.

30. Ibid., 393.

31. Ibid., 289.

32. Ibid.

33. Ibid., 230.

34. See Dodaro, *Christ and the Just Society*, 182–214.

35. Herdt, *Putting on Virtue*, 45. See also Stout, *Democracy and Tradition*, 103.

36. *City of God*, 5.12.

37. Ibid., 1.15, 1.24. For a helpful discussion, see Herdt, "Theater of the Virtues," 124.

38. *City of God*, 5.18. Augustine writes, "Even in matters of human honour, however, we may profit from the kindness of the Lord our God by considering what great things those Romans despised, what they endured, and what lusts they subdued. They did all this for the sake of merely human glory, so that they might come to merit such glory as a reward for their virtue. Let this consideration, then, be useful to us in subduing pride. For that City in which it is promised that we shall reign is as far removed from Rome as heaven is from earth, as eternal life is from temporal joy, as solid glory from empty praise, as the fellowship of angels from that of mortal men, and as the light of the sun and moon from the light of Him Who made the sun and

moon. We who are citizens of so great a fatherland, therefore, should not look upon ourselves as having accomplished any great thing if we have performed some good works or endured some evils in order to attain it" (5.17).

39. Markus, *Saeculum*, 57.

40. *City of God*, 5.16–18. Herdt describes this as "a striking form of mimesis, which works in part through contrast and in part through assimilation" ("Theater of the Virtues," 116)

41. Herdt, "Theater of the Virtues," 123.

42. Ibid. For a discussion of other non-Christian exemplars in Augustine's texts, see Menchaca-Bagnulo, "Deeds and Words," and "Rome and the Education of Mercy," esp. 27.

43. *City of God*, 5.18. Dyson translates *uirtutes . . . similes* as the "same virtues," which might suggest an equivalence between Roman and Christian virtue. However, *uirtutes similes* can also be translated as "similar virtues," which might allow a differentiation between Roman and Christian virtue that better accords with the rest of Augustine's argument. I am grateful to William Morgan for this point. Highlighting Augustine's praises of Regulus, Griffiths suggests that the "implication of these and other similar statements is that some of what Christians and pagans undertake as rulers and subjects and citizens is substantively the same even when it is understood and explained differently" ("Secularity," 36).

44. *City of God*, 5.13.

45. Ibid., 5.13–14.

46. Ibid., 5.13.

47. Ibid. Citing this passage, von Heyking suggests that the "love of praise, as a part of the love of glory, can perform a form of social sanction in preventing people from engaging in shameful acts" ("Disarming," 178).

48. For an alternative interpretation that challenges this view of a continuum of perfect and imperfect virtue, see Dodaro, *Christ and the Just Society*, 184–186. I am not convinced that Augustine elevates Roman leaders "only as counter-examples," as Dodaro suggests (185). While Augustine sometimes elevates Roman statesmen as counter-examples, he also seems to highlight them to encourage Christians to pursue virtue, even if for eternal rewards rather than temporal ones (*City of God*, 5.16–18; Herdt, "Theater of the Virtues," 123–129).

49. *City of God*, 5.15; see also 5.18.

50. Ibid., 5.15.

51. Ibid., 5.19.

52. Ibid., 19.19; *Letter* 130.6.12.

53. *City of God*, 5.19.

54. See von Heyking, "Disarming," 178–179. For a contemporary account of esteem's potential role in politics, see Brennan and Pettit, *Economy of Esteem*; and Sabl, *Ruling Passions*.

55. *City of God*, 5.19.

56. My argument about the possibility of genuine but incomplete virtue is indebted to Irwin's account, which I discuss in detail below. See also Markus, *Christianity and the Secular*, 43–44; and Gregory, *Politics*, 52–53. One may wonder how this account fits with Augustine's explicit claim in *City of God* 5.19 that for "one who possesses the virtues . . . it is a great virtue to despise glory." The opening caveat provides a clue: those who *already* possess the virtues do not need glory to provide an external motivation to act virtuously; they act for the sake of virtue itself. But for those who do *not* already possess virtue, glory can be a powerful

motivation for them to act virtuously and eventually cultivate a more virtuous set of dispositions.

57. *City of God*, 5.19.

58. Ibid.

59. Ibid.

60. Ibid., Bettenson translation, emphasis added.

61. Letter 138.17, in *Political Writings*, 40–41.

62. Letter 138.10–12, in *Political Writings*, 35–37.

63. Letter 138.17, in *Political Writings*, 40.

64. Letter 138.10, in *Political Writings*, 35.

65. My interpretation of Augustinian tolerance and forbearance is indebted to Bowlin, "Tolerance among the Fathers," 3–36, and *Tolerance among the Virtues*.

66. Letter 138.11, in *Political Writings*, 36.

67. Letter 138.12–13, in *Political Writings*, 36–37.

68. Bowlin, "Tolerance among the Fathers," 3–10, 12, 30–31. Here, Bowlin focuses on Augustine's tolerance and forbearance of Donatist dissenters in the Christian community, but I think a similar argument also extends to membership in the political community. Ogle, *Politics and the Earthly City*, 58–59, makes a similar point about the importance Augustine places on seeking friendship with the wicked, in part, to correct them with love.

69. Bowlin, "Tolerance among the Fathers," 6–10, 12.

70. Letter 138.17, in *Political Writings*, 40–41, emphasis added. Note the subtext of this claim: Augustine again places the history of Roman Empire under God's providence, thereby desacralizing an empire that had promoted itself as the "eternal city."

71. Ibid. According to Atkins and Dodaro, "Augustine does not deny the value of civic virtues for purely earthly purposes: Christians and pagans alike benefit from just, peaceful and orderly societies" (introduction to *Political Writings*, xvi–xvii). For a slightly different reading of Letter 138, see Weithman, "Augustine's Political Philosophy," 243.

72. Irwin, "Splendid Vices?"

73. Irwin describes them analytically as follows: "(1) A moderately strict criterion: S has a virtue if S acts on the morally correct conception of the ultimate end. (2) An extremely strict criterion: S has a virtue if S's virtuous action is guided by a wholly correct conception of the ultimate end" (ibid., 112). On Augustine's ambiguity and imprecision, see ibid., 117.

74. Ibid., 112.

75. Ibid.

76. Ibid., 116–117.

77. Irwin typically describes these as "true but imperfect" virtues, but I prefer "incomplete" since it has the same meaning in Latin but avoids some of the negative connotations that "imperfect" can have in contemporary usage.

78. Ibid., 116. See *City of God*, 18.41, 19.1–5.

79. Irwin, "Splendid Vices?," 116–117.

80. Ibid., 121.

81. Ibid.

82. Ibid., 114.

83. Ibid., 120.

84. Ibid., 108.

85. Aquinas, *Summa Theologica*, II–II.23.7. Irwin cites this passage but does not include quotations. I have provided them to expand the argument.

86. Ibid.

87. Ibid., II–II. 23.7.1. Decosimo, *Ethics as a Work of Charity*, 132–134, 262, 267, notes that, in *Summa Theologica*, I–II.63.2 and I–II 65.2, Aquinas makes his account of pagan virtue compatible with Augustine's by adding a distinction between infused and acquired virtue that Augustine does not have. This distinction allows Aquinas to say that Augustine only denies true *infused* virtue to pagans, not true *acquired* virtue.

88. Irwin, "Splendid Vices?," 123. For a different analysis of Aquinas's engagement with Augustine on "pagan virtue," see Decosimo, *Ethics as a Work of Charity*, which offers a nuanced account of how Aquinas appropriates and adapts an Augustinian account of charity to acknowledge non-Christian virtue as true but imperfect virtue.

89. For a similar critique of reading Augustine through a two-tiered Thomism, see Smith, *Awaiting the King*, 43–48.

90. Irwin, "Splendid Vices?," 121.

91. Ibid., 117.

92. Letter 138.17, in *Political Writings*, 41, emphasis added.

93. Dodaro emphasizes the way that theological virtues "transform" the civic virtues (*Christ and Just Society*, 208–211).

94. Milbank, *Theology and Social Theory*, 411.

95. For a thoughtful engagement with Milbank's critique of "pagan virtues," see Wetzel, "Splendid Vices."

96. *City of God*, 5.18.

97. Ibid., 19.25.

98. For contemporary philosophical accounts, see Anscombe, *Intention*; and Vogler, *Reasonably Vicious*.

99. *Expositions of the Psalms*, 31(2).5.

100. *Faith in the Unseen*, 1.2–2.4. For discussion, see chapter 4.

101. Letter 155.13, in *Political Writings*, 97, emphasis added.

102. *City of God*, 11.28, emphasis added.

103. *Enchiridion*, 31.117.

104. I say "simply" here to emphasize that knowledge and love are not completely separate. Augustine, for example, recognizes a link between knowing, loving, and willing in *City of God*, 11.28.

105. See chapter 2.

106. See *City of God*, 21.27, 9.17; *Homilies on the First Epistle of John*, 9.10.

107. *City of God*, 15.22.

108. See, e.g., Sermon 56.2.

109. Gregory, *Politics*, 321, emphasis added. See also Ogle, *Politics and the Earthly City*, 71–72n6, who emphasizes the "refer-ability" of customs. For a similar account of referability related to Aquinas, see Decosimo, *Ethics as a Work of Charity*, 198–202, 241–242.

110. This claim fits with Herdt's suggestion that the "perfect life is something objective, not a subjective state" (*Putting on Virtue*, 55).

111. Gregory, *Politics*, 321.

112. See Herdt, "Theater of the Virtues," 111, 117–119.

113. *City of God*, 19.25. For a helpful account, see Herdt, *Putting on Virtue*, 48–50.

114. See Augustine's critique of Stoic and Epicurean virtue in Sermon 150.9.

115. See Herdt, *Putting on Virtue*, 46–50.

116. Irwin, "Splendid Vices?," 124. See also Letter 155.2, in *Political Writings*, 90.

117. *City of God*, 5.19.

118. Irwin, "Splendid Vices?," 125.

119. Ibid., 125–126.

120. Ibid., 120.

121. In an endnote, Herdt presses a similar point: "While I agree with Irwin that Augustine can and should grant that pagans can pursue virtue for its own sake . . . we fail to understand Augustine's critique unless we understand his suspicion that pagan eudaimonism's formal assumption that our final good is something fundamentally up to us *predisposes* or even *dooms* pagan virtue to corruptions like the magnanimous person's falsifying denial of dependency" (*Putting on Virtue*, 363–364n12).

122. Decosimo, *Ethics as a Work of Charity*, 313n9, offers a similar criticism of Irwin. A subtler way to capture the kind of mixed ends that Irwin has in mind would be to recognize, as Decosimo does in relation to Aquinas, that a "final end conception" can include a number of beliefs about ends and their relations, some of which may be false and some of which may be true. Some acts and their corresponding virtues can be good if they are ordered to good ends, even if one's final ends conception contains some false beliefs. This account enables some "pagans" to possess true but imperfect virtue if they order some of their acts to genuine goods that are not against charity, such as the welfare of the political community, even if they hold other false beliefs about religion (208–235).

123. *City of God*, 22.24; see also 15.22.

124. Irwin recognizes the relation between virtue and the "good use of freewill" early in the article ("Splendid Vices?," 108), but his final solution is not as sensitive to its implications for Augustine's account of pagan virtue.

125. Ibid., 113n25, citing *Trinity*, 6.6, and Letter 167.5, 7. Kent, "Augustine's Ethics," 226–229, offers a helpful discussion of which versions of this ancient doctrine Augustine affirms and rejects.

126. Dodaro makes a similar point about the structural importance of "faith" and "humility" as being necessary virtues to overcome human ignorance and emphasizes the connection between "piety" and "humility" as being necessary for true virtue (*Christ and the Just Society*, 27–71, 196, 211–212).

127. This neglect may reflect Irwin's occasional equation of pagan *conceptions of virtue* with the *possession of actual virtues* themselves. One might possess a proper *conception* of virtue's noninstrumental ends without the possessing the actual *virtues*, *habits*, or *dispositions* that reliably enable one to achieve these praiseworthy ends. The possession of the virtues, unlike a correct conception of virtue, requires an internal ordering of the affections to ensure that one wills these praiseworthy ends in proper measure. The virtues of humility and piety promote this proper ordering.

128. Herdt, "Theater of the Virtues," 117–122, also recognizes "pagan virtue" as a "problem of pride" and describes "humility" as the Augustinian antidote.

129. *City of God*, 5.19.

130. Ibid., 1.31.

131. Letter 189.8, in *Political Writings*, 218.

132. *City of God*, 10.1.

133. *City of God*, 10.1; see also 10.6.

134. Cicero, *On the Commonwealth*, 6.16; also Pref 1–2, 1.8; *On the Laws*, 1.43. On piety toward the gods, see ibid., 2.19–20, 2.26–28.

135. Ibid., 2.19, 2.28.

136. *Miscellany of Eighty-Three Questions*, 31.1, citing Cicero, *On Invention*, 2.161.

137. *City of God*, 10.3–4.

138. Letter 220.8, in *Political Writings*, 222.

139. *City of God*, 10.3.

140. For insightful discussions of Augustine on exemplification and emulation, see Herdt, *Putting on Virtue*, 66–71; and Dodaro, *Christ and the Just Society*.

141. *Confessions*, 5.13.23, 5.14.24, 6.3.4.

142. Ibid., 8.6.15, 8.12.29.

143. Ibid., 8.5.10.

144. Ibid., 3.11.20, 9.12.29.

145. Reading is pivotal in Augustine's development of virtue. Ambrose, for example, helped to foster virtue by teaching Augustine a new way to read, a way to interpret Scripture metaphorically and not simply literally (ibid., 5.14.24). And just as Victorinus converted because of his "habit of reading" scripture, Augustine came to "pick it up and read" because St. Antony provided a model for such inspired reading (8.2.4, 8.12.29). It is no surprise, then, that reading takes on special significance for Augustine, who provides a detailed treatise on interpretation, signs, and symbols in *On Christian Teaching*. Brian Stock devotes an entire book to *Augustine the Reader* (see esp. 1–2, 6). The practice of reading, however, is not the same in Augustine's time as in ours. Today, we take for granted that reading is a private, silent, and solitary act of an individual with a text. In late antiquity, reading was often a *communal, public*, and *performative* practice. Many philosophical and theological texts were usually recited aloud rather than read in solitude. As a result, Patricia Hampl argues, reading became "a kind of team sport" (preface to *Confessions*, xvii; see also Stock, *Augustine the Reader*, 5–6).

146. Confession is perhaps the primary Augustinian practice. Throughout *Confessions*, Augustine confesses both his sin and dependence on God, envisioning confession not simply as an individuated act but as a sustained practice, a habit and way of being in the world that forces us to observe ourselves. Confession increases self-knowledge, chastens prideful self-sufficiency, and fosters humility by providing a truer description of our capacities and limits. In turn, it encourages us to recognize our dependence on God and others and thereby supplements humility with piety. For insightful discussions of Augustine's practice of confession, see Dodaro, "Augustine's Secular City"; *Christ and the Just Society*, 172–179; Mathewes, *Theology of Public Life*, 87; "Book One"; and Coles, *Self/Power/Other*, 34–37. For an account of confession's connection to hope, see especially Brooks, "What May I Hope For?," 180–185.

147. That Augustine's most powerful and decisive conversion at Ostia happened not while he was silent and alone but when he was engaged in conversation with Monica is significant

(*Confessions*, 9.10.23). The dialogical and discursive nature of this experience shows how God can work through human conversation.

148. *City of God*, 10.1.

149. Ibid.

150. Sermon 349.2.

151. Ibid.

152. *Faith in the Unseen*, 2.4.

153. In *Putting on Virtue*, Herdt suggests that "Augustine's own worries about pagan virtue might have been alleviated by the recognition that while pagans do fail to acknowledge the utter dependency of their agency on God, they can at least acknowledge their agency as fundamentally socially dependent and socially constituted. Pagans do not, then, necessarily order all things to self; they can in fact act for virtue's own sake. Such a concession would have moved Augustine's attitude toward pagan virtue closer to that of Aquinas, for whom pagans pursue true if proximate ends and possess true if imperfect virtues" (2–3). Here, I have tried to uncover Augustinian resources to construct such a view.

154. Keys argues that, in Book 3 of *City of God*, Augustine suggests an implicit connection between humility and familial piety by denoting how the lack of humility—pride—"demotes or even severs these bonds, whereas humility acknowledges them gladly" ("Augustinian Humility," 102). The mutually reinforcing relationship between piety and humility mirrors the "upward spiral" between gratitude and humility described in Kruse, Ruberton, and Lyubomirsky, "Gratitude and Humility."

155. *City of God*, 1.Pref.

156. Ibid., translation altered.

157. See Keys, "Augustinian Humility," on the "dialectic" of pride and humility in *City of God*, Books 1–5.

158. Ibid., 110.

159. Ibid., 98.

160. *City of God*, 5.26.

161. Ibid.

162. Ibid., 5.19, 1.35.

163. Ibid., 18.52. Markus notes Augustine's views on "conjecture" in *Saeculum*, 54.

164. Matthew 7:3–5.

165. For an argument that pride is a "natural wrong" and humility is a "natural right," see Keys, "Augustinian Humility." Keys's argument supports the idea that humility can be an incomplete virtue of those who do not profess explicit belief in God.

166. See Dodaro, "Secret Justice." See also Augustine's discussion of Job, compared to whom "no man of his time is his equal in righteousness and piety" (*City of God*, 18.47). For discussion of Job, see Menchaca-Bagnulo, "Deeds and Words," 78–81.

167. Sermon 198.36. For discussion, see Dodaro, "Secret Justice," 85.

168. Ibid.

169. Ibid.

170. Sermon 198.59–61; see also 198.15, 32. According to Dodaro, "The character of salvation is grounded in humility, Augustine believes, because creaturehood was violated in Adam's proud assertion of a private selfhood in which man could hide from God's watch. It was to

overcome this human, conditioned response that God became man and died in Christ. It is true that the *via humilitatis* that God embraced by entering into history is the *sole* pathway to salvation; however, it is also a universal pathway. As such, humility becomes a criterion for evaluating all soteriologies, while it also provides something of a common ground between them, should there be other, valid explanations for salvation than that provided by the Christian religion" ("Secret Justice," 8,). See also Keys, "Elitism and Secularism," on the importance of humility in Augustine's engagement with Platonist philosophers, and Menchaca-Bagnulo, "Deeds and Words," on examples of non-Christians who demonstrate humility, piety, and mercy.

171. On the connection between humility and right perception, see Keys, "Augustinian Humility," 100, 103–104.

172. Bowlin, "Augustine Counting Virtues," 298. See also Keys, "Augustinian Humility," 110.

173. For an overview, see Button, "'Monkish Kind of Virtue,'" 841–849.

174. Ibid., 841.

175. Ibid., 850–851.

176. Ibid., 850.

177. Ibid., 859.

178. Ibid., 856.

179. Ibid., 861.

180. While Button mentions Augustine as an inspiration for his account and draws on Bernard's "Augustinian notion" (ibid., 843–844, 850), he includes an endnote (866n56) acknowledging the limits of the Augustinian account, citing Romand Coles's claim that Augustinian politics relies on "an imagination profoundly blind to the possible being and value of radical alterity in people who live resolutely outside the Christian story" (see Coles, *Rethinking Generosity*, 2–3). If my alternative account of Augustine's approach to pagan virtue is compelling, however, then Button's virtue of humility might find even more resonance with an Augustinian account of humility, particularly one that is connected fundamentally to piety and recognizes the "relations of mutual dependency" that Button seeks to honor (855).

181. Stout, *Democracy and Tradition*, 20–41, esp. 24–29. On the value of piety in a pluralistic, democratic context, see also Bretherton, *Resurrecting Democracy*, 96–99.

182. Stout, *Democracy and Tradition*, 28–30, at 30.

183. Ibid., 21–29.

184. See ibid., 34–35, 63–91.

185. Ibid., 20. Against those who harden divisions based on exclusively religious or secular pieties, Stout suggests the possibility of "more common ground here than the proponents of naturalism and supernaturalism tend to notice when they get caught up in diagnosing the illusions and sins they impute to one another. If being justified in believing something is a contextual affair, and if differences in upbringing and life experience are relevant contextual factors, then perhaps our religious opponents are justified in believing what they believe. This recognition ought at least to give us pause before we propose an uncharitable diagnosis of our religious differences. The default position will be that our neighbors are justified in believing what they believe. If we are charitable interpreters, we will view those who differ from us religiously, in the absence of clear evidence to the contrary, as people doing their best to offer appropriate acknowledgment of their dependence. Insofar as they do acknowledge that dependence

appropriately, given their own conceptions of the sources of our existence and progress through life, they may be said to exhibit an attitude that is worthy of our respect, if not our full endorsement. We can praise this aspect of character as a virtue for the same reason that we can praise the courage, temperance, or wisdom of someone we oppose in battle or debate. We can then leave open whether it satisfies the highest standard of excellence one might want to apply in this area, whether it is a virtue in the strongest sense" (33–34). This account fits with the default and challenge structure of reasoning analyzed in chapter 4.

186. Stout also highlights how democrats like Ralph Waldo Emerson and Ralph Waldo Ellison can converge with Augustinians on "reasons for hope in the here and now" (*Democracy and Tradition*, 58–59).

187. Herdt, *Putting on Virtue*, 58–61, 70–71. See, e.g., *City of God*, 15.1, 19.4, 22.23. As Herdt writes elsewhere, "[T]here is finally no bright line to mark off graced from ungraced, even if Augustine gave way at times to the temptation to try to provide one. Hence, we should not map the divide between splendid vice and true virtue onto a contemporary distinction between Christian and non-Christian or Christian and secular. In the end, Augustine not only holds up pagan heroes for corrective Christian emulation, but—despite his own dismissal of the possibility of true pagan virtue—gives us grounds to keep looking for pagans who do after all see the beauty of a self-emptying compassion, who do recognize in some form the dependent character of their own agency, just as Christians continue to recognize their own sinful pride" ("Theater of the Virtues," 128–129). Aquinas, *Summa Theologica*, I–II.5.3, makes a similar point about all being subject to sin in this life, citing Augustine, *City of God*, 19.4. For discussion, see Decosimo, *Ethics as a Work of Charity*, 248–249.

188. *City of God*, 21.15.

189. Ibid.

190. Sermon 87.10.

Conclusion: Augustine and the Politics of Hope

1. Sermon 80.8, as translated and cited by Markus, *Saeculum*, 40–41.

2. See chapter 6.

3. González, *Mestizo Augustine*, 13–19, 167–171.

4. I am grateful to Jeffrey Stout for this point. See also Green, "Political Theory as Both Philosophy and History."

5. Although what follows goes beyond what Augustine could potentially endorse or imagine, the method follows his precedent. He frequently recovers resources from ancient writers to advance his own constructive vision, and he encourages others to do the same, even for purposes the original authors could not have intended (e.g., *On Christian Teaching*, 2.40.60–61). He explicitly endorses Cyprian's idea that we should return to our authorities and "turn the channel of truth [from them] to our own times" (*On Baptism, Against the Donatists*, 5.26.37, referencing the apostolic tradition). Markus, *Saeculum*, xxiii, also cites this passage but offers a different translation.

6. See, e.g., Ehrenreich, "Pathologies of Hope"; Scruton, *Uses of Pessimism*; "When Hope Tramples Truth"; Runciman, *Confidence Trap*, xi–xix, 41, 52–53, 234, 304.

7. I offer a similar analysis in relation to Aquinas in Lamb, "Passion and Its Virtue," 69–71, 85, and "Aquinas and the Virtues of Hope," 302–303, 325.

8. See Lamb, "Aquinas and the Virtues of Hope," 325–326.

9. For influential accounts of civic virtues, see, e.g., Dagger, *Civic Virtues*; Galston, *Liberal Purposes*, 213–237; Macedo, *Liberal Virtues*; Sabl, "Virtue for Pluralists." Notable exceptions of philosophers who see hope as a virtue include Mittleman, *Hope in a Democratic Age*; and Snow, "Hope as a Democratic Civic Virtue." I make a similar point in Lamb, "Passion and Its Virtue," 71, and "Aquinas and the Virtues of Hope," 303.

10. Lloyd, *Problem with Grace*, 71.

11. *City of God*, 19.17, 18.54. See also chapter 8.

12. King, "Letter from Birmingham City Jail," 295. See also Burroughs, *Christianity, Politics, and the Predicament of Evil*, 10.

13. See *City of God*, 19.13; and chapter 8.

14. Tocqueville, *Democracy in America*, 514.

15. Honig, *Public Things*, 80, 90, 6–7, 24. To develop her defense of "public things," Honig draws on Arendt's *Human Condition*, which offers an account of how public "things" can constitute and shape our "common world" (37–57; Arendt, *Human Condition*, 50–58). Coincidentally, Arendt sets her account against Augustine's vision of Christian love and community, which she criticizes for its "worldlessness" and "unpolitical, non-public character" (53). One upshot of my efforts to defuse Arendt's anxieties about Augustine's otherworldly love in chapter 2 and elevate his vision of a commonwealth united around common objects in chapter 8 is that it brings Augustine and Arendt closer together, all the while recognizing their quite different politics of secular immortality and divine eternity. For more on Arendt's engagement with Augustine, see Gregory, *Politics*, 197–240.

16. Ibid., 61–66.

17. Ibid., 61–66, 13.

18. Ibid., 92, 56.

19. On "incompletely theorized agreement," see Sunstein, "Practical Reason," 268–269. On its application to Augustine, see chapter 8.

20. Maritain, *Man and the State*, 111, as cited by Sacks, *Politics of Hope*, 217.

21. Sacks, *Politics of Hope*, 217.

22. See Ali, Jamoul, and Vali, "New Covenant of Virtue," cited and discussed in Bretherton, *Resurrecting Democracy*, 88.

23. Ali, Jamoul, and Vali, "New Covenant of Virtue," 9.

24. Ibid.

25. See Bretherton, *Resurrecting Democracy*, esp. 76–110.

26. See Pope Francis's *Laudato Si'*; Islamic Declaration on Global Climate Change; Hindu Declaration on Climate Change; Lambeth Declaration; Evangelical Climate Initiative, "Climate Change"; Jewish Climate Action Network; Alliance of Religions and Conservation, "About ARC."

27. Wilson, *Creation*, 163–168, 4.

28. E.g., Markus, *Saeculum*, 69–71, 151. For discussion, see chapter 8.

29. See Rawls, *Political Liberalism*, 9–11, 211–254, 435–490.

30. See Stout, *Democracy and Tradition*, 63–91; Wolterstorff, "Role of Religion"; Biggar, *Behaving in Public*, 45–78; and chapter 8.

31. See Lamb, "Augustine and Republican Liberty," 154–155, and "Augustine and Political Theory," 101–102.

32. Feinberg and Willer, "From Gulf to Bridge."

33. Willer and Feinberg, "Key to Political Persuasion."

34. See Mathewes, *Theology of Public Life*, 261–307; Johnson, *Theology*, 82–173; and chapter 8.

35. See chapter 8. See also Bretherton, *Resurrecting Democracy*, 93, 108; Honig, *Public Things*, 12–15; Johnson, *Theology*, 237–240.

36. Here my account aligns with the Augustinian analysis offered by Smith, *Awaiting the King*.

37. See, e.g., Djupe and Gilbert, *Political Influence of Churches*; Stout, *Blessed Are the Organized*; Bretherton, *Resurrecting Democracy*.

38. Dreher, *Benedict Option*.

39. Ibid., 13, 86, 90, 104–105. In encouraging Christians to embrace a "strategic withdrawal" from "mainstream society" to "*be the church*," Dreher echoes Augustinian communitarians such as MacIntyre and Hauerwas (2–4, emphasis in original).

40. For another powerful Augustinian response to Dreher, see Smith, "Benedict Option or the Augustinian Call?" and *Awaiting the King*, xii, 54n3, 212.

41. See Mathewes, *Theology of Public Life*, 143–146; Bretherton, *Christianity and Contemporary Politics*, 3, 72; Smith, *Awaiting the King*, 43–52.

42. Dodaro, "Between the Two Cities," 111.

43. *City of God*, 19.17.

44. Stout, *Blessed Are the Organized*, 259; see also *Democracy and Tradition*, 55–60.

45. Burke, "Semantic and Poetic Meaning," 160. See chapter 7. Smith identifies Augustine as an example of the "pastor as political theologian," whose twofold function is to help the faithful, first, to diagnose, criticize, and resist political idolatries and, second, to cultivate their virtues as citizens (*Awaiting the King*, 194–197). Smith's analysis supports the one offered here.

46. For a similar Augustinian analysis, see Mathewes, *Theology of Public Life*, 236–238.

47. Hochschild, "Left Pessimism and Political Science," 6. Hochschild focuses on "left pessimism" but notes that, historically, pessimism has been more commonly associated with conservativism (11).

48. Ibid., 11–17.

49. hooks, *Teaching Community*, xiv.

50. Ibid.

51. For an analysis, see Lamb, "Difficult Hope."

52. A prominent example is David Wallace-Wells, "Uninhabitable Earth."

53. See, e.g., Moser, "More Bad News"; O'Neill and Nicholson-Cole, "'Fear Won't Do'"; Moser and Dilling, "Communicating Climate Change," 164–165; Stern, "Fear and Hope in Climate Messages"; McQueen, "Wages of Fear?"

54. See, e.g., Markowitz and Sharif, "Climate Change and Moral Judgment"; Moser, "More Bad News," 73; Ojala, "Hope and Climate Change"; Stern, "Fear and Hope in Climate Messages." For an insightful discussion of both fear and hope appeals in climate communication, see McQueen, "The Wages of Fear?" Applying the work of Michael William Pfau, McQueen draws on Aristotle's account of "civic fear" to encourage fear appeals that also elicit hope. Recognizing that these emotions must be regulated properly to result in action, she also proposes the need for a virtue but focuses on courage instead of hope (165–170). This emphasis may

reflect the fact that McQueen's main source, Aristotle, includes courage, but not hope, among the virtues. My account complements McQueen's by drawing on Augustine's rhetoric and virtue of hope.

55. Wendell Berry offers a similar structure of encouragement in his environmental writing. See Lamb, "Difficult Hope."

56. Nabi, Gustafson, and Jensen, "Framing Climate Change."

57. Dodaro, "Between the Two Cities," 99–100. See chapter 9.

58. Sermon 80.8, as translated and cited by Markus, *Saeculum*, 41.

59. See Sermon 80.8, 198.2, 345.6, and 352A.5.

BIBLIOGRAPHY

Augustine's Texts and Translations

Unless otherwise noted, I have followed R. W. Dyson's translation of *City of God* (1998) and the translations of other texts listed below. Most translations from the New City Press editions of The Works of Saint Augustine were accessed electronically via InteLex's Past Masters online catalogue. Where I have occasionally altered a translation or used an alternative translation, I have indicated it in the notes. All Latin references are from *Corpus Augustinianum Gissense*, edited by Cornelius Mayer (Basel: Schwabe, 1995).

The Advantage of Believing. Translated by Ray Kearney. In *Trilogy on Faith and Happiness*, edited by Boniface Ramsey, 81–141. Hyde Park, NY: New City Press, 2010.

Against the Academicians. In *Against the Academicians and The Teacher*, translated by Peter King, 1–93. Indianapolis, IN: Hackett, 1995.

Answer to Faustus, A Manichean. Translated by Roland J. Teske, edited by Boniface Ramsey. Hyde Park, NY: New City Press, 2007.

The Augustine Catechism: The Enchiridion on Faith, Hope, and Charity. Translated by Bruce Harbert, edited by Boniface Ramsey. Hyde Park, NY: New City Press, 1999.

The Catholic Way of Life and the Manichean Way of Life. In *The Manichean Debate*, translated by Roland Teske, edited by Boniface Ramsey, 15–103. Hyde Park, NY: New City Press, 2006.

The City of God against the Pagans. Edited by R. W. Dyson. New York: Cambridge University Press, 1998.

Concerning the City of God against the Pagans. Translated by Henry Bettenson. New York: Penguin, 1972.

Confessions. Translated by Maria Boulding. New York: Vintage Books, 1998.

The Excellence of Marriage. In *Marriage and Virginity*, translated by Ray Kearney, edited by David G. Hunter, 29–61. Hyde Park, NY: New City Press, 1999.

The Excellence of Widowhood. In *Marriage and Virginity*, translated by Ray Kearney, edited by David G. Hunter, 111–136. Hyde Park, NY: New City Press, 1999.

Expositions of the Psalms, 1–32. Vol. III/15. Translated by Maria Boulding, edited by John E. Rotelle. Hyde Park, NY: New City Press, 2000.

Expositions of the Psalms, 33–50. Vol. III/16. Translated by Maria Boulding, edited by John E. Rotelle. Hyde Park, NY: New City Press, 2000.

Expositions of the Psalms, 51–72. Vol. III/17. Translated by Maria Boulding, edited by John E. Rotelle. Hyde Park, NY: New City Press, 2001.

Expositions of the Psalms, 73–98. Vol. III/18. Translated by Maria Boulding, edited by John E. Rotelle. Hyde Park, NY: New City Press, 2002.

Expositions of the Psalms, 99–120. Vol. III/19. Translated by Maria Boulding, edited by Boniface Ramsey. Hyde Park, NY: New City Press, 2003.

Expositions of the Psalms, 121–150. Vol. III/20. Translated by Maria Boulding, edited by Boniface Ramsey. Hyde Park, NY: New City Press, 2004.

Faith and the Creed. In *Augustine: Earlier Writings*, translated by John H. S. Burleigh, 353–375. Philadelphia, PA: Westminster Press, 1953.

Faith in the Unseen. Translated by Michael G. Campbell. In *Trilogy on Faith and Happiness*, edited by Boniface Ramsey, 55–79. Hyde Park, NY: New City Press, 2010.

The Gift of Perseverance. In *Selected Writings on Grace and Pelagianism*, translated by Roland J. Teske, edited by Boniface Ramsey, 465–523. Hyde Park, NY: New City Press, 2011.

The Happy Life. In *Trilogy on Faith and Happiness*, translated by Roland J. Teske, edited by Boniface Ramsey, 9–53. Hyde Park, NY: New City Press, 2010.

Homilies on the First Epistle of John. Translated by Boniface Ramsey, edited by Daniel E. Doyle and Thomas Martin. Hyde Park, NY: New City Press, 2008.

Homilies on the Gospel of John 41–124. Vol. I/13. Translated by Edmund Hill, edited by Allan D. Fitzgerald. Hyde Park, NY: New City Press, 2020.

Letters 1–99. Vol. II/1. Translated by Roland Teske, edited by John E. Rotelle. Hyde Park, NY: New City Press, 2001.

Letters 100–155. Vol. II/2. Translated by Roland Teske, edited by Boniface Ramsey. Hyde Park, NY: New City Press, 2003.

Letters 156–210. Vol. II/3. Translated by Roland Teske, edited by Boniface Ramsey. Hyde Park, NY: New City Press, 2004.

Letters 211–270, 1*–29*. Vol. II/4. Translated by Roland Teske, edited by Boniface Ramsey. Hyde Park, NY: New City Press, 2005.

The Literal Meaning of Genesis. In *On Genesis*, translated by Edmund Hill, edited by John E. Rotelle, 159–581. Hyde Park, NY: New City Press, 2002.

Miscellany of Eighty-Three Questions. In *Responses to Miscellaneous Questions*, translated by Boniface Ramsey, edited by Raymond Canning, 13–157. Hyde Park, NY: New City Press, 2008.

Of True Religion. In *Augustine: Earlier Writings*, translated by John H. S. Burleigh, 225–283. Philadelphia, PA: Westminster Press, 1953.

On Baptism, Against the Donatists. Translated by J. R. King. In *A Select Library of the Nicene and Post-Nicene Fathers of the Christian Church*. Vol. 4, *St. Augustin: The Writings against the Manicheans, and against the Donatists*, edited by Philip Schaff, 407–514. Buffalo, NY: Christian Literature Company, 1887.

On the Catechising of the Uninstructed. Translated by S.D.F. Salmond. In *A Select Library of Nicene and Post-Nicene Fathers of the Christian Church*. Vol. 3, *St Augustin on the Holy Trinity, Doctrinal Treatises, Moral Treatises*, edited by Philip Schaff, 277–314. Buffalo, NY: Christian Literature Company, 1887.

On Christian Teaching. Translated by R.P.H. Green. Oxford: Oxford University Press, 1997.

On the Free Choice of Will. In *On the Free Choice of Will, On Grace and Free Choice, and Other Writings*, edited and translated by Peter King, 3–126. Cambridge: Cambridge University Press, 2010.

On Grace and Free Choice. In *On the Free Choice of Will, On Grace and Free Choice, and Other Writings*, edited and translated by Peter King, 141–184. Cambridge: Cambridge University Press, 2010.

On Order. Translated by Silvano Borruso. South Bend, IN: St. Augustine's Press, 2007.

On Reprimand and Grace. In *On the Free Choice of Will, On Grace and Free Choice, and Other Writings*, edited and translated by Peter King, 185–228. Cambridge: Cambridge University Press, 2010.

Political Writings. Edited by E. M. Atkins and R. J. Dodaro. New York: Cambridge University Press, 2001.

The Predestination of the Saints. In *Selected Writings on Grace and Pelagianism*, translated by Roland Teske, edited by Boniface Ramsey, 381–464. Hyde Park, NY: New City Press, 2011.

Quaestiones in Heptateuchum. Edited by Iosephus Zycha. Vienna: Leipzig, 1895.

The Retractions. Translated by Mary Inez Bogan. Washington, DC: Catholic University Press, 1968.

Sermons (1–19) on the Old Testament. Vol. III/1. Translated by Edmund Hill, edited by John E. Rotelle. Hyde Park, NY: New City Press, 1990.

Sermons (20–50) on the Old Testament. Vol. III/2. Translated by Edmund Hill, edited by John E. Rotelle. Hyde Park, NY: New City Press, 1990.

Sermons (51–94) on the Old Testament. Vol. III/3. Translated by Edmund Hill, edited by John E. Rotelle. Brooklyn, NY: New City Press, 1991.

Sermons (94A–147A) on the Old Testament. Vol. III/4. Translated by Edmund Hill, edited by John E. Rotelle. Brooklyn, NY: New City Press, 1992.

Sermons (148–183) on the New Testament. Vol. III/5. Translated by Edmund Hill, edited by John E. Rotelle. New Rochelle, NY: New City Press, 1992.

Sermons (184–229Z) on the Liturgical Seasons. Vol. III/6. Translated by Edmund Hill, edited by John E. Rotelle. New Rochelle, NY: New City Press, 1993.

Sermons (230–272B) on the Liturgical Seasons. Vol. III/7. Translated by Edmund Hill, edited by John E. Rotelle. New Rochelle, NY: New City Press, 1993.

Sermons (273–305A) on the Saints. Vol. III/8. Translated by Edmund Hill, edited by John E. Rotelle. Hyde Park, NY: New City Press, 1994.

Sermons (306–340A) on the Saints. Vol. III/9. Translated by Edmund Hill, edited by John E. Rotelle. Hyde Park, NY: New City Press, 1994.

Sermons (341–400) on Various Subjects. Vol. III/10. Translated by Edmund Hill, edited by John E. Rotelle. Hyde Park, NY: New City Press, 1994.

Sermons (Newly Discovered). Vol. III/11. Translated by Edmund Hill, edited by John E. Rotelle. Hyde Park, NY: New City Press, 1997.

Soliloquies. Translated by Kim Paffenroth. Hyde Park, NY: New City Press, 2000.

The Spirit and the Letter. In *Selected Writings on Grace and Pelagianism*, translated by Roland Teske, edited by Boniface Ramsey, 215–292. Hyde Park, NY: New City Press, 2011.

The Teacher. In *Against the Academicians and The Teacher*, translated by Peter King, 94–146. Indianapolis, IN: Hackett, 1995.

The Trinity. Translated by Edmund Hill, edited by John E. Rotelle. 2nd ed. Hyde Park, NY: New City Press, 2012.

Other Primary and Secondary Sources

Adams, Robert Merrihew. "The Theological Ethics of the Young Rawls and Its Background." In *A Brief Inquiry into the Meaning of Sin and Faith*, by John Rawls, edited by Thomas Nagel, 24–101. Cambridge, MA: Harvard University Press, 2009.

Ali, Ruhana, Lina Jamoul, and Yusufi Vali. "A New Covenant of Virtue: Islam and Community Organizing." London: CitizensUK and IAF, 2012. http://www.theology-centre.org.uk/wp-content/uploads/2013/04/Islam-and-Community-Organising-V3-singles.pdf.

Alimi, Olaoluwatoni. "Slaves of God: Augustine and Other Romans on Religion and Politics." Unpublished manuscript, last modified January 10, 2022. Adobe PDF file.

Alliance of Religions and Conservation. "About ARC." http://arcworld.org/about_ARC.asp.

Anscombe, G.E.M. *Intention*. 2nd ed. Cambridge, MA: Harvard University Press, 1963.

Antonaccio, Maria. "Contemporary Forms of *Askesis* and the Return of Spiritual Exercises." *Annual of the Society of Christian Ethics* 18 (1998): 69–92.

Appiah, Kwame Anthony. *The Honor Code: How Moral Revolutions Happen*. New York: Norton, 2010.

Aquinas, Thomas. *Compendium of Theology*. Translated by Richard J. Regan. New York: Oxford University Press, 2009.

———. *Summa Theologica*. Translated by Fathers of the English Dominican Province. 3 vols. New York: Benziger Brothers, 1948.

Arena, Valentina. *Libertas and the Practice of Politics in the Late Roman Republic*. Cambridge: Cambridge University Press, 2012.

Arendt, Hannah. "Augustine and Protestantism." In *Essays in Understanding, 1930–1954*, edited by Jerome Kohn, 24–27. New York: Harcourt Brace, 1994.

———. *Between Past and Future*. New York: Penguin, 1968.

———. *Eichmann in Jerusalem: A Report on the Banality of Evil*. New York: Penguin, 1994.

———. *The Human Condition*. Chicago: University of Chicago Press, 1998.

———. *The Life of the Mind*. Vol. 2, *Willing*. New York: Harcourt Brace, 1978.

———. *Love and Saint Augustine*. Edited by Joanna Vecchiarelli Scott and Judith Chelius Stark. Chicago: University of Chicago Press, 1996.

———. *The Origins of Totalitarianism*. New York: Harvest Book, 1973.

———. "Understanding and Politics (The Difficulties of Understanding)." In *Essays in Understanding, 1930–1954*, edited by Jerome Kohn, 307–327. New York: Harcourt Brace, 1994.

Arendt, Hannah, and Karl Jaspers. *Correspondence, 1926–1969*. Edited by Lotte Kohler and Hans Saner, translated by Robert and Rita Kimber. New York: Harcourt Brace, 1992.

Aristotle. *On Rhetoric: A Theory of Civic Discourse*. Translated by George A. Kennedy. 2nd ed. New York: Oxford University Press, 2007.

Asmis, Elizabeth. "The State as a Partnership: Cicero's Definition of *Res Publica* in His Work *On the State*." *History of Political Thought* 25, no. 4 (2004): 569–598.

Atkins, E. M. "'Domina et Regina Virtutum': Justice and Societas in 'De Officiis'." *Phronesis* 35 (1990): 258–289.

Atkins, E. M., and R. J. Dodaro. Introduction to *Political Writings*, by Augustine, edited by E. M. Atkins and R. J. Dodaro, xi–xxvii. New York: Cambridge University Press, 2001.

Audi, Robert. "Belief, Faith, Acceptance, and Hope." In *Rationality and Religious Commitment*, 51–88. Oxford: Oxford University Press, 2011.

Auerbach, Erich. *Literary Language and Its Public in Late Latin Antiquity and in the Middle Ages.* Translated by Ralph Manheim. Princeton, NJ: Princeton University Press, 1965.

Avramenko, Richard. "The Wound and Salve of Time: Augustine's Politics of Human Happiness." *Review of Metaphysics* 60 (June 2007): 779–811.

Baer, Helmut David. "The Fruit of Charity: Using the Neighbor in *De doctrina Christiana.*" *Journal of Religious Ethics* 24, no. 1 (Spring 1996): 46–64.

Baier, Annette. "Unsafe Loves." In *Moral Prejudices: Essays on Ethics,* 33–50. Cambridge, MA: Harvard University Press, 1995.

Bathory, Peter Dennis. *Political Theory as Public Confession: The Social and Political Thought of St. Augustine of Hippo.* New Brunswick, NJ: Transaction Books, 1981.

Bearsley, Patrick. "Augustine and Wittgenstein on Language." *Philosophy* 58, no. 224 (1983): 229–236.

Bellah, Robert N., Richard Madsen, William M. Sullivan, Ann Swidler, and Steven M. Tipton. *Habits of the Heart.* Berkeley: University of California Press, 1985.

Biden, Joseph R., Jr. "Inaugural Address." United States Capitol, Washington, DC, January 20, 2021. https://www.whitehouse.gov/briefing-room/speeches-remarks/2021/01/20 /inaugural-address-by-president-joseph-r-biden-jr/.

Biggar, Nigel. *Behaving in Public: How to Do Christian Ethics.* Grand Rapids, MI: William E. Eerdmans, 2011.

———. "Is Stanley Hauerwas Sectarian?" In *Faithfulness and Fortitude: In Conversation with the Theological Ethics of Stanley Hauerwas,* edited by Mark Thiessen Nation and Samuel Wells, 141–160. Edinburgh: T&T Clark, 2000.

Bilgrami, Akeel. "Why Does Liberalism Find It So Hard to Cope with Religious Identity?" Religion in Liberal Political Philosophy Conference, Religion and Political Theory Centre, University College London, June 11, 2015.

Billings, David. "Natality or Advent: Hannah Arendt and Jürgen Moltmann on Hope and Politics." In *The Future of Hope: Christian Tradition amid Modernity and Postmodernity,* edited by Miroslav Volf and William Katerberg, 125–145. Grand Rapids, MI: William E. Eerdmans, 2004.

Bitzer, Lloyd F. "The Rhetorical Situation." *Philosophy and Rhetoric* 1 (1968): 1–14.

Bluhm, Heinz. "Nietzsche's Final View of Luther and the Reformation." *Publications of the Modern Language Association* 71, no. 1 (1956): 75–83.

———. "Nietzsche's Religious Development as a Student at the University of Bonn." *Publications of the Modern Language Association* 52, no. 3 (1937): 880–891.

Bok, Nico den. "Peter Lombard." In *The Oxford Guide to the Historical Reception of Augustine,* edited by Karla Pollmann and Willemien Otten, vol. 3, 1527–1530. New York: Oxford University Press, 2013.

Bowlin, John R. "Augustine Counting Virtues." *Augustinian Studies* 41, no. 1 (2010): 277–300.

———. "Augustine on Justifying Coercion." *Annual of the Society of Christian Ethics* 17 (1997): 49–70.

———. "Tolerance among the Fathers." *Journal of the Society of Christian Ethics* 26, no. 1 (2006): 3–36.

———. *Tolerance among the Virtues.* Princeton, NJ: Princeton University Press, 2016.

Brandom, Robert B. *Making It Explicit: Reasoning, Representing, and Discursive Commitment.* Cambridge, MA: Harvard University Press, 1998.

————. *Tales of the Mighty Dead: Historical Essays in the Metaphysics of Intentionality*. Cambridge, MA: Harvard University Press, 2002.

Brennan, Geoffrey, and Philip Pettit. *The Economy of Esteem: An Essay on Civil and Political Society*. New York: Oxford University Press, 2004.

Bretherton, Luke. *Christianity and Contemporary Politics: The Conditions and Possibilities of Faithful Witness*. Malden, MA: Wiley-Blackwell, 2010.

————. *Resurrecting Democracy: Faith, Citizenship, and the Politics of a Common Life*. New York: Cambridge University Press, 2015.

Breyfogle, Todd. "Citizenship and Signs: Rethinking Augustine on the Two Cities." In *A Companion to Greek and Roman Political Thought*, edited by Ryan K. Balot, 501–526. Malden, MA: Wiley-Blackwell, 2009.

————. "Toward a Contemporary Augustinian Understanding of Politics." In *Augustine and Politics*, edited by John Doody, Kevin L. Hughes, and Kim Paffenroth, 217–235. Lanham, MD: Lexington Books, 2005.

Brooke, Christopher. "Rousseau's Political Philosophy: Stoic and Augustinian Origins." In *The Cambridge Companion to Rousseau*, edited by Patrick Riley, 94–123. Cambridge: Cambridge University Press, 2001.

Brooks, David. "How Movements Recover." *New York Times*, March 14, 2013. https://www.nytimes.com/2013/03/15/opinion/brooks-how-movements-recover.html.

————. *The Road to Character*. New York: Random House, 2015.

Brooks, Edward W. R. L. "What May I Hope For? Modernity and the Augustinian Virtue of Hope." Doctoral Dissertation, University of Oxford, 2018.

Brown, Charles C. *Niebuhr and His Age: Reinhold Niebuhr's Prophetic Role and Legacy*. Harrisburg, PA: Trinity Press International, 2002.

Brown, Peter. "Augustine and a Crisis of Wealth in Late Antiquity." *Augustinian Studies* 36, no. 1 (2005): 5–30.

————. *Augustine of Hippo: A Biography*. Berkeley: University of California Press, 2000.

————. *Authority and the Sacred: Aspects of the Christianisation of the Roman World*. Cambridge: Cambridge University Press, 1995.

————. "Political Society." In *Augustine: A Collection of Critical Essays*, edited by R. A. Markus, 311–335. Garden City, NY: Doubleday, 1972.

————. *Power and Persuasion in Late Antiquity: Towards a Christian Empire*. Madison: University of Wisconsin Press, 1992.

————. "St. Augustine's Attitude to Religious Coercion." *Journal of Roman Studies* 54 (1964): 107–116.

————. *Through the Eye of a Needle: Wealth, the Fall of Rome, and the Making of Christianity in the West, 350–550 AD*. Princeton, NJ: Princeton University Press, 2012.

Brown, Robert McAfee. Introduction to *The Essential Reinhold Niebuhr: Selected Essays and Addresses*, by Reinhold Niebuhr, edited by Robert McAfee Brown, xi–xxiv. New Haven, CT: Yale University Press, 1986.

Bruno, Michael J. S. *Political Augustinianism: Modern Interpretations of Augustine's Political Thought*. Minneapolis, MN: Fortress Press, 2014.

Bullock, Jeffrey. "Augustinian Innovation: A Spokesperson for a Post-Classical Age." *Journal of Communication and Religion* 20, no. 1 (March 1997): 5–13.

Bultmann, Rudolf. "Pisteūo." In *Theological Dictionary of the New Testament*, edited by Gerhard Kittel and Gerhard Friedrich, translated by Geoffrey W. Bromiley, vol. 6, 174–228. Grand Rapids, MI: William B. Eerdmans, 1968.

Burke, Kenneth. *The Rhetoric of Religion: Studies in Logology*. Berkeley: University of California Press, 1970.

———. "Semantic and Poetic Meaning." In *The Philosophy of Literary Form: Studies in Symbolic Action*, 3rd ed., 138–167. Berkeley: University of California Press, 1973.

Burnaby, John. *Amor Dei: A Study of the Religion of St. Augustine*. London: Hodder & Stoughton, 1938.

Burnyeat, M. F. "Postscript on Silent Reading." *Classical Quarterly* 47, no. 1 (1997): 74–76.

———. "Wittgenstein and Augustine *De Magistro*." *Proceedings of the Aristotelian Society, Supplementary Volumes* 61 (1987): 1–24.

Burroughs, Bradley B. *Christianity, Politics, and the Predicament of Evil: A Constructive Theological Ethic of Soulcraft and Statecraft*. Lanham, MD: Lexington Books/Fortress Academic, 2019.

Burt, Donald. "Courageous Optimism: Augustine on the Good of Creation." *Augustinian Studies* 21 (1990): 55–66.

Bussanich, John. "Goodness." In *Augustine through the Ages*, edited by Allan D. Fitzgerald, John Cavadini, Marianne Djuth, James J. O'Donnell, and Frederick van Fleteren, 390–391. Grand Rapids, MI: William E. Eerdmans, 1999.

Button, Mark. "'A Monkish Kind of Virtue'? For and against Humility." *Political Theory* 33, no. 6 (2005): 840–868.

Byers, Sarah Catherine. *Perception, Sensibility, and Moral Motivation in Augustine: A Stoic-Platonic Synthesis*. New York: Cambridge University Press, 2013.

Calvin, John. *De Aeterna Dei praedestinatione qua in salutem alios ex hominibus elegit alios suo exitio reliquit*. In *Ioannis Calvini Opera quae Supersunt Omnia*, edited by Guilielmus Baum, Eduardus Cunitz, and Eduardus Reuss, vol. 8, 249–366. Brunsvigae: C. A. Schwetschke, 1870.

Cameron, Averil. *Christianity and the Rhetoric of Empire: The Development of Christian Discourse*. Berkeley: University of California Press, 1991.

Camus, Albert. *Christian Metaphysics and Neoplatonism*. Translated by Ronald D. Srigley. Columbia: University of Missouri Press, 2007.

Canning, Raymond. *The Unity of Love for God and Neighbor in St. Augustine*. Heverlee, Belgium: Augustinian Historical Institute, 1993.

Cartwright, John. "From Aquinas to Zwelethemba: A Brief History of Hope." *Annals of the American Academy of Political and Social Science: Hope, Power, and Governance* 592 (2004): 166–184.

Cary, Phillip, John Doody, and Kim Paffenroth, eds. *Augustine and Philosophy*. Lanham, MD: Lexington Books, 2010.

Cavadini, John C. "Simplifying Augustine." In *Educating People of Faith: Exploring the History of Jewish and Christian Communities*, edited by John Van Engen, 63–84. Grand Rapids, MI: William E. Eerdmans, 2004.

Chadwick, Amy E. "Toward a Theory of Persuasive Hope: Effects of Cognitive Appraisals, Hope Appeals, and Hope in the Context of Climate Change." *Health Communication* 30, no. 6 (2015): 598–611.

Chadwick, Henry. *Augustine*. Oxford: Oxford University Press, 1986.

Charry, Ellen T. *By the Renewing of Your Minds: The Pastoral Function of Christian Doctrine.* Oxford: Oxford University Press, 1999.

Christine de Pizan. *The Book of the Body Politic.* Edited and translated by Kate Langdon Forhan. Cambridge: Cambridge University Press, 1994.

———. *The Book of the City of Ladies.* Translated by Earl Jeffrey Richards. Rev. ed. New York: Persa Books, 1998.

Cicero. *The Best Kind of Orator.* In *On Invention, Best Kind of Orator, Topics,* by Cicero, translated by H. M. Hubbell, 347–373. Loeb Classical Library No. 386. Cambridge, MA: Harvard University Press, 1949.

———. *How to Be a Friend: An Ancient Guide to True Friendship.* Translated by Philip Freeman. Princeton, NJ: Princeton University Press, 2018.

———. *On the Commonwealth and On the Laws.* Edited and translated by James E. G. Zetzel. Cambridge: Cambridge University Press, 1999.

———. *On Duties.* Edited by M. T. Griffin and E. M. Atkins. Cambridge: Cambridge University Press, 1991.

———. *On the Ideal Orator.* Translated by James M. May and Jakob Wisse. Oxford: Oxford University Press, 2001.

———. *On Invention.* In *On Invention, Best Kind of Orator, Topics,* by Cicero, translated by H. M. Hubbell, vii–346. Loeb Classical Library No. 386. Cambridge, MA: Harvard University Press.

———. *Orator.* In *Brutus, Orator,* by Cicero, translated by H. M. Hubbell, 295–509. Loeb Classical Library No. 342. Cambridge, MA: Harvard University Press, 1962.

Cipriani, Nello. "Rhetoric." Translated by Matthew O'Connell. In *Augustine through the Ages,* edited by Allan D. Fitzgerald, John Cavadini, Marianne Djuth, James J. O'Donnell, and Frederick van Fleteren, 724–726. Grand Rapids, MI: William E. Eerdmans, 1999.

Clair, Joseph. *Discerning the Good in the Letters and Sermons of Augustine.* Oxford: Oxford University Press, 2016.

———. *On Education, Formation, Citizenship and the Lost Purpose of Learning.* New York: Bloomsbury Academic, 2018.

———. "Wolterstorff on Love and Justice: An Augustinian Response." *Journal of Religious Ethics* 41, no. 1 (2013): 138–167.

Clark, Gillian. "City of Books: Augustine and the World as Text." In *The Early Christian Book,* edited by William E. Klingshirn and Linda Safran, 117–138. Washington, DC: Catholic University of America Press, 2007.

Clark, Kenneth W. "Realized Eschatology." *Journal of Biblical Literature* 59, no. 3 (1940): 367–383.

Clark, Mark Edward. "Spes in the Early Imperial Cult: 'The Hope of Augustus.'" *Numen* 30 (1983): 80–105.

Coats, Wendell John, Jr. *Oakeshott and His Contemporaries: Montaigne, St. Augustine, Hegel, et al.* Selinsgrove, PA: Susquehanna University Press, 2000.

Cohen, Joshua, and Thomas Nagel. Introduction to *A Brief Inquiry into the Meaning of Sin and Faith,* by John Rawls, edited by Thomas Nagel, 1–23. Cambridge, MA: Harvard University Press, 2009.

Coleman, Janet. "St Augustine." In *A History of Political Thought: From Ancient Greece to Early Christianity,* 292–340. Malden, MA: Blackwell, 2000.

Coles, Romand. *Rethinking Generosity: Critical Theory and the Politics of Caritas.* Ithaca, NY: Cornell University Press, 1997.

———. *Self/Power/Other: Political Theory and Dialogical Ethics.* Ithaca, NY: Cornell University Press, 1992.

Connolly, Joy. *The Life of Roman Republicanism.* Princeton, NJ: Princeton University Press, 2015.

Connolly, William E. *The Augustinian Imperative: A Reflection on the Politics of Morality.* New York: Rowman & Littlefield, 1993.

Conybeare, Catherine. "Augustine's *The City of God* (fifth century A.D.): Patriarchy, Pluralism and the Creation of Man." In *Patriarchal Moments: Reading Patriarchal Texts,* edited by Cesare Cuttica and Gaby Mahlberg, 43–48. New York: Bloomsbury, 2016.

———. "*Terrarum Orbi Documentum*: Augustine, Camillus, and Learning from History." In *History, Apocalypse, and the Secular Imagination: New Essays on Augustine's "City of God,"* edited by Mark Vessey, Karla Pollmann, and Allan D. Fitzgerald, 59–74. Bowling Green, OH: Philosophy Documentation Center, 1999.

Cook, Molly Malone, and Mary Oliver. *Our World.* Boston: Beacon Press, 2007.

Cooper, John M. *Pursuits of Wisdom: Six Ways of Life in Ancient Philosophy from Socrates to Plotinus.* Princeton, NJ: Princeton University Press, 2012.

Corey, Elizabeth Campbell. *Michael Oakeshott on Religion, Aesthetics and Politics.* Columbia: University of Missouri Press, 2006.

Crouter, Richard. *Reinhold Niebuhr on Politics, Religion, and Christian Faith.* New York: Oxford University Press, 2010.

Daley, Brian E. *The Hope of the Early Church: A Handbook of Patristic Eschatology.* Grand Rapids, MI: Baker Academic, 2002.

Daly, Christopher T., John Doody, and Kim Paffenroth, eds. *Augustine and History.* Lanham, MD: Lexington Books, 2007.

Dauphinais, Michael, Barry David, and Matthew Levering, eds. *Aquinas the Augustinian.* Washington, DC: Catholic University of America Press, 2007.

Davidson, Arnold I. "Introduction: Pierre Hadot and the Spiritual Phenomenon of Ancient Philosophy." In *Philosophy as a Way of Life: Spiritual Exercises from Socrates to Foucault,* by Pierre Hadot, edited by Arnold I. Davidson, translated by Michael Chase, 1–45. Malden, MA: Blackwell, 1995.

Davidson, Donald. "On the Very Idea of a Conceptual Scheme." In *The Essential Davidson,* 196–208. New York: Oxford University Press, 2006.

———. "Radical Interpretation." In *The Essential Davidson,* 184–195. New York: Oxford University Press, 2006.

Deane, Herbert A. *The Political and Social Ideas of St. Augustine.* New York: Columbia University Press, 1963.

Decosimo, David. *Ethics as a Work of Charity: Thomas Aquinas and Pagan Virtue.* Stanford, CA: Stanford University Press, 2014.

Deneen, Patrick J. *Democratic Faith.* Princeton, NJ: Princeton University Press, 2005.

Dienstag, Joshua Foa. *Pessimism: Philosophy, Ethic, Spirit.* Princeton, NJ: Princeton University Press, 2006.

Dionne, E. J., Jr. "A Kinder Mix of Religion and Politics during Holy Week." *Washington Post,* April 4, 2012. https://www.washingtonpost.com/opinions/a-kinder-mix-of-religion-and -politics-during-holy-week/2012/04/04/gIQAuH26vS_story.html?utm_term=.7e57c70 a01cb.

———. *Souled Out: Reclaiming Faith and Politics after the Religious Right*. Princeton, NJ: Princeton University Press, 2008.

Dixon, Sandra, John Doody, and Kim Paffenroth, eds. *Augustine and Psychology*. Lanham, MD: Lexington Books, 2012.

Dodaro, Robert. "Augustine on the Statesman and the Two Cities." In *A Companion to Augustine*, edited by Mark Vessey, 386–397. Malden, MA: Wiley-Blackwell, 2012.

———. "Augustine's Secular City." In *Augustine and His Critics: Essays in Honour of Gerald Bonner*, edited by Robert Dodaro and George Lawless, 231–259. New York: Routledge, 2000.

———. "Between the Two Cities: Political Action in Augustine of Hippo." In *Augustine and Politics*, edited by John Doody, Kevin L. Hughes, and Kim Paffenroth, 99–115. Lanham, MD: Lexington Books, 2005.

———. *Christ and the Just Society in the Thought of Augustine*. New York: Cambridge University Press, 2004.

———. "Church and State." In *Augustine through the Ages*, edited by Allan D. Fitzgerald, John Cavadini, Marianne Djuth, James J. O'Donnell, and Frederick van Fleteren, 176–184. Grand Rapids, MI: William E. Eerdmans, 1999.

———. "The Secret Justice of God and the Gift of Humility." *Augustinian Studies* 34, no. 1 (2003): 83–96.

Dodaro, Robert, and George Lawless, eds. *Augustine and His Critics: Essays in Honour of Gerald Bonner*. New York: Routledge, 2000.

Dodd, C. H. *Parables of the Kingdom*. London: Nisbet, 1936.

Doody, John, Adam Goldstein, and Kim Paffenroth, eds. *Augustine and Science*. Lanham, MD: Lexington Books, 2012.

Doody, John, Kevin L. Hughes, and Kim Paffenroth, eds. *Augustine and Politics*. Lanham, MD: Lexington Books, 2005.

Doody, John, Kim Paffenroth, and Mark Smillie, eds. *Augustine and the Environment*. Lanham, MD: Lexington Books, 2016.

Dougherty, Richard J., ed. *Augustine's Political Thought*. Rochester, NY: University of Rochester Press, 2019.

Doyle, Daniel. "The Bishop as Teacher." In *Augustine and Liberal Education*, edited by Kim Paffenroth and Kevin L. Hughes, 81–94. Lanham, MD: Rowman & Littlefield, 2008.

Dreher, Rod. *The Benedict Option: A Strategy for Christians in a Post-Christian Nation*. New York: Sentinel, 2017.

Duin, Julia. "Catholics Rap Pelosi's Abortion Remarks." *Washington Times*, August 27, 2008. https://www.washingtontimes.com/news/2008/aug/27/catholic-bishops-assail-pelosi-over-her-remarks-on/.

Dunbabin, Katherine M. D. *The Mosaics of Roman North Africa: Studies in Iconography and Patronage*. Oxford: Clarendon Press, 1978.

Dupe, Paul A., and Christopher P. Gilbert. *The Political Influence of Churches*. New York: Cambridge University Press, 2009.

Dylan, Bob. "I Dreamed I Saw St. Augustine." Recorded October 17, 1967. Track 3 on *John Wesley Harding*. Columbia Records, 1967.

Dyson, R. W. Introduction to *The City of God against the Pagans*, by Augustine, edited by R. W. Dyson, x–xxix. New York: Cambridge University Press, 1998.

Ehrenreich, Barbara. "Pathologies of Hope." *Harper's Magazine*, February 2007. https://harpers .org/archive/2007/02/pathologies-of-hope/.

Elia, Matthew. "Ethics in the Afterlife of Slavery: Race, Augustinian Politics, and the Problem of the Christian Master." *Journal of the Society of Christian Ethics* 38, no. 2 (2018): 93–110.

———. "Slave Christologies: Augustine and the Enduring Trouble with the 'Form of a Slave' (Phil 2:5–7)." *Interpretation: A Journal of Bible and Theology* 75, no. 1 (2021): 19–32.

Elm, Susanna. "Sold to Sin through *Origo*: Augustine of Hippo and the Late Roman Slave Trade." *Studia Patristica* 98, no. 24 (2017): 1–21.

Elshtain, Jean Bethke. "Augustine." In *The Blackwell Companion to Political Theology*, edited by Peter Scott and William T. Cavanaugh, 35–47. Malden, MA: Blackwell, 2007.

———. *Augustine and the Limits of Politics*. Notre Dame, IN: University of Notre Dame Press, 1998.

———. "But Was It Just? Reflections on the Iraq War." *NEXUS* 9 (2004): 69–77.

———. *Just War against Terror: The Burden of American Power in a Violent World*. New York: Basic Books, 2003.

———. *Public Man, Private Woman: Women in Social and Political Thought*. Oxford: Martin Robertson, 1981.

———. "Reflection on the Problem of 'Dirty Hands.'" In *Torture: A Collection*, edited by Sanford Levinson, 77–90. Oxford: Oxford University Press, 2004.

Eno, Robert B. "Authority." In *Augustine through the Ages*, edited by Allan D. Fitzgerald, John Cavadini, Marianne Djuth, James J. O'Donnell, and Frederick van Fleteren, 80–82. Grand Rapids, MI: William E. Eerdmans, 1999.

Evangelical Climate Initiative. "Climate Change: An Evangelical Call to Action." http://www .christiansandclimate.org/statement/.

Farneth, Molly. "A Politics of Tending and Transformation." *Studies in Christian Ethics* 32, no. 1 (2019): 113–118.

Feinberg, Matthew, and Robb Willer. "From Gulf to Bridge: When Do Moral Arguments Facilitate Political Influence?" *Personality and Social Psychology Bulletin* 41, no. 12 (2015): 1665–1681.

Fiedrowicz, Michael. Introduction to *The Advantage of Believing*, by Augustine. In *Trilogy on Faith and Happiness*, edited by Boniface Ramsey, 83–92. Hyde Park, NY: New City Press, 2010.

———. Introduction to *Faith in the Unseen*, by Augustine. In *Trilogy on Faith and Happiness*, edited by Boniface Ramsey, 57–64. Hyde Park, NY: New City Press, 2010.

Finley, Moses. *Politics in the Ancient World*. Cambridge: Cambridge University Press, 1983.

Fitzgerald, Allan D., John Cavadini, Marianne Djuth, James J. O'Donnell, and Frederick Van Fleteren, eds. *Augustine through the Ages: An Encyclopedia*. Grand Rapids, MI: William B. Eerdmans, 1999.

Fleischacker, Samuel. *A Short History of Distributive Justice*. Cambridge, MA: Harvard University Press, 2004.

Foot, Philippa. *Natural Goodness*. Oxford: Oxford University Press, 2001.

Forhan, Kate L. "Christine de Pizan." In *The Oxford Guide to the Historical Reception of Augustine*, edited by Karla Pollmann and Willemien Otten, vol. 2, 779–780. New York: Oxford University Press, 2013.

Fortin, Ernest. "Augustine and the Problem of Modernity." In *Classical Christianity and the Political Order*, edited by J. Brian Benestad, 137–150. Lanham, MD: Rowman & Littlefield, 1996.

———. "St. Augustine." In *History of Political Philosophy*, edited by Leo Strauss and Joseph Cropsey, 3rd ed., 176–205. Chicago: University of Chicago Press, 1987.

Fox, Richard Wightman. *Reinhold Niebuhr: A Biography*. Ithaca, NY: Cornell University Press, 1996.

Friere, Paulo. *Pedagogy of Hope: Reliving Pedagogy of the Oppressed*. Translated by Robert B. Barr. New York: Bloomsbury, 1994.

Freyburger, Gérard. *Fides: Études sémantique et religieuse depuis les origines jusqu'à l'époque Augustéenne*. 2nd ed. Paris: Société d'Édition Les Belles Lettres, 2009.

Galisanka, Andrius. *John Rawls: The Path to a Theory of Justice*. Cambridge, MA: Harvard University Press, 2019.

Galston, William A. "Augustine or Emerson?" *Commonweal* 131, no. 2 (2004): 24–25.

———. *Liberal Purposes: Goods, Virtues, and Diversity in the Liberal State*. New York: Cambridge University Press, 1991.

———. "When in Doubt." *Democracy*, no. 5 (Summer 2007): 31–37.

Gamble, Harry Y. *Books and Readers in the Early Church: A History of Early Christian Texts*. New Haven, CT: Yale University Press, 1995.

Garsten, Bryan. *Saving Persuasion: A Defense of Rhetoric and Judgment*. Cambridge, MA: Harvard University Press, 2006.

Gavrilov, A. K. "Techniques of Reading in Classical Antiquity." *Classical Quarterly* 47, no. 1 (1997): 56–73.

George, Timothy. "Benedict XVI, the Great Augustinian." *First Things*, February 19, 2013. https://www.firstthings.com/web-exclusives/2013/02/benedict-xvi-the-great-augustinian.

Glatz, Carol. "Holy, Holy, Holy: Pope Talks about His Favorite Saints." *Catholic Accent*, October 24, 2013. https://www.mydigitalpublication.com/publication/?m=27941&i=278812&p=20&ver=html5.

González, Justo L. *The Mestizo Augustine: A Theologian between Two Cultures*. Downers Grove, IL: IVP Academic, 2013.

Green, Jeffrey E. "Political Theory as Both Philosophy and History: A Defense against Methodological Militancy." *Annual Review of Political Science* 18 (2015): 425–441.

Green, R.P.H. Introduction to *On Christian Teaching*, by Augustine, vii–xxiii. New York: Oxford University Press, 1997.

Greenleaf, Robert K. *Servant Leadership: A Journey into the Nature of Legitimate Power and Greatness*. Mahwah, NJ: Paulist Press, 2002.

Gregory, Eric. "Before the Original Position: The Neo-orthodox Theology of the Young John Rawls." *Journal of Religious Ethics* 35, no. 2 (2007): 179–206.

———. "Modern Politics in the Shadow of Augustine." President's Lecture Series, Princeton University, April 9, 2013.

———. *Politics and the Order of Love: An Augustinian Ethic of Democratic Citizenship*. Chicago: University of Chicago Press, 2008.

———. "Sympathy and Domination: Adam Smith, Happiness, and the Virtues of Augustinianism." In *Adam Smith as Theologian*, edited by Paul Oslington, 33–45. New York: Routledge,
2011.

———. "Taking Love Seriously: Elshtain's Augustinian Voice and Modern Politics." In *Jean
Bethke Elshtain: Politics, Ethics, and Society*, edited by Debra Erickson and Michael Le Che-
vallier, 177–190. Notre Dame, IN: University of Notre Dame Press, 2018.

———. "What Hippo and Grand Rapids Have to Say to Each Other." *Studies in Christian Ethics*
32, no. 1 (2019): 119–123.

Gregory, Eric, and Joseph Clair, "Augustinianisms and Thomisms." In *The Cambridge Companion
to Christian Political Theology*, edited by Craig Hovey and Elizabeth Phillips, 176–195. Cambridge: Cambridge University Press, 2015.

Griffiths, Paul J. "Secularity and the *Saeculum*." In *Augustine's "City of God": A Critical Guide*,
edited by James Wetzel, 33–54. Cambridge: Cambridge University Press, 2012.

Grosse, Patricia L. "Love and the Patriarch: Augustine and (Pregnant) Women." *Hypatia* 32,
no. 1 (2017): 119–134.

Grummett, David. "Arendt, Augustine, and Evil." *Heythrop Journal* 41 (2000): 154–169.

Hadot, Pierre. *Philosophy as a Way of Life: Spiritual Exercises from Socrates to Foucault.* Translated
by Michael Chase, edited by Arnold Davidson. Malden, MA: Blackwell, 1995.

———. *What Is Ancient Philosophy?* Translated by Michael Chase. Cambridge, MA: Harvard
University Press, 2002.

Hairston, Eric Ashley. *The Ebony Column: Classics, Civilization, and the African American Recla-
mation of the West.* Knoxville: University of Tennessee Press, 2013.

Hamilton-Bleakley, Holly. "Linguistic Philosophy and *The Foundations*." In *Rethinking the Foundations of Modern Political Thought*, edited by Annabel Brett, James Tully, and Holly-
Hamilton Bleakley, 20–33. Cambridge: Cambridge University Press, 2006.

Hampl, Patricia. Preface to *Confessions*, by Augustine, translated by Maria Boulding, xiii–xxvi.
New York: Random House, 1998.

Hanoune, R. "Le paganisme philosophique de l'aristocratie municipale." In *L'Afrique dans
l'Occident romain (Ier siècle av. J.-C. IVe siècle ap. J.C.)*, Collection de l'Ecole francaise de
Rome 134, 3–75. Rome: Palais Farnese, 1990.

Hardt, Michael, and Antonio Negri. *Empire.* Cambridge, MA: Harvard University Press,
2000.

Harmless, William. *Augustine and the Catechumenate.* Collegeville, MN: The Liturgical Press,
1995.

———. *Augustine in His Own Words.* Washington, DC: Catholic University of America Press,
2010.

Harries, Jill. *Law and Empire in Late Antiquity.* Cambridge: Cambridge University Press, 1999.

Harrison, Carol. *Augustine: Christian Truth and Fractured Humanity.* New York: Oxford University Press, 2000.

———. "The Rhetoric of Scripture and Preaching: Classical Decadence or Christian Aesthetic?" In *Augustine and His Critics: Essays in Honour of Gerald Bonner*, edited by Robert
Dodaro and George Lawless, 214–230. New York: Routledge, 2000.

Hartle, Ann. *The Modern Self in Rousseau's Confessions: A Reply to St. Augustine.* Notre Dame,
IN: University of Notre Dame Press, 1983.

Hauerwas, Stanley. *After Christendom? How the Church Is to Behave if Freedom, Justice, and a Christian Nation Are Bad Ideas*. Nashville, TN: Abingdon Press, 1991.

———. *A Community of Character: Toward a Constructive Christian Social Ethic*. Notre Dame, IN: University of Notre Dame Press, 1981.

———. *The Peaceable Kingdom: A Primer in Christian Ethics*. Notre Dame, IN: University of Notre Dame Press, 1983.

———. "Where Would I Be without Friends?" In *Faithfulness and Fortitude: In Conversation with the Theological Ethics of Stanley Hauerwas*, edited by Mark Thiessen Nation and Samuel Wells, 313–332. Edinburgh: T&T Clark, 2000.

Hauerwas, Stanley, and Charles Pinches. *Christians among the Virtues: Theological Conversations with Ancient and Modern Ethics*. Notre Dame, IN: University of Notre Dame Press, 1997.

Hauerwas, Stanley, and William H. Willimon. *Resident Aliens: A Provocative Christian Assessment of Culture and Ministry for People Who Know That Something Is Wrong*. Nashville: Abingdon Press, 1989.

Hay, David M. "Pistis as 'Ground for Faith' in Hellenized Judaism and Paul." *Journal of Biblical Literature* 108, no. 3 (1989): 461–476.

Herdt, Jennifer A. *Putting on Virtue: The Legacy of the Splendid Vices*. Chicago: University of Chicago Press, 2008.

———. "*Reditus* Reformed: Eudaimonism and Obligation in Aquinas and Calvin." Warfield Lectures, Princeton Theological Seminary, March 18–21, 2013.

———. "The Theater of the Virtues: Augustine's Critique of Pagan Mimesis." In *Augustine's "City of God": A Critical Guide*, edited by James Wetzel, 111–129. Cambridge: Cambridge University Press, 2012.

Hill, Edmund. "Unless You Believe, You Shall Not Understand: Augustine's Perception of Faith." *Augustinian Studies* 25 (1994): 51–64.

Hindu Declaration on Climate Change. 2015. Accessed on August 14, 2021. http://www.hinduclimatedeclaration2015.org/english.

Hobsbawn, Eric. *The Age of Extremes: A History of the World, 1914–1991*. New York: Vintage, 1995.

Hochschild, Jennifer L. "Left Pessimism and Political Science." *Perspectives on Politics* 15, no. 1 (2017): 6–19.

Hollerich, Michael J. "John Milbank, Augustine, and the 'Secular.'" *Augustinian Studies* 30, no. 2 (1999): 311–326.

Hollingworth, Miles. *Pilgrim City: St. Augustine of Hippo and His Innovation in Political Thought*. New York: T&T Clark, 2010.

———. *Saint Augustine of Hippo: An Intellectual Biography*. New York: Oxford University Press, 2013.

Honig, Bonnie. *Public Things: Democracy in Disrepair*. New York: Fordham University Press, 2017.

hooks, bell. *Teaching Community: A Pedagogy of Hope*. New York: Routledge, 2003.

Hordern, Joshua. "Loyalty, Conscience and Tense Communion: Jonathan Edwards Meets Martha Nussbaum." *Studies in Christian Ethics* 27, no. 2 (2014): 167–184.

———. *Political Affections: Civic Participation and Moral Theology*. Oxford: Oxford University Press, 2012.

Howard-Snyder, Daniel. "Propositional Faith: What It Is and What It Is Not." *American Philosophical Quarterly* 50, no. 4 (October 2013): 357–372.

Innocenti, Beth. "Towards a Theory of Vivid Description as Practiced in Cicero's *Verrine* Oration." *Rhetorica* 12, no. 4 (1994): 355–381.

Irwin, T. H. "Splendid Vices? Augustine for and against Pagan Virtue." *Medieval Philosophy and Theology* 8 (1999): 105–127.

Isidore. *Opera Apendices*. In *Patrologiae Cursus Completus, Series Latina*, vol. 83, edited by J.-P. Migne. Paris: Garnier, 1862.

Islamic Declaration on Global Climate Change. Accessed on August 13, 2021. https://www.ifees .org.uk/wp-content/uploads/2020/01/climate_declarationmmwb.pdf.

Jackson, M. G. St. A. "Faith, Hope and Charity and Prayer in St. Augustine." In *Studia Patristica: Papers Presented to the Tenth International Conference on Patristic Studies Held in Oxford 1987*, edited by Elizabeth A. Livingstone, 265–270. Leuven: Peeters Press, 1989.

Jenson, Matt. *The Gravity of Sin: Augustine, Luther, and Barth*. New York: T&T Clark, 2006.

Jewish Climate Action Network. "Mission." Accessed August 14, 2021. https://www .jewishclimate.org/.

Johnson, Kristen Deede. *Theology, Political Theory, and Pluralism: Beyond Tolerance and Difference*. New York: Cambridge University Press, 2007.

Jones, David Albert. "Not Good for Anyone: Death in the Thought of Augustine of Hippo." In *Approaching the End: A Theological Exploration of Death and Dying*, 38–56. Oxford: Oxford University Press, 2007.

———. "Thomas Aquinas, Augustine, and Aristotle on 'Delayed Animation.'" *Thomist* 76, no. 1 (2012): 1–36.

Kabala, Boleslaw Z., Ashleen Menchaca-Bagnulo, and Nathan Pinkoksi, eds. *Augustine in a Time of Crisis: Politics and Religion Contested*. Cham, Switzerland: Palgrave Macmillan, 2021.

Kateb, George. Foreword to *Political Thought and Political Thinkers*, by Judith N. Shklar, edited by Stanley Hoffmann, vii–xix. Chicago: University of Chicago Press, 1998.

Kaufman, Peter Iver. "Augustine's Dystopia." In *Augustine's "City of God": A Critical Guide*, edited by James Wetzel, 55–74. Cambridge: Cambridge University Press, 2012.

———. "Hopefully, Augustine." *Augustinian Studies* 53, no. 1 (2022): 3–27.

———. *Incorrectly Political: Augustine and Thomas More*. Notre Dame, IN: University of Notre Dame Press, 2007.

———. *On Agamben, Arendt, Christianity, and the Dark Arts of Civilization*. New York: Bloomsbury Academic, 2020.

———. "Patience and/or Politics: Augustine and the Crisis at Calama, 408–409." *Vigiliae Christianae* 57, no. 1 (February 2003): 22–35.

———. *Redeeming Politics*. Princeton, NJ: Princeton University Press, 1990.

Kelly, Joseph F. "Carolingian Era, Late." In *Augustine through the Ages*, edited by Allan D. Fitzgerald, John Cavadini, Marianne Djuth, James J. O'Donnell, and Frederick van Fleteren, 129–132. Grand Rapids, MI: William B. Eerdmans, 1999.

Kengor, Paul. "Pelosi v. Augustine." *National Catholic Register*, September 9, 2008. http://www .ncregister.com/site/article/pelosi_v_augustine.

Kennedy, George A. "Christianity and Classical Rhetoric." In *A New History of Classical Rhetoric*, 257–270. Princeton, NJ: Princeton University Press, 1994.

———. *Classical Rhetoric and Its Christian and Secular Tradition from Ancient to Modern Times.* 2nd ed. Chapel Hill: University of North Carolina Press, 1999.

———. *New Testament Interpretation through Rhetorical Criticism.* Chapel Hill: University of North Carolina Press, 1984.

Kennedy, Robert P., Kim Paffenroth, and John Doody, eds. *Augustine and Literature.* Lanham, MD: Lexington Books, 2005.

Kent, Bonnie. "Augustine's Ethics." In *The Cambridge Companion to Augustine*, edited by Eleonore Stump and Norman Kretzmann, 205–233. Cambridge: Cambridge University Press, 2001.

———. "Reinventing Augustine's Ethics: The Afterlife of *City of God.*" In *Augustine's "City of God": A Critical Guide*, edited by James Wetzel, 225–244. Cambridge: Cambridge University Press, 2012.

———. *Virtues of the Will: The Transformation of Ethics in the Late Thirteenth Century.* Washington, DC: Catholic University Press, 1993.

Kerr, Fergus. *Immortal Longings: Versions of Transcending Humanity.* Notre Dame, IN: University of Notre Dame Press, 1997.

Keys, Mary M. "Augustinian Humility as Natural Right." In *Natural Right and Political Philosophy: Essays in Honor of Catherine Zuckert and Michael Zuckert*, edited by Ann Ward and Lee Ward, 97–113. Notre Dame, IN: University of Notre Dame Press, 2013.

———. "Elitism and Secularism, Old and New: Augustine on Humility, Pride, and Philosophy in *City of God* VIII–X." In *Augustine in a Time of Crisis: Politics and Religion Contested*, edited by Boleslaw Z. Kabala, Ashleen Menchaca-Bagnulo, and Nathan Pinkoksi, 227–246. Cham, Switzerland: Palgrave Macmillan, 2021.

Keys, Mary M., and Colleen E. Mitchell. "Augustine's Constitutionalism: Citizenship, Common Good, and Consent." In *Christianity and Constitutionalism*, edited by Ian Leigh and Nicholas Aroney. Oxford: Oxford University Press, forthcoming.

King, Martin Luther, Jr. "Letter from Birmingham City Jail." In *A Testament of Hope: The Essential Speeches and Writings of Martin Luther King, Jr.*, edited by James Melvin Washington, 289–302. New York: Harper Collins, 1986.

———. "Pilgrimage to Nonviolence." In *A Testament of Hope: The Essential Speeches and Writings of Martin Luther King, Jr.*, edited by James Melvin Washington, 35–40. New York: Harper Collins, 1986.

King, Peter. "Augustine on Knowledge." In *The Cambridge Companion to Augustine*, edited by David Vincent Meconi and Eleonore Stump, 2nd ed., 142–165. Cambridge: Cambridge University Press, 2014.

King, Peter, and Nathan Ballantyne. "Augustine on Testimony." *Canadian Journal of Philosophy* 39, no. 2 (June 2009): 195–214.

Kinneavy, James L. *Greek Rhetorical Origins of Christian Faith: An Inquiry.* New York: Oxford University Press, 1987.

Klosko, George. *History of Political Theory: An Introduction.* Vol. 1, *Ancient and Medieval.* New York: Oxford University Press, 2012.

Kolbet, Paul R. *Augustine and the Cure of Souls: Reviving a Classical Ideal.* Notre Dame, IN: University of Notre Dame Press, 2010.

———. "Freedom from Grim Necessity: Correcting Misreadings of Augustine on Torture." *Studia Patristica* 117 (2021): 139–147.

Krey, Philip D. "Luther, Martin." In *Augustine through the Ages*, edited by Allan D. Fitzgerald, John Cavadini, Marianne Djuth, James J. O'Donnell, and Frederick van Fleteren, 516–518. Grand Rapids, MI: William B. Eerdmans, 1999.

Kruse, Elliot, Joseph Chancellor, Peter M. Ruberton, and Sonja Lyubomirsky. "An Upward Spiral between Gratitude and Humility." *Social Psychological and Personality Science* 5, no. 7 (2014): 805–814.

Lamb, Michael. "Aquinas and the Virtues of Hope: Theological and Democratic." *Journal of Religious Ethics* 44, no. 2 (2016): 300–332.

———. "Augustine and Political Theory." In *T&T Clark Handbook of Political Theology*, edited by Rubén Rosario Rodríguez, 89–116. London: T&T Clark, 2020.

———. "Augustine and Republican Liberty: Contextualizing Coercion." *Augustinian Studies* 48, nos. 1–2 (2017): 119–159.

———. "Augustine on Hope and Politics: A Response to Peter Iver Kaufman." *Augustinian Studies* 53, no. 1 (2022): 29–45.

———. "Between Presumption and Despair: Augustine's Hope for the Commonwealth." *American Political Science Review* 112, no. 4 (2018): 1036–1049.

———. "Beyond Pessimism: A Structure of Encouragement in Augustine's *City of God*." *Review of Politics* 80, no. 4 (2018): 591–624.

———. "Biden's Augustinian Call for Concord." In *Breaking Ground: Charting Our Future in a Pandemic Year*, edited by Anne Snyder and Susannah Black, 267–269. New York: Plough Publishing House, 2022.

———. "Difficult Hope: Wendell Berry and Climate Change." In *Hope*, edited by Nancy E. Snow. New York: Oxford University Press, forthcoming.

———. "A Passion and Its Virtue: Aquinas on Hope and Magnanimity." In *Hope*, edited by Ingolf U. Dalferth and Marlene A. Block, 67–88. Tübingen: Mohr Siebeck, 2016.

Lambeth Declaration 2015 on Climate Change. Accessed August 14, 2021. https://www.churchofengland.org/sites/default/files/2021-05/CCB_Lambeth-declaration-2015-on-climate-change-updated.pdf.

Lamoreaux, John C. "Episcopal Courts in Late Antiquity." *Journal of Early Christian Studies* 3, no. 2 (1995): 143–167.

Lane, Anthony N. S. "Calvin, John." In *The Oxford Guide to the Historical Reception of Augustine*, edited by Karla Pollmann and Willemien Otten, vol. 2, 739–743. New York: Oxford University Press, 2013.

Lane, Melissa S. *Method and Politics in Plato's "Statesman"*. New York: Cambridge University Press, 1998.

———. *Plato's Progeny: How Plato and Socrates Still Captivate the Modern Mind*. London: Duckworth, 2001.

Langan, John P. "Augustine on the Unity and the Interconnection of the Virtues." *Harvard Theological Review* 72, nos. 1–2 (1979): 81–95.

Lee, Peter. "Selective Memory: Augustine and Contemporary Just War Discourse." *Scottish Journal of Theology* 65, no. 3 (2012): 309–322.

Leibniz, G. W. *Theodicy*. Edited by Austin Farrar. Translated by F. M. Huggard. Chicago: Open Court, 1985.

Lepelley, Claude. "Facing Wealth and Poverty: Defining Augustine's Social Doctrine." *Augustinian Studies* 38, no. 1 (2007): 1–17.

Lewis, Charlton T. *An Elementary Latin Dictionary*. Oxford: Oxford University Press, 2000.

Leyser, Conrad. "Augustine and the Problem of Authority." In *Authority and Asceticism from Augustine to Gregory the Great*, 3–32. New York: Oxford University Press, 2000.

Lloyd, Vincent W. *The Problem with Grace: Reconfiguring Political Theology*. Stanford, CA: Stanford University Press, 2011.

Longfellow, Henry Wadsworth. "The Ladder of St. Augustine." Poetry Foundation. https://www.poetryfoundation.org/poems/44636/the-ladder-of-st-augustine.

Lovin, Robin W. *Reinhold Niebuhr and Christian Realism*. New York: Cambridge University Press, 1995.

Luban, David. "What Would Augustine Do? The President, Drones, and Just War Theory." *Boston Review*, June 6, 2012. http://bostonreview.net/david-luban-the-president-drones-augustine-just-war-theory.

Lunn-Rockliffe, Sophie. "Early Christian Political Philosophy." In *The Oxford Handbook of the History of Political Philosophy*, edited by George Klosko, 142–155. New York: Oxford University Press, 2011.

Luther, Martin. *D. Martin Luthers Werke: Kritische Gesammtausgabe*. Vol. 9. Weimar: Hermann Böhlau, 1893.

———. *Lectures on Hebrews*. Translated by Walter A. Hansen. In *Luther's Works*, vol. 29, *Lectures on Titus, Philemon, and Hebrews*, edited by Jaroslav Pelikan, 107–241. St. Louis, MO: Concordia, 1968.

———. *The Ninety-Five Theses: A Disputation to Clarify the Power of Indulgences*. In *The Ninety-Five Theses and Other Writings*, translated and edited by William R. Russell, 1–13. New York: Penguin, 2017.

Lyons, John D. *Exemplum: The Rhetoric of Example in Early Modern France and Italy*. Princeton, NJ: Princeton University Press, 1989.

Macedo, Stephen. *Liberal Virtues: Citizenship, Virtue, and Community in Liberal Constitutionalism*. New York: Oxford University Press, 1991.

MacIntyre, Alasdair. *God, Philosophy, Universities: A Selective History of the Catholic Philosophical Tradition*. Lanham, MD: Rowman & Littlefield, 2009.

———. *Whose Justice? Which Rationality?* Notre Dame, IN: University of Notre Dame Press, 1989.

MacMullen, Ramsey. "Judicial Savagery in the Roman Empire." In *Changes in the Roman Empire*, 204–217. Princeton, NJ: Princeton University Press, 1990.

Mandouze, André. *Saint Augustin: L'aventure de la raison et de la grâce*. Paris: Études Augustiennes, 1968.

Marchesi, Simone. *Dante and Augustine: Linguistics, Poetics, Hermeneutics*. Toronto: University of Toronto Press, 2011.

Maritain, Jacques. *Man and the State*. Chicago: University of Chicago Press, 1951.

Markowitz, Ezra M., and Azim F. Shariff. "Climate Change and Moral Judgement." *Nature Climate Change* 2, no. 4 (2012): 243–247.

Markus, R. A. *Christianity and the Secular*. Notre Dame, IN: University of Notre Dame Press, 2006.

———. "City or Desert? Two Models of Community." In *The End of Ancient Christianity*, 157–179. New York: Cambridge University Press, 1990.

———. *Saeculum: History and Society in the Theology of St Augustine*. Cambridge: Cambridge University Press, 1970.

———. *Signs and Meanings: World and Text in Ancient Christianity*. 2nd ed. Eugene, OR: Wipf & Stock, 1996.

Marrou, Henri. *A History of Education in Antiquity*. Translated by George Lamb. London: Sheed & Ward, 1956.

———. *Saint Augustine and His Influence through the Ages*. Translated by Patrick Hepburne-Scott. London: Longmans, 1957.

Marsden, George. "Jonathan Edwards, American Augustine." *Christianity Today*, November 1, 1999, accessed May 24, 2014. http://www.christianitytoday.com/bc/1999/novdec/9b6010.html?start=3.

Marshall, David J. "Calvin, John." In *Augustine through the Ages*, edited by Allan D. Fitzgerald, John Cavadini, Marianne Djuth, James J. O'Donnell, and Frederick van Fleteren, 116–120. Grand Rapids, MI: William B. Eerdmans, 1999.

Martin, Thomas F. "'An Abundant Supply of Discourse': Augustine and the Rhetoric of Monasticism." *Downside Review* 116, no. 402 (January 1998): 7–25.

———. "Augustine and the Politics of Monasticism." In *Augustine and Politics*, edited by John Doody, Kevin L. Hughes, and Kim Paffenroth, 165–186. Lanham, MD: Lexington Books, 2005.

———. "Augustine's *Confessions* as Pedagogy: Exercises in Transformation." In *Augustine and Liberal Education*, edited by Kim Paffenroth and Kevin L. Hughes, 25–51. Lanham, MD: Rowman & Littlefield, 2008.

Mathewes, Charles T. "An Augustinian Look at Empire." *Theology Today* 63 (2006): 292–306.

———. "Book One: The Presumptuousness of Autobiography and the Paradoxes of Beginning." In *A Reader's Companion to Augustine's "Confessions,"* edited by Kim Paffenroth and Robert P. Kennedy, 7–23. Louisville, KY: Westminster/John Knox Press, 2003.

———. *Evil and the Augustinian Tradition*. New York: Cambridge University Press, 2001.

———. "The Liberation of Questioning in Augustine's *Confessions*." *Journal of the American Academy of Religion* 70, no. 3 (September 2002): 539–560.

———. *The Republic of Grace: Augustinian Thoughts for Dark Times*. Grand Rapids, MI: William B. Eerdmans, 2010.

———. *A Theology of Public Life*. New York: Cambridge University Press, 2007.

Mays, Benjamin E. "Love of God and Love of Man—Inseparable." In *Seeking to Be Christian in Race Relations*, 16–23. New York: Friendship Press, 1957.

McCarthy, Michael C. "An Ecclesiology of Groaning: Augustine, the Psalms, and the Making of Church." *Theological Studies* 66 (2005): 23–48.

McConnell, Terrance C. "Augustine on Torturing and Punishing an Innocent Person." *Southern Journal of Philosophy* 17, no. 4 (1979): 481–492.

McGeer, Victoria. "The Art of Good Hope." *Annals of the American Academy of Political and Social Science: Hope, Power, and Governance* 592 (2004): 100–127.

McGrath, Alister E. *Iustitia Dei: A History of the Christian Doctrine of Justification*. Cambridge: Cambridge University Press, 1972.

———. "Last Things: Christian Hope." In *Christian Theology: An Introduction*, 3rd ed., 553–577. Oxford: Blackwell, 2001.

McKaughan, Daniel J. "Action-Centered Faith, Doubt, and Rationality." *Journal of Philosophical Research* 41 (2016): 71–90.

———. "Cognitive Opacity and the Analysis of Faith: Acts of Faith Interiorized through a Glass Only Darkly." *Religious Studies* 54 (2018): 576–585.

———. "On the Value of Faith and Faithfulness." *International Journal of the Philosophy of Religion* 81 (2017): 7–29.

McQueen, Alison. "The Wages of Fear? Toward Fearing Well about Climate Change." In *Philosophy and Climate Change*, edited by Mark Budolfson, Tristam McPherson, and David Plunkett, 152–177. New York: Oxford University Press, 2021.

Meacham, Jon. "The End of Christian America." *Newsweek*, April 3, 2009. http://www.newsweek.com/meacham-end-christian-america-77125.

Meconi, David Vincent. "Heaven and the *ecclesia perfecta* in Augustine." In *The Cambridge Companion to Augustine*, 2nd ed., edited by David Vincent Meconi and Eleonore Stump, 251–272. Cambridge: Cambridge University Press, 2014.

Meilaender, Gilbert C. *Friendship: A Study in Theological Ethics*. Notre Dame, IN: University of Notre Dame Press, 1981.

Menchaca-Bagnulo, Ashleen. "Deeds and Words: *Latreia*, Justice, and Mercy in Augustine's Political Thought." In *Augustine's Political Thought*, edited by Richard J. Dougherty, 74–104. Rochester, NY: University of Rochester Press, 2019.

———. "Rome and the Education of Mercy in Augustine's *City of God*." In *Augustine in a Time of Crisis: Politics and Religion Contested*, edited by Boleslaw Z. Kabala, Ashleen Menchaca-Bagnulo, and Nathan Pinkoksi, 17–36. Cham, Switzerland: Palgrave Macmillan, 2021.

Milbank, John. "Evil: Darkness and Silence." In *Being Reconciled: Ontology and Pardon*, 1–25. New York: Routledge, 2003.

———. "'Postmodern Critical Augustinianism': A Short *Summa* in Forty Two Responses to Unasked Questions." *Modern Theology* 7, no. 3 (April 1991): 225–237.

———. "The Poverty of Niebuhrianism." In *The Word Made Strange: Theology, Language, Culture*, 233–254. Oxford: Blackwell, 1997.

———. *Theology and Social Theory: Beyond Secular Reason*. 2nd ed. Malden, MA: Blackwell, 2006.

Miller, David. "A Tale of Two Cities; or, Political Philosophy as Lamentation." In *Justice for Earthlings: Essays in Political Philosophy*, 228–249. New York: Cambridge University Press, 2013.

Miller, Perry. *The New England Mind: The Seventeenth Century*. Cambridge, MA: Harvard University Press, 1939.

Milton, John. *Complete Prose Works of John Milton*. Edited by Don M. Wolfe. 8 vols. New Haven, CT: Yale University Press, 1953–1982.

Mitchell, Colleen E., and Mary M. Keys. "Love's Labor Leisured: Augustine on Charity, Contemplation, and Politics." In *Pensando il Lavoro: Contributi a Carattere Prevalentemente Filosofico*, edited by Giorgio Faro, vol. 2, 315–332. Rome: EDUSC, 2018.

Mittleman, Alan. *Hope in a Democratic Age: Philosophy, Religion, and Political Theory.* New York: Oxford University Press, 2009.

Mommsen, Theodor E. "St. Augustine and the Christian Idea of Progress: The Background of the *City of God." Journal of the History of Ideas* 12, no. 3 (June 1951): 346–374.

Montás, Roosevelt. *Rescuing Socrates: How the Great Books Changed My Life and Why They Matter for a New Generation.* Princeton, NJ: Princeton University Press, 2021.

Moran, Richard, and Martin J. Stone. "Anscombe on the Expression of Intention: An Exegesis." In *Essays on Anscombe's "Intention,"* edited by Anton Ford, Jennifer Hornsby, and Frederick Stoutland, 33–75. Cambridge, MA: Harvard University Press, 2011.

Morgan, Teresa J. "Response to My Commentators." *Religious Studies* 54 (2018): 592–604.

———. *Roman Faith and Christian Faith: Pistis and Fides in the Early Roman Empire and Early Christian Churches.* Oxford: Oxford University Press, 2015.

Moser, Susanne C. "More Bad News: The Risk of Neglecting Emotional Responses to Climate Change Information." In *Creating a Climate for Change: Communicating Climate Change and Facilitating Social Change,* edited by Susanne C. Moser and Lisa Dilling, 64–80. New York: Cambridge University Press, 2007.

Moser, Susanne C., and Lisa Dilling. "Communicating Climate Change: Closing the Science–Action Gap." In *The Oxford Handbook of Climate Change and Society,* edited by John S. Dryzek, Richard B. Norgaard, and David Schlosberg, 161–174. New York: Oxford University Press, 2011.

Murphy, Andrew. "Augustine and the Rhetoric of Roman Decline." *History of Political Thought* 26, no. 4 (Winter 2005): 588–606.

Murphy, James J. "St. Augustine and the Debate about a Christian Rhetoric." *Quarterly Journal of Speech* 46, no. 4 (1960): 400–410.

Nabi, Robin L., Abel Gustafson, and Risa Jensen. "Framing Climate Change: Exploring the Role of Emotion in Generating Advocacy Behavior." *Science Communication* 40, no. 4 (2018): 442–468.

Nelson, Eric. *The Theology of Liberalism: Political Philosophy and the Justice of God.* Cambridge, MA: Harvard University Press, 2019.

Niebuhr, Reinhold. "Augustine's Political Realism." In *The Essential Reinhold Niebuhr: Selected Essays and Addresses,* edited by Robert McAfee Brown, 123–141. New Haven, CT: Yale University Press, 1986.

———. *The Children of Light and the Children of Darkness: A Vindication of Democracy and a Critique of Its Traditional Defense.* New York: Charles Scribner's Sons, 1944.

———. *The Essential Reinhold Niebuhr: Selected Essays and Addresses.* Edited by Robert McAfee Brown. New Haven, CT: Yale University Press, 1986.

———. *Faith and History: A Comparison of Christian and Modern Views of History.* New York: Scribner's, 1949.

———. "How Faith and Reason Are Related." Reinhold Niebuhr Audio Tape Collection. Union Theological Seminary, 1950.

———. *Leaves from the Notebook of a Tamed Cynic.* New York: World Publishing, 1929.

———. "Love and Law in Protestantism and Catholicism." In *The Essential Reinhold Niebuhr: Selected Essays and Addresses,* edited by Robert McAfee Brown, 142–159. New Haven, CT: Yale University Press, 1986.

———. *Man's Nature and His Communities: Essays on the Dynamics and Enigmas of Man's Personal and Social Existence.* Eugene, OR: Wipf and Stock, 1965.

———. *Moral Man and Immoral Society: A Study in Ethics and Politics.* Louisville, KY: Westminster John Knox Press, 2001.

———. "Reply to Interpretation and Criticism." In *Reinhold Niebuhr: His Religious, Social, and Political Thought,* edited by Charles W. Kegley and Robert W. Bretnall, 429–451. New York: Macmillan, 1956.

Nietzsche, Friedrich. *The Anti-Christ: A Curse on Christianity.* In *The Anti-Christ, Ecce Homo, Twilight of the Idols, and Other Writings,* edited by Aaron Ridley and Judith Norman, translated by Judith Norman, 1–68. Cambridge: Cambridge University Press, 2005.

———. *Beyond Good and Evil: Prelude to a Philosophy of the Future.* Edited by Rolf-Peter Horstmann, translated by Judith Norman. Cambridge: Cambridge University Press, 2002.

———. *The Gay Science: With a Prelude in German Rhymes and an Appendix of Songs.* Edited by Bernard Williams, translated by Josefine Nauckhoff and Adrian Del Caro. Cambridge: Cambridge University Press, 2001.

———. *The Portable Nietzsche.* Edited and translated by Walter Kaufman. New York: Viking Penguin, 1968.

———. *Sämtliche Werke. Kritische Studienausgabe.* 3rd ed. Edited by Giorgio Colli and Mazzino Montinari. 15 vols. Munich: De Gruyter, 1999.

———. "To Franz Overbeck [Nice, March 31, 1885]." In *Selected Letters of Friedrich Nietzsche,* edited and translated by Christopher Middleton, 239–240. Chicago: University of Chicago Press, 1969.

———. *Twilight of the Idols.* In *The Portable Nietzsche,* edited and translated by Walter Kaufman, 463–563. New York: Viking Penguin, 1968.

Nussbaum, Martha C. *Love's Knowledge: Essays on Philosophy and Literature.* New York: Oxford University Press, 1990.

———. *The Therapy of Desire: Theory and Practice in Hellenistic Ethics.* Princeton, NJ: Princeton University Press, 1994.

———. *Upheavals of Thought: The Intelligence of the Emotions.* New York: Cambridge University Press, 2001.

Nygren, Anders. *Agape and Eros.* Chicago: University of Chicago Press, 1982.

Oakeshott, Michael. *Lectures in the History of Political Thought,* edited by Terry Nardin and Luke O'Sullivan. Exeter, UK: Imprint Academic, 2006.

Oberhelman, Steven M. *Rhetoric and Homiletics in Fourth-Century Christian Literature: Prose Rhythm, Oratorical Style, and Preaching in the Works of Ambrose, Jerome, and Augustine.* Atlanta, GA: Scholars Press, 1991.

O'Collins, Gerald. "St. Augustine as Apologist for the Resurrection of Christ." *Scottish Journal of Theology* 69, no. 3 (2016): 326–340.

O'Connor, William Riordan. "The *Uti/Frui* Distinction in Augustine's Ethics." *Augustinian Studies* 14 (1983): 45–62.

O'Daly, Gerard. *Augustine's "City of God": A Reader's Guide.* Oxford: Oxford University Press, 1999.

———. "Thinking through History: Augustine's Method in the *City of God* and Its Ciceronian Dimension." *Augustinian Studies* 30, no. 2 (1999): 45–57.

O'Donnell, James J. *Augustine: A New Biography*. New York: HarperCollins, 2005.

———. "The Authority of Augustine." *Augustinian Studies* 22 (1991): 7–35.

———. "Bible." In *Augustine through the Ages*, edited by Allan D. Fitzgerald, John Cavadini, Marianne Djuth, James J. O'Donnell, and Frederick van Fleteren, 99–103. Grand Rapids, MI: William B. Eerdmans, 1999.

———. "*Doctrina Christiana, De.*" In *Augustine through the Ages*, edited by Allan D. Fitzgerald, John Cavadini, Marianne Djuth, James J. O'Donnell, and Frederick van Fleteren, 278–280. Grand Rapids, MI: William B. Eerdmans, 1999.

O'Donovan, Oliver. *Common Objects of Love: Moral Reflection and the Shaping of Community*. Grand Rapids, MI: William B. Eerdmans, 2002.

———. "The Political Thought of *City of God* 19." In *Bonds of Imperfection: Christian Politics, Past and Present*, edited by Oliver O'Donovan and Joan Lockwood, 48–72. Grand Rapids, MI: William B. Eerdmans, 2004.

O'Neill, Saffron, and Sophie Nicholson-Cole. "'Fear Won't Do It': Promoting Positive Engagement with Climate Change through Visual and Iconic Representations." *Science Communication* 30, no. 3 (2009): 355–379.

Oliver, Mary. "Don't Worry." In *Felicity*, 3. New York: Penguin, 2015.

Ogle, Veronica Roberts. "Healing Hope: A Response to Peter Iver Kaufman." *Augustinian Studies* 53, no. 1 (2022): 47–50.

———. "*Latreia* and Its Parodies: Political Reflections on Augustine's Theological Anthropology." In *Augustine in a Time of Crisis: Politics and Religion Contested*, edited by Boleslaw Z. Kabala, Ashleen Menchaca-Bagnulo, and Nathan Pinkoksi, 73–89. Cham, Switzerland: Palgrave Macmillan, 2021.

———. *Politics and the Earthly City in Augustine's "City of God."* New York: Cambridge University Press, 2021.

———. "Sheathing the Sword: Augustine and the Good Judge." *Journal of Religious Ethics* 46, no. 4 (2018): 718–747.

Ojala, Maria. "Hope and Climate Change: The Importance of Hope for Environmental Engagement among Young People." *Environmental Education Research* 18, no. 5 (2012): 625–642.

Paffenroth, Kim, and Kevin L. Hughes, eds. *Augustine and Liberal Education*. Lanham, MD: Lexington Books, 2008.

Paolucci, Henry. Introduction to *The Political Writings of St. Augustine*, by Augustine, edited by Henry Paolucci, vii–xxiii. Chicago: Henry Regnery, 1962.

Pascal, Blaise. *Pensées*. Translated by A. J. Krailsheimer. New York: Penguin, 1995.

Pecknold, C. C. "Joe Biden Misreads Augustine." *First Things*, January 22, 2021. https://www.firstthings.com/web-exclusives/2021/01/joe-biden-misreads-augustine.

Pelosi, Nancy. Interview on *Meet the Press*, NBC News, August 24, 2008. http://www.nbcnews.com/id/26377338/ns/meet_the_press/t/meet-press-transcript-august/.

Perler, Othmar. *Les voyages de Saint Augustin*. Paris: Études augustiniennes, 1969.

Peters, Jason R. *The Logic of the Heart: Augustine, Pascal, and the Rationality of Faith*. Grand Rapids, MI: Baker Academic, 2009.

Peterson, Christopher, and Martin E. P. Seligman. *Character Strengths and Virtues: A Handbook and Classification*. New York: Oxford University Press, 2004.

Phelan, Thomas W. "St. Augustine and the Recent Excavations of the Christian Monuments of Hippo." *Theological Studies* 20, no. 3 (1959): 422–431.

Pieper, Josef. "On Hope." In *Faith, Hope, Love*, translated by Mary France McCarthy, 87–138. San Francisco, CA: Ignatius Press, 1997.

Plantinga, Alvin. *Warranted Christian Belief.* Oxford: Oxford University Press, 2000.

Pollmann, Karla. "The Proteanism of Authority: The Reception of Augustine in Cultural History from his Death to the Present." In *The Oxford Guide to the Historical Reception of Augustine*, edited by Karla Pollmann and Willemien Otten, vol. 1, 3–14. New York: Oxford University Press, 2013.

Pollmann, Karla, and Willemien Otten, eds. *The Oxford Guide to the Historical Reception of Augustine.* 3 vols. Oxford: Oxford University Press, 2013.

Pollock, John L. *Knowledge and Justification.* Princeton, NJ: Princeton University Press, 1974.

———. "Self-Defeating Arguments." *Minds and Machines* 1 (1991): 367–392.

Pope Francis. *Laudato Si': On Care for Our Common Home.* Encyclical Letter, Vatican Press, March 24, 2015. https://www.vatican.va/content/francesco/en/encyclicals/documents/papa-francesco_20150524_enciclica-laudato-si.html.

Possidius. "The Life of Saint Augustine." Translated by F. R. Hoare. In *Soldiers of Christ: Saints and Saints' Lives from Late Antiquity and the Early Middle Ages*, edited by Thomas F. X. Noble and Thomas Head, 31–73. University Park: Pennsylvania State University Press, 1995.

Povoledo, Elisabetta. "Pope Visits Assisi, Bearing the Message of a Favored Saint." *New York Times*, October 4, 2013. https://www.nytimes.com/2013/10/05/world/europe/pope-francis-assisi.html.

Quinn, Philip L. "Disputing the Augustinian Legacy: John Locke and Jonathan Edwards on Romans 5:12–19." In *The Augustinian Tradition*, edited by Gareth B. Matthews, 233–250. Berkeley: University of California Press, 1999.

Quintilian. *The Orator's Education.* Vol. III, Books 6–8, edited and translated by Donald A. Russell. Loeb Classical Library No. 127. Cambridge, MA: Harvard University Press, 2001.

Qvortrup, Matt. "Rousseau, Jean-Jacques." In *The Oxford Guide to the Historical Reception of Augustine*, edited by Karla Pollmann and Willemien Otten, vol. 3, 1675–1677. New York: Oxford University Press, 2013.

Ramirez, J. Roland E. "The Priority of Reason over Faith in Augustine." *Augustinian Studies* 13 (1982): 123–131.

Ramsey, Boniface. Introduction to *The Augustine Catechism: The Enchiridion on Faith, Hope, and Charity*, by Augustine, translated by Bruce Harbert, edited by Boniface Ramsey, 9–27. Hyde Park, NY: New City Press, 1999.

Ratzinger, Joseph. *Volk und Haus Gottes in Augustins Lehre von der Kirche.* Munich: Zink, 1954.

Rawls, John. *A Brief Inquiry into the Meaning of Sin and Faith.* Edited by Thomas Nagel. Cambridge, MA: Harvard University Press, 2009.

———. "Justice as Fairness: Political not Metaphysical." *Philosophy & Public Affairs* 14, no. 3 (1985): 223–251.

———. *Lectures on the History of Political Philosophy.* Edited by Samuel Freeman. Cambridge, MA: Harvard University Press, 2007.

———. "On My Religion." In *A Brief Inquiry into the Meaning of Sin and Faith*, edited by Thomas Nagel, 259–70. Cambridge, MA: Harvard University Press, 2009.

————. *Political Liberalism*. Expanded edition. New York: Columbia University Press, 2005.

————. *A Theory of Justice*. Cambridge, MA: Belknap Press, 1971.

Riley, Patrick. *The General Will before Rousseau: The Transformation of the Divine into the Civic.* Princeton, NJ: Princeton University Press, 1986.

————. "Michael Oakeshott, Philosopher of Individuality." *Review of Politics* 54, no. 4 (1992): 649–664.

Rist, John M. *Augustine: Ancient Thought Baptized.* New York: Cambridge University Press, 1994.

————. *Augustine Deformed: Love, Sin and Freedom in the Western Moral Tradition.* Cambridge: Cambridge University Press, 2014.

————. "Faith and Reason." In *A Cambridge Companion to Augustine*, edited by Eleonore Stump and Norman Kretzmann, 26–39. Cambridge: Cambridge University Press, 2001.

Roberts, Veronica. "Augustine's Ciceronian Response to the Ciceronian Patriot." *Perspectives on Political Science* 45, no. 2 (2016): 113–124.

Rorty, Richard. "Religion as a Conversation-Stopper." In *Philosophy and Social Hope*, 168–174. New York: Penguin, 1999.

Ruether, Rosemary Radford. "Augustine and Christian Political Theology." *Interpretation: A Journal of Bible and Theology* 29, no. 3 (1975): 252–265.

Runciman, David. *The Confidence Trap: A History of Democracy in Crisis from World War I to the Present.* Princeton, NJ: Princeton University Press, 2013.

Russell, Bertrand. *The History of Western Philosophy.* New York: Simon & Schuster, 1972.

Ryan, Alan. *On Politics: A History of Political Thought from Herodotus to the Present.* Vol. 1. New York: Liveright, 2012.

Saak, Eric L. "Luther, Martin." In *The Oxford Guide to the Historical Reception of Augustine*, edited by Karla Pollmann and Willemien Otten, vol. 3, 1341–1345. Oxford: Oxford University Press, 2013.

Sabl, Andrew. *Ruling Passions: Political Offices and Democratic Ethics.* Princeton, NJ: Princeton University Press, 2002.

————. "Virtue for Pluralists." *Journal of Moral Philosophy* 2, no. 2 (2005): 207–235.

Sacks, Jonathan. *The Politics of Hope.* London: Jonathan Cape, 1997.

Savoie, John. "Milton, John." In *The Oxford Guide to the Historical Reception of Augustine*, edited by Karla Pollmann and Willemien Otten, vol. 3, 1397–1399. Oxford: Oxford University Press, 2013.

Schall, James V. "The 'Realism' of St. Augustine's 'Political Realism.'" In *The Mind That Is Catholic: Philosophical and Political Essays*, 193–207. Washington, DC: Catholic University Press of America, 2008.

Schenkeveld, Dirk M. "Philosophical Prose." In *Handbook of Classical Rhetoric in the Hellenistic Period (330 B.C.–A.D. 400)*, edited by Stanley E. Porter, 195–264. Leiden: Brill, 1997.

Schlesinger, Arthur, Jr. "Forgetting Reinhold Niebuhr." *New York Times*, September 18, 2005. https://www.nytimes.com/2005/09/18/books/review/forgetting-reinhold-niebuhr.html.

Schofield, Malcolm. "Cicero's Definition of *Res Publica*." In *Cicero the Philosopher: Twelve Papers*, edited by J. G. F. Powell, 63–84. Oxford: Clarendon Press, 1995.

————. "Epilogue." In *The Cambridge History of Greek and Roman Political Thought*, edited by Christopher Rowe and Malcolm Schofield, 661–671. Cambridge: Cambridge University Press, 2005.

Scott, Joanna Vecchiarelli. "Hannah Arendt's Secular Augustinianism." *Augustinian Studies* 30, no. 2 (1999): 293–310.

———. "Political Thought, Contemporary Influences of Augustine's." In *Augustine through the Ages*, edited by Allan D. Fitzgerald, John Cavadini, Marianne Djuth, James J. O'Donnell, and Frederick van Fleteren, 658–661. Grand Rapids, MI: William E. Eerdmans, 1999.

Scott, Joanna Vecchiarelli, and Judith Chelius Stark. "Rediscovering Hannah Arendt." In Hannah Arendt, *Love and Saint Augustine*, edited by Joanna Vecchiarelli Scott and Judith Chelius Stark, 113–211. Chicago: University of Chicago Press, 1996.

Scruton, Roger. *The Uses of Pessimism and the Dangers of False Hope*. New York: Oxford University Press, 2010.

———. "When Hope Tramples Truth." *New York Times*, March 24, 2013. http://opinionator .blogs.nytimes.com/2013/03/24/when-hope-tramples-truth/.

Sen, Amartya. *The Idea of Justice*. New York: Penguin, 2010.

Shklar, Judith N. "Giving Injustice Its Due." *Yale Law Journal* 98, no. 6 (April 1989): 1135–1151.

———. "Liberalism of Fear." In *Political Thought and Political Thinkers*, edited by Stanley Hoffmann, 3–20. Chicago: University of Chicago Press, 1998.

Siedentop, Larry. *Inventing the Individual: The Origins of Western Liberalism*. New York: Penguin, 2014.

Siebert, Matthew Kent. "Augustine's Development on Testimonial Knowledge." *Journal of the History of Philosophy* 56, no. 2 (2018): 215–237.

Skerrett, Kathleen Roberts. "The Indispensable Rival: William Connolly's Engagement with Augustine of Hippo." *Journal of the American Academy of Religion* 72, no. 2 (2004): 487–506.

———. "Sovereignty and Sadness: Tragic Vision and Wisdom's Grief." *Augustinian Studies* 41, no. 1 (2010): 301–314.

Skinner, Quentin. *The Foundations of Modern Political Thought*. Vol. 1, *The Renaissance*. New York: Cambridge University Press, 1998.

———. *Reason and Rhetoric in the Philosophy of Hobbes*. New York: Cambridge University Press, 1996.

Smith, James K. A. *Awaiting the King: Reforming Public Theology*. Grand Rapids, MI: Baker Academic, 2017.

———. "The Benedict Option or the Augustinian Call?" *Comment*, March 16, 2017. https:// www.cardus.ca/comment/article/the-benedict-option-or-the-augustinian-call/.

———. "A Response to Critics." *Studies in Christian Ethics* 32, no. 1 (2019): 129–134.

———. *You Are What You Love: The Spiritual Power of Habit*. Grand Rapids, MI: Brazos Press, 2016.

Smith, Thomas W. "The Glory and Tragedy of Politics." In *Augustine and Politics*, edited by John Doody, Kevin L. Hughes, and Kim Paffenroth, 187–213. Lanham, MD: Lexington Books, 2005.

Smith, Wilfred Cantwell. *Believing: An Historical Perspective*. Oxford: Oneworld Publications, 1998.

Smits, Luchesius. *St. Augustin dans l'oeuvre de Jean Calvin*. 2 vols. Assen: Van Gorcum, 1956–1957.

Snow, Nancy E. "Hope as a Democratic Civic Virtue." *Metaphilosophy* 49, no. 3 (2018): 407–427.

Sommer, Andreas Urs. "Nietzsche, Friedrich." In *The Oxford Guide to the Historical Reception of Augustine*, edited by Karla Pollmann and Willemien Otten, vol. 3, 1450–1452. Oxford: Oxford University Press, 2013.

Spellman, W. M. *A Short History of Western Political Thought*. New York: Palgrave Macmillan, 2011.

Stalnaker, Aaron. "Spiritual Exercises and the Grace of God: Paradoxes of Personal Formation in Augustine." *Journal of the Society of Christian Ethics* 24, no. 2 (2004): 137–170.

Stark, Judith Chelius, ed. *Feminist Interpretations of Augustine*. University Park: Pennsylvania State University Press, 2007.

Stevenson, Seth William, C. Roach Smith, and Frederic W. Madden. *A Dictionary of Roman Coins*. London: George Bell & Sons, 1889.

Stewart-Kroeker, Sarah. *Pilgrimage as Moral and Aesthetic Formation in Augustine's Thought*. Oxford: Oxford University Press, 2017.

———. "Resisting Idolatry and Instrumentalisation in Loving the Neighbour: The Significance of the Pilgrim Motif for Augustine's *Usus-Fruitio* Distinction." *Studies in Christian Ethics* 27, no. 2 (2014): 202–221.

———. "World-Weariness and Augustine's Eschatological Ordering of Emotions in *enarratio in Psalmum 36*." *Augustinian Studies* 47, no. 2 (2016): 201–226.

Sting. "Saint Augustine in Hell." Recorded June–December 1992. Track 7 on *Ten Summoner's Tales*. A&M, 1993.

Stock, Brian. *Augustine the Reader: Meditation, Self-Knowledge, and the Ethics of Interpretation*. Cambridge, MA: Harvard University Press, 1996.

———. "Ethical Values and the Literary Imagination." *New Literary History* 29, no. 1 (1998): 1–13.

Stout, Jeffrey. *Blessed Are the Organized: Grassroots Democracy in America*. Princeton, NJ: Princeton University Press, 2010.

———. *Democracy and Tradition*. Princeton, NJ: Princeton University Press, 2004.

———. "The Transformation of Genius into Practical Power: A Reading of Emerson's 'Experience.'" *American Journal of Theology and Philosophy* 35, no. 1 (January 2014): 3–24.

Strand, Daniel. "Augustine's Privation, Arendt's Banality." In *Augustine in a Time of Crisis: Politics and Religion Contested*, edited by Boleslaw Z. Kabala, Ashleen Menchaca-Bagnulo, and Nathan Pinkoksi, 409–426. Cham, Switzerland: Palgrave Macmillan, 2021.

Studer, Basil. "Augustine and the Pauline Theme of Hope." In *Paul and the Legacies of Paul*, edited by William S. Babcock, 201–225. Dallas, TX: Southern Methodist University Press, 1990.

Sunstein, Cass R. "Practical Reason and Incompletely Theorized Agreements." *Current Legal Problems* 51 (1998): 267–298.

Taylor, Charles. *A Secular Age*. Cambridge, MA: Belknap Press, 2007.

———. *Sources of the Self: The Making of the Modern Identity*. Cambridge, MA: Harvard University Press, 1989.

TeSelle, Eugene. "Faith." In *Augustine through the Ages*, edited by Allan D. Fitzgerald, John Cavadini, Marianne Djuth, James J. O'Donnell, and Frederick van Fleteren, 347–350. Grand Rapids, MI: William E. Eerdmans, 1999.

Thistlewaite, Susan B. "The Iraq War: How Our Nation Lost Its Soul." *Washington Post*, March 18, 2013. https://www.washingtonpost.com/national/on-faith/the-iraq-war-how-our-nation-lost-its-soul/2013/03/18/259e6406-8fe5-11e2-9cfd-36d6c9b5d7ad_story.html?utm_term=.6d0c2405f4bb.

———. "'Just War,' or Is It Just a War?" *Chicago Tribune*, October 15, 2002. http://articles
.chicagotribune.com/2002-10-15/news/0210150104_1_war-theory-cold-war-iraq.

Tocqueville, Alexis de. 2000. *Democracy in America*. Translated by George Lawrence, edited by
J. P. Mayer. New York: Perennial Classics.

Torrell, Jean-Pierre. *Saint Thomas Aquinas*. Vol. 1, *The Person and His Work*, rev. ed., translated
by Robert Royal. Washington, DC: Catholic University of America Press, 2005.

Tran, Jonathan. "Assessing the Augustinian Democrats." *Journal of Religious Ethics* 46, no. 3
(2018): 521–547.

Treggiari, Susan. *Roman Marriage: Iusti Coniuges from the Time of Cicero to the Time of Ulpian*.
Oxford: Clarendon Press, 1991.

Vasaly, Ann. *Representations: Images of the World in Ciceronian Oratory*. Berkeley: University of
California Press, 1993.

Van der Meer, Frederick. *Augustine the Bishop*. Translated by B. Battershaw and G. Lamb. London: Sheed and Ward, 1961.

Van Deusen, Nancy. "*Rhetorica, De*." In *Augustine through the Ages*, edited by Allan D. Fitzgerald,
John Cavadini, Marianne Djuth, James J. O'Donnell, and Frederick van Fleteren, 726. Grand
Rapids, MI: William E. Eerdmans, 1999.

Van Fleteren, Frederick. "Augustine and Philosophy." *Augustinian Studies* 41, no. 1 (2010): 255–274.

———. "Authority and Reason, Faith and Understanding in the Thought of St. Augustine."
Augustinian Studies 4 (1973): 33–71.

Vanderjagt, Arjo. "Political Thought." In *The Oxford Guide to the Historical Reception of Augustine*,
edited by Karla Pollmann and Willemien Otten, vol. 3, 1562–1569. New York: Oxford University Press, 2013.

Velde, Rudi te. "Thomas Aquinas." In *The Oxford Guide to the Historical Reception of Augustine*,
edited by Karla Pollmann and Willemien Otten, vol. 3, 1798–1803. New York: Oxford University Press, 2013.

Vessey, Mark. "The History of the Book: Augustine's *City of God* and Post-Roman Cultural
Memory." In *Augustine's "City of God": A Critical Guide*, edited by James Wetzel, 14–32. Cambridge: Cambridge University Press, 2012.

Viroli, Maurizio. *Machiavelli*. New York: Oxford University Press, 1998.

Vogler, Candace. *Reasonably Vicious*. Cambridge, MA: Harvard University Press, 2002.

Von Harnack, Adolf. *History of Dogma*. Vol. 5. Translated by James Miller, edited by T. K.
Cheyne and A. B. Bruce. London: Williams & Norgate, 1898.

Von Heyking, John. *Augustine and Politics as Longing in the World*. Columbia: University of
Missouri Press, 2001.

———. "Disarming, Simple, and Sweet: Augustine's Republican Rhetoric." In *Talking Democracy: Historical Perspectives on Rhetoric and Democracy*, edited by Benedetto Fontana, Cary J.
Nederman, and Gary Remer, 163–186. University Park: Pennsylvania State University, 2004.

Von Jess, Wilma Gundersdorf. "Reason as Propaedeutic to Faith in Augustine." *International
Journal for Philosophy of Religion* 5, no. 4 (1974): 225–233.

Wallace-Wells, David. "The Uninhabitable Earth." *New York*, July 10, 2017. https://nymag.com
/intelligencer/2017/07/climate-change-earth-too-hot-for-humans.html.

Ward, John O. "Roman Rhetoric and Its Afterlife." In *A Companion to Roman Rhetoric*, edited
by William Dominik and Jon Hall, 354–366. Oxford: Blackwell, 2007.

Webb, Melanie. "'On Lucretia Who Slew Herself': Rape and Consolation in Augustine's *De civitate dei.*" *Augustinian Studies* 44, no. 1 (2013): 37–58.

Weithman, Paul J. "Augustine's Political Philosophy." In *The Cambridge Companion to Augustine*, edited by Eleonore Stump and Norman Kretzmann, 234–252. Cambridge: Cambridge University Press, 2001.

———. "Toward an Augustinian Liberalism." In *The Augustinian Tradition*, edited by Gareth B. Matthews, 304–322. Berkeley: University of California Press, 1999.

West, Cornel. "Called Far and Wide to Touch Minds." By Cara Buckley. *New York Times*, January 22, 2010. https://www.nytimes.com/2010/01/24/nyregion/24routine.html.

———. "Power Is Everywhere, but Love Is Supreme." By George Yancey. *New York Times*, May 29, 2019. https://www.nytimes.com/2019/05/29/opinion/cornel-west-power-love.html.

Wetherbee, Winthrop. "Dante Alighieri." In *The Oxford Guide to the Historical Reception of Augustine*, edited by Karla Pollmann and Willemien Otten, vol. 2, 856–858. New York: Oxford University Press, 2013.

Wetzel, James, ed. *Augustine's "City of God": A Critical Guide.* New York: Cambridge University Press, 2012.

———. "Prodigal Heart: Augustine's Theology of the Emotions." In *Parting Knowledge: Essays after Augustine*, 81–96. Eugene, OR: Cascade Books.

———. "Snares of Truth: Augustine on Free Will and Predestination." In *Augustine and His Critics: Essays in Honour of Gerald Bonner*, edited by Robert Dodaro and George Lawless, 124–140. New York: Routledge, 2000.

———. "Splendid Vices and Secular Virtues: Variations on Milbank's Augustine." *Journal of Religious Ethics* 32, no. 2 (2004): 271–300.

———. "Wittgenstein's Augustine: The Inauguration of the Later Philosophy." In *Parting Knowledge: Essays after Augustine*, 225–247. Eugene, OR: Cascade Books.

Willer, Robb, and Matthew Feinberg. "The Key to Political Persuasion." *New York Times*, November 13, 2015. https://www.nytimes.com/2015/11/15/opinion/sunday/the-key-to -political-persuasion.html.

Williams, Brian A. *The Potter's Rib: Mentoring for Pastoral Formation.* Vancouver, BC: Regent College, 2005.

Williams, Michael. *Problems of Knowledge: A Critical Introduction to Epistemology.* Oxford: Oxford University Press, 2001.

Williams, Rowan. "Language, Reality and Desire in Augustine's *De Doctrina.*" *Journal of Literature & Theology* 3, no. 1 (1989): 138–150.

———. *On Augustine.* New York: Bloomsbury, 2016.

Wills, Garry. *Augustine's "Confessions": A Biography.* Princeton, NJ: Princeton University Press, 2011.

———. *Saint Augustine.* New York: Viking, 1999.

Wilson, Edward O. *The Creation: An Appeal to Save Life on Earth.* New York: W.W. Norton & Company, 2006.

Wittgenstein, Ludwig. *Philosophical Investigations: The German Text, with a Revised English Translation.* Translated by G. E. M. Anscombe. Oxford: Wiley Blackwell, 2001.

Wolin, Sheldon S. *Politics and Vision: Continuity and Innovation in Western Political Thought.* Princeton, NJ: Princeton University Press, 2004.

———. *Tocqueville between Two Worlds: The Making of a Political and Theoretical Life*. Princeton, NJ: Princeton University Press, 2001.

Wolterstorff, Nicholas. *Justice: Rights and Wrongs*. Princeton, NJ: Princeton University Press, 2008.

———. *Practices of Belief: Selected Essays*. Edited by Terrence Cuneo. Vol. 2. Cambridge: Cambridge University Press, 2010.

———. "The Role of Religion in Decision and Discussion of Political Issues." In *Religion in the Public Square: The Place of Religious Convictions in Political Debate*, by Robert Audi and Nicholas Wolterstorff, 67–120. Lanham, MD: Rowman and Littlefield, 1997.

Worthen, Molly. "Is There a Way to Dial Down the Political Hatred?" *New York Times*, June 11, 2021. https://www.nytimes.com/2021/06/11/opinion/god-religion-politics-partisanship.html.

Worthington, Glenn. "Michael Oakeshott and the City of God." *Political Theory* 28, no. 3 (2000): 377–398.

INDEX

abolitionist movement, 194

abortion, x–xi

Academic skepticism, 77, 85, 97, 318n133

Adam (biblical), 39–40, 180, 324n260, 359n82, 385n170

The Advantage of Believing (Augustine), 67, 79, 85, 87, 130, 318n133, 322n213

agonism, 188–90, 270

Alimi, Olaoluwatoni, 145–46

Alypius, 84, 110, 212, 214

Ambrose, xii, 74, 78, 108, 150, 205, 251, 316n119, 318n151, 346n18, 384n145

antitheses (oppositions), 131–33, 135, 138, 146, 154, 159, 195, 215, 219, 243, 338nn122–23, 356n42, 362n139

Antony (saint), 84, 251, 323n246, 184n145

Appiah, Kwame Anthony, 193–94

Aquinas, Thomas: Augustine's influence on, ix; on certitude of faith, 79, 318–19n152; on hope and the Lord's Prayer, 294n6; on hope and love, 23, 296n34; on hope as virtue, 19; on "lifeless" and "living" faith, 297n64; on magnanimity, 307n57; on pagan virtue, 241–42, 382nn87–88; 382n122, 385n153, 387n187; on participation in divine goodness, 301n57; on twofold object of hope, 48; on virtue, 241–42, 336n84

Arendt, Hannah, 2, 4–5, 32, 124, 202, 216, 285n26, 287n15, 388n15; on Augustine's eschatology, 37, 170, 171; on Augustine's impact on Luther and Protestantism, 7, 290n69; on Augustine's Platonic influences, 121, 157; on evil, 288n37;

Jaspers on, 333n60; on love of neighbor and temporal goods, 35

Aristotle, ix, 54, 88, 92, 204, 336n84, 389–90n54

ascent, 54, 119, 121, 157–58, 299n23, 331n29

Audi, Robert, 311n13, 312n32

authority, 13, 66–67, 70–72, 84–88, 188, 210, 311n14, 317–318n126, 320n195; forms of, 72–73; legitimate, 211; reason and, 73–79, 87–88, 93, 98, 100–102, 130, 314n69, 316n105, 316n122, 316–317n123, 320–21n197, 322n213

Babylon, 105, 226–27, 359n89

Baier, Annette, 1

Ballantyne, Nathan, 316n123

Benedict (saint), 271

Benedict XVI (pope). *See* Ratzinger, Joseph

Berlin, Isaiah, 4

Bernard of Clairvaux (saint), 257

Berry, Wendell, 390n55

Bettenson, Henry, 238

Biden, Joe, xi

Biggar, Nigel, 183, 187–89, 366–67n229

Bilgrami, Akeel, 304n102

Billings, David, 2, 32–33, 36–37, 44, 171

Boniface, 214–15, 216, 224, 225, 249–250, 321n205, 373n110

Bowlin, John: on coercion, 210; on tolerance, 239; on truthful description, 41–42, 255

Brandom, Robert, 293–94nn114–115, 316–317n123, 320–21n197

Bretherton, Luke, 200, 227, 269, 368n249

Breyfogle, Todd, 159, 358n79, 370n30

421

Brooks, David, x

Brooks, Edward, 107

Brown, Charles C., 288n39, 288n40, 290–91nn74–75

Brown, Peter, 293n101, 338n121, 348n45; on Augustine's sermons, 106, 111, 329nn5–6, 344n209; on *City of God,* 148, 345n4; on coercion of Donatists, 210; mosaic described by, 106; on political action by bishops, 213; on state, 358–59n82

Brunner, Emil, 8–9, 291n76

Bruno, Michael J. S., 287–88n28, 352n117, 353n120, 357n55

Bullock, Jeffrey, 143, 344n208

Burke, Kenneth, 148, 160, 349n65

Burnaby, John, 367n234

Burt, Donald, 352n117, 353n124

Button, Mark, 257–58, 386n180

Byers, Sarah Catherine, 121, 157–58, 331n32, 349n72

Calvin, John, ix–x, 2, 9, 80, 287n14, 291n46

Cameron, Averil, 323n246, 329n14, 337n101, 339n129, 342n178, 351n102; on Augustine's audience, 140, 341n170; on early Christian rhetoric, 139–40, 330n20, 338n122, 342n181

Camus, Albert, 311n14

Canning, Raymond, 44

capital punishment, 208

Carneades, 77

Cassiciacum, xii, 219; dialogues, 86, 124, 335n72

Cato, Marcus, 213, 234

Cavadini, John, 139, 142

Chadwick, Henry, 304–5n112

charity, 42, 136, 198, 238, 252, 296–97n54, 301n57, 313n41; *Enchiridion* on, 20, 295n24; Pauline epistles on, 27, 29, 138; piety and, 252; and public service, 216. *See also* love

Christ, 44–45, 89, 171, 214–15, 255, 343n200; belief in, 313n41; as exemplar, 61–62, 127–28, 217, 228, 239, 310n123, 322n213; faith in, 93–94; as mediator, 37–38, 92–93, 324n270, 337n89; miracles attributed to, 320n195

Christine de Pizan, x, 284n17

church, 136, 169, 172–73, 189, 212, 271, 336n84, 355nn39–40; authority of, 72–73, 78, 85, 102, 315n90; Catholic, 70, 72, 148, 207–8; Hauerwas on, 3, 206, 355–56nn41–42, 356n44, 357n55; institutional church and true church, 172–73, 236, 264–64, 355n55; Milbank on, 3, 205, 233, 355n42, 357n55, 365n197; as political society, 206, 369n23; power in and service to, 216–18; as school, 140–42; Smith on, 225–26; and state, 173–77, 206, 273, 358n76. *See also* ecclesiology

Cicero, ix, 120–22, 141, 194, 196, 206, 294n15, 348n55, 368n1, 369n11; on antitheses, 154, 362n139; on the commonwealth, 177, 179, 180, 182–83, 192; on concord, 184–85, 188; on *dispositio,* 351n101; on faith (*fides*), 66, 312n16, 313n33; on justice, 182, 250, 362n143; on the mean (intermediate course), 54; in Nectarius's and Augustine's correspondence, 192; on piety, 250; political philosophy of, 176, 182, 361n116, 362n143; on rhetoric, 91, 122, 332n43, 368n8, 369n8, 369nn11–12; on vivid description (*illustratio, evidentia*), 158

Circumcellions, 210, 371n49

citizenship, 14–15, 205–7, 261, 271, 273–74, 293n96; liturgy of, 223–27, 271; and slavery, 145, 372n94; in the two cities, 174

City of God (Augustine), 148–51; attributions of optimism and pessimism to, 156–64; on citizenship, 224; eschatology of, 171–72; forms of peace in, 183; on good and evil, 151–56; on human sin, 57; on torture, 209; varying translations of, 238; on war between virtue and vice, 261; on weight of love, 28

civic virtue, 15, 192, 231, 233–42, 260–61, 267, 381n71, 382n93; of hope, 260–261; of piety and humility, 248–59

Clair, Joseph, 57, 206, 308n79, 308n82; on Boniface, 214–15

Clark, Gillian, 343n193, 345n2, 346n15, 346–47n23, 365–66n211